Instructor's Manual to Accompany

LITERATURE

An Introduction to Fiction, Poetry, and Drama

Sixth Edition

X. J. Kennedy

Dorothy M. Kennedy

Dana Gioia

HarperCollins*CollegePublishers*

Instructor's Manual to accompany *Literature: An Introduction to Fiction, Poetry, and Drama*, Sixth Edition

Copyright © 1995 by X. J. Kennedy, Dorothy M. Kennedy, and Dana Gioia

ISBN: 0-673-54154-1

96 97 98 99 9 8 7 6 5 4 3 2

ACKNOWLEDGMENTS

"Introduction to Poetry" from *The Apple That Astonished Paris*, poems by Billy Collins. Copyright © 1988 by Billy Collins. Reprinted by permission of The University of Arkansas Press. "Buck It" by Jerald Bullis. Reprinted by permission of the author.

Contents

SUPPLEMENT: WRITING

Preface

This manual pretends to be no more than a sheaf of notes to supply you—if you want them—with classroom strategies, comments by critics, and a few homemade interpretations. These last may be wrong, but we set them down in hopes of giving you something clear-cut with which to agree or disagree. Wherever it seemed pertinent, facts about a literary work and its background are also supplied.

Every story, poem, and play is dealt with, except for several brief poems given in the text as illustrations.

In the "Fiction" section of the book itself, the "Stories for Further Reading" have no questions after them. This manual supplies some questions, and, most of the time, tentative answers. To be sure, other answers are likely and possible.

To help you refer quickly to the parent book, page numbers are given at the top of each page in this manual. These correspond to pages in the book itself.

We've always found, before teaching a knotty piece of literature, no preparation more helpful than to sit down and discuss it with a colleague or two. If this manual supplies you with such a colleague at inconvenient hours, such as 2:00 A.M., when there's no one in the faculty coffee room, it will be doing its job.

PLAN OF THE BOOK

•There is a plan, but it does not oblige you to follow it. Chapters may be taken up in any sequence; some instructors like to intersperse poetry and plays with stories. Some may wish to teach Chapter 25, on "Myth and Narrative," immediately before teaching *Oedipus the King*. Many find that "Imagery" is a useful chapter with which to begin teaching poetry.

If, because you skip around in the book, students encounter a term unknown to them, let them look it up in the "Index of Terms." They will be directed to the page where it first occurs and where it will be defined and illustrated.

In "Poetry," the sections entitled "For Review and Further Study" do not review the whole book up to that moment; they review only the main points of the chapter. Most of these sections contain some poems that are a little more difficult than those in the body of that chapter.

CHANGES TO THIS EDITION

The major changes in this edition are discussed in the book's preface, but a great many other renovations have been made. For anyone interested, we will list a few new features in detail.

Some changes have been made in *Literature* to afford you greater flexibility as a teacher. For example, we have added *Hamlet* to the book while keeping *Othello*, not because most instructors will have time to teach both tragedies, but to provide the option of using either play (as well as giving students an additional play for a paper or independent study). Likewise, there are now two long works of fiction in Chapter 9, "Reading

Long Stories and Novels." Franz Kafka's *The Metamorphosis* has been added to Leo Tolstoi's *The Death of Ivan Ilych.*

Chapter 10, "A Writer in Depth," now focuses entirely on Flannery O'Connor. The chapter provides three stories as well as two excerpts from her critical writing. Most users of the previous edition felt little need to present three writers in depth, and so the section has been cut back to concentrate entirely on O'Connor, who has consistently been among the most popular writers in the book. O'Connor, however, is not the only short story writer represented by multiple selections. The book contains two stories each by Kate Chopin and William Faulkner. The book also presents critical excerpts by Edgar Allan Poe, Anton Chekhov, James Joyce, Katherine Mansfield, William Faulkner, Nadine Gordimer, and Raymond Carver to accompany their fiction.

Once again, the book's representation of minority writers has been strengthened, as well as the number of women writers past and present. Added to this edition are new stories by Chuang Tzu, James Baldwin, Alice Walker, Amy Tan, Jorge Luis Borges, Ursula Le Guin, Sandra Cisneros, Charlotte Perkins Gilman, Nadine Gordimer, Zora Neale Hurston, Doris Lessing, Gabriel García Márquez, Bobbie Ann Mason, Alice Munro, Eudora Welty, and Virginia Woolf. A few of these selections, like Walker's "Everyday Use," Le Guin's "The Ones Who Walk Away from Omelas," and Lessing's "A Woman on a Roof," long-time users may recognize from earlier editions. They have been reinstated by instructor requests.

In "Poetry," many renovations have been made, while retaining the best-liked material. A whole new chapter has been added: "Poetry and Personal Identity," exploring ways in which poets have defined themselves in personal, social, sexual, generational, and ethnic terms. Please review the new chapter—its impact will be stronger than this summary can explain. An opening section examines how a poet's cultural heritage can inform his or her work; and the chapter includes fifteen teachable new poems that explore diversity.

Many changes also came from instructors requesting that we reinstate favorite selections from previous editions. Instructors who missed Browning's "My Last Duchess," Keats's "Ode on a Grecian Urn," or Frost's "Mending Wall" will find them back in the volume along with a dozen other "golden oldies." In our effort to update and freshen *Literature* with the best of the new, we do not want to neglect the best-liked and most useful classroom materials.

About a fifth of the poems in this edition are new. There are now considerably more women and minority poets, among them Carole Satyamurti, Wendy Cope, Carolyn Forché, Alice Fulton, Julia Alvarez, Shirley Geok-lin Lim, Emma Lazarus, Louise Glück, Anne Stevenson, Emily Grosholz, Nina Cassian, N. Scott Momaday, Claude McKay, Alberto Ríos, Derek Walcott, José Emilio Pacheco, Yusef Komunyakaa, and many more.

Those interested in the Cowboy Poetry movement will now find a cowboy poem, Wallace McRae's "Reincarnation." We have also incorporated a rap lyric for the first time—both to engage students with a contemporary example of verse and to demonstrate how much rap resembles certain types of traditional poetry.

Veteran users of the book, however, need not feel abandoned. It now has *two* of Keats's major odes, and more John Donne, Robert Frost, Edna St. Vincent Millay, Edwin Arlington Robinson, and Philip Larkin than ever, as well as both "Lycidas" and "Elegy Written in a Country Churchyard."

The "Drama" section has been changed to reflect instructor requests. In addition to *Hamlet*, we have also reinstated (by popular demand) the Dudley Fitts and Robert Fitzgerald translations of *Oedipus the King* and *Antigonê.* We have streamlined some minor selections while adding a new section of contemporary drama at the end. "New Voices in American Drama" presents four diverse approaches to recent American theater from Beth Henley, David Hwang, Terrence McNally, and August Wilson. The Wilson play appeared in the previous edition and received strong approval; the other selections are new to *Liter-*

ature. This section can be taught in itself or it can be used to supplement other sections of "Drama" (some specific teaching suggestions can be found in the headnote to "New Voices in American Drama," on page 338 of this manual.)

ANOTHER NEW FEATURE

The final section, "Critical Approaches to Literature," is entirely new. This special supplement presents nine of the most widely used critical methods. It can be taught independently as a mini-introduction to literary theory, or instructors can incorporate selections into the discussion of particular works.

Theory and criticism have become such important aspects of undergraduate study that many instructors asked us to create an accessible and informed beginner's guide. We have tried to present this anxiety-provoking area intelligently and clearly. Our chief objective was not to confuse the student.

Each critical method is explained briefly with a minimum of specialist terminology. Then, two examples of the critical approach are presented. Whenever the critics examine a specific text, it is a work found in *Literature.* In that way, students can relate these approaches to works they are currently studying. Among the works discussed by one critic or another are Browning's "My Last Duchess," Elizabeth Bishop's "One Art," Faulkner's "A Rose for Emily," Sophocles's *Oedipus the King,* and Shakespeare's *Othello.*

Take a look at this new feature. It may give you some new ways of teaching familiar works.

STATISTICS ON POETRY

This edition of the book includes 456 whole poems, counting translations, haiku, clerihews, and anonymous examples. (Fragments were not counted.) There are 301 poems in the body of the text, 153 in the "Poems for Further Reading," and 3 in the "Supplement: Writing."

Many poets are represented by multiple selections. In case you wish to teach an individual poet's work in greater depth or assign a paper on a writer, these are the poets most heavily represented in the current edition (listed by number of poems):

Robert Frost	13
Emily Dickinson	10
William Shakespeare	9
W. B. Yeats	9
William Blake	8
Thomas Hardy	8
W. C. Williams	8
Walt Whitman	7
Langston Hughes	6
John Keats	6
William Wordsworth	6

John Donne	5
T. S. Eliot	5
Gerard M. Hopkins	5
A. E. Housman	5
Wallace Stevens	5
Alfred, Lord Tennyson	5
Richard Wilbur	5
W. H. Auden	4
Elizabeth Bishop	4
Gwendolyn Brooks	4
E. E. Cummings	4
George Herbert	4
Philip Larkin	4
Alexander Pope	4
Adrienne Rich	4
Theodore Roethke	4

Also, there are now three poems each by Wendy Cope, Robert Herrick, Ben Jonson, Denise Levertov, Edna St. Vincent Millay, John Milton, Sylvia Plath, Ezra Pound, and James Wright. Many other poets are represented doubly.

TEXTS AND EDITORIAL POLICY

Spelling has been modernized (*rose-lipped* for Campion's *ros-lip'd*) and rendered American, unless to do so would change the sound of a word. However, the *y* has remained in Blake's strange "Tyger," and Whitman has been left with his *bloom'd* on the conviction that *bloomed* would no more resemble Whitman than a portrait of the poet in a starched collar. Untitled poems are identified by their first lines, except for those that have titles assigned by custom ("The Twa Corbies"). Chaucer's poem is given as edited by F. N. Robinson, and the poems of Emily Dickinson, as edited by Thomas H. Johnson.

It would have been simpler to gloss no word a student could find in a desk dictionary, on the grounds that rummaging through dictionaries is good moral discipline; but it seemed best not to require the student to exchange text for dictionary as many as thirty times in reading a story, poem, or play. Glosses have been provided, therefore, for whatever seemed likely to get in the way of pleasure and understanding.

The spelling *rime* is used instead of *rhyme* on the theory that rime is easier to tell apart from *rhythm*.

A NOTE ON LIVE READINGS

Many find that, for drumming up zeal for poetry, there is no substitute for a good live poetry reading by a poet whose work students have read before. Anyone who wants to order a live poet is advised to send for *A Directory of Live Poets and Fiction Writers* from Poets and Writers, Inc., 72 Spring Street, New York, NY 10012. The price of the 1993-94 edition is $23.95 plus $2.00 for postage. Not all poets give stirring performances, of course, so ask your colleagues on other campuses for suggestions, lest you get stuck with some mumbling prima donna.

If you want the poet to visit classes or confer with student writers, be sure to specify your expectations ahead of time. Some poets, especially media figures whose affairs are managed by agents, will charge for extra services; less-known visitors grateful for a reading are often pathetically happy to oblige (they may even walk your dog). All poets, if they are to do their best for you, need an occasional hour of solitude to recharge their batteries.

THANKS

Many instructors, most of whose names appear in this manual, generously wrote us with their suggestions and teaching experiences. Other instructors are noted in the "acknowledgments" section of the textbook itself. We thank them all for their pragmatic and informed help. We would finally like to thank Mary Gioia whose formidable planning and editorial skills kept this manual in running order.

ON TEACHING LITERATURE

We'll close with a poem. It is by Billy Collins, from his collection *The Apple That Astonished Paris* (University of Arkansas Press, 1988), and it sets forth an experience that may be familiar to you.

INTRODUCTION TO POETRY

I ask them to take a poem
and hold it up to the light
like a color slide
or press an ear against its hive.

I say drop a mouse into a poem
and watch him probe his way out,

or walk inside the poem's room
and feel the walls for a light switch.

I want them to waterski
across the surface of a poem
waving at the author's name on the shore.

But all they want to do
is tie the poem to a chair with rope
and torture a confession out of it.

They begin beating it with a hose
to find out what it really means.

As you might expect, Billy Collins is a professor of English himself—at Lehman College of the City University of New York.

May this manual help you find ways to persuade your students to set aside rope and hose, and instead turn on a few lights.

XJK, DMK, and DG

FICTION

Stories Arranged by Type

If you prefer to teach a *different* story to illustrate an element of fiction—to discuss style, say, with the aid of "Cathedral" or "A Haunted House" instead of the examples in Chapter 5—you will find the substitution easy to make. Many choices are at your disposal in "Stories for Further Reading," and other stories in the book lend themselves to varied purposes. The following list has a few likely substitutions. If you teach other elements of fiction (plot, humor, fantasy) or specific genres, you will find some nominations here.

FABLE
The Parable of the Prodigal Son

TALE
The Tell-Tale Heart
On the Road

PLOT
A Rose for Emily
The Five-Forty-Eight
Barn Burning
The Lottery
An Occurrence at Owl Creek Bridge
The Story of an Hour
How I Met My Husband
The Catbird Seat

POINT OF VIEW
First-person narrator as central character:
A & P
Gimpel the Fool (innocent narrator)
Greasy Lake
A Pair of Tickets
Araby (mature narrator recalling boyhood view)
Cathedral
Barbie-Q
The Yellow Wallpaper
How I Met My Husband
The Use of Force

First-person narrator removed from action:
The Ones Who Walk Away from Omelas

Third-person, all-knowing narrator:
The Storm
A Good Man Is Hard to Find

The Rocking-Horse Winner
Where Are You Going, Where Have You Been? (paragraphs 1-13)

Third person, limited omniscience (with narrator seeing into one major character):
The Jilting of Granny Weatherall
The Five-Forty-Eight
To Build a Fire
Barn Burning
The Gospel According to Mark
The Open Boat
Young Goodman Brown
Everything That Rises Must Converge
Revelation
An Occurrence at Owl Creek Bridge
The Story of an Hour
Shiloh
The Catbird Seat

Third person, limited omniscience (with narrator seeing into one minor character):
The Death of Ivan Ilych (Part I only)

Objective or fly-on-the-wall point of view:
A Clean, Well-Lighted Place (paragraphs 2-75)
The Chrysanthemums

CHARACTER
Miss Brill
Sonny's Blues
Barn Burning (Sarty Snopes: a dynamic character, one who develops within the
    story)
The Chrysanthemums
The Death of Ivan Ilych
The Metamorphosis
A Good Man Is Hard to Find
Revelation
Paul's Case
Where Are You Going, Where Have You Been?

SETTING
A & P
A Rose for Emily
Miss Brill
The Five-Forty-Eight
Gimpel the Fool
A Clean, Well-Lighted Place
Araby
The Gospel According to Mark
The Open Boat
Young Goodman Brown

The Chrysanthemums
A Good Man Is Hard to Find
Paul's Case
The Yellow Wallpaper
Sweat
A Woman on a Roof
A Visit of Charity

TONE
The Tell-Tale Heart
Gimpel the Fool
Greasy Lake
Everything That Rises Must Converge
Barbie-Q
Where Are You Going, Where Have You Been?
First Confession
The Catbird Seat

STYLE
A Rose for Emily
The Tell-Tale Heart
The Jilting of Granny Weatherall
Greasy Lake
The Open Boat
Young Goodman Brown
Cathedral
Revelation
I Stand Here Ironing
A Haunted House

IRONY
The Appointment in Samarra
A Rose for Emily
The Tell-Tale Heart
The Jilting of Granny Weatherall
The Storm
To Build a Fire
The Open Boat (irony of fate)
The Lottery
Everything That Rises Must Converge
An Occurrence at Owl Creek Bridge
The Story of an Hour
The Rocking-Horse Winner
How I Met My Husband
The Conversion of the Jews
The Catbird Seat

SYMBOL
A Rose for Emily
The Tell-Tale Heart

The Jilting of Granny Weatherall
Greasy Lake (the lake itself)
A Clean, Well-Lighted Place
Araby
The Gospel According to Mark
The Open Boat
Young Goodman Brown
Cathedral
The Yellow Wallpaper
Sweat

MYTH, FOLKLORE, AND ARCHETYPE

The Appointment in Samarra
Godfather Death
Gimpel the Fool
Young Goodman Brown
The Lottery
On the Road
Where Are You Going, Where Have You Been?

SCIENCE FICTION

The Ones Who Walk Away from Omelas

FANTASY AND THE SUPERNATURAL

The Appointment in Samarra
Godfather Death
Gimpel the Fool
The Gospel According to Mark
Young Goodman Brown
The Parable of the Prodigal Son
The Lottery
The Ones Who Walk Away From Omelas
The Métamorphosis
On the Road
The Rocking-Horse Winner

HUMOR

Independence
A & P
Gimpel the Fool
Greasy Lake
Barbie-Q
How I Met My Husband
First Confession
The Conversion of the Jews
The Catbird Seat

Stories Arranged by Subject and Theme

In case you prefer to teach fiction according to its subjects and general themes, we have provided a list of stories that may be taken up together. Some instructors who arrange a course thematically like to *begin* with Chapter 6, "Theme," and its four stories.

DEFIANCE OF FATE
The Appointment in Samarra
Godfather Death
The Open Boat

DISABILITIES
Cathedral
Shiloh

DIVINE REVELATION
Gimpel the Fool
The Gospel According to Mark
The Death of Ivan Ilych
Revelation
On the Road

EPIPHANIES AND ILLUMINATIONS
Miss Brill
Greasy Lake
A Pair of Tickets
Araby
The Parable of the Prodigal Son
The Story of an Hour
The Use of Force
(See also *Divine revelation*)

FACING ONE'S OWN DEATH
The Jilting of Granny Weatherall
The Five-Forty-Eight
To Build a Fire
The Gospel According to Mark
The Open Boat
The Death of Ivan Ilych
A Good Man Is Hard to Find
An Occurrence at Owl Creek Bridge

FAMILIES
The Jilting of Granny Weatherall

Everyday Use
The Storm
A Pair of Tickets
Barn Burning
The Parable of the Prodigal Son
The Metamorphosis
A Good Man Is Hard to Find
The Defeated
The Rocking-Horse Winner
I Stand Here Ironing

FATHER-CHILD RELATIONSHIPS
The Storm
A Pair of Tickets
Barn Burning
The Parable of the Prodigal Son
The Death of Ivan Ilych
The Metamorphosis
Misery

FRIENDSHIP AND CAMARADERIE
Greasy Lake
The Open Boat
Cathedral

GENERATION GAPS
A & P
Greasy Lake
Araby
Everything That Rises Must Converge
The Defeated
Barbie-Q
Where Are You Going, Where Have You Been?
I Stand Here Ironing

HOLDING A JOB, WORK
A & P
The Five-Forty-Eight
A Clean, Well-Lighted Place
The Death of Ivan Ilych
Metamorphosis
Revelation
Sweat
How I Met My Husband
The Catbird Seat

HUMANITY AGAINST THE ELEMENTS
To Build a Fire
The Open Boat

ILLUSION AND REALITY

The Tell-Tale Heart
Greasy Lake
Gimpel the Fool
Araby
The Gospel According to Mark
Young Goodman Brown
The Chrysanthemums
The Death of Ivan Ilych
An Occurrence at Owl Creek Bridge
Paul's Case
On The Road
The Yellow Wallpaper
A Haunted House

INDIVIDUAL VERSUS SOCIETY

w/ 1984

Independence
A & P
A Rose for Emily
Gimpel the Fool
Barn Burning
Young Goodman Brown
The Lottery
The Ones Who Walk Away from Omelas
Paul's Case
The Conversion of the Jews

INGENIOUS DECEPTIONS

The Tell-Tale Heart
Young Goodman Brown
The Catbird Seat

LONELINESS

Miss Brill
The Five-Forty-Eight
A Clean Well-Lighted Place
The Chrysanthemums
Paul's Case
Misery

LOVE AND DESIRE

The Jilting of Granny Weatherall
Gimpel the Fool
The Storm
Araby
The Chrysanthemums
The Story of an Hour
A Woman on a Roof
The Woman Who Came at Six O'Clock

9

Shiloh
How I Met My Husband

MACHISMO AND SEXIST BEHAVIOR

A & P
The Five-Forty-Eight
Greasy Lake
Sweat
A Woman on a Roof

MAGIC AND THE OCCULT

The Appointment in Samarra
Godfather Death
Young Goodman Brown
The Rocking-Horse Winner
A Haunted House

MARRIAGES (THE GOOD, THE BAD, AND THE UGLY)

Gimpel the Fool
Cathedral
The Story of an Hour
The Yellow Wallpaper
Shiloh
Sweat
A Haunted House

MEDICINE, SICKNESS, AND HEALTH

The Yellow Wallpaper
The Use of Force

MOTHER-CHILD RELATIONSHIPS

The Jilting of Granny Weatherall
Everyday Use
A Pair of Tickets
Everything that Rises Must Converge
Revelation (the "ugly girl" and her mother)
The Rocking-Horse Winner
I Stand Here Ironing

MULTICULTURAL PERSPECTIVES

Independence
Sonny's Blues
Everyday Use
Gimpel the Fool
A Pair of Tickets
The Defeated
On the Road
Sweat
First Confession

The Conversion of the Jews

MURDER

A Rose for Emily
The Tell-Tale Heart
The Gospel According to Mark
A Good Man Is Hard to Find
Sweat

PRIDE BEFORE A FALL

The Five-Forty-Eight
Barn Burning
Everything That Rises Must Converge
Revelation

RELIGIOUS TRAINING IN CHILDHOOD

First Confession
The Conversion of the Jews

RICH PEOPLE AND POOR

Barn Burning
The Defeated

SEEING BEHIND PUBLIC FACES

A Rose for Emily
Young Goodman Brown
The Death of Ivan Ilych

SIBLINGS

Sonny's Blues
Everyday Use
A Pair of Tickets
The Parable of the Prodigal Son
The Metamorphosis

THE STRENGTH OF OLD PEOPLE

The Jilting of Granny Weatherall

VICTIMS AND VICTIMIZERS

The Tell-Tale Heart
The Five-Forty-Eight
A Good Man Is Hard to Find
The Yellow Wallpaper
Sweat
Where Are You Going, Where Have You Been?

WAR

An Occurrence at Owl Creek Bridge

THE WISH TO ABANDON EVERYTHING AND RUN AWAY

The Parable of the Prodigal Son
The Chrysanthemums
Paul's Case

WOMEN'S ASPIRATIONS

The Chrysanthemums
The Yellow Wallpaper
Shiloh
I Stand Here Ironing

1 *Reading a Story*

For a second illustration of a great detail in a story, a detail that sounds observed instead of invented (besides Defoe's "two shoes, not mates"), you might cite a classic hunk of hokum: H. Rider Haggard's novel of farfetched adventure, *She* (1887). Describing how the Amahagger tribesmen wildly dance by the light of unusual torches—embalmed corpses of the citizens of ancient Kor, left over in quantity—the narrator, Holly, remarks, "So soon as a mummy was consumed to the ankles, which happened in about twenty minutes, the feet were kicked away, and another put in its place." (Pass down another mummy, this one is guttering!) Notice the exact specification "in about twenty minutes" and the unforgettable discarding of the unburned feet, like a candle stub. Such detail, we think, bespeaks a tall-tale-teller of genius. (For this citation, we thank T. J. Binyon's review of *The Private Diaries of Sir Henry Rider Haggard* in *Times Literary Supplement*, 8 Aug. 1980.)

When you introduce students to the *tale* as a literary form, you might point out that even in this age of electronic entertainment, a few tales still circulate from mouth to ear. Ask them whether they have heard any good tales lately (other than dirty jokes). This tale reportedly has been circulated in Israel:

> Two Israeli agents, captured in an Arab country, are tied to stakes to be shot. While the firing squad stands in readiness, the Arab commander asks one of the captured men if he has any last request. For answer, the captive spits in the commander's face. From the other captive comes a wail: "For God's sake, Moishe, don't cause *trouble!*"

FABLE AND TALE

W. Somerset Maugham
THE APPOINTMENT IN SAMARRA, page 4

Maugham's retelling of this fable has in common with the Grimm tale "Godfather Death" not only the appearance of Death as a character, but also the moral or lesson that Death cannot be defied. Maugham includes this fable in his play *Sheppey* (1933), but it is probably best known as the epigraph to John O'Hara's novel *The Appointment in Samarra* (New York: Random House, 1934).

Students may be asked to recall other fables they know. To jog their memories, famous expressions we owe to Aesop ("sour grapes," "the lion's share," "dog in the manger," and others) may suggest the fables that gave them rise. At least, the fable of the hare and the tortoise should be familiar to any watcher of old Bugs Bunny cartoons.

Jakob and Wilhelm Grimm
GODFATHER DEATH, page 6

For all its brevity, "Godfather Death" illustrates typical elements of plot (discussed in the text on pages 9–11). That is the main reason for including it in this chapter (not to mention its intrinsic merits!). It differs from Updike's contemporary "A & P" in its starker characterizations, its summary method of telling, its terser descriptions of setting, and its element of magic and the supernatural. In its world, God, the Devil, and Death walk the highway. If students can be shown these differences, then probably they will be able to distinguish most tales from most short stories.

"Godfather Death" may be useful, too, in a class discussion of point of view. On page 19, you will find some ways in which this tale is stronger for having an omniscient narrator. If you go on to deal with symbolism, you may wish to come back to this tale for a few illustrations of wonderful, suggestive properties: the magical herb, Death's underground cave, and its "thousands upon thousands" of flickering candles.

This is a grim tale even for Grimm: a young man's attentions to a beautiful princess bring about his own destruction. In a fairy tale it is usually dangerous to defy some arbitrary law; and in doing so here the doctor breaks a binding contract. From the opening, we know the contract will be an evil one—by the father's initial foolishness in spurning God. Besides, the doctor is a thirteenth child—an unlucky one.

Possible visual aids are reproductions of the "Dance of Death" woodcuts by Hans Holbein the younger. Have any students seen Ingmar Bergman's film *The Seventh Seal*, and can they recall how Death was personified?

Anne Sexton has a sophisticated retelling of "Godfather Death," in which the doctor's guttering candle is "no bigger than an eyelash," in her *Transformations,* a collection of poems based on Grimm (Boston: Houghton, 1971). "Godfather Death" is seldom included in modern selections of fairy tales for children. The splendid translation by Lore Segal appeared in *The Juniper Tree and Other Tales from Grimm,* selected by Segal, with four tales translated by Randall Jarrell (New York: Farrar, 1973), where a fine drawing by Maurice Sendak accompanies it. Bruno Bettelheim has nothing specific to say about "Godfather Death" but has much of interest to say about fairy tales in his *The Uses of Enchantment* (New York: Knopf, 1976). Though Bettelheim's study is addressed primarily to adults "with children in their care," any college student fascinated by fairy tales would find it stimulating.

Chuang Tzu
INDEPENDENCE, page 8

Chuang Tzu's parables are famous in Chinese culture, both as works of intrinsic literary merit and as pithy expressions of Taoist philosophy. Parables are important literary genres in traditional societies. They reflect a cultural aesthetic that appreciates the power of literary artistry while putting it to the use of illustrating moral and religious ideas. Clarity is a key virtue in a parable or moral fable. Its purpose is not merely to entertain but also to instruct.

Chuang Tzu's celebrated parable suggests the uneasy relationship between philosophy and power in ancient China. It was not necessarily a safe gesture to decline the public invitation of a king, and the refusal of employment could be construed as an insult or censure. Chuang understands that the only safe way to turn down a monarch is with wit and charm. He makes his moral point, but with self-deprecating humor.

In his indispensable book, *Essentials of Chinese Literary Art* (Belmont, CA: Duxbury, 1979, p. 46), James J. Y. Liu of Stanford University comments on the sly rhetoric of this parable:

Instead of solemnly declaring that worldly power and glory are all in vain, Chuang Tzu makes us see their absurdity by comparing them to a dead tortoise. At the same time, life unburdened with official duties is not idealized, but compared to the tortoise dragging its tail in the mud.

The *Tzu* following Chuang's name is an honorific meaning *master*. The philosopher's historical name was Chuang Chou. The Chinese surname is conventionally put first, so Chuang is the proper term to use for the author.

This parable was a favorite of the Argentinean writer Jorge Luis Borges, who was fascinated by the Chinese fabular tradition.

Jesus's "Parable of the Prodigal Son" (Luke 15: 11–32) is found on page 222 in the chapter on "Theme." It may be interesting for students to compare the differing techniques of these two classic parables from different traditions.

PLOT

THE SHORT STORY

John Updike
A & P, page 12

Within this story, Sammy rises to a kind of heroism. Despite the conventional attitudes he expresses in the first half of the story (his usual male reactions to girls in two-piece bathing suits, his put-down of *all* girls' minds: "a little buzz like a bee in a glass jar"), he comes to feel sympathy for the girls as human beings. He throws over his job to protest against their needless humiliation, and in so doing he asserts his criticism of supermarket society, a deadly world of "sheep" and "houseslaves" whom dynamite couldn't budge from their dull routines. What harm in a little innocent showing off—in, for once, a display of nonconformity?

Sammy isn't sophisticated. He comes from a family of proletarian beer drinkers and thinks martinis are garnished with mint. His language is sometimes pedestrian: "Really, I thought that was so cute." But he is capable of fresh and accurate observations—his description of the way Queenie walks on her bare feet, his comparison of the "clean bare plane" of her upper chest to "a dented sheet of metal tilted in the light." (Could Sammy be capable of so poetic an observation, or is this Updike's voice?)

Carefully plotted for all its seemingly casual telling, "A & P" illustrates typical elements. The *setting* is clear from Updike's opening paragraph ("I'm in the third checkout slot . . . with my hand on a box of HiHo crackers"). Relatively long for so brief a story, the *exposition* takes up most of the story's first half. Portraying Queenie and the other girls in loving detail, this exposition helps make Sammy's later gesture of heroism understandable. It establishes, also, that Sammy feels at odds with his job, and so foreshadows his heroism. He reacts against butcher McMahon's piggishness: "patting his mouth and looking after them sizing up their joints." *Dramatic conflict* arrives with the appearance of Lengel, the manager, and his confrontation with the girls. Lengel catches Sammy smiling—we can guess the clerk is in for trouble. Crisis and climax are practically one, but if you care to distinguish them, the *crisis* may be found in the paragraph "I thought and said 'No' but it wasn't about that I was thinking," in which Sammy hovers on the brink of his decision. The *climax* is his announcement "I quit"; the *conclusion* is his facing a bleaker future. The last sentence implies not only that Sammy will have trouble getting another job, but that if he continues to go through life as an uncompromising man of principle, then life from now on is going to be rough.

15

In "A & P" and the fairy tale "Godfather Death," the plots are oddly similar. In both, a young man smitten with a young woman's beauty, makes a sacrifice in order to defend her against his grim overlord. (It is far worse, of course, to have Death for an overlord than Lengel.) If this resemblance doesn't seem too abstract, it may be worth briefly pursuing. The stories, to be sure, are more different than similar, but one can show how Updike is relatively abundant in his descriptions of characters and setting and goes more deeply into the central character's motivation—as short-story authors usually do, unlike most writers of tales.

For a fresh explication of this story, see Janet Overmeyer, "Courtly Love in the A & P," in *Notes on Contemporary Literature* for May 1972 (West Georgia College, Carrollton, GA 30117).

Updike himself reads this story and five others on *Selected Stories,* a set of two audiotape cassettes (169 minutes, $15.95) produced by Random House (ISBN 0-394-55040-4), and available in shops or from American Audio Prose Library, whose phone number is (800) 447-2275. This is a crisp, dry reading that brings out the humor of "A & P."

2 Point of View

For other illustrations of the relatively scarce second-person point of view, see Richard Hugo's poetry collection, *31 Letters and 13 Dreams* (New York: Norton, 1977): "In Your Fugitive Dream," "In Your War Dream," "In Your Young Dream," and others. These also appear in Hugo's collected poems, *Making Certain It Goes On* (New York: Norton, 1984).

William Faulkner
A Rose for Emily, page 25

In his opening sentence, the narrator speaks for the whole town of Jefferson, Mississippi, and throughout the story he always says *we*, never *I*, and he is never named. He is an interested bystander, not a participant in the story's main events, some of which presumably took place before he was born. Telling the story from the point of view of such an observer gives Faulkner advantages. The narrator can report events with detachment, and the tone of his story, often matter-of-fact and gossipy ("the Griersons held themselves a little too high for what they really were"), seems earthbound and convincing. It prepares us to accept on trust his later, more surprising, disclosures. Told from, say, the point of view of the central character herself, "A Rose for Emily" would be a radically different story: one without murder or necrophilia (because Miss Emily cannot acknowledge death), without mystery and suspense, and without a final revelation.

Students will want to make sure of exactly what happens in the story. From the detail that the strand of hair is *iron-gray*, it appears that Emily lay beside Homer's body recently, long after it was rotten; probably lay beside it many times, for her pillow is clearly indented. Just as she had clung to her conviction that her father and Colonel Sartoris were still alive, she had come to believe that Homer Barron had faithfully married her, and she successfully ignored for forty years all the testimony of her senses. The conclusion of the story is foreshadowed by Emily's refusal to allow her father to be buried, by her purchase of rat poison, by the disappearance of Homer Barron, and by the pervasive smell of decay. In fact, these foreshadowings are so evident it is a wonder that, for those reading the story for the first time, the ending is so surprising. Much of the surprise seems due to the narrator's back-and-forth, unchronological method of telling. We aren't told that (1) Emily buys poison, (2) Homer disappears, and (3) there is a mysterious odor—which chain of events might immediately rouse our suspicions. Instead, we hear about (in order) odor, poison, and disappearance. By this arrangement, any connection between these events is made to seem a little less obvious.

Having satisfied their natural interest in the final horror of the story, students can be led to discuss why "A Rose for Emily" isn't a mere thriller. Why (they may be asked) is the story called "A Rose"? No literal rose appears in it, although there may be two serious puns in paragraphs 5 and 6 ("a faint dust rose," "They rose when she entered"), and in the final description of the bedroom there are "curtains of faded rose color" and "rose-shaded lights." Perhaps Emily herself is the white rose of Jefferson (like the heroine of *The White Rose of Memphis*, a novel by Faulkner's scribbling grandfather). But the usual connotations of roses will apply. A rose is a gift to a loved one, and the whole story is the narrator's tribute to Emily.

But, some may object, how can anyone wish to pay tribute to a bloated old poisoner who sleeps with a corpse? The narrator patiently gives us reasons for his sympathy. As a girl, Emily was beautiful, a "slender figure in white," fond of society. But her hopes were thwarted by her domineering father, whose horsewhip discouraged suitors from her door. Her strength and pride vanquished all who would invade her house: the new Board of Aldermen who tried to collect her taxes, the Baptist minister sent to lecture her on her morals, the relatives from Atlanta who eventually departed. "It is important," Ray B. West writes, "to realize that during the period of Emily's courtship the town became Emily's allies in a contest between Emily and her Grierson cousins, 'because the two female cousins were even more Grierson than Miss Emily had ever been'" ("Atmosphere and Theme in Faulkner's 'A Rose for Emily,'" *Perspective* Summer 1949: 239–45).

Suggestions abound. Emily's refusal to recognize change is suggested in the symbol of her invisible watch (paragraph 7), with its hint that she lives according to a private, secret time of her own. Her house seems an extension of her person in its "stubborn and coquettish decay" (2). Now it stands amid gasoline pumps, refusing (like its owner) to be part of a new era. The story contains many such images of stasis: when Emily confronts the aldermen, she looks bloated, "like a body long submerged in motionless water"—a foreshadowing, perhaps, of the discovery of Homer's long-guarded dust.

Some have read the story as an allegory: Homer Barron is the crude, commercial North who invades, like a carpetbagger. Emily, with her faithful ex-slave, is the Old South, willing to be violated. In an interview with students at the University of Virginia, Faulkner played down such North-South symbolism. "I don't say that's not valid and not there," he said, "but . . . [I was] simply writing about people." (The whole interview in which Faulkner discusses this story, not very helpfully, is in *Faulkner in the University,* ed. Frederick Gwynn and Joseph Blotner, University Press of Virginia, 1959.)

Still, it is clear that Emily, representing an antebellum first family, receives both Faulkner's admiration and his criticism for resisting change. "The theme of the story," according to C. W. M. Johnson, "can be stated: 'If one resists change, he must love and live with death,' and in this theme it is difficult not to see an implied criticism of the South" (*The Explicator* VI [No. 7] May 1948: item 45). But Faulkner's criticism, Ray B. West, Jr., feels, is leveled at the North as well. West makes much of the passage in which Faulkner discerns two possible views of Time (55). If, for the South, Time is "a huge meadow which no winter ever quite touches," then for the North it is a mere "mathematical progression" and "a diminishing road." West would propose, for a statement of the story's theme: "One must neither resist nor wholly accept change, for to do either is to live as though one were never to die; that is, to live *with* Death without knowing it" (*The Explicator* VII [No. 1] Oct. 1948: item 8).

Studying "A Rose for Emily" may help prepare students for Faulkner's "Barn Burning" (Chapter 5), whose central character, the son of a sharecropper, is Colonel Sartoris Snopes. "A Rose for Emily" clearly is in the tradition of the Gothic story, for it has a crumbling mansion, a mysterious servant, and a hideous secret. For comparison, one might have students read Poe's "The Tell-Tale Heart," if they don't know it already: another story of violence and madness, but told (unlike "A Rose") from the point of view of the violent madman.

For a valuable discussion of the story's point of view see John Daremo, "Insight into Horror: The Narrator in Faulkner's 'A Rose for Emily,'" in Sylvan Barnet, ed., *A Short Guide to Writing about Literature,* 5th ed. (Boston: Little, Brown, 1985). A more superficial view of the story is expressed in this limerick by a celebrated bard, Anonymous:

Miss Emily, snobbish and cranky,
Used to horse around town with a Yankee.
    When she'd wake up in bed

With the dust of the dead,
She would sneeze in her delicate hanky.

When discussion of the story flagged, JoAnna Stephens Mink of Illinois State University, Normal, hit upon a way to rouse her students to fresh attention. She conducted a mock murder trial. Dividing a class of twenty-five into three groups (defense, prosecution, judge-and-jury), she spent half a class period letting each group prepare its evidence (admitting only faithful references to the story), and then devoted the other half to presentation and arguments. It was assumed, of course, that Emily was still alive and able to stand trial. After animated debate, judge and jury found Emily not guilty on grounds of insanity—but other outcomes might be possible. For Professor Mink's full account of this experiment, see "We Brought Emily Grierson to Trial" in *Exercise Exchange,* Spring 1984: 17–19.

Another instructor, after reading about Professor Mink's bright idea in a previous edition's manual, tried it and reported great success with it. He is Saul Cohen of County College of Morris. He assigned the story to be read and told students to prepare their cases for trial. When the day arrived to bring Emily before the bar of justice, he devoted fifteen minutes to letting the opposing counsel compare notes, determine strategy, and select their spokespersons. After the presentation of briefs, each side was allotted three minutes for rebuttal. The jury then deliberated before the rest of the class so that all could appreciate their discussions and their balloting. He himself served as judge and textual *raisonneur,* summing up positions taken by each side and transcribing on a blackboard summaries of arguments raised, in language acceptable to all, for counsel and jury to consider. The defense argued that reason existed to suspect Emily's faithful, highly protective, fast-disappearing servant of having done the deed and, having raised this uncertainty, persuaded the jury to find the defendant not guilty. For Mr. Cohen's full account of his experience, see *Exercise Exchange* for October 1990.

Faulkner's story resembles a riddle, argues Charles Clay Doyle of the University of Georgia in a recent article. The resemblance lies not so much in the story's structure or rhetoric "as in the tricky way it presents clues, clues that tell the truth but at the same time mislead or fail to enlighten. The pleasure of discovery experienced by readers of the story resembles the pleasure we take in learning the answer to a riddle: we are astonished that the solution, which now seems so obvious, so inevitable, could have eluded us."

Furthermore, Doyle finds an allusion to a well-known riddle in Faulkner's final description of Emily's chamber: Homer's "two mute shoes and the discarded socks." The riddle is, "What has a tongue but can't speak?" (Answer: a shoe.) Taking the phrase *mute shoes* to echo the riddle, Doyle thinks the shoes a pair of silent witnesses who, in their way, resemble the narrator himself, who shows us the truth but does not state it outright ("Mute Witnesses: Faulkner's Use of a Popular Riddle," *Mississippi Folklore Register* 24 [1990]: 53–55).

Katherine Mansfield
MISS BRILL, page 33

For discussion, we present here some possible answers to the questions on pages 36–37. You may not agree with all of them.

QUESTIONS

1. *What is the point of view in "Miss Brill"? Why is the story the better for this method of telling?* "Miss Brill" is written with selective omniscience: from the third-person viewpoint of a nonparticipant, but one who sees events through the eyes of the story's protagonist. In paragraph 5, Miss Brill notices that there is "something funny" about her fellow park sitters: "They were odd, silent, nearly all old, and from the way they stared they looked as though they'd just come from dark little rooms or even—even cupboards!" (That she might look the same to them never enters her head—until she is forced to see herself as others see her.) Because we as readers experience the day's happenings from the perspective of Miss Brill, we come to understand and to sympathize with the sweet old dear, even go along with her sudden view of herself as an actress in a play performed every Sunday. To an intense degree we share her dismay and hurt when she overhears herself called a "stupid old thing" and her furpiece ridiculed as "exactly like a fried whiting."

2. *Where and in what season does Mansfield's story take place? How do we know? Would the effect be the same if the story were set, say, in a remote Alaskan village in the summertime?* In the opening paragraph Mansfield makes clear that Miss Brill is in the Jardins Publiques and, therefore, somewhere in France: in a small town, it seems, since the Sunday band concert is a big feature of local life. In paragraph 6 we learn that the sea is visible from the park. We also know that the season is autumn. Miss Brill has taken her fur out of its box for the first time in a long while. The trees are covered with "yellow leaves down drooping" (6). A chill in the air foreshadows the chill of Miss Brill's dashed spirits at the end of the story.

3. *What details provide revealing insights into Miss Brill's character and life-style?* Miss Brill lives frugally, alone in a small room, eking out a meager living by teaching English and reading the newspaper aloud to an invalid gentleman four afternoons a week. She seems happy with her lot even though her daily activities are drab by most standards and her pleasures are small ones. Her well-worn fur delights her, and an almond in the Sunday honey-cake is cause for rejoicing.

4. *What draws Miss Brill to the park every Sunday? What is the nature of the startling revelation that delights her on the day this story takes place?* Because she lives on the fringes of life in her small French town, Miss Brill regards her solitary Sundays in the park as the highlight of her week. Here, watching the people who come and go and eavesdropping on their conversations, she feels a connection with her fellow human beings. The smallest details about them excite her interest. She comes to feel herself one of them, an actor in life's drama. So caught up does she become in the sudden revelation that all the world's a stage and that she, like everyone else, has a part to play, that she has a mystical experience. In her mind, she merges with the other players, and "it seemed to Miss Brill that in another moment all of them, all the whole company, would begin singing" (10).

5. *Comment on the last line. What possible explanations might there be for Miss Brill's thinking that she "heard something crying?"* Miss Brill, who loves her fur as if it were a living pet or companion, is probably capable of thinking it was that "little rogue" she heard crying over the cruelty of the young couple in the park. It's possible, too, for the reader to believe that Miss Brill actually does hear a sound and that the "something crying" is herself. Perhaps she has, as Eudora Welty surmises in "The Reading and Writing of Short Stories," suffered a defeat that "one feels sure . . . is forever" (*The Atlantic Monthly*, Feb.-Mar. 1949).

James Baldwin
SONNY'S BLUES, page 37

The narrative structure of "Sonny's Blues" is more complex and interesting than it may seem at first glance. The story reads so smoothly that it is easy to overlook the fact that it begins *in medias res*. "Sonny's Blues" opens with the title character's arrest for the sale and possession of heroin; it ends in a jazz club with the older brother's ultimate understanding and acceptance of Sonny. This linear narrative is interrupted, however, by a long flashback that describes the uneasy earlier relation between the brothers. Since their parents are dead when the story opens, we meet the father and mother only in the flashback. The mother is the central moral figure of the story. Her last conversation with the narrator ultimately becomes a crucial part of his impetus to reconcile with Sonny. (The other, more immediately compelling motivation is the death of the narrator's small daughter from polio: "My trouble," the narrator confesses, "made his real.") When the narrator promises to take care of his kid brother, his mother warns him it will be hard. She has seen enough of the world's trouble to be fatalistic. "You may not be able to stop nothing from happening," she tells him, before adding, "But you got to let him know you's *there*." In one sense, "Sonny's Blues" is essentially the story of the narrator's slow, difficult process of living up to the promise he gave his mother.

The basic conflict of the story, which is—it is essential to remember—*the older brother's story,* is the narrator's inability to understand and respect the life of the younger brother he so clearly loves. Baldwin carefully establishes the brothers as opposites. The narrator is a cautious, respectable family man. He teaches math and is proud of his professional standing. Living in a Harlem housing project, he consciously protects himself from the dangers that surround him. Notice how intensely he appears to dislike Sonny's friend, the drug addict, when he encounters him in the school courtyard at the beginning of the story. However, the narrator is also compassionate, and it is important to see, in the same episode, how quickly he recognizes and responds to the addict's battered humanity. That gesture prefigures his reconciliation with his brother. Sonny, by contrast, is a romantic artist who is not afraid of taking risks to pursue the things he desires. His passion for music makes him impatient with everything else. He drops out of school. In his brother's view he is "wild" but not "hard or evil or disrespectful."

The outer story of "Sonny's Blues" is the title character's rehabilitation from drug addiction, reconciliation with his estranged brother, and recognition as a jazz pianist. The inner story is the narrator's spiritual and emotional growth into a person who can understand his younger brother's unorthodox, but nonetheless valuable, life. There should be no doubt that Baldwin, the former boy preacher, saw the narrator's inner growth as in some sense religious. The final scene in the nightclub ends with a religious vision of the blues. Listening to the group leader, Creole, play, the narrator says:

> He hit something in all of them, he hit something in me, myself, and the music tightened and deepened, apprehension began to beat the air. Creole began to tell us what the blues were about. They were not about anything very new. He and his boys up there were keeping it new, at the risk of ruin, destruction, madness, and death, in order to find new ways to make us listen. For, while the tale of how we suffer, and how we are delighted, and how we may triumph is never new, it always must be heard. There isn't any other tale to tell, and it's the only light we've got in all this darkness.

That passage not only offers as good an explanation of the blues and jazz as one is likely to find anywhere; it speaks cogently on the purpose of all art. It is worth having students pause over it. The final scene of "Sonny's Blues" is set in a dark, smoky nightclub, and its lyric quality marks a noticeable shift in tone from the realistic narrative style that preceded it. As the closing episode gains force along with the music it describes, it becomes a kind of vision for the narrator. In intellectual terms (for, after all, the narrator is a reflective math teacher), the vision brings him to a deep understanding of the human importance of art and the terrible cost of its creation. In emotional terms, his comprehension of jazz is inseparable from his sudden and profound understanding of Sonny's identity and motivations as an artist.

Unless the reader can accept the narrator's capacity for this transforming insight, the story is flawed by the sudden change of tone. Several critics have expressed their problem with the conclusion. They feel that Baldwin's authorial voice has replaced the narrator's. As Joseph Featherstone said in an initial review of *Going to Meet the Man*, the volume in which "Sonny's Blues" first appeared:

> The terms seem wrong; clearly this is not the voice of Sonny or his brother, it is the intrusive voice of Baldwin the boy preacher who has turned his back on the store front tabernacles but cannot forget the sound of angels' wings beating around his head. (*New Republic*, Nov. 27, 1965)

[reprinted in Kenneth Kinnamon's "Twentieth Century Views" collection, cited below]

On one level, Featherstone's criticism makes sense. The tone of the final scene is elevated and religious. It is quite unlike the narrator's opening voice. However, a reader, wrapped up in the power of the final scene, is entitled to respond that the entire story up until then exists to justify this passage. "Sonny's Blues" is not merely the story of the narrator's experiences; it is the tale of his inner transformation. The final scene is the demonstration of the older brother's spiritual growth which his earlier experiences of death and loss have motivated. In understanding and accepting Sonny, he has enlarged his soul enough to understand Sonny's music, too.

There is a large, interesting body of criticism on James Baldwin's work. Kenneth Kinnamon's "Twentieth Century Views" critical collection, *James Baldwin* (Englewood Cliffs, NJ: Prentice Hall, 1974) remains extremely useful. John M. Reilly's cogent sociological essay, "'Sonny's Blues': James Baldwin's Image of Black Community," will be interesting for students writing on the story. Sherley Anne Williams's "The Black Musician: The Black Hero as Light Bearer" examines the metaphoric role of the musician in Baldwin's work with special attention given to "Sonny's Blues." Bruce Bawer's insightful overview of Baldwin's fiction, "Race and Art: James Baldwin," in his critical collection, *The Aspect of Eternity* (St. Paul, MN: Graywolf, 1993) will be very useful for students planning a paper on the author. Bawer surveys Baldwin's career in a biographical context and candidly evaluates the strengths and weaknesses of the novels. Quincy Troupe's *James Baldwin: The Legacy* (New York: Simon and Schuster, 1989) contains memoirs, tributes, and appreciations by fellow writers, including Maya Angelou, William Styron, Toni Morrison, and Chinua Achebe. Carolyn Wedin Sylvander's *James Baldwin* (New York: Ungar, 1980) also provides a reliable survey of the author's work, though her discussion of "Sonny's Blues" is brief.

Before students plunge into the secondary material on Baldwin, however, they should be encouraged to read the author's own essays. Baldwin was one of the finest essayists of his time, and there is no better introduction to his work than the title piece of *Notes of a Native Son*, Baldwin's passionate memoir of his Harlem youth.

A lively interview with Baldwin in which the author comments on race relations in America and on the cultural role of black and white artists is available on audiotape cassette from the American Audio Prose Library, Inc., Box 842, Columbia, MO 65205; phone number for orders, (800) 447-2275.

Edgar Allan Poe

THE TELL-TALE HEART, page 61

Poe's story abounds with details that identify his narrator as unreliable, and students will probably enjoy pointing them out. Even in paragraph 1, when he admits to being "very, very dreadfully nervous" and mentions his "disease," the storyteller seems overwrought. By paragraph 2, when he confesses that he made up his mind to kill an old man because of his eye, the narrator's looniness is obvious. Ironically, his madness seems especially clear when he praises his own wisdom, caution, and foresight (paragraph 3).

A rational explanation for the terrifying heartbeat may occur to some students: the madman hears the pounding of his *own* heart. Who knows? All that matters to the story is the narrator's leap to the conclusion that he hears his victim's heart still going strong.

What suggestions do we get from the old man's baleful eye? Is it the all-seeing gaze of the Almighty? Daniel Hoffman has argued that the old man is a father-figure, perhaps even a Father-Figure, and that in striking the old man's eye "the young madman strikes, symbolically, at his sexual power." Perhaps, too, the vulture eye belongs to Time, the narrator's mortal enemy. (See *Poe Poe Poe Poe Poe Poe Poe* [New York: Anchor, 1973] 221-27.)

If Hoffman is right, then perhaps there is a theme in Poe's story; although perhaps it isn't essential to find any. (XJK comments: Once, after a class had read a Poe tale, a wonderful controversy broke out when someone complained, "This story doesn't really say anything." All of us tried to sum up the story's theme, failed miserably, and at last decided that there is a place in literature for stories that don't say anything in particular, but supply their readers with memorable nightmares and dreams.)

Fairy tales, too, often do without clearly discernible themes and stir us powerfully. Bruno Bettelheim contends that fairy tales are therapeutic in his study of them, *The Uses of Enchantment* (New York: Knopf, 1976). Bettelheim urges that people who read fairy tales to children not talk about what the tales mean. Is Poe, perhaps, also good for your mental health, and not to be analyzed endlessly?

3   Character

Katherine Anne Porter
THE JILTING OF GRANNY WEATHERALL, page 70

Suggested here are some possible answers to the questions at the end of "The Jilting of Granny Weatherall." Other answers, of equal merit, may occur to you and your students. Other questions may occur as well.

QUESTIONS

1. *In the very first paragraph, what does the writer tell us about Ellen (Granny Weatherall)?* That Ellen Weatherall is feisty, accustomed to having her way, and unwilling to be treated like the sick old woman she is, all comes through the story from the start.

2. *What does the name of Weatherall have to do with Granny's nature (or her life story)? What other traits or qualities do you find in her?* Granny has "weathered all"—unrequited love, marriage, the birth of five children, early widowhood, backbreaking labor, "milk-leg and double pneumonia," the loss of her favorite daughter, and the frustrations of old age. Her victories over adversity have made her scornful of her daughter Cornelia, who seems to her weak and inadequate. Granny is tough and inclined to hold a grudge. She has never forgiven the man who jilted her. So overweening is her pride, in fact, that at the moment of her death, when she wants a sign and fails to perceive one, she decides she will "never forgive."

3. *"Her bones felt loose, and floated around in her skin, and Doctor Harry floated like a balloon" (paragraph 6). What do you understand from this statement? By what other remarks does the writer indicate Granny's condition? In paragraph 56, why does Father Connolly tickle Granny's feet? At what other moments in the story does she fail to understand what is happening, or confuse the present with the past?* Granny is very ill, her sense of reality distorted by lengthening periods of confusion. The story quite convincingly ushers Granny Weatherall by fits and starts into an altered state of consciousness preceding death. Granny's weakened grasp on reality is again apparent: when the doctor "appeared to float up to the ceiling and out" (paragraph 7); when "the pillow rose and floated under her" and she thought she heard leaves, or newspapers, rustling (8); when she pondered her impossible plans for "tomorrow" (17 and 26), in her belief that she could, if she wanted to, "pack up and move back to her own house" (24); in the distortions that creep into Granny's sense of the passage of time (28, 29, 36, 37, 42, 43, 50, 56, and 57); when she feels the pillow rising again (29); in Granny's sporadic inability to hear (31 and 32); in her belief that there are ants in the bed (40); in Granny's occasional inability to speak clearly enough to be understood (40 and 53); when Granny has hallucinations in which she confronts her daughter Hapsy (41, 50, and 60); in the doctor's "rosy nimbus" (51); in Granny's failure to comprehend that Father Connolly is not tickling her feet but administering the last rites of the Catholic Church (56). (In the anointing of the sick, formerly known as Extreme Unction, the priest makes a sign of the cross with oil upon the eyes, ears, nose, mouth, hands, and feet of the person in danger of death, while praying for his or her soul.)

4. *Exactly what happened to Ellen Weatherall sixty years earlier? What effects did this*

event have on her? George, the man she was to marry, had failed to show up for the wedding. This blow to Ellen's pride had left permanent scars even though Ellen had subsequently lived a full and useful life. It is hard to say whether her exacting, imperious, unforgiving ways resulted from the jilting—or caused it!

5. *In paragraph 49, who do you guess to be the man who "cursed like a sailor's parrot"? In paragraph 56, who do you assume is the man driving the cart? Is the fact that these persons are not clearly labeled and identified a failure on the author's part?* The most likely guess about the man who "cursed like a sailor's parrot" is that he was John, the man Ellen eventually married. Presumably John had always loved her and was angry because she had been so deeply hurt. The identity of the man driving the cart is more nebulous. Was he George? John? A confused amalgam of the two? That the reader remains unsure is not a fault in the story. The dreamlike haze surrounding the man's identity beautifully reflects Granny's loosening hold on reality.

6. *What is "stream of consciousness" (the term is discussed on page 24)? Would you call "The Jilting of Granny Weatherall" a stream of consciousness story? Refer to the story in your reply.* The story's point of view is one of selective omniscience. The events are reported in the third person by a narrator who can see into Granny Weatherall's mind. When Granny is lucid, the story proceeds in tidy chronological order. In the story's most interesting passages—especially in paragraphs 17–18 and 24–31—Porter uses stream of consciousness with great skill to present the randomly mingled thoughts and impressions that move through Granny's dying mind. By fragmenting Granny's thoughts, by having her shuttle back and forth between reality and fantasy, by distorting her sense of the passage of time, the author manages to persuade us that the way Granny experiences dying must be nearly universal.

7. *Sum up the character of the daughter Cornelia.* Cornelia, evidently the oldest of Granny's children, is a dutiful daughter—a fact resented by her cantankerous mother (10). Granny feels demeaned by her knowledge that Cornelia often humors her to keep peace. And, like mothers everywhere, Granny regards her daughter as far less competent than herself. Cornelia is tenderer, less tough than Granny. She weeps beside the deathbed. The old woman fails to appreciate her daughter's care and compassion because she scorns her own need of them.

8. *Why doesn't Granny's last child, Hapsy, come to her mother's deathbed?* Hapsy, the youngest child and her mother's favorite, died young. Paragraph 41 suggests that she may have died giving birth to a son.

9. *Would you call the character of Doctor Harry "flat" or "round"? Why is his flatness or roundness appropriate to the story?* A "flat" character, the doctor is little more than a prop in this account of Granny's dying. There is no reason for him to be more than that, for it is Granny's life and death that we are meant to focus on.

10. *How is this the story of another "jilting"? What is similar between that fateful day of sixty years ago (described in paragraphs 29, 49, and 61) and the time when Granny is dying? This time, who is the "bridegroom" who is not in the house?* Before talking about the final paragraph, why not read aloud to your students the parable of the wise and foolish virgins (Matthew 25:1-13)?

> Then shall the kingdom of heaven be likened unto ten virgins, which took their lamps, and went forth to meet the bridegroom.
>
> 2   And five of them were wise, and five were foolish.
> 3   They that were foolish took their lamps, and took no oil with them:

4   But the wise took oil in their vessels with their lamps.
5   While the bridegroom tarried, they all slumbered and slept.
6   And at midnight there was a cry made, Behold, the bridegroom cometh; go ye out to meet him.
7   Then all those virgins arose, and trimmed their lamps.
8   And the foolish said unto the wise, Give us of your oil, for our lamps are gone out.
9   But the wise answered, saying, Not so; lest there be not enough for us and you: but go ye rather to them that sell, and buy for yourselves.
10 And while they went to buy, the bridegroom came; and they that were ready went in with him to the marriage: and the door was shut.
11 Afterward came also the other virgins, saying, Lord, Lord, open to us.
12 But he answered and said, Verily I say unto you, I know you not.
13 Watch therefore; for ye know neither the day nor the hour wherein the Son of Man cometh.

Evidently, the bridegroom Granny awaits at the end of the story is Christ. When he does not appear, she feels jilted for a second time. Why doesn't he come? Why does Granny not receive the sign she asks for? Is it because her pride is so overweening ("I'll never forgive it") as to keep her from salvation? Is it because of her refusal to stay prepared for death (18)? Or did she receive her sign (the last rites of the Church) and merely fail to perceive it? Students may object to the apparent grimness of the ending. Some of them are likely to insist that Granny gets worse than she deserves, that Porter has allowed her symbolism to run roughshod over her humanity. Divergent opinions may spark a lively discussion.

11. *"This is the story of an eighty-year-old woman lying in bed, getting groggy, and dying; I can't see why it should interest anybody."* How would you answer this critic? Such a critic will be hard to convince. But perhaps discussion can show that the story is remarkable for its condensation of a long life into a few pages. How does it feel to die? All of us find the question interesting, and Porter answers it. Although Edith Wharton has argued that it is not the nature of a short story to develop a character (in *The Writing of Fiction* [New York: Scribner's, 1925]), "The Jilting of Granny Weatherall" certainly makes character its central concern. We finish the story persuaded that we know Ellen Weatherall very well indeed—better than she knows herself.

Here is a bleak reading of the story for possible discussion: For sixty years Ellen Weatherall has suppressed the memory of George, the man she loved, who jilted her. She prays not to remember him, lest she follow him down into the pit of Hell (29). If she remembers him, she herself will be damned—yet she remembers him. She longs to see him again (42), imagines him standing by her deathbed (30). In the end she beholds the pit: a darkness that will swallow up light. For the sake of a man, she has lost her soul.

But is the story so grim an account of one woman's damnation? It seems hardly a mortal sin to remember a person and an event so crucial in one's life; damnation seems undeserved. We sense that the author actually admires Granny's defiance in blowing out the light at the end. To say the least, the story is splendidly ambiguous.

"Granny Weatherall" may be a good means to approach Tolstoi's *The Death of Ivan Ilych* (page 269). The leading fact of each story is death, or preparation for it. Ivan Ilych, despite his useless career, overcomes pride and dies in joyous illumination. Ellen Weatherall's life has been fruitful and full; but, proud to the end, she dies in spiritual anguish.

"The Jilting of Granny Weatherall" lent itself effectively to the PBS television film series "The American Short Story," obtainable on videotape for classroom viewing. Anyone interested in writing for television might care to see Corinne Jacker's excellent script, reprinted in *The American Short Story,* Volume 2 (New York: Dell, 1980), together with a revealing interview with the scriptwriter on the problems of adapting "Granny"—such as a dearth of physical action in the present—and Carolyn G. Heilbrun's short critical essay on the Porter story.

Porter's familiarity with illness and the threat of death may have been drawn from memory. As Joan Givner recounts in her biography, *Katherine Anne Porter* (New York: Simon, 1982), Porter had to struggle for years against bronchial troubles and tuberculosis. Defiantly, she endured to age ninety.

John Cheever
THE FIVE-FORTY-EIGHT, page 78

The power of this remarkable story comes from the depth and complexity of its two main characters. Cheever creates a cold, manipulative, egotistic figure in Blake. He is a man who is outwardly capable but inwardly empty. He understands with keen clarity the public behavior of people, but he has almost completely lost touch with the emotional needs that drive them. He is, to put the matter tersely, a heartless bastard. Cheever carefully explores the chilling details of his private life, but he never judges Blake. The genius of his presentation is to let Blake's character reveal itself in dozens of telling specifics—like the bookshelves he builds in the doorway between his and his wife's bedrooms or his inability in the Madison Avenue bar to remember Miss Dent's name. Blake is an unusual creation for Cheever. As William Peden pointed out in *The American Short Story: Continuity and Change 1940–1975* (Boston: Houghton Mifflin, 1975), "Except for the sadistic organization man of the merciless 'The Five-Forty-Eight,' most of Cheever's nonheroes are essentially amiable men."

Cheever creates an equally complex and troubling character in Miss Dent. His presentation of her is dramatically masterful. At first, we see her only as a vulnerable, shy, and unstable young woman. She is "undistinguished in every way." However, as the story reaches its climax, her underlying strength and courage become evident. If one uses E. M. Forster's two categories of "flat" and "round" characters (see explanation on page 68), Miss Dent is unquestionably a round character. Her behavior surprises us. Each action reveals something new about her. Blake—we are not surprised to observe—fails to understand the individuality and depth of her character. To him, she is a flat character, just another of the women he has picked deliberately "for their lack of self-esteem." He can see but not assimilate the unusual details of her life, like the piano squeezed into her small room with its Beethoven sonatas on the music rack.

"The Five-Forty-Eight" could easily have become pure melodrama. Imagine a barebones plot summary: abused and spurned secretary exacts revenge on heartless boss. Doesn't that sound like something from a soap opera like "The Young and the Restless" or "One Life to Live"? Melodrama, of course, is not all bad; it offers an emotional force and directness that subtler literary forms sometimes lack. Cheever borrows the narrative drive and gripping emotionalism of the mode while transcending its limitations largely through the richness of his two leading characters. The relatively simple plot acquires deep emotional resonance because both Blake and Miss Dent, despite their unusual and disturbing qualities, seem like genuinely real people.

"The Five-Forty-Eight" is told by an omniscient third-person narrator (who knows, for instance, why an unanswered phone is ringing in the Shady Hill station), but the narrator articulates the story mainly from Blake's perspective. We see Miss Dent only from the outside, but we follow Blake's inner life moment by moment. "The Five-Forty-

Eight" is predominately his story, even if Miss Dent comes to control events. Blake is an intelligent and observant, if utterly uncompassionate, man. Cheever's style reflects the quickness of Blake's mind as well as the cruel selfishness of his concerns. It is interesting to note how wonderfully Cheever evokes Blake's heightened consciousness on the train. Confronting the possibility of his own death, he sees everything beyond the train window with an almost lyric poignancy:

> Out of the window he saw the river and the sky. The rain clouds were rolling down like a shutter, and while he watched, a streak of orange light on the horizon became brilliant. Its brilliance spread—he could see it move—across the waves until it raked the banks of the river in dim firelight. Then it was put out. Help would come in a minute, he thought.

Extraneous description? No, the passage puts the reader in Blake's consciousness. We experience the nervous, silent, brooding moments with him. He worries that he may be killed. He remembers the horrifying dead bodies he saw in the war. He watches the daylight die, and implicitly ponders his own mortality. Although the train ride with Miss Dent only takes a few pages, Cheever places us so vividly in Blake's mind that we, too, experience its awful duration.

The names of the characters are interesting. Neither is given a first name—only generic WASP-y surnames. Blake's lack of a first name suggests his lack of intimacy and amiability. He is curt, distant, and businesslike. "Miss" Dent always carries her formal title. Since the story is told largely from Blake's perspective (though in the third person), one might also surmise that the title reflects his wish to keep her at a safe distance. Indeed, Blake keeps most of the world at a considerable emotional distance. He thinks of his neighbors as *Mr.* Watkins and *Mrs.* Compton. There is also an appropriate symbolism in Miss Dent's name. She has been bruised and injured by life.

On the train, the balance of power shifts from Blake to Miss Dent. At the office she had been in Blake's power. He had used it to exploit, hurt, and discard her. Now, pressing a gun against his stomach, *she* exercises absolute power over him. She also will humiliate and discard him, but her actions, though tinged with insanity and desperation, fundamentally differ from his. Blake's cruel treatment of Miss Dent was unreflective and dispassionate. The encounter left so little impact on his hardened nature that he cannot even remember her name exactly when she begins to stalk him. For Miss Dent, however, her retaliation has a paramount importance. It provides her with the self-esteem that she hopes may lead her to sanity.

It would be easy for a reader who does not look too closely at the text to glamorize Miss Dent into a feminist heroine avenging the wrongs of her sex against a piggish male. That would be the melodramatic version of the story. In a manner a bit reminiscent of Flannery O'Connor, Cheever makes Miss Dent a much more uncomfortable heroine. While not perhaps insane, Miss Dent is deeply disturbed. She has visionary dreams and she considers herself clairvoyant, she even quotes the Book of Job as if she were God's messenger. She lives in almost complete isolation ("I have never had a true friend in my life"). Her letter to Blake begins, "Dear Husband." Yet out of this confusion arises a deep humanity and a frighteningly lucid self-knowledge. Miss Dent understands her own sickness better than the doctors. She needs love and self-esteem in a world that refuses her both.

The ending of "The Five-Forty-Eight" is especially powerful because it provides both narrative surprise and symbolic appropriateness. The journey that seemed to have begun in revenge ends in redemption. By sparing Blake's life, Miss Dent affirms her own compassion while also demonstrating the power that she could wield. She purges her spirit of the harm Blake did her (and Blake sees that she has been successful). She also

28

seeks to disrupt Blake's life in a way that will make him realize how shallow, cruel, and loveless it is, although she understands that it may be impossible to reach his humanity in any genuine way. ("I really don't want to harm you, I want to help you, but when I see your face it sometimes seems to me that I can't help you.") Miss Dent is surely transformed by the encounter. A difficult but essential question for readers to ponder, however, is whether the incident will change Blake in any important way. In her study, *John Cheever* (New York: Twayne, 1979), Lynne Waldeland writes that the matter-of-fact last line "leaves us believing that no rude awakening into an enlarged humanity has taken place for Blake." What do your students think?

Students wishing to write on Cheever might find it interesting to compare "The Five-Forty-Eight" to another of the stories first published in the same volume, *The Housebreaker of Shady Hill* (1958). Two excellent stories you might recommend are "The Country Husband" (which won the O. Henry Award in 1955, the same year that "The Five-Forty-Eight" won a Benjamin Franklin Award) and the title story, "The Housebreaker of Shady Hill." The protagonists of both stories are considerably more sympathetic men than Blake. Francis Weed, in "The Country Husband," also has a brush with death when his airplane makes a crash landing. An interesting paper might compare him to Blake. The title character of "The Housebreaker of Shady Hill" loses his job and begins to burglarize his wealthy neighbors to pay the bills. His excruciating moral consciousness makes a stark contrast to Blake's self-absorption. Both stories can also be found in *The Stories of John Cheever* (New York: Random House, 1978), which is available in a Ballentine paperback.

Most of the best writing on Cheever is biographical. The body of criticism on his work remains relatively small. In addition to Lynne Waldeland's study, one might consult George W. Hunt's interesting work, *John Cheever: The Hobgoblin Company of Love* (Grand Rapids, MI: Eerdman, 1983). Hunt's book is an excellent appreciation of Cheever's artistry, and it subtly reveals the essentially religious nature of the stories. Scott Donaldson's *John Cheever: A Biography* (New York: Random House, 1988) provoked complaints from the Cheever clan when it first appeared, but it remains indispensable. It is both well researched and well written. Equally useful is Donaldson's collection of Cheever's many interviews, *Conversations with John Cheever* (Jackson: University of Mississippi Press, 1987).

Alice Walker
EVERYDAY USE, page 90

"Everyday Use" is a genuinely funny story ("Ream it out again," the mother says as she tries to learn her daughter's new name, and she keeps—possibly with tongue in cheek—slipping the new name in throughout the story) with serious undertones. Narrated by the mother, whose wry good sense contrasts vividly with her older daughter's pretensions, the story highlights not only a generation gap, but a contrast between two sharply different attitudes toward the idea of heritage.

Dee, having suddenly discovered that old quilts and dashers are potentially interesting decorations, accuses her mother and sister of not understanding their heritage because they fail to appreciate the artistic value of such objects. However, she herself is so divorced from her heritage that she does not know which member of the family made the dasher. It may be true, as Dee accuses, that Maggie and her mother don't "understand" their heritage—at least not in an intellectual way. The story suggests, however, that by using the quilt, and by having learned the traditional skills passed from generation to generation required to make one, Maggie, the homely, uneducated sister, knows more about her African-American heritage than does Dee (Wangero). Maggie and her mother *live* their cultural heritage; they are nourished by it through everyday use and versed in the craftsmanship needed to pass it on to future generations.

That the mother loves Dee is clear. Although she's aware of the unattractive elements in Dee's nature, her dream of Dee showing her appreciation for her mother on a television show reveals wistfulness: the older woman longs for Dee to return her love. Instead, Dee is scornful. "You ought to try to make something of yourself, too, Maggie," she says as she departs, as if she herself were a superior being, to be emulated. Dee, in spite of her education, has never learned to imagine how she appears to others.

"Everyday Use" is an accessible story for students that explores powerful issues. Although the setting is specifically African-American, the themes of family identity, intergenerational conflict, cultural heritage, and self-esteem are universal. The basic narrative situation—the educated daughter returning on a family visit to criticize her mother and stay-at-home sister—is also particularly relevant to many college students, and most students find it interesting to see this situation from the mother's perspective. Do your African-American students like this story, or are they offended by it? Do any of them feel that the story reinforces undesirable stereotypes? Do any of your black students side with Dee, who is trying so hard to leave poverty and ignorance behind? If the black students in your class are willing to be drawn out on this subject, the discussion might be lively and valuable.

Nadine Gordimer's "The Defeated" (page 437) presents a similar generational conflict, though the parents in Gordimer's story lack the spunk and resiliency of Dee's mother. An interesting student paper could be written by contrasting the two stories. Students wanting critical perspectives on Walker should consult *Alice Walker* (New York: Amistad, 1993), edited by Henry Louis Gates, Jr. and K. A. Appiah, which collects a representative crosssection of reviews, essays, and interviews with the author.

Isaac Bashevis Singer
GIMPEL THE FOOL, page 98

Is Gimpel an antihero? Not for Singer:

> I don't think I write in the tradition of the Yiddish writers' "little man," because their little man is actually a *victim*—a man who is a victim of anti-Semitism, the economic situation, and so on. My characters, though they are not big men in the sense that they play a big part in the world, still they are not little, because in their own fashion they are men of character, men of thinking, men of great suffering . . . . Gimpel was not a little man. He was a fool, but he wasn't little (interview in *The Paris Review* 44 [Fall 1968]).

Like Flannery O'Connor's "Revelation," Singer's story grows from a vision—Gimpel's dream of Elka, with her counsel, "Because I was false is everything false too?" (Several critics have pointed out similarities between Singer and Flannery O'Connor, two writers working with a conflict between new and traditional cultures. See Melvin J. Friedman, "Isaac Bashevis Singer: The Appeal of Numbers," in *Critical Views of Isaac Bashevis Singer,* edited by Irving Malin [New York: New York University Press, 1969].) Singer was an avid reader of Spinoza, whose concept of the lesser or inferior reality of this world probably influenced the famous statement at the end of "Gimpel the Fool," "No doubt the world is entirely an imaginary world." But, in another sense,

> The world [Singer] recoils from is the world of the market place, of human passions, of vain ambitions, of misguided aspirations, and of all the human relationships

which result from them. This is the world of Gimpel the Fool, where the simple and the sensitive are gulled, deprived, humiliated, and despised. It is the world in which the poverty of Frampol distorts the perspective of its people. (J. A. Eisenberg, "Isaac Bashevis Singer: Passionate Primitive or Pious Puritan?" in Malin's collection).

Much of Singer's best fiction, including "Gimpel the Fool," takes place in the *shtetl* or Jewish village of Eastern Europe, a place of rutted streets and tumbledown houses— Singer doesn't romanticize it. He writes, according to Ben Siegel, "compassionate fables of Jews who cling tenaciously to their traditions but who otherwise interest no one but God, the devil, and themselves. And God's interest is never certain" ("Sacred and Profane: Isaac Bashevis Singer's Embattled Spirits," *Critique* 5 [Spring 1963]). Phantoms, demons, *dybbuks,* and the devil figure in Jewish folklore and popular stories; in Singer's fiction, a supernatural personage often embodies a character's passions or obsessions. And so in "Gimpel the Fool," when the Spirit of Evil speaks, he voices Gimpel's resentment against Frampol and his momentary distrust of humankind.

An incisive comment on Gimpel's wife Elka comes from Professor Stan Sulkes of Raymond Walters College.

Do we agree that Gimpel's ability to love his wife emanates from his own goodness rather than hers? (An echo, perhaps, of the prophet Hosea's being commanded to marry a whore so he could appreciate God's love for the errant Israel.) On her deathbed she tells him the truth. (More of her selfishness, I think, since she is anxious over her impending fate rather than his feelings.)

Suggested writing assignment: "A Defense of Elka."
The character of the "simple creature of God," or holy simpleton, ridiculed in this world, rewarded only in afterlife, is a familiar figure in Jewish folk literature. Another famous story with such a character is I. L. Peretz's "Bontsha the Silent." That as a work of storytelling, "Gimpel the Fool" is both traditional and original, Sol Gittleman shows in *From Shtetl to Suburbia: The Family in Jewish Literary Imagination* (Boston: Beacon, 1978) 103–7.
Still, some readers have been bothered by Gimpel's passivity, among them Professor Sulkes. His letter deserves further quotation.

I recall being dismayed when I first read this story. How could a post-holocaust Jewish writer, I wondered, defend the literary convention of the holy fool? Wouldn't someone as naive and accommodating as Gimpel find himself in the Nazi ovens? . . . How could I even be amused by him? Was Singer blinking away the holocaust?
Rereading the story, I realized that it does belong in the context of that horror, though the horror is never mentioned. The holocaust lurks in the background of this tale. As a result I think that Singer is more distanced from Gimpel's simple goodness than he might be if he were a Christian author. He probably *admires* the gullible Gimpel of the first half of the story more than he *approves* of him.
At the end, Gimpel embarks on a journey which reveals to him the evil of the world (events like the holocaust), but he does not allow it to destroy his sweetness and his faith. My class was particularly eager to discuss this point: how does one remain hopeful in light of the atrocities so prevalent in the world? I assume that Singer offers Gimpel's post-journey piety as one response [of] the post-holocaust Jew. But Gimpel's quietism disappoints me, so far removed as it is from the mainstreams of modern Jewry. . . .

Your class might care to discuss this serious objection.

Still another objection might be raised to Gimpel's conclusion, "No doubt the world is entirely an imaginary world." Is, then, the evil in the world only a dream? Isn't this assumption dangerous?

Sol Gittleman, cited above, reads the story to mean that Gimpel, whatever his philosophy, finds truth in his wanderings. Discovering that the world beyond Frampol is less malicious and cruel, Gimpel in the end reaffirms his belief in humanity. Would your students agree or disagree with this paraphrase?

Dr. Eleanor Carducci of Sussex County Community College (New Jersey) has shared with us an assignment that she finds works well for teaching Singer's story. She divided her class into two groups: one consisting of the townspeople and the other, of those sympathetic to Gimpel. The task of the former group was to demonstrate that Gimpel is a fool; the task of the latter, to defend him against the charge. Students were asked to indicate specific passages in the story as evidence. "The townspeople found their task easier, at first," Carducci reports. She continues:

> The others had to delve deeper, but found the search a challenge. After compiling sufficient evidence, the groups tried to convince each other. . . . Students were allowed to join the opposite group, if they were so convinced. It was interesting to note that many townspeople, after thinking more deeply, joined those who felt Gimpel was not a fool. At any rate, the discussion was quite lively and no one remained passive.

This translation of "Gimpel the Fool" offers the work of one Nobel Prize winner rendered into English by another. First published in *Partisan Review* for May 1953, Saul Bellow's translation was the first appearance in English of any Singer story.

In his speech on accepting the Nobel Prize, Singer said he regarded the award as a recognition of the Yiddish language. The language and its speakers—their conduct, their outlook on life—have been for him always identical.

> There is a quiet humor in Yiddish and a gratitude for every day of life, every crumb of success, each encounter of love. The Yiddish mentality is not haughty. It does not take victory for granted. It does not demand and command but it muddles through, sneaks by, smuggles itself amid the powers of destruction, knowing somewhere that God's plan for Creation is still at the very beginning (*Nobel Lecture* [New York: Farrar 1978] 8).

Comic actor Theodore Bikel reads "Gimpel the Fool" on an audiocassette (SWC 1200) available from American Audio Prose Library, Box 842, Columbia, MO 65205. For current price call (800) 447-2275.

4 Setting

Kate Chopin
THE STORM, page 113

French names and carefully recorded dialect place Chopin's story in the bayou country of Louisiana. Setting and plot reinforce each other, the storm in nature precipitating and paralleling the storm of passion that engulfs Calixta and her old lover. In Part I we learn that when the storm begins, Calixta's husband and four-year-old son are trapped in the store. Calixta is home alone. Bibi remembers that Sylvie, who apparently helps out with the housework from time to time, is not with Calixta this evening. We realize later that these details matter: Calixta and Alcée will not be interrupted until the storm is over.

What causes Calixta's infidelity? Her husband loves her, in his way. He buys a can of shrimp because he knows she likes it. He stands in awe of her scrupulous housekeeping, but he seems to know nothing of her sensuality. We're told that after he buys the shrimp, he sits "stolidly." It is this stolidness, perhaps, that has prevented his ever having plumbed his wife's passionate nature.

Doesn't Calixta love her husband? She does, apparently: she worries about him and her son when the storm comes up. She seems genuinely glad to be reunited with them when they come home. But passions, Chopin seems to say, cannot be denied. Their force is equal to that of a storm, and the marriage bed is not the likeliest place for release of that force. The author indeed hints that marriage and sexual pleasure are incompatible in Parts IV and V of the story, where Alcée urges his absent wife to stay away another month and we learn that for Clarisse, "their intimate conjugal life was something which she was more than willing to forgo for a while." Marriage is dull companionship at best, bondage at worst. Without stating this theme, Chopin clearly suggests it. Do students care to argue with her?

Students might like to ponder whether the story would be as powerful if it took place in Chicago on a sunny fall day. If the setting were changed, would we have any story at all?

Compare another wry view of marriage: Chopin's "The Story of an Hour" in Chapter 11, "Stories for Further Reading."

Jack London
TO BUILD A FIRE, page 117

The point of view in "To Build a Fire" is that of an omniscient narrator able to see into the man's mind—even into the dog's. In this powerful story, London lavishes upon the setting the amount of detail usually reserved for a story's characters. Indeed, the Arctic weather functions as if it *were* a character, an unrelenting adversary doing battle with the man. That the man is left nameless seems to emphasize his insignificance in the fight against his mighty enemy.

Skillfully, London builds up almost unendurable suspense. Our hopes, like the protagonist's, are kept alive almost to the end. Detail is piled upon detail as the struggle is gradually lost. The frost on the man's face, the numbing of his extremities and exposed skin, his mental confusion, and, finally, his inability to use his fingers to keep his feeble fire going, presage the drowsy calm that signals his end.

Along the way the man makes us aware of the fatal mistakes he has made, the most serious no doubt being his decision to venture alone into the wilderness. Underestimating his adversary, he also fails to ascertain the temperature and to cover his face. Finally, suffering from mental confusion, he gets his feet wet and then builds a fire in the wrong place. By that time it is too late to rectify what has gone wrong. The dog, protected by his instincts, survives.

Students with some firsthand experience in snow country will respond heartily to this story. But to respond to it, a firsthand acquaintance with freezing cold isn't necessary. In painful and painstaking detail, which repays close scrutiny, London's account does our imagining for us.

Frivolous writing assignment, perhaps for doing in class: Retell this story in 500 words, from the dog's point of view.

T. Coraghessan Boyle
GREASY LAKE, page 129

It is rebellious adolescence in general that Boyle describes in his opening paragraph; but he's also talking about the late 1960s, when adolescents were in plentiful supply, "bad" behavior was much admired, and "courtesy and winning ways went out of style." In 1967 when the American attack on Khe Sanh (mentioned in paragraph 7) took place, Boyle himself was nineteen years old. We can only guess that's about the year in which "Greasy Lake" is set. Not only the epigraph but also the title of the story come from that bard of a slightly later era, Bruce Springsteen, whose first album appeared in 1973.

Are Digby and Jeff really "bad"? Well, no, and neither is the narrator. They're just engaging in the kind of behavior they think is expected of them (1, 3, 4). When, on the night of the story, their rebellion backfires, throwing them into a grimmer world than they had bargained for, they feel revulsion. As is clear at the end, they have had enough of being "bad." Like the boy in James Joyce's "Araby," they have grown up painfully. (For other stories of a young man's initiation into maturity, see "A & P," "Araby," and "Barn Burning." Young women who are similarly initiated, or who seem about to be, appear in "How I Met My Husband" and "Where Are You Going, Where Have You Been?")

That the narrator of "Greasy Lake" grows and changes during his adventures is apparent from the two views of "nature" he voices, one in paragraph 2 and one in paragraph 32. Early in the story, "nature" was wanting "to snuff the rich scent of possibility on the breeze, watch a girl take off her clothes and plunge into the festering murk, drink beer, smoke pot, howl at the stars, savor the incongruous full-throated roar of rock and roll against the primeval susurrus of frogs and crickets." By the end of the story, these swinish pleasures have lost their appeal. When, at dawn, the narrator experiences the beauties of the natural world as if for the first time, he has an epiphany: "This was nature."

Students can have fun demonstrating how Greasy Lake is the perfect setting for Boyle's story. Like the moral view of the narrator (at first), it is "fetid and murky, the mud banks glittering with broken glass and strewn with beer cans and the charred remains of bonfires. There was a single ravaged island a hundred yards from shore, so stripped of vegetation it looked as if the air force had strafed it" (2). The lake is full of "primordial ooze" and "the bad breath of decay" (31). It also hides a waterlogged corpse. Once known for its clear water, the unlucky lake has fallen as far from its ideal state as the people who now frequent its shores have fallen from theirs. (If you teach the chapter on symbol, hark back to Greasy Lake once more.)

Still, in its way, Greasy Lake is a force for change. Caught trying to rape the girl in the blue car, the narrator and his friends run off into the woods, into the water. Waiting in the filthy lake, the narrator is grateful to be alive and feels horror at the death of the "bad older character" whose body he meets in the slime. His growth has begun. When at the end of the story, two more girls pull into the parking lot, the subdued narrator and his friends are harmless. Cold sober, bone tired, they know they have had a lucky escape from consequences that might have been terrible. Also, the narrator knows, as the girls do not, that Al is dead, his body rotting in the lake. He won't "turn up"—except perhaps in the most grisly way. It is this knowledge and the narrator's new reverence for life that make him think he is going to cry.

Students might enjoy spelling out the change in the narrator's outlook. By what hints does Boyle show us that some time has elapsed since the events of the fateful night? Surely the story displays little admiration for the narrator's early behavior, which he now regards with sarcasm, as when he says, "Digby wore a gold star in his right ear and allowed his father to pay his tuition at Cornell" (3), or when he speaks of "new heights of adventure and daring" (6). Other ironic remarks abound, showing his altered view. The maturity the narrator acquired that night seems to have been permanent.

Critics have cited Boyle as a writer socially and politically disengaged; but satire, he points out, can be corrective. "It can hold up certain attitudes as being fraudulent, and in doing that suggest that the opposite might be an appropriate way to behave. And I hope that if my work is socially redemptive, it is in that way" (interview with David Stanton in *Poets & Writers,* January/February 1990). Surely "Greasy Lake," a story some readers find shocking, is socially redemptive.

Candace Andrews of San Joaquin Delta College argues that, while on the surface "Greasy Lake" seems merely to recount the misadventures of a nineteen-year-old delinquent, a careful reading will show that much of the story retells the narrator's experience in Vietnam—"It is a tale of a young man who has been to war and back." For a writing assignment, she had her students list every reference or allusion to war, and told them, "Then bring your 'research' together into some kind of coherent statement which supports the idea that the narrator is a Vietnam veteran." We do not believe, ourselves, that Boyle's several references to war necessarily require the narrator to be an ex-GI. He would have followed the war news and come to feel that the war was senseless violence—like the action out at Greasy Lake on a Saturday night. When he tells us (in paragraph 40) that he and Digby looked at the girl "like war veterans," we take that to be a metaphor: he too feels a sort of battle fatigue. However, you may care to check out Ms. Andrews's provocative theory for yourself. What do your students think of it?

Amy Tan
A PAIR OF TICKETS, page 138

"A Pair of Tickets" is a story of self-discovery—born in pain but eventually resolved in joy. Pain unites characters from different countries and decades. The narrator's still-fresh sorrow at her mother's death, the mother's abiding despair at losing her twin daughters on the war-torn road to Chungking, and the daughters' ache at losing their mother not once, but twice (first as babies in 1944 and then again as adults after they learn their mother is dead) are all caused by the same tragic historical circumstance and its far-reaching consequences. Joy, however, eventually links June with her two half sisters. Acknowledging what they have lost, they find that much remains.

QUESTIONS

1. *How is the external setting of "A Pair of Tickets" essential to what happens internally to the narrator in the course of this story?* "A Pair of Tickets" is a story that grows naturally out of its setting. June's journey to China is one of both external and internal discovery. Finding China, she also finds part of herself. Tan announces the theme at the end of the first paragraph: "I am becoming Chinese." China becomes a spiritual mirror for the narrator, just as her glimpse of her half-sisters's faces provides a living mirror of her own and her late mother's face. One might say that "A Pair of Tickets" is the story of Americanized June May Woo (born, as her passport says, in California in 1951) becoming Jing-mei Woo by discovering her ethnic and cultural roots in her ancestral homeland.

2. *How does the narrator's view of her father change by seeing him in a different setting?* Although June's mother haunts the story, her father is also a quiet, important presence. As the title says, this story is about a *pair* of tickets. June's seventy-two-year-old father, Canning Woo, accompanies her on the trip to China. He is returning after four decades. He is June's physical as well as psychological link with the homeland, as well as her living link with the family history that she (like most children) only half knows. His revelations teach her about both her mother and herself. Seeing him in China, June gets a glimpse of his past, what he was like as a young man before she was born. "He's a young boy," she observes on the train to Shenzen, "so innocent and happy I want to button his sweater and pat his head."

3. *In what ways does the narrator feel at home in China? In what ways does she feel foreign?* June is Chinese-American, which means that she experiences the two cultures from both the inside and the outside. Just as going to China helps her understand how she is Chinese, it also reminds her how much she has been shaped by America. She understands Mandarin Chinese but cannot speak it well. She does not know the Cantonese of her relatives or her father's Mandarin dialect. Although she is purely Chinese in ancestry, not only her clothes betray her American upbringing—she is also too tall. "I stand five-foot-six," June observes, "and my head pokes above the crowd so that I am eye level only with other tourists." And yet she physically resembles her half-sisters. As she realizes at the end of the story: "And now I also see what part of me is Chinese. It is so obvious. It is my family. It is in our blood."

4. *What do the narrator and her half sisters have in common? How does this factor relate to the theme of the story?* She and her half sisters share a biological and spiritual link to their common mother, and through her they share a bond to one another. "Together we look like our mother," June observes. "Her same eyes, her same mouth." Their fates are interrelated, as reflected by their names. In China, June asks her father the meaning of her Chinese name, Jing-mei, and he interprets her name to signify the younger sister who is the essence of the other lost daughters. As she discovers on meeting them, she does share their essence—they are all daughters of the same mother.

5. *In what ways is the story interesting because it explores specifically Chinese-American experiences? In what other ways is the story grounded in universal family issues?* Although "A Pair of Tickets" is saturated in Chinese history and culture, and its plot reflects a situation unlikely to be repeated in other contexts, it also explores nearly universal themes of self-discovery, cultural awareness, and family history. One might say that Tan's broader theme is dual identity—an especially relevant theme for many Americans who come from immigrant families. Tan explores this quintessentially American experience with humor, compassion, and imagination.

Amy Tan reads an abridged version of her novel *The Joy Luck Club* on audio-cassette tape available from the American Audio Prose Library, Inc., Box 842, Columbia, MO 65205; phone number for orders (800) 447-2275. ("A Pair of Tickets" is the last chapter in this book.) Wayne Wang's 1993 film version of *The Joy Luck Club* will probably disappoint most of Tan's readers as much as it did movie critics. The subject matter is so interesting that it carries the film along, but Wang sentimentalizes and sensationalizes the story into a sort of Asian-American soap opera. The final episode (drawn from "A Pair of Tickets") is condensed and simplified. The *pair* of tickets is, alas, reduced to a single passage: June flies to China alone, and poor Canning Woo gets left in the States. The film may nonetheless be useful to students who need help in visualizing the American and Chinese milieus of the story. Under pressure, one might assign a particularly movie-struck student the task of comparing and contrasting the movie's version of "A Pair of Tickets" to the original story.

5 Tone and Style

Ernest Hemingway
A CLEAN, WELL-LIGHTED PLACE, 158

This celebrated story is a study in contrasts: between youth and age, belief and doubt, light and darkness. To the younger waiter, the café is only a job; to the older waiter, it is a charitable institution for which he feels personal responsibility. Of course, he himself has need of it: it is his refuge from the night, from solitude, from a sense that the universe is empty and meaningless, expressed in his revised versions of the Hail Mary and the Lord's Prayer. The older waiter feels kinship for the old man, not only because the waiter, too, is alone and growing old, but because both men are apparently atheists. Willing to commit suicide, the old man (unlike his pious daughter) evidently doesn't think he has any immortal soul to fear for. Robert Penn Warren is surely right in calling Hemingway, at least in this story, a religious writer. "The despair beyond plenty of money, the despair that makes a sleeplessness beyond insomnia, is the despair felt by a man who hungers for the sense of order and assurance that men seem to find in religious faith, but who cannot find grounds for his faith" ("Ernest Hemingway," in Warren's *Selected Essays* [New York: Random House, 1951] 80–118). What values are left to a man without faith? A love of cleanliness and good light, of companionship, of stoic endurance, and above all, of dignity. (Another attempt to state the theme of the story is at the beginning of Chapter 7.)

At the heart of the story is the symbol of the café, an island of light and order surrounded by night and nothingness. Contrasting images of light and darkness begin in the opening paragraph: the old man, not entirely committed either to death or to life, likes to sit in the shadow of the leaves. Every detail in the story seems meaningful: even, perhaps, as L. Rust Hills points out, "the glint of light on the soldier's collar . . . an attribute of sexual potency" (*Writing in General and the Short Story in Particular* [Boston: Houghton, 1977] 85).

The story has been much admired for Hemingway's handling of point of view. The narrator is a nonparticipant who writes in the third person. He is all-knowing at the beginning of the story: in the opening paragraph we are told how the old man feels, then what the waiters know about him. From then on, until the waiters say "Good night," the narrator remains almost perfectly objective, merely reporting visible details and dialogue. (He editorializes for a moment, though, in observing that the younger waiter employs the syntax of "stupid people.") After the waiters part company, for the rest of the story the narrator limits himself to the thoughts and perceptions of the older waiter, who, we now see, is the central character.

It is clear all along, as we overhear the conversation of the two waiters, that Hemingway sides with the elder's view of the old man. The older waiter reveals himself as wiser and more compassionate. We resent the younger man's abuse of the old man, who cannot hear his "stupid" syntax, his equation of money with happiness. But the older waiter and Hemingway do not see things identically—a point briefly discussed in the text on pages 176–177 in a comment on the story's irony.

A small problem in reading the story is to keep the speakers straight. Evidently it is the younger waiter who has heard of the old man's suicide attempt and who answers the questions at the beginning of the story. Hemingway's device of assigning two successive speeches to the same character without identifying him (paragraphs 20-21 and probably 32-33) has given rise to much confusion among readers—also to twenty or more scholarly articles on the correct reading of the story. David Kerner's "The Foundation of the True Text of 'A Clean, Well-Lighted Place'" settles the question. Demonstrating that the device appears many times in Hemingway's novels and stories, Kerner suggests—with evidence—that Hemingway may have learned it from Turgenev or Joyce (*Fitzgerald/Hemingway Annual* 1979: 279-300). Later, Kerner examined manuscripts of books Hemingway saw through press, and found thirty-eight clear instances of the device ("The Manuscripts Establishing Hemingway's Anti-Metronomic Dialogue," *American Literature* 54 [1982]: 385-96).

How original Hemingway's style once seemed may be less apparent today, after generations of imitators. Ford Madox Ford described the famed style: "Hemingway's words strike you, each one, as if they were pebbles fetched fresh from a brook" (introduction to *A Farewell to Arms* [New York: Modern Library, 1932]). Students may be asked to indicate some of the more prominent pebbles: the repetitions of such words as *night, light, clean, late, shadow, leaves,* and (most obviously) *nada.* The repetitions place emphasis. Students may be asked, too, to demonstrate whether Hemingway's prose seems closer to formal writing or to speech. It might help to have them notice the preponderance of one-syllable words in the opening paragraph of the story and to compare Hemingway's first paragraph with that of Faulkner's "Barn Burning." Faulkner's second sentence is a 117-worder, clearly more recondite in its diction (*dynamic, hermetic*). Most of Hemingway's story is told in dialogue, and usually we notice that a character *said* (unlike Faulkner's characters, who often *whisper* or *cry* their lines).

Frank O'Connor comments adversely on the Hemingway style:

> As practiced by Hemingway, this literary method, compounded of simplification and repetition, is the opposite of what we learned in our schooldays. We were taught to consider it a fault to repeat a noun and shown how to avoid it by the use of pronouns and synonyms. This led to another fault that Fowler christened "elegant variation." The fault of Hemingway's method might be called "elegant repetition" (*The Lonely Voice* [Cleveland: World, 1963]).

This criticism may be well worth quoting to the class. From "A Clean, Well-Lighted Place," can students see what O'Connor is talking about? Do they agree with him?

In a preface written in 1959 for a selection of his stories that did not materialize as a book, Hemingway congratulated himself for his skill at leaving things out. In his story "The Killer," he had left out Chicago; in "Big Two-Hearted River," the war. "Another time I was leaving out good was in 'A Clean, Well-Lighted Place.' There I really had luck. I left out everything. That is about as far as you can go, so I stood on that one and haven't been drawn to that since" ("The Art of the Short Story," *The Paris Review* 79 [1981]: 100).

Hemingway himself had reason to empathize with the older waiter. "He was plagued all his adult life by insomnia and in sleep by nightmares," notes biographer Carlos Baker (*Ernest Hemingway: A Life Story* [New York: Scribner's, 1969] viii-ix).

Among its other practical uses, literature provides great names for businesses. Taking a leaf from Hemingway, three California bookshops (in Cupertino, Larkspur, and San Francisco) bear the name "A Clean Well-Lighted Place." Their giveaway bookmark states: "We are of those who like to stay late at a bookstore. . . . Each night we are reluctant to close because there may be someone who needs to relax in A Clean Well-Lighted Place."—or perhaps, someone who needs to seek relief from insomnia?

William Faulkner
BARN BURNING, page 162

From the opening paragraph, we can tell that the tone of the story will be excited and impassioned—at least in the moments when we see through the eyes of the boy, Colonel Sartoris Snopes. Even the boy's view of canned goods in the general store (where court is being held) is tinged with intense emotion. Fear, despair, and grief sweep over Sarty because his father is on trial as an accused barn burner.

The ten-year-old boy's wonder and dismay are conveyed in a suitably passionate style. Whenever Sarty is most excited, Faulkner's sentences grow longer and more complex and seem to run on like a torrent. The second sentence of the story is a good illustration; or the sentence in which Sarty jumps out of the way of Major de Spain's galloping horse and hears the barn going up in flames (at the climax of the story, the long sentence in paragraph 107). A familiar student objection is that Faulkner embodies the boy's feelings in words far beyond a ten-year-old's vocabulary (and Sarty can't even read, we learn from paragraph 1). You might anticipate this objection and get students to realize that a story about a small boy need not be narrated by the boy himself (on page 156 in the remarks on the quotation from *As I Lay Dying*). Evidently, "Barn Burning" is told by a nonparticipating narrator who sees things mainly through the eyes of Sarty Snopes, the main character.

Lionel Trilling wrote a good defense of the style in this story: the complexity of Faulkner's rhetoric reflects the muddlement and incompleteness of the boy's perceptions and the boy's emotional stress in moving toward a decision to break away from father and family (*The Experience of Literature* [New York: Holt, 1967] 745-48).

Now and again, the narrator intrudes his own insights and larger knowledge. At times Faulkner rapidly shifts his perspective from outside Sarty's mind to inside it. Two such shifts take place in a sentence in paragraph 7 ("For a moment . . ."), in which, first, we get the boy's thoughts and then an exterior look at his crouched figure ("small for his age . . . with straight, uncombed, brown hair and eyes gray and wild as storm scud"), and then a return to the boy's perceptions. In the paragraph telling how Ab Snopes's "wolflike independence" impressed strangers (25), Faulkner makes a judgment far beyond the boy's capacity. In paragraph 26, the narrator again separates his view from the boy's to tell us what Sarty would have thought if he were older—"But he did not think this now." The narrator is again clearly in evidence in the story's last two paragraphs.

The effect of these intrusions is, perhaps, to make the reader see that the boy can't quite understand his situation. He is perplexed and innocent, and we realize that somehow he loves his terrible father. In the next-to-last paragraph, Sarty's impressions of his father's war service are set beside the grim truth—which only the father (and the narrator) could know. Wayne C. Booth comments on this passage: "We can say with some confidence that the poignancy of the boy's lonely last-ditch defense of his father is greatly increased by letting us know that even that defense is unjustified" (*The Rhetoric of Fiction* [Chicago: University of Chicago Press, 1961] 308).

"Barn Burning" may be taken together with "A Rose for Emily" (Chapter 2) to demonstrate that point of view, in a masterly story, is an essential determinant of the style in which the story is told. "Barn Burning" is the more difficult story, and so you may want to take up "A Rose for Emily" first and to spend a little while getting students into the universe of Faulkner. Any brief discussion of the Civil War and its effects will help prepare them for "Barn Burning." Compared with the latter story, "A Rose" seems more lucid in style and more cool, detached, and wryly humorous in tone—like its narrator, a spokesman for the town, who (unlike the narrator in "Barn Burning") does not enter the leading character's mind and who is somewhat distantly recalling events of years gone by.

Though her perch in society is loftier, Miss Emily, like Ab Snopes, is fiercely proud, capable of violent revenge, and she too holds herself above the law. (Faulkner, of course, thinks both Emily and Ab appalling and loves them dearly.)

"A Rose for Emily" also introduces the legend of Colonel Sartoris, war hero, mayor, and first citizen, whose fame and influence linger. Coming to "Barn Burning," students may then appreciate the boy hero's given name. Addressing the boy (in 10), the Justice foreshadows the story's conclusion: "I reckon anybody named for Colonel Sartoris in this country can't help but tell the truth, can he?" Truthfully, Sarty warns Major de Spain that his father is going to burn the major's barn; in so defying Ab, Colonel Sartoris Snopes rises to his namesake's nobility.

Question 1 directs the student to paragraph 107, a crucial passage that repays close attention. From the roar Sarty hears, and from the detail that the night sky is "stained abruptly," it is clear that Ab Snopes and Sarty's older brother succeed in setting fire to de Spain's barn. We had long assumed that, although a total of three shots ring out, the barn burners get away, for they turn up in a later volume of Faulkner. But Joseph L. Swonk of Rappahannock Community College, North Campus, persuades us that the outcome is grimmer. Sarty cries "Pap! Pap!"—then trips over "something," looks back, and sobs "Father! Father!" "I contend," says Professor Swonk, "that he tripped over the bodies of his father and brother, that he was looking backward at the bodies, and that his shift from 'Pap' to 'Father' was eulogistic. Furthermore, he continues in this manner: *'Father. My Father . . . He was brave! . . . He was! He was in the war!'"* Now referring to his father in the past tense, Sarty is delivering a final tribute over Ab's corpse.

"Barn Burning," to place the story in the chronicles of Yoknapatawpha County, is a prelude to the Snopes family history later expanded in Faulkner's trilogy *The Hamlet* (1940), *The Town* (1957), and *The Mansion* (1959). At the conclusion of "Barn Burning," Sarty Snopes turns his back on his father and his clan; so, in the trilogy, the primary figure is Flem, Sarty's brother, who remained. Meeting Flem Snopes, whose father Ab is still well known as a barn burner, Jody Varner in *The Hamlet* says dryly, "I hear your father has had a little trouble once or twice with landlords."

"Barn Burning" yields valuable illustrations for any discussion of symbolism: certainly the neat, "shrewd" fire (26) which reflects Ab's cautious nature. Fire is Ab's weapon of revenge, hence to be "regarded with respect and used with discretion." Memorable also are the rug (emblem of the whole social hierarchy that Ab defies and won't make amends to) and Ab's cruddy boots (suggesting his contempt for his employer, his mechanical indifference, his cruddiness).

"Barn Burning" was adapted for television in the PBS television series "The American Short Story," and is available on videotape. A paperback, *The American Short Story, Volume 2* (New York: Dell, 1980), includes short scenes from Horton Foote's television script based on Faulkner's story.

For a stimulating attack on Faulkner's style, see Sean O'Faolain, *The Vanishing Hero* (Boston: Little, Brown, 1957) 101–3, 111–12, 133. Charging that Faulkner can't write plain English because "his psyche is completely out of his control," O'Faolain cites lines of Faulkner that he thinks rely on pure sound instead of sense ("the gasoline-roar of apotheosis"); and complains that Faulkner needlessly uses "second-thought words" ("He did not know why he had been compelled, or anyway needed, to claim it . . ."; "This, anyway, will, shall, must be invulnerable . . ."). In O'Faolain's view, when Faulkner begins a sentence, "I mean," he doesn't know what he means and won't know until he says it. O'Faolain's objections might be entertaining to discuss.

IRONY

James Joyce
ARABY, page 177

Set in the city Joyce called "dear old dirty Dublin," "Araby" reveals a neighborhood so dreary that it seems no wonder a sensitive boy would try to romance his way out of it. In paragraphs 1-3, details stack up tellingly, painting a scene of frustration and decay. We see the dead-end street with an abandoned house at its "blind end"; the boy's house where the priest had died, its room full of "musty air" and "old, useless papers"; dying bushes, a rusty bicycle pump; a street of shadows and dark, dripping gardens lit by somber violet light. Still, the description is not unrelievedly sad. Playing in the cold, the boys feel their bodies glow. From "dark, odorous stables" comes the "music" of jingling harnesses. And for the boy, Mangan's sister lends the street enchantment.

Most students won't need help to see that "Araby" is told by its main character. They may need class discussion, though, to realize that the narrator is a man who looks back on his boyhood memories. One indication of the narrator's maturity is his style. In the first paragraph, he remarks, in unboyish language, that the houses, "conscious of decent lives within them, gazed at one another with brown imperturbable faces." Besides, this mature storyteller is about to step back and criticize his younger self: "her name was like a summons to all my foolish blood" (paragraph 4).

Mangan's sister, whose name is never told, seems an ordinary young woman who summons her kid brother to tea. She is a vague figure: the boy glimpses her from afar, sometimes while peering at her from shadow. John J. Brugaletta and Mary H. Hayden suggest that the conversation in which the boy promises to bring her a gift takes place only in his mind. Mangan's sister, they argue, may never have set foot in the room where the priest died (6), into which the boy retreats to have his visionary experience. In this musty shrine, his senses swoon. He clasps his hands in an attitude of prayer, murmurs an incantation over and over (*O love! O love!*), and conjures her face before him—"At last she spoke to me." Even the spikes he sees her clasping are unreal, for they couldn't be there in the dead priest's drawing room. In the end, at the bazaar, the image of Mangan's sister fades before the physical presence of the banal, flirtatious English salesgirl who says, "O, I never said such a thing." Neither did Mangan's sister say a word to the narrator that bound him to his imagined promise ("The Motivation for Anguish in Joyce's 'Araby,'" *Studies in Short Fiction* Winter 1978: 11-17).

The boy's daydreams of Mangan's sister are difficult to take seriously. Amid barrels of pigs' cheeks, he carries her image in his mind as a priest carries a chalice. He regards her with "confused adoration" and feels himself a harp on which she plays (5). From early in the story, the boy has projected a dazzling veil of romance over the commonplace. At the end, he realizes with shock that illusion has had him in thrall. Araby, the enchanted fair, turns out to be merely a drab charity bazaar where gimcracks are peddled, men count money, and a scatterbrained salesclerk makes small talk till the lights go out. The boy's intense anguish seems justified.

Nearly everything Joyce wrote has a thread of allegory, and "Araby" may be no exception. Making much of the identity of Mangan's sister, William York Tindall remarks: "Since [James Clarence] Mangan, one of Joyce's favorite poets, dedicated 'Dark Rosaleen,' his most famous poem, to his country, it seems likely that Mangan's sister is Ireland herself, beckoning and inviting." Tindall thinks the boy's frustrated quest is for Ireland's Church, toward which Joyce, too, felt bitter disillusionment. Rather than pursue Dark Rosaleen, the mature Joyce (and his protagonist Stephen Dedalus) chose exile.

"Araby" makes a good introduction to *Portrait of the Artist as a Young Man*. (Tindall discusses the story in *A Reader's Guide to James Joyce* [New York: Noonday, 1959] 20.)

Araby, the bazaar with the "magical name," is paramount. Besides, the apple tree in the unkempt garden (2) hints of the tree in some lost Eden. Dublin, clearly, is a fallen world. Other items also suggest sterility and decay: the "blind" or dead-end street and its "uninhabited house ... detached from its neighbors" (1); the dead priest's rusty bicycle pump (2). Counting coins on a tray like that used to serve communion, the men in paragraph 25 perform a little act with symbolic overtones. The darkening hall has seemed to the boy "a church after a service," and the two money changers are not driven out of the temple—they drive out the boy.

Elizabeth A. Flynn compares reactions to this story by twenty-six male and twenty-six female college students in "Gender and Reading," *College English* 45 (Mar. 1983): 236-53. Some men felt uncomfortable with the boy's solipsistic infatuation. Recalling similar experiences of their own, they had trouble attaining distance. Several men, Flynn reports, were harsh in their judgment on Mangan's sister. They saw the girl as manipulating the boy for her own ends: "just using him," "playing him along." Most of the women students made better sense of the story. They didn't condemn Mangan's sister, and they understood the ending. They recognized that as the lights of the bazaar go out, the boy passes a painful judgment on himself: he has been a vain fool. Some women saw him gaining from his experience. Freed from his delusion, he can now reenter reality. If your men students have trouble understanding the story, you might have them take a good look at the last line.

On the popular poem "The Arab's Farewell to His Steed," which the uncle remembers, Matthew A. Fike of the University of Michigan writes, citing an insight by Stanley Friedman: "Joyce's reference to this poem, a work notable for its sentimentality, directs attention to the main significance of 'Araby': the assault on sentimentality and illusion" (Friedman, *The Explicator* 24:5 [Jan. 1966], item 43). There seems more than a little resemblance between the boy's worship of Mangan's sister for "the white curve of her neck" and the Arab's devotion to his horse, with its "glossy neck." Ironically, the Arab's glamorized view of his steed contrasts with the awareness that Joyce's narrator achieves, or as Mr. Fike puts it, "The nomad never parts with his horse, but the boy abandons his illusion." (Thanks to Mr. Fike for prompting XJK to greater precision in his footnote on "The Arab's Farewell.")

Jorge Luis Borges
THE GOSPEL ACCORDING TO MARK, page 183

Jorge Luis Borges, who considered himself primarily a poet, is almost certainly the most influential short story writer of the last half century. His mix of fantasy and realism was the catalyst to the Latin American literary "boom" of magical realism. His use of nonfiction forms—like the essay, book review, or scholarly article—as vehicles for the short story not only inspired experimental writers of metafiction; it also helped challenge, among literary theorists, the traditional distinctions between fiction and factual writing. Writers as diverse as John Barth, Italo Calvino, Gabriel García Márquez, John Updike, Thomas Disch, Donald Barthelme, J. G. Ballard, Michel Foucault, and Angela Carter all reflect Borges's influence.

Many Borges stories—including "The Gospel According to Mark"—operate simultaneously on two levels. The surface of the story usually offers a conventional narrative, often with a surprise ending. Borges's masters in fiction were traditional storytellers like Robert Louis Stevenson, Rudyard Kipling, and G. K. Chesterton. (He was also particularly fond of mystery and supernatural tales.) Borges frequently employed old-fashioned narrative devices borrowed from their work, but he was equally fascinated by the literature of mysticism and the occult, not only the Christian and Jewish traditions but also the Islamic and Chinese. From these mystics and metaphysicians, he developed an obsession for speculating on secret patterns in reality. For Borges, the search for hidden significance was not a literary game; it was an essential undertaking, part of humanity's attempt to uncover God's plan, and the temporal world's means of understanding eternity. Not surprisingly, one of Borges's favorite modern writers was Kafka.

Borges's fascination with hidden significance leads to a consciously constructed second level of meaning in many of his stories in which surface details can be discovered to have secret implications. The amazing thing about Borges's stories is the sheer density of meaning the careful reader will find embedded in the text. One need not catch or understand all these hidden clues to appreciate his stories, but discovering them does enrich one's experience. They are not trivial details, but the individual threads to a complex pattern of expression.

"The Gospel According to Mark" is an example of how tightly interwoven Borges's symbolic subtext can be. In this story, his main technique is irony, the traditional way of saying one thing while meaning another. Virtually everything that happens in the story has an ironic significance. The questions addressed below elucidate some, but by no means all, of the ironic underpinnings of this haunting story.

QUESTIONS

1. *What is about to happen to Baltasar Espinosa at the end of this story?* If students don't understand Borges's surprise ending—the point, that is, where the overt and ironic narratives meet—they will not be able to figure anything else out. Most students will catch the ending at once—Baltasar Espinosa is about to be crucified by the Gutres family. However, it may be worth asking this basic question to make sure no one misses it.

2. *How old is Espinosa? What is ironic about his age?* Espinosa is thirty-three, the age at which Jesus is traditionally thought to have been crucified.

3. *What is the background of the Gutre family? How did they come to own an English Bible? Why is it ironic that they own this book?* Like America, Argentina is a country populated largely by immigrants. (Borges himself was a mixture of English, Italian, Jewish, Uruguayan, and Argentinean stock.) The Gutre family are the descendants of Scottish immigrants, but they have lived on the Argentinean pampas so long that they have forgotten not only their English but even their ancestry. Their name is a corruption of the name *Guthrie.* Significantly, Borges links their Scottish ancestry to Calvinism, with its belief in absolute predestination. (In retrospect, Espinosa's sacrificial death seems fated.) The irony of their owning an English Bible is multiple: they cannot read; they know no English; they are seemingly ignorant of Christianity; they have forgotten their Scottish roots. However, there is, of course, a deeper irony. Although they have forgotten everything else, the Gutres have unconsciously maintained a Calvinistic sensibility that leads them to interpret the Gospel with absolute literalism.

4. *The narrator claims that the protagonist, Espinosa, has only two noteworthy qualities: an almost unlimited kindness and a capacity for public speaking. How do these qualities become important in the story?* Espinosa's two qualities seal his fate. His gift for public speaking makes his renditions of the Gospel particularly effective to the illiterate Gutre family. He even rises to his feet when reading the parables. His unlimited kindness makes Espinosa a perfect Christ figure—the gentle man who sacrifices himself to redeem

others. (One can find significance to virtually all of Espinosa's other attributes, as listed in the first paragraph.)

5. *When Espinosa begins reading the Gospel of Saint Mark to the Gutres, what changes in their behavior does he notice?* Once Espinosa begins reading the Gospel, he suddenly makes an intense connection with the Gutres family. Until then conversation had proved difficult. They treat him with ever-greater respect and follow his orders. He catches them talking about him respectfully, but he does not understand the significance of their change in behavior until too late.

6. *What other action does Espinosa perform that earns the Gutres's gratitude?* Espinosa helps treat the Gutre girl's injured pet lamb. (Borges's choice of that symbolic animal is surely not coincidental.) The family seem to consider his intercession miraculous, although Espinosa does not understand their reaction. There is a consistently ironic gap between what he notices in their behavior and what their actions really signify. It is a good exercise to have students list as many ironic episodes or situations as possible.

7. *Reread the last paragraph. Why is it ironic that the Gutres ask Espinosa's blessing and the daughter weeps?* The irony is that the three people asking his blessing are about to murder him. The weeping girl is both one of his assassins and a Mary (or, perhaps more appropriately, a Mary Magdalene) figure crying at the crucifixion.

8. *Why do the Gutres kill Espinosa? What do they hope to gain?* The Gutres kill Espinosa to achieve salvation. The father questions Espinosa quite explicitly on that point the morning before his execution. For obvious reasons, old Gutres is particularly anxious to know if the soldiers who executed Christ were also saved.

9. *Is the significance of Espinosa's death entirely ironic? Or does he resemble Christ in any important respect?* The central question in interpreting Borges's story is whether it merely depicts a grotesquely ironic misunderstanding or rather suggests a deeper religious vision. Whatever one's conclusions, it is certain that Borges had a lifelong fascination with the idea of Christ and redemption. Some of his best stories, like "Three Versions of Judas" and "The Circular Ruins," explicitly concern the Incarnation. Borges never used the Christian mythos carelessly. A narrowly ironic reading of "The Gospel According to Mark" is easy to make. It is an ironic horror story in which the protagonist unwittingly creates the conditions for his own ritual murder. Read this way, the story is quite satisfactory—like a superior episode of "The Twilight Zone." The story, however, also allows a deeper, though still ironic religious reading. Here, too, Espinosa is an unwitting Christ-figure, but one understands him not to represent real Christianity, but a shallow parody of it. He is a Christ without divinity, a figure whose teaching lacks moral weight and whose death will save no one. When quizzed by the Gutre father about particular points in the Gospel, Espinosa asserts things he does not believe in order to save face. His theology is "rather dim," and so he answers other questions without examining their logical or theological consistency. In his bewildered way, Espinosa enjoys the authority of his divine position, but he neither understands nor deserves it. He is a well-meaning sham, quite unable to comprehend that the Gutres (whom he unmaliciously, but also un-Christianly, considers beneath him) might take matters of salvation seriously. He is a dilettante unsuitably cast in the role of a deity. Although he seems to accept his death meekly (we do not know for sure what follows his realization), he has only the outward features of a redeemer. His dabbling in the divine has not only destroyed him, but morally corrupted his followers. Espinosa may be a Christ-figure, but he is no Christ.

Students wishing to do a paper on Borges might profitably compare "The Gospel According to Mark" with Borges's ingenious tale, "Three Versions of Judas." For more sophisticated students, a comparison between "The Gospel According to Mark" and Flannery O'Connor's "A Good Man Is Hard to Find" could be an absorbing project. Both stories end in senseless murders, and both depict complex and heretical reaction to the Gospels.

6 Theme

Instructors who wish to teach all the stories in the book according to themes (not just the stories in this chapter) will find suggestions on page 7 in "Stories Arranged by Subject and Theme."

Stephen Crane
THE OPEN BOAT, page 192

It may interest students to know that "The Open Boat" is based on Crane's own experience of shipwreck (as the note on page 192 informs them), but they may need some discussion to realize that factuality does not necessarily make a story excellent. Newspaper accounts may be faithful to the fact, but few are memorable; on the other hand, fine stories often are spun out of imagined experience—as was Crane's novel *The Red Badge of Courage*, a convincing evocation of the Civil War by a writer who had only heard of it.

For what other reasons is "The Open Boat" a superb story? Its characters are sharply drawn and believable; captain, cook, oiler, and correspondent are fully realized portraits, etched with great economy. Crane deeply probes the mind of his primary character, the correspondent, from the point of view of limited omniscience. The author knows all but prefers to confine what he reports to what he sees through the correspondent's eyes.

The story seems written with intense energy; alert students will find many phrases and figures of speech to admire. In a vigorous simile, Crane conveys the motion of the boat and a sense of its precarious balance: "By the very last star of truth, it is easier to steal eggs from under a hen than it was to change seats in the dinghy" (paragraph 31). In the same passage, a man changing places in the boat picks himself up and moves his body as carefully as though he were a piece of delicate china. One way to get students to sense the degree of life in a writer's style is to have them pick out verbs. In the opening sentence of Part II (21): "As the boat *bounced* from the top of each wave the wind tore through the hair of the hatless men, and as the craft *plopped* her stern down again the spray *slashed* past them."

Building suspense, Crane brings the men again and again within sight of land and then drives them back to sea. He aligns enemies against them: sharks, the ocean current, the weight of water that sloshes into the boat and threatens to swamp it. The climax of the story—the moment of greatest tension, when the outcome is to be decided—comes in paragraph 204, when the captain decides to make a run through the surf and go for shore.

The situation of having one's nose dragged away before he can "nibble the sacred cheese of life" (70,143) is a clear instance of irony of fate, or cosmic irony. (These slightly ponderous terms are defined as briefly as possible on page 177.) Crane, who sees Fate as an "old ninnywoman" (70), knows that the rain falls alike on the just and the unjust. There is no one right way to state the theme of this rich story, but here are some attempts by students, each with some truth in it:

The universe seems blind to human struggles.

Fate is indifferent, and doesn't always give the brave their just rewards.

It's an absurd world; only people are reasonable.

This theme (however it is stated) may be seen also in the symbol of the giant tower (204) and Crane's remarks on what it suggests: "The serenity of nature amid the struggles of the individual," a presence not cruel or beneficent or treacherous or wise. Students who like to hunt for symbols sometimes want to see the boat as the universe, in which man is a passenger. A very decent case can be made for reading the story in this way. But everything in the story (ocean, waves, shark, beach, lighthouse), however full of suggestions, is first and foremost a thing concrete and tangible.

Although the secondary theme of comradeship is overtly expressed only in paragraph 43 ("the subtle brotherhood of men that was here established"), it informs the entire story. Until they quit the boat, the men are willing to spell one another at the oars; and even in the water, the captain still thinks of the correspondent's safety. The word heroism remains unspoken but understood: in "The Open Boat" a hero seems to be one who faithfully does what needs to be done. All four men thus qualify for the name.

Remembering the scrap of verse by Victorian bard Caroline Norton (179), the correspondent finds himself drawn into sympathy with any sufferer who, like himself, has to die in a remote place. The sentimental lines give rise to a feeling that, under the circumstances, seems heartfelt and real. In their time, the stormy life and dashing Byronic ballads of Caroline Norton (1808–1877), granddaughter of Richard Brinsley Sheridan, attracted wide notice. Joyce mentions another poem in "Araby," paragraph 23. She signed herself "Hon. Mrs. Norton," having married George Norton, a commissioner of bankruptcy who later went bankrupt himself. Michael R. Turner supplies two of her poems and a biographical note in *Parlour Poetry* (London: Michael Joseph, 1967) 71–72, 228–29.

For its view of people as pawns of nature, Crane's story has been classified as an example of American naturalism. Clearly, "The Open Boat" also has elements in common with recent fiction and drama of the absurd: its notion of Fate as a ninny, its account of Sisyphean struggles in the face of an indifferent universe. For critical comment on these aspects of the story, see Richard P. Adams, "Naturalistic Fiction: 'The Open Boat,'" *Tulane Studies in English* 4 (1954): 137–47; and Peter Buitenhuis, "The Essentials of Life: 'The Open Boat' as Existentialist Fiction," *Modern Fiction Studies* 5 (1959): 243–50.

William Maxwell, novelist and for many years a *New Yorker* fiction editor, was asked in a recent interview, "As an editor, in deciding whether or not to read a story how much weight do you place on the first sentence?" "A great deal," Maxwell replied. "And if there is nothing promising by the end of the first page there isn't likely to be in what follows. . . . When you get to the last sentence of a [story], you often find that it was implicit in the first sentence, only you didn't know what it was." Asked for his favorite opening lines in fiction, Maxwell's first thought was of "None of them knew the color of the sky," from "The Open Boat" ("The Art of Fiction," *Paris Review* 82 [December 1982]). Students may be asked what this first line reveals. (That the sea compels the survivors' whole attention.) How does the final sentence in the story hark back to the first?

Nathaniel Hawthorne
YOUNG GOODMAN BROWN, page 211

"Young Goodman Brown" is Hawthorne's most frequently reprinted story and probably the most often misunderstood. Some students will take the devil's words for gospel, agree that "Evil is the nature of mankind," and assume that Brown learns the truth about all those hypocritical sinners in the village, including that two-faced Faith.

One likely point of departure is the puns on *Faith* in Brown's speeches:

"I'll cling to her skirts and follow her to heaven" (paragraph 5).

"Faith kept me back awhile" (12).

"Is there any reason why I should quit my dear Faith . . . ?"

"with Heaven above, and Faith below, I will yet stand firm against the devil" (46).

"My Faith is gone!" (50)

What Faith does Hawthorne mean? Surely not Puritanism—in this story, hardly a desirable bedfellow. More likely Brown's Faith is simple faith in the benevolence of God and the essential goodness of humankind. Brown's loss of this natural faith leads him into the principal error of the Salem witch-hangers: suspecting the innocent of being in league with the devil. At first, Brown assumes that his Faith is a pretty little pink-ribboned thing he can depart from and return to whenever he feels like it—he, Brown, the strongman, who will pass a night in the woods and then return to the bosom of his faithful spouse. Of course this is an attitude of blind pride, and it works Brown's ruin.

We realize that this story is often interpreted as highly ambiguous, highly ambivalent in its attitude toward Puritanism and the notion of innate depravity. But we read it as another of those stories in which the Romantic Hawthorne sets out to criticize extreme Puritanism and to chide the folly of looking for evil where there isn't any. In this regard, the story seems much like "Ethan Brand," in which the protagonist sets out to find the unpardonable sin, only to receive God's pardon anyway; and like "The Minister's Black Veil," in which Mr. Hooper makes himself miserable by seeing the world through a dark screen. (The latter is, admittedly, a more ambivalent tale: Hawthorne also finds something to be said in favor of that black veil and its wearer's gloomy view.) Brown's outlook has been tainted by dark illusion, conjured up, it would seem, by the devil's wiles.

Some initial discussion of the story's debt to American history may be helpful—most students can use a brief refresher on the Salem witchcraft trials, in which neighbor suspected neighbor and children recklessly accused innocent old women. The hand of the devil was always nearby, and it was the duty of all to watch for it. From Cotton Mather's *Wonders of the Invisible World* (1693), Hawthorne drew details of his imagined midnight Sabbath. In revealing to Brown the secret wickedness of all the people he knew and trusted, the story seems to illustrate the Puritan doctrine of innate depravity. Humankind was born tarred with the brush of original sin and could not lose the smudge by any simple ritual of baptism. Only the elect—communicants, those who had experienced some spiritual illumination which they had declared in public—could be assured of salvation. Brown's unhappy death at the end of the story seems conventional: Puritans held that how one died indicated his chances in the hereafter. A radiantly serene and happy death was an omen that the victim was Heaven-bound, while a dour death boded ill. The devil's looking like a blood relative may reflect another Puritan assumption. Hawthorne's great-grandfather, the witch trial judge, would have agreed that the devil often appears in disguise. The Salem trials admitted "spectral evidence"—testimony that the devil had been seen in the form of some innocent person. Spectral evidence was part of the case against Goody Cloyse, Goody Cory, and Martha Carrier—all named in Hawthorne's story, all of whom Judge John Hawthorne condemned to death. For more on Puritan doctrines (and how they eroded with time), see Herbert W. Schneider's classic study *The Puritan Mind* (University of Michigan Press, 1958). Of Hawthorne's tales and *The Scarlet Letter,* Schneider observes: "[Hawthorne] did not need to believe in Puritanism, for he understood it. . . . He recovered what the Puritans professed but seldom practiced—the spirit of piety, humility, and tragedy in the face of the inscrutable ways of God" (262-63).

Why does Brown go out to the woods? Apparently he has promised the devil he will go meet him, but go no farther. By meeting the devil he has "kept covenant" (15). The initial situation—that Brown has a promise to keep out in the woods—is vague, perhaps deliberately like the beginning of a dream.

And was it all a dream? Hawthorne hints that the devil's revelations to Brown and the midnight Sabbath are all one grand illusion. When Brown staggers against the supposedly flaming rock, it proves cold and damp, and a twig that had been on fire suddenly drips cold dew. (We are indebted here to F. O. Matthiessen's discussion in *American Renaissance* [Oxford University Press, 1941] 284.) If we read him right, Hawthorne favors the interpretation that Brown dreamed everything ("Be that as it may . . ."). Leave it to the devil to concoct a truly immense deception.

Still, some ambiguity remains. As Hawthorne declared in a letter to a friend in 1854, "I am not quite sure that I entirely comprehend my own meaning in some of these blasted allegories." In the end, Hawthorne leaves the interpretation of the story open; he will not pronounce absolutely. If what Brown saw at the witches' Sabbath really did take place, then his gloom and misery at the end of the story seem understandable. Some have read the story to mean that Brown has grown up to have a true sense of sin, and therefore ends a good Puritan; he has purged himself of his boyish good cheer. (Personally, we find the morose Brown deluded, not admirable, and suspect that Hawthorne does too.)

Students will not have met the term *allegory* in this book unless you have already dealt with the chapter "Symbolism," but some will know it already. Not only Faith can be seen as a figure of allegory, but Young Goodman Brown himself—the Puritan Everyman, subject to the temptation to find evil everywhere. For a class that has already begun symbol-hunting, "Young Goodman Brown" is a fair field. Among the more richly suggestive items are the devil's snaky staff or walking-stick (13), with its suggestions of the Eden snake and the serpentine rods of the Egyptian magicians (Exodus 7:8-12). When the devil laughs, it squirms happily (22). It works like seven-league boots, and its holder enjoys rapid transportation. The devil gives it to Goody Cloyse and then plucks Brown a fresh stick from a maple (38-41); when Brown grasps it in despair (51), it speeds him on to the unholy communion. Other symbolic items (and actions) include the forest—entering it is to be led into temptation, and Brown keeps going deeper and deeper; the withering of the maple branch at the devil's touch (38); and the proffered baptism in blood or fire at the evil meeting (67).

But the richest symbol of all is Faith's lost pink ribbon that flutters to the ground, prompting Brown to conclude that Faith too is a witch and let fall her ribbon while riding on a broomstick to the midnight Sabbath. (Many students, unless you help them, will miss this suggestion.) Sure enough, when Brown arrives, Faith is there too. The ribbon, earlier suggesting youthful beauty and innocence, becomes an ironic sign of monstrous evil and duplicity. This terrible realization causes Brown to decide to follow the devil after all— even though, presumably, the fluttering ribbon was another diabolical trick. When Brown meets the real Faith once more, she is still all beribboned, as if she hasn't lost anything. (A Freudian explanation would find the ribbon a kind of maidenhead, which Faith loses on losing her innocence.)

What are we to make of the resemblance between the devil and Brown's grandfather? Taken literally, perhaps it suggests that evil runs in Brown's family, or in the Puritan line as the devil asserts (18-19). Or that wickedness lurks within each human heart (as well as good) and that each can recognize it in himself, as if he had looked into a mirror. Of course, donning the family face may be one more trick of the devil: an attempt to ingratiate himself with Brown by appearing as a close relative.

Hawthorne published this story in a magazine in 1835 but, omitting it from *Twice Told Tales* (1837), did not reprint it until eleven years later in *Mosses from an Old Manse* (1846). Did he hesitate to give permanence to this bold blast at the faith of his fathers? The story implies that the Puritan propensity for hunting out hidden sin was inspired by the devil. Perhaps Hawthorne may have had this story in mind when he wrote, in his dedication to a later collection of tales, *The Snow Image* (1851): "In youth, men are apt to write more easily than they really know or feel; and the remainder of life may be not idly spent in realizing and convincing themselves of the wisdom which they uttered long ago."

How to state the theme? Surely not "Evil is the nature of mankind" or "Even the most respected citizens are secretly guilty." That is what the devil would have us believe. A more defensible summing-up might be "Keep your faith in God and humankind" or "He who finds evil where no evil exists makes himself an outcast from humanity."

Compare this story with Shirley Jackson's "The Lottery." There, too, a whole town takes part in a blood-curdling rite—but public, not clandestine.

Luke 15: 11–32.

THE PARABLE OF THE PRODIGAL SON, page 222

The original setting of this famous parable may help clarify its principal theme. Jesus has been preaching in the towns and villages along the road to Jerusalem. He has attracted great crowds, including many disreputable people whom Jewish religious leaders would traditionally have avoided or spurned. The Pharisees (strict practitioners of Jewish dogma) and the Scribes (doctors of religious law) expressed shock that Jesus would be willing to receive and even dine with sinners (not to mention tax collectors). In Luke 15, Jesus answers their criticism with three parables: the lost sheep, the lost coin, and the prodigal son. These parables implicitly preach compassion and concern for sinners. The righteous, Jesus implies, don't reject sinners; they seek to bring them back to virtue.

Most parables from the Gospels have a slightly abstract quality. Short, simple, and allegorical, they illustrate their morals through exemplary but deliberately generalized characters and action. The characters in "The Parable of the Prodigal Son," however, feel like individual human beings. We experience their motivations, emotions, and thoughts. The parable reads like a short story. The philosopher George Santayana called it "a little masterpiece."

The human theme of the parable might be summarized as "genuine virtue includes the power to forgive" or "true goodness requires love and compassion, not just outward virtue." The elder son has led an outwardly virtuous life, but when his erring brother returns home, he cannot put aside his jealousy to greet him. He resents his father's joy as well as his brother's behavior. His external righteousness has not nourished his heart: he feels neither joy nor compassion. The father, however, rejoices in the younger son's safe return. Santayana thought that the parable also had a psychological theme: "There is more joy in finding what was lost than there would be in merely keeping it."

We tend to remember this parable as the story of the younger son. (Its traditional title, "The Parable of the Prodigal Son," surely contributes to this overly narrow focus.) However, the parable is more richly complex; it is, as the opening line tells us, the story of two brothers: "A certain man had two sons." In his excellent commentary on the Gospel, *Saint Luke* (London: Penguin, 1963), G. B. Caird points out that the loving and generous father has actually lost both sons, "one in a foreign country, the other behind a barricade of self-righteousness. The elder contrived, without leaving home, to be as far away from his father as ever his brother was in a heathen pigsty. Both brothers are selfish, though in totally different ways." [p. 182] The theme of the parable would be less dramatically presented if we did not see (and probably feel some sympathy with) the older brother's uncharitable reaction to the prodigal's return.

The father refuses to be drawn into an argument with his older son. When the son complains to him, he answers with, to quote G. B. Caird again, "the gentlest of rebukes": "Son, thou art ever with me, and all that I have is thine. It was meet that we should make merry, and be glad: for this thy brother was dead, and is alive again; and was lost, and is found."

It may be worthwhile to point out a few memorable details along the way. Ask for someone to define the word *prodigal.* You will be surprised how few students know what it means. (On second thought, maybe you won't be surprised.) You may want to point out that tending pigs—unclean animals, according to Jewish belief—was a horribly degrading job for the younger son. You may also wish to store up the prodigal's phrase, "I will arise and go to my father" in your memory for the next time you teach William Butler Yeats's "The Lake Isle of Innisfree" (which appears in the chapter on "Reading a Poem" on page 585). Yeats's poem begins, " I will arise and go now, and go to Innisfree," and the poet intends a biblical echo to let us know that his return to this spot is no mere weekend holiday. Finally, you might want to point out how the image of killing "the fatted calf" has become a traditional symbol for extravagant and joyful feasting. (Students in the Boston area may recognize it as the name of a local restaurant.)

A good writing exercise is to ask students to retell the parable from the older brother's perspective. Can they present his version of the story without losing the original theme? (For a comic retelling of the parable from just this slant, see Garrison Keillor's satiric skit, *The Prodigal Son,* in the Drama section on page 1095.)

Another version of the prodigal son's story occurs in Rainer Maria Rilke's novel, *The Notebooks of Malte Laurids Brigge* (1910). Rilke's powerful retelling of the parable appears as the last few pages of the book, and it can be easily understood by someone who has not read the rest of the novel. (In the German-speaking world, his parable is frequently anthologized separately.) In Rilke's version, the younger brother is "a man who didn't want to be loved," a person who could not bear the weight and responsibility of another's affection. A savvy student could write an excellent term paper on comparing Rilke's parable to the Gospel original.

Raymond Carver
CATHEDRAL, page 223

On the surface, "Cathedral" is a simple story told in the flattest possible style by a not-too-bright narrator. His wife has invited a blind friend to stay with them. The encounter is awkward because the narrator has never met a blind person before. His misgivings are spelled out most clearly in paragraphs 1, 5, 9, 17, and 31. As the evening advances, a hearty meal, several drinks, and a few puffs of marijuana put the wife to sleep. The men stay awake and end up drawing a cathedral, the blind man's hand guided by the narrator's.

What does it all mean? Students will have to examine with uncommon thoughtfulness Carter's detailed account of this episode. In the story, one man's preconceptions about blind people are demolished. At the end, he has a revelation in which he experiences what it's like to be blind. How does this new understanding come about? From the start, the wife's behavior toward Robert is accepting and natural. If ever she felt any awkwardness toward blind people, it has long since disappeared. She sees Robert as a valued friend rather than as merely a blind man. In fact, she and Robert seem to know more about one another's thoughts and feelings than she and her husband do. Perhaps sensing this, the narrator exhibits a bit of jealousy mingled with his other negative reactions, especially in paragraph 46.

At first the husband blunders wretchedly, trying to make small-talk by asking the blind man what side of the train he had sat on (25). He notices with some surprise that Robert doesn't wear dark glasses or use a cane (31) and that he smokes (44). Is it just thoughtlessness, or is it a wish to cover an uncomfortable silence that impels him finally to turn on the TV?

The wife grows sleepy. Still wanting to be a good hostess, she suggests that Robert might like to go to bed. When he shows no inclination to do so, she falls asleep in spite of herself. Left alone with Robert, the narrator, too, suggests bed. Robert is, after all, his wife's guest. When Robert expresses a desire to stay up and talk with the husband, a turning point is reached. Perhaps surprised, the husband suddenly realizes that he's lonely, and in a new spirit begins explaining to the blind man what's happening on the TV screen. The story ends with a startling revelation. The narrator learns from the blind man not only how to draw a cathedral, but what it's really like to be blind.

Students have phrased the story's theme in different ways: "Barriers tend to break down when people try to communicate with one another," or "Even those not physically blind sometimes need to be taught to see," or "Stereotypes render sighted people blind to the common humanity we all share." (Obviously, the story itself is light-years better than any possible statements of its theme.)

For a writing topic, a student might be asked to read D. H. Lawrence's "The Blind Man" (in *Complete Short Stories,* Volume II [Penguin Books], or in many anthologies) and compare the characters of the blind man and the sighted man with the similar pair in "Cathedral."

Shortly after Carver's death, Jay McInerney, who had been his student of fiction writing at Syracuse University in the early 1980s, published a warmly affectionate memoir, "Raymond Carver: A Still, Small Voice," in the *New York Times Book Review* for August 6, 1989. McInerney recalls Carver as a man given to quiet understatement, so shy and soft spoken that an interviewer once had to put the tape recorder in the author's lap and still found his responses almost inaudible. His harshest criticism to a writing student was, "I think it's good you got that story behind you."

Carver talks with frankness and humor about his work in an interview now available on audiotape cassette from the American Audio Prose Library (AAPL) (51 minutes, $13.95). Among other things, he says he chose to write short stories because he found he lacked time to write novels when, at age nineteen, he found himself a father. You may order by phone: (800) 447-2275. AAPL's whole catalog is worth a look.

7 Symbol

John Steinbeck
THE CHRYSANTHEMUMS, page 239

In the sight of the flower pot and its contents, discarded in the road, Elisa sees the end of her brief interlude of hopes and dreams. Once, the chrysanthemums had embodied fulfillment: living proof of her ability to make things grow and bloom. As the title of the story indicates, they are the primary symbol—and when we state their meaning, we are close to stating the story's theme.

Elisa is a complex study in frustration, a frustration that stems in part from her being a woman in a world of men. That she is a strong, intense woman with far more energy than she can put to use is made clear at once, when we learn that "even her work with the scissors was over-eager, over-powerful" and that her house is "a hard-swept looking little house, with hard-polished windows."

Trapped under a "grey-flannel fog" that encloses the valley like a lid on a pot, Elisa works inside a symbolic barrier: a wire fence "that protected her flower garden from cattle and dogs and chickens" and that also protects her, because she is a woman, from the wider world. Custom denies her and her restless energy the adequate outlets that men enjoy. She cannot buy and sell cattle as Henry does. She cannot drift about the countryside mending utensils as the traveling repairman does, though his gypsy life-style powerfully appeals to her. "That sounds like a nice kind of a way to live," she declares on meeting him. "I wish women could do such things," she tells him later, and adds, "I can sharpen scissors, too. . . . I could show you what a woman might do." But she will never be given such an opportunity.

Besides her frustration at the passive role thrust upon her, Elisa is thwarted because her considerable gifts for nurturing—her "planting hands"—have little value in the wider world. It seems clear that the remarkable chrysanthemums are richly symbolic of her feminine talents. Yet the practical and shortsighted Henry, because the flowers are not a cash crop, says, "I wish you'd work out in the orchard and raise some apples that big." The traveling repairman feigns an interest in the chrysanthemum shoots for his own gain and then throws them on the road and saves the pot. So much for Elisa's creativity. Mordecai Marcus, in his critical comment, sees Elisa's flowers as substitutes for the children she (now thirty-five) was apparently unable to have ("The Lost Dream of Sex and Childbirth in 'The Chrysanthemums,'" *Modern Fiction Studies* 11 [1965]: 54–58). The suggestion, though likely, is not clearly confirmed in the story. "Elisa's need is definitely sexual," according to Elizabeth E. McMahan, "but it does not necessarily have anything to do with a longing for children" ("'The Chrysanthemums': Study of a Woman's Sexuality," *Modern Fiction Studies* 14 [1968]: 453–58).

Given to speaking in impassioned poetry ("Every pointed star gets driven into your body"), Elisa is further thwarted by having to live a life devoid of romance. Although kind enough and considerate enough, Henry is dull. When he tries to turn a compliment, the best he can do is, "Why—why Elisa. You look so nice!"—and when pressed for details, falls into grossness: "You look strong enough to break a calf over your knee, happy enough to eat it like a watermelon."

Sleazy as he is, the gypsy repairman has a touch of the poet about him. He can describe a chrysanthemum as "a quick puff of colored smoke." Elisa's short-lived belief that he values her flowers (and by extension, recognizes her womanliness) releases in her a long-pent eroticism for which the repairman is ill prepared. He changes the subject.

Elizabeth McMahan finds, in the bath-and-pumice scene that follows, "a purification ritual." Elisa "felt shame after her display of passion before the stranger. Now she cleanses herself before returning to her husband, the man to whom she should lawfully reach out in desire." And so Elisa punishes herself with the abrasive pumice until her skin is "scratched and red" in atonement for her imagined infidelity.

In the end, Elisa tries to satisfy her spiritual and erotic cravings by a feeble gesture: by asking Henry if they might order wine with their dinner. "It will be enough if we can have wine. It will be plenty." It isn't enough, of course, and she cries "weakly—like an old woman"—she who had briefly thought herself strong. Her new interest in prize fights, in the spectacle of blood-letting she had formerly rejected, manifests Elisa's momentary wish for revenge on men: her desire to repay them for her injured femininity. At least, this is the interpretation of Marcus and of McMahan.

Elisa's battle with her stifled sexuality is conveyed in detail ("her hand went out toward his legs in the greasy black trousers. . . . She crouched low like a fawning dog"). A textual critic, William R. Osborne, demonstrates that Steinbeck, in revising the story, heightened Elisa's earthiness and the sexual overtones of her encounter with the repairman (*Modern Fiction Studies* 12 [1966]: 479-84). Of the two extant texts of the story, this book prints the revised version as it appeared in *The Long Valley* (New York: Viking, 1938).

Like his early model, D. H. Lawrence, Steinbeck is fond of portraying people swept by dark forces of the unconscious. A curious book for additional reading: Steinbeck's Lawrencian novel *To a God Unknown* (New York: Viking, 1933). "The Chrysanthemums" invites comparison with Lawrence's "The Blind Man," which also conveys a woman's struggle for intellectual survival while living with a mindless husband on a farm. Henry Allen is no match, though, for Lawrence's impressive Maurice. If the two stories are set side by side for evaluation, Lawrence's may well seem (in our opinion) the deeper and more vivid. Though finely perceptive, "The Chrysanthemums" has something methodical about it, as if the young Steinbeck were deliberately trying to contrive a short-story masterpiece. But this is to dissent from the judgments of Mordecai Marcus, who thinks it indeed "one of the world's great short stories," and of André Gide, who in his *Journals* finds it in a league with the best of Chekhov (Vol. IV. [New York: Knopf, 1951] 79).

"The Chrysanthemums" is a rare illustration of an unusual method: the objective point of view, or "the fly on the wall." After some opening authorial remarks about the land, Steinbeck confines himself to reporting external details. Although the reader comes to share Elisa's feelings, we do not enter her mind; we observe her face and her reactions ("Elisa's eyes grew alert and eager"). This cinematic method of storytelling seems a hardship for the author only in paragraph 109, when to communicate Elisa's sadness he has to have her whisper aloud.

Shirley Jackson
THE LOTTERY, page 248

Shirley Jackson's famous story shocks us. By transferring a primitive ritual to a modern American small town and by making clear in passing that the same ritual is being carried out in surrounding towns, the author manages to create in us a growing sense of horror over what is happening. Very early—in paragraphs 2 and 3—she mentions the stones that have been gathered in preparation for the day's events. Not until much later in the story does the importance of the stones begin to dawn.

Students might be asked to sum up the rules of Jackson's lottery, which are simple and straightforward. The head of each household—or, if he is absent, another representative of the family—draws a slip of paper out of a big black box. One householder pulls out a piece of paper that has a black circle crudely penciled on it. Each member of his family is then obliged to participate in a second drawing. This time the unlucky recipient of the black circle is stoned to death by the other townspeople, including the members of his or her own family. Whatever justification might ever have existed for the ritual has long since been forgotten. The people simply accept the proceedings as an annual civic duty, the up-to-date version of an ancient fertility ritual ("Lottery in June, corn be heavy soon").

What is spine-chilling in Jackson's story is the matter-of-factness with which the ritual is carried out. Each June the townspeople assemble to murder one of their neighbors. The discrepancy between ordinary, civilized, modern behavior and the calm acceptance of something as primitive as human sacrifice gives "The Lottery" a terrible power. Among the story's many ironies, some of the most notable are:

1. The point of view. An objective narrator tells the story, remaining outside the characters' minds, yet the narrator's detachment contrasts with the attitude of the author, who presumably, like the reader, is horrified. That the day's happenings can be recounted so objectively lends them both credence and force.

2. The setting. The beauty of the June day is out of keeping with the fact that what takes place on the town green is a ritual murder.

3. The misplaced chivalry. Though women can be stoned to death in these yearly proceedings, they are whenever possible protected from having to take part in the general drawing (paragraph 13).

4. The characters. The townspeople are perfectly ordinary types, "surveying their own children, speaking of planting and rain, tractors and taxes" (3). Mr. Summers is in charge because he "had time and energy to devote to civic activities" (4). Old Man Warner is a stickler for tradition. Neighbors chat amiably. Children play. All are grateful that the proceedings will be over in time for them to enjoy their noon meal.

As a matter of course, even the small son of the victim is given some stones to throw at his mother. That is perhaps the most horrifying detail of all.

The story's very outrageousness raises questions about unexamined assumptions in modern society. Do civilized Americans accept and act upon other vestiges of primitive ritual as arbitrary as the one Jackson imagines? Are we shackled by traditions as bizarre and pointless as the lottery in Jackson's story? What determines the line between behavior that is routine and that which is unthinkable? How civilized in fact are we?

In *Private Demons: The Life of Shirley Jackson* (New York: Putnam's, 1988), Judy Oppenheimer gives a good account of the story's genesis. Jackson wrote "The Lottery" in 1948 while pregnant with her third child. She had been reading a book on ancient customs of human sacrifice and had found herself wondering how such a rite might operate in the village of North Bennington, Vermont, where she lived.

Peter Hawkes of East Stroudsburg University finds an obstacle to teaching "The Lottery" in that many students think its central premise totally unrealistic and absurd. How, they assume, can this story have anything to do with me? Hawkes dramatizes the plausibility of the townspeople's unswerving obedience to authority. With a straight face, he announces that the Dean has just decreed that every English teacher give at least one F per class to reduce grade inflation, passes around a wooden box, and tells students to draw for the fatal grade! "While I pass the box around the room, I watch carefully for, and indirectly encourage, the student who will refuse to take a slip of paper. When this happens, I ask the class what should be done. Invariably, someone in the class will say that the person who refused to draw deserves the F. Hearing this, the student almost always draws." See Mr. Hawkes's account in "The Two Lotteries: Teaching Shirley Jackson's 'The Lottery,'" *Exercise Exchange* for Fall 1987. We would expect a class to greet this trick with much skepticism! But what if you were to try it on them *before* assigning the story?

Jackson once remarked that in writing "The Lottery" she had hoped "to shock the story's readers with a graphic demonstration of the pointless violence and general inhumanity in their own lives" (quoted by Lenemaja Friedman, *Shirley Jackson* [New York: Twayne, 1975]). For class discussion: What is the point of Jackson's comment? Is it true? In our own society, what violent behavior is sanctioned? How are we comparable to Jackson's villagers? Don't we too casually accept the unthinkable?

"The Lottery" invites comparison with Hawthorne's "Young Goodman Brown": in each, an entire community is seen to take part in a horrifying rite.

Yet another interpretation is possible. Jackson ran into parental opposition when she announced her intention of marrying fellow Syracuse University student Stanley Edgar Hyman, and some of her housemates warned her of the perils of living with a Jew. Shocked by these early run-ins with anti-Semitism, Jackson once told a friend (according to Judy Oppenheimer) that "The Lottery" was a story about the Holocaust.

There are dangers, of course, in reading more meaning into the story than it will sustain. Jackson herself, in *Come Along with Me* (New York, Viking, 1968), insists that we accept the story at face value. After its debut in *The New Yorker* in 1948, Jackson was surprised by the great amount of mail she received about the story. Some letter writers demanded to know what "The Lottery" meant, others supplied interpretations that they wished confirmed, others angrily abused the author for writing such a story. She even had letters from people asking where these lotteries were held, that they might go and watch the drawings.

Ursula K. Le Guin
THE ONES WHO WALK AWAY FROM OMELAS, page 255

Ursula Le Guin's "The Ones Who Walk Away From Omelas" may be the most unusual story in the book in its relation to the conventions of storytelling. It does not describe the actions of a particular character or small group of characters. It has no plot or protagonist in the usual sense. A skeptical critic of old-fashioned taste might even claim that it is not truly a short story—a fiction, yes, but not a story. Le Guin's central character is an imaginary society. Her plot is a survey of the civilization that leads up to a single shocking revelation. Yet this unusual work has been recognized as a small classic from the beginning. It won a Hugo (science fiction's most prestigious award) after its first magazine appearance, and it has been frequently anthologized in both science fiction and mainstream anthologies. We welcome it back to this anthology after an absence of several editions.

"The Ones Who Walk Away From Omelas" seems only slightly less unusual when seen in the context of science fiction. The story belongs to a standard genre of science fiction that presents an imaginary civilization in order to criticize some aspect of our own culture, and yet even when viewed against such science fiction conventions, Le Guin's story is an unusually plotless, subtly ironic, and intellectually complex piece. This story's genre is often called utopian fantasy (after Thomas More's 1516 *Utopia*), though some readers might claim that she actually describes a dystopia, a conspicuously flawed society. (Some famous dystopian fictions would include George Orwell's *1984*, Aldous Huxley's *Brave New World*, and Anthony Burgess's *A Clockwork Orange*.) Actually, Le Guin's story borrows elements from both the utopian and dystopian traditions. Le Guin's narrator fervently believes that Omelas is a perfect society; the narrator intends the story to be a utopian vision. The reader, however, sees the horrifying moral compromise at the center of the society, and, as the story's title suggests, the author also sees Omelas as a covert dystopia.

Le Guin's story is overtly disturbing—and all the more so because the narrator blithely accepts the undeserved suffering that shocks the reader. Her penetrating parable raises the same ethical issue as Dostoyevsky's famous tale of "The Grand Inquisitor" from *The Brothers Karamazov:* would it be morally acceptable to purchase universal happiness at the cost of injustice to one innocent child? Le Guin appears to say that no society should rest on such injustice. Surely, it is not coincidental that by the time the narrator tells this story, the happy civilization of Omelas has apparently ceased to exist. In this detail, Le Guin suggests perhaps that Omelas has rotted from within and that any civic or cultural achievements purchased at such a price will not endure.

Although Le Guin admits she knew *The Brothers Karamazov*, she claims in a note on this story in her collection, *The Wind's Twelve Quarters* (New York: Harper and Row, 1975) that she got the idea for the story from William James's essay, "The Moral Philosopher and the Moral Life":

> Or if the hypothesis were offered us of a world in which . . . utopias should all be outdone, and millions kept permanently happy on the one simple condition that a certain lost soul on the far-off edge of things should lead a life of lonely torment, what except a specific and independent sort of emotion can it be which would make us immediately feel, even though an impulse arose within us to clutch at the happiness so offered, how hideous a thing would be its enjoyment when deliberately accepted as the fruit of such a bargain? ("The Moral Philosopher and the Moral Life," in *Collected Essays and Reviews* [London: Longmans, Green, 1920])

Le Guin remarked; "The dilemma of the American conscience can hardly be better stated" (*The Wind's Twelve Quarters*). She adds, in the same note on her story:

> Of course, I didn't read James and sit down and say, Now I'll write a story about that "lost soul." It seldom works that simply. I sat down and started a story, just because I felt like it, with nothing but the word "Omelas" in mind. It came from a road sign: Salem [Oregon] backwards. . . . Salem equals schelomo equals salaam equals Peace. Melas. O melas. Homme hélas.

Shades of *Finnegans Wake*!

William James stated his idea differently (and more facetiously) when on another occasion, he told a Harvard class, "This universe will never be completely good as long as one being is unhappy, as long as one poor cockroach suffers the pangs of unrequited love" (quoted by Gilbert Highet in *The Art of Teaching* [New York: Vintage Books, 1953] 207).

There are two dominant symbols in "The Ones Who Walk Away From Omelas" that deserve discussion. The first is the city of Omelas itself, "bright-towered by the sea." What does Omelas symbolize? At the very least, it suggests the dream of human happiness. ("They were not simple folk, you see," the narrator tells us, "though they were happy.") The citizens of Omelas are "Joyous!" as well as "mature, intelligent, passionate adults whose lives are not wretched." To the narrator at least, Omelas represents a happiness no longer possible in a cheerless time. In a moral sense, however, Omelas symbolizes the hidden compromises that prosperous societies must make. "It is the existence of the child, and their knowledge of its existence," the narrator claims, "that makes possible the nobility of their architecture, the poignancy of their music, the profundity of their science."

The unforgettable symbol of Le Guin's story, however, is the filthy, feeble-minded child locked in the dark cellar. The symbolic significance of this pathetic figure and its grim setting ramifies in many directions. The child is imprisoned in the basement of "one of the beautiful public buildings of Omelas." It is the hidden injustice on which the city is built. The child symbolizes all the evil that citizens in a society must learn to accept without question in order to enjoy their own position. "They all know that it is there, all the people of Omelas," the narrator assures us. The child does not suffer because the good citizens of Omelas are ignorant: it suffers because the citizens are willing to trade its "abominable misery" for their peace, pleasure, and prosperity. Although the child is universally known, it is also kept out of sight. In psychological terms, the child symbolizes the horrible knowledge the conscious mind wishes to repress in order to maintain its happiness.

Students planning to write on Le Guin's story might compare it to Dostoyevsky's powerful "The Grand Inquisitor" (*The Brothers Karamazov,* Volume I, Book 5, Chapter 5). How does Le Guin's parable differ from Dostoyevsky's? How does her work resemble his? Le Guin's other fiction will also provide fruitful areas for research. Her finest work is her novels, especially *The Left Hand of Darkness* (1969), *The Lathe of Heaven* (1971), and *The Dispossessed* (1974). (Her "Earthsea" trilogy of novels for young adults is also superb.) *The Dispossessed* would be a particularly interesting book to compare and contrast to "The Ones Who Walk Away From Omelas," since the novel presents two radically different societies, each with conspicuous strengths and weaknesses that puzzle the narrator, who wrestles with the ethical issue of which to consider superior.

8 *Evaluating a Story*

Most students find it a lighter task to place two stories side by side and to decide which is superior than to hold one story before them and evaluate it. This is why we suggest—if you have time for evaluation—assigning pairs of stories in some way comparable. For more suggestions of stories that may be paired, see the two sections at the beginning of the "Fiction" section, "Stories Arranged by Type," and "Stories Arranged by Subject and Theme," pages 3–12.

9 Reading Long Stories and Novels

Leo Tolstoi

THE DEATH OF IVAN ILYCH, page 269

Students might respond to the questions like this:

QUESTIONS

1. *Sum up the reactions of Ivan's colleagues to the news of his death. What is implied in Tolstoi's calling them not friends but "nearest acquaintances"?* "The first thought of each of the gentlemen in that private room was of the changes and promotions [Ivan's death] might occasion among themselves or their acquaintances" (paragraph 5). Then, after these selfish hopes, they thought of their boring duties: to attend the funeral, to visit Ivan's widow (paragraph 18). Tolstoi suggests Ivan had no true friends but only "so-called friends" (18) and "nearest acquaintances" (19).

2. *What comic elements do you find in the account of the wake that Peter Ivanovich attends?* Comic elements include the Church Reader with his imperious tone (paragraph 24), Peter Ivanovich's struggles with the rebellious springs of the couch (33, 37), and his longing to escape to a card game—fulfilled at the end of Chapter I. The widow haggles over the price of a cemetery plot (33–35) and utters the great comic lines (in 40) congratulating herself on enduring Ivan's screams.

3. *In Tolstoi's description of the corpse and its expression (paragraph 27), what details seem especially revealing and meaningful?* See paragraph 27, especially the statement that the corpse's expression contains "a reproach and a warning to the living."

4. *Do you think Tolstoi would have improved the story had he placed the events in chronological order? What if the opening scene of Ivan's colleagues at the Law Courts and the wake scene were to be given last? What would be lost?* Tolstoi's arrangement of events seems masterly. We see from the first the selfish, superficial circle of colleagues among whom Ivan lived and his rather obtuse, querulous, self-centered wife. As the story unfolds, we follow Ivan's progress from total absorption in his petty affairs to his final illumination. We begin with an exterior view of the contex of Ivan's society and end with one man, all alone, confronting eternity. *like Svidrigailov*

5. *Would you call Ivan, when we first meet him, a religious man? Sum up his goals in life, his values, his attitudes.* Ivan seems a usual, sensual man, able to minimize his feelings of guilt (paragraph 59). His life centers in the official world, and he believes it should flow "pleasantly and properly" (82). "The pleasures connected with his work were pleasures of ambition; his social pleasures were those of vanity" (108).

6. *By what "virtues" and abilities does Ivan rise through the ranks? While he continues to succeed in his career, what happens to his marriage?* Ivan performs his official duties with "exactness and incorruptible honesty" (81), he is decorous and rule-abiding, wields power objectively and does not abuse it (65). As he succeeds in the world, his marriage deteriorates (82), and improves only when Ivan and his wife see little of each other (98).

7. *"Every spot on the tablecloth or the upholstery, and every broken window-blind string, irritated him. He had devoted so much trouble to arranging it all that every disturbance of it distressed him"* *(paragraph 104). What do you make of this passage? What is its tone? Does the narrator sympathize with Ivan's attachment to his possessions?* Ivan's excessive concern with every spot on the tablecloth seems part of his fussy overemphasis on material possessions. Tolstoi is suggesting, of course, that Ivan's insistent worldliness goes together with a neglect for the welfare of his soul.

8. *Consider the account of Ivan's routine ("He got up at nine . . . ," paragraph 105). What elements of a full life, what higher satisfactions, does this routine omit?* Ivan's routine (paragraph 105) omits love, worship, and any profound involvement with his friends and family. His social consciousness is confined to a little chat about politics; his interest in art and science to a little chat about "general topics." Ivan devotes himself only to superficial courtesies and appearances—to maintaining "the semblance of friendly human relations" without any deeper fondness or compassion.

9. *What caused Ivan's illness? How would it probably be diagnosed today? What is the narrator's attitude toward Ivan's doctors?* The illness might be diagnosed as cancer of the abdomen caused by falling off a ladder while hanging curtains. (The fall is casually described in paragraph 99.) Tolstoi detested physicians and implies (in paragraphs 115–120, 128, 152–153) that Ivan's doctors are know-nothings. In 247, Ivan submits to an examination that he sees as "nonsense and pure deception," like the speeches of certain lawyers to whom he had listened as a judge. The "celebrated specialist" (258–259) seems a quack.

10. *In what successive stages does Tolstoi depict Ivan's growing isolation as his progressive illness sets him further and further apart?* See especially paragraphs 308–11. (Tolstoi's story has a theme in common with Thomas Mann's *The Magic Mountain:* the sick and the healthy are races set apart.)

11. *What are we apparently supposed to admire in the character and conduct of the servant Gerasim?* From our first meeting with him, Gerasim radiates generosity, warm sympathy, cheerful acceptance of God's will. All men shall come to death, even Ivan Ilych, he affirms (in 50). Gerasim is the good peasant, faithful and devoted, willing to sit all night holding his master's legs (285).

12. *What do you understand from the statement that Ivan's justification of his life "prevented his moving forward, and it caused him most torment of all" (paragraph 346)?* By his reluctance to acknowledge that his life "was not all the right thing" (as he finally admits in paragraph 348), Ivan is hindered in his advance toward enlightenment.

13. *What is memorable in the character of Ivan's schoolboy son? Why is he crucial to the story? (Suggestion: Look closely at paragraphs 349–50).* Ivan's son, though only briefly sketched, is unforgettable. Early in the story (in 48), Peter Ivanovich finds in his eyes ("tearstained" from genuine grief) "the look . . . of boys of thirteen or fourteen who are not pure-minded." As in all masturbators (according to popular lore), "terribly dark shadows showed under his eyes" (268). Yet it is the schoolboy, alone among Ivan's immediate family, who loves Ivan and feels sorry for him. By kissing his father's hand (349), the boy brings on Ivan's illumination.

14. *What realization allows Ivan to triumph over pain? Why does he die gladly?* It is revealed (in paragraph 350) that although Ivan's life has been futile, he still can set it right. "He whose understanding mattered" (351) now understands him. Able to love at last, Ivan feels sorry not for himself but for his wife and son. When at last he is willing to relinquish the life to which he has desperately clung, death holds no fear.

15. *Henri Troyat has said that through the story of Ivan Ilych we imagine what our own deaths will be. Is it possible to identify with an aging, selfish, worldly, nineteenth-century Russian judge?* Randall Jarrell seems right in his observation that "we terribly identify ourselves with" Ivan Ilych. "Ivan Ilych's life has been a conventional falsehood; *The Death of Ivan Ilych* is the story of how he is tortured into the truth. No matter how alien they may have seemed to him to begin with, in the end the reader can dissociate neither from the falsehood, the torture, nor the truth: he *is* Ivan Ilych" ("Six Russian Short Novels," *The Third Book of Criticism* [New York: Farrar, 1965]).

"Beyond any doubt," said Tolstoi's biographer Henri Troyat, writing of *The Death of Ivan Ilych*, "this double story of the decomposing body and the awakening soul is one of the most powerful works in the literature of the world."

Completed in 1886, when its author was fifty-seven, this short novel stands relatively late in Tolstoi's literary career. *War and Peace* had appeared in 1863–1869; *Anna Karenina*, in 1875–1877. Still to come were *The Kreutzer Sonata* (1889) and *Resurrection* (1899–1900). Tolstoi undertook *The Death of Ivan Ilych* as a diversion from writing his earnest sociological treatise *What Then Must We Do?*—a work that few readers have preferred. Apparently, however, he became deeply involved in the story, for he toiled over it for nearly two years. It was to be (he told a correspondent) an account of "an ordinary man's ordinary death." This irony is stressed in the opening words of Part II: "Ivan Ilych's life had been most simple and most ordinary and therefore most terrible"—a sentence that Jarrell called one of the most frightening in literature.

Tolstoi based details of his story upon actual life: his memories of the agonizing death of his brother Nikolai, whom he dearly loved; and a description of the final illness of one Ivan Ilych Mechnikov, public prosecutor of the Tula district court, which he had heard from Mechnikov's brother.

Embedded in Ivan's story is another story: Praskovya's story, equally convincing as a study of character development. This insight comes to us from Nancy Adams Malone of Mattatuck Community College, who writes:

Question: How does the girl described in paragraph 68–70 as "attractive, clever" and "sweet, pretty" turn into the appalling woman we meet at the beginning of the story?

To a twentieth-century reader, it's a story as startlingly recognizable as Ivan's own. Praskovya's story begins in paragraph 72 with her first pregnancy. Like any thoughtless, well-meaning, ignorant young couple of our own time, they are not prepared for a change in emotional balance. The successful bride turns into an insecure woman rather suddenly. She's worried about losing her looks, she needs reassurance that her husband still loves her—in short, paragraph 73. Like many another young husband, Ivan is dismayed by the new whiny, tearful, demanding wife, and does the natural (not the necessary) thing: he retreats. This move naturally increases the insecurity and the demands, a predictably vicious circle. . . .

Paragraphs 80–81 show another recognizable pattern: the family moves, and although the husband may be absorbed in his work, the wife has been uprooted from whatever emotional supports she has had earlier, family or friends or both. Money troubles, of course, don't help. And two children died. Even in a century that didn't expect to raise all its children (as we do), this loss couldn't help being an emotional wound. Paragraph 82 shows how Ivan dealt with all these troubles: "His aim was to free himself more and more from unpleasantness . . . by spending less and less time with his family. . . ."

Without making any kind of point of it, Tolstoi shows clearly how Ivan contributes to his wife's emotional and spiritual deterioration. I suppose, in today's climate, I should point out that this is not a feminist accusation that her deterioration is all Ivan's fault.

Jarrell's essay supplies further insights. Ilych is a man whose professional existence—being absurd, parasitic, irrelevant, and (to take a term from Sartre) unauthentic—has swallowed up his humanity and blinded him to the real. A life so misled is terrible, more to be dreaded than "real, serious, all-absorbing death." Revealingly, Jarrell quotes from Tolstoi's autobiographical *Confessions,* in which the author tells how he felt himself, like Ivan Ilych, shaped by society into an artificial mold, encouraged in his "ambition, lust of power, selfishness." Tolstoi himself had experienced a season of grave illness; it had given him time to reflect on his life (before his conversion to Christianity) and to find it meaningless.

In his *Confessions,* Tolstoi also tells of the death of his brother, who "suffered for more than a year, and died an agonizing death without comprehending what he had lived for, and still less why he should die." Some of the details in *Ivan Ilych* are believed to have been taken from Tolstoi's memory of his brother's struggle against disease and futile search for a cure.

For other useful discussions, see Philip Rahv, *Image and Idea* (Norfolk, CT: New Directions, 1949) 111-27; and Irving Halderin, "The Structural Integrity of 'The Death of Ivan Ilych,'" *Slavic and East European Journal 5* (1961) 334-40.

More clearly, perhaps, than any other modern writer, Tolstoi succeeds in raising an ordinary man to tragic dignity. As a critic observes, writing not of Tolstoi's story but of the nature of tragedy, "To see things plain—that is *anagnorisis,* and it is the ultimate experience we shall have if we have leisure at the point of death . . . . It is what tragedy ultimately is about: the realization of the unthinkable." The statement, from *Tragedy* by Clifford Leech (London: Methuen, 1969), seems closely applicable. Only when Ivan Ilych accepts the unthinkable truth that his life has been lived in vain can he relinquish his tightfisted grip on life, defeat pain, and, on the brink of death, begin to live. Whether or not we accept Tolstoi's religious answer, the story compels us to wonder what in our own lives is valuable—what is authentic beyond petty, selfish, everyday cares.

Tolstoi's subtle, complex history of a spiritual awakening may take awhile to sink in. When she dealt with the story in class, Dr. Edna H. Musso of Daytona Beach Community College found her students' reaction to it "so lackluster" that she decided that they didn't like the story. The dissenters made a fair case. "[Ilych's] life was so drawn out," wrote one student, "that I was almost relieved when he finally died." In the end, however, the class voted by a margin of two to one that the story should remain in the book. Most students felt that "the interpersonal relationships are true to life" and decided (as one put it), that "it will wake somebody up to see their own life paralleling Ivan's."

Robert Frost's poem "Out, Out—" may be compared with Tolstoi's story successfully, reports Jonathan Aldrich of Maine College of Art. Both works touch on the theme that death is an incredible event that arrives unexpectedly; although, unlike Ivan, Frost's protagonist has no time to meditate on the meaning of his death in advance of it.

Franz Kafka
THE METAMORPHOSIS, page 311

Few works of fiction have attracted more critical commentary than Franz Kafka's *The Metamorphosis.* This troubling, mysterious story leaves few readers unmoved, and the tale is a regular favorite among students, who generally find its nightmarish premise and tight family focus gripping. Teachers rarely have trouble getting students to talk about the story; the challenge is to keep the classroom discussion from becoming entirely impressionistic. Kafka has a famously strange effect on readers: they tend to project their own concerns and obsessions into his stories. While it may be impossible to come to one conclusive reading of *The Metamorphosis,* that impossibility should not prevent readers from working toward careful and consistent readings.

Originally issued as a separate volume in 1916, *The Metamorphosis* is a particularly interesting work to examine because it is the longest piece of fiction that Kafka completed and published during his lifetime. (All three of his novels are in some sense unfinished, and all were published posthumously.) Although the obsessively self-critical Kafka considered the work "imperfect almost to its very marrow," *The Metamorphosis* shows his literary artistry at its most ambitious, powerful, and assured.

To what genre does *The Metamorphosis* belong? One can legitimately describe it as a long short story or a short novel. German readers would generally consider it a novella (a fictional tale of intermediate length), a form they see as one of their central literary traditions including masters like Heinrich Von Kleist, E. T. A. Hoffmann, and Hermann Hesse. Famous novellas include Thomas Mann's *Death in Venice,* Henry James's *Daisy Miller,* and Leo Tolstoi's *The Death of Ivan Ilych* (the companion selection in this book). In America, there is no distinct tradition for the novella—despite the missionary efforts of James—so our critics usually consider *The Metamorphosis* a long short story. In any event, both terms imply an extended narrative that combines the concentrated focus of a short story with the novel's insistence on following a course of action to its end. A novella—unlike a novel—almost inevitably centers on a single character (e.g., Gregor Samsa, Ivan Ilych) in the same way that most short stories do, but the author need not compress the narrative into a few exemplary incidents; there is room for the story to unfold more fully. *The Metamorphosis* plunges us into the consciousness of its protagonist, Gregor Samsa, in the way a novel might. There is no sense that Kafka is curtailing the narrative at any point. Instead, the story unfolds at its own deliberate pace.

The instructor may want to point out the overall structure of the story, which is unique in Kafka's fiction. *The Metamorphosis* is divided into three equal sections. Many critics have noticed that this structure resembles a three-act play. In his introduction to *The Complete Stories of Franz Kafka* (New York: Viking, 1983), John Updike observes that in each "act," "the metamorphosed Gregor Samsa ventures out of his room, with tumultuous results." The British scholar Ronald Gray elaborates how each section ends with a climactic moment:

> In the first, Gregor Samsa awakens to the realisation that he has turned into an insect and emerges from his bedroom to be driven back by his infuriated father. In the second, he tries to accommodate himself to his absurdly hideous predicament . . . again, a brief sally into the living room is repulsed by the father, this time even more violently, as he pelts Gregor with apples. In the third, Gregor comes out while his sister is playing the violin, entranced by the music which seems to be the "food" he has so long been unable to find, but a third attack drives him back to die alone and untended. . . . After Gregor's death they turn with relief to the happier life that now awaits them. (reprinted in *Franz Kafka's The Metamorphosis* in Harold Bloom's "Modern Critical Interpretations" series)

Although Gray is wrong in citing a third "attack" on Gregor (he returns the last time to his room unmolested—at least physically), he does clarify the basic structure of the story. Heinz Politzer offers a more schematic structure in his *Franz Kafka: Parable and Paradox* (Ithaca, NY: Cornell University Press, 1966): "The first part shows Gregor in relation to his profession, the second to his family, and the third to himself." This structure does not become annoying, Politzer claims, "because the three parts are united by Gregor's fate, which is and remains an enigma."

The long list of questions at the end of the story is designed to focus students on interesting aspects of the plot and situation they may have overlooked in the initial reading. Considering these narrative details may suggest themes and interpretations that may not have initially occurred to them.

QUESTIONS

1. *What was Gregor's occupation before his transformation? How did he come to his particular job? What keeps him working for his firm?* The question of Gregor's employment is crucial to understanding the story. Gregor works as a traveling salesman—a situation he dislikes. He wants to quit his job, but the pressure to support his family and pay off his bankrupt father's business debts keeps him trapped in his career. Gregor's boss holds the father's debts, so his job reinforces his sense of obligation to his family. The influential Kafka scholar, Walter H. Sokel, has observed that *Schuld,* the German word for *debt,* also means *guilt* in German. The symbolism of its double meaning has not been lost on Freudian and Marxist critics. Both family debts and family guilt force Gregor into intolerable employment.

2. *When Gregor wakes to discover he has become a gigantic insect, he is mostly intent on the practical implications of his metamorphosis—how to get out of bed, how to get to his job, and so forth. He never wonders why or how he has been changed. What does this odd reaction suggest about Gregor?* The only fantastic element present in *The Metamorphosis* is its opening sentence. After that unexplained event, the subsequent action unfolds in a bizarrely realistic fashion. Perhaps the strangest detail of all is Gregor's matter-of-fact acceptance of his transformation into a monstrously large insect. He never wonders why or how he has been changed from a young man into vermin. Although he worries about a great many other things, he accepts his new situation absolutely. This narrative detail is surely part of what gives Kafka's tale its uniquely brooding mystery. For some unstated reason, Gregor acknowledges the inevitability of his fate. Establishing why Gregor and his family so naturally accept his transformation into a despicable creature is central to any interpretation of the story. (See comments on question 10 for some common interpretations of Gregor's metamorphosis.)

3. *When Gregor's parents first see the gigantic insect (page 319), do they recognize it as their son? What do their initial reactions suggest about their attitude about their son?* Although Gregor's parents are horrified to see his new shape, they never doubt that the huge insect is their son. They do not, for instance, fear that some supernatural monster has occupied their son's room. They instinctively recognize the vermin as Gregor. The mother's first reactions seems to be horror or—some critics claim—deep shame. His father is angry and then starts to weep. The family is already publicly embarrassed that Gregor appears to have barricaded himself in his room and has missed his business trip. The suspicious chief clerk from his office has arrived to check on him. Kafka never explains why the parents recognize their transformed son, but the implication seems to be that his new monstrous form manifests something latent in the old Gregor. What that characteristic is has become the crux of most critical debates.

4. *How does each family member react to Gregor after his transformation? What is different about each reaction? What is similar?* Each of the family members acts differently to him although they all feel ashamed of his condition. His sister initially shows the most concern for him. Her loving care sustains him, and when she abandons him (in Part III), he loses his grip on life. Gregor's mother is full of sympathy for her son but, old and asthmatic, she is ineffective in helping or defending him. Gregor's father lacks all compassion for his son's situation. He mercilessly drives Gregor back into his room the first two times he emerges. He resents having to work again, and subsequent events suggest that he had earlier been exploiting his son by forcing Gregor to pay off the family debts.

5. *What things about Gregor have been changed? What seems to have remained the same? List specific qualities.* While Gregor has undergone a complete physical metamorphosis, he changes very little mentally—at least at first. He is still beset by all his usual

worries. Gradually, however, Gregor seems to regress. He accepts his own ineffectiveness and passivity; he also accepts his own monstrous unworthiness and repulsiveness. He becomes childlike in his complete dependence on his family, whereas earlier he had supported them. He not only becomes filthy but slowly loses any shame about his squalid condition. Eventually, he even accepts his own death. "The decision that he must disappear was one that he held even more strongly than his sister, if that were possible," Gregor thinks as he starts to die. He has no resentment for his family; he thinks of them "with tenderness and love." Monstrous and dying, he remains an obedient son.

6. The Metamorphosis *takes place entirely in the Samsa family apartment. How does the story's home setting shape its themes?* Except for the final scene, all of *The Metamorphosis* takes place in the Samsa family apartment. This claustrophobic setting underscores the domestic nature of the story. Kafka's psychological and mythic focus is on the family—especially the relationship between child and parents. It is worth noting that the two Samsa children have Christian names—Gregor and Grete—whereas Mr. and Mrs. Samsa lack first names. In fact, the parents are usually called by the archetypal names of *Father* and *Mother*. (Curiously, although Kafka himself was Jewish, he makes the Samsas Christian—notice the reference to Christmas and how the family makes a sign of the cross over Gregor's dead body; the story suggests Christian as well as Jewish readings.) As Gregor hides in his room, he listens to his family. He becomes a passive witness to their lives. Some critics feel that the central action of the story involves the family more than Gregor; his transformation is only the catalyst to their drama. It might be worth asking the class if they agree or disagree with this emphasis.

7. *What family member first decides that they must "get rid" of the insect? What rationale is given? In what specific ways does the family's decision affect Gregor?* Gregor's sister ultimately decides that "we must get rid of it." Her attitude has gradually changed from one of solicitous concern to hostility. She does not refer to Gregor by name; he is now an *it*. "I won't utter my brother's name in the presence of this creature," she declares. At this point Gregor starts to lose his human identity. She argues that they have been mistaken to think that this creature is her brother. Why? "If this were Gregor," she maintains, "he would have realized long ago that human beings can't live with such a creature, and he would have gone away on his own accord." Gregor, in other words, would not have added to the family burden but would have eased it. His role, she implies, is a provider, not an embarrassing dependent. The sister's announcement provides a turning point in the story. Already weak and injured, Gregor declines into death.

8. *How does the family react to Gregor's death?* When the charwoman announces that Gregor is dead, the parents rush out of bed to check the evidence in their son's room. "Well," says Gregor's father, "now thanks be to God." They cross themselves, but only Grete shows some sympathy. "Just see how thin he was," she observes. When Gregor's mother invites her daughter to sit beside them in their bedroom, Mrs. Samsa already has "a tremulous smile." When they finally emerge from the bedroom, they appear to have been crying, but their grief is short-lived. They are openly relieved that Gregor is gone. They soon appear more vigorous and determined. They make plans for the future. When the charwoman disposes of the body, she is grinning. The family is now openly confident and affectionate for the first time.

9. *Does Grete change in the course of the story? If so, how does she change?* One of the strangest features of *The Metamorphosis* is its closing paragraph. Having lost their only son, the Samsas undergo a quiet transformation into a secure and loving family. The final image is quite unexpected. The parents notice Grete's "increasing vivacity." In spite of all their recent troubles, "she had bloomed into a pretty girl with a good figure." It is time,

they decide, "to find a good husband for her." Immediately after Gregor's unceremonious funeral, they are already planning a marriage. At least one critic has claimed that the title, *The Metamorphosis,* refers to Grete rather than Gregor; she has been transformed from a girl into a young woman. Her transformation brings the promise of new life while Gregor's brought only death.

10. *In what ways is Gregor's metamorphosis symbolic?* The chief concern in interpreting *The Metamorphosis* with students is to read Kafka's story as symbolic rather than allegorical. Kafka resists conventional interpretation; no one, tightly consistent reading will fit all the facts of the tale. Part of Kafka's particular genius was in creating seemingly allegorical situations (as in *The Castle* and *The Trial*) that refuse to fall into neat patterns. Allegory's central technique—like Kafka's—is the extended metaphor, but whereas allegory consistently equates the metaphor with a specific meaning, Kafka's metaphors suggest multiple interpretations. The thrill and mystery of reading Kafka's fiction is the sense that one is always on the brink of understanding everything followed by the discovery of some new fact that changes or contradicts one's own theory.

There are a great many interpretations of Gregor Samsa's metamorphosis. One inarguable observation is that his transformation is horrible. He has become a huge insect that everyone finds disgusting; he himself is ashamed of his new form and hides when his sister enters his room to feed him. One can read the entire story as an extended metaphor, an anti-allegory that no single interpretive key will unlock, in which Gregor's metaphorical identity as a revolting insect becomes literally true. This line of inquiry stills begs the question of *why* Gregor became an insect. Kafka's text is famously silent on this crucial point; it can only be approached by implication. The two most common interpretations are that Gregor's transformation is a *retribution* for some unstated crime (whether it is his own crime, his father's, his family's, or society's, depends on the critic's orientation) or that his change reflects a *wish fulfillment* on his part to abandon his job and be cared for by his family (whether this is a self-asserting wish for freedom or a shameful regression to childhood also depends on the critic's approach).

There is an immense amount of commentary available on *The Metamorphosis.* Harold Bloom's "Modern Critical Interpretations" series contains a volume of essays on the story, *Franz Kafka's The Metamorphosis* (New York: Chelsea, 1988). This compilation includes particularly interesting essays by Martin Greenberg, Stanley Corngold, Ronald Gray, and Walter H. Sokel. For a general study of the author, Erich Heller's *Franz Kafka* (Princeton, NJ: Princeton University Press, 1974) remains a fine short introduction. Page for page, however, Walter H. Sokel's pamphlet, *Franz Kafka* (New York: Columbia University Press, 1966) is probably the best introduction in English; moreover, it provides a compelling psychological reading of *The Metamorphosis.* Roy Pascal's *Kafka's Narrators* (Cambridge University Press, 1982) provides an extremely insightful discussion of how the impersonal narrator of *The Metamorphosis* submerges the reader in Gregor's consciousness in subtle and unexpected ways.

Students curious to know exactly what sort of bug poor Gregor became should consult Vladimir Nabokov's lively *Lectures on Literature* (New York: Harcourt, 1980). Nabokov, who was not only a magisterial novelist but also a renowned entomologist, explores the nature of the *"ungeheures Ungeziefer"* (Kafka's German phrase for Gregor's new shape, which can be translated either as *gigantic insect* or *monstrous vermin*). No one has been able to identify precisely what sort of insect Kafka had in mind—a mystery that almost certainly was the author's intention. Nabokov, however, discusses what sort of bug he was not. Gregor, Nabokov resolves, was definitely not, as some readers often assume, a cockroach. Not all critical issues in Kafka are, it appears, beyond resolution.

One final note: an intriguing tribute to Kafka, one that sums up the powerful appeal of his stories, is that of dramatist Vaclav Havel, former president of Czechoslovakia:

> In Kafka I have found a portion of my own experience of the world, of myself, and of my way of being in the world. I will try . . . to name some of the more easily defined forms of this experience. One of them is a profound, banal, and therefore utterly vague sensation of culpability, as though my very existence were a kind of sin. Then there is a powerful feeling of general alienation, both my own and relating to everything around me, that helps to create such feelings; an experience of unbearable oppressiveness, a need constantly to explain myself to someone, to defend myself, a longing for an unattainable order of things. (From a lecture on Kafka delivered at Hebrew University in Jerusalem in April 1990; *New York Review of Books,* September 27, 1990)

Has the mind of Gregor Samsa ever been more concisely or more accurately described? For a writing assignment, students might be given a copy of Havel's remarks and asked to show, by referring to particulars in the story, how they apply to *The Metamorphosis.*

FLANNERY O'CONNOR

If you think Flannery O'Connor's world, and her theology, are likely to strike your students as remote and unfamiliar, you might begin by telling the class a little about them. Should your library own a copy of Barbara McKenzie's book of photographs, *Flannery O'Connor's Georgia* (Athens, U of Georgia P, 1980), by all means bring it in and show it around. McKenzie recalls John Wesley's remark in "A Good Man Is Hard to Find," "Let's drive through Georgia fast so we won't have to look at it much," and supplies a series of pictures of some "oppressive" landscapes. Besides, there is a stone marker announcing Toomsboro, a town whose name foreshadows the ending of "A Good Man. . . .", a glimpse of a pig parlor of which Mrs. Turpin might have been proud, and a shot of some urban black people who might be waiting for a bus, like passengers in "Everything That Rises Must Converge."

An essay worth quoting aloud is Alice Walker's sympathetic tribute "Beyond the Peacock: The Reconstruction of Flannery O'Connor," *In Search of Our Mothers' Gardens* (New York: Harcourt, 1983). "She was for me," declares Walker, "the first great modern writer from the South," and she praises O'Connor for not trying to enter the minds of her black characters, not insisting on knowing everything, on being God. "After her great stories of sin, damnation, prophecy, and revelation, the stories one reads casually in the average magazine seem to be about love and roast beef."

O'Connor's *Collected Works* has been accorded the honor of appearing in the Library of America series. This volume, along with three new works of O'Connor criticism, was reviewed by Frederick Crews in the April 26, 1990 issue of *The New York Review of Books*. Crews has interesting things to say about O'Connor's debt not only to New Criticism, but also to Edgar Allan Poe and Nathanael West. He offers insight as well into what he calls her "stern fanaticism" and her "twisted feelings about segregation."

EVERYTHING THAT RISES MUST CONVERGE, page 347

Julian's mother, though living in pathetically reduced circumstances, never forgets that she is the granddaughter of a governor and slaveowner, the daughter of a prosperous landowner. Her belief in the innate nobility of her forebears is unshakable. Ancestral values with their emphasis on the importance of "graciousness," of "knowing who you are," still dictate her often wrong and foolish behavior.

Even so, the mother is a more sympathetic character than is her son. There is an innocence about her that mitigates her faults. Julian, on the other hand, is a hypocrite, for all his pretensions to broadmindedness. (The author's ironic view of him is especially clear in paragraph 62.) Despising his mother for her sacrifices, he yet accepts her money and support. He thinks that sitting down next to a Negro on the bus or trying to strike up a conversation with "the better types, with ones that looked like professors or ministers or lawyers," makes him morally superior to his mother. In truth, such efforts seem undertaken only for the smug sense of virtue he derives from them, and the opportunities they provide for needling his mother. Meanwhile, without ever acknowledging his own aristocratic leanings, he secretly longs for the "threadbare elegance" of the now defunct family mansion, "the house that had been lost for him." He is a snob masquerading as a progressive.

Julian is delighted to find on the bus the black woman wearing a hat identical to his mother's. Apparently he regards the black woman's hat with the same amused contempt. "He could not believe that Fate had thrust upon his mother such a lesson" (82). He expects his mother suddenly to realize that her pride is foolish, that black people are her equals. It seems clear that Julian would like nothing better than a painful shattering of the pathetic illusions that sustain his mother. Only then might she learn to appreciate her son's moral superiority. That never happens, of course. Note the chilling line in paragraph 120, which describes her collapse: "The other [eye] remained fixed on him, raked his face again, *found nothing* [italics ours] and closed." But perhaps her death represents a turning point for Julian. At least he seems suddenly aware that he loves her and needs her still.

We are told in paragraph 90 that Julian's mother directs at Carver's mother "the smile she used when she was being particularly gracious to an inferior." Her offer of a penny to the small boy seems motivated not by bigotry but by the habit of condescension she has cultivated in her fantasy world. For Julian's mother, O'Connor writes, "the gesture would be as normal . . . as breathing" (95) and, we suspect, might just as easily have been directed at a white child. But Carver's belligerent mother apparently finds condescension as hard to take as outright bigotry.

The title of this story evidently contradicts the mother's belief that black people "should rise, yes, but on their own side of the fence" (24). That isn't how it works, O'Connor seems to be saying.

What is the theme of "Everything That Rises Must Converge"? Perhaps that spiritual pride is the worst sin of all. Or, to put it another way, that those who sneer at their supposed moral inferiors may not be so lofty as they think.

A GOOD MAN IS HARD TO FIND, page 359

Without some attention to its Christian (specifically Catholic) assumptions, this story won't make much sense to students, who might read it for a tale of meaningless violence. Their seeing what O'Connor is driving at depends on their reading with great care the conversation about Jesus between the Misfit and the grandmother, and the account of the old woman's epiphany and death (paragraph 136).

O'Connor loves to pick unlikely, ordinary people and show how, by the sudden and unexpected operation of God's grace, they are transformed into saints: the nit-witted grandmother who dies loving (and presumably forgiving) the Misfit, the awful Mrs. Turpin in "Revelation." In the course of the story, the grandmother grows and changes. At first, she seems a small-minded biddy, selfish or at least self-centered, capable of dumb remarks like "Oh look at the cute little piccaninny!" (18) and "People are certainly not nice like they used to be" (35), capable of blaming Europe for "the way things were now" (44), of regretting that she hadn't married Mr. Teagarden "because he was a gentleman and had bought Coca-Cola stock when it first came out" (26).

In the end when we are told that "her head cleared for an instant," the grandmother becomes newly perceptive. She reveals—and offers to the Misfit—her vast, compassionate heart. We have no reason to doubt the Misfit's shrewd remark, "She would have been a good woman . . . if it had been somebody there to shoot her every minute of her life." In slaying her, the Misfit has done her a tremendous favor: he has made a martyr of her. For one moment just before she dies, the old lady doubts Jesus, or at least feels forsaken: "Maybe he didn't raise the dead" (135). It is an understandable reaction, after the colossal shock she has undergone: she knows that her family has been massacred. But this moment of confusion passes. The grandmother is headed straight to heaven for her marvelous

Christ-like act of love a moment before she dies, when she realizes that there is a chance that the Misfit will repent and she reaches out to him lovingly, as though he were a child. By this time, she already knows that the Misfit's gang has murdered her son and daughter-in-law and all the children. The Misfit may be a ruthless murderer, but that doesn't prevent her (in the end) from loving him and hoping for his redemption. Symbolically, in death the old woman's body lies with legs in the form of a cross, a look of childlike sweetness on her face. The Misfit, naturally, is glum, having just declined a chance for salvation.

An insightful and outspoken student might raise this objection: "Isn't it a shame to impose Catholic terms of redemption on all these Protestants?" (That the eight-year-old is named John Wesley suggests that the family is at least nominally Methodist.)

The story may draw other objections. O'Connor's use of familiar racist epithets will outrage some African-American students unless they see that O'Connor is only reporting faithfully how the characters think and talk, not condoning it or thinking that way herself. This will be a problem, too, in teaching "Revelation" (or most Faulkner novels or *Huckleberry Finn*).

Who is the central character? Some will say the Misfit, some the grandmother. This is mainly, we think, the grandmother's story from beginning to end—we take it to be the story of her moral and spiritual growth. She causes things to happen; the Misfit merely reacts to her. She persuades the family to depart from the main road to see the old plantation, she causes the accident by letting the cat out of the basket, she dooms the family when she recognizes the Misfit, and her final gesture incites him to murder her.

The scene at Red Sammy's Barbecue is no mere filler, but an essential. It tightens the suspense and enforces the hint that the much talked-about Misfit is bound to show his face. In his highway signs, Red Sammy boasts of his uniqueness: NONE LIKE FAMOUS RED SAMMY'S. He considers himself a hard-to-find good man. In calling him a good man (37), the grandmother first introduces a theme. The barbecue proprietor agrees with her, even declares, thinking of how many bad characters are on the loose these days, "A good man is hard to find" (43).

In the end, what has the platitudinous title indicated? We are left to think: how true, a good man (a saint) certainly is hard to find. We find, at the end, a serenely good woman whose salvation has been achieved only through traumatic suffering and the amazing arrival of grace.

For O'Connor's own reading of this famous story, see her critical comments on page 386. Her interpretation will certainly startle many students reading the story for the first time. If you choose to consider O'Connor's comments in class, it may be worth asking how authoritative a writer's interpretation of her own work is. Are there limitations or inherent biases in a writer's self-assessments?

In an incisive essay on Flannery O'Connor, Clara Claiborne Park points out that while O'Connor may have objected to readers' attempts to reduce her stories to literal meanings or themes, she herself tended to do so in her own commentaries on the stories. Despite their excellence, the stories, when so reduced, may be faulted as over-simplified fables of Christian salvation through suffering. "A Good Man Is Hard to Find" seems vulnerable to this charge. Park observes: "As incursions of grace through arson and through murder and through sudden stroke become familiar to the point of predictability, all moral ambiguity evaporates, leaving the stories that puzzled us all too clear" (*Rejoining the Common Reader,* Chicago: Northwestern University Press, 1991). A question for class discussion is: can O'Connor be defended against this charge? (Perhaps she intends no ambiguity.)

For those who wish to explore this complex story further, a volume containing critical essays by various hands is available in *A Good Man Is Hard to Find,* edited by

Frederick Asals (in a new series, "Women Writers: Texts and Contexts," New Brunswick, NJ: Rutgers University Press, 1993).

REVELATION, page 371

Epiphanies, Flannery O'Connor finds, are imminent in the drabbest, most ordinary life. And so she makes the doctor's waiting room the setting for prophecy; a pigpen, the doorstep of beatitude. Mrs. Turpin, bigoted and smugly self-congratulatory, seems an unlikely recipient for a revelation direct from God; and yet even she is capable of accepting such a revelation and by it being transformed and redeemed. Like Malamud's Angel Levine, Mary Grace, a pimpled Wellesley girl with emotional difficulties, seems an unlikely messenger of the Lord. But Mary Grace—an agent of redemption, as her name indicates—announces herself as a kind of biblical prophet: with "churning face," she goes into a trance. Her eyes change color, and Mrs. Turpin knows that the girl is about to utter some profundity meant for Mrs. Turpin alone.

Like the handwriting on the wall, Mary Grace's utterance is baffling and mysterious. Sorely troubled, Mrs. Turpin revolves it over and over in her mind all afternoon. She knows from Whom the message came: "What do you send me a message like that for?" (paragraph 179), and her impulse is to defend herself, to argue back at God. Her irate challenge to the Almighty, "Who do you think you are?" is exactly the question God is asking *her*. God replies immediately: He is Lord of all creation, whose natural world "burned for a moment with a transparent intensity." He is the giver of life and of death, as Mrs. Turpin realizes when she sees Claud's truck, whose driver and passengers at any moment could be destroyed. Then, in the final revelation, God shows her exactly who *she* is: just another sinner, whose pride in her virtues must perish in eternal light. For Mrs. Turpin, the hard road toward sainthood lies ahead.

"Revelation," a beautifully plotted story, builds slowly to its crisis or turning point: Mary Grace's assault on Mrs. Turpin in the doctor's office or, more specifically, the moment when she declares, "Go back to hell where you came from, you old wart hog." The climax we take to be Mrs. Turpin's challenge to God, "Who do you think you are?"; and the conclusion, her shocked acceptance of the final revelation—the vision of the bridge to heaven.

Symbolism pervades the story, although not obviously. The waiting room suggests a microcosm, or human society in capsule form: old man and child, white-trash woman and Wellesley girl. Significantly, the book that strikes Mrs. Turpin and shatters her view of herself is called *Human Development*. The hogs are fat with meanings. They resemble Mrs. Turpin, who is overweight, with eyes small and fierce, and whom Mary Grace calls a wart hog. In her perplexity, Mrs. Turpin is herself like the old sow she blinds with the hose. Her thoughts about pigs resemble her thoughts on the structure of society, "creating a hierarchy of pigs with a pig astronaut at the top"—Josephine Hendin writes in *The World of Flannery O'Connor* (Bloomington: Indiana University Press, 1970). Mrs. Turpin gazes into her pig parlor "as if through the very heart of mystery." As darkness draws near—and the moment of ultimate revelation—the pigs are suffused with a red glow. Contemplating them Mrs. Turpin seems to absorb "some abysmal life-giving knowledge." What is this knowledge? Glowing pigs suggest, perhaps, the resurrection of the body. As Sister Kathleen Feeley says in her excellent discussion of this story, "Natural virtue does as much for fallen men as parlor treatment does for pigs: it does not change their intrinsic nature. Only one thing can change man: his participation in the grace of Redemption" (*Flannery O'Connor: Voice of the Peacock* [New Brunswick, NJ: Rutgers University Press, 1972]).

"I like Mrs. Turpin as well as Mary Grace," said O'Connor in a letter to a friend.

"You got to be a very big woman to shout at the Lord across a hogpen. She's a country female Jacob. And that vision is purgatorial" (letter to Maryat Lee, May 15, 1964, in *The Habit of Being: Letters of Flannery O'Connor,* ed. Sally Fitzgerald [New York: Farrar, 1979] 577).

One of the last stories Flannery O'Connor finished, "Revelation" appeared in her posthumous collection *Everything That Rises Must Converge* (New York: Farrar, 1965). Walter Sullivan believes that Mrs. Turpin's vision of the bridge of souls, with its rogues, freaks, and lunatics, is the author's vision of humanity and her favorite cast of characters. The story stands as "a kind of final statement, a rounding off of her fiction taken as a whole" ("Flannery O'Connor, Sin, and Grace," in *The Sounder Few: Essays from the Hollins Critic,* ed. R. H. W. Dillard, George Garrett, and John Rees Moore [Athens: U of Georgia P, 1971]).

Joyce Carol Oates, in a comment on "Revelation," finds the story intensely personal. Mary Grace is one of those misfits—"pathetic, overeducated, physically unattractive girls like Joy/Hulga of 'Good Country People'"—of whom the author is especially fond. "That O'Connor identifies with these girls is obvious; it is *she,* through Mary Grace, who throws that textbook on human development at all of us, striking us in the foreheads, hopefully to bring about a change in our lives" ("The Visionary Art of Flannery O'Connor," in *New Heaven, New Earth* [New York: Vanguard, 1974]). In a survey of fiction, Josephine Hendin also stresses O'Connor's feelings of kinship for Mary Grace. As the daughter of a genteel family who wrote "distinctly ungenteel books," O'Connor saw herself as an outsider: "She covered her anger with politeness and wrote about people who did the same." In "Revelation," Mary Grace's hurling the book is an act of violence against her mother, for whom Mrs. Turpin serves as a convenient stand-in ("Experimental Fiction," *Harvard Guide to Contemporary Writing* [Cambridge, MA: Harvard University Press, 1979]).

At least one African-American student has reacted in anger to the language of this story. Writing from Glassboro (N.J.) State College, she called "Revelation" the "most disgusting story I've ever read" and objected to "the constant repetition of the word *nigger.*" O'Connor never uses the word when speaking in her own voice, but it occurs several times in the thoughts and speeches of Mrs. Turpin (also in one speech of the "white-trash woman," [paragraph 51]). Such a reaction deserves a hearing—if possible, in class. African-American students given to signal reactions are in for some painful shocks unless alerted that they will meet this word in much fiction written twenty years ago or earlier, including *Huckleberry Finn* and Faulkner's stories. In "Revelation," how are we supposed to react to the characters who say or think the word? How is Mrs. Turpin limited and narrow in her views of African-Americans (and of herself)? Where does Flannery O'Connor stand? How does she expect *us* to feel? What do you make of the African-American people in the story? In what ways are they more perceptive than Mrs. Turpin? Should the word be expunged from literature? Or is a writer ever justified in using it to show how certain whites used to think and talk—and unfortunately, still do?

"People talk about the theme of a story," Flannery O'Connor wrote, "as if the theme were like the string that a sack of chicken feed is tied with. They think that if you can pick out the theme, the way you pick the right thread in the chicken-feed sack, you can rip the story open and feed the chickens. But this is not the way meaning works in fiction. . . . A story is a way to say something that can't be said any other way, and it takes every word in the story to say what the meaning is" ("Writing Short Stories," in *Mystery and Manners: Occasional Prose,* selected and edited by Sally and Robert Fitzgerald [New York: Farrar, 1980]).

74

THE ELEMENT OF SUSPENSE IN "A GOOD MAN IS HARD TO FIND," page 386

O'Connor's comments came from a reading she gave in 1963 (the remarks were reprinted in her posthumous critical collection, *Mystery and Manners* [New York: Farrar, 1969] 107-14).

Southern students, she had learned, tended to recognize the grandmother as exactly like one of their own relatives, "and they knew, from personal experience, that the old lady lacked comprehension, but that she had a good heart." When her head clears for an instant, the grandmother

> realizes, even in her limited way, that she is responsible for the man before her and joined to him by ties of kinship which have their roots deep in the mystery she has merely been prattling about so far. At this point, she does the right thing, she makes the right gesture. I find that students are often puzzled by what she says and does here, but I think myself that if I took out this gesture and what she says with it, I would have no story.

It is important to note O'Connor's warning against equating the Misfit with the devil. Rather, he is a potential saint gone terribly wrong. She even claims that the grandmother's gesture, "like the mustardseed, will grow to be a great crow-filled tree in the Misfit's heart" and redeem him. Can we accept O'Connor's statement that "in this story you should be on the lookout for such things as the action of grace in the grandmother's soul, and not for the dead bodies"?

Frederick Asals points out in a fruitful critical reading that it remains hard to ignore all those dead bodies. In Asals's view no other O'Connor story sets up such extreme tension between matters sacred and profane, between comedy and violence. See *Flannery O'Connor: The Imagination of Extremity* (Athens, GA: University of Georgia Press, 1982), 142-54.

THE SERIOUS WRITER AND THE TIRED READER, page 389

QUESTIONS

1. *What is Flannery O'Connor's opinion of book clubs? Explain her remark on this subject in the second paragraph.*

2. *Does O'Connor condemn people who want fiction to leave them "lifted up"? What is her attitude toward them?* Bemused contempt.

3. *By what means can writers write the great novels of the future?* By looking into their own hearts, exploring themselves and their native regions, and writing not conventional realistic fiction but a poetic kind of fiction inspired by individual visions.

11 Stories for Further Reading

Ambrose Bierce

AN OCCURRENCE AT OWL CREEK BRIDGE, page 392

QUESTIONS

1. *What has brought Peyton Farquhar to the brink of hanging?* Incited by the Federal Scout, he has apparently tried to burn down Owl Creek Bridge, which is in the hands of the Union Army.

2. *One student, after reading Bierce's story, objected to it on the grounds that the actions of the Federal Scout (paragraphs 9–17) are not believable. "Since when do military men dress up like the enemy and incite civilians to sabotage?" was her question. How would you answer it?* One possible answer might be that Farquhar, "a slave owner and like other slave owners a politician," has managed in his own way to engineer damage to the enemy and so has become a marked man. A believer in "at least a part of the frankly villainous dictum that all is fair in love and war" (8), Farquhar is lured into a fatal trap by someone in the enemy camp who assents to the same view.

3. *Are you surprised by the story's conclusion? Can you find hints along the way that Farquhar's escape is an illusion? At what point in the story does the illusion begin?* Bierce lays in enough hints to make most readers accept the surprise ending, though they may want to reread the story just to make sure. In paragraph 5, though Farquhar makes a conscious effort to think about his wife and children, he has already begun to experience an alteration in his sense of time. Recall the old general belief that at the moment of death we see our whole lives pass by again in a flash. As soon as an escape plot forms in Farquhar's mind (6), the sergeant moves off the plank and the noose tightens around the doomed man's neck. Since we know from the ending that the rope does not break, what happens to Farquhar after the flashback (8–17)—except for the physical sensations of hanging—has to be a fast-moving hallucination in the mind of a dying man.

Bierce has planted clues that this is so. With "superhuman" effort Farquhar manages to free his bound hands. His senses are "preternaturally keen and alert" (20). His ability to dodge all the bullets fired at him seems miraculous. The forest through which he walks is unfamiliar and menacing; the stars above him are "grouped in strange constellations"; he hears "whispers in an unknown tongue" (34). Soon "he could no longer feel the roadway beneath his feet" (35). His wife greets him with "a smile of ineffable joy" (36)—then he is dead.

4. *From what point of view is "An Occurrence at Owl Creek Bridge" told?* In the third person by a nonparticipating narrator able to see into Farquhar's mind.

5. *At several places in the story Bierce calls attention to Farquhar's heightened sensibility. How would you explain those almost mystical responses to ordinary stimuli?* They are the out-of-body sensations of a dying man. Much has been written about such experiences in the popular press. For some interesting, serious comments on the subject see Elisabeth Kubler-Ross, *On Death and Dying* (New York: Macmillan, 1969). Dr. Ross quotes the testimony of persons who, after being declared clinically dead, were resusci-

tated. Some reported finding themselves floating in space, gazing down upon their own bodies.

6. *Where in Bierce's story do you find examples of irony?* There is irony in the contrast between the understated title and the extravagant style of the narrator. Ironic, too, is the mention of Farquhar's belief that "all's fair in love and war"—a belief shared by the Federal Scout who lures Farquhar to his capture and death. Verbal irony occurs in "Death is a dignitary who when he comes announced is to be received with formal manifestations of respect, even by those most familiar with him" (paragraph 2), and "The liberal military code makes provision for hanging many kinds of persons, and gentlemen are not excluded" (3). Students may find other examples as well.

7. *Do you think the story would have been better had Bierce told it in chronological order? Why or why not?* In defense of the way the story is told, we'd argue mainly that Bierce's use of flashback heightens the suspense created by the opening scene on the bridge.

A topic for writing: Compare this story with either Tolstoi's *The Death of Ivan Ilych* (page 269) or with Borges's "The Gospel According to Mark" (page 183). All three stories deal with men on the brink of death and their inner experiences.

Willa Cather
PAUL'S CASE, page 400

QUESTIONS

1. *What is it about Paul that so disturbs his teachers? Recall any of his traits that they find irritating, any actions that trouble them. Do they irritate or trouble you?* The boy's dandyism, his defiance, and his unconcealed contempt disturb his teachers beyond all reason. They also disturb many readers, who find a discrepancy between their own negative feelings about Paul and the fondness Cather seems to feel toward him. The school principal and Paul's art teacher are able to muster sympathy for the boy (paragraphs 7-8), but they don't claim to understand him.

2. *What do the arts—music, painting, theater—mean to Paul? How does he react when exposed to them? Is he himself an artist?* Oddly, when he hears a concert, it's "not that symphonies, as such, [mean] anything in particular to Paul" (11). The romance and beauty in the air excite him to hysteria. He reacts in the same way to fine food and wine, good clothes, a lavishly decorated room. For all his sensitivity, he is not an artist, and he doesn't respond to art as an artist would. It's the *idea* of art and beauty, the pleasure they afford his senses, that evoke a response in him. In *Willa: The Life of Willa Cather*, Phyllis C. Robinson points out that Paul "may have had the sensitivity of an artist but, unlike his creator, he was without discipline, without direction and, saddest and most hopeless of all, he was without talent." In that fact lies his private tragedy.

3. *In what different places do we follow Paul throughout the story? How do these settings (and the boy's reactions to them) help us understand him, his attitudes, his personality?* Cather shows us Paul in school, at home, in the art gallery, in the theater, and, finally, in the big city. Everywhere, he functions apart from the ordinary beings who surround him. Isolated and unhappy, Paul regards his esthetic longings as evidence of his superiority to other human beings. Absence of hope and cool disdain for the ordinary

ways of attaining wealth and finery and an invitation to New York drive him to one grand, suicidal fling in the beautiful, glamorous world where he imagines he belongs.

4. *Does Cather's brief introduction into the story of the wild Yale freshman from San Francisco (in paragraph 54) serve any purpose? Why do you suppose he and Paul have such a "singularly cool" parting? What is Cather's point?* In New York Paul expects to find wealthy persons of taste and temperament similar to his own. He finds instead the disappointing Yale student who, far from sharing Paul's reverence for beauty, seems to the boy hopelessly crass. Ironically, though he seems to have grown up with all the advantages Paul has lacked, this worldly student disappoints Paul as much as do his family and friends at home. Who could measure up to Paul's impossible standards? For the rest of his stay, Paul is content to observe his fellow guests from afar.

5. *Is Paul a static character or a dynamic one? If you find him changing and developing in the course of the story, can you indicate what changes him?* The only change in Paul's character during the story seems to be the fairly minor one mentioned in paragraphs 42–43. Once settled in at the Waldorf, he realizes he is no longer "dreading something." Is this change enough to justify our calling him a dynamic character? The change seems to signal in Paul a deepening involvement in an unreal world rather than any growth. We think he's a static character.

6. *Comment on some of the concrete details Cather dwells on. What, for instance, do you make of the portraits of Washington and John Calvin and the motto placed over Paul's bed (paragraph 18)? Of the carnation Paul buries in the snow (paragraph 64)?* Paul's sensibilities recoil from all that is ugly, even ordinary. His room, featuring pictures of those austere and well-disciplined heroes George Washington and John Calvin, is hateful to him. Working-class Cordelia Street, where he lives, induces in him "a shuddering repulsion for the flavorless, colorless mass of every-day existence; a morbid desire for cool things and soft lights and fresh flowers" (19). By paragraph 64, after Paul has run away from New York, he realizes that fresh flowers do not stay fresh forever. He sees the parallel between "their brave mockery" and his own "revolt against the homilies by which the world is run" and characterizes both as "a losing game in the end." He dies like the flowers, his "one splendid breath" spent.

7. *What implications, if any, does the title "Paul's Case" have for this story? Is Paul mentally ill, or does Cather place the roots of his malaise elsewhere?* Robinson has this to say about Cather's view of Paul:

> As if to underscore her own intuition in regard to the story, Willa gave it the subtitle "A Study in Temperament," and to the modern reader the pathological attributes of Paul's malaise are more persuasive than the romantic aspects. Willa told George Seibel that she drew on two boys who had been in her classes for the character of Paul, but to others she confessed how much of her own hunger and frustration were embodied in the unhappy boy's flight from the drab reality of his daily life and in his instinctive reaching out for beauty.

In other words, we today tend to think Paul seriously disturbed, but apparently Cather didn't see him that way. In conflict with school, neighbors, and family, Paul seems to her an admirable victim. Cather often sticks up for the lonely, sensitive individual pitted against a philistine provincial society—as in her famous story "The Sculptor's Funeral."

"Paul's Case" may be available for classroom viewing on videotape; it was featured in the PBS television film series *The American Short Story.* Short scenes from the script of Ron Cowen's adaptation are included in *The American Short Story, Volume 2* (New York: Dell, 1980), and invite comparison with the original.

A detailed plan for teaching "Paul's Case" is offered by Bruce E. Miller in *Teaching the Art of Literature* (Urbana, IL: NCTE, 1980). To get students involved in the story before they read it outside of class, Miller suggests reading passages from the early part of the story (before Paul flees to New York) and summarizing what happens, and then asking students how they'd imagine Cather would continue the story. He advises the instructor to show the class a few photographs of adolescent boys and to ask how closely the pictures reflect students' mental images of Paul. The point is to spark a discussion of Paul's complex character. Is he a cheat? A victim? A hero? Various opinions are likely to emerge, and students may come to see "that the different views of Paul are not necessarily incompatible with each other, and that Cather has accomplished the difficult feat of delineating a complex character who, though flawed, engages the reader's sympathy."

Anton Chekhov

MISERY, page 415

In 1987, when Daniel Halpern asked twenty-five of the noted writers featured in his collection, *The Art of the Tale: An International Anthology of Short Stories 1945–1985* (New York: Viking, 1987) to name the most crucial influences on their own work, Anton Chekhov's name appeared more often than that of any other author. Ten writers—including Eudora Welty, Nadine Gordimer, and Raymond Carver—mentioned Chekhov. (James Joyce and Henry James tied for a distant second place, with five votes each.) Chekhov's preeminent position among contemporary writers is not accidental; no other author so greatly influenced the development of the modern short story. As the late Rufus Matthewson once observed, Chekhov fully articulated the dominant form of twentieth-century short fiction: "the casual telling of a nuclear experience in an ordinary life, rendered with immediate and telling detail." Chekhov was the first author to consciously explore and perfect this literary method in his vast output of short stories.

"Misery," first published in 1886, is one of the first small masterpieces of Chekhov's maturity. Chekhov began writing professionally at twenty in 1880 to make money for himself and his impoverished family. He started by penning humorous sketches—publishing over three hundred short pieces in five years. Being confined to one hundred lines per story in his early journalistic work, Chekhov learned to compress a complex story into a short space. In 1885 he finished his medical training, and his relative financial security gave him the opportunity to deepen as an artist. Encouraged by an admiring editor, he explored more serious themes. "Misery," written when he was twenty-six, shows the young writer discovering the understated but compassionate perspective that characterizes his finest fiction.

Students sometimes find Chekhov a difficult author—not so much because they do not understand what is going on in the stories as because they do not know how to react to his compressed and subtle treatment. Perhaps Chekhov's strongest influence on the tradition of short fiction was in revolutionizing what writers considered an adequate plot for a short story. He seldom used the clever narrative twists of the traditional tale; instead, he focused on the drama of the basic situation. The Russian author Ivan Bunin reported that Chekhov advised him that in writing short stories, one should eliminate the beginning and the end. "Misery" reflects that method. The beginning of the story (the son's death) is revealed only as the story progresses; the outcome of Iona's suffering is left to the reader's imagination. If students take some time in adjusting to this concise approach, they are in good company. Virginia Woolf, who admired Chekhov immensely, initially experienced the same difficulty. "Our first impressions of Chekhov," she wrote in *The Common Reader,* "are not of simplicity but of bewilderment. What is the point of it, and why does he make a story out of this?" Learning to appreciate Chekhov, Woolf felt, was a fitness test for readers.

Iona Potapov, the protagonist of "Misery," is a cab driver in St. Petersburg whose only son has died the week before. Throughout the story he is surrounded by people, but he remains utterly alone. He "thirsts" for the opportunity to talk about his grief, but no one will share the burden of his misery. Each of his fares brushes off his overtures for conversation. The hunchbacked young man, who one might think would be more compassionate to a fellow person's affliction, is particularly cruel; after he hears Iona's news, he strikes the cabby. Iona's fellow lodgers offer no comfort either; a young cabman falls asleep when Iona tries to discuss his loss. Unable to sleep, the tormented Iona goes out to the stable. In Chekhov's famous ending, Iona tells his mare the story of his misery.

A revealing question for students to consider in Chekhov's story is whether the final scene of "Misery" is purely pathetic or whether it contains an element of affirmation. The pathetic element is easy to see: poor Iona can find no human compassion for his suffering. In the populous city of St. Petersburg, he is utterly alone. Yet there is something nobly humane in Iona's decision to go to the stable to visit his mare. Iona's pain has not shrunk his own compassion. Earlier that night, when he realized how little he had earned from his lonely night's work, he worried about his horse as well as himself. When he tells the mare they cannot afford oats, he speaks in the first person plural: "*we* will eat hay" (our italics). In speaking of his grief to his horse, he affirms his human need to articulate his own suffering. Characteristically, Iona explains his grief in a way that includes the mare. "Now, suppose you had a little colt," he tells it. In his excellent survey, *Anton Chekhov, A Study of the Short Fiction* (New York: Twayne, 1993), Ronald L. Johnson of Northern Michigan University notices the irony that "the cabby thus finds relief from his despair not in his fellow man, but in this fellow creature."

Students intending to write a paper on Chekhov's fiction should be steered toward Johnson's clear, insightful book. It is a fine primer. The secondary literature on Chekhov is immense. Ronald Hingley's *A New Life of Anton Chekhov* (New York: Knopf, 1976) remains useful, as does Edmund Wilson's 1952 essay, "Seeing Chekhov Plain," which is collected in *A Window on Russia* (New York: Farrar, 1972). Ernest J. Simmons's *Chekhov* (Boston: Atlantic, 1962) is valuable, readable, compact, and rich in critical intelligence. Any student willing to write a long paper on Chekhov might want to read at least one of the plays as well. Most of Chekhov's stories have lately been reissued in Constance Garnett's translations by Ecco Press. See also *The Unknown Chekhov,* translated by Avrahm Yarmolinsky (New York: Farrar, 1954) for stories Garnett left out. The Norton Critical Edition of *Anton Chekhov's Short Stories* (New York: Norton, 1979), which contains thirty-four stories as well as some of Chekhov's wonderful letters, is also useful. V. S. Prichett's *Chekhov: A Spirit Set Free* (New York: Vintage, 1988) provides a graceful and engaging biographical study by this notable English man of letters.

Chekhov's observations on writing short stories appear on page 573, in the "Criticism: On Fiction" section. His comments on natural description and the need to focus on few characters are particularly applicable to "Misery."

Kate Chopin
THE STORY OF AN HOUR, page 419

QUESTIONS

1. *Is Mrs. Mallard's sorrow at the news of her husband's death merely feigned? Try to account for her sudden changes of feeling.* Undoubtedly her grief is sincere. Caught

within a conventional marriage, she has not realized the freedom she has been denied. Notice that her rush of new joy, her looking forward to a whole new life, begins when she observes that spring is bursting forth, too, in the natural world.

2. *Some stories—for instance, "An Occurrence at Owl Creek Bridge"—are noted for their surprise endings. How can it be claimed that "The Story of an Hour" has a triple surprise ending?* Surprise ending #1: Mrs. Mallard realizes that her husband's death has left her unexpectedly happy. Surprise ending #2: Her husband is still alive. Surprise ending #3: She dies herself.

3. *"Chopin's little gem gives us a fresh and unconventional view of love and marriage." Discuss, refuting or supporting this opinion by specific references to the story.*

Compare this story with Chopin's "The Storm" in Chapter Four—another realistic, unconventional view of love and marriage that, in Chopin's day, undoubtedly helped annul her reputation. "The Story of an Hour" has been criticized for having a rigged ending that strikes some readers as a cheap trick. A student essay by Jane Betz responds to this charge; it is included in X. J. and Dorothy M. Kennedy, *The Bedford Guide for College Writers,* 2nd ed. (Boston: Bedford Books, 1990).

Sandra Cisneros
BARBIE-Q, page 422

Sandra Cisneros began as a poet, and there are moments when "Barbie-Q" seems as much a prose poem as a short story. The narrative is slight, though in a few pages Cisneros finds time for a clever plot twist. What makes "Barbie-Q" interesting is its language and its psychology—which are cunningly interwoven. In this story, Cisneros explores the language of advertising and marketing. She understands how advertising exploits and excites the desires and fantasies of its target consumers. Barbie and her friends become projections of the narrator's appetite for romance and glamour. Observe how exquisitely the narrator remembers every detail of dress and appearance of each doll. In the flea market, she does not merely see boxes of Barbie clothes; she observes two small fantasy worlds:

> One with the "Career Gal" ensemble, snappy black-and-white business suit, three-quarter-length sleeve jacket with kick-pleat skirt, red sleeveless shell, gloves, pumps, and matching hat included. The other, "Sweet Dreams," dreamy pink-and-white plaid nightgown and matching robe, lace-trimmed slippers, hairbrush and hand mirror included. How much? Please, please, please, please, please, please, please, until they say okay.

The hyperbolic language of toy marketing reflects the psychology of the narrator and her friend. On the edge of adolescence, they explore the traumas of love and experience through play. Notice how their games always end with the two Barbies fighting over a nonexistent Ken. The girls may be young, but they already understand that romance can be divisive to friendship. It might be worthwhile to ask students how old the narrator and her friend are. There is no right answer, of course, but the question will focus them on the psychological and behavioral changes behind the story.

There is also a social dimension to the story. The narrator and her friend are not well-to-do. They cannot afford a Ken doll. They must wait until Christmas to get a new Barbie outfit. They shop at a decidedly downscale Chicago flea market ("tool bits, and platform shoes with the heels all squashed"). Cisneros does not bemoan their pecuniary plight; she simply states it as the condition of their daily lives. Without compromising her stinging social subtext, Cisneros makes "Barbie-Q" a happy story. The girls get their fantasy outfits at fire-sale prices.

Cisneros is not alone in finding Barbie interesting. The vast popular appeal of the character Barbie—700 million units sold worldwide—has enabled Barbara Bell of San Anselmo, California, to publish a *Barbie Channeling Newsletter.* So serious are some of her readers that Ms. Bell is able to charge them a fee for "channeling the spirit of Barbie" and answering their questions such as: "Dear Barbie, should I get involved with this man?" "Should I quit my job?" (So Steve Rubinstein reports in a *San Francisco Chronicle* feature article reprinted in other newspapers in April 1993.)

Thirty serious writers, not all of whom take Barbie seriously, appear in *Mondo Barbie,* edited by Lucinda Ebersole and Richard Peabody (New York: St. Martin's Press, 1993), an anthology of stories and poems, all Barbie-inspired. "As icons go," notes Robert Plunket, "Barbie is right up there with Elvis" (review of *Mondo Barbie* in the *New York Times Book Review,* April 18, 1993). Plunket goes on to observe that Barbie "is a totemic object through which a certain kind of feminine knowledge is passed along from older girls to younger girls." A question for class discussion is: Good grief, why?

Sandra Cisneros reads from her books, *The House on Mango Street* and *Woman Hollering Creek,* on audiocassette tape available from the American Audio Prose Library, Inc., Box 842, Columbia, MO 65205; phone number for orders (800) 447-2275. (The story "Barbie-Q" is not recorded.)

Charlotte Perkins Gilman
THE YELLOW WALLPAPER, page 424

"The Yellow Wallpaper" is now such a famous short story that it is interesting to recall how recently it was rescued from oblivion. The facts behind the original creation of the tale and its modern rediscovery are worth recounting. Gilman completed the story in 1890 after the breakup of her first marriage. Based on her own experience with depression and the debilitating effects of her medical treatment of the condition, "The Yellow Wallpaper" was written, she later claimed, to "save people from being driven crazy." Gilman sent the story to William Dean Howells, then the most influential critic in American fiction. Admiring it, he sent the story to Horace Scudder, the editor of the *Atlantic Monthly,* who turned it down on the basis of its stark and unsettling contents. As Howells later commented, it was "too terribly good to be printed" there. The story was eventually published in *New England Magazine* in 1892, where it stirred up a minor controversy. Howells later reprinted it in his 1920 anthology, *The Great American Short Stories.* For the next fifty years the story remained out of print. In 1973, the Feminist Press reissued it as a separate pamphlet with an admiring afterword. Six years later, Sandra Gilbert and Susan Gubar discussed it in their pioneering feminist study, *The Madwoman in the Attic* (1979). Soon thereafter, "The Yellow Wallpaper" became one of the most widely discussed texts in feminist criticism of American literature.

"The Yellow Wallpaper" lends itself to many different readings, but most obviously it invites—some critics might say *demands*—a feminist approach. Gilbert and Gubar explore the rich subtext of the story. The narrator is not only physically imprisoned in her comfortable, airy room; she is spiritually and intellectually confined in a patronizing male world that reduces her to childish dependency. Whatever critical approach one adopts, the important thing is not to simplify Gilman's complex and richly ambiguous narrative.

The first issue for students to deal with is the narrative situation. "The Yellow Wallpaper" is told by a woman undergoing a nervous breakdown. She suffers visions and is plagued by obsessions. Forbidden to write by her concerned but patronizing husband, she secretly jots down her thoughts and experiences. Her prose is conspicuously anxious and disconnected. Not only is the narrator unreliable, her reports are complicated further by the untrustworthy behavior of her husband and his sister, who take care of her. With good but misguided intentions, they talk down to her, and much of what they say appears to be deliberately misleading. A chief irony of the story is that the further the narrator sinks into madness the more clearly she understands the hypocrisy and paternalism of her keepers. Nothing anyone says in the story can be accepted uncritically.

A good way to acclimatize students to the uncertainty of the narrative situation is to ask them to recount everything they know about the room the narrator shares with her husband in the rented mansion. (The husband, however, has also selected the room because it has another bedroom nearby that he can move into if need be.) The narrator initially describes it as follows:

> It is a big, airy room, the whole floor nearly, with windows that look all ways, and air and sunshine galore. It was a nursery first and then playroom and gymnasium, I should judge; for the windows are barred for little children, and there are rings and things in the walls.

No one in the story ever questions that the room was once a nursery, but as later details pile up (the stripped wallpaper, the bolted-down bed, the stairway gate), the alert reader wonders if it was not really once a genteel cell for an affluent lunatic. Like many other things in the story, a pleasant surface covers an authoritarian reality. Students should be encouraged to examine every aspect of this story with equal care and skepticism.

Another question to ask students is, who is the woman the narrator sees in the wallpaper? If this were a supernatural tale, the reader might eventually assume that it was a ghost or demon who inhabited the yellow wallpaper, and there are overtones of the macabre in Gilman's story. However, Gilman—like Poe before her—uses the outward narrative forms of Gothic and supernatural fiction to explore uncomfortable psychological territory. The woman imprisoned in the wallpaper is the narrator's double, probably the parts of her being confined and repressed by her suffocating life. Only as the narrator sinks into madness do her own inhibitions drop sufficiently that she can liberate these forbidden or unacknowledged aspects of her psyche.

In "The Yellow Wallpaper," Gilman uses the traditional figure of the *Doppelgänger* (a German term that, translated literally, means "double-goer"), in an original, feminist way. In Romantic literature the double usually represented an evil self that had broken free of the dominant, moral, conscious self. The evil double often battles the "real" self for control of the person's life. In Gilman's story, the repressed self that is finally liberated also wants to take over the narrator's life, but the double is neither obviously evil or morally dangerous. Once free, the double seems to merge into the narrator. "I wonder if they all come out of the wallpaper as I did?" she suddenly comments. Although the narrator's outer life is crumbling, she is achieving a new authenticity in her inner life. Robert Louis Stevenson's classic *Doppelgänger* story, *The Strange Case of Dr. Jekyll and Mr. Hyde,* was published with immense acclaim in 1886—only four years before Gilman wrote "The Yellow Wallpaper." One wonders if Gilman knew it. She seems to take Stevenson's conventional moral themes and revise them radically from a feminist perspective.

Finally, students may want to explore the complex central image of Gilman's story, the yellow wallpaper. The "repellent, almost revolting," "smouldering unclean" yellow wallpaper resists neat allegorical interpretation; it is a troubling, changing symbol of the forces that haunt, imprison, and torment the narrator. At first its "bloated curves and flourishes" seem to have no shape, but gradually the obsessively observant narrator starts to comprehend its shape. In a probing essay, "Feminist Criticism, 'The Yellow Wallpaper,' and the Politics of Color in America" (*Feminist Studies* 15:3 Fall 1989) Susan S. Lanser compares the narrator's analysis of the wallpaper to deciphering the text of her own imprisoned female identity:

> The narrator is faced with an unreadable text, a text for which none of her interpretative strategies is adequate. . . . But from all this indecipherability, from this immensely complicated text, the narrator—by night, no less—finally discerns a single image, a woman behind bars, which she then expands to represent the whole.

Students wishing to write on Gilman may want to read her feminist utopian novel, *Herland* (1915), which describes a trio of American men visiting an all-female country. Gilman was, first and foremost, a writer on social issues. Even her champions concede that none of her other short stories is up to the level of "The Yellow Wallpaper." *Herland*, a novel of ideas, shows Gilman at her best—it is a radical, progressive questioning of the traditional assumptions of her age. They may also wish to consult Carol Farley Kessler's long, interesting essay on Gilman's life and work in *Modern American Women Writers* (New York: Scribners, 1991).

There are two stories in this book that could provide students with particularly interesting topics to compare and contrast with "The Yellow Wallpaper." Poe's "The Tell-Tale Heart" (page 61) uses Gothic conventions and an unreliable narrator to depict the consequences of a mental breakdown. (One might also consider Poe's "The Fall of the House of Usher" with its meticulously described house, neurasthenic protagonist, and *Doppelgänger* motif.) William Faulkner's "A Rose for Emily" (page 25) provides interesting parallels to Gilman's story. Faulkner's mad Emily Grierson is also trapped in an old house by different sorts of male presences.

"The Yellow Wallpaper"/Charlotte Perkins Gilman, a volume devoted to "The Yellow Wallpaper," edited by Thomas L. Erskine and Connie L. Richards, appeared in 1993 from "Women Writers: Text and Context," a new series of casebooks about short fiction from Rutgers University Press. It includes historical documents and critical commentaries on the story by various critics including Elizabeth Ammons, Sandra M. Gilbert and Susan Gubar, Susan S. Lanser, and others with an introduction by the editors.

Nadine Gordimer
THE DEFEATED, page 437

"The Defeated" is an early story by Nadine Gordimer. It appeared in *The Soft Voice of the Serpent*, which was first published in New York in 1952. This volume was Gordimer's second book; an earlier collection of stories, *Face to Face*, had been published in Johannesburg in 1949 (some of which were reprinted in the American volume). Gordimer is a white South African writer, and her work grows out of the complex social, political, and cultural situation of her country. Although Gordimer's story should be clear to American students, you may want to make a few comments on its setting so that they understand its social context.

The setting of "The Defeated" is a "small mining town" somewhere near Johannesburg. Gold and diamond mines have supported the South African economy since the late nineteenth century, and their development attracted immigrants from both within and beyond Africa. The town in Gordimer's story reflects this complex mix of cultures. It is not accidental that the narrator notes the race of everyone; her society has taught her to do so. The narrator is the daughter of well-to-do parents. Her ancestry is at least partially Scotch. Her father is presumably a manager of one of the mines. Miriam is the daughter of Eastern European Jewish immigrants. Her parents run a Concession store in the mining town. (The South African government sold exclusive concessions to operate stores in mining towns to sell goods and services to the workers.) Her two uncles run the stores next door. The narrator also notices the natives, who are also mostly immigrants driven by economic necessity to the mines. Notice how the workers are from different tribes (a Swazi and a Shangaan). The story of "The Defeated" concerns the early lives of two white girls, but the situation of the black African workers hovers uncomfortably in the background, as the final image of the story makes explicit. Although Gordimer never states explicitly that the town is racially segregated, the story's opening paragraphs implicitly make the situation clear. The Concession stores serve the natives; little white girls should keep away. If students are asked to analyze the opening paragraph (which is only two sentences long) they will eventually work out much of this social context for themselves.

An obvious question to ask students is how to explain the story's title. Who are the defeated? In a narrow sense, the defeated are Miriam's parents, who have sacrificed a great deal to educate their daughter, only to lose her. The only thing Mr. Saiyetovitz says in the story is, "It doesn't come out like you think." Although they have succeeded in their plans to give their daughter a better life than they enjoyed, they do not share in that success. Their prosperous daughter now considers them a social embarrassment. They feel the pain of this rejection without fully understanding how it came about, and their incomprehension makes their defeat more bitter. But at the end of the story Gordimer suddenly links the Saiyetovitzes' condition to the broader social situation. Looking at the old shopkeeper and his Swazi customer, the narrator calls them "Defeated, and without understanding in their defeat." Neither of these immigrants, she implies, fully understand the losses they have suffered by coming into this new, unrooted society.

In his political reading of Gordimer's work, *The Novels of Nadine Gordimer: History from the Inside* (London: Allen and Unwin, 1986), Stephen Clingman analyzes the South African writer's early fiction that focuses on the theme of betrayal. Clingman observes:

> Children "betray" parents in emerging from the economic and social world that the latter inhabit into new and developing environments. In "The Defeated" a daughter betrays her parents, who run a concession store. They have given the daughter everything they have; she hardly ever comes to see them, and more or less forgets them. . . . In "The Defeated" it [Gordimer's early work] also pays attention to a characteristic manifestation of the white *nouveaux riches* of South Africa, whatever their origins: the way in which, lacking other tradition, and needing to deny their own history, they conveniently tend to forget the past. (pp. 23–24)

A good topic for a student paper would be to compare "The Defeated" to Alice Walker's "Everyday Use" (page 90). Both stories present intergenerational conflicts involving upwardly mobile young women who are ashamed of their family backgrounds. Walker's story reflects the perspective of a decidedly undefeated parent and would provide an illuminating contrast to Gordimer's darker tale.

Students interested in writing on Gordimer might try reading some of the other stories in *The Soft Voice of the Serpent*, which explores the same milieu as "The Defeated." Gordimer's essays have been collected in *The Essential Gesture: Writing, Politics, and Places* (New York: Viking, 1988). Gordimer's comments on "How the Short Story Differs from the Novel" are found in the "Criticism: On Fiction" chapter on page 576.

Langston Hughes
On the Road, page 448

QUESTIONS

1. *Is "On the Road" a fantasy, or is it a realistic story that contains a dream or vision? Defend your answer with evidence from the story.* Students are likely to express sharply differing views. Some will stoutly maintain that the story is a fantasy in which a man pulls down a church and Christ gets off his cross, takes a walk with the man, then heads for Kansas City—an engaging detail! Others will insist with equal fervor that the white cops, who arrive just as the church door is giving way, club the black man into unconsciousness, and that from this unconscious state arises the dream that begins in paragraph 20. This, they will maintain, explains Sargeant's waking up in jail without knowing how he got there (54–56). We ourselves are divided on the question, XJK seeing the story as a tale that reveals the marvelous, DMK and DG as a realistic story containing a vision. It is, in any case, a story about racial prejudice.

2. *Where and when is Hughes's story set?* The time is the Great Depression of the thirties, the place a city big enough to have relief shelters for the destitute and far enough north to have snow. Homelessness being the problem it is today, the story seems curiously timely, though hordes of people no longer ride freight trains as they did back in the thirties.

3. *From what point of view is "On the Road" told?* The narrator is omniscient. Mostly he looks at the action through the black man's eyes, even speaks like Sargeant ("He never did see Christ no more," 51), but in paragraph 18 also sees into the thoughts of the people on the street.

4. *To what extent does this story resemble "Godfather Death" and "The Appointment in Samarra" in Chapter One?* All three stories center around a divine or supernatural being. The characters are flat rather than round; there is no appreciable character development. In all three, plot is perhaps the most important element.

Zora Neale Hurston
Sweat, page 452

Hurston's stark tale of a bitter marriage turned murderous first appeared in the one and only issue of the Harlem arts journal, *Fire!!* in November 1926. *Fire!!*, which carried the subtitle, "A Quarterly Devoted to the Younger Negro Artists," presented some of the leading talents of the new generation, including Langston Hughes, Countee Cullen, and Arna Bontemps. "Sweat," with its use of authentic black dialect and folkways, its forthright presentation of harsh subject matter, and (to quote Alice Walker) its "sense of black people as complete, complex, *undiminished* human beings," makes it a representative work of the Harlem Renaissance.

QUESTIONS

1. *What importance does the setting of "Sweat" have to its action?* The story takes place mostly in a house on the outskirts of a small Florida town (which critics identify with Hurston's hometown of Eatonsville). The isolation of Delia's home is essential to the plot. Its distance from town means that she has no protection there from Sykes's violence, just as its isolation ultimately gives Sykes no escape from his slow, painful death by

snakebite. The setting is also important to the story's motivation. Delia has bought the house with her own hard work. Sykes wants to kill her for the house so that he can bring another woman home to it. The house also becomes a symbol to the otherwise disappointed Delia of what she has managed to accomplish in her hard, painful life. ("It was lovely to her, lovely.")

2. *What has Delia and Sykes's marriage been like?* Delia married out of love. Sykes, she believes, brought only lust to the union ("a longing after the flesh"). Two months after the wedding, he gave her the first of many brutal beatings. In town, he is notorious for beating her and she for surviving his savage assaults. Sykes has frequently disappeared to squander his irregular earnings while Delia has worked as a laundress to pay their bills. Delia's hard work wounds Sykes's masculine pride: it reminds him that he cannot support her. Sykes is now adulterously involved with Bertha. Delia is not surprised to discover that he is trying to kill her.

3. *What is the significance of the story's title?* Hurston's title describes Delia's existence. Trapped in a brutal, loveless marriage and getting no help from Sykes in supporting the two of them, Delia has almost nothing in her life except work. Defending herself against Sykes's threats, she summarizes her life as "Sweat, sweat, sweat! Work and sweat, cry and sweat, pray and sweat!" The title also suggests why Delia is deaf to Sykes's pleas at the end of the story: love and compassion have been sweated out of her.

4. *Is Delia right to let Sykes die at the end of the story?* This may be an uncomfortable question for students, but the point of Hurston's story is to make us consider uncomfortable issues. It may be important to remind students that Delia is not responsible for Sykes being bitten by the snake; he has fallen into his own trap. If she is guilty of anything, it is only of not trying to help her husband—a sin of omission rather than commission. There is little question that a jury would acquit her of any charge. If ever a woman could claim extenuating circumstances, it is Delia. The more interesting question is whether Delia is morally culpable. In this regard, Hurston seems to suggest that Sykes has made Delia a person callous enough to watch coldly her own husband die. The ending has led one critic, Robert Bone, in his *Down-Home: Origins of the Afro-American Short Story* (New York: Columbia University Press, 1988) to call "Sweat" a self-indulgent "revenge fantasy." But most critics have agreed with Lillie P. Howard, who viewed "Sweat" as a complex moral investigation of a good woman in an extreme situation:

> Delia could have warned him, saved him, but she understandably does not. She has been hardened by his constant abuse and has built up a "spiritual earthworks" against him. Poetic justice has been rendered. (*Zora Neale Hurston:* New York, Twayne, 1980, p. 65)

What do your students think?

5. *How does the language of "Sweat" contribute to the story's effect?* There are two different levels of language employed in the story. Hurston presents the narration in sharp and evocative standard English, whereas the dialogue is written in the rural black dialect of her native Central Florida. Their constant alternation heightens the story's considerable nervous energy and suspense. The dialect also adds realism to the story: it evokes real people and a real region. Students sometimes experience some initial difficulty in reading dialogue in dialect because it looks different from conventional English. It is important to get them to hear it. You might ask the class why Hurston chose to write the dialogue in dialect. Would the story be different if the dialogue were written in standard American English?

A volume of critical essays dealing with "Sweat," edited by Cheryl Wall, is forthcoming from Rutgers University Press (in its new series dealing with short fiction, "Women Writers: Texts and Contexts"). Students planning to write on Hurston will find it helpful to read Laura M. Zaidman's comprehensive article on the author in *Dictionary of Literary Biography 86: American Short-Story Writers, 1910–1945,* edited by Bobby Ellen Kimbel (Detroit: Gale, 1989), which provides an insightful and highly readable introduction to her life and work.

D. H. Lawrence
THE ROCKING-HORSE WINNER, page 462

QUESTIONS

1. *The family members in Lawrence's story harbor a number of secrets. What are they?* The mother's secret is that "at the center of her heart was a hard little place that could not feel love, no, not for anybody" (paragraph 1). Paul's secret is that, by furiously riding his wooden rocking-horse, he is often able to predict which horses will win races. Bassett's secret, and Uncle Oscar's, is that they profit from Paul's predictions, even while the boy is on his deathbed. Their winnings are kept secret. Paul gives his mother 5,000 pounds, but does it anonymously. The house itself whispers a secret, "There must be more money" (5, 6, 181). The three children hear the whisper, but no one talks about it.

2. *What motivates each main character? What sets Paul's quest apart from that of the others?* It is the desire for more money that motivates them all. Perhaps the most blatant evidence of the family's obsession with riches appears in Uncle Oscar's attempt to console his sister after her son's death: "My God, Hester, you're eighty-odd thousand to the good and a poor devil of a son to the bad" (244)—as if he were enumerating her assets and liabilities on an imaginary balance sheet.

Paul's frenzied pursuit of money differs from the greed of the others in that he wants wealth not for himself but for his mother. Clearly he hopes that, by being "luckier" than his father, he will win his mother's love and attention.

3. *Some details in Lawrence's story are implausible. What are they?* Those students who can appreciate Lawrence's particular blend of reality and fantasy will like "The Rocking-Horse Winner." A house that whispers is unusual, but even a hard-headed realist can probably accept it at least as a metaphor. That a boy can learn to predict the winner in a horse race by riding his rocking horse is perhaps harder to believe.

4. *At what places in his story does Lawrence make use of irony?* Paul, intent upon stopping the whispers in the house, anonymously gives his mother 5,000 pounds as a birthday present. Ironically, his gift has the opposite effect. The whispers grow louder. Given his mother's insatiable greed for money, this result comes as less of a surprise to the reader than to Paul.

There is irony in the story's title. Paul, the rocking-horse winner, loses his life.

Ironic, too, are Paul's final words: "I *am* lucky" (241). In his mother's definition of luck, in paragraph 18 ("It's what causes you to have money"), Paul *is* lucky, of course—or was.

5. *In what sense may Paul's periodic rides on the rocking horse be regarded as symbolic acts?* The single-minded frenzy with which Paul rides his rocking horse parallels the intensity of the money-lust that dominates Paul's family. There is no joy in his riding, as there is no joy in his house.

6. *What is the theme of "The Rocking-Horse Winner"?* The love of money is destructive of all other love, and even of life itself.

Doris Lessing
A WOMAN ON A ROOF, page 474

As Joyce does in "Araby," Doris Lessing tells a tale of a young man who moves from fantasy to disillusionment. What happens in her story proceeds directly from its setting: the record-breaking heat wave that increases the worker's frustrations. The weather is so vividly present that it seems to become one of the characters. Lessing demonstrates how the summer's weather (and dizzying rooftop) can motivate the characters. As the heat mounts, young Tom's erotic fantasies grow more intense; he becomes like a man in a desert who stares through shimmering heat at a mirage. In the end, after he accosts the woman and is rebuffed, Tom feels irrational hatred and resentment. From the story's last line we know that he and his fellow roof menders want only to finish their job and quit this building.

It might be worthwhile to begin the discussion by asking: Who is the protagonist? Although the woman on the roof is the character around which all the action turns, Tom is the protagonist, the one who acts. Lessing begins the story from the general point of view of all three men and then centers on Tom—the only character whose thoughts we know. As Tom's illusion—and disillusionment—seem central, to tell the story from the woman's point of view would make it a completely different story. The suggestion that this is a modern Lady Godiva story seems only partly accurate. Tom, like Peeping Tom, is punished; but unlike Godiva, the woman has made no particular gesture of charity to others—unless one wants to regard her as a defender of sunbathers.

Although the story centers on Tom, it may be helpful to ask students to characterize each of the three men in relation to the situation. The oldest man, Harry, is relatively well behaved and tolerant towards the sunbather. Stanley is loud, rude, and aggressive. Ophia Jane Allen observes, "In Stanley [the sunbather] evokes the fear that he might fail to possess his wife, whom he would not permit to 'lay about like that'" ("Structure and Motif in Doris Lessing's 'A Man and Two Women,'" *Modern Fiction Studies*, 26:1 Spring 1980). In Tom, however, the sunbather arouses amorous fantasies that combine tender intentions along with his annoying advances.

It may also be interesting to examine the character of Mrs. Pritchett, the woman who gives the workers tea. What does her presence contribute to the story? What contrast does the author draw between her and the woman on the roof?

The theme of this story, in the view of Rosemary Dinnage, is that a woman can evoke shock and anger by appearing stripped of her pretty frills and trappings. "That a woman should belong so much to her surface, to the way she colors and shapes and arranges it, that this surface should be the focal point for male fantasy quite unconnected with the person beneath the surface, is an affront to her" (Review of Lessing's *Stories* in *The New York Review of Books* [Sept. 29, 1978] 12–13).

Another story for comparison is: John Updike's "A & P." In the supermarket, the narrator's fellow workers seem to be voyeurs, like Lessing's roof repairmen, and Updike takes umbrage with macho males who ignore the person below a woman's surface. (Of course, Updike's narrator, too, admires Queenie's surface.) Lessing perhaps goes deeper: her general message in this, as in much of her fiction, is, to quote Rosemary Dinnage again, "our complete moral and social bankruptcy . . . particularly in the relation between men and women. "

Lessing has insisted, however, that she has never written from a consciously feminist perspective. "What the feminists want of men," she told an interviewer,

> is something they haven't examined because it comes from religion. They want me to bear witness. What they would really like me to say is, "Ha, sisters, I stand with you side by side in your struggle toward the golden dawn where all those beastly men are no more." Do they really want people to make oversimplified statements about men and women? In fact they do. I've come with great regret to this conclusion. (quoted by Lesley Hazleton in "Doris Lessing on Feminism, Communism, and 'Space Fiction,'" *New York Times Magazine* [July 25, 1982] 21)

Bob Baron of Mesa Community College, who argued for restoring this story to the sixth edition of *Introduction to Literature,* found that his students "really enjoyed analyzing what the author was saying about contemporary male-female relationships and how they could be bettered." A discussion question for your students: does the author suggest or imply any ways in which men and women might better understand each other?

Gabriel García Márquez
THE WOMAN WHO CAME AT SIX O'CLOCK, page 481

Gabriel García Márquez's story is highly cinematic. It takes place in a single setting, and the action moves forward mainly in dialogue between the two main characters and careful description of their physical actions. Simple and straightforward on the surface, the story suggests complex psychological motivations for both characters.

QUESTIONS

1. *Why does José put up with the woman's insults? Why does he not react to her taunts?* The obvious reason is that José has fallen in love with her—and yet his infatuation doesn't necessarily explain his patience with her cruel teasing and insults. José is fat, unattractive, and presumably somewhat older than the woman. He runs a restaurant so dully regular that he can predict when his customers will arrive. He finds the woman immensely attractive but also disreputable. (In fact, he may even find her attractive *because* she is disreputable.) José understands that there is something slightly ridiculous and embarrassing in his hopeless attachment, though he cannot disentangle himself from it. Perhaps he feels a need to suffer for his folly, or perhaps the woman's ridicule has always been a condition of their relationship. The insults evidently hurt him. He sometimes remains silent after she mocks him, while at other times he tries to brush them aside by changing the subject, but he never insults her back or openly expresses his anger.

2. *How does the woman feel about José? Does she manipulate him cold-heartedly or does she feel some genuine affection for him?* Since we only view the woman from the outside, we cannot know her true feelings with any assurance. We can only draw implications based on her actions. We know that she is dependent on José. She comes into his restaurant every evening at six o'clock for a free dinner. We sense, however, that she depends on him for more than food. Her arrival on this evening—after she has presumably killed a man—betrays an emotional dependence as well. He seems to be the only person she can trust. Her cruel remarks may be her clumsy way of testing the depth of his affection. Whatever her emotions toward him are, however, they do not include sexual attraction—she makes that point painfully clear to the doting José. He seems to be her only reliable protector in a moment of real danger.

3. *Will José lie for her?* Once again, the answer is impossible to give with accuracy. We

only know for sure what happens within the action of the story. The implication is, however, that José will keep his promise. It is the only way beyond feeding her each evening that he can demonstrate his affection—his one chance to be a romantic protector rather than a surrogate father. He has already said he would kill a man because he loves her so much. Her request is the only available consummation for his affection.

4. *José repeatedly tells the woman that he does not understand why she wants him to lie about the time of her arrival. Does he really not understand?* José seems to know that the woman has just killed a man. Since he is jealous of her lovers, he seems to feel no sympathy toward the victim, but his sense of propriety appears to be offended. He does not want to acknowledge her crime openly. That action would be too morally compromising for his conservative nature, but he loves the woman too much in his hopeless but protective way not to take her side. He can only acknowledge her crime silently (with "a fearful compromise of complicity").

Bobbie Ann Mason
SHILOH, page 490

In reviewing Bobbie Ann Mason's *Love Life*, critic Robert McPhillips summarizes the special appeal of her first book, *Shiloh and Other Stories* (1982). "In one volume," McPhillips observes, "Mason had populated a literary landscape almost as distinctive as Sherwood Anderson's Winesburg, Ohio." He goes on to say:

> Formerly ordered by the rhythms of farm life, these lives are now lived against the manufactured hum of television shows, rock and country music and MTV. Mason is at her best when evoking the confusion—sometimes comic and sometimes troubling—that this radical cultural upheaval creates in people who have lost touch with their past but who suddenly face a dizzying number of options—educational, occupational and sexual—from which they must try to piece together their present lives. (*New York Post,* March 19, 1989)

Although McPhillips was discussing the entire collection, he could have been specifically addressing the title story.

QUESTIONS

1. *"Shiloh" is told by a third-person narrator who observes both Leroy and Norma Jean Moffitt. Does the narrator present one character more deeply than the other?* Although the narrator appears initially to be impersonal, the story presents Leroy's thoughts and feelings more deeply than Norma Jean's. We see Norma Jean mainly from the outside. We follow her actions closely but don't always understand her motivations. Leroy's psychology is much more clearly presented—perhaps because he himself understands it. Having been partially crippled in a truck accident, Leroy has been forced to reexamine his life. He has discovered things about himself that his formerly busy schedule did not allow—his newfound passion for building things, for example, and his new appreciation for his wife. He also sees how much his hometown has changed. He seems to see his life up close for the first time. "He has begun to realize that in all the years he was on the road," Mason writes, "He never took time to examine anything. He was always flying past scenery."

2. *What role does the electric organ play in Norma Jean and Leroy's relationship? Does it in any way influence the breakup of their marriage?* Leroy enjoys his wife's obsession with the electric organ he bought her for Christmas. He loves the music, though

he mainly uses it to drift off into his daydreams. For Norma Jean, however, the music unleashes her frustrations. She buys a "Sixties Songbook" and, playing through these old tunes, she feels dissatisfied with what she has done with her youth. "I didn't like these old songs back then," she tells her husband. "But I have this crazy feeling I missed something." Characteristically, Leroy cuts off the conversation. "You didn't miss a thing." In the background is the real hole in their life—their son, Randy, who died in infancy. They never speak about him, a silence that is symptomatic of the couple's inability to address and resolve the real issues in their marriage. The couple has had no other children. Possibly, motherhood and family life is one of the other things Norma Jean has missed and that might have offset her sense of having missed being young. Norma Jean's new smoking habit is surely also significant. Is it the sign of delayed adolescent rebellion in a woman approaching middle age?

3. *What does the story's title contribute to its meaning? Isn't the Shiloh battleground incidental to the couple's situation?* The trip to the Shiloh battleground becomes a symbol for the failure of the Moffitt's marriage. As the British writer Francis King observed in a review of *Shiloh and Other Stories,* when Leroy takes Norma Jean "to the Civil War battlefield of Shiloh, she in effect, vanishes out of sight, leaving him with the desolating sense that, just as he never understood the inner workings of history that erupted in so much carnage, so he has never understood the inner working of the marriage that is now causing his own inner death" (*The Spectator,* August 20, 1983). Norma Jean's mother has urged them to visit the battleground as she did on her honeymoon. Now that Leroy is injured, he has warmed to the idea, but his notion that their aimless visit to Shiloh would remedy or improve their relationship reflects how poorly he understands his wife. Leroy has good intentions, he wants to improve their marriage. But he has grown so remote from his wife's inner life that his solutions—building a log cabin she does not want or having a picnic in Shiloh—have no connection to her still only half-realized aspirations.

Bobbie Anne Mason discusses her aims as a writer on an audiocassette interview available from the American Audio Prose Library, Inc., Box 842, Columbia, MO 65205; phone number for orders, (800) 447-2275.

Alice Munro
HOW I MET MY HUSBAND, page 501

Alice Munro's ingeniously plotted story would make an interesting alternative selection to use in the discussion of plot in "Reading a Story" (Chapter 1). The development in the plot of this story reflects the young narrator's growing awareness of how love and infatuation operate. "How I Met My Husband" would also work well in discussion of "Point of View" (Chapter 2). Munro's story shows how even a sensible and observant narrator can misjudge people and events, especially when she is involved in the action. Munro is also masterful in portraying Edie's opinions of her neighbors and employers. Edie is a richly realized narrator—engaging, complex, and human. At fifteen, she is, ironically, too smart to appreciate how innocent she still is. She does not yet understand the sexual feelings she experiences. Previously in control of most social situations, she stumbles through this comic romance mostly in embarrassed confusion.

QUESTIONS

1. *How would you judge Edie as a narrator? Do we feel she is being objective about the people and events she describes? Take one character or incident and comment on her*

depiction of it. Edie is smart and sensible for her age, but she has a highly critical kind of intelligence and is apt to find fault with most people. She generally keeps her mouth shut in situations, but as a narrator, she speaks candidly to the reader. An amusing illustration of Edie's narrative "objectivity" is her treatment of the gossipy Loretta Bird. Edie views Loretta Bird with delightful disdain and constantly comments on the hypocrisy or pretension behind everything Loretta Bird says. Her candor might be less agreeable if she was not equally candid in confessing her own failings. She readily admits how many dumb things her young self did or said simply because she could not think of anything better. Her narration may be subjective, but it is not overtly self-serving.

2. *How does Munro present Chris Watters as a character? What do we know about him?* The important thing for students to realize is that we see Chris Watters through Edie's eyes. When she first meets him, Watters seems poised and charming. He flirts with her so suavely that at first, she does not even understand he is flirting. Nonetheless, she is affected by his compliments. ("I wasn't even old enough then to realize how out of the common it is, for a man to say something like that to a woman . . . for a man to say a word like *beautiful.*") She begins to fall in love with him without at first admitting it openly in her narrative, and she observes him with the obsessive attentiveness that characterizes sexual attraction. When his unglamorous fiancée, Alice Kelling, arrives, Edie does not waver in her affection. Observing Watters and his fiancée together, she senses that he has little attraction left for the woman. Her infatuation with Watters leads her (and probably the reader) to excuse the lapses in his character. Edie is utterly sympathetic to his flight (in both senses of the word) from the apparently unsuitable Alice Kelling. It is not until long after Watters has flown away, and Edie realizes that he is not going to write (and by implication, never going to see her again), that the reader begins to appreciate how untrustworthy he was. We actually know very little about Watters (except his exciting profession) beyond what Alice and Edie tell us, and both women have a vested interest in him.

3. *Does the story have a climax? If so, when does it occur?* Students may find this a surprisingly difficult question. Many of them will say the climax of the story occurs in the final paragraph when Edie starts dating Mr. Carmichael, the mailman. That moment may be the story's unexpected conclusion, but the climax occurs a few pages earlier, when the women in the story are having dinner and after Chris Watters has flown away. Trouble erupts when Edie admits to being "intimate" with the pilot. That uproarious scene is the moment of greatest tension when the real outcome of the story is being decided. Edie's public humiliation pushes her into maturity, and her fervent loyalty to her errant airman will prove sadly misplaced, even though she does not fully understand its effects for some time. Mrs. Peebles protects her from the worst of the gossip by getting rid of Alice Kelling and keeping Edie on as help, but the key events that will affect Edie's future life have now been set in place.

4. *What effect does Munro achieve by titling her story "How I Met My Husband"? Isn't that title misleading?* Munro's title is both accurate and misleading. Edie indeed tells the story of how she met her husband, but he is probably not the character the reader at first assumes she will marry. If the title is a trick, it is a brilliant and insightful one, because by assuming that Chris Watters will eventually marry Edie, the reader shares Edie's own romantic illusions. We tend to give Watters the benefit of the doubt when, in retrospect, we see he was only a charming cad. Notice how Munro keeps other eligible males out of the first three quarters of the story. We—like Edie—have nowhere to fasten our romantic assumptions except on this exotic pilot (exotic to Edie, that is: "I only knew he wasn't from around here" is how she describes him from their initial meeting. That may not sound like much to us, but to a fifteen-year-old farm girl, her words connote a world of

mystery). Munro's teasing title, therefore, is a psychological ploy that makes readers identify more closely with the narrator's emotions than they themselves initially realize. Munro's story is a good example for students of how a work's title is an essential part of the text and contributes to its total meaning.

There is an excellent interview with Alice Munro in Volume 3 of *Short Story Criticism* (Detroit: Gale, 1989). This useful volume, which will be found in most large libraries, also contains excerpts from reviews and essays on Munro's short fiction. Munro has an interview available on audiocassette, in which she discusses the influences on her work, the state of Canadian literature, and her identity as a woman writer. Contact the American Audio Prose Library, Inc., Box 842, Columbia, MO 65205; phone number for orders, (800) 447–2275.

Joyce Carol Oates
WHERE ARE YOU GOING, WHERE HAVE YOU BEEN? page 515

QUESTIONS

1. *Describe Connie as you see her in the first few paragraphs of the story. In what ways is she appealing? In what respects is she imperceptive and immature?* Connie, Oates implies, is still growing and doesn't know whether to act "childlike" or "languid." Still discovering her identity, she behaves one way at home and another way elsewhere. Her mind is "filled with trashy daydreams," and the first caresses of love seem to her just "the way it was in movies and promised in songs."

2. *Describe the character of Arnold Friend. In what ways is he sinister? What do you make of his strangely detailed knowledge of Connie and her family, of his apparent ability to see what is happening at the barbecue, miles away? Is he a supernatural character?* Perhaps Arnold's knowledge was obtained merely by pumping Connie's friends for information and by keeping close watch on her house, and perhaps his reported vision of the barbecue is merely feigned for Connie's benefit. Much about him seems fakery: his masklike face and "stage voice," his gilded jalopy, his artificially padded boots, his affecting the speech, dress, and music of the youth culture (although he is over thirty). Still, there are hints that he is a devil or a warlock. Perhaps Ellie Oscar, the "forty-year-old baby," is his imp or familiar; perhaps his bendable boot conceals a cloven hoof. He works a kind of magic: on first spying Connie he draws a sign in the air that marks her for his own. He threatens to possess her very soul: he will enter her "where it's all secret" and then, after the sex act, she will give in to him (paragraph 104). A charismatic like Charles Manson, he seeks young girls to dominate. According to Oates, the character of Arnold Friend was inspired by the author's reading a newspaper story about a traveling murderer in the Southwest.

3. *Why doesn't Connie succeed in breaking loose from Arnold Friend's spell?* She seems in a trance, like a dazed and terrified bird facing a snake. Everything appears unreal or "only half real" (94). Like a practitioner of brainwashing, Arnold Friend denies reality: "This place you are now—inside your daddy's house—is nothing but a cardboard box I can knock down any time" (152). Arnold suggests that Connie's beating heart isn't real ("Feel that? That feels solid too but we know better") and soon she thinks her body "wasn't really hers either" (155). Perhaps, some male student will suggest, Connie really wants to give in to Arnold Friend—after all, she loves to flirt with danger and when

Friend first looked at her in the parking lot, she looked back. But Connie's terror seems amply justified; Friend after all has threatened to kill her family unless she submits to him.

4. *What seems ironic in the names of the leading characters?* Friend is no friend; a better name for him would be Fiend. Ellie Oscar, like his first name, seems asexual. His last name suggests a trophy from the Motion Picture Academy—fitting for a media-slave who keeps his ear glued to his transistor radio. His androgynous name perhaps recalls that of another assassin, Lee Oswald. Connie is a connee—one who is conned.

5. *What is the point of view of this story? How is it appropriate?* Limited omniscience, with the author seeing into only one character's mind. Besides, the author perceives more than Connie does and observes Arnold Friend and Ellie more shrewdly than Connie could observe them.

6. *Explain the title. Where is Connie going, where has she been?* She has been living in a world of daydreams, and now, at the end, she is going out into a sunlit field to be raped. In the beginning of the story, we are shown that Connie lives mainly in the present; in the opening paragraph she sees "a shadowy vision of herself as she was right at the moment." She doesn't seem bothered by the ultimate questions asked in the title of the story. Arnold Friend answers the questions in paragraph 152: "The place where you came from ain't there any more, and where you had in mind to go is cancelled out." She has been no-where, she is going nowhere—for in his view, there is no reality.

7. *What significance, if any, do you find in this story's being dedicated to Bob Dylan?* No doubt some of Dylan's music flows through Connie's mind, and some of Friend's repartee seems a weak-minded imitation of Dylanese: surreal and disconnected, as in his tirade to Ellie (133): "Don't hem in on me . . ." Arnold Friend bears a faint resemblance to Dylan: he has "a familiar face, somehow," with hawklike nose and hair "crazy as a wig," and he talks with a lilting voice "as if he were reciting the words to a song." His approach is "slightly mocking, kidding, but serious and a little melancholy" and he taps his fists together "in homage to the perpetual music behind him" (77). Joyce Carol Oates has remarked that Dylan's song "It's All Over Now, Baby Blue" (1965) was an influence on her story. Dylan's lyric addresses a young girl, Baby Blue ("My sweet little blue-eyed girl," Arnold calls Connie), who must make a hasty departure from home across an unreal, shifting landscape. A vagabond raps at her door, and she is told, "Something calls for you / Forget the dead you've left." Oates's title recalls a line from another Dylan song, "Mr. Tambourine Man": "And there is no place I'm goin' to."

8. *Consider this evaluation by a student: "All this story is is a sophisticated cheap thrill. Reading it is sort of like watching a kitten thrown to an octopus."*

In teaching this story to her students at the University of Georgia, Professor Anne Williams had "a couple of minor epiphanies." She has written to share them with us:

"Ellie" may be a diminutive of "Beelzebub," lord of the flies. The story is certainly full of references to flies. I also noticed a series of comic allusions to various fairy tales, all of which, according to Bettelheim, concern the difficulties of coming to terms with adult sexuality:

"Snow White" (in reference to the mother's jealousy over Connie's looks, so much like her own faded beauty [1–2]);

"Cinderella" (the pumpkin on Arnold's car [36]);

"Little Red Riding Hood" (here, there seems a fundamental structural parallel—and Arnold is described: "the nose long and hawk-like, sniffing as if she were a treat he was going to gobble up" [46]).

In spite of *hawk-like*, we agree the description makes Arnold sound distinctly like a wolf. Professor Williams refers, of course, to Bruno Bettelheim's *The Uses of Enchantment* (New York: Knopf, 1976). Perhaps Oates's story might be taken up together with the Grimm tale "Godfather Death."

Joyce Carol Oates reads an excerpt from this story on an audiocassette (order no. AMF-26) available from American Audio Prose Library, Box 842, Columbia MO 65205. For current price, call (800) 447-2275.

A film has been based on Oates's story: *Smooth Talk* (1987), directed by Joyce Chopra, with screenplay by Tom Cole. In an interview, Oates remarked that although she had nothing to do with making the movie, she respects the "quite remarkable" results. "The story itself is a Hawthornian parable of a kind, 'realistic' in its surface texture but otherwise allegorical" (interview with Barbara C. Millard, *Four Quartets*, Fall 1988). Is it, then, an account of a confrontation with the Devil, comparable with "Young Goodman Brown"?

Frank O'Connor
FIRST CONFESSION, page 528

QUESTIONS

1. *Does the narrator of this story seem a boy—an innocent or naive narrator—or a grown-up looking back through seven-year-old eyes? At what moments do you sense an ironic discrepancy between the boy's view of things and Frank O'Connor's?* The latter, as we can tell from the story's knowing selection of details. The small boy's horror, for instance, at the fact that his grandmother drinks porter seems exaggerated; so does his reaction to Mrs. Ryan's yarn about the spirit with burning hands. Why was the priest silent for so long after the boy confesses his murder plot? We assume he was doubled up in silent mirth. Jackie's plan to get rid of the body seems a childish power-fantasy, a solution quite beyond his abilities, as the narrator is evidently well aware.

2. *In what ways is Jackie not entirely naive, but sometimes shrewd and perceptive?* Suggestion: Take a close look at what he says about Mrs. Ryan and about his sister Nora. Most readers feel that the boy's resentment of Nora seems fair and justified. A truly pious girl wouldn't box her brother's ears in church or stick out her tongue at him while he says penance at the altar. Furthermore, the priest sides with him in his opinion. Shrewdly, Jackie notices Mrs. Ryan's overfondness for Hell and her tenacious clinging to her half-crown.

3. *What traits of character do you find in the priest? How does he differ from Mrs. Ryan as a teacher of children?* The easygoing, good-humored priest has a better understanding of child psychology. Unlike Mrs. Ryan, he suggests that wrongdoers are sometimes punished in the here and now. Is he deplorable in trying to implant in Jackie a horror of the gallows? Jackie's reaction is gratitude and relief from his fears of the fiery furnace. Hanging is at least definite and easy to imagine and has an end to it.

4. *Do you believe Frank O'Connor to be saying—as Nora says in the conclusion—that there is no use in trying to lead a virtuous life?* Evidently, Nora's closing speech is meant to be funny: she congratulates herself on living a life of virtue, though in her brother's eyes she is a "raging malicious devil" (paragraph 14) and a hypocrite (17). O'Connor makes no general statement about the virtuous life but strongly implies that the priest shows the way: by looking at the world with humor, compassion, and forgiveness. In Mrs. Ryan's view, on the other hand, to live a good life is a grim and terrible chore.

This appealing story may be useful as a clear illustration of an ironic point of view: the naive boy's impressions as recalled by the grown-up narrator. It is hard to imagine the story told from any other point of view and remaining so effective, or so hilarious.

The boy's intended murder victim is apparently drawn from childhood memory. In his autobiography *An Only Child* (New York: Knopf, 1970), O'Connor relates that his paternal grandmother, an abrasive old soul who swigged porter and ate with her fingers, became a widow and moved in with his family.

Tillie Olsen
I STAND HERE IRONING, page 534

QUESTIONS

1. *What is the point of view in "I Stand Here Ironing"? Who is the "you" in Olsen's story?* The story is told in the first person by the mother of a gifted young woman. The author never identifies the "you" in so many words. We can only deduce from internal evidence (in paragraphs 2, 50, 52) that the mother's interior monologue is in response to a call from a counselor or teacher—in college probably, because Emily is nineteen years old—requesting a conference with the mother. The narrator makes clear in paragraph 55 that she has no intention of going in to see the caller.

2. *Briefly describe the circumstances into which Emily was born.* Emily's childhood was one of poverty and deprivation, perhaps best summed up by her mother in paragraph 55. That Emily was a child whose mother loved her fiercely is poignantly evident in paragraph 8: "She was a miracle to me, but when she was eight months old I had to leave her daytimes with the woman downstairs to whom she was no miracle at all."

3. *What are we to make of Emily's telling her mother not to awaken her the next morning even though she has midterms (53)?* By the time she is nineteen, her daughter is apparently over the terrible "goodness" the mother remorsefully recalls as characteristic of Emily when she was a little girl. Emily indicates that she will skip her midterms—not out of lighthearted laziness, however, but out of a sense of futility brought on by the uncertainties of modern life, the conviction that "in a couple of years . . . we'll all be atom-dead." It is perhaps Emily's neglect of her school work that has occasioned the phone call from her teacher or counselor.

4. *Is there any justification for the mother's determination not to accept the invitation to come in and talk about her daughter?* The mother now realizes that whenever in the past she consulted "experts," their advice caused needless pain. She ignored her own common sense and breastfed her daughter on a rigid schedule because "the books" so decreed (6). "They" said Emily was ready for nursery school at age two (12). The mother, rendered helpless by her need to work for a living, therefore sent her daughter to nursery school. "They"—the people at the clinic—persuaded Emily's mother to send her to a convalescent home to recover from the measles (26). In retrospect the mother realizes her daughter would have been far better off at home. The best advice she ever received came from a man with no special credentials, who kindly entreated her to smile more when she looked at Emily. The happiest moments she remembers are those when, following her own instincts, she kept her children home from school even when they weren't really sick.

5. *What makes "I Stand Here Ironing" more than just a case study of a talented but deprived young woman? What besides the task at hand is suggested by Olsen's use of iron and ironing board in her story?* "I Stand Here Ironing" is enriched by the symbolism of

iron and ironing board. The fervent plea that ends the story is the mother's hope that her daughter will know "that she is more than this dress on the ironing board, helpless before the iron." The iron here suggests fate, heredity, environment—all those forces that limit any individual's aspirations. The mother, who is herself an intelligent, perceptive, sensitive person, has been thwarted by poverty. Like mothers everywhere, she wants a better life for her child. This longing permeates the story. Indeed, her daughter at nineteen leads a very different life from her own at the same age.

6. *One student has called "I Stand Here Ironing" "a very modern story. It could have been written yesterday." What elements in the story support that assessment?* Though few people iron anymore and no one rides the streetcar, and in spite of its references to the Depression of the thirties and to World War II, Olsen's story strikes many a contemporary note. Single parents who have to entrust their children to inadequate day-care so that they can hold down jobs are less the exception now than they were when Olsen wrote her story. The author, by demonstrating that the thoughts of a housewife are fit matter for a story, has in a way written a feminist document. There is a sturdy insistence, too, on the part of the narrator-mother, that parents cannot be held eternally accountable for their children's inadequacies. "She has lived for nineteen years. There is all that life that has happened outside of me, beyond me" (3). Only now has popular psychology begun to concede as much. That sad little Emily, "a child of anxious, not proud, love," should have blossomed into a beautiful, popular comedienne—not troublefree, but at least functioning normally—says something important about the resilience of the human spirit.

An interview with Tillie Olsen is available on cassette from the American Audio Prose Library, Inc., Box 842, Columbia, MO 65205; phone number for orders, (800) 447-2275.

Philip Roth
THE CONVERSION OF THE JEWS, page 541

QUESTIONS

1. *What is the story saying?* Ozzie himself probably best states the theme in paragraph 176: "You should never hit anybody about God." "The Conversion of the Jews" is a comic story, but its theme is serious.

2. *What is the story's major conflict?* Friction between Rabbi Binder and the irrepressible Ozzie. By extension, it is a conflict between the rabbi's strong faith and the boy's, which in its unorthodox way is perhaps even stronger. Ozzie is full of questions. The rabbi has answers, but the boy insists that they don't go with the questions he asks. The irony is that the naive child ascribes to God more power than the devout rabbi is able to. The rabbi's explanations arise from religious tradition—a tradition whose truths he has so far been unable to persuade Ozzie to believe. It is surely no coincidence that Roth gave his rabbi the suggestive name of Binder, and the boy, the name of Freedman. "We may also recognize the name," writes Charles Clay Doyle of the University of Georgia, "as an anglicized spelling of Friedman, 'peaceable man'—an appropriate epithet for one who proclaims, 'You should never hit anybody about God.'"

3. *What chief differences do you find between the character of Ozzie and that of his friend Itzie?* Itzie is straightforward and practical. He knows how to stay out of trouble. "Itzie preferred to keep *his* mother in the kitchen; he settled for behind-the-back subtleties such as gestures, faces, snarls and other less delicate barnyard noises" (6). Clearly he

regards Ozzie as more than a little crazy for bringing up the Christian belief in God as the father of Jesus. He gets sidetracked from Ozzie's argument by the comedy of Rabbi Binder's using the word *intercourse* in Hebrew School. And when the lively-minded Ozzie rhapsodizes about God's having created light, "Itzie's appreciation was honest but unimaginative: it was as though God had just pitched a one-hitter" (21). Itzie is the perfect foil for Ozzie Freedman, whose rebelliousness and intellectual curiosity keep getting him into trouble. "What Ozzie wanted to know was always different" (31).

4. *What part do Ozzie's mother and Yakov Blotnik play in Roth's story?* Both exert pressure to conform. Ozzie accuses his mother of calling a plane crash a tragedy only because it had killed eight people with Jewish names (32). When Ozzie explains to her why she has to come in for yet another conference with Rabbi Binder, thinking she will understand because when she lit candles she looked "like a woman who knew momentarily that God could do anything" (39), she responds by slapping him (40).

As for Yakov, Ozzie suspects him of having "memorized [his] prayers and forgotten all about God" (42). "For Yakov Blotnik life had fractionated itself simply: things were either good-for-the-Jews or no-good-for-the-Jews" (85). Ozzie gets back at both of them, and at the rabbi, by making them say what to them was blasphemy: first, that God can make a child without intercourse (165) and then that they believe in Jesus Christ (173).

5. *For discussion: Is Ozzie a martyr or a spoiled brat?* Probably most students will see things from the boy's point of view. Certainly the author does. He makes sure that when Ozzie jumps he lands in "the center of the yellow net that glowed in the evening's edge like an overgrown halo" (183).

In an interview with Italian critic Walter Mauro, Roth comments on this story.

"The Conversion of the Jews," . . . a story I wrote when I was twenty-three, reveals at its most innocent stage of development a budding concern with the oppressiveness of family feeling and with the binding ideas of religious exclusiveness which I had experienced first-hand in ordinary American-Jewish life. A good boy named Freedman brings to his knees a bad rabbi named Binder (and various other overlords) and then takes wing from the synagogue into the vastness of space. Primitive as this story seems to me now—it might better be called a daydream—it nonetheless evolved out of the same preoccupations that led me, years later, to invent Alexander Portnoy, an older incarnation of claustrophobic little Freedman, who cannot cut loose from what binds and inhibits him quite so magically as the hero I imagined humbling his mother and his rabbi in the "The Conversion of the Jews" ("Writing and the Powers That Be," *Reading Myself and Others* [New York: Penguin, 1985]).

Peter Shaw made a provocative attack on Roth's work (in *Commentary;* quoted in *Contemporary Authors*):

Roth's insistence that he is a friend to the Jews can only theoretically be squared with the loathing for them that he displays in his work. . . . The real message here, or rather the real aspiration, is not to sweep away anti-Semitism, but to transcend being Jewish. If only you try hard enough, Roth's books tell us, it can be done. This is a message that will not do the Jews any more damage than other specious advice that they have received from time to time, so that one has to agree with Roth that his books are not harmful as charged. But if he has not been bad *for* the Jews, he has decidedly been bad *to* them—and at the expense of his art. . . . Roth has been a positive enemy to his own work, while for the Jews he has been a friend of the proverbial sort that makes enemies unnecessary.

You might care to ask students to consider, in class discussion or in writing, whether they think that Shaw's criticism can be justly applied to "The Conversion of the Jews."

James Thurber
THE CATBIRD SEAT, page 552

Discussion of this story might begin with the question, What is Mr. Martin's true character? To his fellow workers at Fitweiler and Schlosser, Martin is a drab, harmless little drudge of seemingly inhuman efficiency ("Man is fallible but Martin isn't"). To his enemy, Ulgine Barrows, he pretends to be a drinker, smoker, heroin addict, and mad bomber. Neither of these images, of course, reflects the Erwin Martin whom the reader comes to know, a character both rounded and complicated. Early in the story, Thurber indicates that Martin is indeed fussy and meticulous: he remembers the very date when Mrs. Barrows first arrived at the office. Secretly, however, he is crafty and imaginative—a dangerous foe and a dirty fighter.

Martin seems a dynamic rather than static character. Within the story he grows from a somewhat ineffectual ditherer to a purposeful man capable of plotting revenge and boldly carrying it out. At first, his schemes seem merely desperate. In Mrs. Barrows's living room, he casts about helplessly for a murder weapon. Then his "strange and wonderful" Machiavellian idea begins to bloom (paragraph 13). In his eccentric way, Martin is a hero, not a passive antihero. He ends as the triumphant captain of his soul. Robert H. Elias points out in a comment on this story that Martin "saves, indeed, the inner life itself, the life that is not to be harnessed like the atom, streamlined like a spaceship, manipulated, calculated, fed to Univac" ("James Thurber: the Primitive, the Innocent, and the Individual," *American Scholar* 27 [Summer 1958]: 355–63).

Thurber skillfully arouses our sympathy for Martin and his empire of filing cabinets. One of the author's strategies is to make Ulgine Barrows, Martin's opponent, as unattractive as possible. He gives her irritating mannerisms: a "quacking voice and braying laugh," a habit of bombarding people with unanswerable questions: "Are you sitting in the catbird seat?" She is Martin's foil, and students may be asked to point out contrasts between the personalities of these two adversaries. Mrs. Barrows is loud, aggressive, and power hungry, an exponent of radical change. Martin, quiet and retiring, seeks only to keep running his inconspicuous department in his own way; he dreads any change at all.

Humor becomes increasingly broad as the story progresses: from the subtly reasoned trial of Mrs. Barrows that Martin conducts in the courtroom of his head to the final slapstick fracas in which Martin is saved by the adept blocking of a former football player. Beautifully plotted, the story lends itself well to examination of its elements. The crisis occurs when Martin, unable to find a murder weapon, is momentarily at a loss but then switches to his new plan. Among the story's abundant ironies, one of the more delectable occurs when Martin sticks out his tongue and tells his foe he's sitting in the catbird seat (14). Not only does he turn her own words against her, he is suddenly aware (as she isn't) that, indeed, now he is sitting pretty. He transforms her tired cliché into a fresh truth. Actually, the whole story has an ironic situation: the discrepancy between the true Erwin Martin and others' view of him. Martin wins his war by turning this discrepancy to his own advantage.

Eudora Welty

A VISIT OF CHARITY, page 559

Eudora Welty's "A Visit of Charity" appeared in her first volume, *A Curtain of Green,* a collection of short stories published in 1941 with an admiring introduction by Katherine Anne Porter. This premiere volume contained some of Welty's most celebrated stories including "A Worn Path," "Why I Live at the P.O.," and "Petrified Man." Somewhat less widely anthologized, "A Visit of Charity" displays all of Welty's characteristic gifts— psychological insight, lucid narrative, sharp social observation, and grotesque humor.

"Eudora Welty's stories are largely concerned with the mysteries of the inner life," writes Ruth M. Vande Kieft in her useful critical introduction, *Eudora Welty* (New York: Twayne, 1987). "A Visit of Charity" is told by an omniscient third-person narrator, but the story describes both the external actions and internal feelings of the fourteen-year-old protagonist Marion, who visits the Old Ladies' Home to gain points in the Campfire Girls. Though the narrator does not editorialize on what Marion learns from her visit, this descent into the world of old age, loneliness, and isolation marks a rite of passage from the innocence of childhood into the hard facts of adulthood. Welty carefully underlines this fall from innocence in her final image of Marion taking "a big bite out of the apple." Welty's symbolic closure can be viewed as either serious or ironic. On the serious side, Marion has faced the harsh realities of old age at its worst. (The first old woman carefully reminds Marion in her "intimate, menacing voice" that she will share their human fate; she says, "When I was a little girl like you . . . ") On the ironic side, once Marion has escaped from the Old Ladies' Home, she shows little evidence of increased maturity. Her fall from childhood Eden has no immediate consequences.

Welty's title is both literal and ironic. Marion's visit is ostensibly charitable. She brings a potted plant and a moment's distraction to impoverished elderly strangers. We should not sneer at such good deeds. Of course, however, it is not charity that compels Marion to this act of kindness; it is her desire for Campfire Girl points. As Elizabeth Evans points out in *Eudora Welty* (New York: Ungar, 1981), Marion "knows nothing of true charity." Evans observes that although Marion brings a potted plant to the old women, she chooses not to bring the Bible. The reactions of the two women she visits reflect this split between outward virtue and inward emptiness. The first woman is desperately grateful for a visitor or gift of any sort. She is so lonely that mere outward show is fine with her. However, the second woman, who appears sick, sees the visit as an annoying intrusion into her already intolerable life.

Discussion of this story might begin by asking students to describe each of the four main characters (Marion, the two old women, and the nurse). What is the chief motive of each character? Where do those motives match and where do they clash? Marion wants to visit the Old Ladies' Home "by the book"—the Campfire Girl rules. She has no sincere desire to assuage the loneliness of these isolated and destitute women. The nurse, who seems emotionally indifferent to the situation, simply wants to keep the institution running according to her rules. She, in fact, personifies the institution; both she and the building are described as cold. Each of the old women has a different governing motive. The first old woman is, in the words of Vande Kieft, "unconvincingly saccharine, flattering and ingratiating." She wants any contact with the outside world that she can get. The other woman, called "Addie" by her roommate, is brutally frank, angry, and bitter. What does she want? At the very least, she longs for privacy, dignity, and peace of mind. Perhaps she wants what her roommate really desires—youth and freedom. Marion's visit may remind them both of what they lost. Robert Penn Warren, one of Welty's early champions, said that "almost all the stories deal with people, who, in one way or another are cut off, alienated, isolated from the world." His insight certainly applies to "A Visit of Charity."

What makes this dark vision not only bearable but even comic is that the story focuses on Marion—who can escape.

Besides asking students about the title, main characters, and closing image, it is illuminating to have them analyze the setting as described in the opening paragraph. What is the weather like? It is cold and bright. What does the Old Ladies' Home look like? (Whitewashed brick, it resembles "a block of ice"—a grimly evocative image in this case.) Where is the Old Ladies' Home located? (It is "on the outskirts of town.") Welty carefully uses this seemingly matter-of-fact paragraph to set her subtext as well as her plot.

One might also ask students about the effects of the animal imagery that Welty uses to describe the two old women, who bleat like sheep and have hands like bird claws. The women, as Elizabeth Evans points out, "are nearly dehumanized." Their basic animal needs have been met, but they have lost their human dignity.

William Carlos Williams
THE USE OF FORCE, page 564

QUESTIONS

1. *To what do you attribute the family's initial wariness toward the doctor? How do you explain the child's refusal to cooperate with him?* Perhaps unaccustomed to doctors, these are new patients unacquainted with the man they have summoned. To be sure, the parents are worried about their daughter. Apparently the child, though she knows she has a sore throat, clamps her mouth shut because she is frightened and suspicious of the doctor.

2. *What is the basic conflict in "The Use of Force"? How is it foreshadowed? How is it resolved?* Foreshadowed in paragraph 4 (where we are made aware of the child's "cold, steady eyes") and again in paragraphs 6–10, the conflict is between the doctor and the little girl who won't open her mouth. The doctor, suspecting that she has diphtheria, cannot make a true diagnosis without seeing her throat. When all else fails, he learns what he needs to know by brutally forcing her mouth open.

3. *In paragraph 22 the doctor calls the parents "contemptible." To what extent are they to blame for such a startling assessment? What does it reveal about the doctor's state of mind?* The poor worried parents are still trying to be conciliatory while, by paragraph 22, the primitive forces underlying the doctor's psyche have already been engaged. The doctor is determined to fight to the finish. In this battle as in all battles, what counts are tenacity and "fury of effort." The doctor increasingly displays these traits as the battle mentality overcomes his professional calm. He sees the little girl as a worthy opponent. Her parents, involved only peripherally in the primal struggle, exist on a separate plane— one that has come to seem irrelevant to the doctor in his altered state.

4. *What makes the narrator persist in his efforts to get the child's mouth open even after it has started bleeding? Is he a sadist, a bad doctor, a potential child molester, or what?* There are two reasons: one rational, the other less so. As the doctor explains in paragraphs 31 and 32, he feels compelled to get a diagnosis immediately, before it's too late, and before the child infects others. But something else explains the ferocity of his assault. He has "got beyond reason. . . . It was a pleasure to attack her." The primitive part of his nature has gained control over him.

5. *What is the doctor's attitude about his behavior toward the little girl? Where in the story is it revealed?* Revealing an awareness of his mixed motives, the narrator confesses to "a blind fury, a feeling of adult shame, bred of a longing for muscular release" (32).

Does he also demonstrate a certain pleasure at having won the battle? By story's end, he has not yet had time to reflect sanely upon the whole awful encounter.

6. *What is the theme of "The Use of Force"?* Perhaps that violence lies ready to erupt through the respectable surface of even the most civilized among us.

In one detail of this story, Bob Gassen of Hutchinson Community College finds a symbolic act that seems central. He notes that Mathilda's first act of resistance to the doctor is to knock off his glasses. "Prior to this incident, the doctor is very calm and professional. Williams writes: 'I smiled in my best professional manner.' After the glasses incident, however, the doctor's smiles cease, and he becomes increasingly aggressive and vindictive. The glasses are a symbol of intellectuality, of the civilized, urbane person. When Mathilda knocks off the glasses, she removes this urbanity [in] a symbolic unmasking."

Virginia Woolf
A HAUNTED HOUSE, page 567

QUESTIONS

1. *Who is telling this story?* One of a couple who now live in an old house, which is haunted by a pair of ghosts.

2. *What does the narrator report that she herself could not have seen or heard? How can she tell us things that she couldn't possibly know?* The ghosts wander the house and talk to each other while the narrator is sleeping (paragraphs 2, 6–10)—"not that one could ever see them" (4). Perhaps she sees and hears them in a dream; perhaps she imagines them.

3. *Who are the ghostly couple? What are they searching for?* A couple of previous tenants, long dead, who seek to recover their "treasure." The narrator, observing them, understands their treasure to be "joy," the happiness they had, "the light in the heart."

4. *"A Haunted House," according to one critic, David Daiches, is not a story at all, but "simply an exercise in the writing of fluid associative prose." What do you think? Can any elements we usually find in a story be found in "A Haunted House"?* Daiches's comment may confirm what some students feel, but are too reticent to say. This brief work reads less like a conventional, plotted story than like a lyric poem in its brevity, its rhythmic language ("The wind drives straightly; the flame stoops slightly"), the slightness of its narrative, and its metaphors (happiness is a treasure; "death was the glass, death was between us"). Still, "A Haunted House" tells a story, whose events we can cast into chronological order. The piece is also animated by characters whose motives make it resemble fiction more than merely "associative prose."

Two or more centuries earlier, two lovers lived in this house, until the death of the woman separated them (5). Now reunited as ghosts, they roam the house and grounds, watching the living couple who have succeeded them. Benevolent prowlers, they draw pleasure from the sight of lovers doing the same ordinary things they once did: sleeping together, reading in the garden, rolling apples in the loft. The living have inherited the dead couple's "treasure": a fund of quiet joy.

At the same time, another story line unfolds: the narrator's attempt to discover what the ghosts are seeking. She knows they search for their "treasure," but what precisely is that precious hoard? She also hears the house repeat to the ghosts that the treasure is "safe." She gradually pieces together that this treasure is emotional rather than material. In the last line, she realizes that it is "the light in the heart."

The structure of the story seems less plot than theme. Can anybody state it? What does the story say? The theme might be put simply: "How happy I am to be living in this house with my loved one." Other statements include: "Happiness can live on after death," "Happiness is a treasure," and "Living lovers take over not only a house, but also the joys of its former occupants."

French critic Jean Guiget draws attention to the story's atmosphere, which "pervades the being who is immersed in it. . . . The inhabitants of the house become one with the ghosts who haunt it" (*Virginia Woolf and Her Works* [London: Hogarth, 1965]). The inhabitants also become one with the house itself: within the narrator, beats, at the same pace—now gently, now wildly—the same "pulse of a heart." The setting of "A Haunted House" profoundly affects the story's characters—both living and dead. It might be interesting for students to compare the setting of "A Haunted House" with the house in Poe's "The Tell-Tale Heart" (page 61). Both stories describe supernatural events in ancient houses. In Poe's story, an uncanny heartbeat is terrifying; in Woolf's, it arouses happiness. For Woolf's narrator, "the pulse of the house beat gladly" (5); also "softly" (4) and "gently" (7), "wildly" and "proudly" (10). To Woolf, the ghosts seem friendly, benevolent, practically lovable. Unlike Poe's dark and oppressive house, Woolf's is full of beauty, love, and light.

If you want to devote a class to Modernist fiction, you might center the discussion on "A Haunted House." Woolf's story displays many of the key features of Modernism and is short enough to read aloud and analyze carefully in class. Some of the Modernist characteristics that you may wish to point out include: its *musical organization* (Modernist literature often aspired to the form of music, with its elaborate repetitions of sound and abstract organization); its *compression* (the story is hardly longer than a page and yet it presents or evokes a great deal of material; the texture of the story is dense and richly detailed); its *associative organization* (Woolf's story moves sideways by implication and nuance rather than in a straightforward narrative manner); and its *self-conscious artistry*. (Modernist fiction revels in its differences from popular fiction; it minimizes the use of conventional devices—like linear plotting—and achieves unity through style and thematic structure.) "A Haunted House" offers a small encyclopedia of high Modernist technique.

12 *Criticism: On Fiction*

To place at your fingertips several famous (or notorious) observations about fiction is the main purpose of this brief anthology. There is nothing you need to do about it, of course—it is here merely to supply you with resources, if you see any use for them.

Among these critical statements, you will find a few that raise topics for larger, more general discussion. Additional topics for writing will arise from some of these remarks. Certain statements raise points applicable to more than one story in this book, perhaps to all of them. You may find them suggesting topics for longer papers. The process of story-telling—interesting not only to aspiring story writers but to most students—is revealed in a few of these comments. Flaubert tells of his slow and agonizing perfectionism—we think his remarks must reading for every freshman who hacks out a term paper the night before it is due.

Here are some questions to which these statements give rise, perhaps useful for either writing topics or class discussion.

Edgar Allan Poe
THE TALE AND ITS EFFECT, page 570

1. *What, according to Poe, does a short prose narrative gain by its brevity?* Absorbed at a sitting, it produces one effect.

2. *Paraphrase Poe's notions of how a skilled writer goes about writing a tale (or a short story). What main purpose does such a writer keep in mind?* To start, the writer imagines one effect upon the reader—say, a feeling of growing terror (as in "The Tell-Tale Heart"). Then the writer carefully invents each incident—indeed, chooses each word—to produce that effect, and not another.

3. *Does Poe strike you as an advocate of "automatic writing," that is, of writing care-lessly at top speed, or getting stoned and letting the wild prose freely flow?* On the contrary, he thinks of the storyteller as a conscious, deliberate craftsman, in control of each incident, calculating every word. Poe's declaration of principles may surprise students who have heard that this author of bizarre tales was a drunk and a dope addict. Why not remind them that, like any other good writer, Poe had to work hard. We suspect, however, that Poe's statements of principles (in "The Philosophy of Composition," too) set up ide-als to which he aspired and don't record his own working habits. No other writer or critic ever so arrogantly reduced the writing of fiction and poetry to the rigorous application of pure mind.

Charlotte Brontë
THE WRITER'S PASSIVE WORK, page 571

1. *Would Charlotte Brontë agree with Poe's view of the fiction writer as entirely in control of the creative process?* On the contrary, she sees the writer as the helpless instru-ment of forces greater than she. (Charlotte is trying to absolve Emily of the guilt of having

invented Heathcliff by suggesting that Emily *had* to invent Heathcliff; she couldn't help herself.)

2. *If you know* Wuthering Heights, *describe Emily Brontë's characterization of Heathcliff. What is he like?* A foundling of obscure origin, perhaps sent "from the Devil," Heathcliff grows up to be a proud, brooding sufferer—a brutal Lord Byron of the Yorkshire moors. He is given to fiery bursts of temper (he throws a knife at old nurse Nelly Dean), to fierce jealousy, and to a love (for Catherine) so passionate and intense it is said to be inhuman—and, in the end, it presumably outlasts his mortal flesh. Cruel and merciless and unforgiving, he takes years to work revenge.

Gustave Flaubert
THE LABOR OF STYLE, page 572

1. *In Flaubert's methods of writing, what strikes you as remarkable?* Flaubert is a perfectionist, a worrier about "two turns of phrase that are still too much alike," a persistent reviser, a seeker after a nearly unattainable ideal prose. He studies a technical book not only to obtain background information for a story, but to observe its style.

2. *From what source, according to Flaubert, may writers draw strong figures of speech?* From technical treatises, from the language of artisans and craftsmen, of blacksmiths and others who work with their hands.

Henry James
THE MIRROR OF A CONSCIOUSNESS, page 572

1. *Put the gist of James's comment into your own words.* This is a difficult morsel of late Jamesian prose, but the following admittedly partial paraphrase might be reasonably fair to it: "In fiction, just as in Shakespeare's tragedies, it's the sensitive characters we most care about—those who can see what's happening and can respond to it—not the unfeeling dopes."

2. *What, in James's view, have great writers of fiction always done?* They have placed in the midst of their stories some fine-minded character ("a consciousness . . . subject to fine intensification and wide enlargement") to take in the meaning of what occurs.

Anton Chekhov
NATURAL DESCRIPTION AND THE CENTER OF GRAVITY, page 573

1. *Point out some "small details" of natural description in Chekhov's own story "Misery" (page 415) that illustrate the sort of writing he considers evocative.*

2. *Chekhov says, "Be sure not to discuss your hero's state of mind," but to present it in "minute particulars." Does "Misery" follow his theory? Agree or disagree, but list specific instances to support your opinion.*

3. *What character or characters are the "center of gravity" in "Misery"?*

James Joyce
EPIPHANIES, page 574

1. *An* epiphany *in fiction (as defined in Chapter 1) is "some moment of insight, discovery, or revelation by which a character's life, or view of life, is greatly altered." Is that the same sense in which Joyce's Stephen Dedalus uses the term here?* Stephen's meaning of the word is much more inclusive: any overheard speech, any observed gesture (however trivial) that the young artist takes to be a sudden spiritual manifestation. Apparently, an epiphany for him can be any perception—or even any thought—that he finds, for any reason, fraught with significance.

2. *What moments in Joyce's "Araby" might Stephen call epiphanies?* For one, compare the overheard conversations between the lady and the gentlemen (paragraphs 26-32) with the trivial conversation Stephen overhears. Why is it an epiphany? Perhaps because the narrator remembers it and thinks it worth recording. In "Araby", the chatters and their English accents suggest (among other things) the controlling British, who sell the Irish dreams.

Katherine Mansfield
WRITING "MISS BRILL," page 575

1. *What do you make of Mansfield's declared attempt to make "the rise and fall of every paragraph" fit Miss Brill? In your own words, explain what you understand the author to be trying. Point to specific passages in the story for examples.*

2. *Select a paragraph from the story that, in style, strikes you as particularly memorable. Read it aloud to the class and, with the aid of other students, try to define what the writer is doing that makes it so effective.*

William Faulkner
"THE HUMAN HEART IN CONFLICT WITH ITSELF," page 575

1. *In Faulkner's first paragraph, what point is he making? What has been the effect upon young writers of living in the nuclear age?*

2. *What, in Faulkner's view, is the duty of the writer today?*

William Faulkner reading his Nobel Prize acceptance speech (from which this excerpt is drawn) is available on cassette tape from the American Audio Prose Library, Inc., Box 842, Columbia, MO 65205; phone number for orders, (800) 447-2275.

Nadine Gordimer
HOW THE SHORT STORY DIFFERS FROM THE NOVEL, page 576

1. *At the time Nadine Gordimer made these remarks, she felt that the short story offered certain advantages over the novel. What were those advantages?*

2. *What "quality of human life" does the short story capture better than the novel? Why is it "the art of the only thing one can be sure of?"*

Raymond Carver
"COMMONPLACE BUT PRECISE LANGUAGE," page 577

1. *What does Raymond Carver's statement tell us about the qualities he prizes in literature? About his personal writing habits?*

2. *Consider "Cathedral." How does it show that this writer practices what he advocates?*

POETRY

Poems Arranged by Subject and Theme

This list sorts out and classifies most of the poems in the entire textbook. Besides subjects or themes, it includes some genres (i.e., elegies, pastoral poems, poems of spring and other seasons).

How to Use This Information. Browse through this list and you will find many poems worth teaching side by side. This list will be particularly helpful to the instructor who wishes to organize a whole poetry course differently from the way the book is structured: to teach poetry not by the elements of poems, but by themes. But, however you prefer to organize your course, you will find this list a ready source of possible writing assignments.

For Writing Topics. You might have students read three or four poems in a group (say, those in the category "Apocalypse," or a few of your choice from "Coming of Age"), then ask them to reply, in a page or two, to the question, "What do these poems have in common?" Or, "How do these poets differ in their expressions of a similar theme?"

What follows is thorough, but not exhaustive. We have left out some categories that sounded unpromising. Would you have cared that the book has four locomotive poems (by Dickinson, Stillman, Whitman, and William Carlos Williams), three (by Yeats, Hollander, and Anonymous) about swans, and three (by Cunningham, Davison, and Tichborne) about persons literally or figuratively decapitated? Not all these themes and subjects are central to their poems, but all will be fairly evident.

APOCALYPSE

Frost	Fire and Ice
MacLeish	The End of the World
Salter	Welcome to Hiroshima
Yeats	The Second Coming

ART

Auden	Musée des Beaux Arts
Keats	Ode on a Grecian Urn
Morgan	The Master
Pastan	Ethics
Stevens	Anecdote of the Jar
W. C. Williams	The Dance
Yeats	Long-Legged Fly

ASIAN EXPERIENCE/ASIAN POETRY

Basho	Heat-lightning Streak
Basho	In the Old Stone Pool
Buson	On the One-Ton Temple Bell
Buson	The Piercing Chill I Feel
Hongo	The Cadence of Silk

Issa	Only one guy and
Khayyam	Rubaiyat
Lim	To Li Po
Shu-ning Liu	My Father's Martial Art
Morgan	The Master
Salter	Welcome to Hiroshima
Satyamurti	I Shall Paint My Nails Red
Uyematsu	Red Rooster, Yellow Sky

BEAST AND BIRD

Blake	The Tyger
Chesterton	The Donkey
Clare	Mouse's Nest
Hall	Names of Horses
Hollander	Swan and Shadow
Hopkins	The Windhover
Layton	The Bull Calf
Lowell	Skunk Hour
Smart	For I will consider my Cat Jeoffrey
Taylor	Riding a One-Eyed Horse
Tennyson	The Eagle
Whitman	A Noiseless Patient Spider

BELONGING TO A MINORITY (see also BLACK EXPERIENCE, INDIAN LIFE)

Alarcón	The X in My Name
Hughes	Dream Deferred
Hughes	Theme for English B
Lim	To Li Po
Shu-ning Liu	My Father's Martial Art
Olds	The One Girl at the Boys Party
Reid	Speaking a Foreign Language
Sellers	In the Counselor's Waiting Room
Stafford	At the Klamath Berry Festival

BLACK EXPERIENCE (see also BELONGING TO A MINORITY)

Anonymous	Scottsboro
Brooks	The Bean Eaters
Brooks	A Street in Bronzeville: Southwest Corner
Brooks	The Rites for Cousin Vit
Brooks	We Real Cool
Cullen	For a Lady I Know
Dove	Daystar
Hayden	Those Winter Sundays
Hayden	The Whipping
Hughes	Dream Boogie
Hughes	Dream Deferred
Hughes	A Negro Speaks of Rivers
Hughes	Theme for English B

Randall	Ballad of Birmingham
Stillman	In Memoriam John Coltrane
Walcott	The Virgins

BOOKS AND READING (SEE ALSO LANGUAGE, WRITING)

Beerbohm	On the imprint of the first English edition . . .
Bradstreet	The Author to Her Book
Keats	On First Looking into Chapman's Homer
Lim	To Li Po
Wallace	The Girl Writing Her English Paper

BORING LIFE STYLES

Eliot	The *Boston Evening Transcript*
Robinson	Miniver Cheevy
Stevens	Disillusionment of Ten O'Clock

CARPE DIEM

Herrick	To the Virgins, to Make Much of Time
Horace	Ode (original "carpe diem" poem)
Housman	Loveliest of trees, the cherry now
Marvell	To His Coy Mistress
Waller	Go, Lovely Rose

CATASTROPHES AND ACCIDENTS

Frost	"Out, Out—"
Hardy	The Convergence of the Twain
Salter	Welcome to Hiroshima
Slavitt	Titanic

CHILDHOOD (see also FATHERS AND CHILDREN, MOTHERS AND CHILDREN)

Bishop	Sestina
Blake	The Chimney Sweeper
Cleghorn	The Golf Links
Cummings	in Just-
Frost	Birches
Hayden	The Whipping
Justice	On the Death of Friends in Childhood
Lawrence	Piano
Nemerov	The Snow Globe
Olds	The One Girl at the Boys Party
Roethke	My Papa's Waltz
Thomas	Fern Hill

CITY LIFE

Blake	London
Brooks	The Rites for Cousin Vit

Brooks	We Real Cool
Eliot	The *Boston Evening Transcript*
Eliot	The Love Song of J. Alfred Prufrock
Eliot	The winter evening settles down
Ginsberg	A Supermarket in California
Hardy	The Ruined Maid
Miles	Reason
Millay	Recuerdo
Simic	Butcher Shop
Swift	A Description of the Morning
Wilbur	Transit
W. C. Williams	The Great Figure
Wordsworth	Composed upon Westminster Bridge

CLERICS

Browning	Soliloquy of the Spanish Cloister
Cunningham	Friend, on this scaffold Thomas More lies dead
Hardy	In Church
Yeats	Crazy Jane Talks with the Bishop

COMING OF AGE

Campion	There is a garden in her face
Carper	Facts
Housman	When I was one-and-twenty
Pastan	Ethics
Phillips	Running on Empty
Shapiro	The Dirty Word

DEATH (see also ELEGIES)

Anonymous	The Three Ravens
Anonymous	The Twa Corbies
Buson	The piercing chill I feel
Cornford	The Watch
Dickinson	Because I could not stop for Death
Dickinson	I heard a Fly buzz–when I died
Frost	Birches
Frost	"Out, Out—"
Hardy	During Wind and Rain
Keats	This living hand, now warm and capable
Knott	Poem (The only response . . .)
Larkin	Aubade
Lennon/McCartney	Eleanor Rigby
Nemerov	The Snow Globe
Owen	Anthem for Doomed Youth
Rossetti	Uphill
Slavitt	Titanic
W. J. Smith	American Primitive
Stevens	The Emperor of Ice-Cream
M. Williams	Thinking About Bill, Dead of AIDS
Wordsworth	A Slumber Did My Spirit Seal

ELEGIES (see also DEATH)

Brooks	The Rites for Cousin Vit
Dryden	To the Memory of Mr. Oldham
Gray	Elegy in a Country Churchyard
Harper	Reuben, Reuben
Housman	For an Athlete Dying Young
Housman	With rue my heart is laden
Hudgins	Elegy for My Father, Who Is Not Dead
Jonson	On My First Son
Justice	On the Death of Friends in Childhood
Merwin	Elegy (quoted in Scholes, How do we make a poem?)
Milton	Lycidas
J. Moore	Little Libby
Poe	Annabel Lee
Ransom	Bells for John Whiteside's Daughter
Roethke	Elegy for Jane
Stillman	In Memoriam John Coltrane
Stuart	Crib Death
Tichborne	Elegy
Whitman	O Captain! My Captain!

FAITH AND DOUBT (see also CLERICS, GLORY BE TO GOD)

Arnold	Dover Beach
Ashbery	The Cathedral Is
Cunningham	This *Humanist,* whom no beliefs constrained
Eliot	Journey of the Magi
Hardy	Hap
Hardy	The Oxen
Hopkins	Thou art indeed just, Lord, if I contend
Hudgins	Elegy for My Father, Who Is Not Dead
Larkin	Aubade
Milton	When I consider how my light is spent
Wordsworth	The World Is Too Much with Us
Wright	Saint Judas
Yeats	The Magi
Zimmer	The Day Zimmer Lost Religion

FAME

Dickinson	Victory comes late
Gray	Elegy in a Country Churchyard
Guiterman	The Vanity of Earthly Greatness
Keats	When I have tears that I may cease to be
Milton	Lycidas (lines 64-84)
Shelley	Ozymandias

FAMILIES (see also FATHERS AND CHILDREN, MOTHERS AND CHILDREN)

Alvarez	The women on my mother's side were known
Bishop	Filling Station
Dove	Daystar

Hardy	During Wind and Rain
Larkin	Home is so Sad
J. Wright	Autumn Begins in Martins Ferry, Ohio

FARM AND COUNTRY

Frost	Birches
Frost	"Out, Out—"
Frost	Stopping by Woods on a Snowy Evening
Gray	Elegy Written in a Country Churchyard
Hall	Names of Horses
Hardy	The Ruined Maid
Hayford	Dry Noon
Layton	The Bull Calf
Mew	The Farmer's Bride
Toomer	Reapers

FATE

Anonymous	The Three Ravens
Anonymous	The Twa Corbies
Hardy	Hap
Hardy	The Convergence of the Twain
Horace	"Carpe Diem" Ode

FATHERS AND CHILDREN

Allen	Night Driving
Carper	Facts
Hayden	Those Winter Sundays
Heaney	Digging
Hecht	Adam
Hudgins	Elegy for My Father, Who Is Not Dead
Jonson	On My First Son
Kees	For My Daughter
Shu-ning Liu	My Father's Martial Art
Phillips	Running on Empty
Plath	Daddy
Roethke	My Papa's Waltz
W. J. Smith	American Primitive
Thomas	Do not go gentle into that good night
Wilbur	The Writer
Winters	At the San Francisco Airport
J. Wright	Autumn Begins in Martins Ferry, Ohio

FRIENDSHIP

Brontë	Love and Friendship
Dryden	To the Memory of Mr. Oldham
W. Whitman	I Saw in Louisiana a Live-Oak Growing

116

GLORY BE TO GOD/RELIGIOUS EXPERIENCE

Blake	Jerusalem
Chesterton	The Donkey
Donne	Batter my heart, three-personed God
Herbert	Easter Wings
Herbert	Love
Herbert	Redemption
Hopkins	God's Grandeur
Hopkins	Pied Beauty
Hopkins	The Windhover

GRIEF (see also ELEGIES)

E. B. Browning	Grief
Jonson	Slow, slow, fresh fount, keep time with my salt tears
Niedecker	Sorrow Moves in Wide Waves
Poe	Annabel Lee
Tennyson	Dark house, by which once more I stand

HAPPINESS

Anonymous	Carnation Milk
Hunt	Rondeau (Jenny kissed me)
Kenyon	The Suitor
Millay	Recuerdo
Pound	The Garret
J. Wright	A Blessing
Yeats	The Lake Isle of Innisfree

HATRED AND INVECTIVE

Anonymous	Edward
Atwood	You fit into me
Betjeman	In Westminster Abbey
R. Browning	Soliloquy of the Spanish Cloister
Ciardi	In Place of a Curse
Frost	Fire and Ice
H. D.	Helen
Randall	Old Witherington
S. Smith	This Englishwoman
Steele	Epitaph
Stephens	A Glass of Beer

HEROES

Anonymous	Sir Patrick Spence 590
Carroll	Jabberwocky
Cummings	Buffalo Bill's 779
Tennyson	Ulysses 1003
Whitman	O Captain! My Captain! 871

INDIAN LIFE

Anonymous	Last Words of the Prophet (Navajo Mountain Chant)
Erdrich	Indian Boarding School: The Runaways
Jeffers	Hands
Merwin	Song of Man Chipping an Arrowhead
Momaday	Simile
Stafford	At the Klamath Berry Festival
Warrior	How I Came to Have a Man's Name

INNOCENCE AND EXPERIENCE

Behn	When maidens are young
Blake	The Chimney Sweeper
Hardy	In Church
Hopkins	Spring and Fall
Nemerov	The Snow Globe
Pastan	Ethics
K. Shapiro	The Dirty Word

LANGUAGE (see also WRITING)

Alvarez	The women on my mother's side were known
Carroll	Jabberwocky
Reid	Speaking a Foreign Language

LEAVE-TAKING

Davison	The Last Word
Donne	A Valediction: Forbidding Mourning
Drayton	Since there's no help, come let us kiss and part
Hughes	Homecoming
Larkin	Poetry of Departures
Levertov	Leaving Forever
Lovelace	To Lucasta

LONELINESS

Anonymous	Western Wind
Eliot	The Love Song of J. Alfred Prufrock
Frost	Desert Places
Frost	Acquainted With the Night
Ginsberg	A Supermarket in California
Hughes	Homecoming
Lennon/McCartney	Eleanor Rigby
Randall	Old Witherington

LOVE

Anonymous	Bonny Barbara Allen
Arnold	Dover Beach
Bridges	Triolet

118

Leda 728

Burns	Oh, my love is like a red, red rose
Chaucer	Your ÿen two wol slee me sodenly
Cope	Lonely Hearts
Donne	A Valediction: Forbidding Mourning —
Drayton	Since there's no help, come let us kiss and part
Frost	The Silken Tent
Hardy	Neutral Tones
Hayden	Those Winter Sundays
Housman	When I was one-and-twenty
Jonson	To Celia *698*
Mason	Disclosure
Marvell	To His Coy Mistress *957*
Millay	Well, I Have Lost You
Pastan	Jump Cabling *793*
Poe	Annabel Lee
Pound	The Garret
Pound	The River Merchant's Wife: a Letter
Roethke	I Knew a Woman *691*
Sellers	In the Counselor's Waiting Room
Sexton	Cinderella
Shakespeare	My mistress' eyes are nothing like the sun
Shakespeare	Not marble nor the gilded monuments
Shakespeare	Shall I compare thee to a summer's day?
Swift	On Stella's Birthday
Waller	Go, Lovely Rose
Waller	On A Girdle
Whitman	I Saw in Louisiana a Live-Oak Growing
Wyatt	With serving still
Yeats	When You Are Old *1022*

LUST AND DESIRE (see also LOVE)

Anonymous	Western Wind
Cope	Lonely Hearts
Donne	The Flea
Graves	Down, Wanton, Down!
Swenson	Four-Word Lines
Stevenson	Sous Entendu
Wyatt	They flee from me that sometime did me sekë
Yeats	Crazy Jane Talks with the Bishop *yow!*

MAGIC AND VISION

Anonymous	The Cruel Mother
Anonymous	The Three Ravens
Anonymous	The Twa Corbies
Blake	Jerusalem
Bogan	The Dream
Coleridge	Kubla Khan
Cornford	All Souls' Night
de la Mare	The Listeners
Hill	Merlin

Sexton	Cinderella
Sexton	Her Kind
Yeats	Sailing to Byzantium
Yeats	The Second Coming
Yeats	Who Goes with Fergus?

MARRIAGE AND DIVORCE

Donne	A Valediction: Forbidding Mourning
Dove	Daystar
Hardy	The Workbox
Heaney	Mother of the Groom
Mason	Disclosure
Mew	The Farmer's Bride
Pound	The River Merchant's Wife: a Letter

MEDICINE

Frost	"Out, Out—"
Stickney	Sir, say no more
W. C. Williams	Spring and All (By the road to the contagious hospital)

MICROCOSMS

Donne	The Flea
Evans	Wing-Spread
Frost	Design
Whitman	A Noiseless, Patient Spider

MOTHERS AND CHILDREN

Alvarez	The women on my mother's side were known
Anonymous	The Cruel Mother
Anonymous	Edward
Bradstreet	The Author to Her Book
Dove	Daystar
Grosholz	Letter from Germany
Gwynn	Scenes from the Playroom
Heaney	Mother of the Groom
Lawrence	Piano
Niedecker	Sorrow Moves in Wide Waves
Olds	Rites of Passage
Olds	The One Girl at the Boys Party
Plath	Metaphors
Randall	Ballad of Birmingham
Stevenson	The Victory

MUSIC

Campion	Rose-cheeked Laura, come
García Lorca	La guitarra
Herrick	Upon Julia's Voice

Stevens	Peter Quince at the Clavier
Stillman	In Memoriam John Coltrane

MYTH AND LEGEND (other than poems in Chapter 13, "Myth and Narrative"; see also SCRIPTURE AND APOCRYPHA)

Anonymous	Silver swan
Atwood	Siren Song
Carew	Ask me no more where Jove bestows
H. D.	Helen
Hill	Merlin
Sexton	Cinderella
Tennyson	Ulysses
Yeats	Leda and the Swan
Yeats	Sailing to Byzantium
Yeats	Who Goes with Fergus?

NATURE (see also BEAST AND BIRD, FARM AND COUNTRY, THE SEASONS)

Bishop	The Fish
Blake	To see a world in a grain of sand
Blake	The Tyger
Clare	Mouse's Nest
Dickinson	A Route of Evanescence
Dickinson	The Lightning is a yellow fork
Frost	Design
Frost	Never Again Would Birds' Song Be the Same
Gioia	California Hills in August
Hopkins	Pied Beauty
Hopkins	Spring and Fall
Hopkins	The Windhover
Housman	Loveliest of trees, the cherry now
Keats	To Autumn
Roethke	Root Cellar
Snyder	Mid-August at Sourdough Mountain Lookout
Stafford	Traveling through the Dark
Steele	Summer
Stephens	The Wind
Stevens	Anecdote of the jar
Stevens	Thirteen ways of Looking at a Blackbird
Tennyson	Flower in a Crannied Wall
Wilbur	In the Elegy Season
W. C. Williams	Spring and All (By the road to the contagious hospital)
Wordsworth	I Wandered Lonely as a Cloud
Wright	A Blessing

OLD AGE

Brooks	The Bean Eaters
Cornford	All Souls' Night
Hayford	Dry Noon
Larkin	Aubade

Niedecker	Sorrow Moves in Wide Waves
Randall	Old Witherington
Shakespeare	That time of year thou mayst in me behold
Tennyson	Ulysses
R. Whitman	Castoff Skin
W. C. Williams	To Waken an Old Lady
Yeats	Sailing to Byzantium

PRISONS, REFORM SCHOOLS, AND LOCK-UPS

Erdrich	Indian Boarding School: The Runaways *920*

POVERTY

Alarcón	The X in My Name
Brooks	The Bean Eaters
Cleghorn	The Golf Links
Niedecker	Popcorn-can Cover
Pound	The Garret
Stallworthy	Sindhi Woman

PROTEST POEMS

Alarcón	The X in My Name
Anonymous	Scottsboro
Axelrod	Once in a While a Protest Poem
Blake	London
Cleghorn	The Golf Links
Cullen	For a Lady I Know
Hughes	Dream Deferred
McKay	America
Owen	Dulce et Decorum Est
Randall	Ballad of Birmingham
Rich	Aunt Jennifer's Tigers
Wordsworth	The World Is Too Much with Us

SCIENCE AND TECHNOLOGY

Eberhart	The Fury of Aerial Bombardment
Frost	Design
Martin	Taken Up
Reed	Naming of Parts

SCRIPTURE AND APOCRYPHA

Blake	Jerusalem
Chesterton	The Donkey
Frost	Never Again Would Birds' Song Be the Same
Hecht	Adam
Hope	Imperial Adam
Meredith	Lucifer in Starlight
Song of Songs	As the apple tree among the trees of wood

Stevens	Peter Quince at the Clavier
J. Wright	Saint Judas

THE SEASONS

Spring

Frost	Nothing Gold Can Stay
Housman	Loveliest of trees, the cherry now
Ríos	Spring in the Only Place Spring Was
Shakespeare	When daisies pied and violets blue
W. C. Williams	Spring and All

Summer

Anonymous	Sumer is icumen in
Gioia	California Hills in August
Lewis	Girl Help
G. Snyder	Mid-August at Sourdough Mountain Lookout
Steele	Summer
Toomer	Reapers

Autumn

Hopkins	Spring and Fall
Keats	To Autumn
Stephens	The Wind
Wilbur	In the Elegy Season
J. Wright	Autumn Begins in Martins Ferry, Ohio

Winter

Bly	Driving to Town Late to Mail a Letter
Frost	Stopping by Woods on a Snowy Evening
Haines	Winter News
Hayden	Those Winter Sundays
Niedecker	Popcorn-can cover
Shakespeare	When icicles hang by the wall

SMALL TOWN LIFE

Lowell	Skunk Hour
Robinson	Richard Cory *70 3*
J. Wright	Autumn Begins in Martins Ferry, Ohio

SPORTS

Francis	Catch
Gildner	First Practice
Hongo	The Cadence of Silk
Housman	To an Athlete Dying Young
Shu-ning Liu	My Father's Martial Art
Updike	Ex-Basketball Player
W. Whitman	The Runner
J. Wright	Autumn Begins in Martins Ferry, Ohio

TIME, THE PASSAGE OF (see also CARPE DIEM, OLD AGE)

Auden	As I Walked Out One Evening
Cummings	anyone lived in a pretty how town
Eliot	The Love Song of J. Alfred Prufrock
Hardy	During Wind and Rain
Horace	"Carpe Diem" Ode
Housman	Loveliest of trees, the cherry now
Jeffers	To the Stone-cutters
Pastan	Ethics
Shakespeare	Not marble nor the gilded monuments
Shakespeare	That time of year thou mayst in me behold
Shelley	Ozymandias
Wordsworth	Mutability
Yeats	Sailing to Byzantium

WAR

Arnold	Dover Beach *890*
Barth	The Insert
Betjeman	In Westminster Abbey
Eberhart	The Fury of Aerial Bombardment *642*
Hughes	Green Memory
Jarrell	The Death of the Ball Turret Gunner *944*
Kees	For My Daughter
Komunyakaa	Facing It
Lovelace	To Lucasta
Owen	Anthem for Doomed Youth
Owen	Dulce et Decorum Est *617*
Reed	Naming of Parts *982*
Salter	Welcome to Hiroshima
W. Whitman	Beat! Beat! Drums!
W. Whitman	Cavalry Crossing a Ford

A WOMAN'S IDENTITY (see also MOTHERS AND CHILDREN)

Alvarez	The women on my mother's side were known
Brooks	The Rites for Cousin Vit
Dove	Daystar
Mew	The Farmer's Bride
Olds	The One Girl at the Boys Party
Plath	Daddy
Rich	Aunt Jennifer's Tigers
Rich	Women
Sexton	Cinderella
Sexton	Her Kind
Warrior	How I Came to Have a Man's Name

WORK

Alarcón	The X in my Name
Blake	The Chimney Sweeper

Cleghorn	The Golf Links
Larkin	Poetry of Departures
Larkin	Toads
Robinson	Miniver Cheevy

WRITING

Belloc	Fatigue
Blake	Her whole life is an epigram
Heaney	Digging
Herrick	The Bad Season Makes the Poet Sad
Hongo	The Cadence of Silk
Jeffers	To the Stone-cutters
Martial	Readers and listeners praise my books
Morgan	The Master
Pope	True Ease in Writing Comes from Art, Not Chance
Shakespeare	My mistress' eyes are nothing like the sun
Shakespeare	Not marble nor the gilded monuments
Wallace	The Girl Writing Her English Paper
Wilbur	The Writer

Poems for Further Reading, Arranged by Elements

Many instructors tell us that they use the poems in the back-of-the-book anthology, "Poems for Further Reading," as an extra reservoir or second fuel tank of illustrations. Others, to be sure, think the book already offers too many examples. If that is your feeling, don't bother with this section.

If, however, you would like a few more poems (or some different poems) to illustrate matters taken up in the body of the book, then the following list can help you put your finger on them. It classifies only poems in the Poems for Further Reading section, and it works through the book chapter by chapter.

Obviously, poems, like any living creatures, are made up of many elements. Far from being exclusive, this list merely points to a few poems in which we think a certain element is prominent, visible to students, and in some instances even likely to spark discussion in class. (Are the poems classified under "Irony" to be taken ironically, or straight? Are the poems listed below under "Literal Meaning" all that simple? Can the Child ballads still be sung? Does "The Convergence of the Twain" have bad spots?)

For Writing Topics. After your students have studied a chapter of the book, you can direct them to certain poems in the Poems for Further Reading. Assign a poem or two and a short paper that springs from their reading. (An essay of two or three paragraphs might be enough: at this stage, overlong papers on topics such as figures of speech, rime and meter, stanza form, etc., might be debilitating.) Topics will occur: The Character of the Soliloquist in Browning's "Spanish Cloister" (after studying *The Person in the Poem);* The Effectiveness of the Repeated Booms and Two-Steps in Stafford's "At the Klamath Berry Festival" (after studying *Sound* and *Rhythm),* The Attitude of the Daughter in Plath's "Daddy" *(Tone),* The Sex Symbolism of Dickinson's Dog-walk *(Symbol,* referring to "I started Early—Took my Dog"), and more.

For suggesting that this manual could use such a classification of the Poems for Further Reading, and for starting to make one of his own, thanks to Prof. Harvey Birenbaum of San Jose State University.

14   Listening to a Voice

TONE

Some poems in which the poet's attitude is especially clear:

Owen	Anthem for Doomed Youth
Plath	Daddy
Tennyson	Dark house, by which once more I stand
Wordsworth	Composed upon Westminster Bridge

Some poems that express, as Auden says, "mixed feelings":

Bishop	Filling Station
Eliot	The Love Song of J. Alfred Prufrock
Hopkins	Thou art indeed just, Lord, if I contend
Larkin	Poetry of Departures
Lowell	Skunk Hour
Snodgrass	Disposal

THE PERSON IN THE POEM

Some poems in which the identity of the speaker is interestingly different from the poet's "I":

R. Browning	Soliloquy of the Spanish Cloister
Chesterton	The Donkey
Levine	Animals Are Passing from Our Lives
Mew	The Farmer's Bride
Pound	The River Merchant's Wife: a Letter

IRONY

(other kinds besides ironic point of view, as in the five poems just listed):

Dickinson	Because I could not stop for Death (a discrepancy between dying and being taken out driving; verbal ironies: "kindness," "Civility," etc.)
Hardy	In Church (irony between the preacher's public and private self)
Hardy	The Convergence of the Twain (irony of Fate)
Reed	Naming of Parts (a discrepancy between the study of a gun and the study of nature, between the voice of the instructor and the view of the soldier; verbal irony in the pun "easing the spring")
Stafford	At the Klamath Berry Festival (a discrepancy between traditional dances and ways of life today)

15 Words

LITERAL MEANING: WHAT A POEM SAYS FIRST

Poems that can be taken at face value, without looking for symbols, endless suggestions, huge significance (not that they won't repay thought and close reading):

Anonymous	Sumer is icumen in
Gioia	California Hills in August
Hall	Names of Horses
Larkin	Poetry of Departures
Millay	Recuerdo
Slavitt	Titanic
Shakespeare	When daisies pied and violets blue
Shakespeare	When icicles hang by the wall
Updike	Ex-Basketball Player
Yeats	The Lake Isle of Innisfree

THE VALUE OF A DICTIONARY

Poems containing two or more brief allusions:

Dryden	To the Memory of Mr. Oldham
Eliot	The Love Song of J. Alfred Prufrock
Hecht	Adam
Moore	The Mind Is an Enchanting Thing
Yeats	Long-Legged Fly

Poems with central allusions:

Auden	Musée des Beaux Arts
Chesterton	The Donkey

Eliot	Journey of the Magi
H. D.	Helen
Keats	On First Looking into Chapman's Homer (the celebrated blooper in the allusion to Cortez)
Milton	When I consider how my light is spent
Stevens	Peter Quince at the Clavier (allusions to Shakespeare and to the story of Susanna and the Elders)
Tennyson	Ulysses
Yeats	The Magi

WORD CHOICE AND WORD ORDER

Poems in dialect:

Anonymous	Edward
Anonymous	The Twa Corbies
Mew	The Farmer's Bride

Poems in Middle English:

| Anonymous | Sumer is icumen in |
| Chaucer | Your ÿen two wol slee me sodenly |

Poems whose diction and syntax depart from those of speech:

Blake	The Tyger
Coleridge	Kubla Khan
Hardy	The Convergence of the Twain
Hopkins	Spring and Fall
Hopkins	Thou art indeed just, Lord, if I contend
Hopkins	The Windhover
Keats	On First Looking into Chapman's Homer (inverted syntax: "Much have I . . . ," "Yet did I never breathe," "Then felt I," etc.)
Keats	To Autumn
Moore	The Mind Is an Enchanting Thing
Thomas	Fern Hill

Poems containing technical words:

| Reed | Naming of Parts |

Poems in colloquial diction:

Frost	Birches
Frost	Stopping by Woods on a Snowy Evening
Hughes	Dream Deferred
Levine	Animals Are Passing from Our Lives
Olds	The One Girl at the Boys Party
Updike	Ex-Basketball Player

Poems containing an interesting mix of formal and colloquial diction:

Bishop	Filling Station
Ginsberg	A Supermarket in California
Larkin	Poetry of Departures
Winters	At the San Francisco Airport

16 Saying and Suggesting

Some poems especially full of words rich in connotations:

Anonymous	The Three Ravens
Anonymous	The Twa Corbies
Coleridge	Kubla Khan
Eliot	The Love Song of J. Alfred Prufrock
Hardy	During Wind and Rain
Keats	To Autumn
Thomas	Fern Hill

17 Imagery

Atwood	All Bread
Bishop	Filling Station
Erdrich	Indian Boarding School: The Runaways
Gioia	California Hills in August
Keats	To Autumn
Moore	The Mind is an Enchanting Thing
Shakespeare	When daisies pied and violets blue
Shakespeare	When icicles hang by the wall
Swift	A Description of Morning
Tennyson	Dark house, by which once more I stand
Thomas	Fern Hill
W. C. Williams	Spring and All
W. C. Williams	To Waken an Old Lady

18 Figures of Speech

METAPHOR AND SIMILE

Poems with central metaphors:

Dickinson	My Life had stood-a Loaded Gun
Hopkins	The Windhover
Jennings	I Feel
Nemerov	The Snow Globe
Phillips	Running on Empty
Rich	Aunt Jennifer's Tigers
W. Whitman	I Saw in Louisiana a Live-Oak Growing
W. C. Williams	To Waken an Old Lady
Wordsworth	Composed upon Westminster Bridge
Yeats	Long-Legged Fly

Other poems with prominent metaphors:

Mason	Disclosure
Randall	Old Witherington
Shakespeare	That time of year thou mayst in me behold
Shapiro	The Dirty Word
Simic	Butcher Shop
Wilbur	The Writer
J. Wright	A Blessing

Poems with prominent similes:

Hongo	The Cadence of Silk
Keats	On First Looking at Chapman's Homer

OTHER FIGURES

Blake	The Sick Rose (apostrophe)
Carew	Ask me no more where Jove bestows (hyperbole)
Dickinson	Because I could not stop for Death (personification)
Dickinson	I started Early—Took my Dog (personification)
Donne	A Valediction: Forbidding Mourning (paradox)
Frost	Birches (understatement)
Keats	To Autumn (apostrophe, personification)
Levine	Animals Are Passing from Our Lives (personification)
Marvell	To His Coy Mistress (hyperbole)
Plath	Daddy (hyperbole)
Reed	Naming of Parts (pun)
Waller	Go, Lovely Rose (apostrophe, personification)
W. C. Williams	Spring and All (personification)

19 Song

SINGING AND SAYING

Some poems originally sung (see also BALLADS):

Anonymous	Western Wind
Shakespeare	When daisies pied and violets blue
Shakespeare	When icicles hang by the wall

BALLADS

Anonymous	Edward
Anonymous	The Three Ravens
Anonymous	The Twa Corbies
Mew	The Farmer's Bride

A balladlike poem:

Auden	As I Walked Out One Evening

20 Sound

SOUND AS MEANING

Poems containing onomatopoeia:

Shakespeare	When daisies pied and violets blue
Shakespeare	When icicles hang by the wall
Stafford	At the Klamath Berry Festival
Stevens	Peter Quince at the Clavier
Wilbur	Transit ("click")

ALLITERATION AND ASSONANCE

Blake	The Tyger
Carew	Ask me no more where Jove bestows
Coleridge	Kubla Khan
Hardy	During Wind and Rain
Hopkins	Spring and Fall
Hopkins	The Windhover
Ransom	Bells for John Whiteside's Daughter ("primly propped"!)
Thomas	Fern Hill
Waller	Go, Lovely Rose

RIME
Poems whose rimes may well repay study:

Bishop	One Art
Blake	The Sick Rose
Dickinson	[all poems: masterworks of off-rime]
Eliot	The Love Song of J. Alfred Prufrock
Lowell	Skunk Hour
Owen	Anthem For Doomed Youth
Plath	Daddy
Stevens	Peter Quince at the Clavier

21 Rhythm

STRESSES AND PAUSES

In any good metrical poem, rhythms matter, of course, and can't be disentangled from meanings. Here are some poems in open or syllabic forms in which rhythms play strong parts:

Hall	Names of Horses
Reed	Naming of Parts
Smart	For I will consider my Cat Jeoffrey
Stafford	At the Klamath Berry Festival (Consider the effect of "he took two steps", repeated four times)
Thomas	Fern Hill

METER

Wyatt	They flee from me that sometime did me sekë (An exercise is suggested in the note after the poem)
Yeats	The Magi (Worth scanning: irregularities battle with regularity for supremacy)

22 Closed Form

FORMAL PATTERNS, SONNETS, EPIGRAMS, OTHER FORMS

Poems in blank verse:

Frost	Birches
Tennyson	Ulysses
Updike	Ex-Basketball Player

Poems in closed (heroic) couplets:

Dryden	To the Memory of Mr. Oldham
Jonson	On My First Son
Rich	Aunt Jennifer's Tigers
Swift	A Description of the Morning

Poems in tercets:

Hardy	The Convergence of the Twain

Poems in tightly structured riming stanzas:

Donne	The Flea
Frost	Stopping by Woods on a Snowy Evening
Hecht	Adam
Herbert	Love

| Keats | To Autumn |
| Moore | The Mind is an Enchanting Thing |

Poems in syllabic stanzas:

| Moore | The Mind is an Enchanting Thing |
| Thomas | Fern Hill |

Sonnets:

E. B. Browning	How Do I Love Thee?
Brooks	The Rites for Cousin Vit
Herrick	The Bad Season Makes the Poet Sad (a sonnet in couplets)
Hopkins	Thou art indeed just, Lord, if I contend
Hopkins	The Windhover
Keats	On First Looking into Chapman's Homer
Keats	When I have fears that I may cease to be
MacLeish	The End of the World
Meredith	Lucifer in Starlight
Milton	When I consider how my light is spent
Nemerov	The Snow Globe
Owen	Anthem for Doomed Youth
Shakespeare	This time of year thou mayst in me behold
Shakespeare	When, in disgrace with Fortune and men's eyes
Wordsworth	Composed upon Westminster Bridge

Villanelles:

| Bishop | One Art |

23   Open Form

A few classics of open form poetry:

Eliot	Journey of the Magi
Ginsberg	A Supermarket in California
H. D.	Helen
Pound	The River Merchant's Wife: a Letter
Roethke	Elegy for Jane
W. Whitman	I Saw in Louisiana a Live-Oak Growing
W. C. Williams	Spring and All
W. C. Williams	To Waken an Old Lady
J. Wright	A Blessing

A prose poem:

| Shapiro | The Dirty Word |

24   Symbol

Ashbery	At North Farm
Blake	The Sick Rose
Bogan	The Dream
Eliot	The Love Song of J. Alfred Prufrock
Lowell	Skunk Hour
Nemerov	The Snow Globe
Rich	Aunt Jennifer's Tigers
Rich	Peeling Onions

25   Myth and Narrative

Atwood	Siren Song
Carew	Ask me no more where Jove bestows
Eliot	Journey of the Magi
Hecht	Adam
H. D.	Helen
Milton	Lycidas
Stafford	At the Klamath Berry Festival
Yeats	The Magi

26   Poetry and Personal Identity

Bishop	One Art
Browning	How Do I Love Thee?
Hayden	Those Winter Sundays (being a son)
Heaney	Digging
Hecht	Adam (fatherhood as an identity)
Hughes	Dream Deferred
Hughes	A Negro Speaks of Rivers
Jonson	On My First Son
Larkin	Poetry of Departures
Liu	My Father's Martial Art
Lowell	Skunk Hour
Mason	Disclosure (divorce)
Milton	When I consider how my light was spent (Milton on his disability)
Owen	Anthem for Doomed Youth (war poem written by a soldier)
Phillips	Running on Empty
Plath	Daddy
Reid	Speaking a Foreign Language (language as identity)
Snodgrass	Disposal
Tennyson	Dark house, by which once more I stand
Thomas	Fern Hill
Uyematsu	Red Rooster, Yellow Sky
Williams	Thinking About Bill, Dead of AIDS

27   Alternatives

TRANSLATIONS

Anonymous	Sumer is icumen in (original and modern version)
Pound	The River-Merchant's Wife: a Letter

28   Evaluating a Poem

TELLING GOOD FROM BAD

Hardy	The Convergence of the Twain (a poem surely bad in parts—e.g., stanza 5—but good in its entirety!)

KNOWING EXCELLENCE

[Your choice]

13   *Reading a Poem*

William Butler Yeats, THE LAKE ISLE OF INNISFREE, page 585

As a young man in London in 1887–91, Yeats found himself hating the city and yearning for the west of Ireland. He recalled: "I was going along the Strand, and passing a shop window where there was a little ball kept dancing by a jet of water, I remembered waters about Sligo and was moved to a sudden emotion that shaped itself into 'The Lake Isle of Innisfree'" (*Memoirs* [New York: Macmillan, 1972] 31). In London (he recalled in his *Autobiography*), he sometimes imagined himself "living in imitation of Thoreau on Innisfree, a little island in Lough Gill." The nine bean rows of the poem were evidently inspired by Thoreau's bean patch.

Yeats's lines provide rich rows of sound for the student to hoe: assonance (from *I . . . arise* in the first through the o-sounds in the closing stanza), onomatopoeia *(lapping)*, initial alliteration, internal alliteration *(arise, Innisfree; hear, heart's core)*. Sound images of bees, cricket, linnet, and lake water are predominate. Whatever noises come from roadway or pavement, however, are left unspecified.

Perhaps, in London, Yeats thought himself one of Ireland's prodigal sons. At least, A. Norman Jeffares has noticed in the first line an echo from the parable of the prodigal son (Luke 15:18): "I will arise and go to my father" (*A Commentary on the Collected Poems of W. B. Yeats* [Stanford: Stanford UP, 1968] 35).

In later years, according to John Unterecker, Yeats was shocked that "The Lake Isle" had become his most popular poem. He had taken a dislike to its "Biblical opening lines." But audiences always demanded it of him, and his sonorous reading of the poem is available on a recording (Spoken Arts, 753).

LYRIC POETRY

D. H. Lawrence, PIANO, page 589

About the first question: it's really a quick writing assignment. Ten minutes of class time might be enough to let students write their paraphrases. To be sure, you could let them wing it and paraphrase the poem out loud, but the results may not be so thoughtful or accurate. A few of the students might then be asked to read their efforts aloud, for others to agree or disagree with.

Reader response theory, if crudely applied, might claim that every paraphrase is valid. But we think it greatly helps a class discussion to assume that it is possible to find an interpretation of a poem that all or most will agree comes closest to it.

"Piano" isn't a flawless poem. Lawrence was seldom at ease in rime, and the strained juxtaposition of *clamor* and *glamor* indicates his discomfort. Still, *glamor* is an accurate word in its context: the mature man knows that the child's eyes endowed the past with an illusory beauty. The quality of Lawrence's poem may be seen in the specificity of its detail: "the boom of the tingling strings," "the small, poised feet." Lawrence enters into the child's perspective, while able to criticize it from outside. The speaker is resisting his urge to cry, as the connotations of his words indicate (the song is *insidious*, it *betrays*). But at last he is unable to hold back his tears and, sensibly, yields to them.

How does Lawrence's poem escape bathos? Robert Pinsky has offered an explanation in "Poetry and Pleasure," in *Threepenny Review* (Fall 1983). The subject of "Piano," Pinsky finds, is a stock source for poems, "as mothers-in-law or airplanes with ethnically various passengers are stock sources for jokes." Yet the poem strikes us with "something fresh, not stock." Its language is vivid, unconventional; its words *insidious* and *betrays* add a "steely spring"; it sets up an energetic tension between present and past.

May Swenson, FOUR-WORD LINES, page 589

Swenson's lovely poem is quintessentially lyric in that it exemplifies almost every feature that a critic might come up with in a definition of lyric poetry: it is brief and subjective; the language is melodic; it celebrates the perceptions and emotions of a single moment; it leaves the reader with a strong and unified impression.

"Four-Word Lines" is essentially one extended and elaborate simile. The speaker compares her lover's eyes to bees. The simile is hardly a conventional one for love poetry; it is, in fact, potentially alarming. How does Swenson turn this swarm of bees into an intimate and sexy image? She subsumes the speaker in her own metaphoric scheme; if her lover's eyes are bees, then she, by extension, becomes the object of those bees' attention—a flower. The rest of the poem explores the relation between those two images, which are both innocently natural and also highly sexual. One might say that taking one's metaphors and similes seriously and pursuing their implications with passionate curiosity is one of the trademarks of real poetry; poets seldom use metaphoric language casually.

The form of Swenson's poem is both interesting and original. "Four-Word Lines" combines some of the qualities of conventionally metric poetry and free verse. Swenson invented her own meter for the poem—four words per line with the number of syllables and accents dependent on the particular words she uses in each case. This inventive form gives the poem both structure and a pleasing unpredictability. There are so many rimes and half-rimes hidden in these twenty-two lines (*flower/power, bees/breeze, gaze/gauze, shade/laid/wade*, etc.) that one wonders if an early draft of the poem was entirely in rime.

NARRATIVE POETRY

Anonymous, SIR PATRICK SPENCE, page 590

On the questions in the book: We really don't think the king's motive can be known for sure from this bare portrait of him; we ask this question mainly to prompt students to pay attention to what they find on the page and be wary of deep extrapolations. As far as we see him in the poem, the king sits around drinking wine, leading a life of ease, and (with a deliberate official gesture) sends his best sea-captain and a loyal contingent of naval officers to their doom. Although the poet takes a sour view of the comfortable life at court, he feels for the Scots nobles, and we too are moved by his spare sketch of the bereaved ladies, futilely waiting for their men, who will never return. The great stanza about the new and old moons, apparently an ill omen, serves further to heighten the tension of the story and foreshadow its conclusion.

Here are two more questions:

Comment on Sir Patrick's character. What do you make of his abrupt transition from laughter to tears (lines 13–16)? (He is not only brave and loyal to obey the king's order; he is a passionate man with quick, open, unconcealed feelings.)

In what lines do you notice a wry comment on the soft life that the nobles led at court? What does this attitude suggest about this anonymous poet? (29–30:

The nobles are loath to get their fine shoes wet. Probably the poet wasn't a noble, but a sarcastic commoner.)

In the famous image of the slim new moon, W. D. Snodgrass finds visual reminders of the king's golden crown and of the gold combs in the ladies' hair. For him, withering scorn for the Scottish lords afraid to dampen their fancy French pumps comes naturally to the singer, who probably went barefoot for much of his life. And he concludes: "This ballad, at least partly because of its scorn for the ignorant court, seems superbly successful in recognizing a more genuine nobility. Not that I need agree with its values: personally, I'd prefer (though not expect to find) a captain with more loyalty to his men than to king and office. Yet while the song lasts, I partake of the Scottish singer's world, and am broadened by entrance to another's experience, another's values." See "Shapes Merging and Emerging," *Shenandoah* (Winter 1991): 58–83.

Robert Frost, "OUT, OUT—," page 592

Like Sir Patrick Spence, the boy's initial reaction to his terrible realization is to laugh—then, almost at once, dismay sets in. And like the folk ballad, "Out, Out—" tells a story of sudden, meaningless death, and does so with spare economy.

Perhaps the "they"—the doctor and the hospital staff—who turn to their own affairs are not merciless. The "watcher at his pulse" grows frightened when the pulse fails; no one wants to believe the boy will die. Radcliffe Squires finds no one to blame for the "faceless accident." In his view, "Simultaneously, one sees the human watchers touched by normal griefs and fears. And yet life must turn to a more important task finally, that of continuing . . . . Only the grand composer could hold together in one poem the two severe and mutually accusing ideas that one must be moved to pity and compassion and that one must coldly and sternly pursue the duty of endurance and survival" (The Major Themes of Robert Frost [U of Michigan P, 1963] 46). Frost's poem offers no comfort, but seems a realistic view of what happens in an emergency ward. Any student interested in a career in medicine might be asked for a response to this poem.

Frost's allusion to *Macbeth is* part of the meaning of the poem, and the students may be asked to think about it. Perhaps Frost suggests that the snarling buzz-saw full of sound and fury, reaching out its friendly handshake, just doesn't make sense. This, as Stanley Burnshaw has noticed, is one among several of Frost's poems that seem to question the existence of a benevolent order in the universe. Others include "A Servant to Servants," "The Housekeeper," "Home Burial," and (we would add) "Design" (*Robert Frost Himself* [New York: Braziller, 1986] 298).

Frost based his poem on an actual incident: an accident that had happened in 1910 to a sixteen-year-old boy he knew in Bethlehem, New Hampshire; five years went by before the poem took form (in 1915-16). See Lawrance Thompson, *Robert Frost: The Early Years* (New York: Holt, 1966) 566-567.

In the article just cited in the previous entry, W. D. Snodgrass contrasts "Sir Patrick Spence" with "Out, Out—." The first poem is about a man who looks unflinchingly at the world's horror ("the buzz-saw of the world"); the second, about a boy who tries to avoid beholding it.

Of Frost's poem, he remarks: "The one thing you must never do while working with machinery is to lift your eyes. The boy does just that—not to count ranges, but perhaps to count time 'saved from work' by his sister's call. A horrifying salvation is granted him: not just a half hour, but a lifetime, saved from work." Why the vision of five mountain ranges on the horizon (lines 4-6) ? "To lift one's view from saw to horizon, reveals a terrifying similarity. We are given one glimpse, ironically lovely, of the edged and jagged teeth of a world only too ready to take us for *its* 'Supper.'" If the poem had a superscription, it ought to come from the old hymn: "Work, for the night is coming when man (or boy) works no more."

DRAMATIC POETRY

Robert Browning, MY LAST DUCHESS, page 594

We have brought this famous dramatic monologue back into the book because of instructor demand; we received more requests to reinstate the poem than any other new selection. Students generally find it fascinating, and instructors consider it an invaluable means of teaching the idea of a persona poem.

Some teachers may want to assign this poem in conjunction with Browning's "Soliloquy of the Spanish Cloister," which is in the "Poems for Further Reading" section on page 902. These two dramatic poems, both uttered by speakers we find unsympathetic, may be taken together as memorable works of character-drawing. In each poem, Browning places us in the midst of a society remote from our own in time, and thoroughly undemocratic. Of the two, only "My Last Duchess" is a typical dramatic monologue. "Soliloquy," as its title indicates, addresses no listener.

"My Last Duchess" may be familiar to students from high school literature courses; and if a show of hands indicates that they have met it before, we would spend less time with it. Whether or not it is familiar, it makes a useful companion to "Soliloquy." Students may be asked to define their feelings toward the Duke, to point to lines in the poem that helped define those feelings. Browning stresses the Duke's arrogance ("I choose / Never to stoop"; "I gave commands; / Then all smiles stopped together") and engages our sympathies for the poor Duchess in lines 21–31, despite the Duke's contempt for her facility to be gladdened. We know one instructor who in teaching this classic takes the tack, "Shouldn't we feel sorry for the Duke, with all his marital troubles?" (Students of both sexes are usually provoked to rise and trounce him.) Another question: to what extent is the Duke's attitude toward women presumably typical of his society? That the Count, the visitor's master, would offer a daughter to a man who had just disposed of his wife, suggests that the Duke is not alone in regarding women as chattel. Still, even for a Renaissance duke he seems cold-hearted: wives and works of art seem identified as objects to collect.

What were the Duke's commands that stopped the Duchess's smiles? "That she should be put to death, or he might have had her shut up in a convent," Browning once explained. But lines 2 ("Looking as if she were alive") and 46–47 ("There she stands / As if alive") seem to hint that she was executed. Hypocrisy is still another aspect of the Duke's character: compare his protest that he lacks skill in speech (lines 35–36) with his artful flattery of the Count (49–53).

Instructors should note that this book now includes Robert Langbaum's insightful commentary on "My Last Duchess" in the new "Critical Approaches to Literature" section on page 1793.

14   *Listening to a Voice*

TONE

Theodore Roethke, MY PAPA'S WALTZ, page 598

Steven Hind of Hutchinson Community College disagreed with last edition's comments on this poem—"It seems to me that the poem is richer than Professor Kennedy's discussion would allow"—and finds its view of Papa ambivalent. "Kennedy hears a 'playfulness' in the slant rhyme *dizzy* and *easy*. Would it be possible to hear that as a slight dissonance? The only other double rhyme in the poem is *knuckle* and *buckle,* which has a hard edge to it, to my ear, [Mother] doesn't seem to be having such a good time. The involuntary response suggests that this isn't a novel experience. She will be the one who picks up the pans, one supposes. *Scraped* is a harsh verb. The ear is a sensitive organ. Certainly the boy loves his father and relishes the recollection of the dear brute's drunken revelry that included him, but these verbs present an unavoidable tension, it seems to me. The father may, as Professor Kennedy says, be 'happily using his son's head for a drum,' but that doesn't mean the drum is entirely comfortable with the impact."

Professor Hind adds a sobering anecdote:

Last year in composition class I taught the recovering alcoholic son of an alcoholic father. He wrote papers about the loving and terrible bond he felt with his father, and some of his experiences reminded me of this poem. I saw Rick in the hall two weeks ago and asked how his summer had gone. "It would have been better if I hadn't learned that my father has been molesting his daughter the past four years and I didn't know about it," he said. They are in therapy. "My mother's countenance / Could not unfrown itself."

Ann Barnard of Blackburn College, in a provocative recent article, also thinks the poem's dark side worth emphasis. She and a colleague had expressed chagrin that half their students had read "My Papa's Waltz" as a poem about child abuse, reducing it to a social tract. But their mutual rediscovery of the poem "included the idea of covert *emotional* abuse." Papa, whose waltz gives the child both pleasure and pain, is a figure of ambivalence. See "'My Papa's Waltz' as a Problem in Pedagogy," *Teaching English in the Two-Year College* 18 (Feb. 1991): 43–47.

Fred Roux of Shippensburg University of Pennsylvania reports that his students' interpretations of "My Papa's Waltz" have differed according to sex. Young men almost unanimously respond to the poem as a happy childhood memory of a loving father's exuberant horseplay. A few young women react negatively. For them, "I hung on like death" and "You beat time on my head," as well as "battered" and "scraped," suggest that the speaker's recollection is unhappy. They also assume that a man with whiskey on his breath must be drunk. None has perceived an ironic parallel between their responses and that of the speaker's frowning mother. "From this," adds Professor Roux, "it would appear that student response to 'My Papa's Waltz' is, to a degree, the result of a difference in socializing experiences during early childhood." Haven't any young women had boisterous fathers? We'd like to hear other classroom experiences.

As Alan Seager discerns in his biography of Roethke, *The Glass House* (New York:

McGraw, 1968) 23, the mature Roethke seems to have felt a certain guilty resentment against his father, a sense of how (as an awkward, chubby, bookish, and sensitive child) the young poet had failed to make the old man proud of him.

"My Papa's Waltz" may have had its genesis in a wish-fulfilling dream. After his father's death Roethke wrote a memoir (calling himself "John"): "Sometimes he dreamed about Papa. Once it seemed Papa came in and danced around with him. John put his feet on top of Papa's and they'd waltz. Hei-dee-dei-dei. Rump-tee-tump. Only babies expected dreams to come true" (qtd. in Seager, 24).

Countee Cullen, FOR A LADY I KNOW, page 599

From Cullen's first book, *Color* (1925), this is one of a series of twenty-nine epitaphs. Compare it with another brief poem that makes a biting social comment: Sarah N. Cleghorn's "The Golf Links" (page 615). Cleghorn's poem seems angrier; the tone of Cullen's poem seems to be wry amusement at stupidity.

Cullen's early biography is sparsely documented. Raised by his grandmother until he was eleven, he was then adopted by the Reverend Frederick A. Cullen, pastor of a Methodist church in Harlem, who gave the future poet not only a name but a new life of books and conversation. Famed as the leading poet of the Harlem Renaissance, Cullen suffered a decline in reputation when militant black critics of the 1960s reevaluated his work and found it wanting in anger and social consciousness. But his wit can bite, as it does in "For a Lady I Know"; and Houston A. Baker has rightly called much of his work an "ironical protest . . . against economic oppression" in his short study of Cullen, *A Many-colored Coat of Dreams* (Detroit: Broadside, 1974).

Anne Bradstreet, THE AUTHOR TO HER BOOK, page 599

The "rags" (line 5) worn by this bastard brat of a book may have been the first edition's abundance of typographical errors. Although Bradstreet patiently revised her work, she did not live to see her "brat" appear in better dress. This poem prefaced the Boston edition published in 1678, six years after the author's death.

Robert Hutchinson, in the introduction to his edition of *Poems of Anne Bradstreet* (New York: Dover, 1969), gives a concise account of the book's publication. Evidently the author's family, proud of her poetry, felt that it deserved more notice than New England could then give. The Reverend John Woodbridge, Bradstreet's brother-in-law, took with him to England the manuscript of the collection. London at the time had sixty printers; New England, one—and so it must have been difficult, even then, to print poetry in America. "The fact," notes Hutchinson, "that Herrick's *Hesperides* had just appeared in England while the latest venture of Samuel Green, the Cambridge, Massachusetts, printer, was a revision of *The Bay Psalm Book* to rid it of its crudities, gives an indication of the intellectual distance between the two countries."

Walt Whitman, TO A LOCOMOTIVE IN WINTER, page 600

Emily Dickinson, I LIKE TO SEE IT LAP THE MILES, page 601

Though both of these great nineteenth-century Americans take almost the same subject, in tone and in form the two poems differ as sharply as opera differs from chamber music. (Some students might argue that the mutual subject isn't a moving locomotive, but the poets' praise of it. While seeing a real similarity, they would be missing the distinction between subject and tone.) Whitman addresses his machine in awe and exultation. In lines 14–19 he practically prays to it (almost like Henry Adams on bended knees before the dynamo in *Education).* Dickinson is evidently more playful in her affectionate view of the locomotive as a great beast. It is horselike in that it neighs and has a stable, but it isn't quite a horse: it crawls and hoots. Both poets, incidentally, see not only a locomotive, but a whole train. Dickinson's seeing it "chase itself" suggests cars trying to catch their locomotive as they roll downhill. Dickinson's allusion to Boanerges means no more, we think, than that the locomotive is a servant, and is thunderous.

Whitman's poem is full of diction from music: *recitative, beat, ringing bell, notes, chant, harp, piano, trills.* The locomotive embodies poetry, too, in its *metrical* pant and roar, and in its ability to serve the Muse. The word *recitative* indicates the form the poem will be cast in. In Italian opera, to which Whitman was devoted, Rossini had introduced the use of the full orchestra to accompany the recitative, the passage of half-sung, half-spoken declamation; and it may be that, as Robert D. Faner has argued, such recitative was a basic model for Whitman's poetry. "The recitative, highly rhythmic and emotional, punctuated by instrumental accompaniment with thrilling effect, and in its chanted delivery giving the impression of the rhythms of speech, he found well adapted to the bulk of his work, which he thought of as a sort of bardic chant" *(Walt Whitman & Opera* [Carbondale: Southern Illinois UP, 1951] 234).

Langston Hughes, HOMECOMING, page 602

The last lines make the speaker's feeling unmistakable: he no longer has a lover, all he has now is vacant space. The title is ironic: *homecoming* usually suggests a warm welcome, not a cold and empty bed. The poem is remarkable for what it leaves unsaid, for the economy with which Hughes portrays utter loneliness.

Weldon Kees, FOR MY DAUGHTER, page 602

Weldon Kees, who was born in Beatrice, Nebraska, in 1914, was one of the most talented artists of his generation. In his short life he managed to do distinguished work in poetry, fiction, painting, film, criticism, and music. In 1955, shortly after the breakup of his marriage, Kees disappeared. Most evidence suggests that Kees killed himself by jumping off the Golden Gate Bridge, but some of his friends believed that Kees faked a suicide so that he could go off to Mexico and start a new life. In either event, Kees was never seen again.

"For My Daughter" usually creates a lively classroom discussion, but the conversation often veers in two different directions—one literary, the other ethical. On the literary side, students are often divided on the question as to whether the poet should mislead the reader for thirteen lines and then reveal the truth (that he has no daughter) only in the final line. Some beginning students may feel that the author isn't playing fair with his readers, that he is exploiting their emotions. This discussion can be important for students, since it dramatizes the fact that literature isn't necessarily considerate of our emotions—it has more important goals than leaving us at ease. Kees was a particularly savage poet in respect to pointing out the cruel and unjust parts of life that most people *want* to overlook. The important point is that the speaker comes clean in the last line, and that admission changes the meaning of everything said before. The first thirteen lines, therefore, can be read in two different ways—once coming up to the end (a father's worst fears for his daughter) and again retrospectively from the end (a man's reasons for not wanting children, especially on the brink of a world war).

The other discussion of "For My Daughter" concerns the ethical responsibilities faced by any parent bringing children into the world. (It may be worth noting here that Kees is not striking a hollow pose in this poem. He and his wife decided not to have children.)

One small technical note is worth mentioning: "For My Daughter" is a Shakespearean sonnet.

THE PERSON IN THE POEM

Trumbull Stickney, SIR, SAY NO MORE, page 603

The death at age 30 of the brilliant Stickney, scholar of Greek and recipient of the only doctorate in letters that the University of Paris had granted to an Anglo-Saxon, silenced one of the finest lyric voices in American poetry. One of his sonnets, "Near Helikon," ends:

> To me my troubled life doth now appear
> Like scarce distinguishable summits hung
> Around the blue horizon: places where
> Not even a traveller purposeth to steer,—
> Whereof a migrant bird in passing sung
> And the girl closed her window not to hear.

Indispensable to anyone who wishes to read further is *The Poems of Trumbull Stickney,* ed. Amberys R. Whittle, with a foreword by Edmund Wilson (New York: Farrar, 1972).

Howard Moss, THE PRUNED TREE, page 604

Anyone who has worked in a garden or orchard knows the paradoxical truth that we can make trees stronger and more fruitful by pruning back their branches. An experienced gardener may also be able to graft branches or vines onto other plants. And, of course, a gardener can prune plants and trees to make them more beautiful (beauty, of course, always being in the eye of the beholder). It may be necessary with urban students to explain what pruning is. (As most literature teachers know, one of the constant challenges in teaching poetry today is explaining the natural imagery and lore that people raised closer to rural life once took for granted; in this case, the problem arises in a contemporary poem.)

"The Pruned Tree" is a wonderfully original soliloquy. Moss projects himself into the alien consciousness of a plant that—and this is a truly unexpected turn in the poem—rejoices in its own mutilation, since dismemberment is the price of its destiny. It is a difficult task to imagine a non-human (and in this case even non-animal) voice. Moss creates a gentle, hauntingly delicate whisper of a voice that speaks in soft images ("a streak of water," "silk," "moonlight"). The poem also loves paradoxes ("my sound has been my healing"), and even the soft imagery often reflects violence. But, in "The Pruned Tree," suffering leads to growth and transcendence ("And I am made more beautiful by losses.").

But this poem is not only about a tree. Resounding with a quiet, almost mystic joy, "The Pruned Tree" works on at least three levels. First, on its literal level, the poem projects human sentimentality by celebrating the naturalistic irony that a tree can be made stronger and more fruitful by most of its branches being cut away. Second, "The Pruned Tree" constitutes an objective correlative for the subjective emotional states found in Moss's early love of poetry. One only has to read the opening stanza without reference to the poem's title to see how clearly, despite the central metaphor, it also expresses the author's theme of the heart's growth through pain and loss. Finally, the poem subtly represents the notion that expression can be more powerful through restraint and order, virtues that are not achieved except through loss and pain.

William Wordsworth, I WANDERED LONELY AS A CLOUD, page 605

To point out the distance between art and reporting, it may be helpful to read Wordsworth's poem aloud—at least part of it. In their rhythm, lines such as "fluttering and dancing in the breeze" and "Tossing their heads in sprightly dance" make the motion of the daffodils come alive. By comparison, Dorothy Wordsworth's record of the incident ("the rest tossed and reeled and danced") seems merely excellent prose.

Actually, Wordsworth's sister was a distinguished poet in her own right, as Hyman Eigerman demonstrates in *The Poetry of Dorothy Wordsworth* (New York: Columbia UP, 1940), an anthology of passages from her journals arranged into formally open verse.

James Stephens, A GLASS OF BEER, page 607

The high regard of the Irish for the magical powers of speech has given them a long and glorious tradition of poetic cursing. In the ancient tales of the Ulster saga, we read of kings who wouldn't go to battle without an accompanying druid: a poet-priest charged with pronouncing magnificent metrical curses upon the enemy. Who knows?—in the pubs of Stephen's native Dublin, curses like the one in "A Glass of Beer" may well have seemed ordinary, even mild.

Although the speaker—some frustrated drinker hard up for cash—is in a towering rage at the barmaid who denied him, the tone of the poem is not anger but high amusement. There is irony, too, in the obvious contrast between the speaker's stupendous hyperboles and the puny occasion for them. Save this poem, if you like, for teaching figures of speech.

There is hardly a better modern poem, however, for reminding students that the feelings expressed in poetry aren't always positive. A poem may be written in rage or chagrin, as well as in love or joy. This seems an essential truth, and one that XJK has tried to demonstrate at some length in *Tygers of Wrath: Poems of Hate, Anger, and Invective* (Athens: U of Georgia P, 1981), an annotated anthology showing the tradition of dark emotion in British, Irish, and American poetry from the Middle Ages to the present. Naturally, in this tradition, "A Glass of Beer" holds an honored place.

"A Glass of Beer" is a free translation from the Irish of Daíbhí Ó Bruadair (c. 1625-98). The original with a translation by Thomas Kinsella ("A Shrewish, Barren, Bony, Nosey Servant") is given by Seán Ó Tuama and Kinsella in *An Duanaire: An Irish Anthology* (Philadelphia: U of Pennsylvania P, 1981) 116-17.

Anne Sexton, HER KIND, page 607

This poem was one of Sexton's favorites, and she usually recited it as the opening of her public readings. (She even named a rock performance group with which she was briefly involved "Anne Sexton and Her Kind.") Published in her first collection, *To Bedlam and Part Way Back* (1960), it became her signature poem.

Who is the speaker? It may help to know that, according to Diane Middlebrook's fascinating *Anne Sexton: A Biography* (Boston: Houghton Mifflin, 1991), the first draft was titled "Night Voice on a Broomstick" and a later draft labeled "Witch." But there really does seem to be two voices in the poem—one a witch, the other a housewife (see lines 9-11 with their "skillets, carvings, shelves, / closets, silks, innumerable goods; / fixed suppers for worms and elves"). Middlebrook calls this technique "the double 'I'," and she points out how at the end of each stanza, the speaker "steps through the frame of 'like that' to witness, interpret, and affirm her alter ego . . . . "

Paul Zimmer, THE DAY ZIMMER LOST RELIGION, page 608

Paul Zimmer writes usually comic, sometimes touching poems featuring a central character who bears his own last name. If Zimmer in this poem is the poet and not a fictitious character, then the speaker may be the mature Zimmer, looking back through his own younger eyes. The "old days" mentioned in line 8 would seem an even earlier time when, as a schoolboy, Zimmer assisted at Mass. Now (as an adolescent?) he has come to doubt—but he still takes a boyish view, expecting Christ, "like the playground bully," to punish him. The last two lines seem the mature Zimmer's view. Only the grown-ups are ready for Christ. Without knowing the actual Zimmer's present convictions, we can assume that the mature poet speaks either as a believer or as one with a deepened respect for belief.

For more Zimmer poems, see *The Zimmer Poems* (Washington: Dryad, 1976). The world in which the character Zimmer moves often seems dreamlike.

William Carlos Williams, THE RED WHEELBARROW, page 609

Evidently many readers have found it easy to admire this poem without feeling a need to know the circumstances in which it was written. For an interesting appreciation, see Louis Untermeyer, *The Pursuit of Poetry* (New York: Simon & Schuster, 1969) 25. Untermeyer views the poem as a kind of haiku that makes us aware of glories in commonplaces. A more sharply critical estimate is that of Roy Harvey Pearce in his fine essay "Williams and the 'New Mode'" in *The Continuity of American Poetry* (Princeton: Princeton UP, 1961) 335–48. Pearce charges the poem with sentimentality: "At its worst this is togetherness in a chickenyard." However, in Pearce's view, the poem also has a better aspect: what "depends" is the poet's vocation as a poet. He needs common objects in order to write poems, and the objects in turn need him to imagine them into poetry.

If the librarian is right about the situation in which the poem was written, "The Red Wheelbarrow" seems a better poem than we had realized: a kind of prayer, a work of compassion. However, that the poem fails to give us an intimation of the reasons for the poet's feelings (and of why we ought to share them) does expose it to Pearce's accusation that it is sentimental. Whatever the instructor's opinion, students may be invited to debate the merits and demerits of the poem.

IRONY

Robert Creeley, OH NO, page 610

"What interests me about 'Oh No' is its tone," Cynthia Edelberg remarks in an interview with the poet. "How would you describe it?" Creeley replies that he sees it as wry irony, the poem being "self-parody," a comment on his feelings at the time. "As Joel Oppenheimer said, that would qualify me to be a Jew. He really liked that poem. It's that kind of humor" (Edelberg's *Robert Creeley's Poetry: A Critical Introduction* [Albuquerque: U of New Mexico P, 1978] 168).

W. H. Auden, THE UNKNOWN CITIZEN, page 611

For making students better aware of irony, Auden's familiar satire remains as dependable as any poem we know. Little seems to have dated in it, other than the praise of the citizen for adding five children to the population. Students are usually good at seeing that, unlike the unknown soldier, the citizen is all too thoroughly identified; and that, nevertheless, his true nature and inmost wants remain unknown. Meaty questions for discussion naturally arise: What are the premises of such a society? It seems dedicated to the proposition that to conform to a norm is the highest virtue—any individual traits, of course, being an annoyance to statisticians. What is a "Modern Man?" One with animal needs, but no aspirations. The epitaph, often overlooked, is worth dwelling on: it tells us at once that the unknown citizen is only a number, and that bureaucrats keep track of him—and, incidentally, like the rest of the poem, the epitaph is in rime.

"The Unknown Citizen" is one of five poems in this chapter in which we hear a voice obviously not the poet's. (The others are the ones by Moss, Betjeman, Stephens, and Blake.)

Sharon Olds, RITES OF PASSAGE, page 612

This poem will not require much explanation. Anyone familiar with six- and seven-year-old boys will understand the situation. The interesting exercise in class is to search out the ironic metaphors and language in the poem ("short men," "small bankers," "celebrating my son's life") and then discussing their effect on our reading of the poem. If some students complain that the poem overstates its case and makes too much of the boys' penchant for mock violence, it will provide a good opportunity to ask the question if a poem (and one might even classify this short descriptive work as "lyric," since it explores a moment's perception) needs to provide a balanced view of life or if it is acceptable to create the sudden, overwhelming, and perhaps unbalanced emotions we feel in a particular moment or situation.

John Betjeman, IN WESTMINSTER ABBEY, page 613

Cadogan Square was an especially fashionable London address around the turn of the century, and the fact that the reader owns stocks (line 30) also indicates her style of life. Her mind, however, is ordinary: her ideals seem bounded by drugstore novels and by plumbing that works properly.

Students usually have a fine time picking out the easy contradictions in the lady's beliefs: that the Lord may allow bombs to hit German women, but not English women; that He protects whites more dutifully than blacks; that it is all very well for the "gallant blacks" to die, but let the Empire remain united; that democracy and class distinction go hand in hand.

The speaker's attitude seems to be: "Let God wait upon my convenience." To call His word a "treat" reduces Scripture to the importance of candy. That Betjeman first printed this ironic blast at smug, hate-mongering chauvinism in the midst of World War II strikes us as a brave and large-minded plea for genuine Christian charity.

Sarah N. Cleghorn, THE GOLF LINKS, page 615

What a great epigram!—no verbal irony in it, just matter-of-fact notation of a social condition that seems ironic in the extreme. As Robert Frost said, in his introduction to Cleghorn's autobiography, *Threescore* (1936), "There is more high explosive for righteousness in the least little line of Sarah Cleghorn's poem about the children working in the mill ... than in all the prose of our radical-bound-boys pressed together under a weight of several atmospheres of revolution." (The conservative Frost didn't like Marxists, but he called Cleghorn "a saint and a reformer" anyway.) For a more recent tribute, see Irving Dilliard, "Four Short Lines," *The Nation* 222 (10 Apr. 1976): 444–45.

Stanley Kunitz and Howard Hayward's *Twentieth Century Authors* (New York: Wilson, 1942), in an article on Cleghorn that she apparently helped write, explains the twenty-year hiatus between her early books and her later ones. "This was caused by the fact that her socialism and pacifism made editors and publishers reluctant to use her later writing, and partly by the fact that in middle age she became a teacher." Among her other works is a novel, *The Spinster* (1916), and a last collection, *Poems of Peace and Freedom* (1945).

Louise Glück, GRATITUDE, page 615

The opening sentence of this short poem is a textbook example of irony. (And this, after all, is a textbook.) The statement can be read literally, and the author affirms that this reading is truthful. But the statement also demands to be read ironically. The speaker's compliment is damning the "you" with faint praise.

But the poem will not rest on so simple an explanation. No sooner does the speaker register the opening ambiguity than she admits that "small kindnesses" have their positive side: they do not leave the receiver indebted to the giver.

The final simile of the "large animal on a rug" (line 6) also won't allow easy interpretation. At first, it seems like an ordinary dog, but the final image of "the bright sun shining on its tusk" gives it a sinister edge. The companionship of this animal is no unmixed blessing.

Don't forget, by the way, to point out the irony of the title.

Thomas Hardy, THE WORKBOX, page 616

Dramatic irony is present in the discrepancy between the carpenter's limited knowledge and the reader's growing conviction that the wife knew John much better than she cares to admit. Her phrase "mere accidental things" contains verbal irony, and in general the whole speech in lines 25–28 is a verbal irony. Cosmic irony may be operating too (and one is sure that it is, knowing Hardy) in the Fate or chance that caused the carpenter to select a piece of poor John's coffin out of all pieces of wood in the world.

To us, the situation in the poem had seemed like that in James Joyce's "The Dead": the wife, by remembering a young man who died of love for her, has a bleak realization that she might have known a joyous life had she married him instead. However, Albert Furtwangler and his students at Mount Allison University found other possible levels of irony, as he kindly wrote to report. For Professor Furtwangler, "The Workbox" is marred by an excess of irony that runs too deep: "it remains fascinating in the long run more as a puzzle than as a clear disclosure of character." Among other readings he considered the two following, which he thinks overingenious and yet consistent with the poem.

The husband, aware of his wife's past, has contrived his present as a cunning torture for her. "He seems to offer it in love, but takes pleasure in drawing out his wife's confused replies . . . thus trapping her in her own hypocrisy."

The husband knows his wife's history; and she knows that he knows it. "But they coexist uneasily with each other by exercising an elaborate fiction of ignorance."

What will you and your students decide?

J. O. Bailey sees in this poem the "ballad-like theme of the lover who died of grief when his beloved married another." Like traditional English and Scottish ballads, the poem has a question-and-answer structure and ends in a surprise. (See *The Poetry of Thomas Hardy* [Chapel Hill: U of North Carolina P, 1970].) Compare "The Workbox" in these respects with "Bonny Barbara Allan" (page 705) and "Edward" (page 886).

FOR REVIEW AND FURTHER STUDY

EXERCISE: *Telling Tone,* page 617

Richard Lovelace, TO LUCASTA, page 617

Wilfred Owen, DULCE ET DECORUM EST, page 617

"To Lucasta" may refer to an actual parting. During the Puritan Revolution of 1642–45, Lovelace fought in the service of Charles I. Students will readily see the poet's theme that Honor (duty to God and King) takes priority over duty to Lucasta; the tone of the poem may give them greater difficulty. The closing line makes a serious affirmation: Honor for Lovelace is not an "old Lie," but a creed. Neither grim nor smug, the poem also has wit and loving tenderness. The witty second stanza seems almost comic in its figures of speech: having renounced Lucasta's nunlike chastity and calm, the speaker will now go whet his sword upon the body of someone wilder.

Owen's theme is apparent: death in battle is hideous, no matter what certain ignorant poets say about it. For us, there seems irony in the fact that Owen himself was to be killed in action in France. Although in a wartime letter he called himself "a conscientious objector with a very seared conscience," Owen in this poem does not question that to die for one's country may be necessary. His attitude is overpowering disgust—with the butchery of war, with those who idealize it.

Bettie Sellers, IN THE COUNSELOR'S WAITING ROOM, page 618

Evidently this student has been referred to the college psychologist. "Home soil" implies that the mothers have been plowed and planted and made to bear, a condition their daughters appear to be resisting.

Still, this "terra cotta" girl is the product of her soil. Unconsciously, her toes furrow the rug as if she is plowing it. Like the mothers, she seems to be one with the earth; but unlike them, she now (in the mothers' view) holds no promise of procreation. In this discrepancy lies the poem's main irony. (Other mildly ironic discrepancies: that a farm girl from a Bible-reading background now studies existentialism; the girl's guilt feelings juxtaposed with existential anguish over the nature of the universe.)

Because the flat-footed girl is the subject, because we witness her unease (toes furrowing the rug as she clutches the comfortless book on existentialism), certainly she receives the larger share of the poet's—and our own—sympathy. She may be an awkward rustic, but she has found love and can't help loving. Sellers regards both student and mothers with (we think) affectionate humor: the girl with her "big flat farm feet," the mothers so eager to see their daughters reproduce that they weep over the prospect of a crop failure.

Yet clearly she understands the feelings of both generations. Without taking sides, she sets forth their conflict with wonderful brevity. Students who see her poem as an editorial for or against gay/lesbian rights will be reading it too narrowly.

Jonathan Swift, ON STELLA'S BIRTHDAY, page 619

Swift's playfully tender birthday gift kids Stella about her size, but artfully turns a dig into a compliment. Imagining her split in two, he declares that even half of her would surpass any other whole woman. For most students, the only difficult lines will be 7–8. Swift's argument seems to be that, while Stella has lost much of the slender beauty she had at sixteen, she hasn't greatly declined in total worth, for an increase of her mental gifts (among them wit) has amply compensated.

José Emilio Pacheco, HIGH TREASON, page 620

Pacheco is a Mexican poet, but he has chosen to work in the United States and currently teaches at the University of Maryland. He writes in Spanish, but he worked with the noted poet-translator Alastair Reid (himself originally an immigrant from Scotland) on the English versions of his poems. Pacheco's presence in the new edition of *An Introduction to Poetry* (along with the inclusion of writers like Octavio Paz, Julia Alvarez, Nina Cassian, Derek Walcott, and Claude McKay—not to mention Alastair Reid) highlights the importance of immigrants and foreign émigrés in our literary culture.

Pacheco's poem should require little gloss, but the effective and subtle irony of the opening probably deserves a moment's consideration in class to show how irony can be used rhetorically. By saying "I do not love my country" in a poem that celebrates his love for his homeland, Pacheco effectively qualifies the nature of his affection. It is not conventional patriotism but love for its particulars.

It is worth noting that although the poem presumably celebrates Mexico, the images of the poem are deliberately universal. It could be describing Finland or China. The title of this poem is also ironic: Pacheco's treason is a personal love for his country.

John Ciardi, IN PLACE OF A CURSE, page 620

The opening line would be hard to top for outrageously swaggering optimism, if we didn't sense that the speaker is well aware that his chances of being elected are slight. (Shades of a line John Updike once put into the mouth of a Greek-letter fraternity lad, "At seventeen, I was elected Zeus.") We say "the speaker," but we believe this to be John Ciardi speaking. The poem reflects his personal attitude—he favored the pugnacious—and it sounds like his speaking voice.

Ciardi, it might be pointed out, doesn't berate the meek whom Jesus blessed (Matthew 5:5), but those who practice meekness as a trade (9), who employ meekness in their calculations (14).

For the very model of hypocritical meekness, recall Uriah Heep in *David Copperfield.*

Since his death, Ciardi's various work as poet, teacher, essayist, lexicographer, critic, translator of Dante, writer for children, lecturer, and broadcaster has been receiving fresh attention and reconsideration. University of Arkansas Press, publisher of Ciardi's *Selected Poems* (1984) and his last collection, *The Birds of Pompeii* (1985), has also brought out Vince Clemente's compilation of critical essays and friendly memoirs, *John Ciardi: Measure of the Man* (1987) and Ciardi's *Saipan: the War* (1988) and *Echoes: Poems Left Behind* (1989). Edward M. Cifelli of County College of Morris (N.J.), has published an edition of the letters and is working on a critical biography.

William Stafford, AT THE UN-NATIONAL MONUMENT ALONG THE CANADIAN BORDER, page 621

This is a wonderful poem that celebrates an even more wonderful event—two neighboring countries who have lived in peace for nearly two hundred years. (It may be worthwhile in class to ask the obvious *factual* question about what this poem celebrates.)

Stafford's poem uses language memorably in at least two unusual ways. First, the poem characterizes the scene mainly by what did *not* happen there—no battles, no deaths, no monument, no memorable historical events of any kind. Second, Stafford consciously invokes the central non-event by borrowing the diction of patriotic oratory—heroic, soldier, battle, monument, ground, hallowed, people, celebrate. (Was Lincoln's "Gettysburg Address" in the back of Stafford's mind? one wonders.) But Stafford uses these words in exactly the opposite way from an old-fashioned commemorative oration.

William Blake, THE CHIMNEY SWEEPER, page 621

Set next to Cleghorn's "Golf Links" (page 615), Blake's song will seem larger and more strange; and yet both poets seem comparable in their hatred of adults who enslave children. Though Blake is not a child, he obviously shares Tom Dacre's wish that the chimney sweepers be freed from their coffinlike chimneys, washed clean, and restored to childhood joys. The punning cry "'weep! 'weep! 'weep! 'weep!" is the street cry of the sweepers, sent through London to advertise their services. Compare the tone of this poem to that of Blake's "London" (page 652); the anger is similar, but in "The Chimney Sweeper," a poem also touching and compassionate, anger is not stated outright, but only implied.

Tom Dacre's dream has a basis in reality: in Blake's time, sweeps were often sent up chimneys naked, the better to climb through narrow spaces (and thus saving the expense of protective clothing). Martin K. Nurmi points out this fact in his essay, "Fact and Symbol in 'The Chimney Sweeper' of Blake's *Songs of Innocence*" (*Bulletin of the New York Public Library* 68 [April 1964] 249–56). "Naked immersion in soot, therefore, is Tom's normal state now, and naked white cleanliness is its natural opposite."

Music to "The Chimney Sweeper" has been supplied by Allen Ginsberg, who sings the resulting song on *Songs of Innocence and Experience* (MGM recording FTS 3083), assisted by Peter Orlovsky.

15 *Words*

LITERAL MEANING: WHAT A POEM SAYS FIRST

Why a whole section on literal meaning? The need first occurred to XJK in a conversation with Robert Reiter and David Anderson of Boston College. Professor Reiter, who had been using the book in a previous edition, averred that, while it was well to encourage students to read poetry for its suggestions, his students tended to go too far in that direction, and sometimes needed to have their attentions bolted down to the denotations of words on a page. Early in a poetry course, the problem seemed especially large—"I try not to let them look for any symbols until after Thanksgiving!" Mr. Anderson had felt the same difficulty. In teaching Donne's "Batter my heart" sonnet, he had had to argue with students who couldn't see how, in a poem of spiritual aspiration, Donne possibly could be referring to anything so grossly physical as rape. They needed to see the plain, literal basis of Donne's tremendous metaphor, that they might then go on to understand the poet's conception of sanctifying grace.

With these comments in mind, the publishers sent a questionnaire to more than one hundred instructors who had used the book, asking them (among other questions) whether they felt the need for more emphasis on denotation. All who replied said that they would welcome such an emphasis (in addition to the old emphasis on connotation)—all, that is, except for one instructor (God help him) who reported that he couldn't persuade his students ever to rise *above* the level of the literal, if indeed he could get them to rise that far.

Most instructors like to discuss imagery fairly early. They will find nothing to hinder them from taking the chapter on imagery ahead of this one. Another procedure would be to defer "Imagery" until after having discussed both denotation and connotation—taking in sequence the present chapter, "Words," and Chapter 16, "Saying and Suggesting."

William Carlos Williams, THIS IS JUST TO SAY, page 625

Williams once recalled that this poem was an actual note he had written to his wife—"and she replied very beautifully. Unfortunately, I've lost it. I think what she wrote was quite as good as this" (conversation with John W. Gerber and Emily M. Wallace in *Interviews with William Carlos Williams,* ed. Linda Welshimer Wagner [New York: New Directions, 1976]).

For parodies of this famous poem, see Kenneth Koch's "Variations on a Theme by William Carlos Williams" in *Contemporary American Poetry,* ed. A. Poulin (Boston: Houghton, 1980) and other anthologies.

Marianne Moore, SILENCE, page 627

This poem appears autobiographical on the surface, but the notes that Marianne Moore scrupulously appended to her poems make it clear that it is a composite, imaginary portrait of a father. (Moore barely knew her father, who had suffered a nervous breakdown shortly after her birth; perhaps, for that reason, imaginary fathers were all the more important to her.) The first five lines were adapted from a "Miss A. M. Homans," according to Moore. "Make my house your inn," is a quote from Edmund Burke, to which Moore added her telling last line. The father in the poem presumably lived in Cambridge, Massachusetts (from references to Longfellow's grave and Harvard), a town in which Moore never resided. We belabor these facts and sources only to demonstrate that poems are often not so autobiographical as they might seem.

A central theme of "Silence" is the eloquence of understatement and restraint. The poet Donald Hall praises this poem in his study *Marianne Moore: The Cage and The Animal* (Pegasus, New York, 1970) saying that by "eschewing the easy words for the ambiguous emotion," Moore displays "a species of honesty and not evidence of lack of depth." Precision is another key term. Notice how important the speaker considers distinctions between related words and situations *(silence/restraint, inn/residence)*.

Henry Taylor, RIDING A ONE-EYED HORSE, page 627

Henry Taylor comments in a letter: "I like the question about the one-eyed horse; the answer is of course, both."

The poem was first published in *Practical Horseman.*

In 1992, Taylor published a superb volume of essays on recent American poets, *Compulsory Figures* (Baton Rouge, Louisiana State U). (The title of the book refers to the circles and squares practiced by serious equestrians.) Taylor's collection includes cogent introductions to the poetry of Gwendolyn Brooks, J. V. Cunningham, Fred Chappell, Anthony Hecht, David Slavitt, William Jay Smith, William Stafford, James Wright, and others. The collection can be recommended to both instructors and students. The essays offer particularly good background essays to any student writing a paper on one of these poets.

Robert Graves, DOWN, WANTON, DOWN!, page 628

This poem can be an astonisher, especially if students haven't read it in advance. One freshman group XJK sprang it on provided a beautiful gamut of reactions: from stunned surprise to hilarity. At first, most didn't know quite what to make of the poem, but they soon saw that its puns and metaphors point to details of male and female anatomy; and, in catching these, they found themselves looking to literal meanings. After further discussion, they decided that the poem, however witty, makes a serious point about the blindness of lust. To get at this point, students may be asked to sum up the contrast Graves is drawing between Love and Beauty and the wanton's approach to them.

The title (and opening line) echo a phrase from Shakespeare in a passage about eels being rolled into a pie (*King Lear,* II, iv, 118–23):

Lear: O me, my heart, my rising heart! But down!

Fool: Cry to it, nuncle, as the cockney did to the eels when she put 'em i' th' paste alive. She knapped 'em o' th' coxcombs with a stick and cried, "Down, wantons down!" 'Twas her brother that, in pure kindness to his horse, buttered his hay.

One instructor at a community college in New Jersey has reported an embarrassing experience. One morning, not having had time to prepare for class, he introduced this poem without having read it first. "What's it about?" he queried, and someone in the class replied, "An erection." "WHAT?" he exploded. "Come on, now, let's look at it *closely....*" But as he stared at the poem before him, a chill stole over him. Luckily, he was saved by the bell.

Peter Davison, THE LAST WORD, page 629

The tangible side of Davison's central metaphor—that to part with a lover is to chop off her head—is plainly enforced by lines 9-13; painful physical actions that end with the *k*-sound of an abrupt crack in *nick ... creak ... block.*

John Donne, BATTER MY HEART, THREE-PERSONED GOD, FOR YOU, page 629

On Donne's last line: the literature of mysticism is full of accounts of spiritual experience seen in physical terms; and any students who wish to pursue the matter might be directed, for instance, to the poems of St. John of the Cross (which have been splendidly translated by John Frederick Nims).

John E. Parish has shown that Donne's poem incorporates two metaphors, both worn and familiar: the traditional Christian comparison of the soul to a maiden and Christ to a bridegroom, and the Petrarchan conceit of the reluctant woman as a castle and her lover as an invading army. Donne brilliantly combined the two into a new whole. In lines 1 to 4, the sinner's heart is like a walled town, fallen to Satan, the enemy. Now God the rightful King approaches and knocks for entrance. But merely to knock won't do—the King must break open the gates with a battering ram. The verbs in these lines all suggest the act of storming a citadel, "and even *blowe* may be intended to suggest the use of gunpowder to blow up the fortress" ("No. 14 of Donne's *Holy Sonnets, College English* 24 [Jan. 1963]: 299-302).

"The paradox of death and rebirth, the central paradox of Christianity" is (according to A. L. Clements in another comment) the organizing principle of the poem. To illustrate the paradox of destroying in order to revive, Donne employs two sorts of figurative language: one, military and destructive; the other, marital and uniting ("Donne's 'Holy Sonnet XIV,' " *Modern Language Notes* 76 [June 1961]: 484-89).

Both the Clements and the Parish articles are reprinted, together with the four other discussions of the poem, in *John Donne's Poetry,* edited by Clements (New York: Norton, 1966).

It is hard to talk for long about rhythm in poetry without citing the opening lines of "Batter my heart." Both in meter and in meaning, they must be among the most powerful lines in English poetry.

THE VALUE OF A DICTIONARY

Richard Wilbur, IN THE ELEGY SEASON, page 631

Rich with imagery, this early Wilbur poem makes a revealing companion piece to Keats's "To Autumn" (page 950). But unlike Keats, the speaker in Wilbur's poem accepts the season neither with mind (which gazes backward, remembering summer) nor with body (which strains ahead, longing for spring). The poem is also wealthy in allusions. Perhaps the "boundless backward of the eyes" echoes Shakespeare's *Tempest:* "the dark backward and abysm of time." The goddess heard climbing the stair from the underworld is Persephone. We are indebted to Donald Hill's reading of the poem in his study *Richard Wilbur* (New York: Twayne, 1967).

A brief glossary of etymologies:

potpourri: rotten pot (denotation: an incongruous mixture)

revenance: a return (denotation: the return of a spirit after death) *circumstance:* condition that surrounds

inspiration: a breathing in

conceptual: taking in (denotations: perceived, apprehended, imagined)

commotion: co-motion, moving together (a wonderful word for what a bird's wings do!)

cordial: pertaining to the heart *(cor* in Latin) (denotations: friendly, stimulating)

azure: lapis lazuli

EXERCISE: *Catching Allusions*, page 633

J. V. Cunningham, FRIEND, ON THIS SCAFFOLD THOMAS MORE LIES DEAD, page 633

Cunningham's epigram states a metaphor: it likens two famous separations decreed by Henry VIII. Separation of the Body (the Church of England) from the Head (the Pope) is like the decapitation of More, who had opposed it. A possible original for Cunningham's epigram, a Latin epigram by John Owen (1606), has been discovered by Charles Clay Doyle:

> Abscindi passus caput est a corpore Morus;
> Abscindi corpus noluit a capite.

In 1659 Thomas Pecke rendered it into English:

> What though Head was from Body severed!
> *More* would not let Body be cut from Head.

Doyle remarks that in fact More played down the role of the Pope as "head" of the Church, preferring the allegorical view (derived from Paul) of Christ as head upon the Church's body ("The Hair and Beard of Thomas More," *Moreana* 18, 71–72 [Nov. 1981]: 5–14).

Nina Cassian, LIKE GULLIVER, page 633

Nina Cassian was born in Romania in 1924. She is one of the major Romanian poets, having published twenty-four volumes of verse and twelve children's books before coming to the United States in 1985 to teach a course at New York University. While in the U.S., the secret police raided a friend's apartment in Romania and found a diary which contained verse by Cassian satirizing the government. Her friend eventually died from police torture, and Cassian sought political asylum in America.

The central simile in "Like Gulliver" is—quite obviously—borrowed from Jonathan Swift's *Gulliver's Travels.* But the Lilliputians in her poem are the speaker's ex-lovers against whose puny attacks she refuses to retaliate.

Henry Wadsworth Longfellow, AFTERMATH, page 633

Like many seemingly abstract words, *aftermath* was originally a concrete descriptive term that referred to the usually meager second-growth of crop in a field that had already been mowed that season *[after & math* (an obsolete word for *mowing)]*. Once you read Longfellow's quietly moving poem, you'll never forget the etymology. "Aftermath" shows how poets usually employ words with careful consideration to their histories.

"Aftermath" provides a literal description of mowing the second growth in a winter field, but his treatment suggests a hidden symbolic meaning. Longfellow is careful not to specify exactly what the subtext is and leaves every reader free to project his or her own private meaning into the poem. The structure of Longfellow's insight, however, is painfully clear: to revisit a scene of the past can be devastating.

Fledged means "having feathers" and refers to young birds who are now old enough to have grown feathers and flown from their nests. *Rowen* is a synonym for *aftermath,* a season's second crop, usually of hay.

James Wright, SAINT JUDAS, page 634

The allusion is obviously to Judas of the Gospels. Wright's twist is in imagining how Judas might have redeemed himself and become the saint of the title. Nearly every line of the poem assumes the reader has some knowledge of the Passion of Jesus. The first line, for example, assumes we know that Judas went off to hang himself after betraying Jesus. Line 8 alludes to the thirty pieces of silver he was paid for leading the armed crowd to Jesus. If your students are familiar with the Gospels, it will be interesting for them to spot as many allusions as possible and then go on to discuss what Wright has added on his own. (Don't let them miss the *bread* and *kiss* in lines 12 and 13 or the *rope* in line 10.)

The last sentence of the poem may require some explication. It is important to remember that Judas believes he has committed an unforgivable sin. His act of compassion toward the beaten man is utterly selfless; he has no notion of being rewarded in this world or the next. He is "without hope." It is in this gratuitous act of generosity—done "for nothing"—that he redeems himself by acting according to Christ's vision; he becomes the Saint in the title.

You might encourage students to look up the story in the Gospels. Luke (Chapter 22) and John (Chapter 18) might be good places for them to search out parallels.

John Clare, MOUSE'S NEST, page 634

The connection between the final couplet and the rest of the poem is one of metaphor. Small trickles of water that "scarce could run" are newborn mice; "broad old cesspools," their mother.

Milton Klonsky has praised the poem in his anthology of graphic and pictorial poetry, *Speaking Pictures* (New York: Harmony, 1975). He admires "the cinematic flow of Clare's imagery, with each picture flashing by to be replaced by the next before its own afterimage has completely faded." This comment might be discussed—do students agree that Clare's poem seems cinematic and contemporary?

A few facts of Clare's heartbreaking life might interest students. Born into grinding poverty, the son of a field laborer in Northamptonshire, Clare enjoyed brief fame for his *Poems Descriptive of Rural Life* (1820). Lionized by Coleridge and other London literati as an untutored genius, he was then forgotten. The latter half of his life was spent in lunatic asylums, where he wrote some remarkable lyrics and (under the delusion that he was Lord Byron) a continuation of *Don Juan.* Theodore Roethke, whose work shows a similar delight in close-up views of living creatures, has paid tribute (in his poem "Heard in a Violent Ward") to "that sweet man, John Clare."

WORD CHOICE AND WORD ORDER

An exercise to make a class more aware of *le mot juste is* suggested by W. Jackson Bate and David Perkins in *British & American Poets* (San Diego: Harcourt, 1986). Print out several lines of a poem, with an admirably chosen word or words left out. Let students suggest ways to fill in the blank, and debate their choices. Then the instructor whips out a trump card: the way the poet filled in the blank—if you're lucky, to "a collective sigh of appreciation."

Josephine Miles, REASON page 637

Only the reference to Gary Cooper's horse at all dates this concise story-poem, a thing of lasting freshness. "The real characters in this story are the fragments of slang, not the speakers," Lawrence R. Smith has noticed. "Their absence is emphasized by the absence of personal pronouns at the beginning of each line. In place of the pronouns, we simply have 'Said.' This is a poem of pure language." ("Josephine Miles: Metaphysician of the Irrational," *A Book of Rereadings,* ed. Greg Kuzma [Lincoln, Pebble and Best Cellar, 1979] 29).

Emma Lee Warrior, HOW I CAME TO HAVE A MAN'S NAME, page 640

No wonder the family didn't change her name, after Yellow Dust's wonderful prayer, after all they endured to reach the hospital. Even if the student struggles over them, the Blackfoot words lend the poem some splendid sounds, not to mention a ring of authenticity.

Why is the poet's name Emma Lee Warrior? Why isn't it Ipisowahs Warrior, or Emma Lee Ipisowahs? It seems she has a Blackfoot name (Ipisowahs—a name for a warrior) and uses her English name as an alternate.

A Peigan Indian born in Brocket, Alberta, Emma Lee Warrior went on to earn her master's degree in English; she has been working on the Blackfoot Reserve in Alberta developing curricula in the Blackfoot language. This poem was first published in *Harper's Anthology of 20th Century Native American Poetry,* ed. Duane Niatum (New York: Harper & Row, 1988).

Thomas Hardy, THE RUINED MAID, page 641

In a London street, an innocent girl from Dorset encounters a friend who has run away from life on the farm. Now a well-paid prostitute, 'Melia calls herself *ruined* with cheerful irony. That this maid has been made, it would seem, has been the making of her. Hardy, of course, is probably less stricken with awe before 'Melia's glamorous clothes than is the first speaker. As the *ain't* in the last line indicates, 'Melia's citified polish doesn't go deep.

For a sequel to "The Ruined Maid," see "A Daughter Returns" in Hardy's last collection of poetry, *Winter Words.* With "Dainty-cut raiment" and "earrings of pearl," a runaway daughter returns to her country home, only to be spurned by her father for having lost her innocence.

Richard Eberhart, THE FURY OF AERIAL BOMBARDMENT, page 642

Dr. Johnson said that technical language is inadmissible to poetry, but in the case of Eberhart's poem, it is hard to agree. We do not need to know the referents of "belt feed lever" and "belt holding pawl" in order to catch the poet's meaning. Indeed, he evidently chooses these terms as specimens of a jargon barely comprehensible to the unlucky gunnery students who failed to master it. At a reading of his poems in public, Eberhart once remarked that he had added the last stanza as an afterthought. The tone (it seems to us) remains troubled and sorrowful but shifts from loftiness and grandeur to matter-of-fact. This shift takes place in diction as well: from the generality of "infinite spaces," "multitudinous will," "eternal truth," and "the Beast" in man's soul down to "Names on a list," "lever," and "pawl." The poem is a wonderful instance of a poet's writing himself into a fix—getting snarled in unanswerable questions—and then triumphantly saving the day (and his poem) by suddenly returning with a bump to the ordinary, particular world.

Wendy Cope, LONELY HEARTS, page 643

Wendy Cope's bittersweet villanelle demonstrates that old forms can easily accommodate new content, as long as the poet has enough imagination and skill.

Students never seem to have trouble understanding this poem. It is a fun exercise to have students write an additional personal ad in the same rime scheme, but, if you use this idea, be prepared for some odd results.

You might suggest that students read the biographical note on Cope in the "Lives of the Poets" section. Her late-blooming career and personal problems may add a personal dimension to this poem. If she is making gentle fun of the authors of personal ads, she also understands their emotional needs.

FOR REVIEW AND FURTHER STUDY

David B. Axelrod, ONCE IN A WHILE A PROTEST POEM, page 644

The crucial word in this disturbing poem is *silicone,* a substance injected into flat bosoms to make them buxom, in order to put up a false front—like those sympathies we merely pretend to feel. Carefully cropped by someone in an advertising agency, the breast of the starving woman (like a breast treated with silicone) is artificially changed and becomes abstract. Although the photograph is supposed to rouse our sympathies (and our contributions), it often has the opposite effect of making us callous. To the poet, it seems meant to "toughen us" (as silicone toughens the bosoms of Playboy bunnies?); it seems meant to "teach us to ignore."

Lewis Carroll, JABBERWOCKY, page 644

"Jabberwocky" has to be heard aloud: you might ask a student to read it, alerting him or her in advance to prepare it, and offering tips on pronunciation. ("The *i* in *slithy* is like the i in *slime;* the *a* in *wabe,* like the *a* in *wave.*")

Although Carroll added *chortled* to the dictionary, not all his odd words are invented. *Gyre* of course means "to spin or twist about"—it is used as a noun in Yeats's "Sailing to Byzantium" (page 866) and the "The Second Coming" (page 813). *Slithy* (sleazy or slovenly), *rath* (an earthen wall), *whiffling* (blowing or puffing), and *callooh* (an arctic duck that winters in Scotland, so named for its call) are legitimate words, too, but Carroll uses them in different senses. *Frabjous* probably owes something to *frab,* a dialect word meaning "to scold, harass, or nag"—as Myra Cohn Livingston points out in her anthology *O Frabjous Day!* (New York: Atheneum, 1977).

Writing in 1877 to a child who had inquired what the strange words meant, Carroll replied:

> I am afraid I can't explain "vorpal blade" for you—nor yet "tulgey wood"; but I did make an explanation once for "uffish thought"—it seems to suggest a state of mind when the voice is gruffish, the manner roughish, and the temper huffish. Then again, as to "burble" if you take the three verbs "<u>b</u>leat," "m<u>ur</u>mur" and "war<u>ble,</u>" and select the bits I have underlined, it certainly <u>makes</u> "burble": though I am afraid I can't distinctly remember having made it that way.

(*Uffish* suggests *oafish* too.)

Students can have fun unpacking other portmanteau words: *gimble* (*gamely, gambol*); *frumious* (which Carroll said is *fuming* plus *furious*); *vorpal* (*voracious, purple*), *galumphing* (*galloping in triumph*), and so on. Some of these suggestions come from Martin Gardner, who supplies copious notes on the poem (as well as translations of it into French and German) in *The Annotated Alice* (New York: Bramhall, 1960).

Jonathan Holden, THE NAMES OF THE RAPIDS, page 645

Jonathan Holden teaches at Kansas State University in Manhattan, Kansas. He has published six volumes of poetry, a novel, *Brilliant Kids* (1992), and three critical collections, most notably *The Fate of American Poetry* (1991). Holden has provided this note on his poem:

> The setting of "The Names of the Rapids" is a stretch of the Arkansas River extending from Salida, Colorado to Royal Gorge—a very populated stretch during the summer.
>
> Rafting is like taking an expensive roller-coaster ride, but instead of ferris wheels, shooting galleries and sawdust, the midway consists of cliffs, blue spruce and hurtling mountain run-off so cold that to fall off the raft is to risk dying of hypothermia in minutes. It's a sport just dangerous enough to make you come alive and suddenly see what's around you with absolute clarity, which is why, I think, people raft—to "see."

E. E. Cummings, ANYONE LIVED IN A PRETTY HOW TOWN, page 646

Trained in the classical languages, Cummings borrows from Latin the freedom to place a word in practically any location within a sentence. The first two lines are easy to unscramble: "How pretty a town anyone lived in, with so many bells floating up [and] down." The scrambling is artful, and pedestrian words call attention to themselves by being seen in an unusual order.

The hero and heroine of the poem are anyone and noone, whose names recall the pronoun-designated principals in Cummings's play "Him"—hero Him and heroine Me. Are they Everyman and Everywoman? Not at all: they're different, they're strong, loving individuals whom the poet contrasts with those drab women and men of line 5, "both little and small," who dully sow isn't (negation) and reap same (conformity). Unlike wise noone and anyone, the everyones of line 17 apparently think they're really somebody.

In tracing the history of anyone and noone from childhood through their mature love to their death and burial, Cummings, we think, gives a brief tour through life in much the way that Thornton Wilder does in *Our Town*. But not all readers will agree. R. C. Walsh thinks that, in the last two stanzas, anyone and noone do not literally die, but grow into loveless and lifeless adults, whose only hope of rejuvenation is to have children ("Explicator 22" [May 1964]: item 72). But it seems unlike Cummings to make turncoats of his individualists. Bounded by the passage of the seasons, the rain, and the heavens, the mortal lives of anyone and noone seem concluded in their burial. But in the next-to-last stanza they go on sleeping in love and faith, dreaming of their resurrection.

EXERCISE: *Different Kinds of English,* page 647

Anonymous, CARNATION MILK, page 647

William Wordsworth, MY HEART LEAPS UP WHEN I BEHOLD, page 648

William Wordsworth, MUTABILITY, page 648

Anonymous, SCOTTSBORO, page 648

Students won't need much help to see that "Carnation Milk" is unschooled speech; that Wordsworth's diction in "My heart leaps up" is plain and unbookish (except for *natural piety*), while his language in "Mutability" is highly formal—not only in diction, but in word order ("Truth fails not"); and that "Scottsboro" is a song in the speech of a particular culture (and, by the way, wonderful in its power to express).

On the difficult "Mutability" (in case anyone cares to read it for its sense) "the tower sublime" may refer to the Bastille, suggests Geoffrey Durant in his excellent discussion of the poem in *Wordsworth and the Great System* ([Cambridge: Cambridge UP, 1970] 82–85). For other poems with the theme of mutability, see Shelley's "Ozymandias" (page 869), Shakespeare's "That time of year . . ." (page 991), Auden's "As I Walked Out One Evening" (page 893), Thomas's "Fern Hill" (page 1005), and (in this same chapter) Cummings's "anyone lived in a pretty how town."

Repercussions from the Scottsboro case lasted long. In October, 1976, the state of Alabama finally granted full pardon to Clarence Norris, last survivor of the nine "Scottsboro boys," at age sixty-four, after he had spent sixteen years in prison, five on death row, and thirty-one years as an escaped fugitive. In 1976, following the television showing of a dramatization, "Judge Horton and the Scottsboro Boys," both alleged rape victims unsuccessfully brought suit against NBC for libel, slander, and invasion of privacy. The last of these suits was dismissed in July, 1977. Clarence Norris died on January 23, 1989. Harper Lee imagines a similar case in Alabama in her novel *To Kill a Mockingbird* (1960), a book which some of your students may know—it is still on some high school reading lists.

16   *Saying and Suggesting*

John Masefield, CARGOES, page 651

Much of the effect of Masefield's contrast depends on rhythms and word-sounds, not just on connotations. In stanza 2, the poet strews his lines with dactyls, producing ripples in his rhythm: *diamonds, emeralds, amethysts, cinnamon.* In the third stanza, paired monosyllables *(salt-caked, smoke stack, Tyne coal, roadrails, pig-lead, firewood)* make for a hard hitting series of spondees. Internal alliteration helps the contrast, too: all those *m*-sounds in the dactyls; and in the harsher lines "Dirty British coaster with a salt-caked smoke stack, / Butting," all the sounds of the *r*, the *t*, and the staccato *k*.

"Cargoes" abounds with lively, meaningful music—and yet Masefield is generally dismissed nowadays as a mere balladeer—a jog-trot chronicler of the lives of the poor and unfortunate. In naming him poet laureate, George V (it is said) mistakenly thought him a hero of the working class; and, unluckily for his later fame, Masefield, like Wordsworth, enjoyed a long senility.

William Blake, LONDON, page 652

Blake's "London" broadens the themes explored in his "The Chimney Sweeper" (page 621). The personal pathos of "The Chimney Sweeper" becomes a general indictment of a society in which such exploitation is possible. In "London," we see Blake as a prophetic poet—not prophesying the future like a tabloid seer, but speaking as a prophet who declares the moral necessity of just change in a time of evil.

In his essay "On Blake and his Critics" (1934), G. K. Chesterton singled out the third stanza of "London" for special praise. He called the images "two lightning-flashes revealing two separate Visions of Judgment." It is important to remember that Blake was a Londoner born and bred who spent most of his life within the city limits. He is not a country poet describing urban squalor; he is a native morally dissecting his own home town. He knows every image from the inside out.

If Blake were to walk the streets of an American city today, would he find any conditions similar to those he finds in "London"? Is this poem merely an occasional poem, with a protest valid only for its time, or does it have enduring applications?

Wallace Stevens, DISILLUSIONMENT OF TEN O'CLOCK, page 654

Stevens slings colors with the verve of a Matisse. In this early poem, he paints a suggestive contrast between the pale and colorless homeowners, ghostlike and punctually going to bed at ten and, on the other hand, the dreams they wouldn't dream of dreaming; and the bizarre and exotic scene inside the drunken head of our disreputable hero, the old seafarer. Who in the world would wear a beaded sash or *ceinture?* (A Barbary pirate? An Arabian harem dancer)? Ronald Sukenick has made a terse statement of the poem's theme: "the vividness of the imagination in the dullness of a pallid reality" *(Wallace Stevens: Musing the Obscure* [New York: New York UP, 1967]). Another critic, Edward Kessler, has offered a good paraphrase: "Only the drunkard, the irrational man ('Poetry must be irrational' [*Opus Posthumous* 162]), who is in touch with the unconscious—represented here, and often elsewhere, by the sea can awake his own passionate nature until his blood is mirrored in the very weather" *(Images of Wallace Stevens* [New Brunswick: Rutgers UP, 19721]).

While they will need to see the contrast between pallor and color, students might be cautioned against lending every color a particular meaning, as if the poem were an allegory.

Stevens expressed further disappointment with monotonous neighbors in a later poem, "Loneliness in Jersey City," which seems a companion piece to this. In Jersey City, "the steeples are empty and so are the people," who can't tell a dachshund from a deer. Both poems probably owe some of their imagery to Stevens's days as a struggling young lawyer, living in rooming houses in East Orange, New Jersey, and Fordham Heights, in New York City.

Gwendolyn Brooks, THE BEAN EATERS, page 655

This spare, understated poem seems one of the poet's finest portraits of poor blacks in Chicago. While "We Real Cool" (page 740) depicts the young, "The Bean Eaters" depicts the old, whose lives are mainly devoted to memories—some happy *(tinklings,* like the sound of their beads) and some painful *(twinges).*

Details are clearly suggestive. The old people are barely eking out a living, eating beans to save money, from *chipware* (chipped tableware, or tableware that chips easily?) set on a creaky old table, using cheap cutlery that doesn't shine.

The long last line, with its extended list, sounds like one of those interminable Ogden Nash lines that Lewis Turco has dubbed Nashers. Why is its effect touching, rather than humorous? Brooks lists the poor couple's cherished, worthless possessions in detail, and each detail matters. Besides, *twinges / fringes,* a fresh rime, achieves a beautiful closure. We end up sharing the poet's respect and affection for this old pair—no mockery.

Richard Snyder, A MONGOLOID CHILD HANDLING SHELLS ON THE BEACH, page 655

This poem, by a longtime teacher at Ashland University in Ohio, has been restored to this book after many instructors lamented its disappearance. With beautiful economy, Snyder elaborates his metaphor: the "unbroken children," those without disabilities, are like surf at the edge of the sea, like seabirds that skim beach and water. Bright as they are, there is something superficial about them, in contrast to the child handling shells. Slow and deliberate as deep ocean currents, she is both "broken," like the shells she fondles, and at the same time whole. As she hums her return message to the sea, she is calm and serene, possessed of a sober happiness.

In using the word *Mongoloid,* the poem betrays its age. To discuss: Should it now be retitled "A Child with Down Syndrome Handling Shells on the Beach"? Would that be as effective?

Timothy Steele, EPITAPH, page 656

"Silence is golden"—but Sir Tact is obviously a coward, afraid to speak his mind. This epigram is included in Steele's first collection of poems, *Uncertainties and Rest* (Baton Rouge: Louisiana State UP, 1979).

Geoffrey Hill, MERLIN, page 656

There is an incantatory quality to this poem that seems to indicate it is Merlin speaking: but then, nearly all of Hill's richly suggestive and highly formal poems tend to sound this way. The dead who might "come together to be fed" recall the souls encountered by Odysseus in the underworld, to whom he fed blood. Once, the towers of Camelot sheltered Arthur and his associates; now, only the pointed tents of piled-up cornstalks (or perhaps growing cornstalks, flying their silklike pennants) stand over the city of the dead.

Walter de la Mare, THE LISTENERS, page 657

This much-loved old chestnut, once a favorite of anthologists, still seems a wonderful demonstration of the value to poetry of hints. The identity of the listeners is by no means clear: the more literal-minded will probably think of bats, mice, and crickets, while others will think of ghosts. The latter theory gains support from the poem: these listeners are *phantom* (line 13), not of the *world of men* (16), strange and mute (21–22). If the Traveller is "the one man left awake" (32), are the Listeners men who have fallen asleep (in death)?

In line 5, *turret* suggests a fortress or castle; but as line 14 makes clear, the scene is a house. Which to believe? Perhaps the scene is set in a kind of Loire Valley chateau: a mansion with castlelike touches.

Attempts to guess what happened before "The Listeners" opens may well be irrelevant, but if students will try, they may find themselves more deeply involved with the poem. This much seems clear: The Traveller has accepted some challenge to visit the house: he has given his promise to someone (more than one person, and someone other than the Listeners, whom the Traveller charges to convey his message to "them"). Perhaps this act is one of the deeds required to lift a curse from a kingdom, as in a fairy tale; or as in the Arthurian story of Sir Percival (or Parsifal), who must spend a night in the terrifying Chapel Perilous.

Robert Frost, FIRE AND ICE, page 658

In his first line, Frost probably refers to those who accept the Biblical prophecy of a final holocaust; and in his second line, to those who accept scientists' forecasts of the cooling of the earth. We admire that final *suffice.* A magnificent understatement, it further shows the power of a rime to close a poem (as Yeats said) with a click like a closing box.

17   *Imagery*

Ezra Pound, IN A STATION OF THE METRO, page 660

Pound recalled that at first this poem had come to him "not in speech, but in little splotches of color." His account is reprinted by K. K. Ruthven in A *Guide to Ezra Pound's Personae* (1926) (Berkeley: U of California P, 1969). Students might like to compare this "hokku-like sentence" (as Pound called the poem) with the more suggestive Japanese haiku freely translated later in this chapter.

For a computer-assisted tribute to this famous poem, see the curious work of James Laughlin and Hugh Kenner, reported in "The Mixpoem Program," *Paris Review* 94 (Winter 1984): 193–98. Following Laughlin's suggestion that the five nouns of "In a Station of the Metro" might interestingly be shuffled, Kenner wrote "a Little program in Basic" that enabled a computer to grind out 120 scrambled versions of the poem, including these:

> The apparitions of these boughs in the face;
> Crowds on a wet, black petal
>
> The crowd of these apparitions in the petal;
> Faces on a wet, black bough.

Kenner then wrote a program in Pascal that would shuffle eight words and produce 40,320 different versions. We don't know what it all demonstrates, except that Pound's original version still seems the best possible.

Kenner's historical account of the London literary scene and its influences on the composition of this poem is found in the "Critical Approaches to Literature" section of this book on page 1799.

Taniguchi Buson, THE PIERCING CHILL I FEEL, page 660

Harold G. Henderson, who translates this haiku, has written a good terse primer in *An Introduction to Haiku* (Garden City: Anchor, 1958). Most of Henderson's English versions of haiku rime like this one; still, the sense of the originals (as far as an ignorant reader can tell from Henderson's glosses) does not seem greatly distorted.

T. S. Eliot, THE WINTER EVENING SETTLES DOWN, page 662

This is the first of the series of four poems called "Preludes," originally published in the July 1915 issue of Wyndham Lewis's *Blast*. It was written during Eliot's days at Harvard. The "Preludes," writes Grover Smith in *T. S. Eliot's Poetry & Plays* (Chicago: U of Chicago P, 1965), belong to the era of "Prufrock." Of "The winter evening settles down," Smith says:

> The first "Prelude" begins with winter nightfall in an urban back street; from indoor gloom and the confined odor of cooking it moves outside into the smoky twilight where gusts of wind whip up leaves and soiled papers, and a shower spatters the housetops. Such adjectives as "burnt out," "smoky," "grimy," "withered," "vacant," "broken," and "lonely" carry the tone.

Some students may point out, though, that the lighting of the lamps seems to end the poem on a note of tranquillity.

Theodore Roethke, ROOT CELLAR, page 662

Probably there is little point in spending much time dividing imagery into touches and tastes and smells; perhaps it will be enough to point out that Roethke's knowledgeable poem isn't all picture-imagery. There's that wonderful "congress of stinks," and the "slippery planks" are both tactile and visual. Most of the language in the poem is figurative, most of the vegetation is rendered animal: bulbs like small rodents, shoots like penises, roots like a forgotten can of fishing worms. Roethke doesn't call the roots lovely, but obviously he admires their tough, persistent life.

Elizabeth Bishop, THE FISH, page 663

This poem is made almost entirely of concrete imagery. Except for *wisdom* (line 63) and *victory* (66), there is no very abstract diction in it.

Obviously the speaker admires this stout old fighter. The image "medals with their ribbons" (line 61) suggests that he is an old soldier, and the "five-haired beard of wisdom" (line 63) suggests that he is a venerable patriarch, of whom one might seek advice.

The poor, battered boat has become magnificent for having the fish in it. The feeling in these lines is joy: bilge, rust, and cracked thwarts are suddenly revealed to be beautiful. In a way, the attitude seems close to that in Yeats's "Sailing to Byzantium" (page 866), in which the triumphant soul is one that claps its hands and louder sings for every tatter in its mortal dress. The note of final triumph is sounded in "rainbow, rainbow, rainbow!" (line 75). The connotations of *rainbow* in this poem are not very different from the connotations often given the word by misty-eyed romantic poets such as Rod McKuen, but we believe Bishop because of her absolutely hard-eyed and specific view of the physical world. (She even sees the fish with X-ray imagination in lines 27–33.)

Anne Stevenson says in *Elizabeth Bishop* (New York: Twayne, 1966):

> It is a testimony to Miss Bishop's strength and sensitivity that the end, the revelation or "moment of truth," is described with the same attention to detail as the rest of the poem. The temptation might have been to float off into an airy apotheosis, but Miss Bishop stays right in the boat with the engine and the bailer. Because she does so, she is able to use words like "victory" and "rainbow" without fear of triteness.

Because the fish has provided her with an enormous understanding, the speaker's letting it go at the end seems an act of homage and gratitude.

Compare "The Fish" with the same poet's richly imaged "Filling Station" (page 896).

The poet reads this poem on a recording, *The Spoken Arts Treasury of 100 Modern American Poets*, vol. 10, SA 1049.

Anne Stevenson, THE VICTORY, page 665

This powerful short poem rejects all of the sentimental versions of childbirth and motherhood. It focuses on the violent physical details and emotional shock of giving birth.

One of the chief strategies of Confessional and Feminist poetry has been to admit personal feelings that conventional "good manners" would consider inappropriate or even shameful. In "The Victory," Stevenson presents a new mother's pain and horror at her newborn son. By admitting these feelings, she implicitly confesses that she is a bad mother in conventional terms. But Stevenson's speaker is unconcerned with keeping up appearances; she is obsessed with getting at the difficult truth of the moment. She is trying to sort through her own unexpected feelings.

It may be worthwhile to stress that as a *lyric* poem, "The Victory" tries to capture the intensity of insight from a particular moment. Stevenson's poem does not imply that the speaker will feel this shocked aversion to her child in the future. In fact, the last two lines of the poem imply that she will—despite her initial reaction—grow to love him.

John Haines, WINTER NEWS, page 666

We are struck by "the stiffening dogs" in this poem. It is possible both to picture such stiffening and to feel it in one's muscles and bones. Haines appeals mostly to the sense of sight ("clouds of steaming breath," "the white- / haired children") and sound ("Oil tins bang," "the voice of the snowman"). Clearly the children's hair, far from manifesting premature aging, is merely covered with snow. Is that snowman a surreal monster, or is his voice another name for the wind?

In 1947 John Haines went to Alaska as a homesteader, and began to write poetry there. This is the title poem from his first collection, *Winter News* (Middletown: Wesleyan UP, 1966).

Emily Dickinson, A ROUTE OF EVANESCENCE, page 666

"A Route of Evanescence" will probably inspire a heated guessing contest. Contestants will need to pay attention to Dickinson's exact words.

Enclosing this poem in a letter to Thomas W. Higginson, Dickinson gave it a title: "A Humming-Bird."

The poet's report of the hummingbird's arrival from Tunis is fanciful. Besides, the creature could hardly fly 4,000 miles nonstop in one morning. New England hummingbirds don't need to cross the Atlantic; to find a warmer climate, they migrate south. If it was a ruby-throated hummingbird that the poet saw, though, it might indeed have come a long distance: from a winter in Mexico or Central America.

The poet's ornithology may be slightly cockeyed, but her imagery is accurate. Hummingbird wings appear to rotate, but they aren't seated in ball joints; in actuality, they merely flap fast.

Jean Toomer, REAPERS, page 667

This ominous poem, with its contrasts between sound and silence, possibly contains a metaphor. The black field hands are being destroyed by something indifferent and relentless, much as the trapped rat is slain under the blade. (Or, as in "Scottsboro" [page 648], as a cat stalks a "nohole mouse"?)

A grandson of P. B. S. Pinchback, the black who served for a short time during Reconstruction as acting governor of Louisiana, Toomer had only a brief public career as a writer. His one book, *Cane* (1923), which experimentally combined passages of fiction with poetry, helped to spearhead the Harlem Renaissance. "Reapers" is taken from it.

That Toomer was a man divided between his profound understanding of blacks and his own desire to pass for white emerges in a recent biography, *The Lives of Jean Toomer: A Hunger for Wholeness,* by Cynthia Earl Kerman and Richard Eldridge (Baton Rouge: Louisiana State UP, 1987). *The Collected Poems of Jean Toomer* (Chapel Hill: U of North Carolina P, 1988) is a slim volume of 55 poems, the best of them from *Cane.*

Gerard Manley Hopkins, PIED BEAUTY, page 667

Sumptuously rich in music (rime, alliteration, assonance), this brief poem demands to be read aloud.

Some students might agree with Robert Frost's objection that the poem "disappoints . . . by not keeping, short as it is, wholly to pied things" (1934 letter to his daughter Lesley in *Family Letters of Robert and Elinor Frost* [Albany; State U of New York P, 1972] 162). But, as question 4 tries to get at, Hopkins had more in mind than dappled surfaces. Rough paraphrase of the poem: God is to be praised not only for having created variegation, but for creating and sustaining contrasts and opposites. In lines 5–6, tradesmen's tools and gear, like the plow that pierces and cuts the soil, strike through the surfaces of raw materials to reveal inner beauty and order that had lain concealed.

For a convincing argument that Hopkins in "Pied Beauty," like Dickens in *Hard Times,* complains about a drab, mechanical, industrial-age uniformity in Victorian England, see Norman H. MacKenzie, *A Reader's Guide to Gerard Manley Hopkins* (Cornell UP, 1981) 85–86. Few students will crave to fathom the poet's notions of *instress* and *inscape,* but if you do, see John Pick's unsurpassed *Gerard Manley Hopkins, Priest and Poet,* 2nd ed. (Oxford UP, 1966) 53–56.

The point of question 5 is that if the images of the poem were subtracted, its statement of theme also would disappear.

Hopkins discovered the form of "Pied Beauty" and called it the *curtal sonnet* (curtal, riming with *turtle:* "crop-tailed"). But, remarks MacKenzie, such sonnets are like a small breed of horse: "compressed, not merely cut short." Instead of two quatrains, the form calls for two tercets; then, instead of a sestet, four lines and brief line more. (Other curtal sonnets by Hopkins: "Peace" and, even more closely cropped, "Ashboughs.")

ABOUT HAIKU

Basho's frogjump poem (page 669) may well be the most highly prized gem in Japanese literature: in Japanese there exists a three-volume commentary on it.

For an excellent discussion of the problems of teaching haiku, and of trying to write English ones, see Myra Cohn Livingston's *When You Are Alone / It Keeps You Capone: An Approach to Creative Writing with Children* (New York: Atheneum, 1973) 152–62. Livingston finds it useful to tell students a famous anecdote. Kikaku, a pupil of Basho, once presented his master with this specimen:

Red dragonflies—
Tear off their wings
And you have pepper pods.

As a haiku, said Basho, that's no good. Make it instead:

Red pepper pods—
Add wings
And you have dragonflies.

A moment of triumph, such as all teachers of poetry hope for but seldom realize, has been reported in a letter to XJK from Maurice F. Brown of Oakland University, Rochester, Michigan:

165

Last year, teaching W. C. Williams in an "invitational" course for a week, I began with "Red Wheelbarrow" . . . and a student hand went up (class of 100): "That's not a poem! That's junk. What if I say, 'Here I sit looking at a blackboard while the sun is shining outside.' Is that a poem?" It was one of those great teaching moments . . . and I did a quick count and wrote it on the board:

Here I sit looking
 At a blackboard while the sun
is shining outside.

Not only a poem . . . a perfect Haiku.

A thorough new guide to this rocky acre of poetry, by William J. Higginson with Penny Harter, is *The Haiku Handbook: How to Write, Share, and Teach Haiku* (New York: McGraw, 1985).

As this example of his work demonstrates, Nicholas A. Virgilio (1928–1989), of Camden, New Jersey, perhaps the most interesting contemporary writer of haiku in English, could give the classic Japanese form a touch of mean American city streets. His *Selected Haiku* (2nd ed., 1988) gathers the best of his life's work ($9.95 from Firefly Books, Ltd., 3520 Pharmacy Ave., Unit 1C, Scarborough, Ontario, Canada M1W 2T8).

Why is John Ridland's "The Lazy Man's Haiku" the work of a slothful soul? Because, according to the poet (in a letter), "he's too lazy to write the proper number of syllables in any line—or to get rid of that occidental end-rhyme à la Harold Henderson's ever-unconvincing translations in that old Anchor book." Henderson, in *An Introduction to Haiku* (Anchor Books, 1956), forced all the haiku to rime like his version from Buson given at the beginning of this chapter. (Reading it as a poem in English, we find it profoundly convincing, and suspect it took work.)

Richard Brautigan, HAIKU AMBULANCE, page 669

This is a Zen poem poking fun at overly thoughty attempts to write Zen poems. Its satire does not seem in the least applicable to the successful haiku-in-English of Paul Goodman, Gary Snyder, and Raymond Roseliep.

There are several small journals that focus on haiku and tanka. If you or your students want to pursue studying (and perhaps even publishing) haiku, you will want to look at some of these magazines. *Modern Haiku* has been in existence for over twenty years. It is now edited by Robert Spiess. The mailing address is *Modern Haiku,* P. O. Box 1752, Madison, Wisconsin, 53701. Meanwhile, the Haiku Society of America publishes *Frogpond* (Haiku Society of America, 333 East 47th Street, New York, N.Y. 10017). If you write these journals asking for information or submitting your own haiku, make sure you enclose a stamped, self-addressed envelope.

FOR REVIEW AND FURTHER STUDY

John Keats, BRIGHT STAR! WOULD I WERE STEADFAST AS THOU ART, page 670

Unlike Petrarchan poets, Keats isn't making the star into an abstraction (Love); he takes it for a visible celestial body, even though he sees it in terms of other things. His comparisons are so richly laden with suggestions (star as staring eye, waters as priestlike), that sometimes students don't notice his insistent negations. The hermit's all-night vigil is *not* what Keats desires. He wants the comfort of that ripening pillow, and (perhaps aware of his impending death) envies the cold star only its imperishability—oh, for unendurable ecstasy, indefinitely prolonged! Compare this to Keats's "To Autumn" (page 950) in which the poet finds virtue in change.

Many readers find the last five words of the poem bothersome. Students might be asked, Does Keats lose your sympathy by this ending? If so, why? If not, how would you defend it? We can't defend it; it seems bathetic, almost as self-indulgent as Shelley's lines in "Indian Serenade":

> Oh, lift me from the grass!
> I die! I faint! I fail!
> Let thy love in kisses rain
> On my lips and eyelids pale.

Thomas Mauch, of Colorado College, intelligently disagrees, and suggests how "or else swoon to death" may be defended. The *or,* he thinks, is what grammarians call an inclusive *or,* not an exclusive.

> I believe that the speaker is saying, not that if he can't be forever in the close company of the beloved he would rather be dead—sort of like what Patrick Henry said about liberty—but rather that, given the closeness to the woman, dying in that condition would be just as good as experiencing it forever, since in either case he would not undergo a separation from her (and still retain his consciousness of it). I think it is the same point he makes in the "Ode to a Nightingale":

> Now more than ever seems it rich to die,
> To cease upon the midnight with no pain,
> While thou art pouring forth thy soul abroad
> In such an ecstasy!

The poem, Mr. Mauch concludes, illustrates the kind of closure that Keats admired when he affirmed that a poem should "die grandly."

Timothy Steele, SUMMER, page 671

Steele's sonnet carefully uses language that evokes—to rearrange his own words—the voluptuous plenty of summer. Most of the images are deliberately still or static—windless lakes, dense orchards, slow creeks, or the person "supine" in the meadow grass. The poem also contrasts nature's immense abundance with the poor striving of humankind. Faced with summer's magnificence, the thoughtful person simply surrenders to it. In this sense, Steele's sonnet works in the tradition of the *carpe diem* poem, but in Steele's world, the consciousness of death is entirely absent. He suggests that we seize the day simply because it is so beautiful.

Instructors may want to note that Horace's original *carpe diem* ode is now found in the "Alternatives" chapter along with three translations.

EXPERIMENT: *Writing with Images,* page 671

To write a poem full of images, in any form, is probably easier for most students than to write a decent haiku. (On the difficulties of teaching haiku writing, see Myra Cohn Livingston, cited under "About Haiku.") Surprisingly, there is usually at least one student in every class who can't seem to criticize a poem to save his neck, yet who, if invited to be a poet, will bloom or at least bud.

167

Walt Whitman, THE RUNNER, page 671

Try reading "The Runner" without the adverbs *lightly* and *partially*. Does the poem even exist without those two delicate modifiers?

T. E. Hulme, IMAGE, page 672

Hulme's poems seem always to have been brief. In his own collection *Personae*, Ezra Pound took two pages to include "The Complete Poetical Works of T. E. Hulme" (in which "Image" does not appear). Pound remarked, "In publishing his *Complete Poetical Works* at thirty, Mr. Hulme has set an enviable example to many of his contemporaries who have had less to say."

William Carlos Williams, THE GREAT FIGURE, page 672

Is the figure a symbol? It looks like one—such intent concentration upon a particular. In an otherwise static landscape, only the 5 moves. It's the one moving thing, like in the eye of the blackbird in Stevens's "Thirteen Ways" (page 783). As far as we can see, however, the 5 has no great meaning beyond itself. Williams just rivets our attention on it and builds an atmosphere of ominous tension. The assumption, as in "The Red Wheelbarrow," is that somehow the figure has colossal significance. But "The Great Figure" is a much more vivid poem than "Wheelbarrow" (page 609) and it contains no editorializing ("so much depends"). Like the poems in the section "Literal Meaning," it's useful for discouraging students from spelling out colossal significance.

In his *Autobiography* (New York: Random House, 1951), Williams recalls how the poem came to be written. As he walked West 15th Street in New York on a summer's day, he heard

> a great clatter of bells and the roar of a fire engine passing the end of the street down Ninth Avenue. I turned just in time to see a golden figure 5 on a red background flash by. The impression was so sudden and forceful that I took a piece of paper out of my pocket and wrote a short poem about it.

Citing this story, Bruce Bawer finds "The Great Figure" a typical poem of Williams's major phase: a quick description of a brief experience. "This is one of many familiar poems in which Williams does not shrink from, but rather observes carefully, celebrates and expresses a childlike wonder at the mechanical, the grubby, the vulgar, the trivial, the homely, the banal, or the grossly physical" ("The Poetic Legacy of William Carlos Williams," *New Criterion*, Sept. 1988, 17–18).

The poem inspired a painting by Charles Demuth, *I Saw the Figure 5 in Gold* (1928, now in New York's Metropolitan Museum of Art).

Robert Bly, DRIVING TO TOWN LATE TO MAIL A LETTER, page 672

No doubt the situation in this poem is real: Bly, who lives in frequently snowbound Minnesota, emits hundreds of letters. Compare this simple poem to Frost's "Stopping by Woods on a Snowy Evening" (page 923), which also has a speaker who, instead of going home, prefers to ogle snowscapes.

Gary Snyder, MID-AUGUST AT SOURDOUGH MOUNTAIN LOOKOUT, page 673

In brief compass, Snyder's poem appeals to the mind's eye (with *smoke haze, pitch glows on fir-cones, rocks, meadows,* and the imagined vista at the end), the sense of moisture *(after five days rain),* of hot *(three days heat)* and of cold *(snow-water from a tin cup).* The *swarms of new flies* are probably both seen and heard.

For more background to this poem and to Snyder's work in general, see Bob Steuding, *Gary Snyder* (Boston: Twayne, 1976). A fictional portrait of Snyder appears in Jack Kerouac's novel *The Dharma Bums* (New York: Viking, 1958).

H. D. [Hilda Doolittle], HEAT, page 673

Heat becomes a tangible substance in this imagist poem, whose power resides mainly in its verbs, all worth scrutiny. Compare this poem and Snyder's: how does each convey a sense of warmth?

H. D.'s work has enjoyed a recent surge of critical attention. For a concise, insightful comment on the lyrics and their originality, see Emily Stripes Watts, *The Poetry of American Women from 1632 to 1945* (U of Texas P, 1977) 153–58. Susan Stanford Friedman's *Psyche Reborn: The Emergence of H. D.* (Indiana UP, 1981) is valuable.

More recently, *Agenda,* that excellent, very serious British magazine of poetry, devoted a 200-page special issue to H. D. (vol. 25, nos. 3–4, Autumn/Winter 1987–88). With contributions by the poet herself, Susan Stanford Friedman, Eileen Gregory, Denise Levertov, Alicia Ostriker ("The Open Poetics of H. D.") and others, it is available from 5 Cranbourne Court, Albert Bridge Road, London SW11 4PE (price in U.S. funds $17.50).

Besides, there is now an *H.D. Newsletter,* edited by Professor Eileen Gregory, Dept. of English, University of Dallas, Irving, TX 75062.

Philip Larkin, TOADS, page 673

"Deprivation is for me," Larkin once joked, "what daffodils were for Wordsworth." Indeed, Larkin's genius came from finding the self-inflicted heartbreak of everyday life. He was the elegist of the humdrum, the poet of the workaday world.

In England, "Toads" is one of the most famous poems of the last half century. In America, it is less well known, but, once read, it is difficult to forget. Most readers do not notice at first that the poem is cast in the form of an internal argument. The first five stanzas outline the case to be made for not working—"No one actually *starves,"* it reasons. In the sixth stanza, the direction of the argument turns, and the speaker begins to admit why he needs to work—"something sufficiently toad-like / squats in me, too."

It may go without saying that Larkin's thematics in this straightforward poem are quietly revolutionary. He is not only exploring the subject matter of work, which, to put it mildly, was not a major theme in English poetry; he is also exploring the middle-class compulsion to work, especially its need for security. Larkin's particular gift was to convey this viewpoint sympathetically while simultaneously satirizing its timidity.

Is it pointless to add that Larkin spent his entire adult life as a hard-working, successful librarian? The target of Larkin's satire is almost always people like himself.

"Toads" can be profitably compared to Larkin's "Poetry of Departures" in the Poems for Further Reading section.

Emily Grosholz, LETTER FROM GERMANY, page 674

Anyone who has lost a parent, spouse, sibling, or child will recognize that this poem does not have a trick ending. It realistically describes the way in which we continue talking to them (or writing imaginary letters) in our minds. It sometimes comes as a shock, as it does in line 27, to remember they are dead.

It might be rewarding for students to pay attention to the last two sentences of the poem (the final eight lines). As the tone shifts from celebratory to elegiac, the images change too—from the loud and earthy ducks in love to the light, airy images of clouds and pollen.

Emily Grosholz is a professor of philosophy at Pennsylvania State University.

Stevie Smith, NOT WAVING BUT DROWNING, page 675

Stevie Smith reportedly got the initial inspiration for this poem from a newspaper item that described a man who drowned in full view of his friends; they mistook his signals for help as playful waving. Smith pursued the fatal irony of this freak accident and found a chilling universal message in it. Students have no trouble understanding how a person's desperate signals for help can be misunderstood or ignored by others.

If you share the story of the poem's genesis with students, you might also point out how the poem's title reads like a tabloid headline.

It never hurts to belabor the obvious with students. You might suggest they read the short biographical note on Smith and discover that the poet is a woman. Any student particularly interested in Smith should be directed to the superb 1978 film *Stevie* starring Glenda Jackson, which contains an especially powerful rendition of this poem.

18 *Figures of Speech*

Why Speak Figuratively?

Alfred, Lord Tennyson, THE EAGLE, page 678

For a hostile criticism of this poem, see Robert Graves, "Technique in Poetry," *On Poetry: Collected Talks and Essays* (New York: Doubleday, 1969) 402–05. Graves finds Tennyson's fragment unable to meet the minimal requirement that a poem should make good prose sense. He complains that if the eagle stands on its hands then its wings must be feet, and he ends up by rewriting the poem the way he thinks it ought to be. Though his remarks are fascinating, Graves reads the poem too literally.

A recent critic has suggested that this poem is a product of Tennyson's hopeless nearsightedness. Celebrating the eagle's 20–20 zoom-lens vision and ability to see a fish from high up, Tennyson yearns for a goal he could not attain: "optical inclusiveness." (See Gerhard Joseph, "Tennyson's Optics: The Eagle's Gaze," *PMLA* 92 [May 1977]: 420–27).

William Shakespeare, SHALL I COMPARE THEE TO A SUMMER'S DAY?
page 678

Howard Moss, SHALL I COMPARE THEE TO A SUMMER'S DAY? page 679

Shakespeare's original—rich in metaphor, personification, and hyperbole—means more, of course, than Moss's tongue-in-cheek desecration. The only figure of speech in Moss's rewrite is the simile in line 1, and even that is denigrated ("Who says?"). Moss manages to condense 115 great words to 78, a sonnet to a mere thirteen lines. It took a poet skilled in handling rimes to find such dull ones.

Shakespeare's nautical metaphor in line 8 may need explaining: a beautiful young person is a ship in full sail; accident or age can untrim the vessel. Compare this metaphor to "bare ruined choirs where late the sweet birds sang" ("That time of year," page 991).

John Stallworthy, SINDHI WOMAN, page 680

The poem contains several examples of figurative language. The woman's grace is compared with that of "the cloth blown back from her face." There is "not a ripple in her tread." But perhaps the most striking figure of speech comes in the last two lines, where *weight* works both literally (referring to the stone jar on the woman's head) and figuratively (in reference to the less tangible weights borne by this woman: filth, poverty, and all the other burdens of slum life). Perhaps the figure of speech can be said to extend to the troubles borne by anyone, anywhere. The weightier they are, the poet suggests, the more character do their bearers display.

METAPHOR AND SIMILE

Richard Wilbur, A SIMILE FOR HER SMILE, page 682

Despite the title, it may be necessary to point out that the detailed and extended comparison that occupies Wilbur's poem isn't between the smile and the approach of a riverboat, but between the latter and the speaker's *experience* of his loved one's smile, or his anticipation of it, or his memory of it.

The graceful ingenuity of this poem, in which the simile is made so explicit, recalls earlier metaphysical poetry. Compare Wilbur's simile with Donne's figure of the two parted lovers in "A Valediction: Forbidding Mourning," (page 912), or to Edmund Waller's central metaphor in "On a Girdle" (page 691).

Alfred, Lord Tennyson, FLOWER IN THE CRANNIED WALL, page 682

Why does Tennyson say "what God and man is" instead of "what God and man *are*"? Apparently, this isn't faulty grammar, but higher pantheism. God and man are one.

William Blake, TO SEE A WORLD IN A GRAIN OF SAND, page 683

Sylvia Plath, METAPHORS, page 683

Students usually are prompt to see that the central fact of the poem is the speaker's pregnancy. The speaker feels herself to be a walking riddle, posing a question that awaits solution: What person is she carrying? The "nine syllables" are like the nine months of gestation. All the metaphors refer to herself or to her pregnancy, except those in lines 4–5, which refer to the unborn baby: growing round and full like an apple or plum, seeming precious as ivory (and with ivory skin?), fine-timbered in sinew and bone like a well-built house.

The tone of the poem is clear, if complicated. Humor and self-mockery are evident in the images of elephant and strolling melon. In the last line, there is a note of wonder at the inexorability of gestation and birth: "The train there's no getting off."

A lively class might be asked to point out any possible connection between what the poem is saying about the arbitrary, fixed cycle of pregnancy and its form—the nine nine-syllable lines.

As Plath records in her Boston journal for 20 March 1959, the pregnancy she had hoped for ended in a miscarriage. Grieving and depressed, she went ahead and finished this poem, then explicitly called "Metaphors for a Pregnant Woman" *(Journals,* New York: Ballantine, 1983) 298–99.

Emily Dickinson, IT DROPPED SO LOW—IN MY REGARD, page 684

The whole poem sets forth the metaphor that someone or something the speaker had valued too highly proved to be like a silver-plated item (a chafing dish? a cream pitcher?) that she had mistaken for solid silver. Its smash revealed that it was made of cheap stuff.

In another version, lines 5–6 read: "Yet blamed the Fate that fractured—*less* / Than I reviled myself." Students may be asked which version they prefer, and why they prefer it. (Personally, we much prefer *reviled* to *denounced* because of its resonance—the sound of the *i*—and its alliteration, the *l* in *reviled* and *self.* Besides, *fractured* seems a more valuable word than *flung:* it gets across the notion of something cracked or shattered, and its *r* sets up an alliterative echo with the words *entertaining, Wares,* and *Silver.)*

N. Scott Momaday, SIMILE, page 684

Momaday is best known as a novelist and prose writer; his *House Made of Dawn* won the 1969 Pulitzer Prize in fiction. But Momaday is also an accomplished poet whose work often combines a compressed formal style with the natural imagery of his native Southwest. The Oklahoma-born author of Kiowa ancestry also often incorporates tribal legends into his verse.

"Simile," true to its title, gives us a single, extended simile, but it withholds the emotional motivation for the choice of this particular image. The reader is forced to interpret the behavior of the metaphorical deer in order to answer the *what* of the opening line. Those familiar with T. S. Eliot's concept of "an objective correlative" ("a set of objects; a situation, a chain of events which shall be the formula" that unleashes a particular emotion in a reader) will recognize Momaday's "Simile" as a classic example of that technique. Momaday lets his image work on the reader's unconscious rather than specify its emotional meaning.

Ruth Whitman, CASTOFF SKIN, page 685

Apparently "crawled away" means that the old woman died, leaving her body behind as a snake sheds a useless skin. "Paper cheek" seems a fine evocation of snakeskin. The simile in line 2 ("small as a twig") also suggests stiffness and brittleness.

EXERCISE: *What is Similar?* page 685

We'd suggest that this exercise be run through rapidly. We wouldn't give students much time to ponder, but would briskly call on people, and if anyone hesitated for long, would skip to someone else. Give them time to cogitate about these items, and they are likely to dredge up all sorts of brilliant, reached-for similarities in each pair of things—possibly logical, but having nothing to do with the lines. Immediate flashes of understanding are the goal of this exercise, not ponderous explication. Do this one for fun, and so it might be; do it slowly and seriously, and it could be deadly.

OTHER FIGURES

On the subject of puns, students familiar with *Hamlet* and other classics of the Bard may be asked to recall other puns of Shakespeare (besides the celebrated lines about golden lads and girls). If such a discussion prospers, Dr. Johnson's well-known observation in his preface to Shakespeare's works may provide an assertion to argue with:

> A quibble is to Shakespeare what luminous vapors are to the traveler: he follows it at all adventures; it is sure to lead him out of his way, and sure to engulf him in the mire. . . . A quibble is the golden apple for which he will always turn aside from his career or stoop from his elevation. A quibble, poor and barren as it is, gave him such delight that he was content to purchase it by the sacrifice of reason, propriety, and truth. A quibble was to him the fatal Cleopatra for which he lost the world, and was content to lose it.

James Stephens, THE WIND, page 686

As a birthday present to Stephens, James Joyce once translated this poem into five other languages (French, German, Italian, Latin, and Norwegian). These versions are reprinted in *Letters of James Joyce*, ed. Stuart Gilbert (New York: Viking, 1957) 318–19.

EXERCISE: *Paradox,* page 688

Chidiock Tichborne, ELEGY, WRITTEN WITH HIS OWN HAND, page 688

"One must admit the possibility that these verses were written by some other poet, rather than by the protagonist himself," note J. William Hebel and Hoyt H. Hudson in *Poetry of the English Renaissance* (New York: Appleton, 1929). Set to music by a later composer, the "Elegy" was sung as a madrigal.

George Herbert, THE PULLEY, page 690

The title may need clarification. Man's need for rest is the pulley by which eventually he is drawn to rest everlasting. The pulley Herbert has in mind is probably not horizontal (like the one with a clothesline), but the vertical kind rigged to hoist a heavy weight. Despite the puns, the tone of the poem is of course devoutly serious, Herbert's concern in it being (in the view of Douglas Bush) "to subdue the wilful or kindle the apathetic self."

Lines 2–10, on the "glass of blessings" and its contents, set forth a different metaphor. As Herbert's editor, F. E. Hutchinson *(Works* [Oxford: Oxford UP, 1941]) and others have remarked, "The Pulley" seems a Christian version of the story of Pandora. At her creation Pandora received gifts from all the gods, mostly virtues and graces—though Hermes gave her perfidy. In some tellings of the myth, Pandora's gift (or vase) held not plagues but further blessings. When she became curious and opened it, they slipped away, all except the one that lay at the bottom—hope.

Herbert's poem, in its fondness for the extended metaphysical conceit, invites comparison with Donne's metaphor of the compasses in "A Valediction: Forbidding Mourning" (page 912). If the instructor cares to discuss metaphysical poetry, "The Pulley" may be taken together with Herbert's "Redemption" (page 802) and "Love" (page 935). ("Easter Wings" [page 788] raises distracting contradictions and may be left for a discussion of concrete or graphic poetry.) Other metaphysical poems, by Waller and Roethke, immediately follow "The Pulley" in this chapter. (See note on Roethke's poem.) Other poems of Donne and of Dickinson can be mentioned. For a recent poem that contains extended conceits, see Wilbur's "A Simile for Her Smile," also in this chapter.

Students might be encouraged to see that poets of the seventeenth century had certain habits of thought strikingly different from our own; but that some of these habits— like the fondness for startling comparisons of physical and spiritual things—haven't become extinct. Perhaps the closest modern equivalent to the conceits of Herbert and Donne may be found in fundamentalist hymns. Two earlier twentieth-century illustrations:

> If you want to watch old Satan run
> Just fire off that Gospel gun!

and

> My soul is like a rusty lock.
> Oh, oil it with thy grace!
> And rub it, rub it, rub it, Lord,
> Until I see thy face!

(The first example is attributed to a black Baptist hymn writer; the second, to the Salvation Army, according to Max Eastman in *Enjoyment of Laughter* [New York: Simon, 1936].) An even more recent illustration, probably influenced by fundamentalist hymns, is a country-and-Western song recorded in 1976 by Bobby Bare, "Dropkick Me, Jesus" ("through the goalposts of life").

Edmund Waller, ON A GIRDLE, page 691

Another way to enter this poem might be to ask:

1. In what words does the poet express littleness or constriction? (In the "slender waist," the rime confined/bind, "pale which held," "narrow compass," "bound.")

2. In what words does he suggest vastness and immensity? (With any luck, students will realize that the entire poem demonstrates the paradox stated in lines 9–10.)

There may be another pun in line 6: *deer.*

What is the tone of "On a Girdle"? Playful and witty, yet tender. You can have fun with this poem by asserting an overly literal-minded reading: somewhere in the world, isn't there probably some ruler who *wouldn't* abdicate just to put his arms around her? If the speaker rejects all the sun goes round, where will that put him and his loved one? If students have trouble objecting to such quibbles, remind them of the definition of a figure of speech. That should help. An overstatement isn't a lie, it's a means of emphasis.

Compare this to another love poem full of hyperbole: Burns's "Oh, my love is like a red, red rose," at the end of this chapter.

Theodore Roethke, I KNEW A WOMAN, page 691

Both outrageous puns occur in line 15. In question 2, the three lines quoted contain overstatement or hyperbole. The speaker's reference to his whole being as "old bones" is synecdoche. "Let seed be grass, and grass turn into hay" are not metaphors, but literal events the speaker hopes for—unless you take the ripening of the grass to be the passage of time. Metaphors occur also in *the sickle* and *the rake,* and in calling lovemaking *mowing.*

"I Knew a Woman" shows Roethke's great affection for metaphysical poetry in its puns, its brief conceits (sickle and rake), and its lovely image out of geometry—"She moved in circles, and those circles moved." Two metaphysical poets of the seventeenth century come immediately before Roethke in this chapter: Herbert and Waller. Here's a good chance to dwell on metaphysical poetry, or at least to mention it. (See the notes on Herbert's "Pulley.")

For more outrageous puns, compare Robert Graves's "Down, Wanton, Down!" (page 628).

FOR REVIEW AND FURTHER STUDY

Robert Frost, THE SILKEN TENT, page 692

Although the word *as* in the opening line might lead us to expect a simile, "The Silken Tent" is clearly an immense metaphor, comparing woman and tent in a multitude of ways. What are the ropes or cords? Not merely commitments (or promises to keep) to friends and family, but generous sympathies, "ties of love and thought," on the part of a woman who cares about everything in the world.

While paying loving tribute to a remarkable woman, the poem is also a shameless bit of showing off by a poet cocksure of his technical mastery. Managing syntax with such grace that the poem hardly seems contrived, Frost has sustained a single sentence into an entire sonnet. "The whole poem is a performance," says Richard Poirier, "a display for the beloved while also being an exemplification of what it is like for a poem, as well as a tent or a person, to exist within the constrictions of space ('a field') and time ('at midday') wherein the greatest possible freedom is consistent with the intricacies of form and inseparable from them" *(Robert Frost: The Work of Knowing* [New York: Oxford UP, 1977] xiv-xv). Poirier points out, too, that the diction of the poem seems Biblical, perhaps echoing "The Song of Songs" (in which the bride is comely "as the tents of Kedar") and Psalm 92 (in which the godly "grow like a cedar in Lebanon"). Not only does the "central cedar pole" signify the woman's spiritual rectitude, it points toward heaven.

In teaching this poem, one can quote Frost's remark to Louis Untermeyer, "I prefer the synecdoche in poetry, that figure of speech in which we use a part for a whole." In 1931 Frost recalled that he had called himself a Synecdochist back when other poets were calling themselves Imagists: "Always, always a larger significance. A little thing touches a larger thing" (qtd. in Elizabeth Shepley Sergeant, *Robert Frost: The Trial by Existence* [New York: Holt, 1960] 325).

Denise Levertov, LEAVING FOREVER, page 693

The man seems glad to go: "stones rolling away" suggests the shedding of some great weight, or possibly even a resurrection (an echo of the rolling away of the stone from the Easter tomb?). But in the woman's view the mountain seems like someone rejected and forlorn. The woman's view, expressed in a metaphor and given force by coming last, seems stronger than the man's simile.

Another question: is the poet right to repeat *away, way, away, away?* The sound reverberates with a terrible flat monotony, it is true—but apparently that is the effect necessary.

Jane Kenyon, THE SUITOR, page 693

This economical poem moves from simile to simile: (1) "like the chest of someone sleeping" (steadily rising and falling); (2) "like a school of fish" (flashing their pale bellies), and (3) "like a timid suitor" (hesitant, drawing back, reluctant to arrive).

Kenyon lives in Danbury, New Hampshire. "The Suitor" is from her first collection, *From Room to Room* (Cambridge: Alice James, 1978).

Robert Frost, THE SECRET SITS, page 694

Besides its personification of the sitting Secret, Frost's poem contains an implied metaphor. To dance round in a ring is to make futile efforts to penetrate a secret—merely going around in circles.

Margaret Atwood, YOU FIT INTO ME, page 694

The first two lines state a simile. In the second couplet, *hook* and *eye* turn out (to our surprise) to be puns.

W. S. Merwin, SONG OF MAN CHIPPING AN ARROWHEAD, page 694

The poem contains an apostrophe to the chips of flint or stone. That the chips are "little children" is also a metaphor; so is "the one you are hiding"—the emerging arrowhead.

John Ashbery, THE CATHEDRAL IS, page 694

Ashbery's unexpected pun on *slated* inspired student Steven B. Stanley of Metropolitan State University to coin "a more contemporary example of a pun" in a one-line poem of his own, "The Spelling Bee Champion":

Studied a spell.

His instructor, Cathy Lewis, took a vote in class: Was Stanley better than Ashbery? Not surprisingly, Stanley triumphed. He adds: "I also came up with: 'The library is booked for demolition.' However, that sounded a little too like Ashbery." Perhaps your students might like to try writing one-liners in this vein, and so realize (as Ashbery does) that it is possible to have fun with poetry.

Robinson Jeffers, HANDS, page 695

This poem can be profitably read with Jeffers's "To the Stone-cutters" (page 945). Both poems show Jeffers's belief in humanity's tenuous position versus nature, and both reveal his interesting view of art—that it is impermanent compared to nature's eternity but that it nonetheless outlives its makers to provide comfort and wisdom to future generations. "Hands," however, is a gentler poem than "To the Stone-cutters," and it shows Jeffers's deep, life-long respect for Native American cultures, whom he admired for living more closely to nature than modern man.

Robert Burns, OH, MY LOVE IS LIKE A RED, RED ROSE, page 695

Figures of speech abound in this famous lyric, similes (lines 1–2, 3–4), a metaphor (*sands o' life*, 12), overstatement (8 and 9, 10), and possibly another overstatement in the last line.

See other professions of love couched in hyperbole, among them Waller's "On a Girdle" (page 691), Roethke's "I Knew a Woman" (page 691), Marvell's "To His Coy Mistress" (page 957), and Auden's "As I Walked Out One Evening" (page 893). Are the speakers in these poems mere throwers of blarney, whom no woman ought to trust?

For a discussion of this poem that finds more in it than figures of speech, see Richard Wilbur, "Explaining the Obvious," in *Responses* (New York: Harcourt, 1976). Burns's poem, says Wilbur, "forsakes the lady to glory in Love itself, and does not really return. We are dealing, in other words, with romantic love, in which the beloved is a means to high emotion, and physical separation can serve as a stimulant to ideal passion." The emotion of the poem is "self-enchanted," the presence or absence of the lady isn't important, and the very idea of parting is mainly an opportunity for the poet to turn his feelings loose. Absurd as this posture may be, however, we ought to forgive a great songwriter almost anything.

19 *Song*

SINGING AND SAYING

"Song" is an unusual chapter. It approaches poetry in ways different from most other textbooks. We urge new instructors to try this chapter. Most students who write comments about this book say this chapter is the most appealing. "It shows that poetry isn't all found in books," is a typical comment; and many students are glad to see song lyrics they recognize. Most important, the chapter talks to them about poetry by using songs—a context they know a great deal about. It also encourages them to hear poems in a way that they might never have done before if their entire experience was seeing poems on the printed page.

Even if there is not time for a whole unit on song, the instructor who wishes to build upon this interest can use at least some of this chapter to introduce the more demanding matters of sound, rhythm, and form (treated in the chapters that follow). Some instructors take the tack that lyric poetry begins with song, and so begin their courses with this chapter, supplemented by folk ballads elsewhere in the text.

Besides Ben Jonson's classic nondrinking song, many other famous poems will go to melodies. The tradition of poems set to music by fine composers is old and honorable. For lists of such poems with musical settings (and recordings), see *College English* for February 1985 and December 1985.

Ben Jonson, CELIA, page 698

Students may not know that in line 2 *I will pledge* means "I will drink a toast." Also, *I would not change for thine* (line 8) in modern English becomes "I would not take it in exchange for yours."

To demonstrate that "To Celia" is a living song, why not ask the class to sing it? Unfortunately, you can no longer assume that the tune is one that everyone knows, so you may need to start them off.

Anonymous, THE CRUEL MOTHER, page 699

Some versions of this ballad start the narrative at an earlier point in time, with a woman discovering that she is pregnant by the wrong man when she is about to marry another. See Alan Lomax's Notes to *The Child Ballads*, vol. 1, Caedmon, TC 1145, which record contains an Irish version.

If the instructor cares to discuss the bottomless but student-spellbinding topic of archetypes, this ballad will serve to illustrate an archetype also visible in the stepmother figure of many fairy stories.

Run D.M.C., from PETER PIPER, page 701

One reason we chose this excerpt from many other rap lyrics was its density of allusion. "Peter Piper" contains as many literary references as Milton's "Lycidas," but most students don't find them intimidating because they come from popular culture and children's literature. It might be helpful to work through the allusions and discuss how they shape the lyrics' effect on the listener; then use this as a model of how allusions to myth and literature work in traditional poetry. (It's nice to see King Midas in a Run D.M.C. lyric.) Rap is a form of oral poetry, and it's interesting to note how these lyrics incorporate many pieces of the central English-language classic of oral poetry—*Mother Goose.*

A metrical note: notice how once the rap settles into its regular rhythm (line 12) it bounces along in a four-stress line, the standard measure of English-language oral poetry from the Anglo-Saxons till today.

William Shakespeare, TAKE, O, TAKE THOSE LIPS AWAY, page 702

In this short madrigal, Shakespeare wrote in the most popular song form of his era. How many popular song lyrics look this good after three hundred years? Shakespeare had the brevity of the madrigal form working to his advantage; singers busy with elaborate counterpoint didn't need extended lyrics found in simpler strophic forms like the ballad. Although this song was presumably sung by a single voice (the boy who enters with Mariana in the fourth act of *Measure for Measure),* it employs the madrigal form usually associated with three or more voices. Madrigals could take flexible forms ranging from four to thirteen lines, but they always end in a couplet.

The fourth line may confuse some students, "Lights that do mislead the morn" means that the lover's eyes are so radiant that they mislead the morning into believing the sun has risen.

Edwin Arlington Robinson, RICHARD CORY, page 703

Paul Simon, RICHARD CORY, page 704

This pair sometimes provokes lively class discussion, especially if someone in the class maintains that Simon converts Robinson into fresh, modern terms. Further discussion may be necessary to show that Robinson's poem has a starkly different theme.

Robinson's truth, of course, is that we envy others their wealth and prestige and polished manners, but if we could see into their hearts we might not envy them at all. Simon's glib song does not begin to deal with this. The singer wishes that he too could have orgies on a yacht, but even after he learns that Cory died a suicide, his refrain goes right on, "I wish that I could be Richard Cory." (Live rich, die young, and make a handsome corpse!)

Some questions to prompt discussion might include:

1. In making his song, Simon admittedly took liberties with Robinson's poem. Which of these changes seem necessary to make the story singable? What suggestions in the original has Simon picked up and amplified?

2. How has Simon altered the character of Richard Cory? Is his Cory a "gentleman" in Robinson's sense of the word? What is the tone of Simon's line, "He had the common touch"? Compare this with Robinson: "he was always human when he talked." Does Robinson's Cory have anything more than "Power, grace and style"?

3. In the song, what further meaning does the refrain take on with its third hearing, in the end, after the news of Cory's suicide?

4. What truth about life does Robinson's poem help us see? Is it merely "Money can't make you happy" or "If you're poor you're really better off than rich people"? Does Simon's narrator affirm this truth, deny it, or ignore it?

Frank J. D'Angelo has noticed that the name Richard Cory is rich in connotations. It suggests Richard Coeur de Lion, and other words in Robinson's poem also point to royalty: *crown, imperially, arrayed, glittered, richer than a king.*

BALLADS

Anonymous, BONNY BARBARA ALLAN, page 705

Despite the numerous versions of this, the most widespread of all traditional ballads in English, most keep the main elements of the story with remarkable consistency. American versions tend to be longer, with much attention to the lovers' eventual side-by-side burial, and sometimes have Barbara's mother die of remorse, too! Commentators since the coming of Freud have sometimes seen Barbara as sexually frigid, and Robert Graves once suggested that Barbara, a witch, is killing Sir John by sorcery. An Irish version makes Barbara laugh hideously on beholding her lover's corpse.

To show how traditional ballads change and vary in being sung, a useful recording is *The Child Ballads,* vol. 1, Caedmon, TC 1145, containing performances collected in the field by Alan Lomax and Peter Kennedy. Six nonprofessional singers are heard in sharply different versions of "Barbara Allan," in dialects of England, Scotland, Ireland, and Wales.

Dudley Randall, BALLAD OF BIRMINGHAM, page 709

Randall's poem is an authentic broadside ballad: it not only deals with a news event, it was once printed and distributed on a single page. "I had noticed how people would carry tattered clippings of their favorite poems in their billfolds," the poet has explained, "and I thought it would be a good idea to publish them in an attractive form as broadsides" (Interview in *Black World,* Dec. 1971). "Ballad of Birmingham" so became the first publication of Randall's Broadside Press, of Detroit, which has since expanded to publish books and issue recordings by many leading black poets, including Gwendolyn Brooks, Don L. Lee, and Nikki Giovanni.

The poem seems remarkably fresh and moving, though it shows the traits of many English and Scottish popular ballads (such as the questions and answers, as in "Edward," and the conventional-sounding epithets in stanza 5). Randall presents without comment the horror of the bombing—in the mother's response and in the terrible evidence—but we are clearly left to draw the lesson that if the daughter had been allowed to join the open protest, she would have been spared.

Four black girls were killed in 1963, when a dynamite blast exploded in Birmingham's Sixteenth Street Baptist Church. In September, 1977, a Birmingham grand jury finally indicted a former Ku Klux Klansman, aged 73, on four counts of first degree murder.

FOR REVIEW AND FURTHER STUDY

John Lennon and Paul McCartney, ELEANOR RIGBY, page 710

"Eleanor Rigby," we think, is a poem. Although swayed by the superstition that priests are necessarily lonely because celibate, Lennon's portrait of Father McKenzie and of Eleanor have details that reflect life. Both music and words contain an obvious beat, and if students pick out those syllables in long lines 4 and 7, 14 and 17, and 24 and 27, they will be getting into the subject of meter. (Each of the lines contains a stressed syllable followed by four anapests.)

Anonymous, THE SILVER SWAN, WHO LIVING HAD NO NOTE, page 711

Don't let students read this madrigal without telling them that it describes the folklore that the swan, a songless bird, breaks forth in song just before it dies. Science has rejected this legend, but it survives in the expression "swan song."

This little poem can be recognized as a madrigal in several ways. First, it is extremely short (only six lines long), and madrigals were rarely longer than a sonnet. Second, the subject of the poem is song. Third, the language breaks up into pithy half lines, just the right size for a singable phrase. (It is interesting to see how the Beatles' "Eleanor Rigby" uses those same short phrases as its basic line, and how its long lines break into two short phrases just as the lines of this madrigal do.)

This madrigal is full of wonderful touches. The phrase "unlocked her silent throat" contains a striking metaphor. Or the way that *silver* and *living* echo each other's sounds in the opening line.

William Blake, JERUSALEM, page 712

The unnamed figure in the opening stanza is God, though not necessarily the deity of orthodox Christianity. Blake is essentially creating a myth in this poem of ancient England (or, as some critics would maintain, pre-industrial Britain) as an earthly paradise. But now the brightness of the Divine Countenance has been clouded, and the heavenly city of Jerusalem replaced by "these dark Satanic Mills."

It is important to remember that while Blake borrows Christian imagery in this poem, he uses them in idiosyncratic ways. His poem is visionary and prophetic: he imagines how the mental, political, and spiritual blight of early-nineteenth-century industrial England might be corrected. His fight, however, is not political or economic (as was Marx's, who critiqued the same English system a half century later); Blake urges a "Mental Fight," a spiritual healing that will eventually redeem society and rebuild Jerusalem "in England's green and pleasant land."

20 *Sound*

SOUND AS MEANING

Alexander Pope, TRUE EASE IN WRITING COMES FROM ART, NOT CHANCE, page 715

Nowadays, looking at the pages of an eighteenth-century book of poetry, we might think the liberal capitalization and use of italics merely decorative. But perhaps Pope wished to leave his readers little choice in how to sound his lines. Most of his typographical indications seem to us to make sense—like a modern stage or television script with things underlined or capitalized, lest the actors ignore a nuance.

Line 12 is deliberately long: an alexandrine or twelve-syllable line that must be spoken quickly in order to get it said within the time interval established by the other shorter, pentameter lines.

William Butler Yeats, WHO GOES WITH FERGUS?, page 717

Originally a song in Yeats's play *The Countess Cathleen,* this famous lyric overflows with euphony. Take just the opening question (lines 1–3): the assonance of the various *o*-sounds; the initial alliteration of *w, d,* and *sh;* the internal alliteration of the *r* in *Fergus, pierce,* and *shore*—musical devices that seem especially meaningful for an invitation to a dance. The harsh phrase *brazen cars* seems introduced to jar the brooding lovers out of their reveries. Unless you come right out and ask what brazen cars are, a few students probably will not realize that they are brass chariots. In ancient Ulster, such chariots were sometimes used for hunting deer—though how you would drive one of them through the deep woods beats us.

If you discuss meter, what better illustration of the power of spondees than "And the WHITE BREAST of the DIM SEA?"

The last line of the poem, while pleasingly mysterious, is also exact. The personification "dishevelled wandering stars" makes us think of beautiful, insane, or distracted women with their hair down: Ophelia in Olivier's film *Hamlet.* That they are wandering recalls the derivation of the word *planet:* Greek for "wanderer." In what literal sense might stars look disheveled? Perhaps in that their light, coming through the atmosphere (and being seen through ocean spray) appears to spread out like wild long hair. For comparable figures of speech, see Blake's "Tyger," (page 899), in which the personified stars weep and throw spears.

EXERCISE: *Listening to Meaning,* page 718

John Updike, RECITAL, page 718

Frances Cornford, THE WATCH, page 718

William Wordsworth, A SLUMBER DID MY SPIRIT SEAL, page 719

Emanuel di Pasquale, RAIN, page 719

Aphra Behn, WHEN MAIDENS ARE YOUNG, page 719

"Recital" shows off Updike as one of America's virtuosos of light verse. The whole poem seems written in imitation of the trochaic "oom-pah" of a tuba, and every line ends in a thumping celebration of the near rime between Mr. Bobo's surname and his chosen instrument. Onomatopoeia is heard even more obviously in Cornford's watch-ticks and Behn's hum-drum. In di Pasquale's lines, the *s*-sounds fit well with our conception of rain, and *hushes* is an especially beautiful bit of onomatopoeia. By the way, di Pasquale's poem is especially remarkable in view of the fact that the poet, born in Sicily, did not learn English until he was sixteen. Di Pasquale is now a professor of English at Middlesex Community College in New Jersey. His first collection of poems, *Genesis,* was published in 1989.

In Wordsworth's Lucy poem, sound effects are particularly noticeable in the first line (the soporific *s*'s) and in the last two lines (the droning *r*'s and *n*'s). If students go beyond the sound effects and read the poem more closely, they might find problems in the first stanza. Is the poet's *slumber* a literal sleep or a figurative one? That is: is Wordsworth recalling some pleasant dream of Lucy (whether the living Lucy he used to know, or the dead Lucy in Eternity), or is he saying that when she was alive he was like a dreamer in his view of her? If so, he was deluded in thinking that she would always remain a child; he had none of the usual human fears of death or of growing old. However we read the poem, there is evidently an ironic contrast between the poet's seeing Lucy (in stanza 1) as invulnerable to earthly years, and his later view that she is affected, being helplessly rolled around the sun once a year with the other inanimate objects. And simple though it looks, the poem contains a paradox. The speaker's earlier dream or vision of Lucy has proved to be no illusion but an accurate foreshadowing. Now she is a "thing," like rocks and stones and trees; and she cannot feel and cannot suffer any more from time's ravages.

Aphra Behn was the first English woman to earn a living by her pen. *Oroonoki* (1688), a tale of slavery in Surinam, is sometimes called the first true English novel. Her colorful life, mostly spent in London's literary bohemia, included a hitch in Holland as a spy for the Crown. In her destitute late years she was pilloried in lampoons ("a lewd harlot"), perhaps because she remained faithful to the Stuarts. She was buried in Westminster Abbey under her poetic pen name—Astrea Behn. Nowadays, she seems to be enjoying a respectful dusting-off. See the extensive treatment given in *Kissing the Rod: An Anthology of 17th Century Women's Verse,* ed. Germaine Greer and others (London: Virago Press, 1988) 240–60.

ALLITERATION AND ASSONANCE

A. E. Housman, EIGHT O'CLOCK, page 721

The final *struck* is a serious pun, to which patterns of alliteration begun in the opening line (*st . . . st, r*), and continued through the poem, have led up. The ticking effect of the clock is, of course, most evident in *the clock collected.*

Compare Housman's strapped and noosed lad with the one in Hugh Kingsmill's parody of Housman (page 850).

Robert Herrick, UPON JULIA'S VOICE, page 721

Julia, apparently, is singing, for the lutes provide accompaniment. At the beginning and end, this brief poem is particularly rich in music: the sibilance of *so smooth, so sweet, so silv'ry;* and the alliteration (both initial and internal) of the *m-* and *l-* sounds in the last line.

The second line seems a colossal hyperbole, meaning, "Julia, your singing is sweet enough to make the damned in Hell forget to wail." In Herrick's poems, such flattery is never out of place. This is the quality of Herrick's work—a lovely deliberate absurdity—XJK has tried to echo (feebly) in a two-line parody:

> When Vestalina's thin white hand cuts cheese,
> The very mice go down upon their knees.

Janet Lewis, GIRL HELP, page 722

A sensitive comment on this poem is that of the poet's husband, Yvor Winters:

> There is almost nothing to it, really, except the rich characterization of a young girl with her life before her and the description of a scene which implies an entire way of life. The meter is curious; one is tempted to call it irregular three-beat accentual, but it seems to be irregular iambic trimeter. On the second basis, the first line starts with a monosyllabic foot, and the fourth line has two feet, both iambic. But *wide* and *broom* are almost evenly accented, and both are long; If one is moved by this to choose the accentual theory, *her* is too lightly accented to count, although it would count as the accented syllable of an iambic foot. There are a few other such problems later in the poem. But there is no problem with the rhythm; the fourth line virtually gives us the movement of the broom, and the seventh and eighth give us the movement of the girl; the movement of the poem is that of indolent summer in a time and place now gone; the diction, like a rhythm, is infallible.

Winters (1900–1969)—see his own poem on page 1016—wrote this analysis in *Forms of Discovery* (Denver: Swallow, 1967) 332.

The poet reads "Girl Help" on her recording *Janet Lewis Reading at Stanford*, News Publications Service of Stanford University, 1975; available from Serendipity Books, 1970 Shattuck Ave., Berkeley CA 94709. "Domestic poetry" is her province, remarks Kenneth Fields in the notes on that record album's sleeve. He cites (in order to disagree with) a review of Lewis's work by Theodore Roethke: "The nursery, the quiet study, the garden, the graveyard do not provide enough material for talent of such a high order."

Janet Lewis, known for *The Wife of Martin Guerre, The Trial of Soren Quist,* and other novels, has brought out *Poems Old and New: 1918–1978* (Athens: Swallow-Ohio UP, 1981).

EXERCISE: *Hearing How Sound Helps*, page 722

Wyatt's version surpasses Surrey's for us, especially in Wyatt's opening line, with its remarkable use of assonance—a good instance of the way vowel-sounds can slow our reading of a line and make us linger over it. The initial alliteration and internal alliteration in these first two lines help besides. In its rhythm, Surrey's version sounds a bit singsong by comparison. The inverted word order in the last line seems awkward.

Alfred, Lord Tennyson, THE SPLENDOR FALLS ON CASTLE WALLS, page 723

If read aloud rapidly, this famous lyric from Tennyson's *The Princess* will become gibberish; and the phrase *Blow, bugle, blow,* a tongue twister. But if it is read with any attention to its meaning, its long vowels and frequent pauses will compel the reader to slow down. Students may want to regard the poem as mellifluous nonsense, but may be assured that the poem means something. In fact, it is based on a personal experience of the poet's. Visiting the lakes of Killarney in 1848, Tennyson heard the bugle of a boatman sound across the still water, and counted eight distinct echoes. "The splendor falls" is the poet's attempt to convey his experience in accurate words.

RIME

William Cole, ON MY BOAT ON LAKE CAYUGA, page 724

This is one of a series of comic quatrains, "River Rhymes," first printed in *Light Year '85* (Case Western Reserve U: Bits Press, 1984).

William Blake, THE ANGEL THAT PRESIDED O'ER MY BIRTH, page 725

Hilaire Belloc, THE HIPPOPOTAMUS, page 727

This short amusing poem requires no commentary. Instructors and students alike, however, might enjoy exploring more of Belloc's light verse found in anthologies such as Kingsley Amis's *The New Oxford Book of English Light Verse* (New York, Oxford UP, 1978).

R. S. Gwynn, SCENES FROM THE PLAYROOM, page 727

This ironic, outrageous poem might be valuable to turn to on a day when a class needs waking up.

How much do we know about these people? That this family is wealthy is suggested by the fact that it's the cook's night off. That these brats are treated indulgently is hinted by the children's having apparently killed a series of unlucky goldfish before this latest one. If Mother were alert enough to notice the monstrous acts of her Gestapo brood, much more than onions would make her cry.

Like the reader, the poet deplores both these children and their parents. His attitude is made plain by his drawing the children as Nazis, their parents as blind or foolish.

Of the younger formalist poets now coming to prominence, Gwynn may be the keenest satirist. This sonnet is from his collection *The Drive-In* (Columbia: U of Missouri P, 1986). He has also written an extended satire on current poets and poetry in the great tradition of Pope's *Dunciad: The Narcissiad* (New Braunfels, TX: Cedar Rock P, 1981). He frequently reviews poetry for *Texas Review, Sewanee Review,* and other literary journals, and is currently a professor of English at Lamar University in Beaumont, Texas.

William Butler Yeats, LEDA AND THE SWAN, page 728

The deliberately awful off-rime *up / drop* ends the sonnet with an approximately jarring plop as the God-swan discards the used Leda and sinks into his postejaculatory stupor.

Other questions that can be raised:

1. What *knowledge* and *power* does Yeats refer to in line 14?

2. Do the words *staggering* (line 2) and *loosening* (line 6) keep to the basic meter of the poem or depart from it? How does rhythm express meaning in these lines? (It staggers on *staggering* and loosens on *loosening.*)

3. Compare this poem to Donne's sonnet "Batter my heart" (page 629). Is the tone of Yeats's sonnet—the poet's attitude toward this ravishing—similar or dissimilar?

For an early draft of the poem, see Yeats's *Memoirs*, ed. Denis Donoghue (New York: Macmillan, 1973) 272–74.

Gerard Manley Hopkins, GOD'S GRANDEUR, page 729

Students who think Hopkins goes too far in his insistence on rimes and other similar sounds will have good company, including Robert Bridges, William Butler Yeats, and Yvor Winters. Still, it is hard not to admire the euphony of the famous closing lines—that ingenious alternation of *br* and *w*, with a pause for breath at that magical *ah!*—and the cacophony of lines 6–8, with their jangling internal rimes and the alliteration that adds more weight to *smeared, smudge,* and *smell.* For Hopkins, of course, sound is one with meaning; and the cacophonous lines just mentioned are also, as John Pick has pointed out, "a summary of the particular sins of the nineteenth century." For a brilliant demonstration that sound effects in Hopkins's poetry have theological meaning, see J. Hillis Miller, *The Disappearance of God* (Cambridge: Harvard UP, 1963) 276–317. Miller finds the poet's theory revealed in his sermons and journals: "Any two things however unlike are in something like"; therefore, "all beauty may by a metaphor be called rhyme."

In the text, it seemed best not to bury the poem under glosses, but to let the instructor decide how thoroughly to explicate it. Here are a few more glosses in case they seem necessary:

7. *man's smudge:* the blight of smoke and ugliness cast over the countryside by factories and mines. As a student for the priesthood in North Wales and as a parish priest in London and Liverpool, Hopkins had known the blight intimately. Another suggestion in the phrase: nature is fallen and needs to be redeemed, like man, who wears the smudge of original sin. 12. *morning . . . springs:* The risen Christ is like the sun at dawn. Eastward is the direction of Jerusalem, also of Rome. (Hopkins cherished the hope that the Church of England and the Pope would one day be reconciled.) 13–14: *bent / World:* Perhaps because of its curvature the earth looks bent at the horizon; or perhaps the phrase is a transferred epithet, attributing to the earth the dove's bent-over solicitude. (And as the world seems to break off at the horizon, line 13 breaks at the word bent.) 14. *broods:* like a dove, traditional representation of the Holy Ghost.

For still more suggestions, see Pick, *Gerard Manley Hopkins, Priest and Poet*, 2nd ed. (Oxford: Oxford UP, 1966) 62–4; Paul L. Mariani, *Commentary on the Complete Poems of Gerard Manley Hopkins* (Ithaca: Cornell UP, 1970); and (not least) the poet's "Pied Beauty."

A sonnet by Wordsworth (page 812) also begins "The world is," and Hopkins no doubt knew of it. In their parallel (though different) complaints against trade and commerce, the two deserve to be compared. Both poets find humanity artificially removed from nature: this seems the point of Hopkins's observation in lines 7–8 that once soil was covered (with grass and trees) and feet were bare; now soil is bare and feet are covered. Clearly we have lost the barefoot bliss of Eden; but in answer to Wordsworth, one almost expects Hopkins to cry, "Great God! I'd rather be a Christian." (Wordsworth by *world* means "worldliness.")

Fred Chappell, NARCISSUS AND ECHO, page 729

Fred Chappell is best known as a novelist and short story writer, but his poetry is exceptionally fine. He has often experimented with old verse forms (like Anglo-Saxon stress meter). In "Narcissus and Echo," he revived a virtually defunct form called "Echo Verse," which had not received much attention since the Renaissance. (Note that "Echo Verse" is described in the footnote to the poem.) To complete his *tour de force*, he uses the form to dramatize the plight of the nymph Echo.

Chappell takes the Echo Verse form one difficult step farther than most earlier poets. He makes his echoes form a vertical poem down the right hand side of the page. (Students will usually miss that aspect of the poem unless you point it out to them.) Likewise, Narcissus's speech can be read in isolation, so there are essentially three different poems in this text: Narcissus's self-absorbed solo, Echo's plaintive response, and the pair's lopsided dialogue.

Robert Frost, DESERT PLACES, page 730

Some possible answers:

1. Terrible pockets of loneliness.

2. The word *snow,* occurring three times. Other *o*-sounds occur in *oh, going, showing, no, so,* and *home.* The *l* of *lonely is* echoed by alliteration in *looked, last,* and *lairs.*

3. It makes us feel a psychic chill! Yet the feminine rime lightens the grim effect of what is said and gives it a kind of ironic smirk.

For an intriguing if far-out appreciation of this poem that makes much of the sibilent SS-sounds, see Marie Boroff, "Sound Symbolism as Drama in the Poetry of Robert Frost," *PMLA* 107 (1992): 131–144.

READING AND HEARING POEMS ALOUD

Here is a comment by William Stafford on why certain poets read their poems with apparent carelessness. Poets spend their energies in writing poems and are not effective public speakers. Unlike the Russian poet Andrei Voznesensky, a great performer, Stafford remarks,

> Most of the poets I know would feel a little guilty about doing an effective job of reading their poems. They throw them away. And I speak as one who does that. It feels fakey enough to be up there reading something as though you were reading it for the first time. And to say it well is just too fakey. So you throw it away. (Interview in *The Literary Monitor* 3, no. 3/4, [1980])

This comment raises provocative questions for discussion. What is the nature of a poetry reading? Should it be regarded as a performance, or as a friendly get-together?

For a symposium on poetry readings, with comments by Allen Ginsberg, James Dickey, Denise Levertov, and twenty-nine other poets, see *Poets on Stage* (New York: Some/Release, 1978).

A rich and convenient source of recorded poetry, no doubt the best in the country, is the Poet's Audio Center, a nonprofit service to the literary community and academe operated by the Watershed Foundation. The center can supply on cassette more than 500 readings by great and minor poets living and dead both commercial and noncommercial productions. They issue a free quarterly catalogue of 280 recordings. Among the cassette offerings are their own Watershed Tapes, an extremely well produced and interesting series of readings by contemporaries. Address: Poet's Audio Center, P.O. Box 50145, Washington, D.C. 20091.

A 1993 catalogue of about 600 radio broadcasts on cassette, including programs featuring poets John Ashbery, Gwendolyn Brooks, John Ciardi, Rita Dove, Allen Ginsberg, Anthony Hecht, Jonathan Holden, Colette Inez, Philip Levine, Paul Zimmer, and many others reading and talking about their work, is available from New Letters on the Air, University of Missouri Kansas City, 5100 Rockhill Road, Kansas City, MO 64110, phone (816) 235-1168.

EXERCISE: *Reading for Sound and Meaning,* page 733

Michael Stillman, IN MEMORIAM JOHN COLTRANE, page 733

William Shakespeare, FULL FATHOM FIVE THY FATHER LIES, page 733

A. E. Housman, WITH RUE MY HEART IS LADEN, page 734

T. S. Eliot, VIRGINIA, page 734

In Michael Stillman's tribute to the great jazz saxophonist, *coal train* is not only a rich pun on Coltrane's name, it also becomes the poem's central image. The poet has supplied this comment:

> One thing about that poem which has always pleased me beyond its elegiac strain— is the way the technique of the lines and phrases corresponds to a musical effect in Coltrane's playing. He was known for his ability to begin with a certain configuration of notes, then play pattern after pattern of variations. The repetition of "Listen to the coal . . . listen to the . . . listen to . . . listen" was one way to capture a feature of his playing. The image of the coal train disappearing into the night comes, particularly, from a place on the James River, west of Richmond, where I happened to be when I heard of Coltrane's death. Like all jazz musicians, I felt the loss very deeply.

Shakespeare's song contains an obvious illustration of onomatopoeia (the bell's sound), obvious alliteration in the *f*-full first line, and (less obviously) internal alliteration (note the *r* and *n* sounds), and assonance galore. Like a drowned man's bones, ordinary language becomes something "rich and strange" in this song.

Housman's lyric will reward the same sort of scrutiny, not that a class will sit still for much scrutiny of this sort!

Eliot's "Virginia" is an experiment in quantitative verse, according to George Williamson *(A Reader's Guide to T. S. Eliot* [New York: Noonday, 1957]). You might read aloud "Virginia" and Campion's quantitative "Rose-cheeked Laura" (page 748) and ask the class to detect any similarity. Ted Hughes has written of "Virginia" with admiration. How is it, he wonders, that Eliot can create so vivid a landscape without specific images? "What the poem does describe is a feeling of slowness, with a prevailing stillness, of suspended time, of heat and dryness, and fatigue, with an undertone of oppressive danger, like a hot afternoon that will turn to thunder and lightning" *(Poetry Is* [New York: Doubleday, 1967]).

21 *Rhythm*

STRESSES AND PAUSES

In the first section of this chapter, rhythm is discussed with as few technicalities as possible. For the instructor wishing to go on to the technicalities, the second part of the chapter, "Meter," will give the principles of scansion and the names of the metrical feet.

Except for one teacher at the University of Michigan, James Downer, who would illustrate the rhythms of Old English poetry by banging on his desk for a drum, we have never known anyone able to spend whole classes on meter without etherizing patients. Meter, it would seem, is best dealt with in discussing particular poems.

EXERCISE: *Appropriate and Inappropriate Rhythms,* page 738

The rollicking anapests of Poe are catchy, but they seem inappropriate and ill-suited to the melancholy and macabre atmosphere the poet wants to create.

Tennyson's monosyllabic words, further slowed by pauses, convey not only the force of the tide, but its repetitiveness.

Finch's meters are in themselves a sort of homage to her subject matter. She has adopted the hymn meter that Dickinson herself loved. She has also deliberately imitated the clean syntax and logical cadences of church hymns to present her images.

Eliza Cook's bouncy anapests seem singularly inappropriate for her grim and ghoulish situation. The tone becomes unintentionally comic.

The rhythms of Shakespeare and Keeler seem suitably rollicking.

Gwendolyn Brooks, WE REAL COOL, page 740

The poet might have ended every line with a rime, as poets who rime usually do:

> We real cool.
> We left school.

The effect, then, would have been like a series of hammer blows, because of so many short end-stopped lines and so many rimes in such quick succession. But evidently Brooks is after a different rhythm. What is it? How to read the poem aloud? Let members of the class take turns trying and compare their various oral interpretations. If you stress each final *We,* then every syllable in the poem takes a stress; and if, besides, you make even a split-second pause at every line break, then you give those final *We*'s still more emphasis. What if you don't stress the *We*'s, but read them lightly? Then the result is a skipping rhythm, rather like that of some cool cat slapping his thighs.

After the class has mulled this problem, read them Brooks's own note on the poem (from her autobiography *Report from Part One* [Detroit: Broadside, 1972] 185):

> The ending WEs in "We Real Cool" are tiny, wispy, weakly argumentative "Kilroy-is-here" announcements. The boys have no accented sense of themselves, yet they are aware of a semi-defined personal importance. Say the "We" softly.

189

Kilroy, as students may need to know, was a fictitious—even mythical—character commemorated in graffiti chalked or penciled by U.S. soldiers wherever they traveled in World War II. KILROY WAS HERE was even scrawled in the sands of Anzio. A small testimonial that the graffitist is a person.

As a student remarked about the tone and theme of this poem, "She doesn't think they're real cool, she thinks they're real fool—to die so young like that."

Brooks has recorded her own reading of the poem for *The Spoken Arts Treasury of 100 Modern American Poets,* vol. 13, SA 1052.

Robert Frost, NEVER AGAIN WOULD BIRDS' SONG BE THE SAME, page 741

He is Adam. In line 9 you say "as MAY be," because the iambic rhythm wants you to. The effect of Frost's closing string of sixteen monosyllables is quietly powerful, in keeping with his final understatement. Much of our pleasure in those lines comes from hearing ordinary, speakable phrases so beautifully accommodated.

Sometimes teachers and critics try to account for the unique flavor of Frost's language by claiming that it is all a matter of his vocabulary. But what rural words are there in this poem, a poem as Yankee-sounding as they come, despite some highly literate diction ("Admittedly an eloquence")? No, what makes the lines memorable is that they embody what Frost called the "sound of sense." He was convinced that certain phrases, customarily spoken with feeling, have a pattern of intonation so distinctive that we can recognize them and catch their meaning even if we hear only the drone of them from behind a closed door. (See Frost's explanations and illustrations in *Selected Letters,* ed. Lawrance Thompson [New York: Holt, 1964] 79-81 and 111-13.)

Reading this poem to an audience in Ann Arbor in March 1962 when he was 88, Frost delivered its closing line with the air of a slowball pitcher hurling a flawless third strike into the catcher's glove to retire the side. The audience caught it and burst out clapping.

Frost's line of monosyllables, by the way, doesn't seem dull either.

Was this sonnet, written in 1942, a dual love poem to both Frost's wife Elinor, who had died in 1938, and to Kay Morrison, who in the same year declined the poet's proposal of marriage but became his secretary? So Matthew A. Fike speculates in his analysis of the poem in *The Explicator* 49 (1991): 2. Like Elinor's influence, Eve's influence persists; like Kay Morrison (who, Frost told a correspondent, "has soothed my spirit like music"), Eve has improved birds' song—and presumably the poet's as well.

Ben Jonson, SLOW, SLOW, FRESH FOUNT, KEEP TIME WITH MY SALT TEARS, page 741

O sounds slow the opening line, whose every word is a monosyllable. Further slowing the line, eight of the ten monosyllables take heavy beats. "Drop, drop, drop, drop" obviously racks up still more stresses, as do the spondees that begin lines 4, 5, and 6. The entire effect is that we are practically obliged to read or sing the poem slowly and deliberately—as befits a lamentation.

Alexander Pope, ATTICUS, page 742

Generosity, kindness, courage, wholeheartedness, and humility seem mainly what Atticus/Addison lacks. As this famous dissection shows, Pope's custom is to break each line after a word that completes not only the line but also a syntactical unit. And so the argument advances in couplets like locked boxes, each box neatly packed with phrases, dependent clauses, things in series, antitheses. Only line 3 is a run-on line, if you go by the book's simple advice that a run-on line doesn't end in a punctuation mark. A sensitive reader, reading the passage aloud, would probably pause slightly after *fires* anyway, for these couplets enforce a rhythm hard to ignore.

For a definition of the heroic couplet and a brief discussion of it, students may be directed to pages 757–758.

EXERCISE: *Two Kinds of Rhythm,* page 743

Sir Thomas Wyatt, WITH SERVING STILL, page 743

Dorothy Parker, RÉSUMÉ, page 743

These two poems differ in rhythm: Wyatt compels a heavy pause only at the end of every quatrain, while Parker end-stops every line. Students may be shown that pauses and meanings go together. Both poems are cast in two sentences, but Wyatt develops one uninterrupted statement throughout the entire poem (in sonnet fashion: first the summary of the speaker's problem in the opening three stanzas, then the conclusion beginning with "Wherefore all ye"). "Résumé," as its punctuation indicates, makes a new self-contained statement in every line.

A question on meaning: Must light verse necessarily be trivial in its theme? State Parker's theme in "Résumé." Surely, it isn't trivial. At least in theme, the poem seems comparable to Hamlet's soliloquy, "To be or not to be. . . . "

After *Not So Deep as a Well,* her collected poems of 1936, Parker brought out no more poetry collections. "My verses," she insisted to an interviewer. "I cannot say poems. Like everybody was then, I was following in the exquisite footsteps of Miss Millay, unhappily in my own horrible sneakers" *(Writers at Work: The Paris Review Interviews,* 1st ser. [New York: Viking, 1959]). Parker's wit, acerbic and sometimes macabre, is as clear from "Résumé" as it is from her celebrated remark on being informed that Calvin Coolidge had just died: "How do they know?"

METER

XJK used to think of a meter as a platonic ideal norm from which actual lines diverge, but J. V. Cunningham's essay "How Shall the Poem be Written?" changed his mind. Metrical patterns (in the abstract) do not exist; there are only lines that poets have written, in which meters may be recognized. "Meter," declares Cunningham, "is perceived in the actual stress-contour, or the line is perceived as unmetrical, or the perceiver doesn't perceive meter at all" *(The Collected Essays of J. V. Cunningham* [Chicago: Swallow, 1976] 262).

Max Beerbohm, ON THE IMPRINT OF THE FIRST ENGLISH EDITION OF THE WORKS OF MAX BEERBOHM, page 744

John Updike has paid tribute to this brilliant bit of fluff:

> The effortless a-b-a-b rhyming, the balance of "plain" and "nicely," the need for nicety in pronouncing "iambically" to scan—this is quintessential-light verse, a twitting of the starkest prose into perfect form, a marriage of earth with light, and

quite magical. Indeed, were I high priest of literature, I would have this quatrain made into an amulet and wear it about my neck, for luck.

("Rhyming Max," a review of Beerbohm's collected verse reprinted in *Assorted Prose* [New York: Knopf, 1965].)

Thomas Campion, ROSE-CHEEKED LAURA, COME, page 748

Campion included this famous lyric in his polemic *Observations on the Art of English Poesie* (1602), in which he argued that English poets ought to adopt the quantitative meters of Greek and Latin. "This cannot be done in English," says John Hollander, "with its prominent word stress, save by assigning Latin vowel lengths to the written English, and simply patterning what amounts to a typographical code which cannot be heard as verse.... 'Rose-cheekt Laura' is therefore merely an unrhymed English trochaic poem, perfectly plain to the ear" (introduction to *Selected Songs of Thomas Campion*, selected by W. H. Auden [Boston: Godine, 1973]).

Walter Savage Landor, ON SEEING A HAIR OF LUCRETIA BORGIA, page 749

In first printing Landor's poem in 1825 in the *New Monthly*, Leigh Hunt explained, "A solitary hair of the famous Lucretia Borgia . . . was given me by a wild acquaintance who stole it from a lock of her hair preserved in the Ambrosian Library at Milan." (Lord Byron could very well have been the wild acquaintance.) According to Hunt, when he and Landor had met in Florence, they had struck up a conversation over the Borgia hair "as other acquaintances commence over a bottle."

EXERCISE: *Meaningful Variation*, page 750

Aside from minor variations from metrical norm (such as the substitution of a trochee for an iamb), the most meaningful departures in these passages seem to occur in these words or phrases:

1. Dryden: *deviates.* (Now there's a meaningful deviation!)

2. Pope: the spondees *snakes, drags,* and *slow length.*

3. Byron: the last line of Byron's stanza is two syllables (or one iambic foot) longer than the earlier lines. These extra syllables give the stanza a strong sense of closure.

4. Longfellow: *autumnal,* and the last line, which we would scan, "The CAT a ract of DEATH FAR THUN der ing from the HEIGHTS." Wonderful arrangement of unstressed syllables in that line! Its rhythm is like that of an avalanche bumbling around for a while before rumbling down.

5. Stevens: *spontaneous, casual, ambiguous.*

EXERCISE: *Recognizing Rhythms*, page 751

Edna St. Vincent Millay, COUNTING-OUT RHYME, page 751

A. E. Housman, WHEN I WAS ONE-AND-TWENTY, page 751

William Carlos Williams, THE DESCENT OF WINTER (SECTION 10/30), page 752

Walt Whitman, BEAT! BEAT! DRUMS! page 752

Langston Hughes, DREAM BOOGIE, page 753

Probably it is more important that students be able to recognize a metrical poem than that they name its meter. The Millay and Housman poems are thoroughly metrical; the Williams and Whitman are not, but include metrical lines when the poets are describing or imitating the sound of something with a regular rhythm: the clank of freight car wheels, the whistle's *wha, wha,* the beating of drums. In Whitman's poem, besides the refrain (lines 1, 8, and 15) there are primarily iambic lines that end each stanza. Hughes's "Dream Boogie" starts out with a metrical beat, then (deliberately) departs from it in the italicized interruptions.

22 Closed Form

Beginning students of poetry often have had a hard time appreciating either a sonnet or a poem in open verse because they have yet to distinguish one variety of poetry from the other. On first meeting an unfamiliar poem, the experienced reader probably recognizes it as metrical or nonmetrical from its opening lines—perhaps even can tell at first glance from its looks on the page (compact sonnet or spaced-out open verse). Such a reader then settles down to read with appropriate expectations, aware of the rules of the poem, looking forward to seeing how well the poet can play by them. But the inexperienced reader reads mainly for plain prose sense, unaware of the rhythms of a Whitmanic long line or the rewards of a sonnet artfully fulfilling its fourteenth line. Asked to write about poetry, the novice reader may even blame the sonnet for being "too rigid," or blame William Carlos Williams for "lacking music" (that is, lacking a rime scheme), or for "running wild." Such readers may have a right to their preferences, but they say nothing about a poem, nor about the poet's accomplishments.

That is why this chapter and the following one seem essential. To put across to students the differences between the two formal varieties, it isn't necessary to deal with every last fixed form, either. One can do much by comparing two poems (closed and open) on the theme of sorrow—Elizabeth Barrett Browning's fine sonnet "Grief" and Stephen Crane's astonishing "The Heart." Before taking up closed form, you might care to teach some song lyrics—those in Chapter 19, or a couple of traditional folk ballads. That way the student isn't likely to regard fixed forms as arbitrary constructions invented by English teachers. A stanza, you can point out, is the form that words naturally take when sung to a tune. That is how stanzas began. Sing a second round of a song, and you find yourself repeating the pattern of it.

FORMAL PATTERNS

John Keats, THIS LIVING HAND, NOW WARM AND CAPABLE, page 757

After Keats's death, these grim lines were discovered in the margin of one of his manuscripts. Robert Gittings has pointed out that the burden of the poem is much like that of two letters Keats wrote late in life to Fanny Brawne, charging her conscience with his approaching death and blaming her for enjoying good health. "This," says Gittings, "marks the lowest depths of his disease-ridden repudiation of both love and poetry" *(John Keats* [Boston: Atlantic-Little, 1968] 403). To discuss: can a repudiation of poetry nevertheless be a good poem?

John Donne, SONG ("GO AND CATCH A FALLING STAR"), page 759

Maybe it is worth pointing out that, in bringing together short stanzas to make one longer one, Donne hasn't simply joined quatrain, couplet, and tercet like a man making up a freight train by coupling boxcars. In sense and syntax, each long stanza is all one; its units would be incomplete if they were separated.

Ronald Gross, YIELD, page 761

Fitting together drab and prosaic materials, Gross leaves them practically unaltered. What he lends them are patterns that seem meaningful. By combining traffic-sign messages in "Yield," he implies that the signs insistently pressure us with their yips and barks. "Yield" states its theme implicitly: we are continually being ordered to conform, to give in, to go along with laws laid down for us. We must heed the signs in order to drive a car but perhaps it is chilling to find their commands so starkly abstracted. Students might wish to discuss whether it is reading too much into the poem to suspect that this theme applies to other areas of our lives, not only to driving.

A discussion of Gross's work may be one of those rare sessions that end with the students' realization that to remove speech from its workaday contexts and to place it into lines is, after all, what most poets do. Many poems, not only found poems, reveal meanings by arranging familiar things into fresh orders.

Nancy Adams Malone of Mattatuck Community College in Waterbury, Connecticut, contributes an insight about "Yield": "Everybody seems to think it's a comment on social conformity, but it seems to me easier and more fun to read it as a seduction."

Jacob Korg of the University of Washington passes on a class assignment that enjoyably makes its point. He asks his students to bring in whatever found poems they can discover. "The best one," he reports, "was the juxtaposition of two shop signs: ADULT ENTERTAINMENT and LIVE BAIT."

EXPERIMENT: *Finding a Poem,* page 762

Timothy F. Walsh, of Otero Junior College in Colorado, discovered another found poem in this book's previous edition:

"The sonnet,"
in the view of Robert Bly,
"is where the old professors
go to die."

"It was fun," he writes, "to discuss found poems following my students' reading about them on page 178, then point to one I found just two pages later."

THE SONNET

Michael Drayton, SINCE THERE'S NO HELP, COME LET US KISS AND PART, page 763

Nay, yea, wouldst, and *mightst* are the only words that couldn't equally well come out of the mouth of a lover in the twentieth century.

There seems to be an allegorical drama taking place, as Laurence Perrine has pointed out in "A Drayton Sonnet," *CEA Critic* 25 (June 1963): 8. Love is also called Passion, and apparently his death is being urged along by the woman's infernal Innocence.

Elizabeth Barrett Browning, GRIEF, page 764

The octave may be forgettable, but the sestet is perhaps one of the eight or ten high moments in English sonnetry. "Grief" antedates the more famous *Sonnets from the Portuguese* (mostly composed in 1845 and 1846). In 1842, when working on "Grief" and some sonnet exercises, Mrs. Browning wrote to her friend Mary Mitford, "The Sonnet structure is a very fine one, however imperious, and I never would believe that our language is unqualified for the very strictest Italian form." But as Alethea Hayter has noticed, "Grief" isn't at all in the strictest Italian form; the shift in its argument comes in the middle of line 8. In her early sonnet, says Hayter, the poet seems to be "arranging roses now in a tall vase, now in a flat bowl, but always in something either too tall or just too shallow" *(Mrs. Browning* [New York: Barnes, 1963]). Still, in gratitude for the sestet of "Grief," we can accept many awkward roses.

Thomas Carper, FACTS, page 765

Thomas Carper is an interesting new arrival on the literary scene. In 1991, at the age of fifty-four, he published his first full-length book of poems, *Fiddle Lane* (Johns Hopkins). One of the remarkable things about this thoroughly engaging collection is that most of the poems are sonnets—with subjects ranging from creation to a pet cockatoo. Many of the sonnets, however, are like "Facts," miniature short stories about the difficulties of family life and the problems of growing into genuine maturity.

Although Robert Bly claims that "the sonnet is where old professors go to die," this contemporary sonnet addresses an issue dear to the heart of the leader of the Men's Movement—how American men are often trained from childhood to repress their expressive, emotional side. Within the confines of the sonnet form, Carper creates a complex and compelling narrative about a father-son relationship that diminishes both parties.

Robert Frost, ACQUAINTED WITH THE NIGHT, page 765

This poem first appeared in *West-running Brook* (1928), Frost's fifth volume, which some critics felt marked a turning in his work toward dark, personal themes. One might argue if Frost's turn to dark themes began here, but it is true that many of his grimmer early poems were cast in a seemingly impersonal narrative form.

"Acquainted with the Night" shows many of the features we associate with Frost's darkly introspective side. Not only is the speaker solitary and alienated from the human community surrounding him; he fatalistically accepts this isolation. The poem begins and ends with the same line, which emphasizes the inescapable quality of the speaker's destiny, though by now *night* has acquired a metaphorical as well as literal meaning.

Although the poem is written in a direct first-person voice, it confides very little to the reader. We know the speaker's desperate isolation but, as William Pritchard observes in his superb study *Frost: A Literary Life Reconsidered* (Oxford, 1984), the poem provides "no clues or provocation to significant action." We know what is happening in the poem but not why. Noting that the poem was written in *terza rima,* Randall Jarrell commented that it possessed "Dante's own form and with some of Dante's own qualities." One might elaborate Jarrell's passing remark by saying that one reading of the poem would describe it as the speech of a lost soul wandering in his own private hell.

For the record, it is worth noting that the moody Frost was a compulsive walker whose late night rambles were legendary, though he liked them best with friends.

EPIGRAMS

Alexander Pope, EPIGRAM ENGRAVED ON THE COLLAR OF A DOG, page 766

Students may be asked: What's the point? Pope makes a devastating comment on society.

With few exceptions (such as His Royal Highness), every man is a dog: owned by some-body, accepting handouts, licking his master's hand, learning to heel.

Martial, Sir John Harrington, William Blake, E. E. Cummings,
Langston Hughes, J. V. Cunningham, John Frederick Nims, Stevie
Smith, Thom Gunn, Bruce Bennett, Hilaire Belloc, Wendy Cope,
A SELECTION OF EPIGRAMS, pages 767–769

Highly various, these twelve examples illustrate the persistence of the epigram since Mar-tial. Blake offers a definition of the epigram, written as epigrams. Not all epigrams come in rimed couplets, as Langston Hughes demonstrates. Whether the form of an epigram is closed or open, its essence consists of brevity and a final dash of wit.

Besides writing "Of Treason," called the best epigram in English, Harrington has another claim to immortality: he invented the water closet.

Cunningham, the American master of the verse epigram in our time, has had few recent rivals. Instructors who wish further examples of this fixed form will find many to quote in his *Collected Poems and Epigrams* (Chicago: Swallow, 1971).

Nims, closest rival to Cunningham, has collected his epigrams, including "Contem-plation," in *Of Flesh and Bone* (New Brunswick: Rutgers UP, 1967). When first printed, in *The New Yorker*, this poem was called "A Thought for Tristram"—suggesting that *you* means Isolde, betrothed of King Mark, with whom Tristan/Tristram shares a love potion.

Those of us who love Henry James's intricate introspective novels will also proba-bly know a few couples like the people in Thom Gunn's "Jamesian." Some students may not get the allusion of the title, but they will probably know the situation all too well.

If the haiku-like brevity of epigrams tempts you to ask your class to write a few, resist the temptation. Even from a bright class the results are likely to depress you. A successful epigrammatist needs, besides the ability to condense, the ability to deliver that final rapier thrust of nastiness. A talented creative writing class, after tackling poems in a few of the less demanding forms (ballads, villanelles, sestinas) might try epigrams, either rimed or rimeless.

If you do ultimately decide to challenge your class with writing an epigram, you might suggest they try the Wendy Cope approach and either update or revise an existing epigram. You'll be surprised how personal some of these revisions can become.

EXERCISE: *Reading for Couplets,* page 769

W. H. Auden, Edmund Clerihew Bentley, Cornelius Ter Maat,
CLERIHEWS, pages 769-770

Keith Waldrop, PROPOSITION II, page 770

Like an epigram, this poem is concise, and the whole poem leads up to a conclusive word: *wind.* Unlike an epigram, its subject isn't human folly, and its apparent purpose may be to express an insight, not to deliver a witty blow.

OTHER FORMS

Dylan Thomas, DO NOT GO GENTLE INTO THAT GOOD NIGHT, page 771

No mere trivial exercise (as a villanelle tends to be), Thomas's poem voices his distress at the decline and approaching death of his father. At the time, the elder Thomas was a semi-invalid, going blind, suffering from the effects of tongue cancer. As a teacher of English at Swansea Grammar School, the poet's father had ruled his class with authority; but those who knew him only in his last years knew a different, humbled man. (See Constantine FitzGibbon, *The Life of Dylan Thomas* [Boston: Atlantic-Little, 1965] 294–95.)

Like many other Thomas poems, this one contains serious puns: *good night, grave.* "Another assumption in this poem," says Amy Mulvahill (in a student paper written at Tufts), "may be Thomas's own self-destructive drive that led him to drink himself to death. It's possible that he preferred to taunt death with his boisterous life—to go down unrepentant and brawling."

Repetitious as a villanelle is, the form suits this poem, making its refrains sound like prayers said over and over. If you have any student poets, they might be challenged to write villanelles of their own. The hard part is to make the repeated lines occur naturally, to make them happen in places where there *is* something to be said. But the repetitious form is helpful. Write the two refrain lines and already your labors are eight nineteenths over.

For another instance of Thomas's fondness for demanding, arbitrary forms, see the poem "Prologue," at the beginning of Daniel Jones's edition of *The Poems of Dylan Thomas* (New York: New Directions, 1971). A poem of 102 lines, its first and last lines rime with each other, as do lines 2 and 101, 3 and 100, 4 and 99, and so on, until two riming lines collide in the poem's exact center. Except for that inmost pair of lines, no reader is likely to notice the elaborate rime scheme—rimes so far apart they can't be heard; but apparently it supplied the poet with obstacles to overcome and with a gamelike pleasure.

Leigh Hunt, RONDEAU, page 771

Jenny (so the story goes) was Jane (Mrs. Thomas) Carlyle, who gave Hunt a buss when he brought word that one of Carlyle's books had been accepted by a publisher.

A true French rondeau has fifteen lines, and follows rules more ingenious than those Hunt set for himself. For specifications, see Lewis Turco, *The Book of Forms* (Hanover: UP of New England, 1986) 215–216.

Robert Bridges, TRIOLET, page 772

The triolet is a form usually associated with light verse, but Bridges's poem demonstrates that it can be used to convey heavier emotional loads, if used with sufficient skill. Bridges's triolet could be used as an example of a short lyric—compressed, evocative, musical, and personal. He also manages to make the opening lines acquire considerable additional force by the end of the poem. We now know both that the couple fell into their passion unawares (they "did not guess") and that love was not only difficult but irretrievably disastrous. Is there a more moving triolet in English?

Elizabeth Bishop, SESTINA, page 772

We would answer the questions like this.

1. That some terrible loss—a death in the family?—causes the grandmother to weep seems a guess that fits the poem. The old woman tries to hide her grief from the child (lines 6, 10, 31–32); she thinks it was somehow foretold (9).

2. We have no authority to read this poem as autobiography, but the figure of the grandmother—the most important person in Bishop's early life—and the stormy setting (such as we might find in a village on the Nova Scotia coast) invite us to do so. The source of grief may have been the death of the poet's father (hence, an irony that the child draws a man with tear-shaped buttons) or it may have been the illness of her mother, hospitalized several times for a mental disorder. When Bishop was eight months old her father died, and according to Robert Giroux, "The first real home Elizabeth knew was in the coastal town of Great Village, Nova Scotia, where her widowed mother returned in order to be with her parents" (introduction to Bishop's *Collected Prose* [New York: Farrar, 1984]). When the poet was five, her mother had a final breakdown, leaving the girl in the care of her grandmother. Apparently Bishop looked back to her days in Nova Scotia with affectionate yearning. When she was six, her father's wealthy parents moved her to Worcester, Massachusetts, for a less happy stay.

3. Small round pieces of paper. Almanacs (such as *The Old Farmer's*) come with punched holes to make them easy to string and hang on a hook or a nail.

4. The playful ingenuity of the sestina, like that of the villanelle, tempts a poet to wax clever; yet Bishop is writing a deeply felt, moving poem in it. The tone is lightly serious, compassionate—yet with touches of gentle humor: the Little Marvel Stove, the child's drawings. Irony, too, informs the poem: a contrast between the grandmother's sorrow and the child's innocent ignorance.

5. Nims's comment seems an apt description of "Sestina." In the six repeated words, we are given the setting *(house)* the characters *(grandmother, child)*, and key symbols *(Stove, almanac, tears)*. "Sestina" weaves all six into a subtle relationship. This poem is full of things that suggest magic: the prophetic almanac, the teacup (with which fortune-tellers divine), the "marvellous stove." It also is full of secret-keepers: the grandmother, the almanac with its powers of prophecy, the concluding reference to the "inscrutable house." The repetitions are worth tracing: *tears,* in particular, accumulates an effect. In stanza 2 the tears arrive like an equinoctial storm; in 3, the kettle also weeps; in 4, tea is tears; in 5, the man in the child's drawing wears tears; in 6, the almanac weeps paper tears; and finally, in the envoy, tears are flowers. "Time to plant tears" may be literal quotation from the almanac, *tears* being (if memory serves) the name of a small white flower favored by rock gardeners.

Bishop's *Complete Poems* contains another intriguing sestina: "A Miracle for Breakfast." At the time it was written Bishop remarked (in a 1937 letter to Marianne Moore):

> It seems to me that there are two ways possible for a sestina—one is to use unusual words as terminations, in which case they would have to be used differently as often as possible—as you say, 'change, of scale.' That would make a very highly seasoned kind of poem. And the other way is to use as colorless words as possible—like Sidney, so that it becomes less of a trick and more of a natural theme and variations. I guess I have tried to do both at once. (Quoted by Nims in his essay, cited in question 5.)

199

In the later "Sestina," the terminal words seem deliberately usual ones.

For poet Eavan Boland's insightful comparison between "Sestina" and Bishop's poem "One Art," which appears in the Poems for Further Reading section, please see the notes on the latter poem in this manual.

EXERCISE: *Urgent Repetition,* page 774

This experiment just might leave you surprised at the quality of some of its results. Whoever writes a sestina has a powerful ally—the form—on his or her side.

In a tour de force, a student in a poetry workshop at Tufts once wrote a fairly successful sestina taking *one, two, three, four, five* and *six* for its repeated words. The result seemed only mildly boring and mechanical!

23 Open Form

In the current edition "Open Form" constitutes a separate chapter. The previous chapter on "Poems for the Eye" has been substantially shortened and incorporated into this chapter. While instructors enjoyed teaching many of the visual poems, most of them felt there wasn't enough time in most course schedules to use a separate unit on the subject.

Denise Levertov, SIX VARIATIONS (PART III), page 775

This poem is discussed fairly extensively in the text. Some instructors may worry that the poem is a little too unusual to start the chapter, but its refusal to rest in normal poetic conventions makes it a strong discussion piece. A provocative question to ask a beginning class is "Why would we consider this text poetry? What features does it have that we would consider poetic?"

E. E. Cummings, BUFFALO BILL'S, page 779

Cleanth Brooks and Robert Penn Warren have taken this poem to be an admiring tribute to William Cody (*Understanding Poetry,* 3rd ed. [New York: Holt, 1960]). But Louis J. Budd, in an interesting dissent, thinks Cummings is satirizing the theatricality of the old sideshow straight shooter and finds Mister Death "a cosmic corporal gathering up defunct tin-gods and stuffed effigies" *(The Explicator* 11 [June 1953]: item 55).

Emily Dickinson, VICTORY COMES LATE, page 780

Of all Dickinson's poems, this is the most formally open, and as a result it sounds almost contemporary. Clearly the poet is in charge of her open form, for each line-break comes after a word that (being essential to meaning) easily stands for the special emphasis. We could imagine a few other possible locations for line-breaks. (After *Love* in the last line?—or would that make the poem seem to end a riming couplet?) But no doubt the poet knew her own mind.

Dickinson's outsized hyphens (or delicate minidashes) usually seem to indicate pauses, little hesitations, as if to give a word or phrase (whether following the dash or preceding it) special emphasis.

If there is time to work further with this splendid poem, both language and meaning deserve a deeper look. Note the pun in line 3: *rapt* for "wrapped." In the next-to-last line, *keep* seems a subjunctive verb: the statement may be a prayer. What sort of "Victory" does the poet mean? Thomas H. Johnson thought she referred to a Civil War battle, but we think this is one of her several poems concerned with reputation and fame. Perhaps the sparrows are minor poets, like Dickinson, unprinted and unacclaimed. Perhaps the Eagle is a famous bard glutted with renown: Ralph Waldo Emerson, maybe. The conclusion seems a bitter acceptance, as if to say: "God is wise not to feed me too generously." Ironically, the poem today seems literally true: Dickinson's victory has indeed come, although she cannot taste it.

William Carlos Williams, THE DANCE, page 781

Scanned, the poem is seen to abound in pairs of unstressed syllables. The result is a bouncing rhythm—anapestic or dactylic, depending on where one wishes to slice the lines into feet. This rhythm seems appropriate to a description of frolicking dancers and helps establish the tone of the poem, which is light, however serious. Williams severs his units of sense again and again in midphrase: placing his linebreaks after *and, the, about, thick, those, such.* In this poem run-on lines predominate, and this is not only a technical device but a way of underlining the poem's meaning. Williams conveys a sense of continuous movement in a syntax that keeps overflowing line units.

By repeating its opening line, the poem, like Breughel's dancers, comes round in a circle to where it began. Another metaphor is possible: like a painting enclosed in a frame, the poem encloses its central scene in a frame of words.

Williams first saw Breughel's painting in Vienna in 1924, but wrote this poem in 1942, some eighteen years later. A French critic, Jacqueline Saunier-Ollier, has speculated on the curious fact that the poem, in describing a vividly colorful tableau, omits all color images. Her work on Williams's Breughel poems is summed up in *William Carlos Williams: Man and Poet*, ed. Carroll F. Terrell (Orono: National Poetry Foundation, 1983) 528–29.

Stephen Crane, THE HEART, page 782

Walt Whitman, CAVALRY CROSSING A FORD, page 782

Two nineteenth-century American poems, the pair seem comparable mainly in brevity and use of narration. The assonance and internal alliteration in Whitman's phrase *silvery river* are echoed in the poem's very opening line: the assonance of the *i*-sound in *line, wind, islands;* the internal alliteration of the *r* in *array, where, green.* But any line of this short poem will repay such inspection. Crane's "The Heart" is obviously less heavy on verbal music, although *Held his heart in his hands* is heavily alliterative; and the second stanza favors the letter *b.* There is rime, too: *it/bitter, bitter/heart.*

Whitman seems to lambaste his poem with sound-effects in his enthusiasm for his grand military spectacle. Crane cares for music, too, and yet his is a subtler, harsher one. Although longer in words, Whitman's "Cavalry" contains fewer pauses than "The Heart" (fifteen compared to Crane's seventeen, if every comma and line-end counts as a pause). The result is, in Crane's poem, a much more hesitant, start-and-stop movement—appropriate, perhaps, to a study of self-immolation. Whitman apparently wants an expansive, continuous progress in his syntax, as in his cavalry.

Wallace Stevens, THIRTEEN WAYS OF LOOKING AT A BLACKBIRD, page 783

Suggestive as blackbirds may be, the theme of the poem is, "Pay attention to physical reality." Stevens chides the thin ascetic men of Haddam who would ignore good blackbirds and actual women for golden phantasms. He also chides that asinine aristocrat who rides about Connecticut (of all places) in a glass coach as if thinking himself Prince Charming. The poem ends in a section whose tone is matter-of-fact flatness, rather as though Stevens were saying, "Well, here's the way the world is; if you don't like it, go read newspapers." Taken as a series of notes for an argument for literalism, this much-discussed poem seems to have unity and to lead to a definite conclusion. For another (and more complicated) view of it, see Helen Hennessy Vendler, *On Extended Wings* (Cambridge: Harvard UP, 1969).

Way-of-looking number 5 recalls Keats's "Grecian Urn": "Heard melodies are sweet. . . ."

Way number 10 eludes final paraphrase. Are the "bawds of euphony" supposed to be, perhaps, crass ex-poets who have sold out their Muses, who utter music to please the box office instead of truth? But blackbirds flying in a green light are so strikingly beautiful that even those dull bawds would be moved to exclaim at the sight of them.

Gary Gildner, FIRST PRACTICE, page 785

Some possible answers to the questions:

1. Hill is a sadist. He is determined to render defenseless boys as bitter as he is.

2. The speaker doesn't want to identify himself with such a worldview; apparently, he wishes to remove it from himself by thrusting the hideous Hill away off in the third person.

3. The broken line indicates a pause—while the boy athletes suck in their breaths and don't dare answer.

4. Closure.

5. The rewrite would make Gildner's appalling poem seem neat, swingy, and jingly.

6. Poems don't have to traffic in moonlight and roses. Nothing in human experience need be alien to them—not even Hill.

In a recent comment on "First Practice," Gildner recalls that the poem came straight from his boyhood in the 1950s. When his parochial school (Holy Redeemer, grades one through eight) started a football team, an ex-Marine who had played ball in the service volunteered to coach it. Practice was held in The Bomb Shelter, a thick-walled basement with a low ceiling. "Some of us later felt slimy and ashamed at hitting out like that—at being *moved* by Cliff's speech. And I know that many of us were more afraid to lose a game than to break a bone. . . . For years I tried to write a short story about this experience, but the attempts always sounded wrong, false. One day I decided to simply 'list' the story's important elements. Except for one unnecessary word, the poem 'First Practice' appeared" (comment in *Poetspeak: In their work, about their work,* ed. Paul B. Janeczko [Scarsdale: Bradbury, 1983] 39–41).

Carolyn Forché, THE COLONEL, page 787

It is possible to argue either way on whether "The Colonel" is a prose poem or a short prose piece, but the stronger case is that it is a poem in prose. Why? First, "The Colonel" displays the compression we usually associate with poetry (prose fiction would unfold more leisurely). Second, by the end of the piece, it becomes apparent that the organization is as much lyric as narrative (the image of the ears pressed to the ground harks back to the *heard* in the opening line and to the auditory images throughout). Third, the density of literary effect (imagery, description, metaphor) has the feel of poetic language. The absence of poetic rhythms and lineation isn't enough to offset these qualities.

The rhetoric of Forché's piece deserves some attention. The effect of the poem depends heavily on the opening sentence ("What you have heard is true.") If we do not—at least initially—accept Forché's piece as reportage, then the poem loses a great deal of its impact. Forché understands this assumption clearly: notice how she dates the incident at the end to increase its verisimilitude. Some critics have questioned whether the episode truly happened as Forché presents it. That is a legitimate historical query, but, in poetic terms, it hardly matters; she has convincingly created the appearance of reality. The exaggerations seem no less credible than the bizarre incidents that fill the newspapers because Forché has captured the tone of factuality.

If you want to study the genre of the prose poem further, look up Karl Shapiro's "The Dirty Word" in the Poems for Further Reading section. It, too, has a quasi-narrative structure filled with memorable images.

VISUAL POETRY

For more examples of graphic poetry, see the anthologies edited by Klonsky and Kostelanetz (cited in footnotes to this chapter). Other useful anthologies include Emmett Williams's *Anthology of Concrete Poetry* (New York: Something Else, 1967), Eugene Wildman's *Chicago Review Anthology of Concretism* (Chicago: Chicago Review, 1967), Mary Ellen Solt's *Concrete Poetry: A World View* (Bloomington: Indiana UP, 1969), and Emmett Williams's selection of "Language Happenings" in *Open Poetry: Four Anthologies of Expanded Poems,* ed. Ronald Gross and George Quasha (New York: Simon Schuster, 1973).

George Herbert, EASTER WINGS, page 788

John Hollander, SWAN AND SHADOW, page 789

The tradition of the shaped poem, or *Carmen figuratum,* seems to have begun in Renaissance Italy, and the form flourished throughout Western Europe in the seventeenth century. English practitioners of the form, besides Herbert, included Robert Herrick (in "The Pillar of Fame") and George Puttenham.

Of "Easter Wings," Joan Bennett has remarked, "The shape of the wings on the page may have nothing but ingenuity to recommend it, but the diminuendo and crescendo that bring it about are expressive both of the rise and fall of the lark's song and flight (Herbert's image) and also the fall of man and his resurrection in Christ (the subject that the image represents)" (qtd. by F. E. Hutchinson in his edition of Herbert's *Works* [Oxford: Oxford UP, 1941]). Visual shape and verbal meaning coincide strikingly when the second stanza dwindles to *Most thin.*

Like Herbert, Hollander clearly assumes that a word-shape has to have a meaningful relation to what is said in it. His reflected swan is one of twenty-five shaped poems collected in *Types of Shape* (New York: Atheneum, 1969). Other graphic poems in the book include a car key, a goblet, a beach umbrella, an Eskimo Pie, and the outline of New York State. Paul Fussell, Jr., discussing "Easter Wings" and Hollander's shaped poems, expresses reservations about this kind of poetry. Most shaped poems, he finds, are directed more to eyes than ears—"or better, we feel that the two dimensions are not married: one is simply in command of the other." But the greatest limitation in the genre is that there are few objects that shaped poems can effectively represent: "their shapes can reflect the silhouettes of wings, bottles, hourglasses, and altars, but where do we go from there?" *(Poetic Meter and Poetic Form* [New York: Random House, 1965] 185–87). Students might be told of Fussell's view and asked to comment. A further disadvantage of most shaped poetry is that it cannot be heard aloud without loss.

Dorthi Charles, CONCRETE CAT, page 791

This trifle first appeared in the second edition of *An Introduction to Poetry* and has been retained out of loyalty to the past. While hunting for an illustration of the sillier kind of concrete poem that simply and unfeelingly arranges words like so many Lincoln Logs, XJK found the very thing in one of William Cole's anthologies of humorous poetry: "Concrete Poem" by the British wit Anthony Mundy. Mundy's work repeats *miniskirt* several times in the form of a miniskirt, and tacks on a couple of *leglegleglegs.* No doubt he was parodying concrete poetry, too. But the cheapskate in XJK rebelled at the thought of paying for permission to reprint such a simple doodad, so decided to cut and paste together a homemade specimen. While constructing the cat, he started having some fun with it, making the tongue a *U,* and so on. As far as we know, however, the pun in the cat's middle stripe (tripes) is the only place where language aspires toward poetry and becomes figurative.

EXERCISE: *Seeing the Logic of Open Form Verse,* page 792

E. E. Cummings, IN JUST-, page 792

Cummings's poem is one of his "Chansons Innocentes," little songs for children. In it, however, we meet a poet who is familiar with the classics and who naturally associates spring with goat-footed Pan. In Greek mythology, the god's pipes heralded the return of Persephone, and caused birds and beasts to start up at his call. In Cummings's view, he seems a kind of Pied Piper who brings children running.

Line-breaks and capital letters in the poem seem designed to emphasize particulars. *Just-spring,* capitalized, is the name of a holiday: the moment when spring begins. Dividing its name with a line-break gives it more importance, perhaps; and *mud - / luscious* similarly takes emphasis. Why are the children's names telescoped (*eddieandbill, bettyandisbel*)? So that these names will be spoken rapidly, pell-mell, the way their owners run and the way children speak about their friends. And when the lame balloonman completes his transformation into Pan, the word *goat-footed is* framed with white space on a line by itself. Except by putting it in capitals, the poet could hardly have thrown more weight on it.

Linda Pastan, JUMP CABLING, page 793

Pastan, in telling us of two cars, divides each line and builds separate columns of words. The last line, all one, fits the proposed action (that the two merge) to the words. Jump cabling we take to be a metaphor for coitus. (For a similar comparison, see E. E. Cummings's well-known "she being Brand / -new," in his *Complete Poems.*) The playful "Jump Cabling" is starkly different in tone from Pastan's "Ethics" (page 973); it was first published in an anthology of light verse, Robert Wallace's *Light Year '85* (Cleveland: Bits, 1984).

A. R. Ammons, THE CITY LIMITS, page 793

Notice that "The City Limits" consists of one extraordinarily long and intricate sentence. Ammons piles up a series of dependent clauses (all beginning with "When you consider") that only resolve themselves grammatically and logically with the *then* in stanza five—ultimately ending with the final word *praise.* "The City Limits" is an idiosyncratic contemporary nature poem, a song of praise to the light that illuminates creation.

Carole Satyamurti, I SHALL PAINT MY NAILS RED, page 794

Satyamurti's poem demonstrates that there are other means than meter for organizing poetic language. In this case, syntax gives the poem a linguistic structure as formal as a sonnet. One might also say the poem has another structure—that of a list, a common genre but not one we usually associate with poetry (though we can upgrade it into the venerable literary device of the *catalogue*, like Homer's catalogue of Greek ships in *The Iliad*). Notice that Satyamurti's lines are grammatically incomplete, unless we read them in conjunction with the title.

All this formal discussion shouldn't blind us, however, to Satyamurti's provocative content. "I Shall Paint My Nails Red" does something that poetry should: it makes us think deeply about part of our everyday world. It asks questions about something we might otherwise take for granted.

Alice Fulton, WHAT I LIKE, page 794

As Fulton observes, the word *friend* contains an *end*, but this poem does not have an ending—at least in the traditional sense. Fulton's poem, however, belongs to a newer tradition of modern art that denies closure. By refusing to answer her own leading statement ("What I like about you," which is also, in part, the poem's title), Fulton forces us to answer the question. We have only two alternatives; we can either fill in the blank with our own notions or we can—and this alternative has more critical forces—say that Fulton has already answered the question in the lines that lead up to the final sentence fragment. Fulton forces us then, in a manner of speaking, to reread the poem backwards.

Notice that the poem has fourteen lines—surely no accident—and that it is chock full of rimes. Fulton intends "What I Like" to be a post-modem sonnet.

Charles Olson, LA CHUTE, page 795

Charles Olson's "La Chute," like "in Just-," can be effective even if merely heard aloud. So many times repeated, the words *drum* and *lute* acquire impressive emphasis; and by repeating phrases and hesitating *(who / will bring it up, my lute / who will bring it up where it fell)*, Olson makes his poem unrehearsed and conversational. White space seems used somewhat cryptically and arbitrarily, but it does throw great weight on *my lute* (line 7) and *They* (line 10), essential words that can take the emphasis. What is the poem saying? We take it to be (like "Gesture") a poem about poetry, with lute and drum representing the poet's talents. Well aware that he was a forefather of a poetic school (the Black Mountain poets), Olson may have foreseen his death and wondered who would carry on his work for him.

24 Symbol

T. S. Eliot, THE BOSTON EVENING TRANSCRIPT, page 797

To help a class see the humor of Eliot's poem, try reading it aloud and pronouncing the name of the newspaper slowly and deliberately, in the dullest tones you can muster. This small gem can serve effectively to introduce an early, longer Eliot poem of spiritual desolation, "The Love Song of J. Alfred Prufrock" (page 916).

Emily Dickinson, THE LIGHTNING IS A YELLOW FORK, page 798

Perhaps the poet would have added more punctuation to this poem had she worked longer on it; a rough penciled draft is its only surviving manuscript. Students may ask, Isn't the fork a symbol? No, it is the other half of a metaphor: what the lightning is like. The lightning (like most literary symbols) is a physical thing or event, reportedly seen. The Apparatus of the Dark (neither fork nor lightning) is whatever dimly glimpsed furniture this cosmic house may hold. The fork seems too simple an instrument to deserve the name of Apparatus. The lightning is doing the revealing, not itself being revealed.

Thomas Hardy, NEUTRAL TONES, page 800

Students usually like to sort out the poem's white, gray washed-out, and ashy things. Can anyone think of a more awful description of a smile than that in lines 9–10? The God in line 2 seems angry and awe-inspiring. He has chided or reproved the sun, and caused it to turn pale in fear (like a schoolboy before a stern headmaster).

Line 8 is a stickler. In Hardy's first draft it read, "On which was more wrecked by our love." Both versions of the line seem awkward, and the present version is obscure, but probably the sense of this and the previous line goes: we exchanged a few words about the question, Which one of us had lost (suffered) the more by our love affair? (That is, after *which* we should mentally insert "of the two of us.")

For speculation about the facts behind "Neutral Tones," see Robert Gittings's fine biography *Young Thomas Hardy* (Boston: Little Brown, 1975) 86–93. Much has been guessed about the possible love affair between young Hardy and his cousin Tryphena Sparks; but if the woman in "Neutral Tones" was indeed real, no one has identified her for sure.

Similar in imagery to "Neutral Tones" is this horrific line from Hardy's novel *The Woodlanders*, chapter 4, when a poverty-stricken woman, Marty South, sees her last hopes expire: "The bleared white visage of a sunless winter day emerged like a deadborn child" (cited by F. B. Pinion in *A Commentary on the Poems of Thomas Hardy* [New York: Barnes, 1977]).

Matthew 13:24—30, THE PARABLE OF THE GOOD SEED, page 801

George Herbert, REDEMPTION, page 802

The old burdensome lease that the speaker longs to cancel is original sin, which Christ, by his sacrifice (lines 12–14) allows humankind to throw off. Who is the speaker? Humanity—or perhaps (like Bunyan's Pilgrim) an individual soul in search of salvation.

What figure of speech is "a ragged noise"? (It's like the "Blue—uncertain stumbling buzz" of the Emily Dickinson poem discussed below.)

Emily Dickinson, I HEARD A FLY BUZZ—WHEN I DIED, page 802

Plump with suggestions, this celebrated fly well demonstrates a symbol's indefiniteness. The fly appears in the room—on time, like the Angel of Death—and yet it is decidedly ordinary. A final visitor from the natural world, it brings to mind an assortment of suggestions, some offensive (filth, stenches, rotting meat, offal, and so forth). But a natural fly is a minor annoyance; and so is death, if one is certain of Eternity. Unsure and hesitant in its flight, the fly buzzes as though faltering. It is another failing thing, like the light that comes through the windows and through the eyes (which are, as a trite phrase calls them, "the windows of the soul"). For other transferred epithets (like "Blue-uncertain stumbling Buzz"), see page 688 of the text, in the chapter on figures of speech.

Most students will easily identify "Eyes around" as those of surrounding friends or relatives, and "that last Onset" as death throes. Is "the King" Death or Jesus? It seems more likely that the friends and relatives will behold death. What is the speaker's assignable portion? Physical things: keepsakes bequeathed to friends and relatives; body, to the earth.

Discussion will probably focus on the final line. It may help students to remember that the speaker is, at the present moment of the poem, in Eternity. The scene she describes is therefore a vision within a vision. Perhaps all the last line means is (as John Ciardi has argued), "And then there was no more of me, and nothing to see with." But the last line suddenly thrusts the speaker to Heaven. For one terrible moment she finds herself, with immortal eyes, looking back through her mortal eyes at a blackness where there used to be light.

Robert Frost, THE ROAD NOT TAKEN, page 803

Stanley Burnshaw writes, in *Robert Frost Himself* (New York: Braziller, 1986), that Frost often said "The Road Not Taken" was about himself combined with Edward Thomas, a Welsh poet and good friend. Knowing this, Burnshaw confessed, didn't contribute much to his understanding of the poem. Still, the story is tantalizing. In *Robert Frost: The Years of Triumph* (New York: Holt, 1970) biographer Lawrance Thompson tells about the "excruciations through which this dour Welshman [Thomas] went each time he was required to make a choice." This amused Frost, who once said to Thomas, "No matter which road you take, you'll always sigh, and wish you'd taken another." "The Road Not Taken" (originally called "Two Roads") was apparently written to poke quiet fun at this failing. When Frost sent the poem in a letter to Thomas, the Welshman apparently missed the joke. He assumed, as have many readers since, that the speaker in the poem was Frost himself. Disappointed, Frost (according to Thompson) "could never bear to tell the truth about the failure of this lyric to perform as he intended it."

Despite the ambiguity that surrounds the poet's intent, the poem succeeds. The two roads are aptly symbolic of the choices we have to make almost every day of our lives. Still, perhaps the poem's essential playfulness is evident in the dramatic "sigh" with which the speaker expects some day to talk about his choice, and in the portentousness of the last line, which seems a bit exaggerated considering that the two roads were "really about the same."

A hard-working introduction to symbolism in poetry is that of Paul Hawkes, of East Stroudsburg University. In a published article, he describes his classroom version of the

TV game show "Family Feud," in which teams of students try to guess which meanings of certain symbols have occurred to most of the class. His aim is to show that a symbol, which may have widely familiar and traditional associations, can mean more or less the same to everyone; its meanings aren't the property of one reader alone. Then, to put this insight to use, he takes up "The Road Not Taken."

"I use this poem," he explains, "because it is simple and straightforward, offering little resistance to any student I may ask to summarize the paraphrasable content of the poem." He asks, "What statements in the poem, what choices of diction, suggest that the two roads are to be understood as something more than literal paths in the woods?" And students tend to reply, "A person wouldn't 'sigh' about a choice made years ago unless it was important," or, "The speaker wouldn't regret it 'ages hence' if it were only a path," or, "Why else would he say the decision 'has made all the difference' unless that decision were life-changing?" (We're paraphrasing and condensing Mr. Hawkes's examples.)

Someone will usually guess that the choice of roads suggests Frost's personal choice of careers: Should he or should he not become a poet? Mr. Hawkes then encourages the class to speculate on other possible life choices: marriage, children, a job, relocation. Perhaps this poem is about decision-making; perhaps the nature of the roads need not be specified. As in *Pilgrim's Progress*, a road or a journey on it is a traditional and conventional symbol for life; a fork or crossroads, a decision or turning-point. "The poem," he concludes, "suggests regret not for the way life has turned out but for the severe limitations life imposes on our desire to explore its possibilities." (See "Fire, Flag, Feud, and Frost: Teaching the Interpretation of Symbols," *Exercise Exchange* [Spring 1991] 6–11.)

Christina Rossetti, UPHILL, page 804

This allegorical poem develops a conventional simile: life is like a journey (shades of *Pilgrim's Progress!*). The road is the path of life; the day, a lifespan; the inn at the end of the road, the grave; other wayfarers, the dead; the door, the mouth of the grave (or perhaps the gate of Heaven); the beds, cold clay (or perhaps Heavenly rest). The title suggests another familiar notion: that life is a struggle all the way.

One possible way to paraphrase line 14: "You'll find the end result of your lifelong strivings: namely, death, and the comfort of extinction." A more happily Christian paraphrase is possible, for Rossetti professed herself a believer: "Your labor shall bring you to your goal, the sight of the Lord." Without admitting the possibility of such a faith, the poem will seem grimmer and more cynical than it is.

Do these two characters seem individuals? Not in the least. This is a straight question-and-answer poem, a dialogue between two stick figures.

"Oh No" (page 610) seems another poem about where you arrive when you die. Creeley, we suspect, kids a conventional notion of Heaven: he makes it a smug, artificial place where the saved sit around smirking at one another.

Gjertrud Schnackenberg, SIGNS, page 805

Signs, in the poet's sense of the word, seem plain indicators of approaching doom, hardship, or loss. In the opening stanza, lines in a hand await a palm reader's interpretation. Students should have little trouble seeing what the other signs foretell.

We wouldn't call these items symbols: their meanings seem too specific and obvious. Dickinson's fly carries a larger cargo of suggestions. (This comparison is not meant to put down "Signs," a poem with a different purpose.)

EXERCISE: *Symbol Hunting,* page 805

Hugo Williams, KITES, page 805

The central symbol of this poem gets at an interesting psychological observation—how often people look at their "lives" as something outside themselves, as something, for example, residing in the future or with a family group. Williams imagines that "our lives" are kites (memorably described as "white specks with faces/Running against the blue"). At first, the metaphor seems playful, but as the lives unravel, the frightening aspect of the symbol becomes apparent.

William Carlos Williams, POEM, page 806

Lorine Niedecker, POPCORN-CAN COVER, page 806

Wallace Stevens, ANECDOTE OF THE JAR, page 806

"Poem" should be taken literally; "Anecdote of the Jar" contains a central symbol. "Popcorn-can cover" uses literal language in a manner reminiscent of Williams, but the title image of the popcorn-can cover screwed to the wall can be taken as a symbol of the house dweller's poverty and pragmatism. Niedecker does not force the symbolism of the image, but it is there for our notice.

Students familiar with Stevens sometimes reason, "The jar is a thing of the imagination, that's why it's superior to the wilderness—it makes order out of formless nature, the way Stevens thinks art is supposed to do." But Stevens is constantly warning us of the dangers of mind divorced from the physical world, and we think he means this gray, bare, dominion-taking jar to be ominous. Who could think a wilderness *slovenly* before it came along? Some critics take the phrase *of a port in air* to mean a portal, "an evanescent entry . . . to order in a scene of disorder" (Ronald Sukenick, *Wallace Stevens: Musing the Obscure* [New York: New York UP, 1967]). We read it differently: *portly,* imposing, pompous. Although it is true that Stevens frequently raises the same philosophic or aesthetic questions, from poem to poem he keeps supplying very different answers. See the brilliant essay on Stevens by J. Hillis Miller in *Poets of Reality* (Cambridge: Harvard UP, 1965).

Jerald Bullis has written an intriguing poem in response to "Anecdote of the Jar." Thanks to Peter A. Fritzell of Lawrence University for discovering it.

BUCK IT

Take a shot-up bucket in a swale of woods—
For years "things" have been adjusting to it:
The deer have had to warp their whylom way
Through the fern to honor the order in their blood
That says not to kick it; the visiting woodcock

Probably take it for some kind of newfangled stump,
And doubtless welcome any addition that offers
Additional cover—especially if its imposition
Provides a shelving stay for worm-rich mulch;
A rivulet of breeze low-eddying the swale

Breaks around it much the way a stress's
Flow gets an increment of curvature
From encounter with an old Singer
Sewing machine; the ferns thereabout have turned
A bit more plagiotropic; if it's upright

And the lid's off it's an urn for leaves, bark-bits,
Bird droppings; but in the scope of the whole
Forty-acre woodpatch is it likely
To take dominion everywhere? no more
Than a barbed-wire tangle of words or a good jar.

25   *Myth and Narrative*

This chapter has been greatly revised in the current edition to make it more accessible to students. Although the chapter still begins with a discussion of what constitutes myth, there is now an attempt to relate the idea of myth to students' experience with popular culture, especially movies and television. This shift may initially annoy some instructors, but we hope that, if they stick with the chapter, they will discover that we have tried to show how similar myths permeate popular and literary culture. We want to make the material of this chapter less threatening to beginning students while still useful to instructors excited by the prospect of teaching Lawrence, Yeats, and Wordsworth.

Besides the poems in this chapter, other poems in the text will readily lend themselves to the study of myth and its pervasiveness in literature.

The story of Adam and Eve figure prominently in the new chapter (Frost's "Nothing Gold Can Stay" and Hope's "Imperial Adam"). Instructors might supplement those poems with Anthony Hecht's "Adam" (in Poems for Further Reading) and William Blake's "Jerusalem," which can also be used to illustrate personal myth.

Personal myths may be found in the poems of Blake; in Hardy's "Convergence of the Twain" (page 927); and in certain poems of Yeats outside this chapter, such as "Leda and the Swan" (page 728) and "Sailing to Byzantium" (page 866).

Poems containing central references to familiar classical myths are Cummings's "in Just-" (page 792), with its reincarnation of the Great God Pan; and Allen Ginsberg's "A Supermarket in California" (page 923). Christian mythos is of course inseparable from the devotional poems of Donne and Herbert; from Hopkins's poems and G. K. Chesterton's "The Donkey" (page 906); from Eliot's "Journey of the Magi" (page 914) and Yeats's "The Magi" (page 1021); from Paul Zimmer's "The Day Zimmer Lost Religion" (page 608); from Milton's sonnet on his blindness and from many more.

In this chapter, Thomas Hardy (in "The Oxen") and William Wordsworth (in "The World Is Too Much with Us") sadly contemplate myths in decline—a theme found also in William Stafford's "At the Klamath Berry Festival" (page 998).

Robert Frost, NOTHING GOLD CAN STAY, page 810

Many of your students may already be familiar with this popular poem. The relevant detail of the poem in this context is how much narrower its meaning would be if the reference to Eden were dropped. This single mythic allusion expands the resonance of the poem from the transience of spring's beauty to the transience of all perfection.

In his excellent study, *Robert Frost: A Literary Life Reconsidered* (reissued with a new preface in 1993 by the University Press of New England), William Pritchard savors the poem's remarkable compression in the following way:

> The poem is striking for the way it combines the easy delicacy of "Her early leaf's a flower" with monumentalities about Eden and the transient fading of all such golden things, all stated in a manner that feels inevitable. It is as if in writing "Nothing Gold Can Stay," Frost had in mind his later definition of poetry as a momentary stay against confusion. The poem's last word proclaims the momentariness of the "gold" that things like flowers and Eden, dawn and poems share. So the shortness of the poem is also expressive of its sense. (Quoted by permission of the author.)

D. H. Lawrence, BAVARIAN GENTIANS, page 811

Written in 1929 when Lawrence was ill and nearing death, this splendid poem has been read as a kind of testament. As Keith Sagar has paraphrased it, "the poet's soul has been invited to the nuptials and accepts with joy." Dissolution offers not mere oblivion but the promise of renewed life, the cyclical rebirth of both the gentians and Persephone. *(The Art of D. H. Lawrence* [Cambridge: Cambridge UP, 1966], 244–45.) Another famous poem of Lawrence's last months, "The Ship of Death," may be read as a companion to this.

Why is "Bavarian Gentians" a better title for the poem than Lawrence's first thought, "Glory of Darkness"?

Thomas Hardy, THE OXEN, page 812

The legend that farm animals kneel on Christmas Eve is widespread in Western Europe. Hardy takes it to suggest the entire Christian mythos, which "in these years" (since Darwin) few embrace as did the "flock" of children and old people remembered in the opening stanza. The *gloom* in line 15 may resemble the gloom of the unbeliever, and its doleful sound is enforced by its riming with *coomb*—like *barton,* a word from older rural speech.

The tone of "The Oxen" is not hostility toward faith, but wistfulness. Not exactly the village atheist Chesterton said he was, Hardy in late life kept going to church and hoping for a reconciliation between the Church of England and science-minded rationalists.

William Wordsworth, THE WORLD IS TOO MUCH WITH US, page 812

As its sense and its iambic meter indicate, the opening line calls for a full stress on the *with.*

Wordsworth isn't arguing, of course, for a return to pagan nature worship. Rather like Gerard Manley Hopkins's blasting tirade in "God's Grandeur" (page 729), he is dismayed that Christians, given to business and banking, have lost sight of sea and vernal woods. They should pay less heed to the world, more to the earth. What "powers" have they laid waste? The ability to open themselves to nature's benevolent inspirations. Modestly, the poet includes himself in the *us* who deserve reproof. The impatient outburst ("Great God!") is startlingly unbookish and locates the break in sense between octave and sestet in an unconventional place.

Compare Wordsworth's "Composed upon Westminster Bridge" (page 1016) for a somewhat similar theme. For another comment on the decline of certain traditional myths, see William Stafford's "At the Klamath Berry Festival" (page 998).

PERSONAL MYTH

William Butler Yeats, THE SECOND COMING, page 813

The brief discussion in the book leaves several points untouched. Students may be asked to explain Yeats's opening image of the falcon and the falconer; to discuss the meaning of the *Blood-dimmed tide* and the *ceremony of innocence;* to explain how the rocking cradle at Bethlehem can be said to "vex" twenty centuries to nightmare; and to recall what they know about the sphinx.

In *A Vision,* Yeats sets forth his notion of the two eras of history (old and new) as two intertwined conelike gyres, revolving inside each other in opposing directions. He puts it succinctly in a note for a limited edition of his poem *Michael Robartes and the Dancer* (1921):

213

The end of an age, which always receives the revelation of the character of the next age, is represented by the coming of one gyre to its place of greatest expansion and of the other to that of its greatest contraction. At the present moment the life gyre is sweeping outward, unlike that before the birth of Christ which was narrowing, and has almost reached its greatest expansion. The revelation which approaches will however take its character from the contrary movement of the interior gyre.

Students can be asked to apply this explanation to "The Second Coming." (In fact, this might be a writing assignment.)

For other evidence of Yeats's personal mythology, direct students to "Leda and the Swan" (page 728) and "Sailing to Byzantium" (page 866). For alternative versions of "The Second Coming," see Yeats's worksheets for the poem as transcribed by John Stallworthy in *Between the Lines: Yeats's Poetry in the Making* (Oxford: Oxford UP, 1963).

Dick Allen, NIGHT DRIVING, page 815

Perhaps we are all, in a sense, night driving—making our way dimly through life buoyed up and kept going by myths old and new, "all the lies / Not really lies." Is this what Allen's poem is about? It can of course be taken literally. The speaker, tired, drives at night from Bridgeport and remembers how his father used to say that the lights of the other cars on the road were cats' eyes. Somehow it gives him pleasure, at least for a while, to contemplate the "images which make / The world come closer, cats' eyes up ahead."

Dick Allen, who teaches at the University of Bridgeport, included this poem in *Flight and Pursuit* (Louisiana State UP, 1987).

Frances Cornford, ALL SOULS' NIGHT, page 815

Cornford's poem combines personal and Christian *mythos*. She takes the Christian feast of All Souls', when one should pray for the well-being of the dead who have not yet found their eternal resting place in Heaven or Hell, and projects her own private purgatory into the scene. The short poem is both a ghost story and a romance.

A question to ask students is why (in line 5) the lover (don't necessarily identify it as a ghost) does not find the speaker as "strange or older." Analyzing that line will unlock the meaning of the entire poem.

MYTH AND POPULAR CULTURE

Charles Martin, TAKEN UP, page 816

"Taken Up" illustrates how a good poet can borrow potentially hackneyed material from popular culture and, by linking it to the underlying myth, can transform it into genuine poetry.

Martin links the popular myth of flying saucers with the eternal human need for the divine. His golden aliens (whose bodies are so fine as to seem incorporeal) are almost godlike. What they offer the humans who waited for them is a version of heaven. (Notice that the aliens mention angels in factual terms; the spiritual and divine are real to them). The situation of the poem on a hill deliberately recalls the Transfiguration and Ascension episodes of the Gospels. The aliens are science fiction versions of angels— perhaps even gods.

One way to start a classroom discussion on the poem is to ask if anyone has seen

Spielberg's *Close Encounters of the Third Kind* and encourage someone to describe the film's ending. Then compare it to the poem and discuss from what mythic sources do they both draw their inspiration.

Edward Field, CURSE OF THE CAT WOMAN, page 817

Edward Field has done several delightful movie poems, including versions of "Franken-stein" and "Bride of Frankenstein." His method is generally to retell the film's story quite faithfully while playing with the tone and imagery to make a wry commentary on its themes. His approach is classically "campy" in that he pokes fun at the sentimentality and melodrama of these old films while obviously adoring their excesses.

This poem might be compared by students to James Wright's "Saint Judas" (page 634). Both poems are short narratives in which the title character achieves redemption. In Wright's poem, however, we see Judas redeem his soul with an act of charity to an injured stranger. The dying Cat Woman, however, achieves a more Hollywood salvation; her love for the man in the poem saves her soul. Field revels in this sentimental ending while slyly underscoring its silliness. By translating a popular medium like film into the verbal medium of poetry, he exposes the delightful illogic of the original.

A. D. Hope, IMPERIAL ADAM, page 819

Alec Derwent Hope is one of the few indisputably great Australian writers. Australians themselves, however, are usually of two minds about their elder poetic statesman: they are dazzled by his virtuosity but openly upset that their first great poet of international repute wrote polished formal poems on universal themes rather than celebrating the roughneck, local particulars of Down Under. Australia's dilemma, however, isn't ours, and we can approach Hope on his own terms without looking for Crocodile Dundee.

"Imperial Adam" is one of several poems in the volume on the story of Eden. Hope's poem focuses on Adam's discovery of Eve, and their mutual discovery of sex (with its consequence—children). The poem ends with a bitter irony: their first child is Cain, who will become the first murderer. The innocence of Adam and Eve's sexual awakening, described in its natural purity, is contrasted to life after their fall from grace.

Adam is "imperial," according to Hope, who wrote an essay on this poem ("The Practical Critic" in *The Cave and the Spring*, published by University of Chicago in 1970) because he was "the founder of the whole empire of man upon the earth." But Hope was also interested in the irony that originally Adam ruled Eden by himself.

Hope's attitude toward sex in this poem is interesting. The poem takes place before the fall, and the sex has the innocence of nature, but it also contains the seeds of Adam and Eve's ruin. The fifth stanza compares their sex to the serpent and the forbidden fruit, and, as the ending makes clear, the human race they engender will not keep the pastoral peace of Eden.

Hope claimed that this poem was "a *jeu d'esprit,* a way of having a little gentle fun with the ancient story," but critics have usually explored it for deeper psychological and theological meaning. In his essay, "The Practical Critic," Hope attacked three critics (all of them his friends) who found too much in the poem. And yet, as Hope admitted, a poet may not be the best judge of his own poems, and there are deeper issues lurking in the poem than Hope admits. The challenge is to recognize them without pushing them too far.

Robert Darling of Keuka College has shared some of his experiences in teaching this poem (in a letter to DG):

Some of the more perceptive students in the class will usually remark about the shock of the last line and comment about how evil seems to follow out of what appeared innocent pleasure. Discussion can lead to what the poet and critic James McAuley termed the Manichean element in Hope, the sense of the world as a battleground between the forces of light and darkness, how sensual love spurs death and decay. Students will often see a parallel in the AIDS epidemic.

Probably the next step is a discussion of whether the poem builds toward the shock of the last line, or if the ultimate line is totally unprepared for in the rest of the poem. There are traces, especially in the description of Eve, that may prepare one for the poem's closing, but I try to give the students almost a free hand in seeking out whatever clues the poem offers about its eventual destination.

Anne Sexton, CINDERELLA, page 820

"Cinderella" was part of Sexton's fifth collection, *Transformations* (Boston: Houghton-Mifflin, 1971). This volume consisted of seventeen long poems that retold fairy tales in idiosyncratic versions. Although earlier poets like Auden and Jarrell had published revisionist fairy tale poems, Sexton's book proved extremely influential by claiming the fairy tale as the special territory of feminist poets. Some critics (as well as Sexton's editor, Paul Brooks) felt these poems represented a falling off from her more compressed earlier poetry (like "Her Kind" on page 607), and there is some truth in that criticism. But the poems have remarkable narrative energy and originality.

"Cinderella" begins like a lyric poem with a series of four rags to riches stories that seem gleaned from the tabloids. But just when it might seem that Sexton would wrap up her short poem, she leaps into an extended narrative. Her version of Cinderella is very close to the Perrault original, although she spices it up with contemporary images and large doses of irony, but, as the story comes to its conclusion, Sexton emphasizes the violent aspects of the original so that it overwhelms the romance. Then in the last stanza, Sexton resumes the original structure of the poem with a bitterly ironic version of "happily ever after."

To use an overworked word, Sexton "deconstructs" the happy ending of a fairy tale; marriage, in her view, is no solution to Cinderella's problems, just the beginning of new ones.

216

This chapter is entirely new. "Poetry and Personal Identity" provides students with an introduction to the ways in which a poet's race, gender, cultural background, age, and other factors influence his or her writing. The chapter explores the different ways that poets have defined their personal, social, sexual, and ethnic identities. It also examines the problematic relationship between the author and the poem.

The first section focuses on autobiography and explores the idea of "confessional" poetry. Having drilled students earlier in this book that poems cannot be read as direct autobiography, we are now relaxing a bit and letting them think about the tricky relationship between life and art. This issue usually generates lively classroom discussion. The challenge will be to keep the discussions on track by focusing on the specific text under examination.

With Julia Alvarez's poem, we broaden the discussion by showing how autobiography includes issues of culture, age, and gender as well as purely individual experience. We then look at different approaches toward ethnic writing by contrasting two important African-American poems by Claude McKay and Langston Hughes. With Samuel Menashe and Francisco X. Alarcón we see poems about Jewish and Mexican-American identity.

Anne Stevenson's short poem, "Sous Entendu," focuses on gender in terms that students should understand from their everyday life, while Adrienne Rich's poem explores it in more general, archetypal terms. Yusef Komunyakaa's powerful Vietnam poem raises questions of identity that transcend racial categories; he is a black veteran, but he seems to speak for all Vietnam vets without losing his personal identity (reflected in the Vietnam Memorial's black stone). With Donald Justice's striking "Men at Forty," we begin looking at issues of age; these questions are explored—with merciless honesty—in Philip Larkin's "Aubade," a poem that will disturb everyone. Andrew Hudgins's poem explores both religion and the gap between generations. Shirley Geok-lin Lim's poem dramatizes the situation of the immigrant (in this case Chinese) caught between cultures but still rooted in the past. Alberto Ríos's poem explores how geography plays a role in our view of the world.

Sylvia Plath, LADY LAZARUS, page 825

This poem was written over seven days in late October, 1962 (about two weeks after the composition of "Daddy" in the Poems for Further Reading section). On February 11, 1963, Plath committed suicide by putting her head in a gas oven.

In her 1989 biography of Plath, *Bitter Fame,* Anne Stevenson described "Lady Lazarus" as a "merciless" self-projection of the author who cast herself as "the central figure of her mythic world." Stevenson continues about several of the poems written that final October:

> "The poems are extraordinary *performances*—not only in their consummate poetic skill, but in that their central figure is giving a performance as though before a single quelled spectator or in a fairground . . ."

Stevenson concludes:

"These poems, penetrating the furthest reaches of disdain and rage, are bereft of all normal 'human' feeling. Hurt has hardened to hate, and death is omnipresent."

Surely the dark anger and aching death-wish is tangible in "Lady Lazarus." This poem is spoken by a voice beyond hope. If Plath is a performer, she performs only a script of her own merciless invention.

One stylistic note: "Lady Lazarus" (like "Daddy") is full of German tags. You might ask students why she uses German so much in these late poems. The Nazi connection will be easy for them to see, but it may be worthwhile to mention that Plath's father, Doctor Otto Plath (Ph.D. in entomology), was a German immigrant who spoke with a heavy accent. In other words, there is something to interest both formalist and biographical critics in this chilling, late poem.

Julia Alvarez, THE WOMEN ON MY MOTHER'S SIDE WERE KNOWN, page 828

This poem is discussed at some length in the text. Interested students (and instructors) are encouraged to look up this poem in its original context, a sequence of thirty-three sonnets written about Alvarez turning thirty-three, in her first book of poems, *The Homecoming* (New York: Grove, 1984). Alvarez is currently a professor of literature at Middlebury College. In 1992 she published a novel, *How the Garcia Girls Lost Their Accents* (Chapel Hill: Algonquin Books).

RACE AND ETHNICITY

Claude McKay, AMERICA, page 829

McKay was one of the first of many black American writers who immigrated from the West Indies. (Students might write an interesting comparison between McKay's sonnet and the later Caribbean poet Derek Walcott's "The Virgins" found in the Poems for Further Reading section). McKay was born in Jamaica in 1891 but emigrated to the U.S. in 1912. Although shaped by black experience, "America" reaches for—and indeed achieves—universality of expression; it articulates the frustrated dreams and overpowering desires of any young immigrant. The speaker in this poem defines himself not by his ethnic identity but by his existential identity—as an outsider—in a heartless, if vital society.

Langston Hughes, THEME FOR ENGLISH B, page 831

This poem demonstrates how a great writer in his maturity can turn a routine homework assignment into a memorable piece of literature. If youth is wasted on the young, so perhaps are writing assignments.

Hughes is so convincing a storyteller that you will probably have to remind them—repeatedly—that this poem is not autobiographical. Hughes was not born in Winston-Salem, but in Joplin, Missouri. He did not go to school in Durham, but in Lawrence, Kansas and Cleveland, Ohio. He did attend Columbia (where, by implication, the poem takes place), but left after a year to travel. (He later completed his college education at Lincoln University in Pennsylvania.) He was nearly fifty when he wrote this poem, not twenty-two as the narrator is.

Samuel Menashe, THE SHRINE WHOSE SHAPE I AM, page 832

Menashe's poem defines Jewishness in a mystical biological way. "Breathed in flesh by shameless love," he was born from his parents' bodies, and his body contains the history of his people. "There is no Jerusalem but this" means, among other things, that his Jewishness is not found in a geographical place but in himself: his body is the lost temple ("the shrine") of his people, his bones the hills of Zion. This poem may seem difficult to students at first, but once they understand the central metaphor, they usually find it fascinating. A good place to start discussing the poem is its title, which contains the central idea.

Menashe's short, compressed poetry has been repeatedly praised by leading critics such as Stephen Spender, Donald Davie, Kathleen Raine, and Hugh Kenner, but it remains little known. Menashe lives in New York City barely above poverty level in a cold-water flat.

Francisco X. Alarcón, THE X IN MY NAME, page 833

Alarcón's poem is about the relation between one's name and one's identity. On a literal level, the X in Alarcón's name stands presumably as an abbreviation for Xavier, (a name that almost always identifies one as being of Catholic background and most commonly Hispanic descent, though many an Irishman bears it, too). But Alarcón sees the name as a symbol for the X an illiterate peasant must sign on the legal documents that control his or her life. Ultimately, Alarcón also implicitly uses the X (in a way perhaps influenced by Malcolm X) as an algebraic symbol for the elements of his identity lost or repressed in America.

Francisco X. Alarcón teaches at the University of California at Davis. He publishes poetry in both Spanish and English.

GENDER

Anne Stevenson, SOUS-ENTENDU, page 834

Students will have no trouble understanding the situation of this poem, but you may need to push them to explore the role of language between the two people. Not only does everything the people say (and don't say) have two meanings—one literal, the other sexual—but the words they speak metaphorically became part of the clothes they undress.

Song of Songs, AS THE APPLE TREE . . ., page 835

The King James Version of the Bible is probably the single most influential book in the English language. For over three centuries it has shaped our notion of literary English. Even the quintessential American poet, Walt Whitman, patterned his notion of our native speech from the English rhythms of this Jacobean translation.

The *Song of Songs* (sometimes called the *Song of Solomon*) is a unique book in the Bible: it is a book of love poems that celebrates the passion and sexuality of marriage. The beautiful poetry of this book has both fascinated and puzzled Biblical scholars for millennia. It seems written in a different voice from the rest of the Old Testament. As Marcia Falk points out in the preface to her powerful contemporary translation, *The Song of Songs* (San Francisco: HarperCollins, 1990), "For centuries, both Jewish and Christian traditions viewed the *Song* as a spiritual allegory, thus justifying its place in the biblical canon." They often ascribed the poems to King Solomon. More recently, scholars have explored its literal side—the celebration of sexual love within marriage.

Today scholars agree that it is unlikely that a single author wrote all of the poem or that the book represents a single, extended narrative. Marcia Falk, for instance, breaks the text into thirty-one separate poems. Feminist scholars, however, have added a new twist; they speculate that some of these authors were women. The poems' perspective, they argue, differs so dramatically from the rest of the Old Testament that it suggests a female authorship. (Such a theory incidentally would not contradict a religious notion of the Bible's divine authorship, since God works through human agents—male or female.)

It is an interesting class exercise to see how students read a text differently based on the assumptions of its author's gender. In this Biblical passage, for instance, do the images of flowers and fruits acquire a different resonance, if spoken by a woman entering marriage?

Yusef Komunyakaa, FACING IT, page 836

This powerful new poem requires little commentary. One feature of the poem requires special mention, since students may overlook it—the *entire* poem describes what the speaker sees on the polished black granite of the Vietnam Veteran's Memorial. What he witnesses there is the combination of the memorial itself and what the mirror-like stone reflects. *Reflection* (line 6) is, therefore, the key word in the poem, which the author uses in both senses, for, as the speaker studies the name on the stone, he reflects back on his wartime experience and flashes back to the death of a fellow soldier. The way the stone both mirrors and transforms the reality around it is the external symbol for the speaker's internal experience.

EXERCISE: *Donald Justice*, MEN AT FORTY, page 837
Adrienne Rich, WOMEN, page 838

As anyone who tries to translate the images and metaphors of either poem into the voice of the opposite gender discovers, these poems are both embedded in the sexual identity of the speaker. But the experiences they describe still speak to the opposite sex. The poems' structures do survive the translation, which demonstrates that good art can be both specific and universal.

FOR REVIEW AND FURTHER STUDY

Shirley Geok-lin Lim, TO LI PO, page 838

Lim's poem explores a common predicament of ethnic Americans: they have lost the language of their ancestors but still feel a deep identification with their family's native land. The last word in the poem—*kin*—is critical to understanding its message.

Lim was born and educated in Malacca, Malaysia, before coming to do a Ph.D. in English at Brandeis. For years she taught at Westchester Community College in New York. She is currently a professor at the University of California at Santa Barbara.

Alberto Ríos, SPRING IN THE ONLY PLACE SPRING WAS, page 839

Westerners will understand this poem immediately. Where we grow up determines our sense of time and the seasons. Those raised in the dry Southwest don't think of the spring (or summer) as lush, green seasons. This poem may be profitably compared to Dana Gioia's "California Hills in August" in the Poems for Further Reading section.

Andrew Hudgins, ELEGY FOR MY FATHER, WHO IS NOT DEAD, page 840

Hudgins's poem explores religious identity—and, by extension, a generation gap. He and his father see death differently. The father has a devout Christian's faith in an afterlife; the speaker, by contrast, is not sure. The son is not against his father's religion; he simply doesn't share its consolations.

Students can compare the father's vision of death in this poem with the bleak view of the speaker in Philip Larkin's "Aubade" at the end of the chapter.

Edna St. Vincent Millay, WELL, I HAVE LOST YOU . . ., page 840

It is a great pleasure to see Millay, one of the great neglected American poets of the century, coming back into fashion. Her work, romantic in tone and formal in style, stood at such an odd angle to the Modernist movement around her that critics often ignored or belittled her achievement. Now that Modernism itself is a historical style, the quality of Millay's work is more readily apparent (though some of us must confess we never stopped loving it). Likewise, her place in an interesting counter-tradition of female lyric poets of a formalist bent (such as Elinor Wylie, Louise Bogan, Elizabeth Bishop, and May Swenson) is also clearer in retrospect.

The relevant aspect of Millay's sonnet in this context is how intimate it feels, although she tells almost nothing specific about the failed love affair. For the record, the poem comes from Millay's sonnet sequence, *Fatal Interview* (1931), which Edmund Wilson called one of the great volumes of poetry of this century. The poems chronicle Millay's tempestuous affair with the poet George Dillon, who was fifteen years younger than her. Like most Millay's ex-lovers, he remained deeply attached to her for the rest of his life.

Those interested in reading more Millay should look up the recent *Selected Poems: The Centenary Edition* (New York: HarperCollins, 1992), edited by the British poet Colin Falck.

Philip Larkin, AUBADE, page 841

"Aubade" was the last substantial poem that Philip Larkin wrote. Except for a few minor short poems and occasional verses, he produced no more poetry in his remaining eight years. "I didn't abandon poetry," he later remarked, "it abandoned me." In this context, it's hard not to see "Aubade" as a kind of summing up and, if so, what a chilling summation.

"Aubade" is a confessional poem about old age and the fear of death. Larkin's poems often begin in observation and only move into a personal tone midway. "Aubade" begins with a surprising personal confession ("I work all day and get half drunk at night.") Waking alone in bed in the middle of the night, the speaker confronts his own mortality and discovers he has no defenses—neither philosophical ("No rational being/Can fear a thing it will not feel" he notes ironically) nor religious ("That vast moth-eaten musical brocade/created to pretend we never die.") Larkin sees death without any illusions and can barely survive the vision. Ultimately, he can only resolve to meet it when he must ("Death is no different whined at than withstood").

The British critic John Bayley sees Larkin's ability to confront this frightening subject so candidly in poetry as a kind of moral victory. Larkin, Bayley claims, "goes on to descant with an almost joyful eloquence on the fear of death and the terror of extinction. The fear is all too genuine but the fact of the poetry overcomes it."

Students may want to compare this poem to Andrew Hudgins's "Elegy For My Father, Who Is Not Dead." In Hudgins's poem, religious faith banishes the fear of death for the father. It would be hard to find a starker contrast in tone or images between the two visions of death.

27 *Alternatives*

TRANSLATIONS

Federico García Lorca, LA GUITARRA (GUITAR), page 844

The translator's liberty with Lorca's lines 23–24 seems well taken: "on the branch" would be weaker as a line by itself than "and the first dead bird on the branch."

Lorca's poem comes from his *Poema del cante Jondo* (1921), an early sequence of brief lyrics based on traditional folk music. The *cante jondo* ("deep song") was an Andalusian form related to *flamenco;* and in 1922 Lorca and composer Manuel de Falla organized a festival of the *cante jondo,* offering prizes for new songs in the old tradition.

Carl W. Cobb has suggested that the "Heart heavily wounded / by five sharp swords" is the guitar itself, struck by the player's five fingers (*Federico García Lorca* [New York: Twayne, 1967]).

Horace, CARPE DIEM ODE (ODES I, 11), page 845

Quintus Horatius Flaccus, whom we remember as Horace, was the son of a freed slave. Although his father was a poor man, he sacrificed a great deal to give his talented son an excellent education in Rome and Athens. Having served as a soldier on the losing side of the Roman civil wars, Horace returned to find his father dead and their small farm confiscated. He managed to find work as a minor financial clerk and gradually established his reputation as a poet. By the end of his life in 8 B.C. he was one of the most honored authors in the Roman empire. He has never lacked readers since.

This famous short ode created a tradition of lyrics we call *carpe diem* poems. Although later poets often use the *carpe diem* line to woo their reluctant lovers, Horace's original is more strictly philosophical. We do not know how long our lives will last, and death is inevitable, so let us enjoy the time we have. (Horace's clear-eyed stoic acceptance of death contrasts interestingly to Larkin's nihilistic terror in "Aubade" in the previous chapter.) Horace finds joy and meaning in life's uncertainty. No wonder it became the framework for later playful poems like Marvell's "To His Coy Mistress" or Herrick's "To the Virgins, to Make Much of Time."

Edwin Arlington Robinson, James Michie, John Frederick Nims, TRANSLATIONS FROM HORACE, pages 845–846

All three translations are excellent—but in different ways. The Robinson (done when he was barely out of school) is straightforward and classical in its approach. The Michie emphasizes the lyric and intimate elements of the Latin. Nims's version does something amazing: it recreates the original Latin meter in snappy conversational English.

Some of the best student poems ever seen by one of the editors of this anthology came from an assignment to "translate this poem into a contemporary American setting, preferably somewhere where you yourself have lived." (None of the students knew Latin, but worked with literal translation plus two poetic versions.) The results were outstanding, and the students were astounded at how many settings appeared to work equally well.

Omar Khayyam, RUBAI, page 847

The phonetic transcription of the Persian may confuse students slightly, if they study the rime scheme, since in this poem all four lines rime (rather than the usual aaba scheme).

But it seems worthwhile to let them study the original of the best-known rubai in English (and almost equally famous in Persian). You might point out to the class the poem's final word in Persian—*soltani*—a word that exists virtually unaltered in English as *sultan.*

Edward FitzGerald, Robert Graves and Omar Ali-Shah, Dick Davis, TRANSLATIONS FROM OMAR KHAYYAM, pages 847–848

FitzGerald's rubaiyat are so intoxicating that we couldn't resist including a few more at the end. But their music should not distract you entirely from Dick Davis's ingeniously faithful version, which even duplicates the original's quadruple rime. (Davis teaches Persian literature at Ohio State University and is a considerable poet in his own right.) By comparison, the Graves/Ali-Shah version seems stiff and unidiomatic.

EXERCISE: *Persian Versions,* page 848

PARODY

Ezra Pound, in his *ABC of Readings*, urges students of poetry to write parodies of any poems they find ridiculous, then submit their parodies to other students to be judged. "The gauging pupil should be asked to recognize what author is parodied. And whether the joke is on the parodied or the parodist. Whether the parody exposes a real defect, or merely makes use of an author's mechanism to expose a more trivial content."

Anonymous, WE FOUR LADS FROM LIVERPOOL ARE, page 849

The origin of this jingle among children who sang it on the streets of Edinburgh, about 1963 when the Beatles became popular, is attested by folklorist James T. R. Ritchie in *The Singing Street* (Edinburgh and London: Oliver & Boyd, 1964). Clearly, even Christmas carols are fair game to jejune British parodists. Another classic, current at the time of the abdication of Edward VIII in 1936, goes, "Hark, the herald angels sing: / Missus Simpson's pinched our king!"

Wendy Cope, from "FROM STRUGNELL'S *RUBAIYAT*", page 849

Wendy Cope has written about how her father would recite FitzGerald's *Rubaiyat* to his family. Loving the poems since childhood, Cope turned her considerable powers of parody to exorcising these resonant poems from her psyche. To parody the old song, "You always hurt the poems you love."

Jason Strugnell is an imaginary second-rate poet invented by Cope. Strugnell leaps on every fashionable and unfashionable bandwagon—thereby allowing Cope endless opportunities for parody. All of the FitzGerald originals parodied by Cope are found earlier in the translation section of this chapter.

Hugh Kingsmill, WHAT, STILL ALIVE AT TWENTY-TWO? page 850

Kingsmill's insistence on dying young suggests "To an Athlete Dying Young" (page 942), but the parodist grossly exaggerates Housman's hint of nihilism. Like bacon, Kingsmill's lad will be "cured"—of the disease of life. (And how often Housman himself says *lad* by the way.) His metaphysical conceit of ink and blotting pad coarsens Housman's usual view of night and day. (Some comparable Housman lines, from "Reveille": "Wake: the silver dusk returning / Up the beach of darkness brims, / And the ship of sunrise burning / Strands upon the eastern rims.")

Bruce Bennett, THE LADY SPEAKS AGAIN, page 851

Bennett's quatrain shows students a different use of parody. Bennett is not making fun of Emma Lazarus's sonnet (the original is found in "Evaluating a Poem''); instead, Bennett is using Lazarus's poem as a departure point for his own satire on how contemporary America has fallen short of the ideals articulated by Lazarus's democratic vision.

George Starbuck, MARGARET ARE YOU DRUG, page 851

"Margaret Are You Drug" is a deliberately crass, lowbrow, American version of Hopkins's "Spring and Fall" (page 939).

28 *Evaluating a Poem*

TELLING GOOD FROM BAD

Ezra Pound long argued for the value of bad poetry in pedagogy. In his *ABC of Reading*, Pound declared that literary education needs to concentrate on revealing what is sham, so that the student may be led to discover what is valid. It is a healthy gesture to let the student see that we don't believe everything contained in a textbook to be admirable. Begin with a poem or two so outrageously awful that the least sophisticated student hardly can take it seriously—some sentimental claptrap such as Cook's "The Old Arm-Chair." From these, you can proceed to subtler examples. It is a mistake to be too snide or too self-righteous toward bad poems, and it is well to quickly turn to some excellent poetry if the classroom starts smelling like a mortuary. There is a certain sadness inherent in much bad poetry; one can readily choke on it. As Allen Tate has said, the best attack upon the bad is the loving understanding of the good. The aim in teaching bad poetry has to be the admiration of good poetry, not the diffusion of mockery.

One further suggestion on bad poetry: a program of really execrable verse orated with straight faces by a few students and members of the faculty can be, with any luck, a fine occasion. For bad poems to work on besides those offered in this chapter, see the dustier stacks in a library of the following anthologies: *Heart Throbs* and *More Heart Throbs*, ed. Joe Mitchell Chapple (New York: Grosset, 1905 and 1911 respectively; many later editions); *The Stuffed Owl: An Anthology of Bad Verse*, ed. D. B. Wyndham Lewis and Charles Lee (London: Dent, 1930; reprinted in the United States by Capricorn paperbacks); *Nematodes in My Garden of Verse*, ed. Richard Walser (Winston-Salem: Blair, 1959); *Worst English Poets*, ed. Christopher Adams (London: Wingate, 1958); *Pegasus Descending: A Book of the Best Bad Verse*, ed. James Camp, X. J. Kennedy, and Keith Waldrop (New York: Macmillan, 1971); and *The Joy of Bad Verse*, ed. Nicholas T. Parsons (London: Collins, 1988).

Anonymous, O MOON, WHEN I GAZE ON THY BEAUTIFUL FACE, page 855

Glorious behind seems inexact, and so does *boundaries* for "boundlessness."

Grace Treasone, LIFE, page 856

Treasone's poem develops a central metaphor, but its language is wildly imprecise. Is the tooth "that cuts into your heart" one's own or somebody else's? (It is probable that the poet means not tooth but "toothache.") Anatomically, the image seems on a par with the "heart's leg" of the tradesman poet quoted by Coleridge. Through the murk of her expression, however, the poet makes clear her theme: the familiar and sentimental notion that life is really all right if you see it through (or have a competent dentist).

Treasone's item first adorned a Dover, New Jersey, newspaper column of local poets called "This Way to Parnassus."

Stephen Tropp, MY WIFE IS MY SHIRT, Page 856

To give this item the benefit of doubt, its metaphor is elaborated consistently but is hard to see anatomically. To compare the shirt-sleeves to the wife's armpits and the shirt's neck to her mouth, rather than to other parts of her, seems arbitrary. In a personification an inanimate object is seen as human. In "My Wife Is My Shirt" a person is seen as an inanimate object.

If this paraphrase of his idea is a fair one, Tropp does not get it across at all. The buttoning of the blood—a thoughty and ingenious figure—seems merely horrible. Tenderness is lost.

This poem appears in *Beat Coast East: An Anthology of Rebellion* (New York: Excelsior, 1960) and may be a relic of a kind of work once fashionable, in which the poet tries to turn off his feelings and to "play it cool." Whatever the poet's intentions, the result is bathetic. All we know about Tropp comes from a note in a poetry magazine that said he lived in New York and had a little boy named Tree.

Emily Dickinson, A DYING TIGER—MOANED FOR DRINK, page 856

This is not, by any stretch of critical imagination, a good poem. Besides the poet's innocent lack of perception that *His Mighty Balls* can suggest not eyeballs but testicles, the concluding statement (that the fact that the tiger was dead is to blame) seems an un-Dickinsonian failure of invention. Perhaps the poet intended a religious allegory (Christ the Tiger). Her capitalization of *He* in the last line doesn't seem sufficient proof of such intent, for her habits of capitalization cannot be trusted for consistency.

The failures of splendid poets are fascinating. As in this case, they often seem to result from some tremendous leap that sails over and beyond its object, causing the poet to crash to earth on the other side.

EXERCISE: *Ten Terrible Moments in Poetry,* page 857

J. Gordon Coogler, a printer by trade, was said to have displayed a sign in the window of his print-shop in Columbia, S.C.: "POEMS WRITTEN WHILE YOU WAIT."

For Byron's rousing lines, we have to thank Walter H. Bishop of Atlanta, for whom this discovery won first prize in a contest to find the worst lame verse by a well-known poet, conducted by John Shelton Reed in *Chronicles.* (The results were reported in the magazine's issue of November 1986.)

Mattie J. Peterson has attracted fierce partisans, some of whom see her battling Julia A. Moore for the crown of Queen of American Bad Verse. Richard Walser has brought out of a modern facsimile of her *Little Pansy, A Novel, and Miscellaneous Poetry* (originally 1890; Charlotte: McNally & Loftin, 1967).

Francis Saltus Saltus is the rediscovery of Nicholas T. Parsons in *The Joy of Bad Verse* (London: Collins, 1988). We lifted these two excerpts from Mr. Parsons's splendid anthology. It was a temptation to lift a third:

> Oh! such a past can not be mute,
>   Such bliss can not be crushed in sorrow,
> Although thou art a prostitute
>   And I am to be hanged tomorrow.

Saltus regarded himself as a rakehell. As C. T. Kindilien has observed, "Although he idealized cigarette-smoking women, looked for pornography in the Bible, and honored Baudelaire, Gerard de Nerval, and Le Marquis de Sade, he never escaped the tone of the boy who expected any moment to be caught smoking behind the barn" *(American Poetry in the Eighteen-Nineties,* Brown UP, 1956, 188-9).

Rod McKuen, THOUGHTS ON CAPITAL PUNISHMENT, page 859

William Stafford, TRAVELING THROUGH THE DARK, page 860

McKuen is still popular with some students, and any dogmatic attempt to blast him may be held against you. There may be value in such a confrontation, of course; or you can leave evaluation of these two works up to the class. Just work through McKuen's effusion and Stafford's fine poem, detail by detail, in a noncommittal way, and chances are good that Stafford will win the contest.

It may not be apparent that Stafford's poem is ordered by a rime scheme from beginning to end: *abcb* stanzas and a final couplet. Stafford avoids obvious rimes in favor of the off-rimes *road / dead* and *engine / listen* and the cutoff rimes *killing / belly, waiting / hesitated,* and *swerving / river*—this last a device found in some folk ballads. McKuen's poem announces an obvious rime scheme but fails to complete it. Unlike Stafford, he throws rime out the window in the end, with the effect that his poem stops with a painful inconclusiveness.

Stafford contributes a long comment on his poem to *Reading Modern Poetry: A Critical Introduction,* ed. Paul Engle and Warren Carrier (Glenview: Scott, 1968).

EXERCISE: *Fine or Shoddy Tenderness,* page 861

Julia A. Moore, LITTLE LIBBY, page 861

Bill Knott, POEM, page 862

Dabney Stuart, CRIB DEATH, page 862

Michael Harper, REUBEN, REUBEN, page 862

Ted Kooser, A CHILD'S GRAVE MARKER, page 863

One horrendously bad poem, followed by four good ones. All five poets tackle a difficult subject: the death of a child or young person, but only Julia Moore ("the Sweet Singer of Michigan") throws off restraint and wallows in a bath of emotion. Perhaps she is sincere, but apparently she has no idea that writing a powerful poem requires anything more than a wish to share a good cry. In truth, lines like "Her Savior called her, she had to go," and "While eating dinner, this dear little child / Was choked on a piece of beef" demonstrate an alarming insensitivity to audience (and to the sound of words). The poet's uncertain handling of rime and rhythm add to the ludicrousness.

Mrs. Moore was the author of *The Sentimental Songbook* (1876), which Mark Twain said he carried with him always. She may have inspired the portrait of poet Emmeline Grangerford and her elegies in *Huckleberry Finn.* Her rimes, though, could be surprising. Given the first three-and-a-half lines of this quatrain, how would you expect it to end? You might read it to the class, and ask them to guess how it finishes:

Many a man joined a club
That never drank a dram,
Those noble men were kind and brave,
They do not care——.

(Wrong. The last two words are "for slang.")

In Bill Knott's poem, on the other hand, freedom from artifice seems to help what is said: a direct, seemingly casual and yet playful statement of grief.

Dabney Stuart focuses quietly but powerfully on the dread which the living feel when they confront a child's death. Perhaps few students will notice that "Crib Death" is an acrostic (we didn't, until the poet pointed out this fact). In a letter to XJK, Stuart wrote, "The poem is particularly close to me since it . . . honors the daughter my wife lost 19 years or so ago. Not my child, as we are newly married (1983), but part of my grief nonetheless."

Michael Harper's poem alternates between direct and indirect treatment of the subject. He begins the poem by stating the subject in direct but abstract terms ("I reach from pain"). He then shifts into metaphors. His sudden shift into jazz may seem odd at first until one realizes that he sees jazz as a great art that was born out of suffering. Only at the end does the speaker specify the source of the pain ("we've lost a son.") Now we start to see the title in a different perspective; it is not only the name of an old folk song—it may also have been the name of the child dead at two days old. The specific metaphors that Harper uses in the poem ("brown berry") as well as the diction ("lovefruit") tell us that the child and the father are African-American, a detail which reinforces the power of jazz as the metaphor of art (and by implication the poem the author has just written with its verbal music) strong enough to bear such pain.

Ted Kooser imagines his way into a grief expressed seventy years ago. The speaker in his tender poem, moved by a clumsy but touching grave marker, acknowledges the love and longing that inspired it. The passage of time supplies the emotional distance necessary.

Wallace McRae, REINCARNATION, page 863

If any recent cowboy poem deserves the name of classic, it's "Reincarnation," probably the most widely recited work by one of the best-known poets of the cowboy school. McRae is a rancher from Forsyth, in eastern Montana, an area where his family settled five generations ago.

"Reincarnation" is no simple thing to evaluate. Its theme of the organic continuity of life seems straight out of *Hamlet:* "Thus may a king pass through the guts of a beggar." But the poem turns out to be a shaggy-dog meditation all leading up to an insulting joke: "Slim, you always were a horse's turd, and you still are." Still, most of us will probably enjoy being taken in. Perhaps we feel relief when a ponderous meditation on life and death turns into a mere comic kick-in-the-teeth.

The poem's language wavers inconsistently between plain speech and bookishness: "life's travails," "rendered mound," "yer vegetative bower." In retrospect, McRae's bookish, ornate phrasings may seem ironic, for apparently even the poet doesn't take them in earnest. They exist only to be punctured with a bang in the last line.

If you teach "Reincarnation," you might find it interesting to tell your students that Wallace McRae actually is a cowboy. He runs a cattle ranch in Montana.

Short of attending the annual Cowboy Poetry Gathering in Elko, Nevada (if you can get a room), the next-best introduction to the field may be two anthologies edited by Hal Cannon: *Cowboy Poetry* and *New Cowboy Poetry* (Salt Lake City: Peregrine Smith Books, 1985 and 1990). *American Cowboy Poetry,* published in Idaho, is a magazine whose motto might well be "Git along, little doggerel, git along." (We are grateful for some advice and a bibliography provided by Jim Hoy of Emporia State University.)

KNOWING EXCELLENCE

William Butler Yeats, SAILING TO BYZANTIUM, page 866

Has XJK implied that this poem is a masterpiece so far beyond reproach that no one in his right mind can find fault with it? That is, of course, not the truth. If the instructor wishes to provoke students to argument, he might read them the withering attack on Yeats's poem by Yvor Winters *(Forms of Discovery* [Chicago: Swallow, 1967] 215-16).

This attack really needs to be read in its entirety. Winters is wrong, we believe, but no one can begin to answer his hard-headed objections to the poem without being challenged and illuminated.

Other discussions of the poem, different from XJK's and also short, include Richard Ellmann's *Yeats: The Man and the Masks* (New York: Macmillan, 1949) and John Unterecker's in *A Reader's Guide to William Butler Yeats* (New York: Noonday, 1959). Those who wish to go deeper still and to read a searching examination (informed by study of Yeats's manuscripts) can be directed to Curtis Bradford, "Yeats's Byzantium Poems," *PMLA* 75 (Mar. 1960): 100-25. For those interested in alternatives, John Stallworthy reprints nearly all the legible manuscript versions in *Between the Lines: Yeats's Poetry in the Making* (Oxford: Clarendon, 1963) 87-112.

A deconstructionist reading of "Sailing to Byzantium," subjecting the poem to relentless questioning, showing where it fails to make sense and how it doesn't work, is offered by Lawrence I. Lipking in "The Practice of Theory" (in *Profession 83: Selected articles from the Bulletins of the Association of Departments of English and the Association of Departments of Foreign Languages,* MLA, 1983). But in his role as a poststructuralist, Lipking confesses himself "a sheep commissioned to say something sympathetic about wolves." He finds deconstructionist tactics offending his students, especially bright idealistic ones who expect their teachers to show them why certain works are great, and who wish poems to "make sense" and to relate to their own lives.

Jean Bauso has used a writing assignment to introduce this challenging poem. "I want you to pretend that you're an old person—someone in his or her eighties," she tells a class. "You've got arthritis, so buttoning or zipping your clothes is slow. Now you will write for ten minutes nonstop in the voice of this old person that you've made yourself into. You want to follow your person's stream of consciousness as he or she sits there thinking about the human condition, about the fact that we human beings have to die." After the students free-write for ten minutes, they read a few of the results, and she picks up on any comments about wishing for immortality. Then she asks for responses to the name Byzantium, perhaps holds up some pictures of the Santa Sophia mosaics. She then reads "Sailing to Byzantium" aloud, gives out reading sheets with points for reading it alone, and dismisses the class. For Bauso's detailed account of this lesson plan and her reading sheets, see "The Use of Free-Writing and Guided Writing to Make Students Amenable to Poems," *Exercise Exchange* (Spring 1988).

EXERCISE: *Two Poems to Compare,* page 868

Arthur Guiterman, ON THE VANITY OF EARTHLY GREATNESS, page 868

Percy Bysshe Shelley, OZYMANDIAS, page 869

The title of Guiterman's bagatelle playfully echoes that of a longer, more ambitious poem: Samuel Johnson's "The Vanity of Human Wishes." If Guiterman's achievement seems smaller than Shelley's "Ozymandias," still, it is flawless. "Ozymandias," although one of the monuments of English poetry, has a few cracks in it. Many readers find line 8 incomplete in sense: the heart that fed what, or fed on what? From its rime scheme, we might think the poem a would-be Italian sonnet that refused to work out.

Nevertheless, Shelley's vision stretches farther than Guiterman's. Ozymandias and his works are placed at an incredibly distant remove from us. The structure of the poem helps establish this remoteness: Ozymandias's words were dictated to the sculptor, then carved in stone, then read by a traveler, then told to the first-person speaker, then relayed to us. Ironies abound, more subtle than Guiterman's. A single work of art has outlasted Ozymandias's whole empire. Does that mean that works of art endure (as in "Not marble nor the gilded monuments")? No, this work of art itself has seen better days, and soon (we infer) the sands will finish covering it. Obviously, the king's proud boast has been deflated, and yet, in another sense, Ozymandias is right. The Mighty (or any traveler) may well despair for themselves and their own works, as they gaze on the wreckage of his one surviving project and realize that, cruel as Ozymandias may have been, time is even more remorseless.

What are the facts behind Shelley's poem? According to the Greek historian Diodorus Siculus, Ozymandias was apparently a grand, poeticized name claimed for himself by the Egyptian pharaoh Rameses II. Diodorus Siculus saw the king's ninety-foot-tall statue of himself, carved by the sculptor Memnon, in the first century B.C. when it was still standing at the Ramesseum in Thebes, a mortuary temple. Shelley and his friend Horatio Smith had read a description of the shattered statue in Richard Pococke's *Description of the East* (1742). Smith and Shelley wrote sonnets expressing their imagined views of the wreckage, both of which Leigh Hunt printed in his periodical *The Examiner* in 1818. This is Smith's effort, and students might care to compare it with Shelley's in quality:

> On a Stupendous Leg of Granite, Discovered
> Standing by Itself in the Deserts of Egypt
>
> In Egypt's sandy silence, all alone,
>   Stands a gigantic leg, which far off throws
>   The only shadow that the desert knows.
> 'I am great Ozymandias,' saith the stone,
>   'The king of kings: this mighty city shows
> The wonders of my hand.' The city's gone!—
>   Nought but the leg remaining to disclose
> The site of that forgotten Babylon.
>
> We wonder, and some hunter may express
> Wonder like ours, when through the wilderness,
>   Where London stood, holding the wolf in chase,
> He meets some fragment huge, and stops to guess
>   What powerful but unrecorded race
>   Once dwelt in that annihilated place.

For more background to the poem, see H. M. Richmond, "Ozymandias and the Travelers," *Keats-Shelley Journal* 11 (1962): 65–71.

William Shakespeare, MY MISTRESS' EYES ARE NOTHING LIKE THE SUN, page 869

Have students state positively each simile that Shakespeare states negatively, and they will make a fair catalog of trite Petrarchan imagery. Poking fun at such excessive flattery is a source of humor even today, as in an old wheeze: "Your teeth are like the stars—they come out at night."

Thomas Campion, THERE IS A GARDEN IN HER FACE, page 870

In tone, Campion's lyric is admiring and tender, and yet there are ironies in it. The street vendor's cry, as Walter R. Davis has pointed out, "undercuts, with its earthy commercialism, the high Petrarchan style of the rest of the song." In Campion's society, a girl of marriageable age was, in a sense, on sale to the highest bidder.

For Campion's music to his song—incorporating the set melody of the street cry "Cherry ripe, ripe, ripe!"—see Davis's edition of Campion's *Works* (New York: Doubleday, 1967). Campion has been called (by W. H. Auden) "the only man in English cultural history who was both a poet and a composer."

Some students, taking the figures of speech literally, may find the last stanza absurd or meaningless. They can be led to see that Campion's angels with bended bows enact his theme that the young girl's beauties are defended. Who defends them? She herself, by her nay-saying frowns and by her immaturity. Throughout the poem run hints of Eden. The garden, that *heav'nly paradise*, holds *sacred cherries*—forbidden fruit—and so the guardian angels seem traditional. John Hollander thinks the Petrarchan cliché of bowlike eyebrows "redeemed" by its new associations. "The courtly compliment now turns out to be found in beautiful sexual attainment, in the plucking of cherries that are not forbidden apples, and just for that reason, such attainment isn't always easy" (introduction to *Selected Songs of Thomas Campion* [Boston: Godine,] 973]).

Walt Whitman, O CAPTAIN! MY CAPTAIN! page 871

This formerly overrated poem is uncharacteristic of Whitman in its neatly shaped riming stanzas and in its monotonously swinging observation of iambic meter, so inappropriate to a somber elegy. The one indication that an excellent poet wrote it is the sudden shift of rhythm in the short lines that end each stanza—particularly in line 5, with the unexpected turning-on of heavy stresses: "Oh heart! heart! heart!"

Carl Sandburg, FOG, page 872

Like Pound's "In a Station of the Metro" (page 660), Sandburg's celebrated minipoem is all one metaphor, all imagery. Not closely detailed, it seems vague when set next to Eliot's agile fog-cat in "Prufrock" (page 916). Eliot can depict even fog without vagueness; evidently cats are right up his alley. Students also might enjoy a look at his *Old Possum's Book of Practical Cats.*

Thomas Gray, ELEGY WRITTEN IN A COUNTRY CHURCHYARD, page 873

Like other critics, students may disagree widely in their statements of Gray's theme. Roger Lonsdale (cited below) sees the main preoccupation of the poem to be "the desire to be remembered after death, a concern which draws together both rich and poor, making the splendid monuments and the 'frail memorials' equally pathetic." Concern with being remembered after death informs the Epitaph as well, making it seem intrinsic to the poem (despite Landor's objections). But Gray also seems to suggest that there is positive virtue in remaining little known.

About question 10: most students will readily see that Gray, Shelley, and Guiterman all state (however variously) a common theme—the paths of glory lead but to the grave. In ranking the three poems in order of excellence, however, they risk getting into a futile debate unless they can agree that (1) Guiterman's excellent comic poem need not be damned for not trying to be an elegy, and (2) Gray's poem is more deep-going, moving, musical, and ultimately more interesting in what it says than Guiterman's.

Of three stanzas found in the earliest surviving version of the poem (the Eton manuscript) and deleted from the published version of 1753, one has been much admired. It followed line 116, coming right before the Epitaph:

> There scatter'd oft, the earliest of the year,
> By hands unseen, are showers of violets found:
> The Red-breast loves to build, and warble there,
> And little footsteps lightly print the ground.

Topic for discussion: Should Gray have kept the stanza?

Topic for a paper of moderate (600- to 1,000-word) length: "Two Views of Anonymity: Gray's 'Elegy' and Auden's 'Unknown Citizen.'"

Kingsley Amis offers a view of the "Elegy" that may trigger discussion: he calls it "a great Rightie poem," and remarks, "No work of literature ever argued more persuasively that the poor and ignorant are better off as they are." (From a note in his *Amis Anthology: A Personal Choice of English Verse* [London: Hutchinson, 1988]). Lest students numbly accept this view and dismiss the poem, you might ask, Does Gray indeed argue in favor of poverty and ignorance? What qualities in the lives and characters of these poor and ill-schooled countryfolk *does* he praise?

Twentieth Century Interpretations of Gray's Elegy, ed. H. W. Starr (Englewood Cliffs: Prentice, 1968), is a convenient gathering of modern criticism. A good deal of earlier criticism is summarized by Roger Lonsdale in his edition of *The Poems of Gray, Collins, and Goldsmith* (New York: Norton, 1969), which provides extensive notes on texts and sources. For a modern poem at least partly inspired by the "Elegy," see Richard Wilbur's "In a Churchyard" in *Walking to Sleep* (New York: Harcourt, 1969). Among the countless parodies, there is an anonymous "Allergy in a Country Churchyard" that begins, "The kerchoo tolls, Nell's 'kerchief swats away."

EXERCISE: *Reevaluating Popular Classics,* page 877

Emma Lazarus, THE NEW COLOSSUS, page 878

Most Americans know at least a line or two of this famous sonnet carved on the pedestal of the Statue of Liberty, but surprisingly few can name the author of the poem. The poem and its author have vanished from most anthologies and textbooks. Yet Lazarus's sonnet seems that rare thing—a truly successful public poem. The images are clear and powerful, the language memorable, and the sonnet avoids the chief danger of public poetry—prolixity. The contrast between the original colossus of the ancient world, which represented might, and the new colossus, which represents freedom, is both an original and effective means of dramatizing the difference between the Old World of European despotism and the New World of American democracy, a popular theme of nineteenth-century patriotic poetry, but one rarely so well expressed.

Edgar Allan Poe, ANNABEL LEE, page 879

Students usually adore this poem. Most modern critics hate it. There is some truth in both camps.

Let's catalogue the faults of the poem first. The poem is sentimental: it asks the reader to be sad while reveling in the beauty of the sadness. The poem is also heavy-handed. When Poe gets a nice line or image going, he can't resist repeating it—more often for the sake of sound than sense. (These repetitions make most of the stanza patterns go awry.) The language is abstract and literary (angels, kingdom, highborn kinsmen, sepulcher, maiden, etc.). It may be unfair to say that these are not authentic *American* images, but, more to the point, the words seem borrowed from a book rather than observed from life.

And yet, with all its faults neatly noted, the poem remains weirdly beautiful. The very irregularity of the stanzas keeps the form of the poem subtly surprising, despite the bouncy anapestic meter. The abstract quality of the language used in this hypnotic meter—all drenched in emotion—eventually gives the poem a dreamlike reality. That placeless "kingdom by the sea" now begins to resemble the world of memory, and the poem lures us back into our own emotion-drenched childlike memories. (*"I* was a child and *she* was a child," as more than one psychological critic has noted, places the poem in a presexual stage; Annabel Lee is a bride only in the future tense.) The childlike innocence of the language and emotions somehow carry the poem into a sphere where adult critical concerns seem less relevant. "Annabel Lee" somehow marries the style and meter of light verse to the themes of elegiac, if not quite tragic, poetry. Whatever its faults, American poetry would be poorer without it.

When told we were including this poem in a new edition, one instructor (a highly regarded critic adept in literary theory) said "Be gentle. I love that poem. Critics keep showing me why it's awful, but I love it anyway." We hope she feels we've been gentle enough.

29   *What is Poetry?*

Robert Francis, CATCH, page 881

Putting a spin on his poem-ball, hurling high ones and sometimes grounders, the poet keeps the reader on his toes, yet sometimes provides an immediate reward. Most students, though they might paraphrase this poem indifferently, will find this much of Francis's comparison easy to pick up—although they might object that the reader doesn't get to hurl one back at the poet. And how does a poet "outwit the prosy?" Playing with swagger and style, the poet doesn't want to communicate in a dull, easily predictable way. A magician of the mound, he or she will do anything to surprise, to make poetry a high-order game in which both poet and reader take pleasure.

Anonymous, EDWARD, page 886

"Edward," with its surprise ending in the last line, is so neatly built that it is sometimes accused of not being a popular ballad at all, but the creation of a sophisticated poet, perhaps working from a popular story. Students might be asked to read the information about ballads in Chapter Nineteen, "Song," either before or after reading this ballad.

QUESTIONS FOR DISCUSSION:

1. In "Edward," why is the first line so effective as an opening? What expectations does it set up in the hearer's mind? How does the last line also display the skill of a master storyteller?

2. Reading a ballad such as "Edward" on the printed page, we notice that its refrains take up much room. Do you find this repetitiousness a hindrance to your enjoying the poem? Is there anything to be said in favor of the repetitiousness?

3. What is the value to the poem of the question-and-answer method of storytelling? ("Edward" proceeds like a courtroom cross-examination in which the mother, by pointed questioning, breaks down her son's story. Dramatically, the method is powerful, and it holds off until the very end the grimmest revelation.)

4. What else could the author of "Edward" conceivably have told us about this unhappy family? Do you find it troublesome that Edward and his mother behave as they do without our quite knowing why? Might the story have suffered if told by a storyteller who more deeply explored the characters' motivations?

Anonymous, THE THREE RAVENS, page 887

Anonymous, THE TWA CORBIES, page 889

QUESTIONS FOR DISCUSSION:

1. In "The Three Ravens," what is suggestive in the ravens and their conversation? How are the ravens opposed in the poem by the hawks and the hounds? (The ravens are selfish eaters of carrion, but the hawks and hounds are loyally standing guard over their dead master's body. Their faithfulness also suggests that of the fallow doe.)

2. Are you persuaded by Friedman's suggestion (quoted in the note under "The Three Ravens") that the doe is a woman who is under some enchantment? What other familiar fairy tales or stories of lovers transformed into animals do you recall?

3. Do you agree that "The Twa Corbies" is "a cynical variation of 'The Three Ravens,'" as it has been called? Compare the two poems in their comments on love and faithfulness.

4. For all the fantasy of "The Three Ravens," what details in the ballad seem realistic reflections of the natural world?

Anonymous, SUMER IS ICUMEN IN, page 889

If you are not an expert in Middle English pronunciation, ask a colleague who is to give you a briefing and take a stab at reading "Summer is icumen in" aloud to the class. Even the experts are only guessing (educatedly) how thirteenth-century English sounded, and your reading need do no more than suggest that the language has not always stood still.

This slight, exquisite, earthy song may be compared with Shakespeare's "When daisies pied," in which the song of the cuckoo suggests cuckoldry (as it doesn't in this innocent, humorless lyric).

For a parody, see Ezra Pound's "Ancient Music," beginning "Winter is icummen in," in his collection *Personae* (New York: New Directions, 1949), and in *Selected Poems* (from the same publisher, 1957).

Anonymous, WESTERN WIND, page 889

Originally a song for tenor voices, "Western Wind" probably was the work of some courtier in the reign of Henry VIII. Untouched by modernization, it reads (in its one surviving manuscript):

Westron wynde when wyll thow blow
the smalle rayne douune can rayne
Chryst yf my love wer in my armys
and I yn my bed agayne

This famous poem, according to contemporary poet Deborah Digges, "demands that we create a context for this speaker who is far from home, waiting, it would appear, for the weather to break so that he can return. Is he at sea? Is he lost on the landscape? Is he dying? The poem refuses to answer, lives only by its breath, its longing" ("Lyrics and Ballads of the 15th Century, *Poetry Pilot,* [monthly newsletter of the Academy of American Poets], January 1989, page 4).

QUESTIONS FOR DISCUSSION:

1. In reading the poem, how does it help to know that the moist, warm west wind of England brings rain and is a sign of spring?

2. What do the first pair of lines and the last pair have to do with each other?

3. Do you agree with a critic who suggested that the speaker is invoking Christ, asking for help in obtaining sex? "By a blasphemous implication Christ is in effect assigned the role of a fertility spirit" (F. W. Bateson, *English Poetry: A Critical Introduction* [London: Longmans, 1966]).

4. Consider another critic's view: the unhappy speaker is stressing his (or her) longing to go to bed with his (or her) loved one, and so the word *Christ* is an exclamation. (We prefer this view; see Arthur O. Lewis, Jr., writing in *The Explicator* 15 Feb. 1957: item 28.)

Anonymous, LAST WORDS OF THE PROPHET (NAVAJO MOUNTAIN CHANT), page 889

This valediction is part of the Mountain Chant of the Navajo translated by Washington Matthews, one of the pioneering linguistic anthropologists. His work helped broaden appreciation for the genius of Native American poetry. The Mountain Chants were performed by the Navajo under the direction of a shaman and contain many archaic words whose meaning was lost even to the priesthood.

Matthew Arnold, DOVER BEACH, page 890

Arnold and his family did such an efficient job of expunging the facts of his early romances that the genesis of "Dover Beach" is hard to know. Arnold may (or may not) have been in love with a French girl whom he called Marguerite, whose egotistic gaiety made her difficult. See Lionel Trilling's discussion of the poem and of Arnold's Marguerite poems in his biography *Matthew Arnold* (New York: Columbia UP, 1949). Marguerite, Trilling suspects, viewed the world as much more various, beautiful, and new than young Arnold did.

A sympathetic reading of "Dover Beach" might include some attention to the music of its assonance and alliteration, especially the *s*-sounds in the description of the tide (lines 12–14). Line 21 introduces the central metaphor, the Sea of Faith. Students will probably be helped by a few minutes of discussion of the historical background of the poem. Why, when the poem appeared in 1867, was religious faith under attack? Darwin, Herbert Spencer, and Victorian industrialism may be worth mention. Ignorant armies (line 37) are still with us. Arnold probably had in mind those involved in the Crimean War of 1853–56, perhaps also those in the American Civil War. For sources of the poem, see C. B. Tinker and H. F. Lowry, *The Poetry of Matthew Arnold* (New York: Oxford UP, 1940) 173–78.

A dour view of the poem is taken by Donald Hall in "Ah, Love, Let Us Be True" (*American Scholar*, Summer 1959). Hall finds "love invoked as a compensation for the losses that history has forced us to sustain," and adds, "I hope there are better reasons for fidelity than disillusion. . . . Like so many Victorian poems, its negation is beautiful and its affirmation repulsive." This comment can be used to provoke discussion. A useful counterfoil to "Dover Beach" is Anthony Hecht's satiric poem "The Dover Bitch," in his collection *The Hard Hours* (New York: Atheneum, 1960) and in many anthologies. For other critical comment, see William E. Cadbury, "Coming to Terms with 'Dover Beach,'" *Criticism* 8 (Spring 1966): 126–38, James Dickey, *Babel to Byzantium* (New York: Farrar, 1968) 235–38 (a good concise general essay); and A. Dwight Culler, *Imaginative Reason: The Poetry of Matthew Arnold* (New Haven: Yale UP, 1966).

Compare Hardy's attitude in "The Oxen" (page 812) with Arnold's wistful view of the Sea of Faith.

John Ashbery, AT NORTH FARM, page 891

It is never easy to decide what an Ashbery poem "means." This one is rich with suggestions about which students may be invited to speculate. Who is this threatening catlike "someone" for whom we set out milk at night and about whom we think "sometimes, / Sometimes and always, with mixed feelings?" Is it the Grim Reaper? And yet Death always knows where to find the person he's looking for. And what are we to make of lines 7–11? How can the granaries be "bursting with meal, / The sacks of meal piled to the rafters" if "Hardly anything grows here"? The poet hints at a terrible sterility underlying the visible abundance at North Farm. Perhaps the farm can be regarded as, among other things, a paradigm of the world, rich in material things but spiritually empty. But that is to reduce the poem to flat words. Because such paraphrases tend to slip from Ashbery's poems like seals from icebergs, this poet's work is a current favorite of critics. It challenges them to make subtler and stickier paraphrases.

Margaret Atwood, SIREN SONG, page 891

Atwood's "Siren Song" is a wonderfully tricky poem that seduces the reader as cleverly as it does its doomed listener. The reader doesn't realize that he or she has been taken in, until it is too late.

The poem is in three parts. The first section (lines 1-9) recounts the sirens and their deadly songs. Many readers will recognize the legendary monsters (half bird, half woman) from Box XII of the *Odyssey*. Their name has become synonymous for any dangerously alluring woman. The second section (lines 10-24) switches gears suddenly, as one of the sirens confesses to us her unhappy plight. She offers to tell us the secret of her irresistible song, but she mainly talks about herself and cries for our help. Then, without knowing it until too late, we are in the final section (the last three lines) in which we realize that we have been lured into the siren's emotional grasp.

Feminist poets have often retold famous myths and legends with a twist. Atwood's "Siren Song" is surely a model of this genre.

W. H. Auden, AS I WALKED OUT ONE EVENING, page 893

This literary ballad, with its stark contrast between the innocent song of the lover and the more knowing song of the clocks, affords opportunities to pay close attention to the poet's choice of words. Auden selects words rich in connotations: the *brimming* of the river (which suggests also the lover's feelings), the *crooked* neighbor (with its hint of dishonesty and corruption as well as the denotation of being warped or bent by Time, like the "diver's brilliant bow"). Figures of speech abound: the opening metaphor of the crowds like wheat (ripe and ready to be scythed by Time the Reaper), the lover's extended use of hyperbole in lines 9-20, the personifications of Time and Justice, the serious pun on *appalling* in line 34 (both awe-inspiring and like a pall or shroud, as in Blake's "London," page 652), the final reconciliation in metaphor between the original "brimming river" and the flow of passing Time. Auden's theme appears to be that as young lovers grow old, their innocent vision is smudged and begrimed by contact with realities—and yet "Life remains a blessing" after all.

The lover's huge promises in stanzas 3 and 4 ("I'll love you Till China and Africa meet . . .") have reminded Richard Wilbur of the hyperbolic boasts of the speaker in Burns's "Oh, my love is like a red, red rose" (page 695). Burns speaks for the romantic lover, wrapped in his own emotions, but Auden's view of romantic love is skeptical. "The poem then proceeds to rebut [the lover's] lines, saying that the human heart is too selfish and perverse to make such promises" *(Responses* [New York: Harcourt, 1976] 144).

This poem may appear to have too little action in it to resemble folk ballads in more than a few touches. Auden himself, according to Monroe K. Spears, did not call this a ballad but referred to it as "a pastiche of folk-song."

"As I Walked Out One Evening" is one of the "Five Lyrics" included in *W. H. Auden Reading* (Caedmon recording TC 1019). For comparison with the poet's own modest delivery, *Dylan Thomas Reading*, vol. 4 (Caedmon, TC 1061) offers a more dramatic rendition.

W. H. Auden, MUSÉE DES BEAUX ARTS, page 895

In Breughel's *Landscape with the Fall of Icarus* reproduced on page 895, students may need to have their attention directed to the legs disappearing in a splash, one quarter inch below the bow of the ship. One story (probably apocryphal) is that Breughel's patron had ordered a painting on a subject from mythology, but the artist had only this landscape painting completed. To fill the order quickly, Breughel touched in the little splash, gave the picture a mythological name, and sent it on its way. Question: How does that story (if true) make Breughel seem a shallower man than Auden thinks he is?

Besides the *Landscape,* Auden apparently has in mind two other paintings of Pieter Breughel the Elder: *The Census,* also called *The Numbering at Bethlehem* (Auden's lines 5–8), and *The Massacre of the Innocents* (lines 9–13). If the instructor has access to reproductions, these works might be worth bringing in; however, the *Landscape* seems central to the poem. This painting seems indebted to Ovid's *Metamorphoses,* but in Ovid the plowman, shepherd, and fisherman looked on the fall of Icarus with amazement. The title of Auden's poem, incidentally, is close to the name of the Brussels museum housing the *Landscape:* the Musées Royaux des Beaux Arts.

Edward Mendelson has remarked on the poem in *Early Auden* (New York: Viking, 1981):

> The poetic imagination that seeks out grandeur and sublimity could scarcely be bothered with those insignificant figures lost in the background or in the crowd. But Auden sees in them an example of Christianity's great and enduring transformation of classical rhetoric: its inversion of the principle that the most important subjects require the highest style. If the sufferings of a carpenter turned preacher mattered more to the world than the doom of princes, then the high style, for all its splendor, was a limited instrument. . . . These casually irregular lines make none of the demands for action and attention that marked Auden's earlier harangues on the urgency of the times, yet beneath the apparent surface disorder a deeper pattern of connectedness gradually makes itself felt. The unassertive rhymes, easily overlooked on a first reading, hold the poem together.

Yet another device of language helps bring unity to Auden's meditation, in P. K. Saha's view. Four clauses begin with *how* and one phrase begins with *anyhow* (line 11). These *hows* vary in meaning; still, the repeated *how* is the crucial word in the linguistic pattern of the poem ("Style, Stylistic Transformations, and Incorporators," *Style* 12 [1978]: 18–22).

R. L. Barth, THE INSERT, page 896

We would sum up Barth's theme: war blunts the sensibilities of the participant. Like one who begins taking heroin, the new soldier is at first eager for excitement; but with every use, the thrill is of shorter duration.

We didn't know exactly what an *insert* was, and asked the poet to define it. He replied: "Dropping troops, in this case recon troops, into an area by helicopter—one never knew if it would be a 'hot' LZ or not and was always ready for the worst."

Barth's poem invites comparison with other poems by another poet with field experience: Wilfred Owen's "Dulce et Decorum Est" (page 617) and "Anthem for Doomed Youth" (page 972). Barth's protest is stated not in the abstract, but in what lies before the observer's senses. Owen, by contrast, for all his vivid detail, seems continually to be editorializing.

Elizabeth Bishop, FILLING STATION, page 896

QUESTIONS FOR DISCUSSION:

1. What is the poet's attitude toward the feeble attempts at beautification detailed in lines 23–33? Sympathy, contempt, or what? How is the attitude indicated? (The attempts

are doomed, not only by the gas station's being saturated with oil, but by the limitations of the family, whose only reading appears to be comic books and whose tastes run to hairy plants and daisy-covered doilies. In line 20, *comfy is* their word, not the poet's own. But the tone of the poem seems to be good-humored amusement. The sons are "quick and saucy"—likable traits. The gas station can't be beautiful, but at least its owners have tried. In a futile gesture toward neatness, they have even arranged the oil cans in symmetry.)

2. What meanings do you find in the last line? (Somebody has shown love for all motorists by arranging the oil cans so beautifully that they spell out a soothing croon, such as what one might say over and over to an agitated child. But the somebody also suggests Somebody Up There, whose love enfolds all human beings—even this oilsoaked crew.)

3. Do you find any similarity between "ESSO—SO—SO—SO" in "Filling Station" and "rainbow, rainbow, rainbow!" in "The Fish" (page 663)? (Both lines stand late in their poems and sound similar; both express the speaker's glimpse of beauty—or at least, in "Filling Station," the only beauty the people can muster and the poet can perceive.)

Helen Vendler, discussing the poem in *Part of Nature, Part of Us* (Cambridge: Harvard UP, 1980), takes the closing statement to mean "God loves us all." But Irvin Ehrenpreis disagrees: "The '—so—so—so' of overlapping labels on stacked cans is supposed to comfort automobiles as if they were high-strung horses, i.e., like a mother, not a god." Doily and begonia indicate that some absent woman has tried to brighten up this gas station for her husband and her sons (review of Vendler's book in *The New York Review of Books,* 29 Apr. 1980).

Edward Cifelli, County College of Morris, passes along an insight from his student Joseph Grana. The message "ESSO—SO—SO—SO" may be an SOS from the same "somebody" who embroidered the doily and waters the plant. Professor Cifelli adds, "The pitiable woman who tries to put traces of beauty into a filthy filling station is unconsciously calling out for help, for rescue. Now *that* engages me!"

Robert Pinsky has also written of "Filling Station" with high esteem. He calls the poem a kind of contest between "the meticulous vigor of the writer" and "the sloppy vigor of the family," both filling a dull moment and scene with "an unexpected, crazy, deceptively off-hand kind of elegance or ornament." He particularly admires the poet's choice of modifiers—including the direct, honest-seeming *dirty.* "Adjectives," he notes, "according to a sound rule of thumb for writing classes, do not make 'good descriptions.' By writing almost as though she were too plain and straightforward to have heard of such a rule, Bishop loads characterizations of herself and her subject into the *comfy* dog, the *dim* doily, the *hirsute* begonia; the quietest possible virtuoso strokes" *(The Situation of Poetry* [Princeton: Princeton UP, 1976] 75–77).

"I've sometimes thought 'Filling Station' would make a good exercise for acting students," observes critic and teacher David Walker, "given the number of different ways the first line—and much of the rest—might be stressed. Is the opening exclamation solemn and childlike, or prissy and fastidious, or enthusiastic? All we can identify with certainty, I think, is the quality of fascination, the intent gaze on the filling station's pure oiliness." Walker is reminded of Frost's "Design" (page 1763) in that both poets seek to discover "a meaningful pattern in apparently random details"—but while Frost points toward a sinister architecture in what he observes, Bishop finds beauty and harmony ("Elizabeth Bishop and the Ordinary," *Field,* Fall 1984).

Brad Leithauser has admired the poem's ingenious sound effects. At its end, "the cans of oil are arranged like cue cards to prompt that concluding sentence, the SO—SO—SO grading toward that 'Somebody loves us all.' Neatly, the message in the oil cans is

241

reinforced by both the *'so'* and the *'softly'* in the fourth line from the end" ("The 'complete' Elizabeth Bishop," *New Criterion* Mar. 1983: 38).

Elizabeth Bishop, ONE ART, page 897

Like Thomas's "Do not go gentle," this villanelle manages to say something that matters while observing the rules of a tricky French courtly form. (For remarks on the villanelle and on writing it, see the entry on Thomas in this manual, page 198). A similar feat is performed in Bishop's ingenious recollection of childhood, "Sestina."

Question: What varieties of loss does the poet mention? (She goes from trivial loss—lost door keys—to lost time, to losing beloved places and homes, to loss of love.)

In recalling that she has lost a continent, the poet may be speaking personally: she lived in Brazil for many years, and wrote this poem after returning to America. Early in life, Bishop knew severe losses. Her father died when she was eight months old; when she was five, her mother was confined to an institution.

Perceptively, the Irish poet and critic Eavan Boland has likened "One Art" to Bishop's "Sestina" (which ends Chapter 22, page 772), remarking that "it is obvious that [the poet] entrusted some of her deepest implications of loss to two of the most intricate game forms in poetry." However, she finds differences between the two works: " 'Sestina' is packed with desolate halftones, dropped hints, and the incantatory shadows of nursery rhymes. It manages to convey, at one and the same time, that there is sorrow, yes, and loss, yes, but that they are imperfectly understood. Therefore the poem operates at two different levels. Within it a terrible sorrow is happening. But the teakettle keeps boiling, the cup is full of tea, the stove is warm. Only we, outside the poem, get the full meaning of it all. 'One Art' is quite different. . . . The tone, which is both casual and direct, is deliberately worked against the form, as it is not in 'Sestina.' Once again, Bishop shows that she is best able to display feeling when she can constrain it most." (We quote from her fine essay on Bishop's work, "Time, Memory, and Obsession," in *PN Review* [Nov.-Dec. 1991] 18–24.)

William Blake, THE SICK ROSE, page 899

William Blake, THE TYGER, page 899

In "The Sick Rose," why is the worm, whose love is rape, *invisible*? Not just because it is hidden in the rose, but also because it is some supernatural dweller in night and storm. Perhaps the worm is unseen Time, that familiar destroyer—is the rose then mortal beauty? Those are usual guesses. For an unusual guess, see E. D. Hirsch, Jr., *Innocence and Experience* (New Haven: Yale UP, 1964). "The rose's sickness, like syphilis, is the internal result of love enjoyed secretly and illicitly instead of purely and openly." In Hirsch's view, the poem is social criticism. Blake is satirizing the repressive order, whose hypocrisy and sham corrupt the woman who accepts it. Still, like all the best symbols, Blake's rose and worm give off hints endlessly, and no one interpretation covers all of them. We noted with interest that "The Sick Rose" is rightly included in *The Faber Book of Seduction* (London, 1988).

"The Tyger," from *Songs of Experience,* is a companion piece to "The Lamb" in *Songs of Innocence.* But while "The Lamb" poses a relatively easy question ("Little lamb, who made thee?") and soon answers it, "The Tyger" poses questions that remain unanswerable. Alert students may complain that some of Blake's questions have no verbs—what dread hand and what dread feet did *what*? While the incompleteness has been explained by some critics as reflecting the agitated tone of the poem, it may have been due to the poet's agitated habits of composition. Drafts of the poem in Blake's notebook show that, after writing the first three stanzas, he began the fourth stanza with the line "Could fetch it from the furnace deep," which would have completed the question in line 12. But then he deleted it, and wrote in stanza four almost as it stands now. (See Martin K. Nurmi, "Blake's Revisions of 'The Tyger,'" *PMLA* 71 [1956]: 669–85.) Other useful discussions include that of Hirsch, who thinks the stars are the rebel angels who threw down their spears when they surrendered; and John E. Grant, "The Art and Argument of 'The Tyger'" in *Texas Studies in Literature and Language* 2 (1960): 38–60.

Louise Bogan, THE DREAM, page 900

In *Louise Bogan: A Portrait* (New York: Knopf, 1985), Elizabeth Frank discusses "The Dream," which Bogan wrote in her late thirties after having suffered a series of breakdowns. Bogan herself described the poem as "the actual transcript of 'a nightmare,' but there is a reconciliation involved with the fright and horror. It is through the possibility of such reconciliations that we, I believe, manage to live." Thus Frank sees the horse (the *night-mare)* as "the accumulated power of terror and rage Bogan had only recently confronted during her breakdowns," and the other woman in the poem, who comes to the rescue, as "Bogan's new self, the 'cured' woman, the emergent adult and artist." The glove, according to Frank, "becomes a symbol of challenge and submission, a token of the poet's strong feminine sexuality—and perhaps many other things as well. Put at the mercy of the beast, who is not only appeased, but in turn enchanted, the glove in the end represents the poet's whole self, triumphant over the lovingly submissive beast."

Emily Brontë, LOVE AND FRIENDSHIP, page 900

This poem (usually a great favorite of students) has been restored to the anthology. Many teachers missed it in the previous edition.

"Love and Friendship" appeared in the Brontë sisters' first published book, *Poems by Currer, Ellis, and Acton Bell*, which came out in 1846. Fannie E. Ratchford, the scholar who found that most of Emily's poems were not reflections of her personal life, as early scholars and biographers had assumed, but rather "pertain to an imaginative country called Gondal, which she created when she was thirteen or fourteen years old and continued to develop as long as she lived," calls "Love and Friendship" a Gondal poem or "unplaced in the story pattern" ("The Gondal Story," in *The Complete Poems of Emily Jane Brontë*, ed. C. W. Hatfield [New York: Columbia UP, 1952]).

In "Love and Friendship" the poet sustains her opening similes to the end. It is clear that the speaker values the holly more than the wild rose briar.

Gwendolyn Brooks, THE RITES FOR COUSIN VIT, page 901

Cousin Vit, a vital, life-loving woman (a prostitute?), is dead. In this contemporary sonnet, the poet depicts her as too lively a presence to be confined by the casket, the "stuff and satin aiming to enfold her, / The lid's contrition nor the bolts before." To the poet, Cousin Vit appears to be still energetically moving about: walking, talking, drinking, dancing as of old. The wonderful *Is* that ends the poem emphatically sums up the dead woman's undying vigor.

Gwendolyn Brooks, A STREET IN BRONZEVILLE: SOUTHEAST CORNER, page 902

This short poem first appeared in Brooks's debut volume, A *Street in Bronzeville* (1944).

The book centered on a group of interrelated poems, including this one, set in Bronzeville, a fictional African-American neighborhood in Chicago. In her autobiography, *Report from Part One* (Detroit: Broadside Press, 1972), Brooks praised Langston Hughes whom she met during the time she was composing the poems in *A Street in Bronzeville:*

> Mightily did he use the street. He found its multiple heart, its tastes, smells, alarms, formulas, flowers, garbage, and convulsions. He brought them to his table-top. He crushed them to a writing paste. He himself became the pen . . .

In that passage, Brooks seems to be describing her own method in these early poems. This selection describes a tavern that was once a School of Beauty. The former owner, still respectfully called Madam, now lies in Lincoln Cemetery where her wealth has bought her a fine tomb and casket. Brooks does not criticize the woman, probably born poor, for posthumously displaying her material success. Brooks seems to revel in the tomb's ironic opulence.

Elizabeth Barrett Browning, HOW DO I LOVE THEE? LET ME COUNT THE WAYS, page 902

If dropping the Brontë poem caused a few troubled queries, dropping this famous sonnet from the last edition broke more than one teacher's heart. The many requests for this poem, "My Last Duchess," "Mending Wall," "Death Be Not Proud," and Poe's work reminds us how much students enjoy reading famous poems—work that an educational theorist like E. D. Hirsch would claim have "cultural utility." They are poems that are still frequently quoted in newspapers, conversation, and electronic media. Anthologists eager for novelty too often forget that these famous poems remain novel to every new generation.

This is the penultimate sonnet of forty-four constituting Elizabeth Barrett Browning's *Sonnets from the Portuguese,* a book that Ezra Pound once called "The second: that is, a sonnet sequence surpassed in English by one other alone. I would argue for that." The sonnets document the poet's growing love for Robert Browning, whom she married, in defiance of her father's wishes, in her fortieth year. "My little Portuguese" was a pet name Robert often used for Elizabeth: hence the title of her book.

Teachers not opposed to biographical interpretations might direct their students to the notes on both Brownings in the "Lives of the Poets" section. Another fine sonnet by Elizabeth Barrett Browning, "Grief," appears on page 764.

Robert Browning, SOLILOQUY OF THE SPANISH CLOISTER, page 902

The "Soliloquy" is a poem especially valuable to combat the notion that poetry can deal only in love and gladness. Here, the subject is a hatred so intense that the speaker seems practically demented. In the last stanza, he almost would sell his soul to the Devil in order to blight a flowering shrub. A little background information on abbeys, their organization, and the strictness of their rules may help some class members. From internal evidence, it is hard to say whether this is a sixteenth-century cloister or a nineteenth-century one; Barbary corsairs (line 31) plied their trade from about 1550 until 1816. The business about drinking in three sips (lines 37–39) may need explaining: evidently it refers to a symbolic observance, like crossing knife and fork.

It might be stressed that the person in this poem is not the poet: the tone isn't one of bitterness, but of merriment. Comedy is evident not only from the speaker's blindness to his own faults, but from the rollicking rhythm and multisyllable comic rimes *(abhorrence/Lawrence; horsehairs/corsairs; Galatians/damnations; rose-acacia/Plena gratia).*

Questions: With what sins does the speaker charge Brother Lawrence? (Pride, line 23—monogrammed tableware belonging to a monk!; lust, 25–32; and gluttony, 40.) What sins do we detect in the speaker himself? (Envy, clearly, and pride—see his holier-than-thou attitude in stanza 5. How persuasive are his claims to piety when we learn he secretly owns a pornographic novel?) "Soliloquy" abounds in ironies, and class members can spend a lively few minutes in pointing them out.

Thomas Carew, ASK ME NO MORE WHERE JOVE BESTOWS, page 904

Carew's poem is an eloquent tribute to a lady whose complexion is so beautiful, the poet says, that it must emanate, with divine assistance, from the very roses. Her hair is made of sunbeams, her voice is like the nightingale's, and the stars twinkle in her eyes. Exaggerated? Yes. Still, what woman, even in the unromantic 1990s, wouldn't relish so lyrical a testimonial to her beauty?

You might want to ask your class to compare "Ask me no more where Jove bestows" with "My mistress' eyes are nothing like the sun" (page 869), where Shakespeare twits the Petrarchan conventions while of course relying as heavily as Carew does upon his readers' ability to appreciate a well-turned conceit.

Herbert J. C. Grierson, in his anthology *Metaphysical Lyrics and Poems of the Seventeenth Century* (Oxford UP, 1921), waxes poetic over the *dividing throat:* "One seems to hear and see Celia executing elaborate trills as Carew sits entranced."

There is a famous anecdote about Carew, which may or may not be true. One evening he was lighting King Charles I to the queen's chamber. Entering the room first, the poet saw the queen in the arms of Lord St. Albans. Before the king noticed that anything was amiss, Carew tactfully stumbled, thus extinguishing his candle long enough for the queen to adjust her position. His quick thinking endeared Carew to the queen from that day forward.

Geoffrey Chaucer, YOUR ŸEN TWO WOL SLEE ME SODENLY, page 905

It can be great fun for students to learn (well, more or less) how to pronounce Chaucer's English, provided one has the time and strength to help them make the attempt. One does much better by Chaucer's lines if one puts on an Irish brogue. (A couple of Guinness stouts before class usually helps.)

Some scholars doubt that Chaucer himself wrote this poem, but if he did not, someone who thoroughly knew Chaucer's work probably did.

"Since I escaped from love, I've grown so fat . . . " is, of course, a crude modernization of another poem from the "Merciles Beaute" series. Carlos Baker offers another modern American version of it in his book of poems, *A Year and a Day* (Nashville: Vanderbilt UP, 1963).

G. K. Chesterton, THE DONKEY, page 906

QUESTIONS FOR DISCUSSION:

1. Who is the speaker—some particular donkey? (No, the generic donkey, looking back over the history of his kind.)

2. To what prehistoric era does Chesterton refer in lines 1–3? (To the original chaos out of which the world was made. The poet apparently imagines it in bizarre, dreamlike imagery: fish with wings, walking forests, fig-bearing thorn.) Chesterton was fascinated by the book of Genesis "because of its beginning in chaos," comments Garry Wills in his introduction to a reprint edition of Chesterton's novel of 1908, *The Man Who Was Thurs-*

day (New York: Sheed, 1975). The novel hints at a playful God who enjoys returning things to chaos every now and then. Writing about the world of dream in a newspaper article in 1904, Chesterton remarked, "A world in which donkeys come in two is clearly very near to the wild ultimate world where donkeys are made."

3. Whose "ancient crooked will" is meant? The will of the devil in perversely designing the donkey, or the donkey's own venerable stubbornness? (We're not certain.)

4. What *fools* does the donkey chide in the last stanza? (Anybody who ever abused a donkey, or who thinks donkeys contemptible.)

5. Explain how the allusion in the last stanza is essential to the meaning of the poem.

6. What devices of sound contribute to the poem's effectiveness?

Samuel Taylor Coleridge, KUBLA KHAN, page 906

The circumstances of this poem's composition are almost as famous as the poem itself, and, for the convenience of instructors who wish to read to their students Coleridge's prefatory note, here it is:

> In the summer of the year 1797, the author, then in ill health, had retired to a lonely farmhouse between Porlock and Linton, on the Exmoor confines of Somerset and Devonshire. In consequence of a slight indisposition, an anodyne had been pre-scribed, from the effects of which he fell asleep in his chair at the moment that he was reading the following sentence, or words of the same substance, in *Purchas's Pilgrimage:* "Here the Khan Kubla commanded a palace to be built, and a stately garden thereunto. And thus ten miles of fertile ground were inclosed with a wall." The author continued for about three hours in a profound sleep, at least of the exter-nal sense, during which time he had the most vivid confidence that he could not have composed less than from two to three hundred lines; if that indeed can be called composition in which all the images rose up before him as *things,* with a parallel production of the correspondent expressions, without any sensation or con-sciousness of effort. On awaking he appeared to himself to have a distinct recol-lection of the whole, and taking his pen, ink, and paper, instantly and eagerly wrote down the lines that are here preserved. At this moment he was unfortunately called out by a person on business from Porlock, and detained by him above an hour, and on his return to his room, found, to his no small surprise and mortification, that though he still retained some vague and dim recollection of the general purport of his vision, yet, with the exception of some eight or ten scattered lines and images, all the rest had passed away like the images on the surface of a stream into which a stone has been cast, but, alas! without the after restoration of the latter!

It is clearly a vulgar error to think the poem a mere pipe dream, which anyone could have written with the aid of opium. The profound symbolism of "Kubla Khan" has con-tinued to intrigue critics, most of whom find that the pleasure-dome suggests poetry, the sacred river, the flow of inspiration, or instinctual life. About the *ancestral voices* and the *caves of ice* there seems less agreement, and students might be invited to venture their guesses. For a valuable modern reading of the poem, see Humphry House, "Kubla Khan, Christable and Dejection" in *Coleridge* (London: Hart-Davis, 1953), also reprinted in *Ro-manticism and Consciousness,* ed. Harold Bloom (New York: Norton, 1970).

Some instructors may wish to bring in "The Rime of the Ancient Mariner" as well—in which case it may be a temptation to go on to Jung's theory of archetypes and to other dreamlike poems such as Yeats's "The Second Coming" (page 813). A fine topic for a term paper might be, after reading John Livingston Lowes's classic source study *The Road to Xanadu* (Boston: Houghton, 1927), to argue whether it is worth trying to find out everything that may have been going on in the back of a poet's mind, and to what extent such investigations can end in certainty.

Emily Dickinson, BECAUSE I COULD NOT STOP FOR DEATH, page 908

QUESTIONS FOR DISCUSSION:

1. What qualities does Dickinson attribute to Death? Why is Immortality going along on this carriage ride? (For the poet, death and immortality go together. Besides, Dickinson is amplifying her metaphor of Death as a gentleman taking a woman for a drive: Immortality, as would have been proper in Amherst, is their chaperone.)

2. Is the poem, as the poet wrote it, in some ways superior to the version first printed? Is *strove* perhaps a richer word than *played?* What is interesting in the phrase *Gazing Grain?* How can grain "gaze"? (It has kernels like eyes at the tips of its stalks. As the speaker dies, the natural world—like the fly in "I heard a Fly buzz" on page 802—is watching.) What is memorable in the rhythm and meaning of the line "The Dews drew quivering and chill?" (At *quivering,* the rhythm quivers loose from its iambic tetrameter. The image of cold dampness foreshadows the next stanza, with its images of the grave.)

3. What is the Carriage ? What is the House?

4. Where is the speaker at the present moment of the poem? Why is time said to pass more quickly where she is now? (Eternity is timeless.)

5. What is the tone of the poem? (Complicated!—seriousness enlivened with delicate macabre humor? Surely she kids her own worldly busyness in the opening line.)

William Galperin reads the poem as a feminist affirmation. Not death, he finds, but immortality is Dickinson's subject. In the end the poet asserts a triumph possible only because she has renounced the proposal of Death, that threatening gentleman caller who might have married her ("Emily Dickinson's Marriage Hearse," *Denver Quarterly,* Winter 1984: 62–73).

Emily Dickinson, I STARTED EARLY—TOOK MY DOG, page 909

It would be unfortunate if students were to regard this poem as nothing more than a sexual fantasy. Handled with frankness and tact, it can be an excellent class-awakener. The poet expresses feelings for the natural world so intense that, like a mystic choosing erotic imagery to speak of the Beatific Vision, she can report her walk on the beach only in the language of a ravishing. The humor of the poem also is essential: the basement-dwelling mermaids, the poet's self-picture as a mouse.

Emily Dickinson, MY LIFE HAD STOOD—A LOADED GUN, page 910

This astonishing metaphysical poem (another hymnlike work in common meter) can be an excellent provoker of class debate. Before trying to fathom it, students might well examine its diction. *Sovreign Woods* ("sovereign" would be the more usual spelling) suggest an estate owned by a king. How do the Mountains *reply?* By echoing the gun's report. Apparently the *smile* is the flash from the gun's muzzle; and the *Vesuvian face,* a glimpse of the flaming crater of the volcano. The Eider-Duck, a sea duck, has particularly soft and silky down which is used in pillows and quilts. The gun's *Yellow Eye* seems, again, its flash: and the emphatic *Thumb* is presumably the impact of the bullet that flattens its victim. (Some will say the thumb is a trigger finger, but you don't pull a trigger with your thumb.)

Argument over the meaning of the poem will probably divide the class into two camps. One will see the poem, like "Because I could not stop for Death," as an account of resurrection, with the Owner being God or Christ, who carries away the speaker, life and all, to the Happy Hunting Grounds of Paradise. Personally, we incline toward the other camp. In that view the Owner seems a mere mortal, perhaps a lover. The last stanza reveals that he can die. So taken, the last two lines make more sense. Not having the power to die, the speaker feels something lacking in her. She doesn't wish to outlive her huntsman and be a lonely killer.

Philip Larkin admits the possibility of both views: "This is a romantic love in a nutshell, but who is its object? A religious poet—and Emily was this sometimes—might even have meant God" *(Required Writing* [New York: Farrar, 1984] 193).

Lately a third camp has appeared, proclaiming a feminist interpretation. The poem, as summed up by Adalaide Morris, "tells about a life packed with a potential that the self was not empowered to activate." From this point of view, the poem is overtly political, exhilarating to teach because it recognizes long suppressed animosities ("Dick, Jane, and American Literature Fighting with Canons," *College English* 47 [1985]: 477).

But the poem remains tantalizingly ambiguous. You won't know until you go into class what a discussion may reveal.

John Donne, DEATH BE NOT PROUD, page 910

During the Renaissance, when life was short, a man of the cloth like Donne would have surprised no one by being on familiar terms with death. Still, "Death be not proud," one of Donne's "Holy Sonnets," is an almost startling put-down of "poor death." Staunchly Christian in its sure expectation of the resurrection, Donne's poem personifies death as an adversary swollen with false pride and unworthy of being called "mighty and dreadful." (For another bold personification, see "Batter my heart, three-personed God" [page 629], also one of the "Holy Sonnets," in which Donne sees God as ravisher.)

In "Death Be Not Proud" the poet accuses death of being little more than a slave bossed around by "fate, chance, kings and desperate men"—a craven thing that keeps bad company, such as "poison, war, and sickness." Finally Donne taunts death with a paradox: "death, thou shalt die."

Of interest, though perhaps of less than immediate usefulness in the classroom, are the articles on Donne's religious poetry by Helen Gardner, Louis L. Martz, and Stanley Archer in *John Donne's Poetry: Authoritative Texts, Criticism,* ed. A. L. Clements (New York: Norton, 1966). All three explore the extent to which Jesuit methods of meditation might have influenced the "Holy Sonnets."

It might be instructive for students to compare two personifications of death: Donne's and Emily Dickinson's in "Because I could not stop for Death" (page 908), where death appears in the guise of a courtly gentleman who stops by to take the poet for a pleasant ride.

John Donne, THE FLEA, page 911

This outrageous poem is a good class-rouser on a dull day, but we don't urge you to use it unless the class seems friendly. (Some women students tend to be offended by Donne's levity; men tend to be put off by his ingenuity.)

A little familiarity with a seventeenth-century medical notion may help make Donne's metaphor clear. Conception, it was thought, took place when the blood of men and women mingled during intercourse. That is why Donne declares in line 11 that "we almost, yea more than married are." Bitten by the flea containing his blood, the woman may already be pregnant.

Instructors fond of Donne's knotty poems will be grateful for Theodore Redpath's valuable crib-book *The Songs and Sonnets of John Donne: An Editio Minor* (London: Methuen, 1956; also New York: University Paperbacks, 1967). Redpath works through the poems line by line, explicating difficulties. He explains line 18: The woman would commit "three sins in killing three" in that she'd commit murder in killing him, suicide in killing herself, and sacrilege in killing the flea. Why sacrilege? Because she would be attacking a "marriage temple."

Patricia Meyer Spacks has treated the poem to scrutiny in *College English* 29 (1968): 593–94.

John Donne, A VALEDICTION: FORBIDDING MOURNING, page 912

In his *Life of Donne,* Izaak Walton tells us that Donne wrote this poem for his wife in 1611, when he was about to depart on a diplomatic mission to France.

Much of the meaning of the poem depends upon the metaphor of the compasses in the last three stanzas. There is probably no better way to make sure students understand it clearly than to bring in a draftsman's compass—even the Woolworth's variety—and to demonstrate the metaphor with it. There'll always be someone who thinks Donne means the kind of compass that indicates north.

QUESTIONS FOR DISCUSSION:

1. What is a *valediction* anyway? (What is a high school "valedictorian"?)

2. Why does the speaker forbid mourning? Do lines 1–4 mean that he is dying? Explain this metaphor about the passing away of virtuous men. (As saints take leave of this world—so sweetly and calmly that one hardly knows they're gone—let us take leave of each other.)

3. In lines 7–8, what is suggested by the words with religious denotations? *Profanation* (the desecration of a sacred thing), *the laity.* What is the idea? (Love seems to the speaker a holy mystery. He and his wife are its priests or ministers.)

4. Explain the reference to astronomy in the third stanza. (Earthquakes shake, rattle, and roll; Ptolemaic spheres revolve gently and harmlessly. This takes us to the notion of *sublunary* lovers in stanza 4. In the medieval cosmos, the heavenly bodies are fixed and permanent, while everything under the moon is subject to change.)

5. Paraphrase stanza 4. (Unlike common lovers, bound to their earthly passions, we have less need of those things that serve sensual love: namely, bodies.)

6. Why is beaten gold an appropriate image in the sixth stanza? What connotations does gold have? (Refined, precious, durable, capable of being extended without breaking.)

7. Comment on the word *hearkens,* line 31. (As a draftsman's compass will illustrate, the fixed central foot leans forward when the compass is extended, as if, in Donne's metaphor, eager for the other mate's return.)

Rita Dove, DAYSTAR, page 913

What suggestions can be found in the title of Dove's poem? The word is a trove of connotations. You may wish to make sure at the start that your students are familiar with the dictionary meaning of *daystar*: the morning star or, poetically, the sun. From the poem's last line, we infer that it was the sun the poet had in mind. Why *daystar* instead of sun? Does the word suggest to the poet, as to us, joy and happiness? Also, a star is a "self-luminous, self-containing mass of gas in which the energy generated by nuclear reactions in the interior is balanced by the outflow of energy to the surface and the inward-directed gravitational forces are balanced by the outward-directed gas and radiation pressures." Perhaps the poet is suggesting that a similar state of balance is what the wife and mother in the poem seeks—and finds—when she sits behind the garage, "building a palace," while her children are taking their naps. The chance to daydream in solitude sustains her not only through her toils but "that night when Thomas rolled over and / lurched into her."

Thomas and Beulah, in which "Daystar" appears, won the 1987 Pulitzer Prize for poetry. The book contains a series of poems about the lives and concerns of an ordinary black couple.

In 1993, Rita Dove became the U.S. Poet Laureate, the first African-American to hold this prestigious position.

John Dryden, TO THE MEMORY OF MR. OLDHAM, page 914

With the aid of Dryden's great short poem (and the selections in the book from Swift, Pope, and Johnson), one at least can acquaint students with a little neoclassical poetry. One can point out, too, that such poetry is not quite dead in America in our own day, as may be seen from the poems of Yvor Winters (page 1016) and J. V. Cunningham (pages 633, 768). The directness and plainness of Dryden's poem are clear from its very opening, and in teaching it one can question the assumption that neoclassical poetry is written only in bookish and Latinate words.

In teaching Dryden's poem, one can also mention (and define) the elegy, and can refer students to other famous elegies in the text: those of Milton (page 962) and Gray (page 873). If one is going to teach "Lycidas," Dryden's succinct poem might well serve as an introduction. It may be readily compared with "Lycidas" in that it mourns the death of a poet, expresses abhorrence for knaves, and observes a few classical conventions.

A. E. Housman's "To an Athlete Dying Young" (page 942) also may be likened to Dryden's poem in that both poets favor classical conventions: footraces with laurels as crowns and the dead hero's descent into the underworld. Both poets find that premature death can confer benefits. What would Oldham have gained had he survived? More polish as a poet, yet he would have lost much of his force. In reading Housman's poem, students can be helped to recognize its metaphors: the comparison in the first two stanzas of victor's chair and dead lad's coffin, the comparison in line 5 of all human life to a footrace, with death at the finish line. Students might be asked if they know of any living proof of Housman's observation that sometimes the name dies before the man (a truth often shown by the wistfulness of old football players at alumni weekends).

T. S. Eliot, JOURNEY OF THE MAGI, page 914

The speaker is a very old man ("All this was a long time ago . . ."), looking forward to his death. As his mind roves back over the past, it is mainly the discomforts and frustrations of his journey that he remembers, and when he comes to the part we have been waiting for, his account of the Nativity, he seems still mystified, as though uncertainly trying to figure out what had happened—"There was a Birth, certainly." Apparently the whole experience was so devastating that he prefers to omit all further details. His plight was to recognize Christ as God and yet to be unable to accept Christ as his savior. Being a king, he did not renounce his people but they henceforth seemed alien to him, clutching their discredited gods like useless dolls.

The passage beginning "Then at dawn" (lines 21-28) is full of foreshadowings, both hopeful and sinister. Besides the symbolic white horse, the vine leaves suggest Christ who said to his disciples, "I am the vine, ye are the branches" (John 15:5). The tavern customers suggest the Roman soldiers who will drink and cast dice at the cross.

Although Eliot's dissatisfied Magus isn't one of the kings portrayed by Yeats in "The Magi" (page 1021)—being dissatisfied for different reasons—it is curious that Eliot may have taken the dramatic situation of his poem from one of Yeats's stories. In "The Adoration of the Magi" in Yeats's prose collection *Mythologies* (reprinted in 1925, two years before Eliot first published his poem), three old men call on the storyteller, and, drawing close to his fire, insist on telling him of a journey they had made when young, and of a vision of Bethlehem. Like Eliot's speaker, who repeats "set down / This set down / This," they demand that their story be taken down word for word.

Among the useful discussions of Eliot's poem are Elizabeth Drew's in *T. S. Eliot: The Design of His Poetry* (New York: Scribner's 1949) 118-22, and Grover Smith's in *T. S. Eliot's Poetry and Plays* (Chicago: U of Chicago P, 1960) 121-25. More recently, Daniel A. Harris has characterized the Magus as a primitive Christian with a "baffled consciousness of mystery." See his article "Language, History, and Text in Eliot's 'Journey of the Magi,'" *PMLA* 95 (1980): 838-56. But Harris's opinions are questioned by William Skaff in a letter in *PMLA* 96: (1981) 420-22: "In 'Journey' Eliot adopts the dramatic mask of the Magus in order to express his own struggles with literal belief, his real 'religious position of 1927.'"

T. S. Eliot, THE LOVE SONG OF J. ALFRED PRUFROCK, page 916

Teaching any basic course in literature, an instructor would have to be desperate for time not to devote to "Prufrock" at least a class or two. Eliot's early masterpiece can open such diverse matters as theme, tone, irony, persona, imagery, figures of speech, allusion, symbolism, and the difference between saying and suggesting. Most students will enjoy it and remember it.

QUESTIONS FOR DISCUSSION:

1. Why the epigraph from Dante? What expectations does it arouse? (Perhaps that this "song" will be the private confession of someone who thinks himself trapped and unredeemable, and thinks it of his hearer, too.)

2. What facts about J. Alfred can we be sure of? His age, his manner of dress, his social circles? What does his name suggest? Can you detect any puns in it? (A prude in a frock—a formal coat.)

3. What do you make of the simile in lines 2-3 ? What does it tell us about this particular evening? (*Etherized* suggests fog, also submission, waiting for something grim to happen.) What does it tell you about Prufrock's way of seeing things? ("A little sick," some students may say, and with reason.)

4. What gnaws at Prufrock? (Not just his sense of growing old, not just his inability to act. He suffers from Prufrock's Complaint: dissociation of sensibility. In line 105, unable to join thought and feeling, he sees his own nerves existing at one remove from him, as if thrown on a screen by a projector.)

5. Who are "you and I" in the opening line? Who are "we" at the end? (Some possibilities: Prufrock and the woman he is attending. Prufrock and the reader. Prufrock and

Prufrock—he's talking to himself, "you" being the repressive self, "I" being the timid or repressed self. Prufrock and the other eggheads of the Western world—in this view, the poem is Eliot's satire on the intelligentsia.)

6. What symbols do you find and what do they suggest? Notice those that relate to the sea, even *oyster-shells* (line 7). (XJK points out blatantly that water has connotations of sexual fulfillment, and quotes "Western Wind" [page 889]. Eliot hints that unlike Prufrock, the vulgar types who inhabit cheap hotels and fish shops have a love life.)

7. Try to explain the last three lines.

8. Now summarize the story of the poem. What parts does it fall into? (Part one: Prufrock prepares to try to ask the overwhelming question. Then in lines 84–86 we learn that he has failed to ask it. In 87–110 he tries to justify himself for chickening out. From 111 to the end, he sums up his static present and hollow future.)

That Eliot may have taken the bones of his plot from Henry James's story "Crapy Cornelia" (1909) is Grover Smith's convincing theory. "This is the story of White-Mason, a middle-aged bachelor of nostalgic temperament, who visits a young Mrs. Worthington to propose marriage but reconsiders owing to the difference in their worlds." (*T. S. Eliot's Poetry and Plays* [Chicago: U of Chicago P, 1960] 15).

"The meter of 'Prufrock' is peculiar," observes John Heath-Stubbs. "It is not simply free verse, as in [Eliot's] earlier Laforgueian pieces, but in its lines of irregular length, many but not all of which rhyme, suggests a free version of the Dantesque Canzone." This suggestion, and the poem's epigraph from the *Inferno*, point to Eliot's growing preoccupation with Dante ("Structure and Source in Eliot's Major Poetry," *Agenda*, Spring-Summer 1985: 24)

T S. Eliot Reading His Poetry (Caedmon recording TC 1045) includes the poet's rendition of "Prufrock."

Cleanth Brooks has written an essay full of wisdom and practical advice, "Teaching 'The Love Song of J. Alfred Prufrock,'" which you can find in *Eliot's Poetry and Plays*, one of the MLA's valuable Approaches to Teaching series (1988).

Louise Erdrich, INDIAN BOARDING SCHOOL: THE RUNAWAYS, page 920

For discussion: Have you ever been somewhere you wanted to run away home from? If so, how does your memory of that experience compare with that of the speaker in this poem ?

This poem is long on wounds: the railroad tracks are scars (6), the runaways' old welts are like roads (15), the names they wrote in wet cement and the leaves they pressed into the sidewalk before it dried recall "delicate old injuries" (22–24). All these things carry powerful connotations of being wounded, mistreated, beaten down—like the runaways themselves.

Jacklight (New York: Holt, 1984), the collection in which this poem appears, contains several other realistic poems of Indian life. Since the success of *Love Medicine* (1984), *The Beet Queen* (1986), and *Tracks* (1988), Louise Erdrich is best known as a novelist, but we think her poetry warrants attention too.

Erdrich, born in Little Falls, Minnesota, grew up in Wahpeton, North Dakota, and now lives in New Hampshire with her husband, Michael Dorris, also a novelist and a nonfiction writer.

Robert Frost, BIRCHES, page 920

"Birches," according to Lawrance Thompson, was written during a spell of homesickness in 1913–14, when Frost and his family were living in Beaconsfield, Buckinghamshire, England *(Robert Frost: The Years of Triumph,* Holt, 1970; 37, 541).

Students may be led to see the poem as much more than a nostalgic picture of boyhood play. From line 43 on, the poem develops a flamboyant metaphor. Richard Poirier has given us a good summary of the poem's theme; "While there are times when the speaker of ["Birches"] would 'like to get away from earth awhile,' his aspiration for escape to something 'larger' is safely controlled by the recognition that birch trees will only bear so much climbing before returning you, under the pressure of human weight, back home" *(Robert Frost: The Work of Knowing* [Oxford UP, 1977] 172).

One line in "Birches" meant most to Frost, the line about feeling lost in the woods, facing too many decisions about which way to go. He pointed it out to audiences on several occasions: "It's when I'm weary of considerations" (line 43). Reading the poem at Bread Loaf in July 1954, he remarked of the line, "That's when you get older. It didn't mean so much to me when I wrote it as it does now" *(Robert Frost: A Living Voice,* ed. Reginald Cook [U of Mass P, 1974] 51). Radcliffe Squires has written interestingly of the birch tree as a path toward heaven fraught with risk, suspense, even a kind of terror. The climbing boy performs his act of birch-bending gracefully, but in doing so goes almost too far, like one filling a cup "even above the brim" *(The Major Themes of Robert Frost* [U of Michigan P, 1963] 55–56).

Sidelights on the poem: Frost wrote to his friend, Charles Madison, in 1950, "'Birches' is two fragments soldered together so long ago I have forgotten where the joint is." Can anybody find it? . . . A particular word he congratulated himself on finding was *crazes* in line 9: "cracks and crazes their enamel" (Cook, 230). Frost's concern for scientific accuracy is well known. He sought evidence to confirm his claim that birches bend to left and right. "With disarming slyness, he said: 'I never go down the shoreline [from Boston] to New York without watching the birches to see if they live up to what I say about them in the poem.' His birches, he insisted, were *not* the white mountain or paper birch of northern New England *(Betula papyrifera);* they were the gray birch *(Betula populifolia)*" (Cook, 232).

Robert Frost, MENDING WALL, page 922

This familiar poem is often misread, or loaded with needless symbolism. Some possible notions you might meet:

1. That the poem is an allegory: the wall stands for some political barrier such as high tariffs, immigration quotas, the Berlin Wall, or the Iron Curtain. But can the text of the poem lend such a notion any support? Frost, according to Louis Untermeyer, frowned on all attempts to add to the wall's meaning: "He denies that the poem says anything more than it seems to say." (Note in *Robert Frost's Poems* [New York: Washington Square Press, 1964].)

2. Frost's theme is that fences should be destroyed. Up with communal land, away with private property! But as Radcliffe Squires points out, none of Frost's other poetry supports such a left-wing view. Neither does "Mending Wall" support it, "for the poet-narrator himself cooperates with the wall-builder, replacing the stones in the spring even as he protests in spirit." *(The Major Themes of Robert Frost* [Ann Arbor: University of Michigan Press, 1963].)

3. The maxim "Good fences make good neighbors" is just a smug platitude for which the speaker has only contempt. This view would make him out to be a cynic. Yet, by cooperating in the wall-mending, the speaker lends the maxim some truth. Although limited in imagination, the neighbor isn't an idiot. (Frost is portraying, by the way, an actual farmer he liked: the cheerful Napoleon Guay, owner of the farm next door to the Frosts'

farm in Derry, New Hampshire. See *New Hampshire's Child: The Derry Journals of Leslie Frost* [Albany: State University of New York Press, 1969].)

At the center of the poem is a contrast between two ways to regard mending a wall. The speaker's view is announced in the first line; the neighbor's is repeated in the last. "The opposing statements," says Untermeyer, "are uttered by two different types of people—and both are right." Students may be asked to define the very different temperaments of speaker and neighbor. A hard-working farmer to whom spring means walls to mend, the neighbor lacks fancy and frivolity. Spring is all around him, yet he *moves in darkness,* as though blind. Lines 30–40 compare him to a man of the Stone Age. A conservative from habit, he mends walls mainly because his father did. The speaker, full of mischief and imagination, is presumably a poet who wants to do no more hard labor than he can help. Speaker enjoys having some fun with neighbor, telling him that apple trees won't invade pines. Mending walls is a kind of spring ritual, and the speaker likes to pretend there is magic in it: using a spell to make stones balance, blaming the wear-and-tear of winter upon elves—or more exactly, upon some Something not to be offended.

Robert Frost, STOPPING BY WOODS ON A SNOWY EVENING, page 923

Students will think they know this poem from their elementary school textbooks, in which it is usually illustrated as though it were about a little horse, but they may need to have its darker suggestions underlined for them. Although one can present a powerful case for seeing Frost as a spokesman for the death wish, quoting other Frost poems such as "Come In," "To Earthward," and "Into My Own," we think it best to concentrate on this familiar poem and to draw the class to state what it implies. The last stanza holds the gist of it. What would he do if he *didn't* keep his promises? There is sense, however, in an objection a student once made: maybe he'd just stay admiring the snow for another fifteen minutes and be late for milking. "People are always trying to find a death wish in that poem," Frost told an audience at the Bread Loaf Writers' Conference in 1960. "But there's a life wish there—he goes on, doesn't he?"

Ask students if they see anything unusual about the rime scheme of the poem (rimes linking the stanzas as in terza rima or as in Shelley's "Ode to the West Wind"), and then ask what problem this rime scheme created for the poet as the poem neared its end. How else would Frost have ended it if he hadn't hit upon that magnificent repetition? In 1950 Frost wrote to a friend, "I might confess the trade secret that I wrote the third line of the last stanza of Stopping by Woods in such a way as to call for another stanza when I didn't want another stanza and didn't have another stanza in me, but with great presence of mind and a sense of what a good boy I was I instantly struck the line out and made my exit with a repeat end" (qtd. in Lawrance Thompson, *Robert Frost: The Years of Triumph* [New York: Holt, 1970] 597–98). On another occasion Frost declared that to have a line in the last stanza that didn't rime with anything would have seemed a flaw. "I considered for a moment winding up with a three line stanza. The repetend was the only logical way to end such a poem" (letter of 1923 to Sylvester Baxter, given by R. C. Townsend, *New England Quarterly* 36 June 1963]: 243).

That this famous poem may be sung to the old show tune "Hernando's Hideaway" (from *The Pajama Game*) was discovered by college students working as waiters at the Bread Loaf Writers' Conference in 1960.

Paper topic: Read Lionel Trilling's speech at Frost's eight-fifth birthday dinner, in which Trilling maintained, "I think of Robert Frost as a terrifying poet" ("A Speech on Robert Frost: A Cultural Episode," *Partisan Review* 26 [Summer 1959]: 445–52; also reprinted in *Robert Frost: A Collection of Critical Essays,* ed. James M. Cox [Englewood

Cliffs: Prentice, 1962]). Referring to "Stopping by Woods" and other Frost poems, state to what extent you agree with Trilling's view or disagree with it.

Frost reads the poem on *An Album of Modern Poetry* (Library of Congress, PL 20) and on *Robert Frost Reading His Own Poems,* record no. 1 (EL LCB 1941, obtainable from the National Council of Teachers of English, 1211 Kenyon Road, Urbana, IL 61801). Both recordings also include "Fire and Ice."

Allen Ginsberg, A SUPERMARKET IN CALIFORNIA, page 923

A comparison of this poem with Walt Whitman's "I Saw in Louisiana a Live-Oak Growing" (page 1010) and "To a Locomotive in Winter" (page 600) demonstrates the extent to which Ginsberg, in his tribute to Whitman, uses very Whitmanlike "enumerations." Ginsberg's long sentences, use of free verse, parentheses, and fulsome phases ("childless, lonely old grubber," "lonely old courage-teacher," etc.) are further indications that he is paying tribute to Whitman in part by echoing his style.

There is in "A Supermarket in California" as well a quality of surrealism that is Ginsberg's own. The existence of a "Neon fruit supermarket," the juxtaposition of past and present, the inclusion of Spanish poet García Lorca (like Ginsberg and Whitman, a homosexual) "down by the watermelons," and the references to Charon and to the River Lethe all hover at the edges of dream.

Questions for discussion: What does Ginsberg mean when he speaks of "the lost America of love"? What does the poem say about loneliness? about death? (Whitman's death, in the poem, is as lonely a journey as Ginsberg imagines his life to have been.)

Dana Gioia, CALIFORNIA HILLS IN AUGUST, page 924

When this poem was first added to this anthology in 1986, Dana Gioia provided the following note (little suspecting he would one day become a co-conspirator in editing the book):

"California Hills in August" was conceived as a defense of the special beauty of the dry landscape of California and the American Southwest. While the poem admits that an outsider might initially find this environment harsh and even hostile in the summer months, it asks that the landscape be seen on its own terms and not judged as some deficient form of conventionally verdant summer scenery.

Strangely, I did not write this poem until I had been living in the Northeast for several years. It was only then that I realized how foreign the sparse August hills of California seemed to most Americans who came from areas which are lushly green and overgrown during the summer. Likewise, living back East, I finally understood how much the symbolic framework of traditional English poetry depended on the particular kind of climate shared by England and Eastern America. Until then the seasonal patterns of this poetry with its snowy winters and green summers had always seemed remote and artificial to a Westerner like me, raised in a climate which endowed a radically different sense of Nature's cycles. I wondered why Western writers had not played with that paradox more forcefully in their poetry.

These thoughts must have been in the back of my mind when suddenly I returned home for a family emergency. Two sleepless days later, after it had been resolved, I took a noontime walk through some nearby hills. In the strangely heightened consciousness of physical exhaustion and dislocating travel, I found myself overwhelmed by the delicate, sun-bleached beauty of the place. This was a landscape which I had left long enough ago both to hunger for as a native and to recoil from as an outsider. Sorting out these contradictions as I walked home, I heard myself say the first few lines of the poem. Writing out the opening stanzas later that day, I realized how image by image this poem had been forming for a long time in my unconscious.

The poem divides into two uneven parts. The first four stanzas view the landscape through the eyes of an imaginary Easterner who sees only the emptiness, deprivation, and savagery of the place. But then in the final stanza the speaker suddenly upsets everything said up to this point by suggesting how a native might see the same place from a different perspective. Isn't one of the purposes of poetry to make us see the unexpected beauty of some person, place or thing we previously took for granted or dismissed? That transformation was what I hoped to accomplish in "California Hills in August."

H. D., HELEN, page 925

What a cold, hate-inspiring queen H. D. portrays! She makes a sharp contrast with the lovable image of Helen as a child in Yeats's "Long-legged Fly."

For a few notes on recent scholarly activity, see the entry on H. D.'s "Heat" in this manual.

Donald Hall, NAMES OF HORSES, page 926

Hall is apparently eulogizing not one horse but a long succession of them, each taking on its predecessors' duties through the years. The poem enumerates the everyday chores the horses had to do, "generation on generation," Sundays included. The "man, who fed you and kept you, and harnessed you every morning" represents not a single farmer, apparently, but all those on this New Hampshire farm who cared for and finally buried their horses in the time-honored way "for a hundred and fifty years." Like all dead animals (including people), the horses when they die become "soil makers," useful even in their graves.

The wonderful list in the poem's last line delivers what the title has promised, names of horses. The last one, Lady Ghost, is the most connotative. You might wish to have students explore its suggestions.

First published in *The New Yorker,* this poem later appeared in Hall's seventh book of poems, *Kicking the Leaves* (New York: Harper, 1978). The farm in New Hampshire where Hall lives was once a working farm run by his grandparents and, before them, his great-grandparents. Hall has written a prose memoir, *String Too Short to Be Saved* (Boston: Godine, 1981), about the boyhood summers he spent there with his grandmother and grandfather. "Names of Horses," too, seems to depend heavily on the poet's fond memories of the farm he still loves.

Thomas Hardy, THE CONVERGENCE OF THE TWAIN, page 927

The discovery in September 1985 of the well-preserved wreck of the *Titanic* in the North Atlantic, and the subsequent squabble over possession of it, has given this old favorite poem a certain immediacy. Many students will be familiar with the history of this great disaster from news reports (or from the popular book and film *Raise the Titanic!*). Still, a few facts may need to be recalled. The fateful day was April 15, 1912. The pride of the British White Star lines, the *Titanic* was the world's largest ship in its day, celebrated for luxurious trappings (including Turkish baths and a fully equipped gym). Many of the unlucky passengers were wealthy and famous. One reason the *Titanic* sank with such cost of life was that the builders, smugly assuming the ship to be unsinkable, had provided lifeboats for fewer than half the 2,200 passengers. (Only 705 survived.) Hardy wrote the poem for the souvenir program of a benefit show for the *Titanic* Disaster Fund (to aid survivors and the bereaved) given at Covent Garden, May 14, 1912.

Hardy has been seen as an enemy of science and industrialism, those spoilers of rural England, but Donald Davie argues that "The Convergence of the Twain" shows no such animosity. The poem censures vanity and luxury, "but not the technology which built the great ship and navigated her" *(Thomas Hardy and British Poetry* [Oxford: Oxford UP, 1972]). Although Hardy personally knew two victims of the disaster, the "Convergence," as J. O. Bailey points out, is not a personal lament; indeed, the drowned are hardly mentioned. The poem is a philosophic argument, with the Immanent Will punishing man for pride: "It acts like the Greek concept of Fate that rebukes *hubris" (The Poetry of Thomas Hardy* [Chapel Hill: U of North Carolina P, 1970]). Fate, however, seems personified in the poem as the Spinner of the Years, a mere agent of the Will.

Students can concentrate profitably on the poet's choice of words: those that suggest the exotic unnaturalness of the *Titanic's* furnishings *(salamandrine, opulent, jewels . . . to ravish the sensuous mind, gilded).* Diction will also point to the metaphor of the marriage between ship and iceberg: the *intimate welding* and the *consummation.* The late Allen Tate was fond of reading this poem aloud to his friends, with mingled affection and contempt, and remarking (according to Robert Kent) that it held "too many dead words, dead then as now, and all the more obtuse for having been long dead in Shelley. 'Stilly,' for example." From Hardy's original printed version of the poem, as given in *The Variorum Edition of the Complete Poems of Thomas Hardy,* ed. James Gibson (New York: Macmillan, 1979), it appears that he originally cast line 6: "The cold, calm currents strike their rhythmic tidal lyres." Isn't *thrid* an improvement, even though it is stiltedly archaic?

Thomas Hardy, DURING WIND AND RAIN, page 929

A view of the passage of time and the coming of death to ordinary people, this great lyric invites comparison with E. E. Cummings's "anyone lived in a pretty how town." It differs, though, in sticking to conventional language and in utterly lacking sentiment. Is there a more blood-chilling line in poetry than "And the rotten rose is ripped from the wall," a powerful example of alliteration that means business?

In *A Commentary on the Poems of Thomas Hardy* (New York: Harper, 1977), F. B. Pinion sees this poem as inspired by Hardy's reading of his wife's reminiscences. The scenes in the poem, he says, depict "two of the homes and gardens of the Gifford family, which Emma remembered from her girlhood at Plymouth. Each of the recollections, bright and happy in itself, is seen through the regret which years and death have brought." Donald Davie, in *Thomas Hardy and British Poetry* (New York: Oxford UP, 1972), calling this poem "one of Hardy's greatest achievements," admires in it "the cunning variations of the accomplished metrist."

In "During Wind and Rain" the variation that is decisive is on the seventh and last line of each stanza:

> "How the sick leaves reel down in throngs!"
> "See, the white storm-birds wing across!"
> "And the rotten rose is ripped from the wall"
> "Down their carved names the rain-drop ploughs."

Rhythmically so various, the lines are metrically identical. Though anapests are twice substituted for iambs in the line about the rose, the expectation of symmetry proves that line too is iambic tetrameter like the others. . . . The effect is that when we reach the refrain at the end of the third stanza, though symmetry is maintained between that stanza and the first two, it is so masked by the rhythmical variation that, instead of checking back to register how this stanza reproduces the earlier ones, we are propelled forward to see what will happen in the last.

Thomas Hardy, HAP, page 930

This early poem summarizes Hardy's bleak view of existence. A lesser artist might have been crushed by this sense of hopelessness, but Hardy filled the theological gap with love, compassion, and humor (as for instance, in the following poem "In Church"). Students might compare this bitterly atheistic poem with the gentler "The Oxen" (on page 812). In "The Oxen" Hardy longs for the Christian faith he had as a child.

Two things are worth noting in the poem (since students sometimes overlook them). First, Hardy would rather have a cruel deity than none at all. It is not the pain of existence he bemoans, it is the meaninglessness of life without some guiding divine plan. Second, Hardy's worldview is so deeply religious that even when he claims there is no God, he ends up personifying the nothingness under which he suffers ("Crass Casualty" and "dicing Time," which he then groups as "purblind Doomsters.")

The vocabulary of "Hap" is interesting. The title word means both a "happening" and "chance." *Hap* is not used much today but is still alive in common terms in "happenstance" and "hapless." *Casualty* is a word we are used to seeing primarily in accident reports and insurance forms. Hardy uses it here in its broader original sense of "chance" in the same way we still use "accident" in the neutral sense of a "chance event." Detective novel fans may remember *Doomsters* from the title of Ross MacDonald's compelling novel; *doomster* is an archaic word for a judge (that survives in the family name Dempster). In Scottish courts the doomster not only read the sentence but also carried out the execution. Finally, you might quiz the class on *purblind,* a perfectly modern term, that many of them won't know.

"Hap" is, by the way, a sonnet. Notice how neatly the meaning turns at the beginning of the sestet ("But not so."). Hardy uses the form so naturally that one might overlook it entirely.

Thomas Hardy, IN CHURCH, page 930

This is a selection from the fifteen "Satires of Circumstance," a sequence that (at the publisher's insistence) lent its title to Hardy's poetry volume of 1914. This major collection appeared in a momentous year for the poet: after his second marriage and shortly after the outbreak of World War I. Hardy himself had voiced doubts about putting these bitter items in a book together with more recent, poignant elegies for his first wife. He called them "caustically humorous productions which had been issued with a light heart before the war"; and later remarked to Edmond Gosse: "The scales had not fallen from my eyes when I wrote them, and when I reprinted them they had" (letter of 16 Apr. 1918).

Robert Gittings, a recent biographer, agrees with reviewers of 1914 that the "Satires" would have been better off as short stories (*Thomas Hardy's Later Years* [Boston: Atlantic-Little, 1978] 161–63). Yet the astute John Crowe Ransom has been fond of these caustic items. "They are satires rather than proper tragedies," he observes, "being poems in which the victims are not entitled to our sympathy. The joke is upon persons who have to be punished because they were foolish; because they were more innocent than anybody can afford to be in this world." The "Satires" show Hardy in a mood of ferocity that enlarges his range, "though the gentle reader may not like him any the better" (Introduction, *Selected Poems of Thomas Hardy* [New York: Collier, 1966]). We admire Hardy's extreme economy in telling these stories, in centering on moral crises so painful that, unless we laugh, we must cringe. Together, the "Satires" form a small gallery of various kinds of irony.

J. O. Bailey has illuminated the title "Satires of Circumstance." Earlier, in a novel of 1876, Hardy had used the phrase in describing a man who "sometimes had philosophy enough to appreciate a satire of circumstance, because nobody intended it" (*The Hand of Ethelberta,* chapter 12). Most of the poems in this series, Bailey notes, present ironic situations that no one intended. Some, like in "In Church," depend on things accidentally noticed or overheard (*The Poetry of Thomas Hardy: A Handbook and Commentary* [Chapel Hill: U of North Carolina P, 1970] 334).

"In Church": Irony lies in a contrast between the pulpit personality of the preacher and the vain, self-satisfied actor he is when behind the scenes. We feel for his disillusioned little pupil: a terrible contrast is implied between her before and after views of her idol.

Robert Hayden, THE WHIPPING, page 931

Hayden's poem chillingly depicts the cycles of family and social violence. The old woman beats the boy to avenge the "lifelong hidings / she has had to bear." The narrator stands outside the action of the poem, but the boy's tears trigger his own memories of being beaten by—in a frightening synecdoche—"the face that I / no longer knew or loved." Notice that Hayden deliberately leaves the relationship between "the boy" and "the old woman" unstated. Is she mother, grandmother, aunt, babysitter, foster mother? It doesn't matter in the poem. She is large and powerful while the boy is small and helpless. One might assign this poem together with the next selection, Hayden's "Those Winter Sundays," for contrasting views of domestic life.

Robert Hayden, THOSE WINTER SUNDAYS, page 932

QUESTIONS FOR DISCUSSION:

1. Is the speaker a boy or a man? How do you know?

2. Summarize the poem's theme—its main idea.

3. What do you understand from "the chronic angers of that house"?

4. How does this poet's choice of words differ from that of most writers of prose? Suggestion: Read the opening five lines aloud.

This brief poem, simple in the word's best sense, has a depth that rewards close reading. That the speaker is a boy is a safe inference: most grown-ups do not lie abed while their fathers polish their shoes. Besides, evidently years have intervened between the speaker today and his previous self—the observing child. Now the speaker understands his father better, looks back on himself, and asks, "What did I know?"

The poem states its theme in its wonderful last line (worth quoting to anyone who distrusts abstract words in poetry). Students can miss Hayden's point unless they understand its vocabulary. *Austere* can mean stern, forbidding, somber, but it can also mean (as it does here) ascetic, disciplined, self-denying. To rise in the freezing house takes steely self-discipline. That the father's life is built on austerity we get from his labor-worn hands. What is an *office*? A duty, task, or ceremony that someone assumes (or has conferred on him): the tasks of shining shoes, of stirring banked fires in a furnace (or a coal-burning stove?). James Wright, a keen admirer of Hayden's poem, has spoken of it in an interview:

> The word *offices* is the great word here. *Office,* they say in French. It is a religious service after dark. Its formality, its combination of distance and immedi-

acy, is appropriate. In my experience uneducated people and people who are driven by brute circumstance to work terribly hard for a living, the living of their families, are very big on formality. *(The Pure Clear Word: Essays on the Poetry of James Wright,* ed. Dave Smith [Urbana: U of Illinois P, 1982] 10).

Perhaps the "chronic angers" belong to the father: the boy gets up slowly and fearfully as though in dread of a tongue-lashing. Yet this reading does not seem quite in keeping with the character of the father as he emerges: stoic, patient, long-suffering, loving. Hayden does not invest these angers in the father exclusively. Perhaps any tenant of this bitterly cold house has reason to dread getting up in it.

When read aloud, the opening stanza reveals strong patterns of sound: the internal alliteration of the *k*-sound in *blueblack, cracked, ached, weekday, banked, thanked* (and, in the next stanza, in *wake, breaking, chronic*)—staccato bursts of hard consonants. Rather than using exact rime at the ends of lines, Hayden strengthens lines by using it internally: *banked/thanked* (line 5), *wake/breaking* (6); perhaps off-rime, too: *labor/weather* (4), *rise/dress* (8). Alliteration and assonance occur in *clothes . . . cold* (2), *weekday weather* (4). If you assign this poem early in your investigation of poetry, probably it matters more that students hear and respond to the rich interplay of repeated sounds than that they be able to give these devices labels.

"Those Winter Sundays" is the most often reprinted poem of Robert Hayden. A black poet who grew up in Detroit and who for many years was an English professor at the University of Michigan, he has written other poems apparently drawn from childhood and memory, among these "Obituary," another moving tribute to his father. Hayden's posthumous *Collected Poems* (New York: Norton/Liveright, 1985) belongs, we think, in every library.

James Hayford, DRY NOON, page 932

This wonderfully concise poem may serve as an example of symbolism: the dry, motionless valley suggesting the characters' stasis and old age. The scene is upstate Vermont, James Hayford's home territory.

Students may need a little class discussion to help them see the art of the poem, its command of meter and rime, its tremendous, bridled energy. Who are these people and what are their circumstances in life? The first couplet identifies them and sets forth their situation: their poverty—the house is "low," not multistoried and imposing—their years, the fact that they dwell in the past. Outside of life, outside of the cycle of the seasons, they are transfixed in a valley where everything is drying, including themselves, and even the wind doesn't move. In language almost painfully flat, the poet recalls an exchange of pleasantries between the old man and someone with business to do, who had passed along the road and is now gone by.

Indeed, all of Hayford's language repays a closer look. How accurately the phrase "rain *or* shine" is chosen and placed, transforming it from cliché to literal truth! The word *nooning* seems an inspired coinage.

What is the poem's tone? Wry, amused, sympathetic. This portrait seems a perfect cameo, well worth comparing with Gwendolyn Brooks's compassionate glimpse of an old couple in "The Bean Eaters."

An octogenarian, James Hayford is only now beginning to win recognition. For a recent appreciation of him, see XJK, "The Least Known Major American Poet," in *Harvard Review* 3 (Spring 1993). In 1992, in his eightieth year, Hayford brought out a new collection, *Uphill Home* ($9.95, paperbound). *Star in the Shed Window,* his remarkable collected poems 1933–1988 ($24.95, hardcover), appeared in 1989. Both books, published by a regional press, may be hard to find in shops, but may be obtained from New England Press, Box 575, Shelburne, VT 05482 ($2 shipping for one book, $2.25 for two).

Seamus Heaney, DIGGING, page 933

When Irish poet Seamus Heaney went to Lewiston, Maine, in 1986 to receive an honorary degree at Bates College, he read "Digging" aloud to the assembled graduates, parents, and friends. It seemed an appropriate choice. Some of the Maine students in his audience must have found expressed in Heaney's poem their own ambition for hardworking forebears whose course through life they had decided not to follow. Is the speaker in the poem uneasy about choosing instead to be a poet? It is clear that he admires the skill and strength his father and grandfather displayed in their work. But the poem ends on a positive note. The poet accepts himself for what he is.

In "Feeling into Words," an essay in his *Preoccupations* (New York: Farrar, 1980), Heaney likens the poetry to digging up archaeological finds. Apparently it is a matter of digging a spade into one's past and unearthing something forgotten. "Digging," written in 1964, was his earliest poem in which it seemed that his feelings had found words. "The pen/spade analogy," he adds, "was the simple heart of the matter and *that* was simply a matter of almost proverbial common sense." As a schoolboy, he was often told to keep studying "because 'learning's easily carried' and 'the pen is lighter than the spade.'"

Seamus Heaney, MOTHER OF THE GROOM, page 933

This tender poem enters the thoughts of someone often forgotten: the mother of the groom. Floating through her mind at the wedding is a vivid memory of her son as a little boy. Now her lap is "voided." Though she "hears a daughter welcomed," she is not yet ready to take part in the welcoming.

> It's as if he kicked when lifted
> And slipped her soapy hold.

The third stanza shifts to another theme: the permanence of marriage—a generation-old Irish Catholic marriage, at any rate—symbolized by the mother's wedding ring, "bedded forever now / In her clapping hand."

Is the poem sentimental? We think not. It sticks to just a few closely observed details, understated but implying volumes.

Anthony Hecht, ADAM, page 934

"Adam" was the title poem (see line 26) of Anthony Hecht's Pulitzer Prize winning collection, *The Hard Hours* (1967). The book is dedicated to Hecht's two sons, Jason and Adam. The poem's title, therefore, has a double resonance—one religious, the other personal. The poem memorably embodies one of the central teachings of the Judeo-Christian tradition, namely that human love emulates God's love for mankind. Hecht parallels God's love for His first "son," Adam, with the poet's love for his own son Adam.

The first stanza is spoken by the God of *Genesis* to Adam who has been created but not yet awakened to find the world fashioned for him. The divine voice announces that "These very words you hear / Compose the fish and starlight." God's word, as the Judeo-Christian tradition believes, becomes reality. While not claiming divine power for his own words, the speaker of "Adam" asserts his right as a poet and father to use the power of language to bless and comfort his son.

It may be worth asking students about the dramatic situation of the poem. Where is the speaker's son when these fatherly words are spoken? (In the beginning of the third stanza, we learn that the son is in a foreign country and the poet speaks "to the empty air.")

There are several other poems that can be profitably compared to "Adam." To pursue the mythic elements, it can be read along with A. D. Hope's "Imperial Adam." This combination will demonstrate how differently two poets can use the same material. To explore the human dimension, "Adam" can be compared to the two Robert Hayden poems earlier in the Poems for Further Reading section. "Those Winter Sundays," especially, provides a son's glimpse of a father to contrast with this father's view of a son. Finally, a dramatic contrast could be made with Weldon Kees's "For My Daughter" (page 602), which is spoken by a man who feels he has no power to bless or protect his child.

George Herbert, LOVE, page 935

Herbert's poem is often read as an account of a person's reception into the Church; the eaten *meat,* as the Eucharist. Herbert's extended conceits or metaphors are also evident in "The Pulley" (page 690) and "Redemption" (page 802).

For discussion: compare "Love" with another seventeenth-century devotional poem, Donne's "Batter my heart" (page 629). What is the tone of each poem? Herbert may seem less intense, almost reticent by comparison. Douglas Bush comments, "Herbert does not attempt the high pitch of Donne's 'Divine Poems.' His great effects are all the greater for rising out of a homely, colloquial quietness of tone; and peace brings quiet endings—'So I did sit and eat'" (*English Literature in the Earlier Seventeenth Century* [New York: Oxford UP, 1945] 139).

Herbert, by the way, is an Anglican saint—the only one who does not also appear in the Roman Catholic calendar.

Robert Herrick, THE BAD SEASON MAKES THE POET SAD, page 936

A poem of interest for several reasons. For one, it makes the ability to write poetry depend on congenital politics. As a priest of the Church of England whom the Puritans ousted from his sinecure, Herrick, of course, was a staunch Royalist. For another, it is a kind of sonnet written in couplets.

The "many fresh and fragrant mistresses"? Perhaps Herrick refers to his poems, perhaps to the Muses, perhaps to the many lovely women his poems portray.

Like so many of Herrick's poems, this one is rich in classical lore. *Tyrian dews* echoes Tibullus; the last line, Horace. In line 7, there's an allusion to the myth of the golden age (the degeneration of the ages of man through gold, to silver, and finally to iron).

The last line strikes us as a quite wonderful description of the poetic experience. Even if it is borrowed from the Latin poet, it still seems fresh and fragrant.

Robert Herrick, TO THE VIRGINS, TO MAKE MUCH OF TIME, page 937

Roses would have suited Herrick's iambic meter—why is *rose-buds* richer? Rosebuds are flowers not yet mature, and therefore suggest virgins, not matrons. There may be a sexual hint besides: rosebuds more resemble private parts than roses. But in this poem, time flies, the rosebuds of line 1 bloom in line 3. Rose-buds is also rhythmically stronger than roses, as Austin Warren has pointed out: it has a secondary stress as well as a primary. Warren has recalled that when he first read the poem in college in 1917, he misread *rose-buds* as *roses,* kept misreading it ever after, and only a half-century later realized his mistake and found a new poem in front of him. "In untutored youth, the sentiment and the rhythm suffice: the exactness of the language goes unnoticed. And in later life a remembered favorite escapes exact attention because we think we know it so well" ("Herrick Revisited," *Michigan Quarterly Review 15* [Summer 1976]: 245–67).

Question for discussion: What do you think of Herrick's advice? Are there any perils in it?

Garrett Hongo, THE CADENCE OF SILK, page 937

Here's one to convince basketball watchers, especially Lakers fans, that the subjects of poetry don't have to be arcane. Not only a poem about sports, "The Cadence of Silk" may refer also to writing poetry: watching the Sonics taught the speaker about cadence, rhythm, and rhetoric (lines 6–14). Appropriately, when the final ball swishes through the net, the poem ends too.

Worth noticing: Hongo's colorful imagery and similes ("sleek as arctic seals," "like a waiter balancing a tray").

Gerard Manley Hopkins, SPRING AND FALL, page 939

Hopkins's tightly wrought syntax may need a little unraveling. Students may be asked to reword lines 3–4 in a more usual sequence ("Can you, with your fresh thoughts, care for leaves like the things of man?") and then to put the statement into more usual words. (An attempt: "Do you, young and innocent as you are, feel as sorry for falling leaves as for dying people?") Lines 12–13 may need a similar going-over and rough paraphrase. ("Neither any human mouth nor any human mind has previously formed the truth that the heart and spirit have intuited.") "Sorrow's springs are the same"—that is, all human sorrows have the same cause: the fact that all things pass away. A world of constant change is "the blight man was born for": an earth subject to death, having fallen from its original state of a changeless Eden. The difficulties of a Hopkins poem result from a swiftly thoughtful mind trying to jam all possible meaning into a brief space (and into words that are musical).

Wanwood is evidently a term the poet coined for pale autumn woods. W. H. Gardner, editor of Hopkins's poems, finds in it also the suggestion of "wormwood"—bitter gall, also wood that is worm-eaten. The term *leafmeal* reminds him of "piecemeal," and he paraphrases line 8: "One by one the leaves fall, and then rot into mealy fragments."

John Crowe Ransom's "Janet Waking" is another poem in which a sophisticated poet contemplates a grieving child. How do the poems differ? Ransom tries to convey the intensity of Janet's grief over her dead hen; Hopkins is content to talk to Margaret, like a priest trying to console her, and to philosophize.

Hopkins's great lyric ought to survive George Starbuck's brilliant travesty (page 851). The two are worth comparing in case students assume that what matters in poetry is the message alone, that particular words have no consequence. Starbuck obviously is having a good time translating "Spring and Fall" into the American vernacular. His parody may be useful as a way into a number of crucial matters: the diction of a poem and how language indicates it. Who or what is the butt of Starbuck's ridicule? Is it Hopkins and his poem; or the speaker himself, his crudeness, his hard-boiled simplemindedness? (Howard Moss performs a comparable reduction of a sonnet of Shakespeare's on page 679.)

Gerard Manley Hopkins, THOU ART INDEED JUST, LORD, IF I CONTEND, page 940

Like Milton in his sonnet on page 968, Hopkins begins with a complaint. Unlike Milton he seems, at last, far from being reconciled to the Lord's will; and tension between his faith and the testimony of his experience threaten to (but do not quite) overpower him. In the octet, to be sure, Hopkins is not merely speaking for himself: he is paraphrasing Jeremiah, who also complains that God lets scoundrels prosper. One of Hopkins's so-called "Terrible Sonnets," the poem ends not with any sense of deliverance, but with a prayer.

In line 1, why is the Lord said to be just? Well, at least he gives the poor suffering mortal a hearing. "When I have a friend like you, who needs an enemy?" seems the near-despairing thrust of lines 5–9. Although in the sestet the speaker sees the possibility of change, drawing hope from the fact that nature is renewed in spring, nature only reminds him once more of his own impotence and sterility. Birds build nests, but he can't.

In this as in other Hopkins poems, close reading is essential, but will reveal a few vexing difficulties. In line 2, "but, sir, so what I plead is just," the *so what* can give trouble—more so than the way Hopkins worded the line originally: "but, sir, what I shall speak is just." Syntax is inverted in lines 12–13 to stress the *no* and the two *nots*.

Norman MacKenzie has suggested that this poem could have been entitled "Bitterness in Spring," and thinks the poet's envy of the *fresh wind* (which shakes those lucky birds) suggests lack of poetic inspiration. (You might contrast this tormented poem with Hopkins's rapturous "Pied Beauty" [page 667] and with "The Windhover" [next], in which the *sheer plod* of the religious life is triumphantly justified.) It is ironic, notes MacKenzie, "that one of [Hopkins's] most enduring poems should be based on the conviction that no work of his would ever endure" (*A Reader's Guide to Gerard Manley Hopkins* [Ithaca: Cornell UP, 1981] 204).

Gerard Manley Hopkins, THE WINDHOVER, page 941

"The best thing I ever wrote," said Hopkins. If your students have enjoyed "Pied Beauty" (page 667) or "God's Grandeur" (page 729) without too much difficulty, then why not try "The Windhover," despite its famous ambiguities? Some students may go afield in reading the opening line, and may take *I caught* to mean that the poet trapped the bird; but they can be told that Hopkins, a great condenser, probably means "I caught a glimpse of."

Dispute over the poem often revolves around whether or not the windhover is Christ and around the meaning of *Buckle!* Most commentators seem to agree that the bird is indeed Christ, or else that Christ is like the bird. (Yvor Winters, who thought the poem "minor and imperfect," once complained, "To describe a bird, however beautifully, and to imply that Christ is like him but greater, is to do very little toward indicating the greatness of Christ.") Some read *Buckle!* as a plea to the bird to descend to earth; others, as a plea to all the qualities and things mentioned in line 9 (*Brute beauty, valor, act*) to buckle themselves together into one. Still others find the statement ending in *Buckle!* no plea at all, but just an emphatic observation of what the poet beholds. If Christ is the windhover (other arguments run), in what sense can he be said to buckle? Two of the answers: (1) in buckling on human nature and becoming man, as a knight buckles on armor; (2) in having his body broken on the cross. Students can be asked to seek all the words in the poem with connotations of royalty or chivalry—suggestive, perhaps, of Christ as King and Christ as noble knight or chevalier. Why the *sheer plod*? Hopkins reflects (it would seem) that if men will only buckle down to their lowly duties they will become more Christ-like, and their spiritual plowshares will shine instead of collecting rust. Hopkins preached a sermon that expressed a similar idea: "Through poverty, through labor, through crucifixion His majesty of nature more shines." The *embers*, we think, are a metaphor: moist clods thrown by the plow going down the sillion. Hopkins likes to compare things to hearth fire: for instance, the "fresh-firecoal chestnut-falls" in "Pied Beauty."

For detailed criticism, one might start with Norman H. MacKenzie, *A Reader's Guide to Gerard Manley Hopkins* (Ithaca: Cornell UP, 1981). MacKenzie provides facts from ornithology and his own kestrel-watching: no other birds are so expert in hovering, body horizontal, tail and head pointing down as they study the ground for prey. To hang stationary in the air over one spot, they must fly into the wind "with rapidly quivering *(wimpling,* line 4) wings, missing a few beats as gusts die, accelerating as they freshen"— responding to variations in the wind with nearly computer speed. Once in about every eight hovers, the kestrel will dive, not inertly but with wings held tense and high—it doesn't "buckle" in the sense of *collapse.* If it finds no victim, the bird swings and banks and takes an upward "stride," to hover once more. Hopkins's "how he rung upon the rein" doesn't mean that the kestrel climbs in a spiral. No gyring Yeats-bird, he.

An interesting view of the religious imagery informing this poem can be found in James Finn Cotter's study, *Inscape: The Christology and Poetry of Gerard Manley Hopkins* (Pittsburgh: U of Pittsburgh Press, 1972). Cotter, who is formidably learned in theology, examines traditional Christian writings to discover how they shaped Hopkins's sense of imagery. Cotter maintains that "Hopkins fashioned a myth of his own making," but that his private vision drew from a wide variety of philosophical and theological sources. In his long, careful reading of "The Windhover" Cotter observes:

> Circular motion and form dominate "The Windhover": the kestrel moves in slow, wide, sharp, and gliding circles which the rhythm and language perfectly mimic. Christ is present here as throughout the other sonnets, in the sun illuminating the scene; he is the dawn drawing the bird to a brilliant expression of itself and hence of its Lord.

Despite his fondness for Old and Middle English, Hopkins luckily refrained from calling the windhover by its obsolete name: *fuckwind* or *windfucker.* (No, that *f* is not a long *s.*) Thomas Nashe in *Lenten Stuffe* (1599) speaks of the "Kistrilles or windfuckers that filling themselves with winde, fly against the winde evermore." See *windfucker* in the *Oxford English Dictionary.* (For this dumbfounding discovery, thanks to David Lynch, who copyedited *Literature,* 4th ed.)

A. E. Housman, LOVELIEST OF TREES, THE CHERRY NOW, page 941

What is Housman's theme? Good old *carpe diem.* If you ask students to paraphrase this poem (it's not hard), a paraphrase might add, to catch the deeper implication, "Life is brief—time flies—I'd better enjoy beauty now."

Not part of the rough poem Housman began with, the second stanza was added last. Lines 9–10 originally read: "And since to look at things you love / Fifty times is not enough." What can be said for Housman's additions and changes? (These and other manuscript variations are given by Tom Burns Haber in *The Making of "A Shropshire Lad"* [Seattle: U of Washington P, 1966].)

A. E. Housman, TO AN ATHLETE DYING YOUNG, page 942

For a comment on this poem, see the note in this manual on Dryden's "To the Memory of Mr. Oldham," page 914 in the text.

Langston Hughes, DREAM DEFERRED, page 943

Simile by simile, Hughes shows different attitudes, including violent protest, that blacks might possibly take toward the long deferral of their dream of equality. Students might be asked what meaning they find in each comparison. The sugared crust (line 7) is probably the smiling face obligingly worn by Uncle Toms.

The angry, sardonic tone of the poem is clearly different from the sorrowful tone of Dudley Randall's "Ballad of Birmingham" (page 709).

Hughes's poem supplied the title for Lorraine Hansberry's long-running Broadway play A *Raisin in the Sun* (1958), in which the Youngers, a family descended from five generations of slaves, come to a Chicago ghetto in hopes of fulfilling their dream.

Donald Ritzhein has written a moving account of what the poem has meant to him, starting when his mother cut it out of a newspaper and pasted it to his bedroom door. "By the time I got to high school . . . I still didn't know a lot about the misery of deferred dreams . . . I knew a little more about them when I heard Martin Luther King, Jr., talk about dreams in Washington. I finally felt a little of what it's like to defer dreams when John F. Kennedy was killed" ("Langston Hughes: A Look Backwards and Forwards," *Steppingstones,* a little magazine published in Harlem, Winter 1984: 55–56). Have you any student who would care to write about what the poem has meant to her or him?

Langston Hughes, THE NEGRO SPEAKS OF RIVERS, page 943

This remarkable poem was written by Hughes while still in his teens. A good discussion question is to ask why Hughes chooses each of the four specific rivers to tell his story of the Negro race. The Euphrates is traditionally the original center of human civilization. By invoking it, Hughes places the Negro at the dawn of humanity. The Congo is the center of black African culture. The Nile represents the source of the most celebrated African culture, and Hughes claims the Negro a role in building this great civilization. Finally, the Mississippi becomes a symbol of the Negro in America, though Hughes selects a joyous moment to represent the race's turbulent place in our history.

Randall Jarrell, THE DEATH OF THE BALL TURRET GUNNER, page 944

The speaker seems an unknown citizen like Auden's (page 611). Jarrell's laconic war poem is complex in its metaphors. The womb is sleep; the outside world, waking; and the speaker has passed from one womb to another—from his mother into the belly of a bomber. His existence inside the ball turret was only a dream, and in truth he has had no mature life between his childhood and his death. Waking from the dream, he wakes only to nightmare. In another irony, the matter-of-fact battle report language of the last line contrasts horribly with what is said in it. How can the dead gunner address us? Clearly the poet had written his epitaph for him—and has done so as Jarrell said he wrote "The Woman at the Washington Zoo," "acting as next friend."

Robinson Jeffers, TO THE STONE-CUTTERS, page 945

If students will compare this poem with Shakespeare's sonnet "Not marble nor the gilded monuments," they'll be struck by a sharp difference of view. Shakespeare, evidently, is the optimist. For him, a poem can confer immortality and inspire love until doomsday. For Jeffers, poems will merely bring a little respite to "pained thoughts"—much as a spoonful of honey helps a hangover, according to one popular belief.

For a short assignment: Write a paraphrase of each of these two poems. Bring your work to class, ready to read it aloud. We'll discuss the poems, taking off from your work on them.

For another pessimistic view of monuments, direct students to Shelley's "Ozymandias." You might ask them to compare its theme with those of Shakespeare and Jeffers.

A sidelight on this poem: Any doubt he may have had that stone monuments last long didn't prevent Jeffers from building, with his own hands, a stone tower next to his home at the ocean's edge in Carmel, California.

Elizabeth Jennings, I FEEL, page 946

This poem has the passionate simplicity of a popular song, and yet it contains a series of complex metaphors. A Renaissance scholar would see the roots of some of these metaphors in Petrarch, but Jennings makes them entirely her own. The images are paired in implied opposition (ice and fire, stone and earth). They also move from intensity of feeling (ice and fire) to unconsciousness (stone and earth), as the speaker longs to escape the pain of her existence.

Ben Jonson, ON MY FIRST SON, page 946

This heartbreaking poem from Jonson's *Epigrammes*, requested by several instructors, repays close reading. What is "the state [man] should envy?" Death. Why the dead child should be envied is made clear in the lines that immediately follow (7–8). The final couplet is difficult in its syntax, and contains a pun on *like* in a sense now obsolete. The speaker vows, or prays (*vow*, along with *votive*, comes from the Greek *euchesthai:* "to pray"), that anyone whom he loves may not live too long. The seriousness of Jonson's wit is shown in this colossal pun: *like* meaning "thrive, do well, get on" as well as "to be fond." See *like* in the *OED* for other illustrations:

> Shallow to Falstaff: "By my troth, you like well and bear your years very well" (*Henry IV*, P.2, 3.2.92).
> "Trees generally do like best that stand to the Northeast wind" (Holland's Pliny, 1600).

"Poems Arranged by Subject and Theme" in this manual lists the book's sixteen other poems about fathers and children. In this section, see especially the father-and-son poems by Anthony Hecht, Robert Phillips, Stephen Shu-ning Liu, and James Wright ("Autumn Begins in Martins Ferry, Ohio").

Donald Justice, ON THE DEATH OF FRIENDS IN CHILDHOOD, page 947

There is more emotional distance, less grief in this poem than in Ben Jonson's. Neither does the speaker in "On the Death of Friends in Childhood" seem to be mourning one specific loss. The "Friends" he mentions suggest friends in general, perhaps other people's as well as his own. Yet, though time has softened the impact of long-ago losses, the narrator urges that we remember dead childhood friends and what was shared with them.

John Keats, ODE ON A GRECIAN URN, page 947

Why is the symbol of the urn so endlessly suggestive? It may help students to recall that Grecian urns are vessels for the ashes of the dead, and that their carved or painted figures (*Of deities, or mortal, or of both*) depict a joyous afterlife in the Elysian fields. The urn being circular, its design appears to continue endlessly. What greater image for eternity, or for the seamlessness of perfected art?

Most good discussions of the "Urn" confront a few of the poem's celebrated difficulties. Some questions to help speed the confrontation:

1. Assuming that the urn is said to be *sylvan* because it displays woodland scenes, in what sense is it a *historian*? What history or histories does it contain, or represent?

2. How can unheard melodies be sweeter than heard ones?

3. Why are youth, lover and loved one, trees, and musicians so lucky to exist upon the urn? (Lines 15–27.)

4. What disadvantages do living lovers labor under? (Lines 28–30.)

5. In stanza four, the procession of thought turns in a new direction. What additional insight occurs to the poet? (That the urn, whose world had seemed perfect, is in some ways limited and desolate. Altar cannot be reached nor sacrifice fulfilled, nor can the unseen little town ever be returned to.)

6. Paraphrase the statement that the urn *doth tease us out of thought / As doth Eternity.* (The urn lures us out of our habit of useless cogitation. Eternity also stops us from thinking because, for us mere mortals, it too is incomprehensible.)

7. How is the urn a *Cold Pastoral*? (Literally, it's lifeless clay; figuratively, it stands aloof from human change and suffering. Compare Stevens's "Jar," page 806.)

8. How then can a Cold Pastoral be called *a friend to man?* (It provides a resting place for human ashes; it inspires and delights; and, as the last lines attest, it teaches us.)

John Keats, ON FIRST LOOKING INTO CHAPMAN'S HOMER, page 948

QUESTIONS FOR DISCUSSION:

1. What are the *realms of gold?* Can the phrase have anything to do with the fact that early Spanish explorers were looking for El Dorado, a legendary city of treasure in South America?

2. Does Keats's boner about Cortez mar the poem?

3. Did you ever read anything that made you feel like a stout Cortez? If so, what?

John Keats, WHEN I HAVE FEARS THAT I MAY CEASE TO BE, page 949

Students will see right away that the poem expresses fear of death, but don't let them stop there: there's more to it. Why does the poet fear death? Because it will end his writing and his loving. The poem states what both loving and writing poetry have in common: both are magical and miraculous acts when they are spontaneous. Besides favoring "unreflect-ing love" for its "fairy power," Keats would write "with the magic hand of chance." And—if you care to open up a profundity—what might the poet mean by those "huge cloudy symbols of a high romance"? Literal cloud shapes that look like Tristram and Isolde's beaker of love-potion, or what?

Note that this poem addresses not Keats's beloved Fanny Brawne, but "the memory of the mysterious lady seen in adolescence one brief moment at Vauxhall long ago in the summer of 1814," according to Robert Gittings in *John Keats* (Boston: Atlantic, 1968) 188. The poem is about a "creature of an hour." (Fanny, of course, occupied not one hour but many.)

Gittings has found in the poem echoes of two sonnets of Shakespeare, both about devouring time: #60 ("Like as the waves make towards the pebbled shore, / So do our minutes hasten to their end") and #64 ("When I have seen by Time's fell hand defaced"). In the copy of the *Sonnets* that Keats co-owned with his friend Reynolds, these two were the most heavily marked.

This poem has had a hefty impact on later poets, notably John Berryman, who took from it the title for an autobiographical collection of his own poems on ambition and desire: *Love and Fame* (1972).

John Keats, TO AUTUMN, page 950

Although "To Autumn" was to prove the last of the poet's greatest lyrics, we have no evidence that Keats (full of plans and projects at the time) was consciously taking leave of the world. On September 21, 1819, three days after writing the poem, Keats in a letter to his friend John Hamilton Reynolds spoke of his delight in the season: "I never lik'd stubble fields so much as now—Aye better than the chilly green of the Spring. Somehow a stubble plain looks warm—in the same way that some pictures look warm—this strikes me so much in my Sunday's walk that I composed upon it."

QUESTIONS FOR DISCUSSION:

1. In the opening stanza, what aspects of autumn receive most emphasis? To what senses do the images appeal?

2. In the first two stanzas, autumn is several times personified (lines 2-3, 12-15,16-18, 19-20, 21-22). Who are its different persons? (Conspiring crony, careless landowner, reaper, gleaner, cider presser.)

3. In the third stanza, how does the tone change? Has there been any progression in scene or in idea throughout the poem? (Tone: calm serenity. In the first stanza, autumn is being prepared for; in the second, busily enjoyed, in the third, calmly and serenely contemplated. There is another stanza-by-stanza progression: from morning to noon to on-coming night. Like the *soft-dying day,* the light wind sometimes dies. The gnats in *wailful choir* also have funereal, mourning suggestions, but the stanza as a whole cannot be called gloomy.)

4. What words in stanza 3 convey sounds? (*Songs, music, wailful choir, mourn, loud bleat, sing, treble, whistles, twitter.* What an abundance of verbs! The lines convey a sense of active music making.)

5. Do you see any case for reading the poem as a statement of the poet's acceptance of the facts that beauty on earth is transitory and death is inevitable? (Surely such themes are present; the poem does not have to be taken to mean that the poet knows he himself will soon perish.)

For an unusually grim reading of the poem, see Annabel M. Patterson, "'How to load . . . and bend': Syntax and Interpretation in Keats's 'To Autumn,'" *PMLA 94* (1979): 449-58. Finding that the poem "undermines" our traditional notion of Autumn, Patterson argues that Keats subversively portrays the goddess as deceptive, careless, and demanding. Her proffered ripeness leads only to *last oozings* and *stubble-plains*—dead ends not to be desired. In the poet's view (as she interprets it), "Nature is amoral and not to be depended upon." Try this argument on the class. Do students agree? Whether or not they side with Patterson, they will have to examine the poem closely in order to comment.

For a good discussion of ways to approach Keats's poem with a class, see Bruce E. Miller, *Teaching the Art of Literature* (Urbana: NCTE, 1980) 75-84. Miller points out that not all students will know how cider is made, and suggests asking someone to explain Keats's reference to the cider-press in stanza 2. He recommends, too, borrowing from our nearest art department some reproductions of landscape paintings: "Constable's work, which was contemporary with Keats, to my mind almost catches the spirit to 'To Autumn,' but it is a little more literal and photographic. . . ."

With this rich poem, you might well start a discussion of imagery, or review this topic if students have met it earlier. "The students," remarks Miller, "need not ask themselves as they read, 'What does it mean?' Rather they should continually ask, 'What do I see?' 'What do I hear and touch?' 'What do I feel?'" (Not that in reading the poem they're actually seeing or touching anything except printed books, of course.)

Philip Larkin, HOME IS SO SAD, page 951

Larkin's considerable achievement in "Home is so Sad" is that he so beautifully captures the ring of ordinary speech within the confines of a tight *a b a b a* rime scheme and iambic pentameter. Note the slant rimes in the second stanza: *as, was,* and *vase.*

In an interview, Larkin has recalled a letter he received from a middle-aged mother who had read his poem: "She wrote to say her children had grown up and gone, and she felt precisely this emotion I was trying to express in the poem" ("Speaking of Writing XIII: Philip Larkin," [London] *Times* 20 Feb. 1964: 16). Bruce Martin finds the poem written not from a mother's point of view, but from that of a son who used to live in this house himself. The speaker projects his own sadness into it: it has remained pathetically changeless. What has changed is himself and others who once lived here (*Philip Larkin* [Boston: Twayne, 1978] 52).

DMK, taking a different view, thinks it quite possible to read the poem as though (as in Larkin's well-known "Mr. Bleaney" from the same collection, *The Whitsun Weddings*) the former inhabitants of this house have died. The speaker is left unidentified, an impersonal seeing-eye; and so your students, too, will probably come up with differing interpretations.

Is Larkin's poem sentimental? Hard-eyed and exact in its observations, aided by the colloquialism of line 7, "A joyous shot at how things ought to be," it successfully skirts the danger. Students might like to discuss the three words that follow: "Long fallen wide." Does Larkin mean that the home was an unhappy one, or merely ordinary in its deviation from the idea? Or is it that the arrow—the "joyous shot"—has fallen merely in the sense that, meant to be full of life, the home is now "bereft / Of anyone to please"?

Philip Larkin, POETRY OF DEPARTURES, Page 952

The speaker wonders why he doesn't break with his dull, tame life, just walk out, chuck everything, launch into the Romantic unknown like a highwayman. What an appealing notion! Question: Have you ever yearned to do that very thing? (Who hasn't?)

Well, why doesn't he take off? Because he sees all too clearly and painfully that such a grandiose gesture would be ridiculous. Commenting on lines 25-27, in which the speaker imagines himself swaggering nut-strewn roads and crouching in the fo'c'sle, David Timms finds him "unconvinced by such daydreams, though sympathetic to the dreamers, for he is one himself." And so he dismisses his Romantic urge as too studied and belabored, ultimately false. Still, just because he sees through those dreams, he won't let himself feel superior. The dreams may be artificial, but so is his own tame life, his room, his specially chosen junk. As he is well aware, at the end, his greatest danger is to be trapped in owning things and neatly arranging them: books, china, all fixed on shelves in an order "reprehensibly perfect." (We have somewhat expanded on Timms's paraphrase, from *Philip Larkin* [Edinburgh: Oliver & Boyd, 1973] 87.)

William H. Pritchard has remarked that Larkin himself expunged Romantic possibilities from his life, the better to entertain them in his writing ("Larkin's Presence," in *Philip Larkin: The Man and His* Work, ed. Dale Salwak [U of Iowa Press, 1989] 74-75).

Irving Layton, THE BULL CALF, page 953

Sentimental poets frequently shed tears over concrete objects, while (in their imagery and diction) failing to open their eyes to the physical world. Such is not the case of Layton's

"The Bull Calf," in which the poet tells us that he weeps only after having portrayed the dead calf in exact detail ("one foreleg over the other").

Layton's poem develops a series of contrasts. In the first section, the calf's look of nobility ("the promise of sovereignty," "Richard II") is set against his immaturity. The "fierce sunlight," in an implied metaphor, is compared to the calf's mother: taking in maize, licking her baby. In line 14, the "empty sky," suggestive of the calf's coming death, seems the turning point of the poem. In the remainder, the calf, which had been portrayed at first as full of life and pride, becomes an inanimate object, "a block of wood," a numb mass that emits ugly sounds when handled ("a sepulchral gurgle"). But in the closing lines, introducing still another contrast, Layton seems to show the calf as a living sleeper, or perhaps a statue or finished work of art.

Probably the best-known living poet in Canada, Layton was born in Rumania and came to Montreal early in life. Standing outside both British and French communities, Layton's perspective often has been that of an outsider, a Jew, a satirist, and a revolution-ary. *The Selected Poems of Irving Layton,* with an introduction by Hugh Kenner (New York: New Directions, 1977), is an attempt to widen his audience south of the border.

Philip Levine, ANIMALS ARE PASSING FROM OUR LIVES, page 954

Remarkable about this poem is its point of view—a pig's—and its insouciant tone, con-sidering the circumstances. This pig is on its way to market, and to death. An intelligent animal with a startlingly human persona (even jauntily condescending to the boy who, it says, thinks it will act "like a beast" [line 22]), it knows exactly the kind of death that awaits, and takes pride in facing its fate with courage. Its English is colloquial ("squeal / and shit like a new housewife / discovering television," "Not this pig"), its manner breezy.

Levine's title seems ironic. It leads us to expect a self-consciously "significant" poem about endangered species and the urgent need to save them. But in fact, it surprises us by focusing instead on meat animals, killed in great numbers every day without our thinking twice. Like Simic in "Butcher Shop," Levine sets forth the unpalatable details of the slaughter and the discomfort sensitive people feel when they reflect on the bloodshed necessary to provide meat for the table. Levine, describing the dreams in which the snouts of slaughtered pigs "drool on the marble," calls attention as well to the hypocrisy of "the consumers / who won't meet their steady eyes / for fear they could see." Given the title and the opening lines, who could predict where this poem was going?

Stephen Shu-ning Liu, MY FATHER'S MARTIAL ART, page 954

Born in China, Stephen Shu-ning Liu has lived in this country since 1952 and currently teaches at Clark County Community College in Las Vegas. In *Breaking Silence, An An-thology of Contemporary Asian American Poets* edited by Joseph Bruchac (New York: Greenfield Review, 1983) he remarks:

> My philosophy in writing poetry is that poetic language should be simple, clear and direct. Like fresh air and wholesome bread, poetry is for the crowd; and the poet, since he is just another human being, does not necessarily have a tattoo or a weird hairdo. A poet should work alone and leave group exercise to the football players.

In "My Father's Martial Art," the father has apparently died ("the smog / between us deepens into a funeral pyre"). His son remembers him and his skill with the martial arts, learned during a three-year stay in a monastery. The poignant final stanza makes evident the speaker's love and longing for his absent father. "But don't retreat into night, my father" calls to mind another elegy for a father, Dylan Thomas's famous "Do not go gentle into that good night" (page 771).

271

Dream Journeys to China, an English-Chinese bilingual edition of his poems (Beijing: New World Press, 1982) is available from the China Publications Center, P. O. Box 399, Beijing, People's Republic of China.

Robert Lowell, SKUNK HOUR, page 955

Students should have no trouble in coming up with the usual connotations of skunk, but they may need help in seeing that the title is a concise expression of Lowell's theme. This is an evil-smelling hour in the speaker's life; and yet, paradoxically, it is the skunks themselves who affirm that life ought to go on. After the procession of dying and decadent people and objects in the first four stanzas, the mother skunk and her kittens form a triumph: bold, fecund, hungry, impossible to scare. Although they too are outcasts (surrounded by their aroma as the poet is surrounded by his madness and isolation?), they stick up for their right to survival.

The poem is rich in visual imagery. In the mind's eye, there are resemblances between the things contained in stanza 5 (the Ford car and the hill's skull), also the objects set in fixed rows (love-cars, tombstones, beached hulls). Water and the sea (by their decline or absence) are to this poem what they are to Eliot's *Waste Land.* Even the Church is "chalk-dry"; its spire has become a spar like that of a stranded vessel.

This poem is intensively analyzed in *The Contemporary Poet as Artist and Critic: Eight Symposia,* ed. Anthony Ostroff (Boston: Little, 1964). Richard Wilbur, John Frederick Nims, and John Berryman comment on the poem, after which Lowell comments on their comments. Lowell calls the opening of the poem "a dawdling, more or less amiable picture of a declining Maine sea town. . . . Sterility howls through the scenery, but I try to give a tone of tolerance, humor, and randomness to the sad prospect." He sees the skunk hour itself as a sort of dark night of the soul and refers readers to the poem by Saint John of the Cross. Lowell's night, however, is "secular, puritan, and agnostical." Lowell notes that the phrase *red fox stain* was intended only to describe the color of vegetation in the fall on Blue Hill, a mountain in Maine.

Elizabeth Hardwick, Lowell's wife when "Skunk Hour" was written, has affirmed that all the characters in the poem were actual—"were living, more or less as he sees them, in Castine [Maine] that summer. The details, not the feeling, were rather alarmingly precise, I thought. But fortunately it was not read in town for some time" (quoted by Ian Hamilton, *Robert Lowell: A Biography* [New York: Random House, 1982] 267).

Sandra M. Gilbert, who sees the poem as "richly magical," reads it for its embodiment of myth. She explores it as a vision of Hell, pointing out that its events happen not on Halloween, but "somewhere in Hallowe'en's ritually black and orange vicinity." (The decorator's shop is "sacramentally orange.") The summer millionaire has departed in fall, like a vegetation deity—Osiris or Attis. Nautilus Island's witchlike hermit heiress is Circe, Hecate, Ishtar, Venus, "the goddess of love turned goddess of death in an All Soul's Night world" ("Mephistopheles in Maine: Rereading Lowell's 'Skunk Hour,'" *A Book of Rereadings,* ed. Greg Kuzma [Lincoln, Neb.: Pebble and Best Cellar, 1979] 254–64).

Archibald MacLeish, THE END OF THE WORLD, page 956

QUESTIONS FOR DISCUSSION:

1. Where does the action of this poem take place?

2. To see for yourself how the sonnet is organized, sum up what happens in the octave. Then sum up what happens in the sestet.

3. How does the tone of the octave contrast with that of the sestet? (If you need to

review *tone,* see pages 597-602). Comment in particular on the clause in line 8: *the top blew off.* How do those words make you feel? Grim? Horrified? Or what?

4. Now read the closing couplet aloud. Try to describe (and account for) its effectiveness. Suppose MacLeish had wanted to write an Italian sonnet; he might have arranged the lines in the sestet like this—

> And there, there overhead, there, there hung over
> Those thousands of white faces, those dazed eyes,
> There in the sudden blackness the black pall,
> There in the starless dark the poise, the hover,
> There with vast wings across the canceled skies
> Of nothing, nothing, nothing—nothing at all.

Would that have been as effective?

What is the tone of this sonnet? Not at all grim, though the poet speaks of the most horrific event imaginable. Our pleasure in the poem comes from many elements besides its subject: its sounds (including rimes), its rhythm (metrical lines of even length), its portrait of a circus frozen in a split second, and its colossal pun in *the top blew off (top* meaning the "big top" or circus tent, perhaps also the lid of the enormous pot of all Creation). Whose are the "vast wings"? Nothingness's.

The octave, with its casual description of routine merriment, stands in contrast to the sestet, which strikes a note of awe. Perhaps the pale faces and dazed eyes of the circus spectators reflect the attitude of stunned wonder that the poet feels—or would have us feel. Obviously, to rearrange MacLeish's lines would be to weaken his poem. For one thing, the closing rimed couplet in the original throws great emphasis on the final *nothing at all.* In both sound and sense, "the black pall / Of nothing, nothing, nothing—nothing at all" seems more powerful than "canceled skies / Of nothing. . . ." In this sonnet, as in Shakespeare's sonnets, the concluding couplet firmly concludes.

Andrew Marvell, TO HIS COY MISTRESS, page 957

QUESTIONS FOR DISCUSSION:

1. "All this poet does is feed some woman a big line. There's no time for romance, so he says, 'Quick, let's hit the bed before we hit the dirt.'" Discuss this summary. Then try making your own, more accurate one. Suggestion: The poem is divided into three parts, each beginning with an indented line. Take these parts one at a time, putting the speaker's main thoughts into your own words.

(There's a grain of truth to this paraphrase, rude though it be. We might question, however, whether Marvell's speaker is trying to hoodwink his loved one. Perhaps he only sums up the terrible truth he knows: that time lays waste to youth, that life passes before we know it. He makes no mention of "romance," by the way—that's the paraphraser's invention. A more nearly accurate paraphrase, taking the three divisions of the poem one by one, might go like this:

Lines 1-20: If we had all the room in the world and if we were immortal, then our courtship might range across the globe. My love for you could expand till it filled the whole world and I could spend centuries in praising your every feature (saving your heart for last). After all, such treatment is only what you deserve.

Lines 21-32: But time runs on. Soon we'll be dead and gone, all my passion and all your innocence vanished.

Lines 33-46: And so, while you're still young and willing, let's seize the day. Let's concentrate our pleasure into the present moment. Although we can't make the sun stand still (like Joshua in the Bible), we'll do the next best thing: we'll joyously make time fly.

Now, obviously, any such rewording of this matchless poem must seem a piddling thing. But if students will just work through Marvell's argument part by part, they may grasp better the whole of it.)

2. In part one, how much space would be "world enough" for the lovers? Exactly how much time would be enough time?

(To point out the approximate location of the Humber and the Ganges on a globe [or a simple circle drawn on a blackboard] can drive home the fact that when the poet says *world enough*, he spells out exactly what he means. A little discussion may be needed to show that in defining "enough" time, Marvell bounds it by events [the conversion of the Jews], numbers the years, and blocks out his piecemeal adoration. Two-hundred years per breast is a delectable statistic! Clearly, the lover doesn't take the notion of such slow and infinitely patient devotion seriously.)

3. What is the main idea of part two? How is this theme similar to that of Housman's "Loveliest of trees"?

(Both Marvell and Housman in "Loveliest of trees" [page 941] are concerned with the passage of time; they differ on what needs to be done about it. Marvell urges action; Housman urges filling one's youth with observed beauty. Of these two expressions of the *carpe diem* theme, Housman's seems the more calm and disinterested.)

4. Paraphrase with special care lines 37–44. Is Marvell urging violence?

(In lines 37–44, Marvell's point seems to be that time works a gradual, insidious violence. It is like a devouring beast (slow-chapped), holding us in its inexorable jaws. Some students will find the imagery odd, even offensive in a love poem: *birds of prey* (who want to eat, not be eaten), the cannonball of strength and sweetness that batters life's iron gates. Violence is not the speaker's counsel, but urgency. His harsh images lend his argument intensity and force.)

5. Considering the poem as a whole, does the speaker seem playful, or serious?

(This fifth question presents an easy dichotomy, but of course Marvell's speaker is both playful and serious. In making clear the tone of the poem, a useful poem for comparison is Marlowe's "Passionate Shepherd." What are the two speakers' attitudes toward love? Marvell's seems more down-to-earth, skeptical, and passion-driven: a lover in a fallen world, not [like Marlowe's shepherd] a lover in a pastoral Eden.

If later on, in teaching figures of speech, you want some great lines for illustrations, turn back to this inexhaustible poem. There's hyperbole in lines 7–20, understatement ["But none, I think, do there embrace"], metaphor, simile, and of course the great personification of chariot-driving time.

Telling a class that Marvell was a Puritan usually shakes up their overly neat assumption. Some may be surprised to learn that one can be a Puritan and not necessarily be puritanical.

Defending the poem against charges that its logic is fallacious, a recent critic, Richard Crider, has shown that "the speaker's appeal is not merely to the lady's passion, . . . but to a more inclusive and compelling value—completion and wholeness." A good student of Aristotle's logic as well as Aristotle's ethics, Marvell's speaker calls on his listener to exercise all her human powers, among them reason. "Although no single net will capture all the resonances of the final couplet, near the heart of the passage is the thought of living life completely, in accordance with natural law" ["Marvell's Valid Logic," *College Literature* (Spring 1985): 113–211].)

David Mason, DISCLOSURE, page 958

The title of Mason's moving poem about the emotional aftermath of divorce has a double meaning. "Disclosure," of course, means revealing information, but it is also a legal term describing the exchange of documents in civil suits. The poem dramatizes the speaker's private memories prompted by the arrival of an official divorce form. The poem jumps back and forth between areas of experience—past and present, private and public, domestic and legal. There is no bitterness in this poem, only painful longing and deep regret. Ultimately, "Disclosure" becomes an elegiac love poem written to a woman lost forever.

"Disclosure" appeared in Mason's first full-length collection, *The Buried Houses* (Brownsville, Oregon: Story Line Press, 1991), which won the Nicholas Roerich Award in poetry. Mason teaches at Moorhead State University in Minnesota.

George Meredith, LUCIFER IN STARLIGHT, page 959

The name Lucifer (Latin for "light-bringing") comes from Isaiah 14:12: "How art thou fallen from heaven, O Lucifer, son of the morning!" Early interpreters of Scripture thought this line referred to the fallen archangel; later translators changed *Lucifer* to *day star*. Students may not be aware that Lucifer is a name both for the Devil and for the planet Venus as the morning star. (Venus is sometimes the evening star, too, but only as the morning star is it called Lucifer.)

Meredith, however, seems well aware of the name's duality. Although his sonnet can be read first as an account of the Miltonic fiend's taking a new flight (and meeting chagrin), it is also satisfying to read the poem as a description of Venus as a planet. We are told that Lucifer *uprose* and *sank*. Amid the stars, *his huge bulk*—a *black planet* crosses Africa and shadows the Arctic, arriving at a *middle height* in the sky. The last two lines are puzzling, but seem to refer both to God's law and to the orderly path each star and planet follows as it circles the sun.

An Italian sonnet, "Lucifer in Starlight" illustrates a clear division in meaning between octave and sestet. In lines 1–8, the fiend appears triumphant and domineering: this is his night to howl. In lines 9–14, however, he crumples in defeat once more; or, if Lucifer is also the morning star, he rises in the octave and sets in the sestet.

James Merrill, CHARLES ON FIRE, page 959

Merrill's poem seems to describe a real incident. It begins casually, as if the reader already knew the characters and location, "Another evening we sprawled out discussing / "Appearances." Indeed, the mystery of appearances becomes the theme of the poem. When the glass of burning cognac breaks and runs down "long-suffering" Charles's arm, his hand is momentarily clothed in an eerie flame. He seems momentarily transformed into a spirit. The strange instant soon passes, but it leaves everyone slightly in awe. A good question to ask a class is why (in line 24) does Charles look in the mirror after he extinguishes the flame?

Charlotte Mew, THE FARMER'S BRIDE, page 960

Mew's thwarted life, marked by insanity in her family, a difficult invalid mother, frustrated lesbian desires, struggles with depression, and her suicide at 59, is documented in Penelope Fitzgerald's biography of the poet, *Charlotte Mew and Her Friends* (Reading: Addison Wesley, 1988)—documented as well as it can be, considering Mew's lifelong reticence about herself and her family. Mew's career as a writer spanned literary movements: her first published story appeared in *The Yellow Book* in 1894; a few years later, as

Imagism bloomed, Ezra Pound was printing her work in *The Egoist.* Her work, as Val Warner points out in his introduction to *Charlotte Mew: Collected Poems and Prose* (New York: Carcanet, 1982), "is a celebration of passion deeply felt, but always denied."

As does the speaker in the Robert Browning's "Soliloquy of the Spanish Cloister" (page 902), Mew's farmer-narrator reveals more than he realizes. Make sure that students understand what has caused the farmer's bride first to shrink from her husband, then run away. They can find abundant evidence in the poem. The farmer admits in the first stanza that she was "too young maybe" when he married her, and that the courtship was brief. Clearly the bride was unprepared for sex, and this well-meaning but unromantic man scared her off. Three years after the wedding she's still afraid—of him and of all men.

Evident throughout the poem is the strength of the farmer's love for "little frightened fay." Untutored he may be, but he has not approached her sexually since she ran away. As lines 40–41 make clear, he longs for a child. It is also apparent that he longs for his beautiful young wife. Especially after line 30, the expression of his desire for her has an intensity that soars to heart-rending lyricism. Mew makes clear that, for the speaker, the physical nearness of his wife in the final stanza is almost unbearable. Note the skill the poet demonstrates in "The Farmer's Bride," a rimed poem that seems effortless, plain speech.

James Wright said of Mew, "The truth is that she wrote maybe six of the best poems of the 20th century. She's a superb poet, and a great woman" (*Poetry Pilot* [newsletter of the Academy of American Poets] Sept. 1978). Thomas Hardy called Mew "far and away the best living woman poet—who will be read when others are forgotten," and in 1918, after reading *The Farmer's Bride,* he invited her to his home at Max Gate and struck up a friendship that endured. In 1924 Virginia Woolf declared Mew "the greatest living poetess," and in her day she was also admired by John Masefield, May Sinclair, Walter de la Mare, and Siegfried Sassoon. Yet, ironically, her poems did not circulate widely and she never received her share of acclaim. Since 1953 there have been sporadic attempts to give the poet her due. Perhaps Warner's edition of her work and Fitzgerald's biography signal a fresh appreciation.

Edna St. Vincent Millay, RECUERDO, page 961

There is probably not much to do with this delightful poem but leave it alone and let students discover it for themselves. The only thing we would find in it to discuss: Would that newspaper vendor really break down into tears of gratitude? We bet she is a mere literary convention here, and in real life would probably be one tough old egg.

Would this highly musical lyric make a good song? Might it be sung?

John Milton, LYCIDAS, page 962

"Lycidas" for many students is formidable, and before teaching the poem, at least a half hour of class time will probably be needed for preparation. At least a smattering of information on the time and place of Milton's elegy is helpful, if students are to see that their own lives (and friendships) and Milton's life at Cambridge are not completely remote from each other. A book useful for background is Louis Porter's *A Preface to Milton* (New York: Scribner's, 1971), especially 122–25. Many students are intrigued by mythology and find that to read up on a flock of classical myths reveals much to them, besides making them able to follow Milton's allusions. You may wish to allow two class hours to the poem itself, enough time to deal with only a few passages. Milton's powerful condemnation of the false shepherds (lines 119–31) is usually a high point of the poem for students, and students generally end with at least some respect for Milton as a mythmaker.

Michael Fixler has seen the poem's multifold allusions to myth as one with its "unheard" or "unexpressive" music. "In myth Orpheus sings even as his severed head, resting on his silent lyre, races down the swift Hebrus. But in 'Lycidas' that song is 'unexpressive' in yet a further sense, being implicit, a part of the allusion" ("'Unexpressive Song': Form and Enigma Variations in *Lycidas,* a New Reading," *Milton Studies 15* [1981]: 213–55).

For the instructor who wishes further aid in reading the poem, the amount of available criticism is, of course, vast. Modern studies we have found valuable include Rosemond Tuve's "Theme, Pattern, and Imagery in *Lycidas,*" in *Images and Themes in Five Poems of Milton* (Cambridge: Harvard UP, 1957); Jon S. Lawry's "'Eager Thought': Dialectic in *Lycidas,*" in *Milton: Modern Essays in Criticism;* ed. Arthur E. Barker (Oxford: Oxford UP, 1965); and Michael Fixler's discussion in *Milton and the Kingdoms of God* (Evanston: Northwestern UP, 1964) 56–60.

John Milton, WHEN I CONSIDER HOW MY LIGHT IS SPENT, page 968

While this famous sonnet is usually taken to refer to the poet's lost eyesight, some critics have argued that it is not about blindness at all. The familiar title "On His Blindness" was not given by Milton, but by a printer a century later.

QUESTIONS FOR DISCUSSION:

1. *If* the poem is not about blindness, what might it be about? (Possible suggestions: Milton's declining powers of poetry; Milton's fame as a Puritan apologist.)

2. Is talent a pun referring to Milton's talent for writing poetry? What other meanings of the word seem appropriate in this poem? In the New Testament parable (Matthew 25: 14–30), the hidden talent is money that should have been earning interest. That Milton is thinking primarily of work and business can be plausibly argued; other words in the poem convey such connotations—*spent, true account, day-labor,* and perhaps *useless,* which suggests the Medieval Latin word for interest, *usura.*

The theme of frustration in life (and reconciliation to one's lot) is dealt with differently in Shakespeare's "When, in disgrace with Fortune and men's eyes" (page 991).

Marianne Moore, THE MIND IS AN ENCHANTING THING, page 968

About this poem the poet has written, "One of the winters between 1930 and 1940, Gieseking gave at the Brooklyn Academy a program of Handel, Bach, and Scarlatti, the moral of this poem being that there is something more important than outward tightness. One doesn't get through with the fact that Herod beheaded John the Baptist, 'for his oath's sake'; as one doesn't, I feel, get through with the injustice of the deaths died in the war, and in the first world war" (note on the poem in Kimon Friar and John Malcolm Brinnin's anthology *Modern Poetry* [New York: Appleton, 1951]).

These remarks, and the poem's appearance in 1944, have led critics to call "The Mind Is an Enchanting Thing" a war poem. What to make of the poet's statement? To put it baldly, perhaps she means that nobody but a bigoted Herod would condemn a superb German musician for being German and for playing splendid German and Italian music, even in the 1930s. The drift of the poem is that it takes the mind to recognize beauty and, to do so, the mind must pierce through the heart's illusions (and prejudices?). Still, one needn't speculate about the poem's wartime relevance in order to see it as a restatement of the poet's favorite poet's theme, "Beauty is truth, truth beauty." Only the mind can apprehend things truly; like Gieseking's violin and like the apteryx's beak, it is a precision instrument.

Class discussions of this poem tend to be slow, but good and ruminative. Many students greatly admire the poem, and some instructors report getting outstanding papers about it.

What form is the poem written in? Syllabics, with lines arranged in a repeated stanza pattern—like Dylan Thomas's "Fern Hill" (page 1005), which students may compare with Moore's poem. In an interview, Donald Hall asked Moore, "Do you ever experiment with shapes before you write, by drawing lines on a page?" "Never, I never 'plan' a stanza," she replied. "Words cluster like chromosomes, determining the procedure. I may influence an arrangement or thin it, then try to have successive stanzas identical with the first." Asked "How does a poem start for you?" she answered, "A felicitous phrase springs to mind—a word or two, say—. . . 'katydid-wing subdivided by *sun* / till the nettings are *legion.*' I like little rhymes, inconspicuous rhymes" (interview in *The Paris Review* [Winter 1961], reprinted in *A Marianne Moore Reader* [New York: Viking, 1961]).

Hall discusses the poem helpfully, too, in his study *Marianne Moore* (New York: Pegasus, 1970). He admires the poet's ability to weave a single word through the length of the poem, subtly changing its meaning: "The word *eye,* for example, is first the eye of the mind, then the eye of the memory, then the eye of the heart, suggesting three ways of 'seeing' that do not involve sight, but insight."

Frederick Morgan, THE MASTER, page 970

Morgan's poem describes an actual painting—Han Kan's "Nightshining White," which is owned by the Metropolitan Museum of Art in New York. The painting is so fragile that it is not always on display, but it is so striking that, once seen, it is never forgotten.

Morgan's poem retells the legendary account of the painting's creation. Han Kan (who was active between 742–756) was a painter of the T'ang dynasty. His depiction of the Emperor Ming-huang's favorite charger is probably the most famous horse painting in Chinese art. It has been considered a masterpiece since its creation. The actual painted scroll is covered with seals and commentaries by scholars.

The theme of Morgan's poem is the artist's dependence on actual experience. Arriving in the capital, Han Kan is invited to study with the imperial court painter. He chooses instead to study from nature itself in the emperor's stables.

Poetry, then, tends to inhere not in abstract editorial stands, but in particulars. William Carlos Williams's brief poem about eating the plums in the ice box (page 625) may not be great, but it is human, and hard to forget. Sources of poems may lie before your eyes. Although poets can learn from reading other poets' work, they can also learn from the testimony of their own senses. In the best poems, as Morgan's poem reminds us, there is always a quality that cannot be distilled from schools and libraries: a freshness that comes only from contact with the living world.

Frederick Morgan is a well-known editor as well as a poet. In 1948, he was one of the founders of *The Hudson Review,* the distinguished journal which has been called "the last of the great quarterlies." Nearly half a century later he still co-edits the journal.

Howard Nemerov, THE SNOW GLOBE, page 970

Is the globe a symbol? If so, what does it suggest? Nemerov calls it an "emblem," one that seems to have changed its meaning for him as he has grown to adulthood. When he was a child, the toy was part of the "brightness" with which his parents "would have wanted [him] beguiled." Now he is older and sadder. When he remembers the snow globe, its coldness rather than its whiteness speaks to him, and it is death of which it speaks.

The tone of the poem is wistful, nostalgic, sorrowful. The real world cannot, like the village in the snow globe, be "frozen forever." Time does not stand still.

Lorine Niedecker, SORROW MOVES IN WIDE WAVES, page 971

Though she published five collections here and in Britain, Niedecker's work has seldom appeared in anthologies. The new wave of feminist criticism seems not yet to have caught up with her. But here and there, her life and distinctive work have won recognition. In 1985 the Jargon Society published her collected writings, *From This Condensery.* In 1989 *Niedecker,* a biographical play by Kristine Thatcher, had a successful Off-Broadway production.

The poet, who spent most of her quiet life on remote Blackhawk Island, Wisconsin, worked for a time as a cleaning person in a hospital. While far from literary capitals, she kept up a lively correspondence with Basil Bunting, Cid Corman, William Carlos Williams, Louis Zukofsky, and other innovative, nonacademic poets of her day.

This poem needs to be heard aloud, and in getting into it, students may need a few pertinent questions. What details render the dying woman real to us? (The thimble, surely; her turning blue, her final plea.) What is the point of view? (An objective view of death, this speaker's perspective contrasts sharply with that of Emily Dickinson's subjective, first-person "I heard a Fly buzz—when I died.") How would you describe the tone of the whole poem? In what words and phrases does it come through?

Sharon Olds, THE ONE GIRL AT THE BOYS PARTY, page 972

This poem whimsically describes a talented little girl, "her math scores unfolding in the air around her," during a pool party at which all the other guests are boys. *They* in lines 2 and 15, *their* in lines 18 and 19 seem to refer only to the boys. In lines 5, 7, and 11, the word *they* apparently includes the girl. You might ask students to note the pairs of adjectives that affirm the child's strength and composure: she is "smooth and sleek" (line 3), her body is "hard and / indivisible as a prime number" (lines 5–6), her face is "solemn and / sealed" (lines 16–17). The adjectives make clear the narrator-mother's respect for her brilliant daughter. Notable too is the metaphor of wet ponytail (itself a by-now-dead metaphor!) as pencil (line 12). That and the "narrow silk suit / with hamburgers and french fries printed on it" remind us that she is in some ways a very typical little girl.

It is the mathematical figures of speech that make this poem unique. Why not ask students to point out and discuss them? Are they apt? Do they ever appear forced? Which ones succeed best?

Wilfred Owen, ANTHEM FOR DOOMED YOUTH, page 972

Metaphorically, this sonnet draws a contrast between traditional funeral trappings and the actual conditions under which the dead lie on the field of battle: with cannon fire instead of tolling bells, rifle bursts instead of the patter of prayers, the whine of shells instead of choirs' songs, the last lights in dying eyes instead of candle-shine, pale brows (of mourning girls, at home?) instead of shrouds or palls, the tenderness of onlookers (such as the poet?) instead of flowers—an early draft of the poem reads, "Your flowers, the tenderness of comrades' minds"—and the fall of night instead of the conventional drawing down of blinds in a house where someone has died.

For another Owen war poem, see "Dulce et Decorum Est" (page 617). For other war poems, see in this manual "Poems Arranged by Subject and Theme."

The poet's revisions for this poem, in four drafts, may be studied in the appendix to C. Day Lewis's edition of Owen's *Collected Poems* (London: Chatto, 1963). In its first draft, the poem was called "Anthem for Dead [not Doomed] Youth," and it went, in our reading of the photographed manuscript:

What minute bells for these who die so fast?
Only the monstrous anger of our guns.
Let the majestic insults of their iron mouths
Be as the priest-words of their burials.
Of choristers and holy music, none;
Not any voice of mourning, save the wail
The long-drawn wail of high, far-sailing shells.
What candles may we hold for these lost souls?
Not in the hands of boys, but in their eyes
Shall many candles shine, and [?] will light them.
Women's wide-spreaded arms shall be their wreaths,
And pallor of girls' cheeks shall be their palls.
Their flowers, the tenderness of all men's minds,
And every dusk, a drawing-down of blinds.

Linda Pastan, ETHICS, page 973

As a student, the narrator, like others in her class, found her teacher's ethical puzzler irrelevant. Now the mature woman pondering the "real Rembrandt" in the museum finds the question still remote from her vital concerns, but for different reasons. The approach of her own old age has shown her that nothing lasts, that with the onflow of years our choices, whatever they may be, fade into insignificance.

One way of entering the poem: students may be asked to sum up its theme. Is it *carpe diem?* Is the poet saying, with Housman in "Loveliest of trees," "Life is fleeting; I'd better enjoy beauty while I can"? No, for the poet seems not to believe in day-seizing. Is it *ars longa, vita brevis est?* No, for both art and life seem pitifully brief and temporary. The point, rather, is that all things pass away despite our efforts to hold on to them. But instead of telling them what the point is, you might ask students to paraphrase the poem's conclusion that "women and painting and season are almost one / and all beyond saving by children."

To discuss: In what ways does "Ethics" differ from prose? Pastan's language seems far more musical. She makes beautiful music of alliteration and assonance. Read the poem aloud. And central to "Ethics" is a huge metaphor: old woman, season, earth, painting, and poet become one—all caught in time's resistless fire.

In our last Instructor's Manual, we wondered: How many times did the speaker have to repeat that ethics course? To our relief, on a recent visit to the University of Arizona in Tucson, Linda Pastan supplied an answer reported to us by Ila Abernathy of the Poetry Center. Pastan went to the Ethical Culture School in New York City, a private school run by the Ethical Culture Society and serving both elementary and high school students. The school's curriculum hits ethics hard: the poet was required to take once-a-week ethics classes for twelve years.

Linda Pastan chose "Ethics" to represent her in *The Poet's Choice,* an anthology of poets' own favorite poems edited by George E. Murphy, Jr. (Green Harbor, MA: Tendril, 1980).

Octavio Paz, WITH OUR EYES SHUT (CON LOS OJOS CERRADOS), page 974

This short poem by Nobel laureate Octavio Paz is simple enough that anyone with basic Spanish can follow it in the original. (The original text will also give any native Spanish speakers in your class a chance to show off their bilingual abilities.) The poem explores a paradoxical conceit—shutting one's self off from physical light, one can experience an inner light. Becoming a "blind stone" to the outside, "You light up from within." The second stanza allows the metaphor to become erotic, although Paz is deliberately ambiguous about whether the lovers are together or apart. "Night by night" the speaker recreates his love with his eyes shut—perhaps carving her features from memory or perhaps touching her with his hands. The final stanza celebrates how the lovers enlarge their existence from knowing one another "with our eyes shut."

Robert Phillips, RUNNING ON EMPTY, page 974

Robert Phillips was born in Delaware. For many years he worked on Madison Avenue as a copywriter. During his advertising career, Phillips published over a dozen volumes of poetry, short stories, and criticism as well as edited several volumes by his late teacher, Delmore Schwartz. Phillips now heads the Creative Writing Department at the University of Houston. Phillips has provided the following comment about his poem:

> "Running on Empty" is fairly autobiographical. I was stunned at how grudgingly my father let me use the family car once I'd obtained my driver's license at age 16. It seemed to me he withheld this symbol of my new freedom and attainment just as he withheld his affection. So when I finally had use of the car, I went hog-wild in celebration and release.
>
> The landscape is Sussex County, Delaware—extremely flat country bisected by Route 13 (nicknamed "The Dual" because it is composed of twin lanes dually parallel in an inexorable straight line). I was pushing my luck speeding and refusing to refuel in an act of rebellion against my father's strictness (which may explain why the 12th line reads "defying chemistry" rather than the more accurate "defying physics"—my father taught high school chemistry, and even in the classroom I was subject to his discipline).
>
> I'm rather pleased with the way the poem picks up rhythm and begins to speed when the car does (5th-7th stanzas). And I hope students relate to the central images of car and boy, one of which can be mechanically refueled and replenished, one of which cannot.

To us the word *chemistry* in line 12 carries additional meaning, as in "behavior or functioning, as of a complex of emotions" *(The American Heritage Dictionary)*. In this sense, too, the narrator was surely in defiance of his father's chemistry.

Sylvia Plath, DADDY, page 975

There are worse ways to begin teaching this astonishing poem than to ask students to recall what they know of Dachau, Auschwitz, Belsen (line 33), and other Nazi atrocities. "Every woman adores a Fascist"—what does Plath mean? Is she sympathizing with the machismo ideal of the domineering male, lashing his whip upon subjugated womankind? (No way.) For an exchange of letters about the rightness or wrongness of Plath's identifying with Jewish victims of World War II, see *Commentary* (July and October 1974). Irving Howe accuses Plath of "a failure in judgment" in using genocide as an emblem of her personal traumas.

Incredible as it seems, some students possess an alarming fund of ignorance about Nazis, and some might not even recognize the cloven foot of Satan (line 53); so be prepared, sadly, to supply glosses. They will be familiar with the story of Dracula, however, and probably won't need much help with lines 71–79. Plath may be thinking of *Nosferatu*, F. W. Murnau's silent screen adaptation of Bram Stoker's novel *Dracula*, filmed in Germany in 1922. Hitler's propagandists seized on the Nosferatu theme and claimed that the old democratic order was drinking the country's blood. Plath sees Daddy as doing the same to his daughter.

Edgar Allan Poe, TO HELEN, page 978

The first version of this poem appeared in Poe's third volume, *Poems* (1831), which was published while the author was a cadet at West Point. (At twenty-two he had already published two earlier books!) Poe circulated a subscription among his fellow cadets to underwrite a volume of his verse. Many of them subscribed in the expectation that Poe would publish the satirical squibs he had written about their teachers and officers. Imagine their surprise on opening the volume to discover delicate lyrics like "To Helen" and "Israfel." Poe later revised it slightly in 1841 to polish its most famous lines to read: "To the glory that was Greece / And the grandeur that was Rome." (It is a worthwhile exercise to ask students to differentiate between the implications of *glory* and *grandeur*.)

Poe (whose comments on his own poems are famously unreliable) claimed that "To Helen" was written in youth "to the first, purely ideal love of my soul." That statement seems uncharacteristically accurate. The woman in "To Helen" seems less a flesh and blood beauty than an object of aesthetic contemplation. Notice how, in the final stanza, Helen becomes transformed in the speaker's mind into a statue, as she stands in the window niche.

Poe's idealized notion of love seems more maternal than sexual—not a surprising thing for a sensitive boy who lost his mother before his third birthday. "To Helen" makes a very interesting comparison piece to "Annabel Lee," which is found on page 879.

Alexander Pope, A LITTLE LEARNING IS A DANG'ROUS THING, page 978

This passage is an excerpt (lines 215–232) from Pope's "An Essay on Criticism," which he published when he was only twenty-three years old. It was this poem, which Joseph Addison immediately proclaimed "a Master-piece in its kind," that made Pope a literary celebrity.

Many teachers object to using excerpts from long works; such selections, they feel, betray the author's original intentions. In general, we agree; we favor including complete poems, so that each part of the work may be seen in relation to the whole. Pope, however, provides a special case. All of his greatest poems are too long to include in total. But it would seem too cruel to deny both teachers and students alike the pleasures of Pope's work, so we have bent the rules several times to introduce this satiric master's work to a new generation. As every teacher knows, one sometimes needs to bend critical rules a bit.

As long as we are bending the rules, we should point out how much this excerpt from a long didactic poem looks like a self-standing lyric in its new form. Examining these eighteen lines in isolation, we see how carefully Pope arranged the images in each line to build toward a cumulative poetic as well as intellectual effect. The final image of the weary traveler looking over the mountaintop at the endless Alps rising ahead is a brilliant stroke that seems closer to a romantic sensibility than a neo-classical one.

Ezra Pound, THE GARRET, page 979

Ezra Pound is best known for his formidably allusive Modernist epic, the *Cantos*, which he worked on for over fifty years. Less well known are Pound's early London poems, which are often funny, tender, and direct. This poem from *Lustra* (1915) celebrates the romantic poverty of bohemian life. (You might begin by asking students what a *garret* is; they frequently know its connotation but not the precise definition.)

This poem begins in a satiric Whitmanian vein, but the second stanza shifts unexpectedly into a soft imagistic style. At the root, most Modernists were secret romantics.

Ezra Pound, THE RIVER-MERCHANT'S WIFE: A LETTER, page 980

After the death of Ernest Fenollosa, a scholar devoted to Chinese language and literature, Pound inherited Fenollosa's manuscripts containing rough prose versions of many Chinese poems. From one such draft, Pound finished his own version of "The River Merchant's Wife." Fenollosa's wording of the first line went:

My hair was at first covering my brows (child's method of wearing hair)

Arthur Waley, apparently contemptuous of Pound for ignoring dictionary meanings of some of the words of the poem, made a translation that began:

Soon after I wore my hair covering my forehead . . .

Pound's version begins:

While my hair was still cut straight across my forehead . . .

Pound, says the recent critic Waj-lim Yip, has understood Chinese culture, while Waley has not, even though he understands his dictionary. "The characters for 'hair/first/cover/forehead' conjure up in the mind of a Chinese reader exactly this picture. All little Chinese girls normally have their hair cut straight across the forehead." Yip goes on to show that Pound, ignorant of Chinese as he was, comes close in sense and feeling to the Li Po original. (*Ezra Pound's Cathay* [Princeton: Princeton UP, 1969] 88–92.)

What is the tone of the poem? What details make it seem moving and true, even for a reader who knows nothing of Chinese culture?

Dudley Randall, OLD WITHERINGTON, page 981

QUESTIONS FOR DISCUSSION:

1. What suggestions do you get from the name Old Witherington?

2. What is meant by "I'll baptize these bricks with bloody kindling" (line 7)?

3. Describe the impact of *tenderly* as it is used in line 19.

4. What possible significance do you see in Old Witherington's *not* cursing "his grinning adversary" (line 18) when he has cursed everyone else?

5. What is the tone of Randall's poem?

Full of withering hate, habitually intent upon cutting people down ("withering" them), Old Witherington himself withers, too. A veteran drunkard, he claims to have died before, a "million times"—presumably of loneliness, neglect, and self-destructive behavior. His neighbors jeer him. The only person who takes him seriously, it seems, is the "crazy bastard" he is about to fight. In a curious way, Witherington's adversary, simply by engaging him in battle, endows the old man with some importance in both men's eyes. Because of this opponent Witherington exists, he somehow matters. For the man with the "jag-toothed bottle," Witherington is the sun.

Complex in its feelings, Randall's poem is about much more than hate. In it we sense compassion for the old man, if not from his neighbors then surely from the poet. In his book *(A Litany of Friends* [Detroit: Lotus, 1981]) Randall has placed "Old Witherington" in the section entitled "Friends."

The scene in Randall's poem is vividly rendered, the imagery exact and alive. The "bloody kindling" in line 7 presumably refers to what the hatchet will look like when the fight is over. *Tenderly* in line 19 suggests an appropriate gingerliness on the part of the adversary. It also suggests love—a connotation equally appropriate in light of the adversary's role in affirming Witherington's worth.

John Crowe Ransom, BELLS FOR JOHN WHITESIDE'S DAUGHTER, page 982

This is an excellent poem with which to set off a discussion of sentimentality—a quality of much bad poetry that Ransom beautifully avoids. What conventional sentiments might be expected in response to a small child's death? Usual expressions of grief. But how does the poet respond? With disbelief and astonishment, delight in remembering the little girl alive, with vexation—even outrage—that she is dead.

Between what Ransom says and what he might have said gapes the canyon of an ironic discrepancy. "It is not a poem," Robert Penn Warren has said, "whose aim is unvarnished pathos of recollection. . . . The resolution of the grief is not on a compensatory basis, as is common in the elegy formula. It is something more modest. The word *vexed* indicates its nature: the astonishment, the pathos, are absorbed into the total body of the mourner's experiences and given perspective so that the manly understatement is all that is to be allowed. We are shaken, but not as a leaf" (see "John Crowe Ransom: A Study in Irony," *Virginia Quarterly Review* 11[1935]: 93–112).

Vivienne Koch has underscored the colloquial phrase *brown study* ("a state of serious absorption or abstraction"—*Webster's New Collegiate). A* child in a brown study seems alien, for her nature includes "speed" and "lightness." "The repetition in the last stanza of 'brown study' in conjunction with the key word *vexed* clinches the unwillingness of the narrator to accept the 'little lady' as departed" ("The Achievement of John Crowe Ransom," *Sewanee Review* 58 [1950]: 227–61). Warren's essay, Koch's, and other good ones are reprinted in *John Crowe Ransom: Critical Essays and a Bibliography,* ed. Thomas Daniel Young (Baton Rouge: Louisiana State UP, 1968).

James Wright has recalled a four-line parody of this poem that he wrote in collaboration with four or five other undergraduates, Ransom's students at Kenyon College (interview with Wright in *The Pure Clear Word,* ed. Dave Smith [Urbana: U of Illinois P, 1982] 12):

BALLS ON JOAN WHITESIDE'S STOGY

There was such smoke in our little buggy
And such a tightness in our car stall—
Is it any wonder her brown stogy
Asphyxiates us all?

Henry Reed, NAMING OF PARTS, page 982

This is one of the most teachable poems ever written. There are two voices: the voice of the riflery instructor, droning on with his spiel, and the voice of the reluctant inductee, distracted by the springtime. Two varieties of diction and imagery clash and contrast: technical terms opposed to imagery of blossoming nature. Note the fine pun in line 24, prepared for by the rapist bees in the previous line. Note also the connotations of the ambiguous phrase *point of balance* (line 27)—a kind of balance lacking from the recruits' lives?

Students need to be shown the dramatic situation of the poem: the poor inductee, sitting through a lecture he doesn't want to hear. One would think that sort of experience would be familiar to students, but a trouble some instructors have met in teaching this poem is a yearning to make out of it a vast comment about Modern Civilization.

The poet himself has recorded the poem for *An Album of Modern Poets,* 1 (Library of Congress, PL 20). Dylan Thomas reads "Naming of Parts" even more impressively in his *Reading, Vol. IV: A Visit to America and Poems* (Caedmon, TC 1061).

Alastair Reid, SPEAKING A FOREIGN LANGUAGE, page 983

Alastair Reid is a Scottish poet who has lived all of his adult life abroad—in Spain, the United States, and now the Dominican Republic. Although he is best known as a translator of Neruda, Borges, and other Latin-American authors and as a *New Yorker* contributor, Reid is a superb poet. "Speaking a Foreign Language" brings a double perspective on the challenge of communicating a second tongue—Reid portrays the roles of both speaker and listener. "What faith / we rest in one sentence," Reid writes, "hoping a smile will follow," as he portrays the role of the speaker. Then in the second stanza he shifts perspective from the speaker to the listener ("And yet, to hear . . .") and affirms how our common humanity helps translate "syntax into love."

Adrienne Rich, AUNT JENNIFER'S TIGERS, page 984

The poet herself has made revealing mention of this poem in a *College English* essay reprinted in *Adrienne Rich's Poetry,* ed. Barbara Charlesworth Gelpi and Albert Gelpi (New York: Norton, 1975):

> Looking back at the poems I wrote before I was 21, I'm startled because beneath the conscious craft are glimpses of the split I even then experienced between the girl who wrote poems, who defined herself in writing poems, and the girl who was to define herself by her relationships with men. "Aunt Jennifer's Tigers," written while I was a student, looks with deliberate detachment at this split. In writing this poem, composed and apparently cool as it is, I thought I was creating a portrait of an imaginary woman. But the woman suffers from the opposition of her imagination, worked out in tapestry, and her life-style, "ringed with ordeals she was mastered by." It was important to me that Aunt Jennifer was a person as distinct from myself as possible—distanced by the formalism of the poem, by its objective, observant tone—even by putting the woman in a different generation.

Rich's feminism clearly was beginning to emerge, however, as far back as 1951, when this poem was first published. It is apparent in the poem that the poet perceived something wrong with the passive role assigned to women. The pride, confidence, and fearlessness ("masculine" virtues, whatever the sex of the tigers) of Aunt Jennifer's imaginary creations contrast sharply with Aunt Jennifer herself—a frail lady with fluttering fingers, *terrified hands.* Worth comment is the poet's use of the word *ringed*—suggesting "encircled"—to refer both to the wedding ring that "sits heavily upon Aunt Jennifer's hand" and to "ordeals she was mastered by," specifically marriage and being expected to conform. Although she goes down in defeat, her tigers triumph.

Question for discussion: Is Aunt Jennifer's plight that of the woman artist in our society? (Because of the wedding ring's weight, she must struggle to ply her instrument, the ivory needle.)

Compare Aunt Jennifer with the dead woman who once embroidered fantails in

Wallace Stevens's "The Emperor of Ice-Cream" (page 1000). For another, in some ways comparable, contrast between a dull world of reality and the colorful life of the imagination, see Stevens's "Disillusionment of Ten O'Clock" (page 654), in which

> Only, here and there, an old sailor,
> Drunk and asleep in his boots,
> Catches tigers
> In red weather.

Mary Slowik discusses this and other early poems of Rich in "The Friction of the Mind," *Massachusetts Review* Spring 1984: 142–60.

Adrienne Rich, PEELING ONIONS, page 985

This poem first appeared in *Snapshots of a Daughter-in-Law* (New York: Norton, 1963), Rich's pivotal third volume. In this collection Rich began moving from formal to free verse and from an often impersonal tone to a candid, intimate voice. Her feminist vision also now starts to find more open forms of expression.

Many poems begin with tears, but "Peeling Onions" opens with a flood of passionless weeping caused only by the onions. The speaker notes the irony of the situation. "There's not a sob in my chest," she remarks and then reminisces on her earlier self when "Crying was labor." She sees her suffering younger self with clinical detachment now. Back then, she could not weep easily, although she had great need to. Now she weeps for no emotional reason, only a physiological reaction. But in the process of retrospection, the present painless tears become the earlier tears she never shed ("These old tears in the chopping bowl"). The speaker, however, is—most emphatically—not giving in to sentimental recollection; she is, instead, acknowledging how much she has outgrown that earlier self.

An excellent discussion question is to ask students to explain the final line. In doing so, they will unpeel all the layers of the poem.

If you have a student interested in both Rich and Ibsen, you might suggest a possible paper topic about why the speaker in "Peeling Onions" compares herself to Peer Gynt, the title character of Ibsen's 1867 play. In the last act of Ibsen's play, Peer has returned to Norway as an old man and scrounges in the forest looking for onions to eat. Finding an onion, he peels away the layers and imagines each one to represent a stage of his life. He looks for the core of the onion to discover the "heart" of his life, but he discovers there are only many layers with nothing at the center.

Adrienne Rich, POWER, page 985

"Power" explores the tragic theme that human insight and achievement often came at the expense of self-destruction. Marie Curie, the great Franco-Polish scientist, discovered polonium and radium, but her research exposed her to the massive doses of radiation that eventually blinded and killed her. Rich underscores the pathos of this situation without sentimentalizing it. She is especially concerned with Curie's denial of the connection between her scientific work and her illness. Curie's intellectual power (and, by implication in the poem, much spiritual and artistic power) derives from the same sources that wound us. On one hand, Rich criticizes Curie's denial, but, on the other hand, she seems also to admire Curie's heroism. Ultimately, however, the poem is not a judgment of Madame Curie but an analysis of power. The energy that drives achievement takes its human toll, the poem implies, and power often finds its source in pain.

Edwin Arlington Robinson, MINIVER CHEEVY, page 986

"Miniver Cheevy" is one of Robinson's great character portraits. These miniature character studies (see also "Richard Cory" on page 703) are a genre that Robinson perfected. Based on the dramatic and narrative poems of poets like George Crabbe and Robert Browning, Robinson compressed the portrait poem into tighter, often lyric structures. His work with its stark realism, bitter antiromanticism, and concise form marks the true beginning of modern (but not Modernist) American poetry.

Mr. Cheevy of the title is a man unable to face reality. He lives in a fantasy world of "the days of old." Cheevy imagines he would have lived a more exciting and fulfilling life in an earlier age, but Robinson makes it clear that Cheevy's fantasies are pure self-deception. Robinson undercuts Cheevy's delusions with irony ("He missed the medieval grace / Of iron clothing.")

Writing the introduction to Robinson's posthumous *King Jasper* in 1935, Robert Frost reminisced about reading "Miniver Cheevy" in London in 1913 with Ezra Pound. They laughed over the fourth *thought* in "Miniver thought, and thought, and thought / And thought about it." "Three 'thoughts' would have been 'adequate,' as the critical praise then was," Frost remembered ". . . the fourth made the intolerable touch of poetry, with the fourth, the fun began."

Theodore Roethke, ELEGY FOR JANE, page 987

By piling up figures of speech from the natural world, Roethke in "Elegy for Jane" portrays his student as a child of nature, quick, thin, and birdlike. A *wren,* a *sparrow,* a *skittery pigeon,* Jane has a *pickerel smile* and neck curls *limp and damp as tendrils.* She waits *like a fern, making a spiny shadow.* She has the power to make shade trees and (even more surprising) mold burst into song. For her, leaves change their whispers into kisses.

Then she dies. The poet acknowledges that for him there is no consolation in nature, in the "sides of wet stones" or the moss; his grief is not assuaged. Because he mourns the girl as teacher and friend, no more, he recognizes a faint awkwardness in his grief as he speaks over her grave:

> I, with no rights in this matter,
> Neither father nor lover.

Roethke, writing about this poem in *On the Poet and His Craft* (Seattle: U of Washington P, 1965) 81–83, reminds the reader that it was John Crowe Ransom (to whose "Bells for John Whiteside's Daughter" [see page 982] this poem has often been compared) who first printed "Elegy for Jane." Roethke discusses his use of enumeration, calling it "the favorite device of the more irregular poem." He calls attention to one "of the strategies for the poet writing without the support of a formal pattern," a strategy he uses in "Elegy for Jane": the "lengthening out" of the last three lines in the first stanza, balanced by the progressive shortening of the three lines at the poem's end.

Some readers have interpreted "Elegy for Jane" as the work of a man who never had children of his own; but in fact Roethke as a young man had fathered a daughter for whom he felt great affection. Although "neither father nor lover" of Jane, he at least could well imagine a father's feelings.

Mary Jo Salter, WELCOME TO HIROSHIMA, page 988

Salter's poem is a meditation on the tragedy of Hiroshima that admits the foreigner's difficulty in understanding the exact nature of the event as the Japanese themselves experienced it. The speaker looks to understand the past cataclysm but repeatedly finds that the contemporary commercial reality impedes her comprehension. The ironic title is made even more mordant by being in English on a sign sponsored by Toshiba. One touristic observation after another distracts, surprises, dismays or confuses the speaker, until an exhibit of a glass shard trapped in a woman's arm for three decades finally provides the mute but eloquent testimony of suffering and redemption on a tangibly human scale.

William Shakespeare, NOT MARBLE NOR THE GILDED MONUMENTS, page 990

To discuss: Is Shakespeare making a wild boast, or does the claim in lines 1–8 seem at all justified? (Time has proved him right. Here we are, still reading his lines, 480 or so years after they were written! Of course, the fact that he happened to be Shakespeare helped his prediction come true.)

For teaching this poem in tandem with Robinson Jeffers's "To the Stone-cutters," see the entry on Jeffers (in the book itself, page 945).

William Shakespeare, THAT TIME OF YEAR THOU MAYST IN ME BEHOLD, page 991

William Shakespeare, WHEN, IN DISGRACE WITH FORTUNE AND MEN'S EYES, page 991

Shakespeare's magnificent metaphors probably will take some brief explaining. How is a body like boughs, and how are the bare boughs like a ruined choir loft? Students will get the general import, but can be helped to visualize the images. "Consumed with that which it was nourished by" will surely require some discussion. Youth, that had fed life's fire, now provides only smothering ashes. The poet's attitude toward age and approaching death stands in contrast to the attitudes of poets (or speakers) in other poems of similar theme: admiration for the exultant sparrows in William Carlos Williams's "To Waken an Old Lady" (page 1015); defiance in Yeats's "Sailing to Byzantium" (page 866).

Figures of speech are central to "That time of year," but rarely enter into "When, in disgrace" until the end, when the simile of the lark is introduced. The lark's burst of joy suggests that heaven, called *deaf* in line 3, has suddenly become keener of hearing. Critical discussion of both sonnets goes on: *Shakespeare's Sonnets,* edited with analytic commentary by Stephen Booth (New Haven: Yale UP, 1977) is especially valuable.

William Shakespeare, WHEN DAISIES PIED AND VIOLETS BLUE, page 991

William Shakespeare, WHEN ICICLES HANG BY THE WALL, page 992

Students are usually pleased to add the word *cuckold* to their vocabularies. (The origin of the word is uncertain, but it evidently refers to the cuckoo's habit of laying its eggs in other birds' nests.) Both songs take birdcalls for their refrains. How is the owl's call evocative of winter? Despite the famous harsh realism of the winter scene, discussion may show that winter isn't completely grim, nor is summer totally carefree.

Bertrand Bronson has a good discussion of these two poems in *Modern Language Notes* 63 (Jan. 1948): 35–38.

Karl Shapiro, THE DIRTY WORD, page 993

Shapiro's theme, which the class may be asked to make explicit, is that the dirty word one secretly loves in childhood is seen in maturity to be powerless. Is it a paradox that the word-bird is said to outlive man, and yet later the speaker tells us he murdered it? It would seem, rather, that at these two moments in his poem Shapiro sees the word from two different points of view. In one sense, the word will continue to live after the speaker's death because (figuratively) it is freed from the cage of his mind and also because (literally) words live longer than their speakers do. In the last paragraph the speaker means that he neutralized the bird's magic. Simply by growing up, he abolished its power over him.

Arranged in paragraphs rather than in conventional lines of poetry, "The Dirty Word" may lead some students to ask why this is poetry, not prose. It is a good opportunity to point out that poetry is a name we can apply to any language we think sufficiently out of the ordinary and that poetry is not determined merely by arranging lines in a conventional order on a page. To a much greater extent than a prose writer usually does, Shapiro expresses himself through metaphor. Besides the central metaphor of word as bird, there are the metaphors of mind as cage, brain as bird food, self as house, skull as room, secret thoughts as closet, vocabulary as zoo, feathers as language. The poem needs to be heard aloud, for it is full of unprosaic sounds: rimes *(sweet meat, bird . . . word);* alliterations *(buried, body, bird; worn, wing; murdered, my, manhood);* and internal alliterations *(ripping and chopping, walls of the skull).* It is also rich in bizarre and startling imagery.

Charles Simic, BUTCHER SHOP, page 993

"Butcher Shop" is a constellation of metaphors. Associating the everyday instruments of a butcher's trade with things we wouldn't expect—things whose connotations are emotionally powerful—Simic works a kind of nighttime transformation. The light recalls a convict struggling to escape. Knives recall church, cripple, and imbecile. Most pervasive of the metaphors in the poem is the river of blood (lines 8 and 14). In a sense, we are nourished by a river of blood when we dine on the flesh of animals. Perhaps (like convict, cripple, and imbecile) the animals too are sufferers. Perhaps all of these victims in chorus lift the mysterious voice that the poet hears in the closing line.

David R. Slavitt, TITANIC, page 994

In "The Convergence of the Twain," Hardy censures the vanity, luxury, and pride that prompted Fate to ram the *Titanic* into an iceberg. Slavitt's poem about the same tragedy takes another tack. He makes dying on the *Titanic* sound almost like fun—all aboard!

If they sold passage tomorrow for that same crossing, who would not buy?

Slavitt's point is that, since we all have to die, it's certainly more glamorous, more desirable to do it "first-class" (note the double meaning of "go" in the last line) than to die less comfortably, in more mundane ways, and soon be forgotten.

Christopher Smart, FOR I WILL CONSIDER MY CAT JEOFFRY, page 994

Telling us more about cats than Carl Sandburg and T. S. Eliot (in "Prufrock," lines 15–22, page 916) put together, Smart salutes Jeoffry in one of several passages in *Jubilate Agno* that fall for a little while into some continuity. This fascinating poem, and the whole work that contained it, have come down to us in a jumble of manuscripts retrieved from the asylum, sorted out brilliantly by W. H. Bond in his edition of Smart's work (Cambridge: Harvard UP, 1954). Some of Smart's gorgeous lines seem quite loony, such as the command to Moses concerning cats (lines 34–35) and the patriotic boast about misinformation: the ichneumon (or *Icneumon*, line 63) is not a pernicious rat, but a weasellike, rat-killing mammal.

Read aloud, Smart's self-contained poem in praise of Jeoffry can build a powerful effect. In its hypnotic, psalmlike repetition, it might be compared with the section of Whitman's "When Lilacs Last in the Dooryard Bloom'd."

Talking with Boswell of Smart's confinement, Dr. Johnson observed:

> I did not think he ought to be shut up. His infirmities were not noxious to society. He insisted on people praying with him; and I'd as lief pray with Kit Smart as with any one else. Another charge was, that he did not love clean linen; and I have no passion for it.

A possible paper topic: "Smart's Cat Jeoffry and Blake's Tyger: How Are These Poems Similar in View?"

William Jay Smith, AMERICAN PRIMITIVE, page 997

We might expect a painter called an American primitive to be naive, unsophisticated, and childlike in his view. So is the speaker who draws this verbal scene. Not only do the references to Daddy seem juvenile, but so does the line "the screen door bangs, and it sounds so funny." (Smith, incidentally, has written much fine verse for children in addition to his more serious poetry, and he understands the way a child thinks and speaks.) There is, of course, an ironic distance between the speaker's point of view and the poet's. Irony is enforced, too, by contrast between the grim event and the bouncy rhythm and use of feminine rimes.

Another possible way of looking at the poem is that Daddy himself is the primitive: the primal dollar-worshipping American. The capitalization of *Dollar* (as in the familiar phrase "the Almighty Dollar") may support this view. We are not told why Daddy died, an apparent suicide, but it is evident that riches did not buy him life. Besides inviting comparison with Sylvia Plath's ironic poem about the death of a terrible "Daddy" (page 975), Smith's mock-elegy may be set beside Wallace Stevens's "The Emperor of Ice-Cream" (page 1000), with students asked to compare the two in tone and in subject matter.

W. D. Snodgrass, DISPOSAL, page 997

This account of the aftermath of a family death is chillingly clinical. The speaker talks matter-of-factly of giving away the clothes of the deceased woman. This disposal provides the simile for the dead woman herself who lies boxed "like a pair of party shoes / That seemed never to find a taker." On the surface, the poem may seem heartless, but the elaborately metaphorical rhetoric holds a strong emotional undercurrent in place, a quiet heartbreak over "life somehow gone out of fashion / But still too good to use."

William Stafford, AT THE KLAMATH BERRY FESTIVAL, page 998

QUESTIONS FOR DISCUSSION:

1. What is ironic in the performance of traditional dances, by a scout troop on an Indian reservation, for an audience including a sociologist? What does the sociologist signify?

What is the significance of the fact that other Indians are gambling outside, turning their backs on the dances? Sum up the poet's theme.

2. Why is the war chief *bashful?* How do you account for his behavior ("listening and listening, he danced after the other stopped")? (Listening past the noise of the gamblers to the quiet of mountains and river, he gets caught up in the old dance in spite of himself, and thoughtfully keeps dancing, forgetful of himself and of the modern world.)

3. How would you scan "He took two steps"? The poet introduces the statement four times—what is the effect of this repetition? (It makes for a row of heavy stresses followed by a pause. The poem is approximately the rhythm of the war chief, who makes heavy footfalls, pauses, and goes on with his dance.)

Wallace Stevens, PETER QUINCE AT THE CLAVIER, page 998

QUESTIONS FOR DISCUSSION:

1. We know that it is Peter Quince who speaks to us in the opening section; what are we to make of what follows? (We are to laugh when he sits down at the clavier. The story of Susanna is to be a tale told by a clown, not a faithful and serious recital, nor are we to take the clown's anguish [lines 5-15] in total earnest.)

2. Point out all the onomatopoeia you can find in the poem. Why is it appropriate to a poem whose imagery is largely taken from music?

3. "Music is feeling, then, not sound" (line 4). How is the truth of this statement demonstrated in the rest of the poem? (Each character in the poem has a theme song. Whenever we hear the music of the elders, as in lines 12-15 and 39-40, it is like that of a coarse jazz band, or like show-off violinists excitedly plucking their violins instead of playing them: "pizzicati of Hosanna"—praise not of God, but of Susanna. The elders are unimaginative men, coarse sensualists bound to the physical world. All they can hear is "Death's ironic scraping," not Susanna's music of immortality. Other theme songs are audible. Susanna, as she lolls in her bath, touches "springs" of melody—an autoerotic suggestion? The simpering Byzantine maids titter like tambourines. All have their appropriate music.)

4. "Beauty is momentary in the mind—/ The fitful tracing of a portrayal; / But in the flesh it is immortal." Is this statement nonsense? What sense can you make of it? (Stevens weaves a metaphor: the beauty of a woman is like music. Not that bodily beauty lasts forever; instead, it becomes a legend, and so continues to inspire works of art that live on in human memory.)

Harold Bloom has found an affinity between "Peter Quince" and Robert Browning's dramatic monologue "A Toccata of Galuppi's." In Browning's poem, a man apparently playing the music of the Venetian composer on the clavichord finds himself remembering Venetian gallants and ladies, and their long vanished lust. But in Stevens's opening lines, says Bloom, "it is Stevens who speaks directly of his own desire." This desire "deprecates itself, by an identification with the desire of the elders for Susanna rather than with the more refined and repressed desire of Susanna herself, in section II" (*Wallace Stevens, The Poems of Our Climate* [Ithaca: Cornell UP, 1977] 36).

The notion that Peter Quince, a Shakespearean clown, need not be taken seriously rubs John N. Serio the wrong way. "Many scholars have made a similar observation," he writes. "However, this has always seemed to me to violate the serious and sensitive tone of the poem. Perhaps a double irony is at work here: if we note Peter Quince's ultimately serious role in Shakespeare's play, perhaps we can attribute to him an equally serious function in Stevens's poem, one more in accord with the clearly dignified tone."

Professor Serio, who teaches at Clarkson University and edits *The Wallace Stevens Journal,* has amplified his view in an article. As so occurs often in the theater of Shakespeare, a clown delivers serious truth in *A Midsummer Night's Dream.* The bumpkins' unintentionally comic play-within-a-play is meant to instruct, and Pyramus and Thisbe are the only lovers in the macroplay (up until then) whose love remains unwavering and eternal. Ironically, the farce that Quince has directed states the whole play's deepest theme and conveys a message for the three couples about to be wed: let love transcend the flesh. (Stevens: "The body dies; the body's beauty lives.") Although Hippolita calls the yokels' play "the silliest stuff I ever heard," the wise Theseus suggests that even these rude characters will be acceptable "if imagination amend them." Reading the poem, says Professor Serio, we do not think Peter Quince a fool, but rather "a serious-minded poet/musician who, in the act of playing the clavier, has discovered a theory of art." See "Stevens, Shakespeare, and Peter Quince" in *Modern Language Studies* 9 (1978–79): 20–24.

Wallace Stevens, THE EMPEROR OF ICE-CREAM, page 1000

Choosing this poem to represent him in an anthology, Stevens once remarked, "This wears a deliberately commonplace costume, and yet seems to me to contain something of the essential gaudiness of poetry; that is the reason why I like it." (His statement appears in *Fifty Poets: An American Auto-Anthology* ed. William Rose Benet [New York: Diffield, 1933].)

Some students will at once relish the poet's humor, others may discover it in class discussion. Try to gather the literal facts of the situation before getting into the poem's suggestions. The wake or funeral of a poor old woman is taking place in her home. The funeral flowers come in old newspapers, not in florists' fancy wrappings; the mourners don't dress up, but wear their usual street clothes; the refreshments aren't catered but are whipped up in the kitchen by a neighbor, a cigar-roller. Like ice cream, the refreshments are a dairy product. Nowadays they would probably be a sour cream chip-dip; perhaps in 1923 they were blocks of Philadelphia cream cheese squashed into cups for spreading on soda crackers. To a correspondent, Stevens wrote that *fantails* refers not to fans but to fantail pigeons (*Letters* [New York: Knopf, 1966] 341). Such embroidery seems a lowbrow pursuit: the poor old woman's pathetic aspiration toward beauty. *Deal* furniture is cheap. Everything points to a run-down neighborhood, and to a woman about whose passing nobody very much cares.

Who is the Emperor? The usual guess is Death. Some students will probably see that the Emperor and the muscular cigar-roller (with his creamy curds) suggest each other. (Stevens does not say that they are identical.) Ice cream suggests the chill of the grave— and what besides? Today, some of its connotations will be commonplace: supermarkets, Howard Johnson's. To the generation of Stevens, ice cream must have meant more: something luxurious and scarce, costly, hard-to-keep, requiring quick consumption. Other present-day connotations may come to mind: sweetness, deliciousness, childhood pleasure. Stevens's personal view of the ice cream in the poem was positive. "The true sense of 'Let be be finale of seem' is let being become the conclusion or denouement of appearing to be: in short, ice cream is an absolute good" (*Letters* 341). An absolute good! The statement is worth quoting to students who have doubts about the poet's attitude toward ice cream—as did an executive of the Amalgamated Ice Cream Association, who once wrote to the poet in perplexity (see *Letters* 501–2). If ice cream recalls sweet death, still (like curds) it also contains hints of mother's milk, life, and vitality.

On a visit to Mount Holyoke, XJK was told that, as part of annual celebration, it is customary for the trustees and the seniors to serve ice cream (in Dixie cups) to the freshman class at the grave of Mary Lyon, founder of the college. In a flash he remembered Stevens's poem, and embraced Jung's theory of archetypes.

Ruth Stone, SECOND HAND COAT, page 1001

QUESTIONS FOR DISCUSSION:

1. Who is the speaker? (A woman, poor or on a tight budget, who has bought a second-hand coat.)

2. What distinguishes "Second Hand Coat" from prose? (Starting with line 6, the poem is an extended metaphor in which both coat and buyer become the woman who previously wore the coat.)

3. What is the tone of Stone's poem? (A little awed, perhaps, but at the same time whimsical, especially in the last two lines.)

This is the title poem of Stone's *Second-Hand Coat: Poems New and Selected* (Boston: Godine, 1987). For several appreciative comments about Ruth Stone and her work by her fellow writers, see pages 323–330 of *Extended Outlooks,* edited by Jane Cooper, Gwen Head, Adalaide Morris, and Marcia Southwick (New York: Collier, 1982).

Jonathan Swift, A DESCRIPTION OF THE MORNING, page 1002

This slice of eighteenth-century London life seems replete with human failings: Betty (a conventional name for a servant) sleeping with her master and trying to hide the evidence, prisoners released from jail in order to steal. Swift's couplets describe not the highborn but the common people, for whom a hackney coach heralded dawn in place of mythology's grander chariot driven across the sky by Phoebus Apollo. Although Swift crams his lines with images of city dirt and human corruption, the humor of his poem implies considerable affection for London's streets and sinners. If students see no humor in his view, let them compare this poem with another poem about eighteenth-century streets, Blake's angry "London" (page 652), or a rhapsodic, Romantic description of a London morning, Wordsworth's "Composed upon Westminster Bridge" (page 1016).

Alfred, Lord Tennyson, DARK HOUSE, BY WHICH ONCE MORE I STAND, page 1002

In Memoriam, section 7. "This is great poetry," wrote T. S. Eliot, "economical of words, a universal emotion related to a particular place; and it gives me the shudder that I fail to get from anything in *Maud"* (Introduction to *Poems of Tennyson* [London: Nelson, 1936]). The dark house was indeed a particular place—"67, Wimpole Street," as Tennyson noted—the house of Henry Hallam. The poem contains at least two allusions, whether or not we are expected to pick them up: "And then it started, like a guilty thing" (Horatio describing the ghost in *Hamlet,* I, i, 148); and "He is not here, but is risen" (Luke 24:6). In line 11 of one manuscript version, Tennyson wrote *dripping* instead of *drizzling.* Why is *drizzling* superior? The highest moment in the poem occurs in the last line in the two spondees, at least equal in their effect to Yeats's "And the *white breast* of the *dim sea"* ("Who Goes with Fergus?" page 717).

For some of these notes we are indebted to Christopher Ricks's matchless edition of *The Poems of Tennyson* (New York: Norton, 1969).

Alfred, Lord Tennyson, ULYSSES, page 1003

The following inadequate précis, meant to make lovers of Tennyson's poem irate, might be quoted to students to see whether they agree with it: A hardy old futzer can't stand life in the old folks' home, and calls on his cronies to join him in an escape, even though the whole lot of them are going to break their necks.

For criticism, see Paul F. Baum, *Tennyson Sixty Years After* (Chapel Hill: U of North Carolina P, 1948) 92–94; and John Pettigrew, "Tennyson's 'Ulysses': A Reconciliation of Opposites," *Victorian Poetry* 1 (Jan. 1963): 27–45.

Dylan Thomas, FERN HILL, page 1005

Fern Hill is the farm of Thomas's aunt, Ann Jones, with whom he spent boyhood holidays. In line 2 the poet cites a favorite saying of his father's, "Happy as the grass is green." The saying is echoed again in line 38. As students may notice, Thomas likes to play upon familiar phrases and transform them, as in line 7, "once *below* [not *upon*] a time."

It came as a great shock when we first realized that this poem, which XJK had thought a quite spontaneous burst of lyric energy, is shaped into a silhouette, and that the poet contrived its form by counting syllables. Such laborious working methods were customary for Thomas. John Malcolm Brinnin has recalled seeing more than 200 separate and distinct versions of "Fern Hill"—a fact worth conveying to students who think poets simply overflow.

We take the closing line to express Thomas's view of his own poetry, lyrical and rule-bound at the same time: a song uttered in chains. Of course, the last line also means that the boy in the poem was held in chains by Time, the villain, who informs the whole poem (except for stanzas 3 and 4, which see childhood as Eden). Students may be asked to trace all the mentions of Time throughout the poem, then to sum up the poet's theme. William York Tindall, who offers a line-by-line commentary, makes a fine distinction: "Not how it feels to be young, the theme of 'Fern Hill' is how it feels to have been young" (*A Reader's Guide to Dylan Thomas* [New York: Noonday, 1962]). And we'd add, "how it would have felt to grow old, if the boy had realized he wouldn't live forever."

According to Tindall (in a lecture), Thomas used to grow huffy whenever asked if he were an admirer of Gerard Manley Hopkins. Still, to hear aloud both "Fern Hill" and Hopkins's "Pied Beauty" (page 667) is to notice much similarity of sound and imagery. Hopkins studied Welsh for a time, while Thomas never did learn the language; but both at least knew of ancient Welsh poetry and its ingeniously woven sound patterns.

Thomas's magnificent (or, some would say, magnificently hammy) reading of this poem can be heard on Caedmon recording TC 1002, cassette 51002, compact disk Z1002. The recording, A *Child's Christmas in Wales and other poems,* also contains "Do not go gentle into that good night."

John Updike, EX-BASKETBALL PLAYER, page 1006

Updike's ex-basketball player suffers the fate that Housman's athlete escapes by dying young. Flick Webb has to live on, unsung, in "fields where glory does not stay." The man whose "hands were like wild birds" now uses those hands to pump gas, check oil, and change flat tires. "Once in a while, / As a gag, he dribbles an inner tube." In his spare time, he sits in Mae's luncheonette and "just nods / Beyond her face toward bright applauding tiers / Of Necco Wafers, Nibs, and Juju Beads." (Are today's students still familiar with those brand names?)

Updike's light tone does not obscure the pathos of Flick's situation. (Students might be asked if they know anyone like Flick Webb.) Though Updike has written notable light verse, he says of this early poem, his second to be accepted by *The New Yorker*, that it "is 'serious' and has enjoyed a healthy anthology life, though its second stanza now reads strangely to students. . . . That is, they have never seen glass-headed pumps, or gas stations with a medley of brands of gasoline, or the word *Esso*" (foreword to a new edition of Updike's first book, *The Carpentered Hen* [New York: Knopf, 1982]).

See how quickly your class can identify the poem's form as blank verse.

Amy Uyematsu, RED ROOSTER, YELLOW SKY, page 1007

This recent poem describes the difficult communication among three generations of Japanese-Americans. Sharing no common language, the grandmother and granddaughter speak through an image—in this case a commercial card brought from Japan to celebrate the Asian Year of the Rooster. Significantly, the card is "drawn in a child's hand." The granddaughter (then as a child and now as an adult) is able to find a message in the card, understanding the rooster's body split "in two uneven parts" nonetheless stands on sturdy feet that bear its own weight.

Mona Van Duyn, EARTH TREMORS FELT IN MISSOURI, page 1008

Van Duyn's poem starts by talking about an earthquake and moves by wonderfully subtle steps into a discussion of love. The outer, geological tremors become a symbol for the private, emotional ones, and gradually several surprising sets of correspondences (between, for instance, the earth turning and people turning toward one another).

In 1992, Mona Van Duyn became America's first female Poet Laureate. Born in Waterloo, Iowa, she currently lives in St. Louis, Missouri. In 1992, she won the Pulitzer Prize for her collection, *Near Changes*.

Derek Walcott, THE VIRGINS, page 1008

Walcott provides an ironic view of the main seaport of the Virgin Islands. The irony begins with the title in which the islands seem waiting to be raped or seduced by outsiders. The sun is like a drug ("sun-stoned"), and the term *free-port* is used sarcastically to underscore how little of any worth freedom has brought this city. The dense images and careful rhetoric of this poem create the impression of a dead place where no genuine life is possible.

Edmund Waller, GO, LOVELY ROSE, page 1009

In some ways quieter than Marvell's "To His Coy Mistress" (page 957) or Herrick's "To the Virgins, to Make Much of Time" (page 937), this poem has the same theme: *carpe diem*. "Go, Lovely Rose" merits admiration for its seemingly effortless grace and for the sudden, gently shocking focus on our mortality in the poem's final stanza.

Students may enjoy reading Ezra Pound's imitative tribute to Waller: the "Envoi" to *Hugh Selwyn Mauberley*, beginning "Go, dumb-born book . . . ," in *Personae*, Pound's collected shorter poems (New York: New Directions, 1949).

Walt Whitman, A NOISELESS PATIENT SPIDER, page 1010

"A Noiseless Patient Spider" isn't a poem about human beings reaching out in love to other human beings, but about the soul trying to form contact with higher reality. It may be used effectively in discussing symbolism in poetry, as well as figures of speech.

Whitman's poem is open in form, and yet certain lines fall into traditional measures (almost into rime, too), as would be indicated by rearranging them:

> Till the bridge you will need be form'd
> Till the ductile anchor hold,
> Till the gossamer thread you fling
> Catch somewhere, O my soul.

Walt Whitman, I SAW IN LOUISIANA A LIVE-OAK GROWING, page 1010

Whitman often regards some other living thing and sees himself reflected in it. In "Live-Oak" (one of the *Calamus* poems), the tree becomes his mirror in line 4; and one might expect the poem, like "A Noiseless Patient Spider," to extend the comparison. But the poem takes a surprising twist: Whitman himself cannot abide the oak's solitude. (This poem has not been shown to refer to any particular friends or events in the poet's life.)

Pablo Neruda's tribute to Whitman may well be applied:

> There are many kinds of greatness, but let me say (though I be a poet of the Spanish tongue) that Walt Whitman has taught me more than Spain's Cervantes: in Walt Whitman's work one never finds the ignorant being humbled, nor is the human condition ever found offended (qtd. in Gay Wilson Allen in *Poetry Pilot [Nov. 1976]*).

Richard Wilbur, TRANSIT, page 1011

In this skillfully metrical poem, Wilbur chooses a subject that might appear simple: the passage of a beautiful woman as she steps from her door, pulls on her gloves, and proceeds down her walk. But the poet's observations are neither simple nor simpleminded. There's a staggering hyperbole in the bit about the sun—a metaphysical conceit that recalls Marvell's "To His Coy Mistress." Why is stanza 2 a rueful question? It seems almost an attempt to mask how bowled over by her beauty the speaker is. His admiration bursts forth again in the startling image of the whip in the last line.

Richard Wilbur, THE WRITER, page 1012

A searching criticism of Wilbur's work, and this poem, is offered by Andrew Hudgins in a review of recent poetry (*Hudson Review,* Winter 1989). Sometimes Wilbur implies that it is possible to master the world and its complicated problems in much the same way that a poet, in a successful poem, masters the language—but it isn't, of course. Wilbur thus places himself in a dilemma, one he is aware of. Hudgins summarizes "The Writer" and interprets it:

> . . . Hearing his daughter as she types a story in her room, he compares the house to a ship and the sound of the typewriter keys to "a chain hauled over a gunwale," while the "stuff" of his daughter's life is "a great cargo and some of it heavy." Then, rather glibly, he wishes her a "lucky passage." As soon as he's completed the metaphor, however, he rejects the "easy figure" because he remembers how difficult the life of a writer can be. The next metaphor he advances is embedded in the anecdote of a "dazed starling" that once became trapped in the same room his daughter is now working in. . . . Though the poem is touching and even powerful, the implied final metaphor, and the ending of the poem, while infinitely better than

the rejected first metaphor of the ship, still have a bit of its premeditated neatness about them.

Whether or not the poem is autobiography, Wilbur does have a daughter, Ellen Wilbur, now a widely published fiction writer, author of *Wind & Birds & Human Voices,* a collection of short stories (Stuart Wright, 1984: NAL paperback, 1985).

Miller Williams, THINKING ABOUT BILL, DEAD OF AIDS, page 1013

Williams's poem presents, with admirable candor, the compassion and confusion of people watching a friend dying of AIDS. They do what love and decency dictate, but nonetheless they feel the painful inadequacy of their own actions. They have no convincing answers with which to face the situation. The speaker's uncertainty and self-critical introspection give the poem both depth and ambiguity while never taking it away from its emotional center.

William Carlos Williams, SPRING AND ALL, page 1014

QUESTIONS FOR DISCUSSION:

1. Why cannot Williams's attitude toward spring be called "poetic" and "conventional"? What is his attitude toward the approaching season? By what means is it indicated? Consider especially lines 14-15 and 24-25, and the suggestion of *contagious* in the opening line. (Spring is stealing over the land as a contagious disease infects a victim. But spring is not a disease: it has a "stark dignity.")

2. An opinion: "This poem clearly draws from the poet's experience as a pediatrician who had attended hundreds of newborns, and whose work was often to describe with clinical exactness the symptoms of his patients." Discuss. (Lines 16-18 especially seem to contain a metaphor of newborn infants. The adjectives *mottled, dried, sluggish* could occur in a physician's report. In lines 9-13 also, the description of bushes, trees, and vines seems painstakingly exact in its detail.)

Recalling his life as writer and physician in an article for a popular magazine, Williams once told how poems would come to him while driving on his daily rounds. "When the phrasing of a passage suddenly hits me, knowing how quickly such things are lost, I find myself at the side of the road frantically searching in my medical bag for a prescription blank" ("Seventy Years Deep," *Holiday* Nov. 1954: 78). "By the road to the contagious hospital" was one such poem, originally recorded on prescription blanks (Roy Miki, "Driving and Writing," in *William Carlos Williams: Man and Poet,* ed. Carroll F. Terrell [Orono: National Poetry Foundation, 1983] 113).

Scholars have speculated that the brief lines of many of Williams's poems may have been decreed by the narrow width of a prescription blank, but we don't buy that guess. Had he wanted longer lines Williams would have turned the blanks sideways, or composed in smaller handwriting.

William Carlos Williams, TO WAKEN AN OLD LADY, page 1015

QUESTIONS FOR DISCUSSION:

1. By which words or phrases does Williams suggest the physical ravages of old age? What very different connotations do the phrases *broken / seedhusks* and *shrill / piping*

carry, as well as the suggestions of feeble and broken senility? (Broken husks suggest a feast, piping suggests merriment.)

2. What is the *dark wind?* Can a wind be literally dark? (No, it can't; Williams means dark in the sense of sinister or menacing. This wind is like the passage of time that buffers or punishes.)

3. What is the dictionary definition of *tempered?* What does the word mean in this poem?

Yvor Winters, AT THE SAN FRANCISCO AIRPORT, page 1016

Students might be asked to compare the language of this poem with that of a neoclassical poem such as Dryden's "To the Memory of Mr. Oldham" (page 914). Both poems demonstrate that it is possible for a poet to write of a subject of personal concern and yet to select a diction relatively devoid of imagery, tending to be general and abstract. (For the result to be good poetry, the abstract words have to be accurate, as in these illustrations.)

Of all the terms in Winters's poem, the most tangible things named are light, metal, planes, and air. It is not to Winters's purpose here to number the streaks on any tulip; his concerns take in knowledge and passion, being and intelligence. At the outset Winters indicates that to see perfectly with one's physical eyes may be, in a sense, to see falsely and imperfectly. The glittering metal of the planes is a menacing distraction. He restates this observation in lines 16–17: "The rain of matter upon sense / Destroys me momently." It is not until the third stanza, when the poet is able to see beyond the immediate moment, that he achieves understanding. In the last line we are back to the original paradox, stated another way: to be awake in a merely physical light is not to be awake at all.

Like Winters's criticism, the poem praises will, reason, and intelligence. We admit, though, to some reservations about it. In lines 18–20, the diction becomes so abstract as to seem grandiose. We might wish to know more about the situation. Why is the girl leaving? Where is she going? But if we accept the poet's lofty tone—in which seeing one's daughter off on an airplane becomes an event as momentous as the launching of Cleopatra's barge—it seems an impertinence to ask.

In his fine study of Winters, the English poet and critic Dick Davis has written sympathetically of this poem:

> The farewell is given the deeper implication of the father's watching his daughter move out of his immediate care and influence into the world of her own life.... "That which you dare not shun" suggests the child's future journey through life, on which the poet cannot accompany her. The understated stoicism of the end is very moving, particularly if we recall that this was virtually Winters's last serious poem ... The closing image is not only a fine evocation of the father left alone, momentarily fixed in private thought, withdrawn from the airport's public glare, but it suggests too that light of the intellect which had become Winters's chief concern, the intellect which sees and understands but knows that it is cut off from the life it loves and watches. *(Wisdom and Wilderness: The Achievement of Yvor Winters* [Athens: U of Georgia P, 1983] 146–47).

This beautiful, knotty, generation-spanning poem has lasted in the *Introduction to Poetry* ever since the book's first edition. Today, as in the 1960s, its appeal to students seems to reach deep.

William Wordsworth, COMPOSED UPON WESTMINSTER BRIDGE, page 1016

Imaginary conversation:

> *Instructor:* What do you make of the title? Is this a poem composed upon the subject of a bridge, or a poem composed while standing on a bridge's sidewalk?
> *Student:* The latter, obviously.
> *Instructor:* How do you know?
> *Student:* His eye is located up on the bridge. Otherwise he wouldn't see with such a wide-angle lens.
> *Instructor:* You genius! To the head of the class!

Whose is the "mighty heart"? Wordsworth is describing the city as a sleeping beauty about to awaken. Of course, the brightness of the scene is increased by the poet's being out for his stroll before a hundred thousand chimneys have begun to smoke from coal fires preparing kippers for breakfast. Charles Lamb, in a letter to Wordsworth, had chided the poet that the urban emotions must be unknown to him, so perhaps this famous sonnet is an answer to the charge.

Compare "The World Is Too Much with Us" (page 812) for a different Wordsworth attitude toward commerce; or compare Wordsworth's London of 1807 with Blake's "London" of 1794 (page 652)—practically the same city, but a different perspective. (Wordsworth up on the bridge at dawn, letting distance lend enchantment; Blake down in the city streets by night, with the chimney sweep, the teenage whore, and the maimed veteran.)

James Wright, A BLESSING, page 1017

At first, students are likely to regard "A Blessing" as "a delicate poem about the kinship between men and horses," as Ralph J. Mills sees it (*Contemporary American Poetry* [New York: Random House, 1965]). They will be right, of course; but to take them a step further, they can be asked what *blessing* the poem refers to, and to ponder especially its last three lines. In a sense, the image of stepping over barbed wire into an open pasture (line 7) anticipates the idea of stepping out of one's body into—what? Any paraphrase is going to be clumsy; but Wright hints at nothing less than the loneliness of every creature alive. Although they are together, the two ponies are lonely to an extreme and are apparently overjoyed to see people. By implication, maybe the speaker and his friend are lonely together as well. In lines 15-21 the speaker, to his astonishment, finds himself falling in love with one of the ponies; he sees her beauty as that of a girl. At this point, we might expect him to recoil and cry, "Good grief! what's the matter with me?"—but he persists and becomes enlightened, at least for a moment. Only his physical body, he realizes, keeps him alone and separated. What if he were to shed it? He'd bloom.

A master of open form, Wright knows how to break off a line at a moment when a pause will throw weight upon sense: "Suddenly I realize / That if I stepped out of my body I would break / Into blossom."

Maybe the best way to teach "A Blessing" is just to read it aloud, and then say nothing at all.

James Wright, AUTUMN BEGINS IN MARTINS FERRY, OHIO, page 1018

Martins Ferry is the poet's native town. "Dreaming of heroes," the speaker sits in the high school stadium, the only place in town where heroes are likely to appear. Certainly the heroes aren't the men portrayed in lines 2-4; beery, gray-faced, ruptured, worn out by their jobs in heavy industry. These are the same "proud fathers" who, ashamed of their failures (including their failures as lovers to their wives), won't go home but prefer to hang around taverns. Without fathers to supply them with hero figures, their sons set out to become heroes themselves on the football field. The season of their "suicidal" ritual is fittingly the season of the death of the year. Will they become heroes? Most likely they'll just break their necks.

Perhaps the fathers were once football heroes themselves, as George S. Lensing and Ronald Moran point out in *Four Poets and the Emotive Imagination* (Baton Rouge: Louisiana State UP, 1976), a study that discusses nearly the whole of Wright's work. "From this there is the suggestion that the futures of the current community heroes may be as bleak as the present time assuredly is for the fathers."

Did Wright mean to protest the violence of football—at least, football of the Martins Ferry kind? Not according to the poet himself, who once played on an Ohio River Valley semipro team. Although the high school games were "ritualized, formalized violence," they had positive qualities: "the expression of physical grace," "terrific aesthetic appeal." Wright's own high school produced not just lads doomed to frustration (like their fathers), but at least one football hero—Lou Groza, placekicker for the Cleveland Browns. (Wright made his remarks in an interview reprinted in *The Pure Clear Word: Essays on the Poetry of James Wright*, ed. Dave Smith [Urbana: U of Illinois P, 1982] 3–4)

In the same critical anthology, Robert Hass sees football in the poem as a harvest ritual, which, like all good harvest rituals, celebrates sexual potency and the fruitfulness of the earth (two positive qualities apparently not conspicuous in Martins Ferry). "Even the stanzaic structure of the poem participates in the ritual. The first two stanzas separate the bodies of the men from the bodies of the women, and the third stanza gives us the boys pounding against each other, as if they could, out of their wills, effect a merging" (210).

Sir Thomas Wyatt, THEY FLEE FROM ME THAT SOMETIME DID ME SEKË, page 1019

Surely Wyatt knew what he was about. Sounding the final *e*'s helps to fulfill the expectations of iambic pentameter in lines 2, 12, 15, 17, 20, and 21, lines that otherwise would seem to fall short. In other lines, however, Wyatt appears to make the rhythm deliberately swift or hesitant in order to fit the sense. Line 7 ("Busily seeking with a continual change") seems busy with extra syllables and has to be read quickly to fit the time allotted it. Such a metrical feast seems worthy of Yeats, as does line 11, in which two spondees ("loose gown," "did fall") cast great stress upon that suddenly falling garment.

What line in English love poetry, by the way, is more engaging than "Dear heart, how like you this?" And when have a lover's extended arms ever been more nicely depicted? (This line may be thrown into the teeth of anyone who thinks that, in descriptive writing, adjectives are bad things.)

William Butler Yeats, CRAZY JANE TALKS WITH THE BISHOP, page 1019

Piecing together a history from this Crazy Jane poem and others, John Unterecker has identified the Bishop as a divinity student who had courted Jane in his youth. She rejected him in favor of a wild, disreputable lover: Jack the journeyman. As soon as he got enough authority, the Bishop-to-be had Jack banished, but Jane has remained faithful to her lover (at least, in spirit). (See *A Reader's Guide to William Butler Yeats* [New York: Noonday, 1959].) In this poem, the Bishop's former interest in Jane has dwindled to a concern for her soul only. Or has it? Perhaps the Bishop, no doubt a handsome figure in his surplice, may be demonstrating Yeats's contention that fair needs foul. Jane is living in lonely squalor. The grave, she says, can affirm the truth that her friends are gone, for it holds many of them; and her own empty bed can affirm that Jack is gone, too. Still, she firmly renounces the Bishop and his advice.

Each word of the poem is exact. Love has *pitched* his mansion as one would pitch a tent. The next-to-last line ends in two immense puns: *sole or whole.* The Bishop thinks that soul is all that counts, but Jane knows that both soul and hole are needed. Such puns may be why Yeats declared (in a letter) that he wanted to stop writing the Crazy Jane series: "I want to exorcise that slut, Crazy Jane, whose language has become unendurable."

What does Yeats mean by the paradoxical statement in the last two lines? Perhaps (1) that a woman cannot be fulfilled and remain a virgin—that, since fair and foul are near of kin, one cannot know Love, the platonic ideal, without going through the door of the physical body; and (2) that the universe is by nature a yin/yang combination of fair and foul (or, as Yeats would have it in *A Vision,* a pair of intertwining gyres). Crazy Jane may be crazy, but in Yeats's view she is a soothsayer.

William Butler Yeats, LONG-LEGGED FLY, page 1020

Is there a finer poem in praise of the beauty of solitary thought? It seems a good anecdote to any excessive yen for togetherness. Questions for discussion: What is the poet's attitude toward solitude? Are you won over by it? How does he try to convince us that solitary thought is beautiful? (By the metaphor of that graceful, swooping fly, riding alone in its skill.)

If students will compare the portrait of Helen of Troy given in Yeats's lines 11–20 with the one in H. D.'s "Helen," they will meet a striking contrast. Yeats makes Helen a very human little girl—a queen and yet a playful child. He also makes his Helen a bit Irish in that she practices a "tinker shuffle," picked up, it would seem, from watching those disreputable gypsy tinsmiths who plied their trade in the Irish countryside and sometimes danced for coppers in a village square.

Yeats's thinkers are three immortals from politics, mythology, and the arts, all figures of greatness in the scheme of Yeats's *A Vision.* As John Unterecker points out, Yeats attributes a strange aphrodisiac power to Michelangelo's art in another late poem, "Under Ben Bulben," in which a globe-trotting woman, having glanced at the fresco of Adam in the Sistine Chapel, finds herself "in heat" (*A Reader's Guide to William Butler Yeats* [New York: Noonday, 1959] 283).

According to A. Norman Jeffares, Yeats is probably thinking once more of Maud Gonne as a child (*A Commentary on the Collected Poems of W B. Yeats* [Stanford UP, 1968] 498). He loves to imagine the childhood of that great object of his unrequited love, notably in "Among School Children."

William Butler Yeats, THE MAGI, page 1021

After writing a lesser poem than this—"The Dolls," in which dolls hurl resentment at a "noisy and filthy thing," a human baby—Yeats had a better idea. "I looked up one day into the blue of the sky, and suddenly imagined, as if lost in the blue of the sky, stiff figures in procession" (Yeats's note at the back of his *Collected Poems*). Like dolls, the Magi seem frozen, somewhat inhuman ("rain-beaten stones"), unfulfilled. They are apparently troubled that Christ, whose birth was a miracle, died as a man. In hopes of regaining the peace of the Nativity, they pursue a second journey.

Bestial will seem to students an odd word to apply to a stable floor, unless they catch its literal sense: "belonging to beasts." But they will also need to see that its connotations of brutality fit the poem and interact with *Calvary's turbulence.* Compare "The Magi" with the rough beast in "The Second Coming" (page 813), a poem written after Yeats had more fully worked out his notion that historical events move in a cycle of endless return. ("Leda and the Swan," page 728, can be brought in, too, if there is time for it.)

In comparing Yeats's unsatisfied wise men to Eliot's in "Journey of the Magi" (page 914), good questions to ask include, Which poet writes as a Christian? How can you tell?

William Butler Yeats, WHEN YOU ARE OLD, page 1022

Yeats wrote this poem to the actress Maud Gonne in October, 1891. It is based very loosely on Ronsard's sonnet, "Quand Vous Serez Bien Vielle," but it is not a translation. Yeats merely took Ronsard's premise (an old woman rereading the verses a poet wrote to her in their youth) and developed it in his own way.

In this gentlest of love poems, the speaker is resigned to not winning the woman he loves. He is merely one of many men who love her. His claim, however, is that his love was not for the surface charms of her grace or beauty; he alone loved her for her searching soul. And he has the satisfaction of being able to preserve the unique quality of his devotion in words. Yeats's lyric, therefore, celebrates the ennobling power of both love and poetry.

To be candidly emotional risks seeming sentimental, but may we end the notes to the Poems for Further Reading by hoping that many years from now a few of our students take down this book to reread a few of the poems we taught them and realize that we spoke to "the pilgrim soul" in them?

31 *Criticism: On Poetry*

This additional anthology is designed not to give you anything more to teach, but to supplement your teaching resources. While there isn't anything you'll *need* to do about it, this anthology of criticism offers additional possibilities for paper topics and some broad, general subjects for discussion. It provides, moreover, brief texts of certain famous critical statements that some instructors have said they would like to have available. These include Plato's account of Socrates's theory of inspiration, Aristotle on imitation, Samuel Johnson on the superiority of universal truths to tulips' streaks, Wordsworth on emotion in tranquility, Coleridge on the imagination, Shelley's view of poets as "unacknowledged legislators," Emerson on the relation of thoughts to form, Poe on long poems, Dickinson on recognizing real poetry, Frost on the "sound of sense," and Eliot on personality. All seem part of the permanent baggage of received critical ideas that the reader who cares deeply for poetry will tote along. Finally, we added two more recent comments by contemporary poets—Rich on Feminist re-vision and Paz on the complex heritage of writers from the Americas.

The anthology is arranged in chronological order. Here are a few topics (for either writing assignments or class discussion) suggested by these selections, including the classic ones.

Plato, INSPIRATION, page 1025

1. According to Socrates, what is the source of poets' inspiration? How is it possible for "the worst of poets" to sing "the best of songs"?

2. Can readers be inspired as well? (Yes, and critics such as Ion.)

Aristotle, TWO CAUSES OF POETRY, page 1026

In your own words, sum up what Aristotle appears to mean by imitation. Can it be charged that he reduces poetry to journalism, poems to mere descriptions of the world? (But mere descriptions don't embody harmony and rhythm—two equally essential sources of a poem.)

Samuel Johnson, THE BUSINESS OF A POET, page 1027

1. Do poets, in Johnson's view, appear to be Muse-inspired utterers of surprising statements not their own? (Look back once more on Socrates's remarks on inspiration.)

2. What, then, is a poet's task as Johnson sees it?

3. Write a one-paragraph review of a book of imagist poetry (including, say, Ezra Pound's "In a Station of the Metro" [page 660], H. D.'s "Heat" [page 673], and Elizabeth Bishop's "The Fish" [page 663]—this last a later poem, but owing much to imagism) as Dr. Johnson might have written it. Would he condemn such poets for numbering the streaks of the tulip instead of articulating universal ideas?

William Wordsworth, EMOTION RECOLLECTED IN TRANQUILLITY, page 1027

1. In Wordsworth's description of the poetic process, how does a poet usually go about writing a poem?

2. Take another look at Wordsworth's poem "I Wandered Lonely as a Cloud" (page 605). What light does this statement cast upon it? What lines in the poem seem to describe the same process of poetic composition?

Samuel Taylor Coleridge, IMAGINATION, page 1028

1. This won't be easy, but try to state in your own words Coleridge's doctrine of the imagination, as you understand it from this passage. What does the mind of a poet *do* in composing a poem? (Coleridge's doctrine is more fully set forth in the *Biographia Literaria*, chapter 13. But this concise description, without special philosophical terms, of the *synthesizing* power of the imagination will serve, perhaps, to give the beginning student the essence of it.)

2. Name a poem, by any poet, in which you find what Coleridge might call "the balance or reconcilement of discordant qualities." (Suggestion: "The Love Song of J. Alfred Prufrock," in which Eliot certainly blends unlikely, conflicting matter—versions of loveliness such as the mermaids with ratty and sordid urban imagery.)

Percy Bysshe Shelley, UNACKNOWLEDGED LEGISLATORS, page 1029

How is Shelley's view of the value of poetry different from that of Socrates in the statement about banishing poets from the Republic? How does Shelley's thinking resemble that of Socrates in the remarks on inspiration?

Ralph Waldo Emerson, METER-MAKING ARGUMENT, page 1029

Are there any poems in this anthology that you think are mostly meter and lack a "meter-making argument"?

Edgar Allan Poe, A LONG POEM DOES NOT EXIST, page 1030

Do you agree or disagree? If Poe is right, should we discard *The Odyssey, The Divine Comedy,* and "Lycidas"? If he is wrong, then how do you account for the fact that certain long poems contain patches of deadly dullness?

Emily Dickinson, RECOGNIZING POETRY, page 1030

It may be worth pointing out to students that this famous passage from Dickinson does not exist in any of her writing. It comes from a letter that T. W. Higginson, a critic and novelist who befriended Dickinson after she wrote him, mailed to his wife during a visit to Amherst. Higginson took notes on his conversation with the poet to share with his wife; these brief notes provide a vivid description of both her genius and her eccentricity.

1. Is Dickinson right about recognizing poetry? Is there any other way to recognize it than by experiencing physical sensation?

2. What poem in the anthology affects you in the way that Dickinson describes? Can you relate the sensations you experience to any particular words or images in the poem?

Robert Frost, THE SOUND OF SENSE, page 1030

1. Experiment: Let someone in the class follow Frost's instructions, go out into the hall, and try speaking these or other sentences in a soft voice through a closed door. What element (if any) can the hearers still recognize?

2. Point to sentences in Frost's poems that sound as though written according to his ideas. Any Frost poem will do.

William Carlos Williams, THE RHYTHM PERSISTS, page 1032

Williams's own poetry is often regarded as an influential model of *vers libre,* or free-form verse. What isn't free or formless about it? How do Williams's remarks help you perceive what he is doing in his poems?

Ezra Pound, POETRY AND MUSIC, page 1032

Do you agree? Or are there any poems you know that aren't particularly musical but are worth reading? Give examples.

T. S. Eliot, EMOTION AND PERSONALITY, page 1032

Why does Eliot think Wordsworth (in his remarks on emotion recollected in tranquillity) is wrong? Compare these two poets' statements.

Adrienne Rich, FEMINIST RE-VISION, page 1033

Can you find a poem in the anthology that allows you to fulfill Rich's demand that it "work first of all as a clue to how we live, how we have been living, how we have been led to imagine ourselves" either as men or women in our society?

Octavio Paz, EUROPEAN LANGUAGES AND THE LITERATURE OF THE AMERICAS, page 1034

1. What does Paz mean by saying that languages "are vast realities that transcend those political and historical entities we call nations?"

2. Why would Paz feel that an American writer without any English blood in his or her ancestry must still have a special relationship with English literature?

32 Lives of the Poets

Instead of being strewn throughout the poetry section, biographical notes on poets are collected in this chapter. The intent is to make them easy to find and to keep them from interrupting the poetry. Biographies are supplied for most poets represented by two or more poems.

DRAMA

In many parts of the country, students rarely if ever see plays other than school or other amateur productions, and the instructor may encounter some resistance to the whole idea of studying drama. But all students are steeped in film and television drama, and it may be useful to point out that such drama begins with playscripts. One might reason somewhat like this. Movies and television, it's true, give plays hard competition in our society, and a camera does have advantages. In moments, film can present whole panoramas and can show details in close-up that theaters (with their cumbersome sets and machinery) cannot duplicate. Movies used to be called "photoplays," but the name implies an unnecessary limitation, for there is no point in confining the camera to recording the contents of a picture-frame stage. But a play—whether staged in a proscenium theater or in a parking lot—has its own distinct advantages. It is a medium that makes possible things a camera cannot do. Unlike movies and television, a play gives us living actors, and it involves living audiences who supply it with their presences (and who can move one another to laughter or to tears). Compared, say, to the laughter of live spectators at a comedy, the "canned" laughter often dubbed into television programs is a weak attempt to persuade television viewers that they are not alone.

A PLAY IN ITS ELEMENTS

Susan Glaspell
TRIFLES, page 1066

The recent comeback of *Trifles* may be due, we think, not only to Glaspell's pioneering feminist views but also to its being such a gripping, tightly structured play. Several instructors have asked for its inclusion in *Literature*. Whether or not you have much time to spend on the elements of a play, we think you will find *Trifles* worth teaching; students respond to it.

Topic for writing or discussion: What common theme or themes do you find in both *Trifles* and *Antigonê*? (A conflict between the law and a woman's personal duty.)

The Provincetown Players, who performed in a theater on an abandoned wharf, had a fertile summer in 1916. Besides *Trifles*, with Glaspell herself playing Mrs. Hale, their season included the first Eugene O'Neill play to be produced, *Bound East for Cardiff*. Glaspell has said that she derived the plot of *Trifles* from a murder case she had investigated as a reporter in Des Moines.

Ruth E. Zehfuss of DeKalb College has pointed out a meaningful way to compare *Trifles* with another classic drama in this book:

> The key idea in *Trifles*, the conflict between outer or legal authority and inner or moral law, was ... more than simply a feminist statement. The universality of the question Glaspell poses can be compared to Sophocles' *Antigonê*. In each play, the question is whether individuals have a right to follow their own moral beliefs when their beliefs conflict with the law of the state. ("The Law and the Ladies in *Trifles*," *Teaching English in the Two-Year College* [Feb. 1992], 42–44).

To compare the themes of *Trifles* and *Antigonê,* and how the characters of the two plays embody them, might be a rewarding topic either for class discussion or for a term paper. (See also the entry on *Antigonê* in this manual, on p. 326, for more ways to set the two plays side by side.)

TRAGEDY AND COMEDY

John Millington Synge
RIDERS TO THE SEA, page 1083

The narrative of Synge's play is gaunt in its simplicity. At the start, old Maurya has already lost six men of her family to the sea: her husband, father-in-law, and four sons. In the course of the play, suspicions are confirmed: a man reported drowned is indeed Michael, son number five. At the end, Maurya has lost Bartley, her sixth and last son, and the sea can do no more.

If you use the play to illustrate the elements of drama, you might point out the *exposition:* the early conversations of the girls and their mother, informing us that Michael is missing, feared drowned, and that Maurya dreads Bartley's going on a journey from which he will never return. While the *major dramatic question* seems plain—Will Bartley survive?—there is also a minor question: Was the missing Michael the man drowned in Donnegal? From the beginning we are given to suspect that he was, and this question is definitively answered in mid-play. The *crisis* occurs when Cathleen gives her mother the bundle and confirms that Michael's body has been found. The *climax* follows almost immediately—two blasts of emotion in a row!—with the bringing in of the dead Bartley. The *resolution,* we would say, is Maurya's rise to nobility. And the *theme?* That the sea is merciless, or perhaps more accurately (since after all, the islanders derive their living from the sea), the sea indifferently gives and takes away. Or it might be argued that Maurya sums up the theme in her memorable closing line. Does the play have a *protagonist?* Some may prefer to see Maurya instead as a central character. She is not a protagonist in the sense that she causes things to happen—she can't even prevent Bartley's journey—unless we regard what happens in this play as mainly what happens inside Maurya herself: her attaining a generous compassion for all humankind.

Riders to the Sea does not fit the mold of classic Greek tragedy, as Aristotle defined it, for its central character is a peasant, not a person of high estate, and she does not bring about her own downfall. Still, unquestionably the play has the tragic spirit. Like *Oedipus the King* and *Antigonê,* it shows the central character facing and accepting the inscrutable workings of the universe, finally rising to serene dignity. Maurya may begin as quarrelsome and complaining, but in the end she becomes as noble as a queen. Beholding these events, hearing the play's wonderful language, the spectator is stirred, perhaps overwhelmed, but far from depressed. And Synge's play is undoubtedly (as Aristotle would expect of a tragedy) serious, complete in itself, of a certain magnitude, and written in a language embellished with artistry. It even has a chorus: the band of keening old women. But you probably won't want to wrestle with how it is similar or dissimilar to a Greek tragedy until your students have read Sophocles. Then, Synge's play will surely reward another glance.

The world of this play—intense, stark, informed with the language of poetry—

seems to turn into a symbol virtually every ordinary object it contains. Even the rope that hangs from a nail hints of death (death by hanging). On one level, Cathleen's halting her spinning wheel merely indicates her sudden fear that Michael has drowned. On another level, her spinning, a routine of daily life, is (like that life itself) suddenly interrupted and shattered by death, or the fear of it. On still another level, a spinning wheel is associated with the famous three mythological Fates, who spin, measure, and cut off the thread of life. In abruptly ceasing to spin, perhaps, Cathleen symbolically breaks Michael's thread. Definite in its hints, the sea-wind that blows open the door, like the sea itself, is hostile, powerful, and irresistible.

Other suggestive objects invite symbol-hunting: the drowned man's clothes, for instance, tied into a sea-soaked bundle with a tight, unopenable black knot—like a terrible, impenetrable secret to be hidden from the old mother. Then, too, there's the bread that Maurya fails to convey to Bartley before his death: life-sustaining food of no use to a dead man, an undelivered good like the blessing that the old mother fails to impart. What of the fine white coffin-boards that ironically cannot be held together for lack of nails? Perhaps Maurya's forgetting them suggests her unconscious wish not to coffin another son. Boards are harbingers of death, for Bartley's body arrives on a plank. Suggestive, too, are the red mare that Bartley rides—red, the color of blood?—and the gray pony that knocks the young man into the sea, the very steed on which Maurya in her vision or waking dream saw the dead Michael ride. Maurya herself, it seems, has beheld riders to the sea—like Egyptians about to be drowned by the wrath of God. (For this Biblical allusion, see in the text the footnote on the title of the play.) A more obvious symbol is the empty, inverted cup that Maurya places on the table with a gesture of finality, as though to signify that all is gone, that the last drop of life (or of suffering) has been drained.

Maurya's vision of her two sons presages the play's resolution. Bartley, to be sure, might not have been a vision—actually, he may have been riding that red mare, and perhaps Maurya did try (and fail) to speak with him. When he passes her and she is unable to utter a sound and fails to give him the bread and her blessing, his doom is sealed. The apparition of Michael riding that fateful gray pony seems a clear foreshadowing—as perhaps Cathleen knows when she cries, "It's destroyed we are from this day." Bartley's death is foreshadowed from early in the play when Maurya hopes the priest will stop him from going on his errand.

Presumably the young priest isn't about to stop Bartley from taking a reasonable risk and making a needed horse sale. But the priest turns out to be a bad prophet, quite mistaken in his confidence that the Lord would not claim an old woman's last remaining son. Maurya never believed the priest's assurances: "It's little the like of him knows of the sea." (We get the impression that the characters in this play are faithful Christians living in an inscrutably pagan universe, or else one run by some cruel Manichean sub-deity.) No one but Maurya strongly feels that Bartley shouldn't take the horses to the Galway fair. The young assume that life must go on, for as Cathleen declares, "It's the life of a young man to be going on the sea." But the old mother has seen enough men claimed by the sea to fear that it is ready to claim one more.

Although Maurya has suffered the trauma of having her worst fears confirmed within minutes—learning of the death of one son and beholding the body of another—and although the sea has robbed her of a husband and six sons, she is not "broken," as Cathleen thinks, but is strong and rises to tragic serenity. In her moving speeches at the play's end, she goes beyond suffering to accept the nature of life and to take a long view of the mortality of all humankind.

For discussion: James Joyce's remark that the play suffers in that disaster is worked by a pony, not by the sea. (This seems to us a quibble: the pony may kick Bartley into the sea, but the sea conveys him out to the rocks and finishes him off.)

Garrison Keillor
PRODIGAL SON, page 1095

Garrison Keillor's amusing revision of the Gospel parable illustrates the basic elements of comedy in a way that many students will find especially engaging. Its form, the short satiric sketch, is one that will be familiar to them from television. The short length and simple structure of Keillor's sketch should make it easy to examine, while its gently satiric relation to the original parable (found on page 222) should reward repeated readings.

QUESTIONS

1. *Divide this play into elements. How much of the play is* exposition? *Who is the protagonist? What is the* climax *of the play, the moment when the tension is at its height?* It may be illuminating to students that even a short comic sketch like this one displays the traditional elements of dramatic structure. The exposition of the play is in the opening, where the principal characters and their motivations are presented—the affectionate and indulgent Dad, the hard-working and critical Dwight, and prodigal, easygoing Wally. The protagonist is Wally, who sets the plot in motion with his request to "get away for a while" to "get his head straight." The climax of the play is a little harder to pinpoint because of Keillor's deliberately understated humor. He gets laughs by underplaying the big moments. Keillor's narrative climax is the same as the original parable's—the moment when the prodigal son, having squandered his money, hits bottom and decides to return to his father. Wally is not one to take on much tension, so his climactic moment is comically brief.

2. *Comedy usually portrays human failings. What weaknesses does Wally have? Do Dad and Dwight also have weaknesses?* Wally is quite likable, but not even his doting Dad would declare him weakness-free. Among his more conspicuous failings are laziness, gullibility, drunkenness, and prodigality. Your students can surely uncover more. Dad and Dwight also have their failings. If the father of the original parable was wisely compassionate, Keillor's Dad is fatuously indulgent to prodigal Wally but takes his hard-working son for granted. Whatever his faults, Dwight is surely the sanest person in the sketch. His faults are modest compared to Wally's. He cares too much about business and has a tendency toward self-pity, though it is hard to blame Dwight for feeling sorry for himself at the play's conclusion.

3. *Does Keillor change any important elements of the plot from the original parable? ("The Parable of the Prodigal Son" is found on page 222.) If so, what part or parts of the plot does he alter?* While Keillor contemporizes the setting of the parable, he changes surprisingly few plot elements. His main alteration is to achieve comic effects by denying the characters any spiritual growth. Wally does not learn anything from his dissipation; he just spends Dad's money and returns home to mooch some more. Dad lacks the parental wisdom of the original father in the parable. The most interesting figure in the sketch is Dwight. He closely resembles the older brother of the original Gospel story. Keillor adds new elements to the plot, however, by introducing satiric versions of characters from other parables—the Stewards, Harry Shepherd and his lost sheep, the wise and foolish virgins, and the pushy Samaritans. Keillor also illustrates the prodigal son's dissipation, which the original parable treats tersely. Keillor's most important change is to end the play on the older brother's complaints rather than the father's attempt at reconciliation. In the original parable, we might assume that the older brother learns to share his father's compassion, but in Keillor's retelling, we have no illusions about Dwight's real feelings. He is seething with the moral indignation only a virtuous big brother can feel.

4. *How does Keillor turn this famous parable into a comedy? What elements of setting, characterization, or tone does he shift to get his comic effects?* There is no doubt that Keillor makes the parable into a comedy—specifically into a farce, a comic form that revels in low humor and ridiculous situations and characters. It may be worth remembering that farce originated as comic interludes in liturgical plays, and so the genre bears a traditional relation to sacred stories, just like Keillor's sketch. Keillor achieves his comic effects by updating the setting, making the characters mix biblical and contemporary language (especially the lingo of self-help books), and by revising the story into purely secular terms. How many comic allusions to the Bible can your students spot?

5. *Is Keillor's parody disrespectful of the original parable, or does he explore the same theme in a different way? Is it possible for a comedy to pursue the same themes as a more earnest work?* Keillor's version is extremely respectful to the original parable. There should be nothing in his sketch to offend the most devout student. He explores the same themes as the original parable, but, being a comic writer, he is less hopeful of humanity's moral improvement. The characters suffer more or less the same tribulations as in the original story, but they achieve no discernible spiritual growth.

6. *How can this play be considered a comedy if Dwight is so unhappy at the end?* Dwight's final, peevish monologue is really just a tantrum. He is not really going to live in the pigpen. Nor is it likely that Wally will get his big brother's room. Dwight indulges in exaggerated self-pity. While the audience will probably sympathize with his emotions, they will also find his angry monologue funny. Comedies are full of unhappy people— usually much less happy than Dwight. Think of what happens to the characters in a typical slapstick comedy. The purpose of comedy is not to make its characters happy, but to amuse the audience by ridiculing human failings. Dwight's final monologue comically portrays the older brother's all-too-human fallibilities.

Sophocles
OEDIPUS THE KING, page 1105

One problem in teaching this masterpiece is that students often want to see Oedipus as a pitiable fool, helplessly crushed by the gods, thus stripping him of heroism and tragic dignity. (A classic bepiddlement of the play once turned up on a freshman paper: "At the end, Oedipus goes off blinded into exile, but that's the way the cookie crumbles.") It can be argued that Oedipus showed himself to be no fool in solving the riddle of the Sphinx or in deciding to leave Corinth; that no god forced him to kill Laïos or to marry Iocastê.

Another problem in teaching this play is that some students want to make Oedipus into an Everyman, an abstract figure representing all humanity. But Oedipus's circumstances are, to say the least, novel and individual. "Oedipus is not 'man,' but Oedipus," as S. M. Adams argues in *Sophocles the Playwright* (Toronto: University of Toronto Press, 1957). On the other hand, Freud's reading of the play does suggest that Oedipus is Everyman—or, better, that every man is Oedipus and like Oedipus wishes to kill his father and marry his mother. A passage from Freud's celebrated remarks about the play is given on page 1805.

Despite Freud's views, which usually fascinate students, critical consensus appears to be that Oedipus himself did not have an Oedipus complex. Sophocles does not portray Oedipus and Iocastê as impassioned lovers; their marriage was (as Philip Wheelwright says) "a matter of civic duty: having rid the Thebans of the baleful Sphinx by answering her riddle correctly, he received the throne of Thebes and the widowed queen as his due reward" (*The Burning Fountain* [Bloomington: Indiana University Press, 1954]). Wheelwright also notes, incidentally, that the title *Oedipus Tyrannus* might be translated more accurately as "Oedipus the Usurper"—a usurper being (to the Greeks) anyone who gains a throne by means other than by blood succession. Actually, of course, Oedipus had a hereditary right to the throne. (Another interpretation of the play sees Laïos and Iocastê as having incurred the original guilt: by leaving a royal prince to die in the wilderness, they defied natural order and the will of the gods.)

For the nonspecialist, a convenient gathering of views will be found in *Oedipus Tyrannus,* ed. Luci Berkowitz and Theodore F. Brunner (New York: Norton, 1970). Along with a prose translation of the play by the editors, the book includes the classic comments by Aristotle, Nietzsche, and Freud, and discussions by recent critics and psychologists. Seth Bernardete offers a detailed, passage-by-passage commentary in *Sophocles: A Collection of Critical Essays,* ed. Thomas Woodard (Englewood Cliffs: Prentice, 1966). Francis Fergusson has pointed out that the play may be read (on one level) as a murder mystery: "Oedipus takes the role of District Attorney; and when he at last convicts himself, we have a twist, a *coup de théâtre,* of unparalleled excitement." But Fergusson distrusts any reading so literal, and questions attempts to make the play entirely coherent and rational. Sophocles "preserves the ultimate mystery by focusing upon [Oedipus] at a level beneath, or prior to any rationalization whatever" (*The Idea of a Theatre* [Princeton: Princeton UP, 1949]). Refreshing, after you read many myth critics, is A. J. A. Waldock's *Sophocles the Dramatist* (Cambridge: Cambridge University Press, 1951; reprinted in part by Berkowitz and Brunner). According to Waldock, the play is sheer entertainment, a spectacular piece of shock, containing no message. "There is no meaning in the *Oedipus Tyrannus.* There is merely the terror of coincidence, and then, at the end of it all, our impression of man's power to suffer, and of his greatness because of this power." Pointing out how little we know of Sophocles's religion, Waldock finds the dramatist's beliefs "meagre in number and depressingly commonplace."

Although the religious assumptions of the play may not be surprising to Waldock, students may want to have them stated. A good summing-up is that of E. R. Dodds, who maintains that Sophocles did not always believe that the gods are in any human sense "just"; but that he did always believe that the gods exist and that man should revere them ("On Misunderstanding the Oedipus Rex," *Greece and Rome* [Oxford: Oxford University Pree, 1966] Vol. 13). This comment is now included in the book ("Criticism: On Drama," page 1717).

"Possibly the best service the critic can render the *Oedipus Rex,*" says Waldock, "is to leave it alone." If, however, other criticism can help, there are especially valuable discussions in H. D. F. Kitto, *Greek Tragedy,* 3rd ed. (London: Methuen, 1961), and *Poiesis* (Berkeley: University of California Press, 1966); Richmond Lattimore, *The Poetry of Greek Tragedy* (Baltimore: Johns Hopkins University Press, 1958); and Patrick Mullahy, *Oedipus, Myth and Complex* (New York: Grove, 1948).

In the "Suggestions for Writing" at the end of the chapter (page 1149, there is one especially challenging topic (number 3): to compare translations of the play. For any student willing to pick up the challenge, we think this topic might produce a great term paper. The differences between versions, of course, are considerable. Sheppard's rendition, or Kitto's, is more nearly literal than that of Fitts and Fitzgerald and much more so than that of Berg and Clay. In the latter team's version of 1978, the persons of the tragedy all speak like formally open lyrics in current little magazines. Lots of monosyllables. Frequent pauses. Understatement. Lush imagery. Berg and Clay perform this service brilliantly, and it might be argued: why shouldn't each generation remake the classics in its own tongue?

Still impressive is the film *Oedipus Rex* (1957), directed by Tyrone Guthrie, a record of a performance given in Stratford, Canada. Although the theater of the play is more Stratfordian than Athenian, the actors wear splendid masks. The text is the Yeats version. The film (88 minutes long, 16 mm, in color) may be bought or rented from Contemporary/McGraw-Hill Films, 1221 Avenue of the Americas, New York, NY 10020, or from their regional distributors.

In July 1984, the Greek National Theater presented a much-discussed *Oedipus Rex* at the Kennedy Center in Washington. Bernard Knox offers an admiring account of it in *Grand Street* for Winter 1985. The director, Minos Volankis, staged the play on a "circular, dark brown plate, tilted toward the audience" and etched with a labyrinth pattern. In Volankis's version, Oedipus and Iocastê cannot see the pattern and ignore it as they move about the stage, but the chorus and Teiresias are aware of the labyrinth and respectfully trace its curves in their movements. Oedipus is a clean-shaven youth, the only young person in the play—"caught in a web spun by his elders."

In a useful recent article on teaching *Oedipus,* W. A. Senior of Broward Community College suggests ways to present the play as meaningful to freshmen who wonder how anything so ancient and esoteric as classical drama can help them in their lives today and advance their pursuit of a C.P.A. degree. His approach is to demythify the character of Oedipus, stressing that the protagonist is no god or superman, but a confused, deceived human being at the center of a web of family relationships (to put it mildly) and political responsibilities. Like a business executive or professional today, Oedipus has to interrogate others, determine facts, and overcome his natural reluctance to face painful realities.

To help students come to terms with the central character, Senior has used specific writing assignments. "I have them compose a letter to Oedipus," he reports, "individually or at times in groups, at the height of the action in the third act to advise him on what to do or to explain to him what he has done wrong so far. In a related essay taking a page from *Antigonê* and its theme of public versus private good, which is foreshadowed in *Oedipus Rex,* I ask them to write an editorial on Oedipus as politician; each student must adopt a position and defend it." ("Teaching Oedipus: The Hero and Multiplicity," *Teaching English in the Two-Year College* [Dec. 1992], 274–79.)

William Shakespeare

THE TRAGEDY OF OTHELLO, page 1153

For commentary on the play, some outstanding sources of insight still include A. C. Bradley's discussion in *Shakespearean Tragedy* (1904; rpt. ed. [New York: St. Martin's, 1965]); and Harley Granville-Barker, "Preface to *Othello,*" in *Prefaces to Shakespeare,* II (Princeton UP, 1947), also available separately from the same publisher (1958). See also Leo Kirschbaum, "The Modern *Othello,*" *Journal of English Literary History* 2 (1944), 233-96; and Marvin Rosenberg, *The Masks of "Othello"* (Berkeley: University of California Press, 1961). A convenient gathering of short studies will be found in A *Casebook on Othello,* ed. Leonard Dean (New York: Crowell, 1961). For a fresh reading of the play, see Michael Black, who in *The Literature of Fidelity* (London: Chatto, 1975) argues that the familiar view of Othello as a noble figure manipulated by the evil Iago is wrong and sentimental. According to Black, we see ourselves and our destructive impulses mirrored in both characters; hence, we are disturbed.

Lynda E. Boose has closely read the confrontation scene between Othello and Brabantio, the father of Desdemona, in front of the Duke (I, iii), and has found in it an ironic parody of the traditional giving away of the bride at a marriage ceremony. Instead of presenting his daughter to Othello as a gift, the thwarted Brabantio practically hurls her across the stage at the Moor. (The scene resembles Lear's casting away of Cordelia in *King Lear,* I, i.) In most of Shakespeare's plays, the father of the bride wants to retain and possess his daughter. Prevented by law and custom from doing so, he does the next best thing: tries to choose her husband, usually insisting on someone she does not desire. But Shakespeare, in both comedy and tragedy, always stages the old man's defeat ("The Father and the Bride in Shakespeare," *PMLA* 97 [May 1982]: 325-47).

Still another opinion that students might care to discuss: "No actress could credibly play the role of Desdemona if the character's name were changed to, say, Sally" (Frank Trippett, "The Game of the Name," *Time,* 14 Aug. 1978).

General question 3: "How essential to the play is the fact that Othello is a black man, a Moor, and not a native of Venice?" That Othello is an outsider, a stranger unfamiliar with the ways of the Venetians, makes it easier for Iago to stir up Othello's own self-doubts; and so the fact seems essential to the plot. (See especially III, iii, 215-23, 244-47, 274-84.) Venice in the Renaissance had no commerce with black Africa but Shakespeare's many references to Othello's blackness (and Roderigo's mention of the Moor's "thick lips," I, i, 68) have suggested to some interpreters that Othello could even be a coastal African from below the Senegal. On the modern stage, Othello has been memorably played by African-American actor Paul Robeson and by Laurence Olivier, who carefully studied African-American speech and body language for his performance at the Old Vic (and in the movie version). A critic wrote of Olivier's interpretation:

> He came on smelling a rose, laughing softly with a private delight; barefooted, ankleted, black. . . . He sauntered downstage, with a loose, bare-heeled roll of the buttocks; came to rest feet splayed apart, hips lounging outward. . . . The hands hung big and graceful. The whole voice was characterized, the o's and the a's deepened, the consonants thickened with faint, guttural deliberation. "Put up yo' bright swords,

or de dew will rus' dem": not quite so crude, but in that direction. It could have been caricature, an embarrassment. Instead, after the second performance, a well-known Negro actor rose in the stalls bravoing. For obviously it was done with love; with the main purpose of substituting for the dead grandeur of the Moorish empire one modern audiences could respond to (Ronald Bryden, *The New Statesman*, I May 1964).

For a fascinating study of the play by a white teacher of African-American students at Howard University, see Doris Adler, "The Rhetoric of *Black* and *White* in Othello," in *Shakespeare Quarterly* 25 (Spring 1974): 248–57. Iago, Roderigo, and Brabantio hold negative and stereotyped views of black Africans which uncomfortably recall modern racial prejudices. In their view, Othello is "lascivious" (I, i, 126), an unnatural mate for a white woman (III, iii, 245–49), a practitioner of black magic (I, ii, 74–75). Under the influence of Iago's wiles, Othello so doubts himself that he almost comes to accept the stereotype forced on him, to reflect that in marrying him Desdemona has strayed from her own nature (III, iii, 243). Such, of course, is not the truth Shakespeare reveals to us, and the tragedy of Othello stems from a man's tragic inability to recognize good or evil by sight alone. "Eyes cannot see that the black Othello is not the devil," Adler observes, "or that the white and honest Iago is."

In answer to general question 4 ("Besides Desdemona and Iago, what other pairs of characters seem to strike balances?"): Alvin Kernan in his introduction to the Signet edition of *Othello* comments,

> The true and loyal soldier Cassio balances the false and traitorous soldier Iago. . . . The essential purity of Desdemona stands in contrast to the more "practical" view of chastity held by Emilia, and her view in turn is illuminated by the workaday view of sensuality held by the courtesan Bianca. . . . Iago's success in fooling Othello is but the culmination of a series of such betrayals that includes the duping of Roderigo, Brabantio, and Cassio.

On general question 5: Thomas Rymer's famous objections to the play will not be easy to refute. At least, no less a critic than T. S. Eliot once declared that he had never seen Rymer's points cogently refuted. Perhaps students will enjoy siding with the attack or coming to the play's defense.

The last general question ("Does the downfall of Othello proceed from any flaw in his nature, or is his downfall entirely the work of Iago?") is a classic (or cliché) problem, and perhaps there is no better answer than Coleridge's in his *Lectures on Shakspere:*

> Othello does not kill Desdemona in jealousy, but in a conviction forced upon him by the almost superhuman art of Iago—such a conviction as any man would and must have entertained who had believed in Iago's honesty as Othello did. We, the audience, know that Iago is a villain from the beginning; but in considering the essence of the Shaksperian Othello, we must perseveringly place ourselves in his situation, and under his circumstances. Then we shall immediately feel the fundamental difference between the solemn agony of the noble Moor, and the wretched fishing jealousies of Leontes. . . . Othello had no life but in Desdemona: the belief that she, his angel, had fallen from the heaven of her native innocence, wrought a civil war in his heart. She is his counterpart; and, like him, is almost sanctified in our eyes by her absolute unsuspiciousness, and holy entireness of love. As the curtain drops, which do we pity the most?

Was the Othello-Desdemona match a wedding of April and September? R. S. Gwynn of Lamar University writes: "Has anyone ever mentioned the age difference between Othello and Desdemona? Othello speaks of his arms as 'now some nine moons wasted.' Assuming that this metaphor means that his life is almost 9/12 spent, he would be over 50! Now if a Venetian girl would have normally married in her teens (think of the film version of *Romeo and Juliet*), that would make about 30 years' difference between him and his bride." This gulf, Othello's radically different culture, his outraged father-in-law, and Iago's sly insinuations, all throw tall obstacles before the marriage.

"If we are to read the play that Shakespeare wrote," maintains Bruce E. Miller, "we must acknowledge that Othello as well as Iago commits great evil." In *Teaching the Art of Literature* (Urbana: NCTE, 1980), Miller takes *Othello* for his illustration of teaching drama and stresses that Othello went wrong by yielding to his gross impulses. In demonstrating why the play is a classic example of tragedy, Miller takes advantage of students' previously having read Willa Cather's "Paul's Case." The latter story illustrates "the difference between sadness and tragedy. Paul's death is sad because it cuts off a life that has never been fulfilled. But it is not tragic, for Paul lives and dies in this world of human affairs." But Othello's death has the grandeur of tragedy. Realizing at last that Desdemona has been true and that in staying her he has destroyed his own hopes of happiness, the Moor attains a final serenity of spirit, intuiting the true order of things.

Henrik Ibsen

A DOLL'S HOUSE, page 1258

At the heart of the play, as its title indicates, is its metaphor of a house of make-believe. In the play's visible symbols, we see Ibsen the poet. In Act I, there is the Christmas tree that Nora orders the maid to place in the middle of the room—a gesture of defiance after Krogstad had threatened her domestic peace and happiness. In the Christmas gifts Nora has bought for the children—sword, toy horse, and trumpet for the boys, a doll and a doll's bed for the girl Emmy—Nora seems to assign boys and girls traditional emblems of masculinity and femininity and (in Rolf Fjelde's phrasing) is "unthinkingly transmitting her doll-identity to her own daughter." When the curtain goes up on Act II, we see the unfortunate Christmas tree again: stripped, burned out, and shoved back into a corner—and its ruin speaks eloquently for Nora's misery. Richly suggestive, too, is Nora's wild tarantella, to merry music played by the diseased and dying Rank. Like a victim of a tarantula bite, Nora feels a kind of poison working in her; and it is ironic that Rank has a literal poison working in him as well. (The play's imagery of poison and disease is traced in an article by John Northam included in Rolf Fjelde's *Ibsen: A Collection of Critical Essays* [Englewood Cliffs: Prentice, 1965]). Significant, too, is Nora's change of costume (page 1309): taking off her fancy dress, she divests herself of the frivolous nonsense she has believed in the past and puts on everyday street attire.

Ibsen's play was first performed in Copenhagen on December 21, 1879; no doubt many a male chauvinist found it a disquieting Christmas present. Within a few years, *A Doll's House* had been translated into fourteen languages. James Gibbons Huneker has described its fame: when Nora walked out on Helmer, "that slammed door reverberated across the roofs of the world." With the rise of feminism, *A Doll's House* gradually became Ibsen's most frequently performed play—not only on the stage but also in television and film adaptations. In 1973, for example, two screen versions were issued almost simultaneously: Joseph Losey's overly solemn version starring Jane Fonda, and Hilliard Elkin's superior adaptation featuring Claire Bloom (expertly assisted by Anthony Hopkins, Ralph Richardson, Denholm Elliott, and Edith Evans).

Ibsen, to be sure, was conscious of sexual injustices. In preliminary notes written in 1878, he declared what he wanted his play to express:

> A woman cannot be herself in contemporary society; it is an exclusively male society with laws drafted by men, and with counsel and judges who judge feminine conduct from the male point of view. She has committed a crime and she is proud of it because she did it for love of her husband and to save his life. But the husband, with his conventional views of honor, stands on the side of the law and looks at the affair with male eyes.

Clearly, that is what the finished play expresses, but perhaps it expresses much more besides. A temptation in teaching Ibsen is to want to reduce his plays to theses. As Richard Gilman says, the very name of Henrik Ibsen calls to mind "cold light, problems, living rooms, instruction" (*The Making of Modern Drama* [New York: Farrar, 1964]).

But is the play totally concerned with the problems of the "new woman"? Ibsen didn't think so. At a banquet given in his honor by the Norwegian Society for Women's Rights in 1898, he frankly admitted,

> I have been more of a poet and less of a social philosopher than people have generally been inclined to believe. I thank you for the toast, but I must decline the honor of consciously having worked for women's rights. I am not even quite sure what women's rights really are. To me it has been a question of human rights.

Elizabeth Hardwick thinks Ibsen made this statement because he had "choler in his bloodstream" and couldn't resist making a put-down before his admirers. She finds Ibsen nevertheless admirable: alone among male writers in having pondered the fact of being born a woman—"To be female: What does it mean?" (*Seduction and Betrayal* [New York: Random, 1974]). Perhaps there is no contradiction in arguing that Ibsen's play is about both women's rights and the rights of all humanity.

Another critic, Norris Houghton, suggests a different reason for the play's timeliness. "Our generation has been much concerned with what it calls the 'identity crisis.' This play anticipates that theme: Ibsen was there ahead of us by ninety years" (*The Exploding Stage* [New York: Weybright, 1971]). Houghton's view may be supported by Nora's declared reasons for leaving Torvald: "If I'm ever to reach any understanding of myself and the things around me, I must learn to stand alone" (p. 1311).

The play is structured with classic severity. Its first crisis occurs in Krogstad's initial threat to Nora, but its greatest crisis—the climax—occurs when Helmer stands with the revealing letter open in his hand (page 1306). We take the major dramatic question to be posed early in Act I, in Nora's admission to Mrs. Linde that she herself financed the trip to Italy. The question is larger than "Will Nora's husband find out her secret?"—for that question is answered at the climax, when Helmer finds out. Taking in more of the play, we might put it, "Will Nora's happy doll house existence be shattered?"—or a still larger question (answered only in the final door slam), "Will Nora's marriage be saved?"

Ibsen's magnificent door slam has influenced many a later dramatist. Have any students seen Stephen Sondheim and Hugh Wheeler's musical *Sweeney Todd, The Demon Barber of Fleet Street* (1979) on stage or on television? At the end, Todd slams a door in the faces of the audience, suggesting that he would gladly cut their throats.

For a dissenting interpretation of Ibsen's play, see Hermann J. Weigand, *The Modern Ibsen* (New York: Dutton, 1960). Weigand thinks Nora at the end unchanged and unregenerate—still a wily coquette who will probably return home the next day to make Torvald toe the line.

A topic for class debate: Is *A Doll's House* a tragedy or a comedy? Much will depend on how students interpret Nora's final exit. Critics disagree: Dorothea Krook thinks the play contains all the requisite tragic ingredients (*Elements of Tragedy* [New Haven: Yale UP, 1969]). Elizabeth Hardwick (cited earlier) calls the play "a comedy, a happy ending—except for the matter of the children."

To prevent North German theater managers from rewriting the play's ending, Ibsen supplied an alternate ending of his own "for use in an emergency." In this alternate version, Nora does not leave the house; instead, Helmer makes her gaze upon their sleeping children. "Oh, this is a sin against myself, but I cannot leave them," says Nora, sinking to the floor in defeat as the curtain falls. Ibsen, however, thought such a change a "barbarous outrage" and urged that it not be used. Students might be told of this alternate ending and be asked to give reasons for its outrageousness.

Citing evidence from the play and from Ibsen's biography, Joan Templeton argues that those critics who fail to see *A Doll's House* as a serious feminist statement have distorted its meaning and unintentionally diminished its worth ("*The Doll House* Backlash: Criticism, Feminism, and Ibsen," PMLA: January 1989).

For a cornucopia of stimulating ideas, see *Approaches to Teaching Ibsen's A Doll's House,* edited by Yvonne Shafer (New York: Modern Language Association, 1985), one of the MLA's likable paperback series "Approaches to Teaching Masterpieces of World Literature." June Schlueter writes on using the play as an introduction to drama, and notes that, unlike *Oedipus,* the play does not create an inexorable progress toward disaster. "At any point, we feel, justifiably, that disaster might be avoided." Irving Deer recommends approaching the play by considering "how it deals with decaying values and conventions." J. L. Styan urges instructors to have a class act out the play's opening moments, before and after discussing them, so that Ibsen's wealth of suggestive detail will emerge, which students might otherwise ignore. Other commentators supply advice for teaching the play in a freshman honors course, in a course on women's literature, and in a community college. Joanne Gray Kashdan, author of this latter essay, reports that one woman student exclaimed on reading the play: "I realized I had been married to Torvald for seven years before I divorced him!"

TRAGICOMEDY AND THE ABSURD

Edward Albee
THE SANDBOX, page 1318

The Sandbox (1960) was not only one of the plays that first brought Edward Albee to national prominence; it is also one of the works that defined the Theater of the Absurd in America. Since the play's action is so overtly unrealistic, the audience is forced to reach for some other sort of significance. What is that significance? Certain obvious themes come to mind: the inability of people to communicate; the meaninglessness of modern existence; the horrible absurdity of death in a universe without divine providence; the hypocritical emptiness of contemporary family life. Whatever interpretation one reads into *The Sandbox,* the play's theatrical creativity, dark humor, and stinging satire still make it lively and uncomfortable viewing.

QUESTIONS

1. *What is unusual about the names of the characters in* The Sandbox? *How does this quality affect our perceptions of the characters?* The names of all the characters are generic—Mommy, Daddy, Grandma, The Young Man, The Musician. The characters, Albee implies, are not individuals as much as archetypes, symbolic characters acting out some representative action. The names also emphasize the familial and generational nature of the action. In "The Theater of Edward Albee" (*Tulane Drama Review,* Summer 1965), Lee Baxandall notes:

> Three generations comprise Albee's archetypal family: *Then,* the epoch of a still-dynamic national ethic and vision; *Now,* a phase which breaks down into several tangents of decay; and *Nowhere,* a darkly prophesied future generation. Only two characters are left over from *Then:* Grandma and a *paterfamilias* or patriarch who is occasionally mentioned but never appears. These establish a polarity based upon the axis of female and male principles. It has been often remarked that Grandma is the sole humane, generous creature in the Albee ménage. She tries to relate to others in a forthright and meaningful fashion, but at her age she no longer commands the requisite social weight. The others, her offspring, do not want Grandma involved in their dubious lives. They ask her to stifle her "pioneer stock" values. Her pleas that

she be put to use—"beg me, or ask me, or entreat me . . . just anything like that" are not heeded, because she is of a different epoch.

As the names suggest, the basic action of *The Sandbox* takes place within the family unit. The names are also one of the many antirealistic elements in the script. Since the play cannot be understood in realistic terms, we tend to view it allegorically or symbolically.

2. *Where does the play take place? What does the presence of the sandbox suggest?* The play takes place on the beach (as Mommy's first line makes clear). The sandbox suggests a number of things, most notably a burial plot or grave. A sandbox also brings to mind early childhood play, an odd association for a dying old woman but also one that suggests both her ironically childlike dependence on Mommy and Daddy, and the absurd playfulness of this play about death.

3. *Does* The Sandbox *contain any traditional elements of plot structure? Does the play have a climax? If so, where?* Although it is absurd in most respects, *The Sandbox* has a visible structure: an *exposition* (when Mommy and Daddy enter, then carry on Grandma); an intentionally hokey *climax* (the violent off-stage rumbles that precede the second day and announce Grandma's death); and a bizarre *dénouement* (in which Grandma discovers that she is dead and that the Young Man is the Angel of Death). It would be hard to think of a more traditional way to end a play than by the central character's death. Albee employs all these elements with deliberate irony.

4. *Describe how Mommy and Daddy treat Grandma. How do they speak to her?* Mommy and Daddy treat Grandma with a polite but merciless detachment. They talk *about* her, but hardly talk *to* her, except to say, "Be quiet, Grandma . . . just be quiet and wait." Mommy reveals no emotional attachment whatsoever to her own mother. Daddy at least worries that Grandma is uncomfortable, but Mommy shuts him up. The outward emotions of concern they display are overtly hypocritical. Grandma, by contrast, seems relatively normal—at least once her initial childish fit is over. Her reactions and comments seem sincere, if not particularly profound.

5. *Albee tells the audience quite specifically that the Young Man is the Angel of Death. What other occupation does he have?* The Young Man is an actor, though apparently not either an experienced or particularly talented one. When he delivers his big line, "I am the Angel of Death," the stage directions state he says it "like a real amateur," and then he muffs his next line. By making The Young Man an actor, Albee pokes fun at his own dramatic scheme while self-consciously reminding the audience that everyone on the stage is an actor. Theater of the Absurd frequently reminds the audience that the performance is an artifice.

6. *What purpose does the Musician serve in the play? Would* The Sandbox *have the same effect without this character?* By bringing The Musician on stage, Albee further heightens the overt artificiality of the play. (Music usually comes from offstage.) He also increases the amusing stage business. The Musician also supports the symbolic atmosphere of the play. Rituals, like funerals, usually have music. *The Sandbox* would lose a great deal without The Musician. (Of course, the play would lose its live music, too.)

7. *What, in your own words, do you think is the theme of* The Sandbox? *What parts of the play support your opinion?* It is hard to state the theme of *The Sandbox* in definitive terms. Albee has made a great deal of his play being deliberately elusive. However, one might suggest a theme like *"The Sandbox* pokes absurd fun at middle-class family values by satirizing the hypocrisy and indifference family members exhibit toward one another."

8. *What aspects of the play seem comic? What aspects appear unpleasant?* The Sandbox

seems simultaneously both comic and unpleasant. The basic dramatic premise of Mommy and Daddy bringing Grandma to the beach to die is rather nasty, but the way Albee presents it (as in the couple unceremoniously dumping the old gal in the sandbox or the Young Man muffing his most dramatic line) is deliberately funny. The way in which Albee intermingles the dark and light aspects of his play seems intrinsic to his style. The Theater of the Absurd characteristically portrays the darkest existential material in slapstick comic terms. We laugh, but part of what we laugh at is the absurdity and ephemerality of our own existence.

37 *Evaluating a Play*

This chapter may be particularly useful for students to read before they tackle a play about whose greatness or inferiority you have any urgent convictions. The chapter probably doesn't deserve to be dealt with long in class, but it might lead to a writing assignment: to comment on the merits of any play in the book.

If you assign students to write a play review (see "Writing about a Play" page 1780), you might like to have them read this chapter first. To help them in forming their opinions, they may consult the list of pointers on pages 1325–26.

Sophocles
ANTIGONÊ, page 1328

QUESTIONS

1. *Some critics argue that the main character of the play is not Antigonê, but Creon. How can this view possibly be justified? Do you agree?* Antigonê disappears from the play in its last third, and we are then shown Creon in conflict with himself. Creon suffers a tragic downfall: his earlier decision has cost him his wife and his son; Eurydicê has cursed him; and in the end, he is reduced to a pitiable figure praying for his own death. Still, without Antigonê the play would have no conflict; surely she suffers a tragic downfall as well.

2. *Why is it so important to Antigonê that the body of Polyneicês be given a proper burial?* "I say that this crime is holy." (Prologue; line 56. See also the footnote on line 3).

3. *Modern critics often see the play as centering around a theme: the authority of the state conflicts with the religious duty of an individual. Try this interpretation on the play and decide how well it fits. Does the playwright seem to favor one side or the other?* The pious Sophocles clearly favors Antigonê and sees divine law taking precedence over human law; but Creon's principles (most fully articulated in Scene I, lines 28-41 and 98-124) are given fair hearing.

4. *Comment from a student paper: "Antigonê is a stubborn fool, bent on her own destruction. Her insistence on giving a corpse burial causes nothing but harm to herself, to Haimon, Eurydicê, and all Thebes. She does not accomplish anything that Creon wouldn't eventually have agreed to do." Discuss this view.*

5. *Explain the idea of good government implied in the exchange between Creon and Haimon:* "My voice is the one voice giving orders in this city!"—"It is no city if it takes orders from one voice." *(Scene III, 105-6).*

6. *What doubts rack Creon? For what reasons does he waver in his resolve to punish Antigonê and deny burial to the body of Polyneicês? In changing his mind, does he seem to you weak and indecisive?* Not at all; he has good reason to pull down his vanity and to listen to the wise Haimon and his counselors.

7. *In not giving us a love scene in the tomb between Antigonê and Haimon, does Sophocles miss a golden opportunity? Or would you argue that, as a playwright, he knows his craft?*

David Grene has pointed out that the plots of the *Antigonê* and the *Oedipus* have close similarities. In both, we meet a king whose unknowing violation of divine law results in his own destruction. In both, the ruler has an encounter with Teiresias, whom he refuses to heed. Creon relents and belatedly tries to take the priest's advice—Oedipus, however, defies all wise counsel (introduction to "The Theban Plays" in *Complete Greek*

Tragedies, ed. David Grene and Richard Lattimore [University of Chicago Press, 1959] II: 2–3).

Charles Paul Segal views the clash between Creon and Antigonê as the result of two conflicting worldviews—one female, the other masculine:

It is again among the tragic paradoxes of Antigone's position that she who accepts the absolutes of death has a far fuller sense of the complexities of life. Creon, who lacks a true "reverence" for the gods, the powers beyond human life, also lacks a deep awareness of the complexities within the human realm. Hence he tends to see the world in terms of harshly opposed categories, right and wrong, reason and folly, youth and age, male and female. He scornfully joins old age with foolishness in speaking to the chorus (267–68) and refuses to listen to his son's advice because he is younger (684–85). . . .

All these categories imply the relation of superior and inferior, stronger and weaker. This highly structured and aggressive view of the world Creon expresses perhaps most strikingly in repeatedly formulating the conflict between Antigone and himself in terms of the woman trying to conquer the man. He sees in Antigone a challenge to his whole way of living and his basic attitudes toward the world. And of course he is right, for Antigone's full acceptance of her womanly nature, her absolute valuation of the bonds of blood and affection, is a total denial of Creon's obsessively masculine rationality. ("Sophocles' Praise of Man and the Conflicts of the *Antigone,*" in *Sophocles: A Collection of Critical Essays,* ed. Bernard Knox [Twentieth Century Views Series: Englewood Cliffs, N.J.: Prentice-Hall, 1966].)

Students with experience in play production might be asked to suggest strategies for staging *Antigonê* today. In their commentary on the play, translators Dudley Fitts and Robert Fitzgerald make interesting suggestions. The Chorus had better not chant the Odes in unison, or the words will probably be unintelligible; let single voices in the Chorus take turns speaking lines. The solemn parados might be spoken to the accompaniment of a slow drumbeat. No dancing should be included; no attempt should be made to use larger-than-life Greek masks with megaphone mouths. More effective might be lifelike Benda-type masks, closely fitting the face. "If masks are used at all, they might be well allotted only to those characters who are somewhat depersonalized by official position or discipline: Creon, Teiresias, the Chorus and Choragos, possibly the Messenger. By this rule, Antigonê has no mask; neither has Ismenê, Haimon, nor Eurydicê" (*The Oedipus Cycle: An English Version* [New York: Harcourt, 1949] 242–43).

Entertaining scraps from our sparse knowledge of the life of Sophocles are gathered by Moses Hadas in *An Ancilla to Classical Reading* (Columbia University Press, 1954). The immense popular success of *Antigonê* led to the playwright's being elected a general, although as he himself admitted, he was incompetent in battle. Many reports attest to his piety, his fondness for courtesans and boys, and his defeat of an attempt by his sons to have him declared an imbecile. Plutarch relates that when Sophocles, then past ninety, read to the jury from his latest work, *Oedipus at Colonus,* he "was escorted from the lawcourt as from a theater, amid the applause and shouts of all." One account of the playwright's death is that he strangled while reading aloud a long, breathless sentence from *Antigonê.*

Suggestions for Writing. Compare and contrast the character of Creon in the two plays. (In *Oedipus the King,* he is the reasonable man, the foil for the headstrong Oedipus.)

How important to the play is Haimon? Ismenê? Eurydicê?

How visibly does the family curse that brought down Oedipus operate in *Antigonê?* Does fate seem a motivating force behind Antigonê's story? (In *Antigonê* fate plays a much less prominent part; the main characters—Creon, Antigonê, and Haimon—seem to decide for themselves their courses of action.)

Ruth E. Zehfuss has noticed that *Antigonê* cries out for comparison with Susan Glaspell's *Trifles*: both are plays in which the protagonists find their moral convictions at odds with the law of the state. Interestingly, Zehfuss sees other parallels. "The settings of both *Trifles* and *Antigonê* emphasize the relative positions of authority figures and those whose lives they control. *Antigonê* is played out in front of the palace, the locus of authority." Similarly, in the stage directions for the beginning of *Trifles*, the Sheriff and the County Attorney are in charge: as guardians of the law, they occupy center stage, near the warm stove, while the women stand off near the cold door. Like Creon, they represent officialdom. Other characters in both plays also reveal similarities. Sophocles's Ismenê, like Glaspell's Mrs. Peters, are both weak characters reluctant to challenge the authority of the law. But both Antigonê and Mrs. Hale have the strength to question it and finally to defy it ("The Law and the Ladies in *Trifles*," *Teaching English in the Two-Year College* [Feb. 1992], 42–44.)

William Shakespeare

HAMLET, page 1359

In 1964 on the quadricentennial anniversary of Shakespeare's birth, the celebrated Polish critic Jan Kott observed, "The bibliography of dissertations and studies devoted to *Hamlet* is twice the size of Warsaw's telephone directory. No Dane of flesh and blood has been written about so extensively as Hamlet." A few years earlier, Harry Levin of Harvard computed from A. A. Raven's 1953 *Hamlet Bibliography* that over a sixty-year period, a new discussion of *Hamlet* had been published every twelve days. No work of world literature has generated as much commentary as this play.

The key to teaching *Hamlet* is not to be intimidated by this Mount Everest of scholarship. Familiarity with some of the criticism will enrich your teaching, but *Hamlet* has never needed commentary to win over an audience. For nearly four hundred years, it has been Shakespeare's most popular tragedy. Nonetheless, it might be worthwhile to review some of the best critical works, especially those that can be recommended to students.

Still indispensable is A. C. Bradley's *Shakespearean Tragedy* (1904), which is available in several inexpensive editions, including a recent Penguin paperback (1991) with a new introduction by John Bayley. This classic book contains Bradley's general observations on Shakespeare's tragedies along with detailed examinations of *Hamlet, Othello, King Lear,* and *Macbeth.* If you have never read this volume, you are in for a treat: there has never been a better general introduction written to these plays. Bradley was not only a superb scholar and critic; he remains an engaging and lucid writer. The book grew out of Bradley's lectures to undergraduates at the University of Glasgow, and in them we see a great teacher in action.

Most libraries will have David Bevington's excellent critical collection, *Twentieth Century Interpretations of Hamlet* (Englewood Cliffs, NJ: Prentice Hall, 1968). This volume will probably be more useful to students than some later compilations because it presents essays written before the rise of literary theory made them too complicated for most undergraduates to follow easily. We now use Professor Bevington's authoritative text and notes for *Hamlet* in the current edition of *Literature.*

Jan Kott's influential *Shakespeare Our Contemporary* (New York: Norton, 1964) is a great pleasure to read. Kott writes about Shakespeare from the perspective of an Eastern European and emphasizes the political nature of the plays. His chapter "*Hamlet* of the Mid-Century" describes how Polish productions of the play reflected the social and political environment around it. "*Hamlet* is like a sponge . . . it immediately absorbs all the problems of our time." Although he grounds his discussions in the history of modern totalitarian states, his comments are extremely illuminating. Describing a performance in Cracow in 1956, he captures a central aspect of *Hamlet* that has eluded most critics:

> In this performance everybody, without exception, was being constantly watched. Polonius, minister to the royal murderer, sends a man to France even after his own son. . . . At Elsinore castle someone is hidden behind every curtain. The good minister does not even trust the Queen. . . .
>
> Everything at Elsinore has been corroded by fear: marriage, love, and friendship. . . . The murderous uncle keeps a constant watchful eye on Hamlet. Why does he not want him to leave Denmark? His presence at court is inconvenient, reminding everybody of what they would like to forget. Perhaps he suspects something? . . .
>
> Ophelia, too, has been drawn into the big game. They listen in to her conversations, ask questions, read her letters. It is true that she gives them up herself. She is at the same time part of the Mechanism, and its victim. Politics hangs here over every feeling, and there is no getting away from it. All the characters are poisoned by it. The only subject of their conversations is politics. It is a kind of madness. (pages 60–61)

The most useful recent study of the play is probably Paul Cantor's *Shakespeare: Hamlet* (Cambridge University Press, 1989), which is part of Cambridge's generally distinguished "Landmarks of World Literature" series. Cantor's volume provides a concise, informed introduction to the tragedy. (The entire text is only 106 pages, including the notes and bibliography.) Taking recent scholarship into account, Cantor places the tragedy in an historical context and examines the central critical problems raised by the drama. It is a savvy, sophisticated volume that both instructors and students will find interesting.

The best way of teaching Shakespeare is through performance—not just watching one, but by doing one. The more the instructor encourages, entices, cajoles, or compels students to perform scenes from the plays, the more deeply they will become involved in Shakespeare's drama. Memorization remains unfashionable in some circles, but few students will regret having to memorize all or part of a famous soliloquy from *Hamlet*. Memorization helps accommodate a contemporary student's ear to Elizabethan speech more quickly than any other method. Most long-term teachers of Shakespeare will have their own stories of classroom productions, but one particularly interesting account can be found in Frederick Turner's fascinating book *Rebirth of Value: Meditation on Beauty, Ecology, Religion, and Education* (Albany: SUNY Press, 1991). Turner uses his experiences teaching a "Shakespeare in Performance" course to develop a broader theory of education. Turner's discussion (pp. 151–70) focuses on *Hamlet*, but his procedures can be applied to any play:

> The class method was as follows. Each student was assigned to direct a scene from Shakespeare, casting it from the class, and recording the rehearsal process for an essay that would be due later. The rest of the class voted on the performance, and the actors, the director, and any other stage personnel would all get the same grade. In other words, the performing group stood or fell together, and the reward system demanded that it please, move, and inspire a real, experienced, and perceptive audience. As the year went on the productions became more and more elaborate, daring, polished (and time-consuming in rehearsal). The students were addicted and some performed many times more than I had required. They began to use costumes, scenery, makeup, even lights and special effects, improvising with great ingenuity in our drab little classroom, and decorating it festively when appropriate. The grading system was soon forgotten, and we had to remind ourselves to keep it going. Some

students even protested their own grades when they thought them too high! (pages 164–165)

Not all classes afford the luxury of time to perform parts of *Hamlet*, but all students should be encouraged to see or hear the play performed. There are several excellent film versions available on video. Laurence Olivier's classic 1948 version won him Academy Awards for best picture and best actor. Olivier's version is heavily cut and highly interpretive (very Freudian), but it remains compelling. Tony Richardson's *Hamlet* (1969) has Nicol Williamson, one of the most celebrated contemporary Hamlets, in the title role, but it never comes entirely alive. Franco Zeffirelli's 1991 version stars Mel Gibson. Anyone who has not seen the film has the right to be skeptical, but Gibson works surprisingly well. Zeffirelli's lushly realistic production occasionally threatens to overwhelm his superb cast (including Glenn Close, Alan Bates, and Paul Scofield), but he trusts Shakespeare's drama. Casting an actor like Gibson, best known for action-hero roles like *Road Warrior* or *Lethal Weapon*, in the title role actually seems very Elizabethan. His cinematic associations as a man-of-action underscore the divided character of the Danish prince, a hero who hesitates to begin.

There is also a new BBC audio recording of the complete text of *Hamlet* (distributed in the United States by Bantam Doubleday Dell Audio publishing, available on four cassettes or three compact discs). This performance lavishly parades the wealth of British theater. Kenneth Branagh takes the title role with Judi Dench as Gertrude and Derek Jacobi as Claudius. Even the minor roles are superbly cast: John Gielgud is the Ghost; Michael Horden the Player King; and Emma Thompson the Player Queen.

Hamlet has one of the most complex plots of any Shakespeare play. There is a large cast. Many characters have different private and public personalities, and Hamlet himself is probably the most multifaceted protagonist in Shakespeare. It is always helpful in class to ask questions that make students think through the basic situation, actions, and characters of the drama. Here are a few possible questions.

QUESTIONS

1. By what means does Shakespeare build suspense before the Ghost's appearances? Why is Hamlet so unwilling to trust what the Ghost tells him? Is it possible to interpret the play so that the Ghost is just a projection of Hamlet's disturbed imagination?

2. What is the play's major dramatic question? (For a discussion of this term, see page 1079.) At what point is the question formulated? Does the play have a crisis, or turning point?

3. How early in the play, and from what passages, do you perceive that Claudius is a villain?

4. What comic elements does the play contain—what scenes, what characters, what exchanges or dialogue? What is their value to a play that, as a whole, is a tragedy?

5. A familiar kind of behavior is showing one face to the world and another to oneself. What characters in *Hamlet* do so? Is their deception ever justified?

6. How guilty is Gertrude? With what offenses does Hamlet charge her (see III, iv)? Is our attitude toward her the same as Hamlet's, or different? Does our sympathy for her grow as the play goes on or diminish?

7. If the characters of Rosencrantz and Guildenstern are cut from the play, as is the case in some productions, what is lost?

8. Consider Hamlet's soliloquies, especially those beginning "O that this too too sullied [or solid] flesh would melt" (I, ii, 129–159); "O, what a rogue and peasant slave am I!" (II, ii, 477–533); and "To be, or not to be" (III, i, 56–89). How do these meditations round out the character of Hamlet? How do they also serve to advance the story?

9. Discuss how Shakespeare differently portrays Hamlet's feigned madness and Ophelia's real madness.

10. Is Laertes a villain like Claudius, or is there reason to feel that his contrived duel with Hamlet is justified?

11. How is Hamlet shown to be a noble and extraordinary person, not merely by birth, but by nature? See Ophelia's praise of Hamlet as "The glass of fashion, and the mold of form" (III, i, 142–153). Are we to take Ophelia's speech as the prejudiced view of a lover, or does Shakespeare demonstrate that her opinion of Hamlet is trustworthy?

12. Discuss Hamlet's treatment of Ophelia (see especially Act III, scene i). Does his behavior seem cruel, in conflict with his supposed nobility and sensitivity?

13. In what respects does *Hamlet* resemble a classical tragedy, such as *Oedipus Rex*? In what ways is Shakespeare's play different? Is Hamlet, like Oedipus, driven to his death by some inexorable force (Fate, the gods, the nature of things)?

For a classroom discussion of Hamlet's character, you might present the poet-critic Jack Foley's radical notion of the character's individuality (written especially for this handbook):

At the beginning of Sir Laurence Olivier's acclaimed film production of *Hamlet,* a disembodied voice, speaking above an image of clouds, says *"This is the story of a man who could not make up his mind."* Someone in the theater at which I saw it answered ironically, "Oh, so *that's* what it's about." The meaning of *Hamlet* and the nature of the central character are by no means as clear as Olivier wished his audience to believe. To call a play *Hamlet* or *King Lear* or *Richard III* or *Othello* is not so different from calling a television program *The Johnny Carson Show* or *The Bill Cosby Show* or *Roseanne.* The title implies, *The Interesting Individual Show.* The Renaissance, the period in which Shakespeare wrote his plays, is often described as the great age of individuality and self-assertion.

Plays with titles like *Hamlet* implicitly promise to "tell all" about some central, charismatic character—someone usually portrayed by the most famous actor in the company—to give us a powerful psychological portrait of a fascinating "individual." Hamlet the character is, we know from hundreds of performances, just such a fascinating "individual"—and he is overwhelmingly real. Yet the moment we try to "explain" his reality—even to explain his essential *problem*—we find ourselves confused, uncertain. The reason for this is that Shakespeare's extremely memorable characters do not behave consistently according to *any* system of psychology, whether Renaissance or Modern. Freud was right. There are moments in the play when Hamlet is exhibiting clear Oedipal characteristics. But not *throughout* the play. Hamlet himself suggests that he is "melancholy"—a psychological condition exhaustively studied by Shakespeare's contemporary, Robert Burton, in *The Anatomy of Melancholy.* It's true, Hamlet is melancholy, but not *throughout* the play. Hamlet also functions as the figure of the Avenger—as in Thomas Kyd's famous revenge drama, *The Spanish Tragedy.* But, again, not *throughout* the play.

The same character who tells his mother that he "knows not seems" displays a considerable interest in theater (an art of "seeming") and announces that he will put on an "antic disposition" and *pretend* to be mad—"seeming" to the max. On the other hand, there are several moments in the play when Hamlet really does appear to be crazy. Nor are such contradictions limited to the character of Hamlet. Polonius is throughout the play nothing but an old fool. Yet his diagnosis of Hamlet as mad for the love of Ophelia is not without some justification in Hamlet's behavior, and his "This above all: to thine own self be true" speech is one of the great set pieces of the play, something far beyond the powers of the foolish old man he is everywhere else. . . . The fact is that Hamlet seems real not because he is a coherent character of "self" or because there is some discoverable "essence" to him but because *he actively and amazingly inhabits so many diverse, interconnecting, potentially contradictory contexts.*

Hamlet is one of the most famous fictional characters ever created. Why is this so? Foley asserts that Hamlet's reality as a character derives from his multiplicity and inconsistency as a character: Hamlet is as difficult to comprehend with a single explanation as a real person. What do your students think?

Arthur Miller
DEATH OF A SALESMAN, page 1476

QUESTIONS

1. Miller's opening stage directions call for actors to observe imaginary walls when the action is in the present, and to step freely through walls when the scene is in the past. Do you find this technique of staging effective? Why or why not?

2. Miller has professed himself fascinated by the "agony of someone who has some driving, implacable wish in him" (*Paris Review* interview). What—as we learn in the opening scene—are Willy Loman's obsessions?

3. What case can be made for seeing Linda as the center of the play: the character around whom all events revolve? Sum up the kind of person she is.

4. Seeing his father's Boston side-girl has a profound effect on Biff. How would you sum it up?

5. Apparently Biff's discovery of Willy's infidelity took place before World War II, about 1939. In this respect, does *Death of a Salesman* seem at all dated? Do you think it possible, in the present day, for a son to be so greatly shocked by his father's sexual foibles that the son's whole career would be ruined?

6. How is it possible to read the play as the story of Biff's eventual triumph? Why does Biff, at the funeral, give his brother a "hopeless" look?

7. How are we supposed to feel about Willy's suicide? In what way is Willy, in killing himself, self-deluded to the end?

8. What meanings do you find in the flute music? In stockings—those that Willy gives to the Boston whore and those he doesn't like to see Linda mending? In Biff's sneakers with "University of Virginia" lettered on them (which he later burns)? In seeds and gardening?

9. Of what importance to the play are Charley and his son Bernard? How is their father-son relationship different from the relationship between Willy and Biff?

10. What do you understand Bernard to mean in telling Willy, "sometimes . . . it's better for a man just to walk away" (page 1522)?

11. Explain Charley's point when he argues, "The only thing you got in this world is what you can sell. And the funny thing is that you're a salesman, and you don't know that" (page 1523). (Miller, in his introduction to the play, makes an applicable comment: "When asked what Willy was selling, what was in his bags, I could only reply, 'Himself.'")

12. What do you make of the character of Ben? Do you see him as a realistic character? As a figment of Willy's imagination?

13. Suppose Miller had told the story of Willy and Biff in chronological order. If the incident in the Boston hotel had come early in the play, instead of late, what would have been lost?

14. Another death of another salesman is mentioned in this play: on page 1514 that of Dave Singleman. How does Willy view Singleman's death? Is Willy's attitude our attitude?

15. In a famous speech in the final Requiem, Charley calls a salesman a man who "don't put a bolt to a nut"; and Charley recalls that Willy "was a happy man with a batch of cement." Sum up the theme or general truth that Charley states. At what other moments in the play does this theme emerge? Why is Willy, near death, so desperately eager to garden?

16. When the play first appeared in 1949, some reviewers thought it a bitter attack upon the capitalist system. Others found in it social criticism by a writer committed to a faith in democracy and free enterprise. What do you think? Does the play make any specific criticism of society?

17. Miller has stated his admiration for Henrik Ibsen: "One is constantly aware, in watching his plays, of process, change, development." How does this comment apply to *A Doll's House*? Who or what changes or develops in the course of *Death of a Salesman*?

Directed by Elia Kazan, with Lee J. Cobb superbly cast as Willy Loman, *Death of a Salesman* was first performed on Broadway on February 10, 1949. Originally, Miller had wanted to call the play *The Inside of a Head,* and he had planned to begin it with "an enormous face the height of the proscenium arch which would appear and then open up." Fortunately, he settled upon less mechanical methods to reveal Willy's psychology. In later describing what he thought he had done, Miller said he tried to dramatize "a disintegrating personality at that terrible moment when the voice of the past is no longer distant but quite as loud as the voice of the present." *Death of a Salesman* has often been called "poetic," despite its mostly drab speech. At first, Miller had planned to make its language more obviously that of poetry and in an early draft of the play wrote much of it in verse. He then turned it into prose on deciding that American actors wouldn't feel at home in verse or wouldn't be able to speak it properly. Miller's account of the genesis of the play is given in his introduction to his *Collected Plays* (New York: Viking, 1959).

In the same introduction, Miller remarks why he thinks the play proved effective in the theater but did not make an effective film. Among other reasons, the movie version transferred Willy literally to scenes that, in the play, he had only imagined, and thus destroyed the play's dramatic tension. It seems more effective—and more disturbing—to show a man losing touch with his surroundings, holding conversations with people who still exist only in his mind. Keeping Willy fixed to the same place throughout the play, while his mind wanders, objectifies Willy's terror. "The screen," says Miller, "is time-bound and earth-bound compared to the stage, if only because its preponderant emphasis is on the visual image. . . . The movie's tendency is always to wipe out what has gone before, and it is thus in constant danger of transforming the dramatic into narrative." Film buffs may care to dispute this observation.

Miller's play is clearly indebted to naturalism. Willy's deepening failure parallels that of his environment: the house increasingly constricted by the city whose growth has killed the elms, prevented anything from thriving, and blotted out human hope—"Gotta break your neck to see a star in this yard." Heredity also works against Willy. As in a Zola novel, one generation repeats patterns of behavior established by its parent. Both Willy and Biff have been less successful than their brothers; presumably both Willy and his "wild-hearted" father were philanderers; both fathers failed their sons and left them insecure. See Willy's speech on page 1499. "Dad left when I was such a baby . . . I still feel—kind of temporary about myself."

The play derives also from expressionism. Miller has acknowledged this debt in an interview:

> I know that I was very moved in many ways by German expressionism when I was in school: . . . I learned a great deal from it. I used elements of it that were fused into *Death of a Salesman.* For instance, I purposefully would not give Ben any character, because for Willy he *has* no character—which is, psychologically, expressionist because so many memories come back with a simple tag on them: something represents a threat to you, or a promise *(Paris Review* 38 [Summer 1966]).

Ben is supposed to embody Willy's visions of success, but some students may find him a perplexing character. Some attention to Ben's speeches will show that Ben does not give a realistic account of his career, or an actual portrait of his father, but voices Willy's dream versions. In the last scene before the Requiem, Ben keeps voicing Willy's hopes for Biff and goads Willy on to self-sacrifice. Willy dies full of illusions. Unable to recognize the truth of Biff's self-estimate ("I am not a leader of men"), Willy still believes that Biff will become a business tycoon if only he has $20,000 of insurance money behind him. One truth gets through to Willy: Biff loves him.

Class discussion will probably elicit that Willy Loman is far from being Oedipus. Compared with an ancient Greek king, Willy is unheroic, a low man, as his name suggests. In his mistaken ideals, his language of stale jokes and clichés, his petty infidelity, his deceptions, he suffers from the smallness of his mind and seems only partially to understand his situation. In killing himself for an insurance payoff that Biff doesn't need, is Willy just a pitiable fool? Pitiable, perhaps, but no mere fool: he rises to dignity through self-sacrifice. "It seems to me," notes Miller (in his introduction to his *Collected Plays),* "that there is of necessity a severe limitation of self-awareness in any character, even the most knowing . . . and more, that this very limit serves to complete the tragedy and, indeed, to make it all possible." (Miller's introduction also protests against measuring *Death of a Salesman* by the standards of classical tragedy and finding it a failure.)

In 1983 Miller directed a successful production in Peking, with Chinese actors. In 1984 the Broadway revival with Dustin Hoffman as Willy, later shown on PBS television, brought the play new currency. Miller added lines to fit the short-statured Hoffman: buyers laughing at Willy call him "a shrimp." The revival drew a provocative comment from Mimi Kramer in *The New Criterion* for June 1984: she was persuaded that Miller does not sympathize with Willy Loman and never did.

> Since 1949 certain liberal attitudes—towards aggression, ambition, and competitiveness—have moved from the periphery of our culture to its center, so that the views

of the average middle class Broadway audience are now actually in harmony with what I take to have been Miller's views all along. In 1949 it might have been possible to view Willy as only the victim of a big, bad commercial system. In 1984, it is impossible not to see Miller's own distaste for all Willy's attitudes and petty bourgeois concerns, impossible not to come away from the play feeling that Miller's real judgment of his hero is that he has no soul.

For a remarkable short story inspired by the play, see George Garrett's "The Lion Hunter" in *King of the Mountain* (New York: Scribner's, 1957).

A natural topic for writing and discussion, especially for students who have also read *Othello* and a play by Sophocles: How well does Miller succeed in making the decline and fall of Willy Loman into a tragedy? Is tragedy still possible today? For Miller's arguments in favor of the ordinary citizen as tragic hero, students may read his brief essay "Tragedy and the Common Man" (in "Criticism: On Drama," page 1726).

For other comments by Miller and a selection of criticism by various hands, see *Death of a Salesman: Text and Criticism,* ed. Gerald Weales (New York: Viking, 1967). Also useful is *Arthur Miller: A Collection of Critical Essays,* ed. Robert W. Corrigan (Englewood Cliffs: Prentice, 1969). In *Arthur Miller* (London: Macmillan, 1982), Neil Carson seeks to relate *Death of a Salesman* to the playwright's early life.

Tennessee Williams
THE GLASS MENAGERIE, page 1548

QUESTIONS

1. How do Amanda's dreams for her daughter contrast with the realities of the Wingfields' day-to-day existence?

2. What suggestions do you find in Laura's glass menagerie? In the glass unicorn?

3. In the cast of characters, Jim O'Connor is listed as "a nice, ordinary, young man." Why does his coming to dinner have such earthshaking implications for Amanda? For Laura?

4. Try to describe Jim's feelings toward Laura during their long conversation in Scene VII. After he kisses her, how do his feelings seem to change?

5. Near the end of the play, Amanda tells Tom, "You live in a dream; you manufacture illusions!" What is ironic about her speech? Is there any truth in it?

6. Who is the main character in *The Glass Menagerie?* Tom? Laura? Amanda? (It may be helpful to review the definition of a protagonist.)

7. Has Tom, at the conclusion of the play, successfully made his escape from home? Does he appear to have fulfilled his dreams?

8. How effective is the device of accompanying the action by projecting slides on a screen, bearing titles and images? Do you think most producers of the play are wise to leave it out?

For Williams's instructions for using the slide projector, see "How to Stage *The Glass Menagerie*" in "Criticism: On Drama," page 1724. Personally, we think the slide projector a mistake. In trying to justify it, Williams underestimates the quality of his play's spoken lines—but what do your students think?

The gracious world of the old South lives on in Amanda's memories. No doubt its glories shine brighter as the years go by, but all three members of the Wingfield family, in their drab little apartment, live at several removes from the real world. Laura is so shy that she cannot face strangers, yet her mother enrolls her in a business school where she is, of course, doomed to failure. Next, quite ignoring the fact that Laura has no contact with anyone outside her own family, Amanda decides that her daughter ought to marry, and cheerfully sets about finding her a gentleman caller. Some students will want to see Amanda as a silly biddy and nothing more, so that it may help to ask: In what ways is she admirable? (See Williams's initial, partially admiring description of her in the cast of characters.)

A kindly, well-intentioned young man, Jim O'Connor, is a self-styled go-getter, a pop psychologist. Like Biff Loman in *Death of a Salesman*, Jim is a high school hero whose early promise hasn't materialized. He was acquainted with Laura in school but now remembers her only when prompted. Laura's wide-eyed admiration for him flatters Jim's vanity, and in her presence he grows expansive. Gradually, Laura awakens in him feelings of warmth and protectiveness, as well as a sense that her fragility bespeaks something as precious and rare as her glass unicorn. It is with genuine regret that he shatters her tremulous, newly risen hopes with the revelation that he is engaged to be married to Betty, a young woman as unremarkable as himself.

Laura's collection of glass animals objectifies her fragility, her differentness, her removal from active life. Significantly, the unicorn is her favorite. "Unicorns, aren't they extinct in the modern world?" asks Jim; and he adds, a few lines later, "I'm not made out of glass." When Jim dances with Laura and accidentally breaks off the unicorn's horn, the mythical creature becomes more like the common horses that surround him, just as Laura, by the very act of dancing, comes a few steps closer to being like everyone else. Although Jim can accept the broken unicorn from Laura as a souvenir, he cannot make room in his life for her. Her fleeting brush with reality does not in the end alter her uniqueness or release her from her imprisonment.

Amanda's charge that Tom manufactures illusions seems a case of the pot calling the kettle black. As we know from Amanda's flighty talk and far-fetched plans for Laura, the mother herself lives in a dream world, but she is right about Tom. A would-be poet, a romantic whose imagination has been fired by Hollywood adventure movies, Tom pays dues to the Merchant Seamen's union instead of paying the light bill. So desperate is he to make his dreams come true, he finally runs away to distant places, like his father before him. In truth, each character in the play has some illusions—even Jim, who dreams of stepping from his warehouse job into a future as a millionaire television executive. And as Tom's commentaries point out, at the time of the play's action all Americans seem dazzled by illusions, ignoring the gathering threat of World War II. "In Spain, there was Guernica! But here there was only hot swing music and liquor, dance halls, bars, and movies, and sex that hung in the gloom like a chandelier and flooded the world with brief, deceptive rainbows" (page 1568).

For a challenging study of the play, see Roger B. Stein, *"The Glass Menagerie* Revisited: Catastrophe without Violence," *Western Humanities Review* 18 (Spring 1964):141–53. (It is also available in *Tennessee Williams: A Collection of Critical Essays,* ed. Stephen S. Stanton [Englewood Cliffs: Prentice, 1977].) Stein finds in the play themes of both social and spiritual catastrophe: the failure of both Christianity and the American dream. Although some of the play's abundant Christian symbolism and imagery would seem just decoration, students may enjoy looking for it. Scene V, in which Tom tells his mother that Laura will have a gentleman caller, is titled on the screen "Annunciation." Laura says she has dreaded to confess she has left business school, because her mother, when disappointed, wears a look "like the picture of Jesus' mother." Amanda is also identified with the music of "Ave Maria." When Tom comes home drunk, he tells Laura of seeing the stage magician Malvolio, an Antichrist who can escape from a nailed coffin and can transform water to wine (also to beer and whiskey). Jim O'Connor is another unsatisfactory Savior: he comes to supper on a Friday night and (symbolically?) is given fish, but unlike the Christ whose initials he shares, he can work no deliverance. Laura is described as if she were a saint, or at least a contemplative. When she learns that Jim is engaged to Betty, "the holy candles in the altar of Laura's face have been snuffed out" (page 1593). Compare Williams's instructions to lighting technicians in his production notes:

> Shafts of light are focused on selected areas or actors, sometimes in contradistinction to what is the apparent center. For instance, in the quarrel scene between Tom and Amanda, in which Laura has no active part, the clearest pool of light is on her figure. This is also true of the supper scene. The light upon Laura should be distinct from the others, having a peculiar pristine clarity such as light used in early religious portraits of female saints or madonnas.

Most suggestive of all, Williams keeps associating candles with lightning. Amanda's candelabrum, from the altar of the Church of the Heavenly Rest, had been warped when the church was struck by lightning. And when Tom, in his final speech, calls on Laura to blow her candles out, he declares that "nowadays the world is lit by lightning." The playwright suggests, according to Stein, that a hard, antireligious materialism now prevails. (At least, this line of reasoning may be worth an argument.)

The character of Laura, apparently, contains traits of Williams's sister Rose. Although the painfully shy Laura is not an exact portrait of his sister (Laura "was like Miss Rose only in her inescapable 'difference,'" Williams has written), the name of Rose suggests Laura's nickname, "Blue Roses." A young woman with "lovely, heartbreaking eyes," Rose felt acute anxiety in male company. She was pressed by her mother to make a painful social debut at the Knoxville Country Club. For a time she was courted by a junior executive, an ambitious young man who soon suspended his attentions. After the breakup, Rose suffered from mysterious illnesses, showed symptoms of withdrawal, and eventually was committed to the Missouri State Asylum. Williams tells her story in his *Memoirs* (New York: Doubleday, 1975) 116-28. Like Tom Wingfield, apparently Williams as a young man was a restless dreamer and aspiring writer who left home to wander the country.

In his own memoir, William Jay Smith, who knew Williams in St. Louis as a fellow college student at Washington University, remarks on the background of the play:

> I am frequently amused by those who take Tom's autobiographical projection of his family in *The Glass Menagerie* literally and picture him as having inhabited a rundown, seedy old house, if not a downright hovel. The house on Arundel Place, with its Oriental rugs, silver, and comfortable, if not luxurious furniture, was located in an affluent neighborhood. . . . Our entire bungalow on Telegraph Road would have fitted comfortably into one or two of its rooms. Mrs. Williams presided over it as if it were an antebellum mansion. (*Army Brat* [New York: Persea, 1980] 190)

Tennessee William reads excerpts from *The Glass Menagerie* on cassette tape, available from the American Audio Prose Library, Inc., Box 842, Columbia, MO 65205; phone number for orders, (800) 447-2275. An excellent reading of the complete play with Montgomery Clift, Julie Harris, and Jessica Tandy is also available on audio cassette from Caedmon (A-301).

This new feature presents a small cross-section of recent American plays to supplement the main selections in the book. The section can be taught as a unit to present new developments in American theater, or instructors can use individual plays to illustrate themes discussed elsewhere in the "Drama" section. Beth Henley's bittersweet but hilarious *Crimes of the Heart* (page 1598) is an engaging and accessible full-length play that could be used for the discussion of comedy in "Reading a Play." David Hwang's one-act play, *The Sound of a Voice,* (page 1647) provides an additional selection for "The Modern Theater," especially in demonstrating contemporary alternatives to realistic theater. Terrence McNally's *Andre's Mother* (page 1662) could serve as an ideal vehicle for an additional discussion on the elements of a play in Chapter 33 ("Reading a Play," page 1063). Less than three pages long, this powerful vignette is guaranteed to provoke a lively classroom discussion, and its brevity permits it to be read aloud in class without taking up more than a few minutes. August Wilson's *Joe Turner's Come and Gone* (page 1665) also makes an excellent text for a discussion of "Modern Theater," since it combines both realistic and symbolist elements. Critical statements by Hwang and Wilson appear at the end of the "Criticism: On Drama" section (pages 1729, 1730). Finally, these new plays provide students with potential subjects for research papers. Possible paper topics are mentioned in the notes on individual plays.

Beth Henley
CRIMES OF THE HEART, page 1598

Beth Henley's "comedy of private disasters," *Crimes of the Heart,* had an extremely unlikely reception for a Pulitzer Prize and New York Drama Critics Circle award-winning play. Premiered in Louisville, it was produced off-Broadway in a small theater. The critics were divided on the play. Henley's dark humor and fast-paced action unnerved several reviewers, and her devotion to an old-fashioned, well-plotted play made the comedy no friends among champions of the avant-garde. Nonetheless, some of the nation's toughest and most discerning theater critics, like John Simon, Edith Oliver, and Stanley Kauffman, championed its quirky qualities. Subsequent productions and the fine 1986 film have demonstrated that *Crimes of the Heart* was one of the most original and enduring plays of its decade. John Simon's original 1981 review still constitutes the best exposition of the play's particular appeal:

> For this is one of those rare plays about a family love that you can believe and participate in, because that love is never sappy or piously cloying, but, rather, irreverently prankish and often even acerb. . . . Laughter is squeezed from anguish as the logical consequence of looking absurd reality in the eye and just plain outstaring it. (*New York Magazine,* Nov. 16, 1981)

Crimes of the Heart can be an enjoyable play to teach for several reasons. First, its contemporary, small-town setting and themes of family love, troubled romance, and frustrated aspirations are accessible and engaging to most students. Second, the play's strongly narrative, realistic treatment offers no barriers to unsophisticated literary readers, while Henley's deep characterizations will sustain the interest of more advanced students.

Finally, *Crimes of the Heart* is very funny—grotesque, irreverent, and daffy. As Brendan Gill commented in *The New Yorker* (Nov. 16, 1981), "We laugh almost from the first moment of the play to the last, and the curious fact of the matter is that what we laugh at is a succession of misfortunes inflicted upon people who lack the capacity to avoid them."

Crimes of the Heart is a quintessentially Southern comedy. More than one critic has compared Henley's play to Eudora Welty's fiction, and a reader of Flannery O'Connor will also recognize her grotesque and cruel humor in Henley's world. Brendan Gill put the matter tersely—and in the process probably explained the hostility of trendy Manhattan reviewers to the play—when he wrote, "Southern writers are masters of the art of exaggeration, of tall tales that consist of a piling up of improbable incidents. Northern writers appear to have inherited a Puritan disinclination to tell whoppers; Southern writers tell little else." Henley owes much to the tradition of Southern women writers—like O'Connor, Welty, Carson McCullers, and perhaps Harper Lee—whose comic vision has a dark, sharp edge. If Henley's vision is gentler, the compassion at the center of *Crimes of the Heart* is part of its attraction.

Crimes of the Heart takes place entirely in the MaGrath family kitchen where the three sisters act out their family drama with assorted friends and relations. Henley's comedy unfolds like a traditional well-made play with a complicated web of plots and subplots that move toward meaningful resolution. However, it is a mistake to consider a play unoriginal simply because it uses traditional elements. Henley employs features of the family drama and the well-made play but in a highly unusual way. As Scott Haller observed in *Saturday Review* (Nov. 11, 1981), "In effect, she has mated the conventions of the naturalistic play with the unconventional protagonists of absurdist comedy." *Crimes of the Heart* often seems to be made of equal portions of Anton Chekhov, Edward Albee, and the Marx Brothers. Its basic method is realism, but, as John Simon commented, it is "chiefly a piece of heightened realism—heightened not into symbolism or expressionism or whatever realism usually gets heightened into, but into a concentrate."

QUESTIONS

1. *Characterize each of the MaGrath sisters. Explain in what ways they are different. Do you see any similarities?* Lenny (Leonora) is the oldest MaGrath sister. She turns thirty the day the play begins. Lenny is almost as eccentric as her sisters, but, unlike them, she ardently desires an entirely normal life. Unmarried and currently unattached, she nurses her aged grandfather. She wants love in her life, but her inability to have children makes her feel unworthy as a potential wife. (Her grandfather feeds this fear and he urged her to turn away her one suitor.) Her eagerness to be liked allows other characters to dominate her. Meg (Margaret) is the "wild" sister who went to Hollywood to be a singer, but she currently works in the billing department of a dog food company. The artist and rebel of the sisters, she is also the most self-assured and independent, although at twenty-seven she is still searching for her place in the world. Babe (Rebecca/Mrs. Zackery Botrelle) remains the indulged little sister at twenty-four. The only married sister, she is "the prettiest and most perfect of the three"—at least on the outside. It is clear, however, that she is also slightly crazy. Babe is sufficiently unhinged to shoot her husband and then offer him a glass of lemonade. Each sister is a well-differentiated individual. What they share is a strong emotional bond to one another and the weight of the past—their father's abandonment and their mother's suicide.

2. *What was unusual about their mother's suicide?* Their mother hung her cat with her. This bizarre detail gave the suicide "national coverage" in the press (to Chick's enduring shame and the sisters' girlish pride). The sisters have been puzzling out their mother's motives since the horrible incident, and they rightly see the cat's murder as an essential part of the mystery. After she was abandoned by her husband, their mother grew so with-

drawn that the girls wondered if she loved them. As Babe remarks, "I thought if she felt something for anyone it woulda been that old cat." It is characteristic of Henley's black humor that the suicide becomes a source of both comedy and pathos in the play. (When the girls remember their mother's funeral, for instance, what they recall most vividly is Babe throwing up into the flower arrangements.) The suicide sixteen years before the play begins is the motive behind the dramatic action: it brought the girls to Hazlehurst; it separated them from other children; and it has left an emotional hole in their lives. It is only when Babe tries to commit suicide in Act III that she realizes why her mother killed her cat—"She was afraid of dying alone." Understanding that her mother loved and needed the cat because she felt she had nothing else, Babe discovers she has more than her mother did: she has her sisters' love.

3. *Why did the young Meg study the library book* Diseases of the Skin, *which was full of "sickening pictures"?* After the pain of her mother's suicide (and her earlier abandonment by her father), Meg trained herself to bear suffering and shut off her natural feelings. "See, I can stand it," she told Babe as she looked at the horrifying medical book. After crying herself to sleep for so long, the young Meg "was afraid of being a weak person." Now as an adult, she keeps many of her deepest feelings at a distance. We see her fear of love in her desertion of Doc after his injury in the hurricane. She runs away to California and leaves him to suffer alone.

4. *There are more characters off-stage in* Crimes of the Heart *than on-stage (e.g., Old Granddaddy, Zackery, Lucille, Willie Joe). What effect does this situation have on the play?* By presenting only six characters (and one set), Henley achieves dramatic focus despite her complex plot. We understand how complicated the MaGrath family situation is, but the dramatic action always rests with the three sisters. Henley is masterful at amusing plot complications, but those narrative turns never rob the play of its emotional intensity.

5. *Why did Babe shoot Zackery?* Babe repeatedly claims she tried to kill him because "I didn't like his looks," but her rationale is more of a symptom of her desperation than an accurate description of the case. Babe shoots her husband because she is excruciatingly unhappy with this abusive, suffocating man. She takes emotional refuge in an escapist affair with Willie Joe which her husband soon discovers. Already on the verge of a nervous breakdown beforehand, she now falls apart. Her bungled attempt to murder Zackery is the only way a slightly deranged Babe can free herself from the marriage. How do we know the action is less than sane? Babe considers it with an equally dire alternate—suicide. In her emotional turmoil more measured solutions elude her. Then, after shooting Zackery, she offers him a glass of lemonade. It is important to note that the sisters mostly treat the shooting as something funny.

6. *How do the sisters change in the course of the play?* Lenny changes the most. She learns to assert her own desires. We see this most dramatically when she chases the disapproving Chick out of the kitchen. She will no longer accept Chick's demeaning version of the MaGrath sisters. "This is my home," she asserts. Her triumph over pushy Chick gives her the confidence to call her old boyfriend and renew their romance. Meg changes more subtly and inwardly; she allows herself to love and be loved—by her sisters and by herself. Meeting Doc again, she realizes she can care about someone deeply, even if it can no longer be Doc, who is happily married. Babe, whose shooting of her husband initiates the plot, changes both externally and internally. Publicly, she ends the marriage that had suffocated her. Privately, she at first surrenders to the psychological fears that plague her, but then, after her suicide attempt, she learns to conquer them. The sisters also change as

a unit. They learn to value one another and not let their natural affection be restrained by the disapproval of others.

The film version of *Crimes of the Heart* is superb. Australian-born director Bruce Beresford displays a foreigner's fascination with the minutiae of Southern life, and his cast could hardly be improved upon. Diane Keaton plays a quirky, vulnerable Lenny, Jessica Lange portrays Meg, and Babe is played by Sissy Spacek. Even the small roles have "luxury" casting. Playwright actor Sam Shephard memorably portrays Doc, and Tess Harper earned an Academy Award nomination for her portrayal of the pesky Chick. Henley wrote the screenplay for the film (which gained another Academy Award nomination). She stayed extremely close to the original play but opened it up visually with many locations. An interesting term paper could be written comparing some element of the film to the original play. Possible topics could include: the portrayals of Zackery Botrelle and Barnette Lloyd; Henley's additions to the plot; and the visualization of scenes that are only verbally related in the play.

Other possible paper topics include the following: describe and discuss one of the characters who never appears on stage—what importance do they have to the drama? Each of the sisters has one love affair presented—how do their attitudes toward their men differ and how are they similar? Discuss Henley's humor—does she ever go too far?

David Henry Hwang
THE SOUND OF A VOICE, page 1647

David Hwang's short play, *The Sound of a Voice*, is simple, direct, and deeply mysterious. The play unfolds like an eerie folktale. A nameless man visits an enigmatic female hermit, who is reputed to be a witch. Although they both recognize that they are potential foes, they fall into a doomed love affair. Eventually, one of them is destroyed. Hwang's treatment combines elements from both the Eastern and Western traditions. *The Sound of a Voice* borrows many features from *Nō* drama, the courtly theater of Japan. Despite their elaborate and allusive language, *Nō* plays have simple narrative structures, and they mostly focus on the interaction of two principle characters (one of whom is usually a ghost haunting some mysterious locale). Like *Nō* drama, *The Sound of a Voice* prominently deploys music to build a brooding atmosphere rife with emotive impact and symbolic significance. *The Sound of a Voice* also resembles the short symbolist plays of William Butler Yeats, J. M. Synge, and August Strindberg. Yeats's plays, which masterfully combine elements of *Nō* drama with English verse tragedy to create a poetic form for folk material, seem particularly influential on *The Sound of a Voice*.

The main reason to outline the rich literary background of *The Sound of a Voice* is not because the play needs such explication. Hwang's play wears its learning lightly; the influences have all been assimilated into a remarkably straightforward and accessibly contemporary style. The importance of Hwang's diverse sources is to demonstrate the complex heritage of an Asian-American playwright. There is sometimes a temptation to reduce the work of minority writers to mere autobiography, but in this short play, Hwang consciously draws from a Japanese genre that has nothing directly to do with either the Chinese heritage of his family or the historical traditions of the author's native language, English. Hwang himself has complained about how narrowly he has been stereotyped as a writer:

> I first became aware of the simplistic nature of this stereotyping when I did the two Japanese plays *The Sound of a Voice* and *The House of Sleeping Beauties*. I thought this work was a departure because these were the first plays I'd written that didn't

deal with being Chinese-American, with race and assimilation; I felt that they were tragic love stories. Yet they were not perceived as being a departure, because they had Asian actors. (*Contemporary Authors*, vol. 132. Susan M. Trosky, ed. Detroit: Gale Research)

While *The Sound of a Voice* draws from Hwang's consciousness as an Asian writer, it is also a work that grows out of the traditions of American experimental theater.

QUESTIONS

1. *How does Hwang's names for his two characters ("Man" and "Woman") affect our reading of the play?* Although the author lets the woman's name (Hanako) slip into the stage directions, he otherwise refers to them only by their generic titles of Man and Woman. The two characters never give one another their true names but only self-evident fictions (Yokiko, Man Who Fears Silence, and Man Who Fears Women). By refusing to name them, Hwang encourages us to see them as archetypal or symbolic characters. The visitor is all men, and Hanako is, implicitly, womankind. Their story, by extension, bears some symbolic significance to all male-female relations. When the Woman suggests "Man Who Fears Women" as a name for her visitor, she underscores the symbolic nature of their relationship. The action generally seems not to be realistic in detail but symbolic in import. Hwang is not trying to recreate the texture of daily reality as a naturalistic dramatist might; instead, he attempts to portray a mythic drama—a folk legend come to life. Although the action of Hwang's play takes place in Japan, one could easily imagine a staged production of it set in rural New England or on the Louisiana bayou. All you would have to change is to substitute a Cajun violin or Vermont fiddle for the *shakuhachi*.

2. *Why does the man visit the woman in her remote house?* We never know *exactly* why he visits, but we gradually learn that he came on a quest or dare to kill her. The woman tells of other men who arrived because "great glory was to be had by killing the witch in the woods." He initially believes (as do the nearby villagers) that she is a witch who enchants and destroys the men who visit her home. He even imagines (scene 7) that her flowers contain the trapped spirits of her previous lovers. As the man falls in love with her, his desire to kill her disappears, but he is nonetheless plagued by guilt at his failure to keep to his quest.

3. *The woman is unsure of the length of time since her last visitor. What effect does that uncertainty have on our sense of the dramatic situation?* This detail contributes to the mythic quality of the action. It seems possible that she is a supernatural being unaffected by human mortality; or, perhaps more to the point, that this particular plot is played again and again between her and generations of young men. Moreover, at the very least, it adds to the sense of mystery that pervades the play.

4. *Does this play have a central conflict?* Like Japanese etiquette, the action of Hwang's play is understated; the real drama is implied mostly in the details. Both the man and the woman understand from the opening scene that they are locked in a potentially mortal combat, but neither of them directly admits their knowledge. Everything concerning the central conflict emerges slowly—and often indirectly—at least insofar as the audience is concerned. But Hwang's deliberately low-key style, however, eventually intensifies the dramatic tension since it creates a heavy sense of mystery we become anxious to resolve. The central dramatic conflict is the symbolic battle that the man and woman play out. The woman seems to win by removing the man's fears and arousing love in him. Ironically, however, the man, who could not defeat her by force, manages to destroy her by love. His decision to abandon her after their professions of devotion drives her to suicide.

5. *When we read a play, we focus mostly on the text. When we see a play in the theater, however, we experience it visually as well as verbally. What nonverbal elements play important roles in Hwang's play?* The Sound of a Voice illustrates the importance of nonverbal elements in achieving theatrical effects. Two complete scenes (scenes 4 and 6), as well as the conclusion, are played without words. Another episode (scene 8) depends on a visual trick (the man balancing his chin on the point of a sword) to create dramatic tension. Likewise, one of the central contests between the two characters is a physical fight with wooden sticks. The play's finale is a visual tableau. Music also plays an important role in establishing and maintaining the mood of the play. Students will be able to find other nonverbal elements of the play. Hwang reminds us of the importance of spectacle, even in a modest, two-character play. A play works by total representation of a drama, not by the words alone.

There are a great many possible topics for papers based on Hwang's play. Students could trace a single image from the play (flowers would be an obvious candidate) and discuss its significance. Another interesting notion would be to discuss the use of music in the play: what does it contribute to the atmosphere and tone that words could not? Another good subject would be to examine the two scenes in the play (scenes 4 and 6) that are played without words: what effect do they have on the structure and feeling of the drama? Students could also discuss the end of *The Sound of a Voice:* is the woman's death tragic? The theme of suicide would also be an illuminating topic since both characters contemplate the idea, and the woman hangs herself at the end of the play. Students could compare the use of archetypal names (Man, Woman) in *The Sound of a Voice* to a similar technique in Edward Albee's *The Sandbox* (page 1318); do both playwrights achieve the same effect or are there significant differences? Finally, students could compare and contrast *The Sound of a Voice* with one of its models—either a *Nō* drama or one of Yeats's short plays. *Nō* plays are generally very brief (around ten pages). Arthur Waley's classic, *The Nō Plays of Japan* (New York: Grove, 1957) provides an excellent starting point. Any play by Seami, such as *Tsunemasa* or *Kumasaka* (both in the Waley book), the most celebrated master of the form, would work well. Several of Yeats's short plays provide excellent contrasts to Hwang's piece, most notably, *Deidre, The Only Jealousy of Emer,* and *Purgatory.*

Hwang's comments on "Multicultural Theater" appear on page 1730, in the "Criticism: On Drama" section.

Terrence McNally
ANDRE'S MOTHER, page 1662

One of the major genres of American theater during the last ten years has been the AIDS play—dramas that explore the painful social, moral, and personal issues that came into public prominence in the epidemic of Acquired Immune Deficiency Syndrome. Terrence McNally has examined these issues with his characteristic mixture of humor and humanity in *Andre's Mother,* a dramatic vignette of extraordinary compression. At the center of this compelling scene is the title character, a role without words. Students find this play provocative. Not only does it address a highly visible public issue, but the play's literary structure focuses the reader's attention on puzzling out what goes on inside Andre's Mother's mind.

QUESTIONS

1. *What relation does Andre's Mother have to the other characters in the play?* Her only connection is through her dead son, but they come from a part of his life she never knew—or at least never acknowledged. She has never met the other three people, although they played important roles in her son's life. She seems to be isolated in her grief and her unspoken disapproval of her son's homosexuality. Arthur, Penny, and Cal are articulate, sophisticated, witty people. Andre's Mother is neither urbane nor worldly (Andre is described by Cal as a "country boy"). There is a social distance between her and them. McNally portrays her intense isolation, confusion, and initial resentment through her silence.

2. *Andre's Mother, the title character of this piece, never says a word in the course of the play. What thoughts and emotions do you think she experiences in the final scene? Give reasons for your opinions.* The dramatic point of this vignette is to make the audience project their feelings onto the silent, suffering mother. McNally does not portray her in an entirely positive light. She refuses to speak, even as Cal desperately begs her for some response. She has also apparently never acknowledged that her son was gay. Her presumed disapproval made it impossible for Andre to speak to her either about his homosexuality or illness, and yet we feel the intensity and isolation of her grief. All we know about her feelings, however, are her external actions, which in the final scene appear understandably ambiguous. She wants to hold on to the balloon. She starts to let it go, then pulls it back to kiss it before finally letting it sail away. Her fixed stare on the balloon, however, suggests she cannot let go of her son or break his "last earthly ties" with her. However harshly we may have judged her earlier in the play, we are probably touched by her evident love and pain in this final moment.

3. *Is the balloon a symbol in* Andre's Mother? *If so, what does it represent?* This becomes the dominant symbol of McNally's vignette. Cal explains what he considers the balloons' significance. "They represent the soul," he explains. "When you let go, it means you're letting his soul ascend to Heaven. That you're willing to let go. Breaking the last earthly ties." It seems uncertain, however, whether Andre's Mother would share Cal's interpretation. When she finally lets go of her balloon, her slow, agonized gestures seem to confirm the permanence of her earthly ties. A more focused interpretation of the balloon is probably in order. The balloons may be intended to represent all the things that Cal claims, but they also come to symbolize the relationship each character has with the deceased. Arthur and Penny let go first; they knew him least well. Each expresses his or her personal perspective on him. Cal's farewell is more deeply complicated, especially since he speaks it to Andre's silent Mother. One might even suggest that the Mother's painful silence suggests all that went unspoken between her and her son. The balloons also become surrogates for Andre, whose presence haunts the play he never enters. Can your students suggest other symbolic associations of the balloons?

A good writing exercise would be to have students create a final speech for Andre's Mother. Ask them to write 500 words for her character to speak alone on the stage about her reactions to Andre's death. An alternate version of the assignment would be to have her speak to Andre's spirit, as if he could hear her.

A more analytical topic would be to compare and contrast the silence of Andre's Mother with the attitudes of the speakers in Miller Williams's poem, "Thinking about Bill, Dead of AIDS" (page 1013).

August Wilson
JOE TURNER'S COME AND GONE, page 1665

QUESTIONS

1. What does Bynum's "shining man" represent? What is the significance of his telling Bynum to rub blood on himself? What action of Loomis's in Act III does this ritual foreshadow?

2. What is implied when, in Act II, Scene 2, Bynum asks Loomis whether he has ever been in Johnstown?

3. Who is Joe Turner? What does he represent?

4. At what moment does the crisis occur in *Joe Turner's Come and Gone*?

5. After reading Wilson's play, what would you say is the Secret of Life that Bynum learns from the shining man?

6. What, if anything, does Wilson's play have to say about religion?

7. For discussion: Do you think the play would have been more effective had Herald Loomis and his wife decided to stay together once they had been reunited?

8. Comment on the spelling of Loomis's name. Is he a herald? If so, what message does he impart?

9. What is the theme of *Joe Turner's Come and Gone*? Is it stated in the play, or only implied?

David Savran remarks about Wilson's play:

Joe Turner's Come and Gone, which takes place in 1911, performs a ritual of purification, setting African religious tradition against American Christianity. It documents the liberation of the spiritually bound Herald Loomis, who years before had been pressed into illegal servitude by the bounty hunter named in the play's title. In the course of the play the details of everyday life in a Pittsburgh boarding house give way to the patterns of African religion and ritual. With the help of Bynum, an African healer, a "Binder of What Clings," Loomis effects his own liberation. He recognizes that his enslavement has been self-imposed; this man "who done forgot his song" finds it again. Bynum explains to him: "You bound on to your song. All you got to do is stand up and sing it, Herald Loomis. It's right there kicking at your throat. All you got to do is sing it. Then you be free" *(In Their Own Words: Contemporary American Playwrights* [New York: Theatre Communications Group, 1989] 289).

The lines Savran quotes, appearing in the play's final scene, are perhaps as good a statement of the play's theme as there is.

The troubled Loomis is a herald, it seems—Bynum's "One Who Goes Before and Shows the Way" (see Bynum's long speech in Act I, Scene 1). What Loomis learns, and shows the others, is that African-Americans, if they search, can find within themselves and their African traditions the power to be free. This is apparently the Secret of Life that Bynum has learned from his "shining man." Everyone has to find his own song. Only then can he make his mark on life.

Bynum, the conjure man, is a pivotal character. At the start of the play, he is the only one who has found his song (though Bertha and Jeremy seem closer to having found theirs than do some of the other characters). Loomis, when he first appears, is still under the influence of Joe Turner, the cruel bounty hunter who personifies all the evils of slavery. Thus Loomis frightens the others, seems to them crazy and unpredictable. Though Seth knows where Martha Pentecost is, he refuses to tell Loomis. In fact, Loomis is a man searching for his song.

Bynum also realizes that, after their long period of slavery and separation, black people have to seek and find one another. That's why his magic is aimed at bringing people together. That's also why he likes the People Finder, and why he encourages Jeremy to go "down to Seefus" to play his guitar, even though Bertha warns him the place might get raided. "That's where the music at," Bynum says. "That's where the people at. The people down there making music and enjoying themselves. Some things is worth taking the chance going to jail about." Several of the characters in Wilson's play are in search of the right person to connect with. What makes this play so life-affirming is that some of them, by reaching out, find what they're looking for.

The turning point in the play seems to come at the end of Act I, when Loomis has his vision, making such a commotion that Seth tells him he'll have to leave the boarding house. Only Bynum realizes how crucial that vision is to Loomis's spiritual health. By this time he clearly believes that Loomis is a shining man. That's why he asks, on the following day, whether Loomis has ever been in Johnstown. It was in Johnstown that Bynum had the experience with the shining man that he tells Selig about in Act I, Scene 1.

By singing the Joe Turner song in Act II, Scene 2, Bynum gets Loomis to unburden himself, to reconnect with his own African roots. As if by instinct, Loomis seems to know he can do so by rubbing himself with his own blood, thus acting out the ritual Bynum has described to Selig in Act I, Scene 1. Wilson is clearly aware that blood functions as a Christian symbol of purification. Martha urges Loomis to be washed in the blood of the Lamb. But Loomis rejects the Christianity that sustains his wife. Purification comes for Loomis and Bynum not through Christianity but through the powerful African rituals of their forefathers. "I don't need nobody to bleed for me!" Herald says. "I can bleed for myself." Loomis's song is "the song of self-sufficiency." When he learns to sing it, he becomes a shining man.

Students need to pay attention to Wilson's prologue ("The Play," preceding Act I, Scene 1). The world of *Joe Turner's Come and Gone* is a now-vanished corner of American society—a world of poor drifters, of migrants from the cotton fields to the booming Pittsburgh steel mills of 1911. But although times have changed, the situation of the characters ("foreigners in a strange land" seeking "a new identity") may recall that of any new settlers in a big city, whether Africans, Hispanics, or Asians. For class discussion: How does the play remind us of the lives (and problems) of minority people today, who find themselves transplanted to an American city from a very different culture?

For another topic for discussion, have students read Wilson's comments to his interviewer, Bill Moyers, in "Black Experience in America" (Chapter 40, "Criticism: On Drama"). How does the play reflect Wilson's views? Particularly interesting may be Wilson's opinion that African-Americans were ill advised to leave the South.

Here are three suggested writing topics:

1. The importance of magic in *Joe Turner's Come and Gone.*

2. Is Wilson a symbolist? (That he imparts a message and that he portrays real and recognizable people does not prevent his play from being richly suggestive. Joe Turner, Bynum's "shining man," and the blood rituals that are part of the quest for an individual song all hint at larger meanings. Students may find others as well.)

3. For a long paper, one entailing some research in a library: In what ways has life for

most African-Americans changed since the 1911 of which Wilson writes? In what ways have problems and conditions of life stayed the same?

Wilson's play was first performed in a staged reading in 1984 at a playwright's conference at the Eugene O'Neill Theater Center. Later, in 1986 and 1987, it had two productions by the Yale Repertory Theater. Shortly thereafter, in 1988, a successful Broadway production received great acclaim: "haunting, profound, indescribably moving" (Frank Rich in *The New York Times)*; "Wilson's best play" (William A. Henry III in *Time*).

Students might be asked to comment on this summing up by Henry in *Time* for April 11, 1988, and if necessary argue with it:

> At the end, when Loomis seems pathetically shorn of his consuming purpose . . . the most spiritual boarder perceives in him instead the "shiny man" of a folkloric religious vision. In that moment, spectators too find themselves transported from pity to admiration: Loomis has transformed his pointless suffering into an ennobling search for life's meaning.

Shortly after Wilson received a second Pulitzer Prize for *The Piano Lesson* in April 1990, he made a few revealing comments to an interviewer. Nothing in his work is autobiographical, he declared; nothing he has written has been taken from his own experience. He has successfully avoided studying other playwrights. He claims to have read nothing by Shakespeare except *The Merchant of Venice* (in high school), nothing by Ibsen, Miller, or Tennessee Williams. The only other playwrights whose work he admits to knowing are Amiri Baraka, Ed Bullins, and Athol Fugard. He doesn't go to the theater himself, hasn't been to a movie in ten years. "Part of this creative isolation is self-protective fear," explains the interviewer, Kevin Kelly. "Wilson is afraid of tampering with those chaotically rich and whimsically independent forces in his head, terrified of confusing their voices and stories with the voices and stories of other writers" ("August Wilson's True Stories," *Boston Globe*, April 29, 1990).

Again, as in the earlier "Criticism" chapters on fiction and poetry, the purpose of this little anthology of critical passages is to supply you with further resources, but only if you wish any. Aristotle's celebrated discussion of the nature of tragedy is here given at greater length than in the chapter on "Tragedy" (where it is only briefly quoted), while the comments of Tennessee Williams and Arthur Miller (both complete essays) may prove useful to assign for reading along with their plays. These selections raise many questions for more general discussion or for writing topics.

QUESTIONS

Aristotle

TRAGEDY, page 1715

1. *According to Aristotle, what sort of man is the most satisfactory subject for a tragedy?* A man neither entirely virtuous nor completely vicious: "a man of great reputation and great prosperity" who comes to grief because of some great error.

2. *Try this description of a man on the character of Oedipus. How well does it fit?* Like a tailor-made sweater. Oedipus may be Aristotle's finest illustration of a tragic hero of middling virtue. Far from perfect, Oedipus is impulsive and imperious.

3. *Consider the advice that any extravagant incidents should be kept outside a tragedy. In* Oedipus the King, *what "extravagant" events in the story are not shown on stage?* The most fantastic is probably the meeting of Oedipus with the Sphinx; we are merely told, in the closing speech of the Chorus, that Oedipus "knew the famous riddle."

E. R. Dodds

SOPHOCLES AND DIVINE JUSTICE, page 1717

1. *What is Dodds's central point? Does it make sense to you? Could you love (or at least worship) an unjust God?*

2. *What evidence can you find in* Oedipus the King *to justify Dodds's view?* Notice that in the closing scene of the play, Oedipus continues to pray, to call on God to be kinder to his children than to him. Creon denies that God hates Oedipus.

Thomas Rymer

THE FAULTS OF OTHELLO, page 1717

1. *What chief complaints against* Othello *does this critic lodge?*

2. *How would you answer them?*

W. H. Auden
IAGO AS TRIUMPHANT VILLAIN, page 1718

1. *What aspects of* Othello *does Auden consider unique? ("I cannot think of any other play . . . ")?*

2. *What character does Auden assert stands at the center of Shakespeare's play? What is unusual about this character?*

3. *What is peculiar about Othello's fall in relation to the fall of most tragic heroes?*

Samuel Johnson
"SHAKESPEARE HAS NO HEROES," page 1719

1. *"Shakespeare has no heroes"—what do you understand from this remark? What is a hero, in Johnson's sense of the word?*

2. *We might expect that Dr. Johnson, a follower of classical "rules of criticism" (as he says), might condemn Shakespeare for mingling tragedy and comedy in one play. But why doesn't he? How does he justify—even praise—Shakespeare's practice?*

3. *Both Johnson and Bernard Shaw (page 1721), find that Shakespeare places his characters in extreme situations, even impossible ones. What does each critic think of Shakespeare for doing so?* Johnson admires the Bard for imagining human nature "in trials to which it cannot be exposed." In Shaw's opinion, the fact that our uncles seldom murder our fathers as in *Hamlet*, renders Shakespeare's plays of less consequence for us.

Anthony Burgess
AN ASIAN CULTURE LOOKS AT SHAKESPEARE, page 1720

1. *In Anthony Burgess's experience, who seemed to be the only British author with universal appeal in Malaysia? How does Burgess account for this fact?*

2. *According to Burgess, what does translation involve besides words?*

Bernard Shaw
IBSEN AND THE FAMILIAR SITUATION, page 1721

1. *How, according to Shaw, does* A Doll's House *reflect Ibsen's originality? In the play's time, what was so new about it?*

2. *How does Shaw explain the origin of drama?*

3. *Which playwright does Shaw prefer: Ibsen or Shakespeare? Why?*

4. *(See Question 3 for Samuel Johnson, above.)*

Virginia Woolf

WHAT IF SHAKESPEARE HAD HAD A SISTER?, page 1722

1. *What are the obstacles, as Woolf presents them, that would have prevented a gifted Englishwoman of the seventeenth century from rising to the heights that Shakespeare attained?*

2. *What positive point is Woolf driving at?* That women, like men, deserve a climate in which their gifts will be free to germinate.

3. *How—and why—has the situation of a gifted woman changed in our own day?*

Edward Albee

THE THEATER OF THE ABSURD, page 1723

1. *What, according to Albee, should a play do besides entertain?*

2. *What paradox does he find in the nature of "the supposed Realistic theater"?*

Tennessee Williams

HOW TO STAGE THE GLASS MENAGERIE, 1724

1. *How do both Albee (above) and Williams feel about theatrical "realism"?*

2. *How does Williams argue for his use of the slide projector? If you were producing* The Glass Menagerie, *would you follow the playwright's instructions and use the projector, or leave it out?*

3. *What other antirealistic devices would Williams employ? Would you expect them to be effective?*

Arthur Miller

TRAGEDY AND THE COMMON MAN, page 1726

1. *In arguing that a tragedy can portray an ordinary man, how does Miller find an ally in Sigmund Freud?* See Miller's second paragraph.

2. *According to Miller, what evokes in us "the tragic feeling"? Compare his view with Aristotle's.* Unlike the Greek theorist, Miller finds the sense of tragedy arising not from pity and fear but from our contemplating a character who would give his life for personal dignity.

3. *In Miller's view, why is not tragedy an expression of pessimism? What outlook does a tragedy express?*

4. *Consider what Miller says about pathos (p. 1728), and try to apply it to* Death of a Salesman. *Does the play persuade you that Willy Loman could have won his battle? That he isn't witless and insensitive? Or is the play (in Miller's terms) not tragic, but only pathetic?*

Maria Irene Fornes
CHARACTERS ARE NOT REAL PEOPLE, page 1729

1. *What dividing line does Fornes draw between a play and real life?* "Characters are not real people. . . ."

2. *What does Fornes see as the purpose of art?*

August Wilson
BLACK EXPERIENCE IN AMERICA, page 1729

1. *What does Wilson see as a part of his purpose in writing plays?* "To see some of the choices that we as blacks in America have made."

2. *How does* Joe Turner's Come and Gone *illuminate any such choice?* Wilson has respect and affection for black folk culture, with its elements of myth and magic. Perhaps, he hints, it risks disappearance when transplanted to the urban North.

3. *What light do Wilson's remarks throw on the line in the play, "Everyone has to find his own song"?* These characters, as the playwright sees them, are looking for their African identities. That they are embarked on any such a quest won't be obvious to most readers. Students will need to do some thinking and discussing in order to make sense of Wilson's claim. What is an African identity? How does Herald Loomis end up with one at the end? Carefully reread the playwright's explanatory stage directions in the last moments of the play.

David Henry Hwang
MULTICULTURAL THEATER, page 1730

1. *What events contributed to Hwang's heightened consciousness of his Asian roots?*

2. *What importance does Hwang feel mythology has in drama?*

3. *On what does Hwang think the notion of "ethnic theater" depends?*

SUPPLEMENT: WRITING

1 *Writing about Literature*

This Supplement is no more than a brief guide and a small work of reference. If you find it useful, you might ask students to read it before they plan their papers. As succinctly as we can, we set forth in the section "Writing About Literature" a few general critical approaches to a story, poem, or play; then we escort the student through the various procedures of finding a topic and organizing, drafting, revising, and finishing a paper.

Such matters need not divert much classroom time from the livelier task of reading literature. Perhaps it would be sufficient, after students have tried "Writing About Literature," to take a few minutes to question them on this material, to make sure at least that they are aware of it. At the same time, you might invite their own questions about essay writing (to which, no doubt, you will have your own answers).

If this Supplement fulfills its purpose, it will save you some breath and spare you from reading many innocent almost-plagiarisms, floating unidentified quotations (of the kind that suddenly interrupt the student's prose with Harold Bloom's prose in quotation marks), and displays of ill-fitting critical terminology.

Some instructors assign few papers and exact from their students rather highly polished prose; others prefer to keep students scribbling away constantly, on the assumption that the practice in writing is valuable (whether or not the instructor reads all their output word by word). Instructors who favor the latter approach report that they simply assign selections in the book that have questions after them, and ask students to answer some questions in writing outside of class. These papers are collected and the instructor later skims through them and selects a few of the livelier points to quote and discuss at the next class. (The papers are not returned.)

Once—at the end of a class in which argument had waxed over the question "Is 'Naming the Parts' an antiwar poem or isn't it?"—XJK made the mistake of cutting off the discussion and telling students to go home and write their opinions down on paper. The result was to cool future class discussions: students were afraid that if they talked animatedly, they would be told to write. A different approach is that of an instructor who would halt a class discussion that had grown driveling, or bad-tempered, or without heart, and cry, "For God's sake, let's all stop talking! Now get out your pencils and write me a paragraph. . . . " He claimed that in the next class the discussion improved markedly.

Robert Wallace
THE GIRL WRITING HER ENGLISH PAPER, page 1746

This fine poem has no purpose here but to interrupt the editorial prose and help put students in a writing mood. But it is worth reading with an eye to its metaphors: Crumpled-up drafts are like the wreakage of Eden (lovely hyperbole!); writing about a poem is like plowing furrows.

In our previous edition, this poem had a different last line, so that it ended, "stars would be overhead, / their light come in." Since then, the poet has rewritten the ending, for reasons he explains in his textbook *Writing Poems, Second Edition* (Boston: Little, Brown, 1987):

A vague dissatisfaction with the last line persisted. I didn't know what the problem was until—again reading the poem to an audience, in Kansas—the right line suddenly came to me. I had been aware, I think, that "their light come in" wasn't really necessary, only emphasizing what line 11 already does: "stars would be overhead." But stopping there would leave the rhythm unfinished, and the stanza pattern uncompleted.

In the instant before I said the line, I knew how it should really go—and changed it. At once the weakness of "their light come in" was also plain. It left the room vaguely in place, with the starlight coming in an unmentioned window, rather than simply overhead. Instead of implying such a limit, the new line extends mysteriously the little world of the farm.

2 *Writing about a Story*

If your students complain, "I've never written about *stories* before—what am I supposed to do?" you can have them read this section. We can't imagine spending whole class hours with this material; it is supplied here mainly to provide students with illustrations of acceptable papers written by each of three usual methods, and a few pointers on format and mechanics. If you like, you can assign this section for outside reading when you first make a writing assignment.

XJK comments: The card report (page 1753) may well be God's gift to the instructor overwhelmed with papers to grade. At least, I can't take credit for its creation. This demanding exercise first impressed me as a student in the one course I took at Teachers College, Columbia. The professor, Lennox Grey, assigned us aspiring literature teachers to pick ten great novels we hadn't read and to write card reports on them. Among the novels were *War and Peace* and *Les Misérables,* and although Grey allowed us as many as two cards to encompass them, I must have spoiled a pack of cards for every novel I encompassed. But the task was an agreeable challenge, and I felt it obliged me to look more closely at fiction than I ever had. Later, as a graduate student in Ann Arbor, I found the same device heavily worked by Kenneth Rowe, Arthur Miller's teacher of playwriting, in a popular course in modern drama. Every week, students were expected to read two full-length plays and to turn in two card reports. Nearly a hundred students swelled the course, and Rowe employed two teaching assistants to do the grading. As one of them, I soon realized the beauty of the method. Even a novice like me could do a decent job of grading a hundred card reports each week without being crushed under the toil, either. For an hour a week Rowe met with the other assistant and me and superintended our labors a little, and we thrashed out any problem cases.

If you care to give such an assignment a try, don't feel obliged to write a card report of your own as a Platonic ideal to hold your students' reports up to. When you gather in the sheaves, you can compare a few of them (looking hard at the reports of any students whom you know to be intelligent and conscientious) and probably will quickly see what a better-than-average report on a story might encompass. In grading, it isn't necessary to read every item on every card: you may read the plot summaries with intermittent attention and concentrate on the subtler elements: symbol, theme, evaluation. Because extensive remarks by the instructor don't seem called for (and anyway, wouldn't fit on the card), your comments may be short and pointed. If a student reporting on "The Tell-Tale Heart" has omitted a crucial symbol, you may simply query, "The eye?" or "The heart-beat?" One can probably grade thirty card reports in less than an hour and do an honest job; whereas a set of thirty essays, even brief ones, takes at least four hours.

By asking students to produce so few words, you need not feel that their writing skills are being slighted. To get the report to fit the card, a good student has to do several drafts and revisions, none of which the instructor has to read. A shoddy job by a student who hasn't thoroughly read the story is painfully obvious. Once in a while, after a surfeit of expansive essays, I have asked a class for a card report just to rest my eyes and to remind them of the virtues of concision. Some students inevitably grumble, but most are in for a reward, some will even be delighted that the assignment is so clearly defined and limited! (Although, as reproduced in the text, the sample card is smaller than 5 by 8 inches, it illustrates exactly the amount of wordage that can be crammed on one card, even if typed with a pica typewriter.)

Warn your students to allow plenty of time to do this job right. Stephen Marcus, of the University of California, Santa Barbara, tells us that some of his students were appalled to find it took them two or three hours to write one card report. That sounds about par for the assignment; if you want to abbreviate it, you can omit some of the required elements.

To read nothing but card reports all term is, however, a mind crusher. Essays, of course, develop different skills of thinking and organization and will probably still seem necessary. In choosing an essay topic, if given a choice, many students have trouble deciding how large a topic to attempt in an assigned word length, and many are tempted to choose a topic larger than they can handle. Some want to make sure they'll have enough ideas to fill the word length. Even if you don't care to assign any of the topics suggested in the text, having students read the list on pages 1757-60 may give them a clearer notion of the right amplitude of topics for papers of various lengths.

If this list, and the "Suggestions for Writing" at the end of most chapters, and your own inspiration don't suffice, still more topics for writing may be quarried from the questions after the stories. (For "Stories for Further Reading," the questions are in this manual.)

3   *Writing about a Poem*

Here are notes on the two poems contained in "Writing about a Poem."

Robert Frost
DESIGN, page 1763

"Design" is fruitful to compare in theme with Walt Whitman's "A Noiseless Patient Spider" (page 1010). One could begin by comparing the early versions of the two poems, Whitman's "The Soul, reaching" and Frost's "In White." What are the themes of these versions? It is more difficult to tell from these vaguer, more general statements. In rewriting, both poets seem not only to have made their details more specific, but also to have defined their central ideas.

If you wish to deal with this section in class, you might have students read "Design," then the two student papers about it (pages 1763 and 1768). What did these writers notice about the poem that you didn't notice? What did you notice about it that they left out?

Besides Jarrell's classic explication, many other good discussions of the poem can be consulted. Elizabeth Drew has a succinct explication in *Poetry: A Modern Guide to Its Understanding and Enjoyment* (New York: Norton, 1959), and there is a more detailed reading by Richard Ohmann in *College English* 28 (Feb. 1967): 359-67.

Abbie Huston Evans
WING-SPREAD, page 1771

The student's evaluation seems just to us. While "Wing-Spread" is not so vivid a cameo as "Design," nor so troubling in its theme, and while it contains trite rimes (except for *beryl/peril*), we think it a decent poem and admirably terse.

Insufficiently recognized (like most poets), Evans (1881-1983) had a long, productive life. Her *Collected Poems* was published in 1970 by the University of Pittsburgh Press. There are dozens of poems better than "Wing-Spread" in it.

SUGGESTIONS FOR WRITING

Here are a few more topics for paper assignments to supplement the list on page 1776 in the book.

TOPICS FOR BRIEF PAPERS (250-500 WORDS)

1. A *précis* (French, from Latin: "to cut short") is a short abstract or condensation of a literary work that tries to sum up the work's most essential elements. Although a précis, like a paraphrase, states the poet's thought in the writer's own words, a paraphrase is sometimes as long as the original poem, if not longer. A précis, while it tends to be much briefer than a poem, also takes in essentials: theme, subject, tone, character, events (in a narrative poem), and anything else that strikes the writer as important. A précis might

range in length from one ample sentence to a few hundred words (if, say, it were condensing a long play or novel, or a complex longer poem). Here, for instance, is an acceptable précis of Robert Browning's "Soliloquy of the Spanish Cloister":

> The speaker, a monk in a religious community, voices to himself while gardening the bitter grudge he has against Brother Lawrence, one of his fellow monks. He charges Lawrence with boring him with dull talk at mealtime, sporting monogrammed tableware, ogling women, drinking greedily, ignoring rituals (unlike the speaker, who after a meal lays knife and fork in a cross—which seems overly scrupulous). Having vented his grudge by slyly scissoring Lawrence's favorite flowering shrubs, the speaker is now determined to go further, and plots to work Lawrence's damnation. Perhaps he will lure Lawrence into misinterpreting a text in Scripture, or plant a pornographic volume on him. So far gone is the speaker in his hatred that he is even willing to sell his soul to the devil if the devil will carry off Lawrence's; and so proud is the speaker in his own wiles that he thinks he can cheat the devil in the bargain. Vespers ring, ending the meditation, but his terrible grudge seems sure to go on.

As the detailed précis makes clear, Browning's poem contains a chronicle of events and a study in character. The précis also indicates the tone of the poem and (another essential) its point of view.

Students might be supplied with a copy of the above material to guide them and be asked to write précis of four or five poems, chosen from a list the instructor compiles of six or eight poems in the Poems for Further Reading.

2. Find a poem that you like, one not in this book so it may be unfamiliar to other members of the class. Insert into it a passage of five or six lines that you yourself write in imitation of it. Your object is to lengthen the poem by a bit of forgery that will go undetected. Type out the whole poem afresh, inserted lines and all, and have copies duplicated for the others in the class. Then let them try to tell your forged lines from those of the original. A successful forgery will be hard to detect, since you will have imitated the poet's language, handling of form, and imagery—indeed, the poet's voice.

TOPICS FOR MORE EXTENSIVE PAPERS (600-1,000 WORDS)

1. Relate a personal experience of poetry: a brief history of your attempts to read it or to write it; a memoir of your experience in reading poetry aloud; a report of a poetry reading you attended; an account of how reading a poem brought a realization that affected you personally (no instructor-pleasing pieties!); or an account of an effort to foist a favorite poem upon your friends, or to introduce young children to poetry. Don't make up any fabulous experiences or lay claim to profound emotions you haven't had; the result could be blatantly artificial ("How I Read Housman's 'Loveliest of trees' and Found the Meaning of Life"). But if you honestly can sum up what you learned from your experience, then do so, by all means.

2. Write an imitation or a parody, as directed in suggestion 1 on page 851. This and the following topic may result in a paper of fewer words than the essay topics, but the amount of work required is likely to be slightly more.

(Note: This assignment will be too much of a challenge for some students and not all ought to be required to do it. But those who possess the necessary skills may find themselves viewing the poet's work as if they were insiders.) The instructor has to insist that the student observe the minimal formal requirements of a good imitation. A convincing imitation of, say, Thomas Hardy can hardly be written in Whitmanic free verse. Students may be urged to read whole collections of work in order to soak up a better sense of the poet. This assignment asks much but the quality of the results is often surprising. Honestly attempted, such an exercise requires far more effort from students than the writing of most critical essays, and probably teaches them more.

3. After you have read several ballads (both folk ballads and literary ballads), write a ballad of your own, at least twenty lines long. If you need a subject, consider some event recently in the news: an act of bravery, a wedding that took place despite obstacles, a murder or a catastrophe, a report of spooky or mysterious happenings. Then in a prose paragraph, state what you learned from your reading of traditional or literary ballads that proved useful to you as a ballad composer yourself.

TOPICS FOR LONGER PAPERS (1,500 WORDS OR MORE)

1. Leslie Fiedler, the critic and novelist, once wrote an essay in which he pretended to be a critic of the last century ("A Review of *Leaves of Grass* and *Hiawatha* as of 1855," *American Poetry Review* 2 [Mar.-Apr. 1973]). Writing as if he subscribed to the tastes of that age, Fiedler declared Whitman's book shaggy and shocking, and awarded Professor Longfellow all the praise. If you can steep yourself in the literature of a former age (or recent past year) deeply enough to feel confident, such an essay might be fun to write (and to read). Write about some poem once fashionable, now forgotten; or about some poem once spurned, now esteemed. Your instructor might have some suggestions.

2. For a month (or some other assigned period of time), keep a personal journal of your reading of poetry and your thinking about it. To give direction to your journal, you might confine it to the work of, say, half a dozen poets who interest you; or you might concentrate on a theme common to a few poems by various poets.

WRITING A POEM: *(Some notes by XJK)*

These notes are provided mainly for the instructor who employs *Literature* in a creative writing course. Some may be of interest, however, to anyone who in teaching composition includes a unit on writing poems. Such an instructor will probably have firm persuasions about poetry and about the teaching of poets. Instead of trying to trumpet any persuasions of my own, let me just set down some hunches that, from teaching poetry workshops, I have come to feel are mostly true.

In reading a student's poem, you have to look at it with your mind a blank, reserving judgment for as long as possible. Try to see what the student is doing, being slow to compare a fledgling effort to the classics. There's no use in merely reading the poem and spotting any influences you find in it—"Ha, I see you've been reading Williams!" You can, however, praise any virtues you discover and you can tell the student firmly, kindly, and honestly any adverse reactions you feel. Point to anything in the poem that causes you to respond toward it, or against it. Instead of coldly damning the poem's faults, you can inquire why the writer said something in such-and-such a way, rather than in some other. You can ask to have anything you don't understand explained. If a line or a passage doesn't tell you anything, you can ask the student to suggest a fresh way of wording it. Perhaps the most valuable service you can perform for a student poet is to be hard to please. Suggest that the student not settle for the first words that flash to mind, but reach deeper, go after the word or phrase or line that will be not merely adequate, but memorable.

The greatest method of teaching poetry writing I have ever heard of was that of the late John Holmes. Former students at Tufts remember that Holmes seldom made comments on a poem, but often would just lay a finger next to a suspect passage and fix the student with a look of expectancy until the silence became unendurable, and the student began explaining what the passage meant and how it could be put better. (I have never made the Holmes method succeed for me. I can't keep from talking too much.)

Most workshop courses in poetry fall into a classic ritual. Students duplicate their poems, bring them in, and show them around to the class. This method of procedure is hard to improve upon. Some instructors find that the effort of screening the work themselves first and deciding what to spend time on in class makes for more cogent class sessions, with less time squandered on boring or inferior material. In general, class sessions won't be any more lively and valuable than the poems that are on hand. (An exception was a workshop I once visited years ago at MIT. The poems were literal, boring stuff, but the quality of the students' impromptu critical analyses was sensational.) Often a great class discussion will revolve around a fine poem with deep faults in it.

The severest challenge for the instructor, incidentally, isn't a *bad* poem. A bad poem is easy to deal with; it always gives you plenty of work to do—passages to delete, purple adjectives to question. The challenge comes in dealing with a truly surprising, original, and competent poem. This is risky and sensitive work because genuine poets usually know what they are doing to a greater degree than you or any other outsider does; and you don't want to confuse them with reactions you don't trust. For such rare students, all a poetry workshop probably does is supply an audience, a little encouragement, and sometimes even an insight.

There are natural temptations, of course, to which teachers of poets fall prey. Like coin collectors, they keep wanting to overvalue the talents they have on hand, to convince themselves that a student is a Gem Mint State poet, when a less personal opinion might find the student just an average specimen, although uncirculated. It's better to be too slow than too quick to encourage a student to seek nationwide publication. It is another temptation, if you have a class with a competent poet in it, to devote most of each session to that poet's latest works, causing grumblings of discontent (sometimes) among the other paying customers. I believe that a more competent poet deserves more time, but you have to conduct a class and not a tutorial.

Poetry workshops can become hideously intimate. They are bound to produce confessional or diary poems that, sometimes behind the thinnest of fictive screens, confide in painful detail the writer's sexual, psychic, and religious hang-ups. I have known poetry workshops where, by semester's end, the participants feel toward one another like the members of a hostile therapy group. That is why I believe in stressing that a poem is not merely the poet's self-revelation. It usually helps to insist at the start of the course that poems aren't necessarily to be taken personally. (See Chapter 14, "The Person in the Poem," if you want any ammunition.) Everybody will know, of course, that some poets in the class aren't capable of detached art and that a poem about a seduction may well be blatant autobiography; but believe me, you and your students will be happier if you can blow the trump in favor of the Imagination. There is no use in circulating poems in class anonymously, pretending that nobody knows who wrote them. Somebody will know and I think that the sooner the members of the class freely admit their identities, the more easy and relaxed and open the situation will be. To know each one personally, as soon as you can, is essential.

As the workshop goes on, I don't always stick to a faithful conference schedule. Some will need (and wish for) more of your time than others, but I like to schedule at least one conference right away, at the beginning of the course. This is a chance to meet with students in private and get a sense of their needs. I tell them to bring in a few poems they've already written, if they've written any. But I make it clear that class sessions will deal only with brand-new poems. At the end of the course, I program another such conference (instead of a final exam), sit down with each student, and ask, "Well, where are you now?"

Some students will lean on you for guidance ("What shall I write about?"); others will spurn all your brilliant suggestions and want to roar away in their own directions. Fine. I believe in offering the widest possible latitude in making assignments—but in having some assignments. Even the most inner-directed poet can learn something from being expected to move in a new direction. Having a few assignments will discourage the customers who think they can get through any number of creative writing courses by using the same old yellowed sheaf of poems. Encourage revision. Now and then, suggest a revision as an assignment instead of a new poem.

In "Writing a Poem" I offer a radical suggestion: that the students memorize excellent poems. Feeling like a curmudgeon for making this recommendation, I was happy to find some support for it in the view of Robert Bly, who remarks in *Coda* (June/July 1981):

> I won't even read a single manuscript now, when I visit a university workshop, unless the poet in advance agrees to memorize fifty lines of Yeats. At the first workshop I visited last fall it cut the number of graduate-student writers who wanted to see me from 15 to 2. Next year I'm changing that to fifty lines of *Beowulf.*

Bly may seem unreasonably stern, but he and I agree on the value of memorization. I believe it helps coax the writing of poetry down out of the forebrain, helps it unite with the pulse.

Bly has sane things to say, in this same article, about the folly of thirsting for publication too early. And incidentally, here's one of his unorthodox exercises for a writing workshop (imparted in an interview in the *Boston Globe Magazine* for April 10, 1988):

> One workshop, I brought in an onion for each of the students. I asked everybody to spend 10 to 15 minutes describing the exterior of the onion, using all of their senses. That requires every bit of observation you have, to remain looking at the onion. Then, in the second part of the exercise, I said, "Now I want you to compare the onion to your mother."

That must have rocked 'em! I wonder if it produced any good results.

For a textbook wholly devoted to the writing of poetry, quite the best thing of its kind, see Robert Wallace's *Writing Poems, Third Edition* (New York, HarperCollins, 1991).

Another book crammed with teaching hints and lively writing exercises for student poets is *The Teachers & Writers Handbook of Poetic Forms,* edited by Ron Padgett (1987), and sold by Teachers & Writers Collaborative, 5 Union Square West, New York, NY 10003. Besides supplying unstuffy definitions and examples of many expected forms, the *Handbook* deals with blues poems, collaborations, ghazals, insult poems, light verse, pantoums, performance poems, raps, renga, and more.

Although knowing something about any element of poetry may benefit a poet-in-training, here is a list, chapter by chapter, of material in *Literature* that may be particularly useful in a creative writing class.

Chapter 14, THE PERSON IN THE POEM, page 603
Novice poets often think of their poems as faithful diary accounts of actual experiences. This section may be useful to suggest to them that, in the process of becoming art, the raw material of a poem may be expected to undergo change.

Chapter 15, *David B. Axelrod,* ONCE IN A WHILE A PROTEST POEM, page 644
Assignment: Write a protest poem of your own.

Chapter 17, ABOUT HAIKU, page 668
    Assignment: Write some haiku, either original or in imitation of classic Japanese haiku.

Chapter 17, *Experiment: Writing with Images,* page 671
    A poetry writing assignment with possible examples.

Chapter 18, *Howard Moss,* SHALL I COMPARE THEE TO A SUMMER'S DAY? page 679
    Assignment: Choosing a different famous poem, write a Mosslike version of it. Then try to indicate what, in making your takeoff, was most painful to leave out. (See also George Starbuck's parody "Margaret Are You Drug," page 851.)

Chapter 18, *Jane Kenyon,* THE SUITOR, page 693
    Assignment: Write a poem similarly constructed of similes, or metaphors.

Chapter 19, *Paul Simon,* RICHARD CORY, page 704
    Assignment: In somewhat the fashion of Simon's treatment of Robinson, take a well-known poem and rewrite it as a song lyric. Try singing the result to a tune.

Chapter 20, *Exercise: Listening to Meaning,* page 718
    Assignment: After reading these examples, write a brief poem of your own, heavy with sound effects.

Chapter 20, READING AND HEARING POEMS ALOUD, page 731
    Assignment: Ponder this section before reading your own poems aloud in class.

Chapter 21: METER, page 744
    Assignment: After working through this section on your own, write a poem in meter.

Chapter 22, CLOSED FORM, page 755
    This chapter may be of particular value to a poetry writing class. Not only does it analyze some traditional forms, it also suggests a rationale for formally open verse.
    Assignment: After considering the definition of *syllabic verse* given in this chapter, carefully read Dylan Thomas's "Fern Hill" (page 1005). Work out the form of the Thomas poem with pencil and paper, then try writing a syllabic poem of your own.

Chapter 23, OPEN FORM, page 775
    This chapter is important for students to read and consider since it tries to suggest why competent verse is seldom entirely "free." It also helps students who are enamored with traditional, formal notions of poetry to open themselves up to new possibilities.
    Assignment: Ponder, not too seriously, Wallace Stevens's "Thirteen Ways of Looking at a Blackbird" (page 783). Then, as the spirit moves you, write a unified series of small poems. Or, on a more modest scale, write a fourteenth way of looking at these poetic fowls.

Chapter 25, MYTH AND NARRATIVE, page 808
    Assignment: Read the final section of the chapter, "Myth and Popular Culture." Retell a popular story (from the Bible, folklore, or the movies) in the form of a poem, but give the story some new twist that allows the reader to see the familiar tale in a novel way.

Chapter 27, TRANSLATIONS, page 843
    Assignment: Consider the translations in this section and decide what you admire or

dislike in each of them. Translate a poem of your choice, from any language with which you are familiar or can follow in a bilingual edition.

Chapter 27, PARODY, page 849
    Assignment: Read these parodists, comparing their work with the originals. Then, choosing some poet whose work you know thoroughly, write a parody yourself.

Chapter 28, EVALUATING A POEM, page 853
    Warning: Although you may care to give "Telling Good from Bad" a try, this is dangerous matter to introduce into a poetry writing class. Young poets already tend to be self-consciously worried that their work will be laughed at. Save this section for late in the course, if you use it at all.

FURTHER NOTES ON TEACHING POETRY *by XJK*

These notes are offered in response to the wishes of several instructors for additional practical suggestions for teaching poetry. They are, however, mere descriptions of a few strategies that have proved useful in his own teaching. For others, he can neither prescribe nor proscribe.

1. To a greater extent than in teaching prose, the instructor may find it necessary to have poems read aloud. It is best if students do this reading. Since to read a poem aloud effectively requires that the reader understand what is said in it, students will need advance warning so that they can prepare their spoken interpretations. Sometimes I assign particular poems to certain people, or ask each person to take his choice. Some advice on how to read poetry aloud is given in Chapter 20. I usually suggest only that students beware of waxing overemotional or rhetorical, and I urge them to read aloud outside of class as often as possible. If the student or the instructor has access to a tape recorder, it may be especially helpful.

2. It is good to recall occasionally that poems may be put back together as well as taken apart. Sometimes I call on a student to read a previously prepared poem, just before opening a discussion of the poem. Then, the discussion over and the poem lying all around in intelligible shreds, I ask the same student to read it over again. It is often startling how the reading improves from the student's realizing more clearly what the poet is saying.

3. I believe in asking students to do a certain amount of memorization. Many groan that such rote learning is mindless and grade-schoolish, but it seems to me one way to defeat the intellectualizations that students (and the rest of us) tend to make of poetry. It is also a way to suggest that we do not read a poem primarily for its ideas: to learn a poem by heart is one way to engrave oneself with the sound and weight of it. I ask for twenty or thirty lines at a time, of the student's choice, then have them write the lines out in class. Some students have reported unexpected illuminations. Some people, of course, can't memorize a poem to save their souls, and I try to encourage but not to pressure them. These written memorizations take very little of the instructor's time to check and need not be returned to the students unless there are flagrant lacunae in them.

4. The instructor has to sense when a discussion has gone on long enough. It is a matter of watching each student's face for the first sign of that fixed set of the mouth. Elizabeth Bishop once wisely declared that, while she was not opposed to all close analysis and criticism, she was against "making poetry monstrous and boring and proceeding to talk

the very life out of it." I used to be afraid of classroom silences. Now, I find it helps sometimes to stop a discussion that is getting lost, and say, "Let's all take three minutes and read this poem again and think about it silently." When the discussion resumes, it is usually improved.

In recent years, the finest, most provocative essays on teaching poetry in college I have seen are these:

Alice Bloom, "On the Experience of Unteaching Poetry," *Hudson Review* (Spring 1979): 7-30. Bloom: "I am interested in the conditions of education that would lead a student to remark, early in a term, as one of mine did, that 'I wish we didn't know these were poems. Then it seems like it would be a lot easier.'"

Clara Clairborne Park, "Rejoicing to Concur with the Common Reader" in her volume *Rejoining the Common Reader: Essays, 1962–1990* (Evanston: Northwestern, 1991). Park is now a professor at Williams College, but for many years she taught in a community college. This essay recounts the joys and disappointments of working with students who were just discovering literature. Park is most concerned by how to relate literature to the lives of her students without condescending to them. She praises a kind of simplicity in approaching literature that "need not mean narrowness." Discussing the teacher's realization that he or she participates "in a process that changes lives," Park writes an essay that proves both moving and enlightening.

ON INTEGRATING POETRY AND COMPOSITION

How do you teach students to read poetry and, at the same time, to write good prose? Instructors who face this task may find some useful advice in the following article, first published in *The English Record,* bulletin of the New York State English Council (Winter 1981). It is reprinted here by the kind permission of the author, Irwin Weiser, director of developmental writing, Purdue University.

THE PROSE PARAPHRASE
INTEGRATING POETRY AND COMPOSITION

Irwin Weiser

Many of us teach composition courses which demand that we not only instruct our students in writing but that we also present literature to them as well. Such courses often frustrate us, since a quarter or a semester seems too brief to allow us to teach fundamentals of composition alone. How are we to integrate the teaching of literature with the teaching of writing? What are we to do with a fat anthology of essays, fiction, poetry, or drama and a rhetoric text and, in some cases, a separate handbook of grammar and usage?

Recently, I tried an approach which seemed to provide more integration of reading and writing than I previously had felt I attained in similar courses. The course was the third quarter of a required freshman composition sequence; the departmental course description specifies the teaching of poetry and drama, but also states "English 103 is, however, primarily a composition, not a literature, course. Major emphasis of the course should be on writing." The approach I will describe concerns the study of poetry.

Because this is a writing course, I explained to my students that we would approach poetry primarily as a study of the way writers can use language, and thus our work on denotation and connotation, tone, irony, image, and symbol should help them learn to make conscious language choices when they write. Chapters in the poetry section of X. J.

Kennedy's *Literature* entitled "Words," "Saying and Suggesting," and "Listening to a Voice" fit nicely with this approach. Further, because this is a writing course, I wanted my students to have frequent opportunities to write without burying myself under an even greater number of formal, longish papers than I already required. An appropriate solution seemed to be to have my students write prose paraphrases of one or two poems from those assigned for each discussion class.

During the first week of the course, we discussed and practiced the paraphrase technique, looking first at Kennedy's explanation of paraphrasing and then at his paraphrase of Housman's "Loveliest of trees, the cherry now." By reading my own paraphrase, not among the ablest in the class, I was able to place myself in the position of coinquirer into these poems, most of which I had not previously taught. This helped establish a classroom atmosphere similar to that of a creative writing workshop, one conducive to the discussion of both the poetry in the text and the writing of the students. In fact, while the primary purpose of assigning the paraphrases was to give my students extra writing practice, an important additional result was that throughout the quarter their paraphrases, not the teacher's opinions and interpretations, formed the basis for class discussion. There was rarely a need for the teacher to *explain* a poem or a passage: someone, and frequently several people, had an interpretation which satisfied most questions and resolved most difficulties.

At the end of this essay are examples of the prose paraphrases students wrote of Emily Dickinson's "I heard a Fly buzz—when I died." Two of the paraphrases, at 90 and 112 words, are approximately as long as Dickinson's 92-word poem; the 160-word third paraphrase is over 75% longer because this student interpreted as she paraphrased, explaining, for example, that the narrator willed her earthly possessions in a futile attempt to hasten death. Such interpretation, while welcome, is not at all necessary, as the two shorter, yet also successful, paraphrases indicate. In fact I had to remind students that paraphrases are not the same as analyses, and that while they might have to interpret a symbol—as these students variously explained what the fly or the King meant—or unweave a metaphor, their major task was to rewrite the poem as clear prose.

The first paraphrase is perhaps the most straightforward of this group. The author's voice is nearly inaudible. He has stripped the poem of its literary qualities—no "Heaves of Storm," only "the air before a storm"; no personification; the author is only present in the choice of the word "sad" to describe the final buzz of the fly. His paraphrase is a prose rendering of the poem with no obvious attempt to interpret it.

Paraphrase II seems to ignore the symbolic importance of the fly, and perhaps in the very casualness of the phrase "and the last thing I was aware of was this fly and its buzz" suggests the same insignificance of death from the perspective of the hereafter that Dickinson does. More interesting is this student's treatment of the willing of the keepsakes: the formal diction of "proper recipients," "standard fashion," and "officially ready to die" suggests death as a ritual. Unexpected interpretations like this appear frequently in the paraphrases, demonstrating the flexibility and richness of language, emphasizing the error in assuming that there is one *right* way to interpret a poem, and sometimes, when the interpretations are less plausible, leading to discussions of what constitutes valid interpretation and how one finds support for interpretations of what one reads.

The third paraphrase, as I suggested before, offers more interpretation as well as a stronger authorial voice than the previous two. The author adds a simile of her own, "as if the winds had ceased temporarily to catch their breaths," and more obviously than the other students uses the fly as a metaphor for death in her final sentence.

I will not take the space for a thorough analysis of these paraphrases, but I think that they suggest what a teacher might expect from this kind of assignment. Clearly, these three students have read this poem carefully and understand what it says, the first step towards understanding what it means. Small group and classroom discussions would allow us to consider these paraphrases individually and comparatively, to point out their merits and weaknesses, and then to return to the original verse with new perspectives.

Most heartening were the comments of several students during the quarter who told me that they felt more confident about reading poetry than they previously had. Though I doubt that my students are any more ardently devoted to poetry now than they were before the course began, they are not intimidated by verse on the page. They have an approach, a simple heuristic, for dealing with any unfamiliar writing. Ideally, my students will remember and use their ability to paraphrase and their ability to use their paraphrases to understand and evaluate what they read when they come upon a particularly difficult passage in their chemistry or history texts during the next three years or in the quarterly reports or technical manuals or journals they will read when they leave the university and begin their careers.

Appendix: Sample Paraphrases

Paraphrase I

I heard death coming on. The stillness in the room was like the stillness in the air before a storm. The people around me had wiped their eyes dry, and they held their breaths waiting for that moment when death could be witnessed in the room. I wrote a will which gave away my possessions—that being the only part of me I could give away. A fly then flew between the light and me making a sad, uncertain buzz. My eyesight faded and I could not see to see.

Paraphrase II

I heard a fly buzz as I was about to die. The sound of the fly broke the quietness in the room which was like the calm before a storm. The people sitting around waiting for me to die cried until they could not cry anymore. They began to breathe uneasily in anticipation of my death when God would come down to the room to take me away. I had willed all of my valuables to the proper recipients in the standard fashion. I was officially ready to die, going through the final dramatic moments of my life, and the last thing I was aware of was this fly and its buzz.

Paraphrase III

I could feel the approach of death just as I could hear the buzz of an approaching fly. I knew death was buzzing around, but I did not know when and where it would land. The stillness of death was like the calmness that exists between storms, as if the winds had ceased temporarily to catch their breaths.

I was aware of the sorrow in the room. There were those who had cried because death was near, and they waited for death to stalk into the room like a king and claim its subject.

I willed all of my earthly possessions, all that could legally be assigned to a new owner, in an attempt to hasten death. But there was no way to control death; I was at the mercy of its timing. And then like the fly that finally lands on its choice place, death fell upon me, and shut my eyes, and I could no longer see.

*   *   *

Mr. Weiser reported in a letter that, once again, he had used the method of poetry paraphrase in his writing course, and remained pleased with it. "My students," he remarked, "no longer treat poems as holy scripts written in some mystical code, but attack them fearlessly." The course had proved fun both for them and for him, and he felt he was paying his dues to both writing and literature.

4 *Writing about a Play*

In an introductory literature course that saves drama for last, there seems never enough time to be fair to the plays available. That is why many instructors tell us that they like to have students read at least two or three plays on their own and write short papers about at least one or two of them.

If you decide to assign any such critical writing but find your time for paper-grading all the more limited as your course nears its end, you might consider assigning a card report (discussed and illustrated on pages 1782–85). Earlier in this manual (in "Writing about a Story"), we trumpet the virtues of card reports—which aren't every instructor's salvation, but which we have found to work especially well for teaching plays. The card report shown in the book—on Glaspell's *Trifles*—manages to cover a one-act play in two card faces. For a longer and more involved play, you might wish to limit the students' obligation to just a few of the play's elements (leaving out, say, *Symbols* and *Evaluation*). Otherwise, they'll need more than one card.

Among the "Topics for More Extended Papers" (page 1788), number 6 invites the student to imagine the problems of staging a classic play in modern dress and in a contemporary setting. If you prefer, this topic could be more general: Make recommendations for the production of any play. In getting ready to write on this topic, students might first decide whether or not the play is a work of realism. Ask them: Should sets, lighting, and costumes be closely detailed and lifelike, or perhaps be extravagant or expressionistic? Would a picture-frame stage or an arena better suit the play? What advice would you offer the actors for interpreting their roles? What exactly would you emphasize in the play if you were directing it? (For a few insights into methods of staging, they might read Tennessee Williams's "How to Stage *The Glass Menagerie*" on page 1724.)

Further topics for writing about plays will be found at the ends of Chapters 33, 34, 35, 36, and 37.

This new feature is designed to introduce students to the variety of possible approaches they can take in analyzing literature. Theory and criticism have become such important aspects of undergraduate literary study that many instructors asked us for an informed beginner's guide to the subject. The objective was to cover the area intelligently without overwhelming or confusing the beginning student.

The new section presents overviews of nine critical approaches. While these nine methods do not exhaust the total possibilities of literary criticism, they represent the most influential and widely used contemporary approaches. Each approach is introduced with an overview designed to explain to beginning students the central ideas of the critical method. The general note does not try to explain every aspect of a critical school or summarize its history; instead, it focuses on explaining the fundamental insights that motivate each approach. While many contemporary critics combine methodologies, it seemed wisest to keep the categories as simple and separate as possible, since students may be wrestling with these ideas for the first time. After each introductory note, we have selected two short excerpts to illustrate the critical approach in action.

Critical methods are always easier to understand when they discuss a poem, play, or story that you know. Consequently, we have tried wherever possible to find noteworthy excerpts that illustrate a particular critical approach and that also focus on a literary text found in the book. This feature allows the instructor the possibility of assigning many of these critical texts as ancillary readings. Robert Langbaum's formalist analysis of "My Last Duchess," for example, makes a good supplementary assignment to reading Browning's poem. Brett Millier's biographical comment on Elizabeth Bishop's "One Art" might broaden a discussion of the villanelle. Hugh Kenner recreates the heady atmosphere of Modernist London in a way that places Ezra Pound's "In a Station of the Metro" in a historical context. Likewise, Daryl Pinckney's discussion of Langston Hughes's "The Negro Speaks of Rivers" articulates the racial issues of the time. Geoffrey Hartman deconstructs Wordsworth's "A Slumber Did My Spirit Seal," while Sandra Gilbert and Susan Gubar analyze the situation of Emily Dickinson, who is represented by ten poems in the textbook.

It was not always possible to find critical excerpts that could do the double duty of illustrating a school of thought while analyzing a text at hand. Sometimes, as in Harold Bloom's discussion of poetic influence or Roland Barthes's announcement of "the death of the author," we chose the clearest exposition available of an influential critical concept. Some of these critical texts are challenging because the ideas are subtle and complex, but we have tried to find the most accessible excerpt possible.

Some instructors may want to use "Critical Approaches to Literature" as a formal part of the course, but more, we suspect, will prefer to use it in a less systematic way as a resource that can be tailored to whatever occasion seems suitable. An excellent way to introduce students to the section is to assign a short paper analyzing a single poem according to the critical approach of their choice. This method allows them to explore the introductory material for each critical school and then learn one approach in depth by trying it on a specific text.

Many poems in the textbook lend themselves to this assignment. Some likely choices (from the first few "Poetry" chapters) include D. H. Lawrence's "Piano," Robert Browning's "My Last Duchess," Theodore Roethke's "My Papa's Waltz," Anne

Bradstreet's "The Author to Her Book," Anne Sexton's "Her Kind," Wilfred Owen's "Dulce et Decorum Est," and Josephine Miles's "Reason." All these poems invite multiple readings from a variety of perspectives.

Certain stories also naturally suggest multiple readings. Poe's "A Tell-Tale Heart," for instance, easily allows formalist, biographical, psychological, mythological, reader-response, and deconstructionist readings. Charlotte Perkins Gilman's "The Yellow Wallpaper" is similarly open to multiple interpretations. Openly autobiographical, it directly addresses issues of gender, sociology, psychology, and myth. Other stories that invite wide approaches include Faulkner's "A Rose for Emily," Cheever's "The Five-Forty-Eight," Tan's "A Pair of Tickets," Joyce's "Araby," Hawthorne's "Young Goodman Brown," O'Connor's "A Good Man Is Hard to Find," Cather's "Paul's Case," and Lessing's "A Woman on a Roof." If you want to assign a single work for students to try the critical approach of their choice, you could probably not do better than Kafka's *The Metamorphosis.*

Plays like *Oedipus the King, Antigonê, Othello,* and *Hamlet* have already been analyzed from every conceivable critical perspective, but there is no reason why a student should not try his or her own hand at them. *A Doll's House, Trifles,* and *Death of a Salesman* are also naturally open to multiple approaches.

If any of your brighter students should start writing papers following any of these critical approaches and you should wish to provide them with models longer than the brief illustrative samples we supply, a new series of paperbacks may be helpful to them. It will be still more helpful if they are familiar with a classic such as *Frankenstein, The Scarlet Letter, Wuthering Heights, Heart of Darkness, Hamlet, Portrait of the Artist as a Young Man, Gulliver's Travels, The Awakening,* or *The House of Mirth.* Titles dealing with each of these classics and others have appeared, or will appear shortly, in the series "Case Studies in Contemporary Criticism," whose general editor is Ross C. Murfin of the University of Miami (Bedford Books). Each book contains five essays on a particular novel, illustrating five different approaches: psychoanalytic criticism, reader-response criticism, feminist criticism, deconstruction, and the new historicism. There are also readable essays that explain each critical school and bibliographies of critical books representing each of them.